HISTORY OF
THE SECOND WORLD WAR

UNITED KINGDOM CIVIL SERIES

Edited by Sir Keith Hancock

The authors of the Civil Histories have been given free access to official documents. They and the editor are alone responsible for the statements made and the views expressed.

CIVIL DEFENCE

BY

TERENCE H. O'BRIEN

LONDON: 1955

HER MAJESTY'S STATIONERY OFFICE

AND

LONGMANS, GREEN AND CO

First published 1955

HER MAJESTY'S STATIONERY OFFICE

London: York House, Kingsway, W.C.2 & 423 Oxford Street, W.1
Edinburgh: 13a Castle Street   Cardiff: 109 St. Mary Street
Manchester: 39 King Street   Bristol: Tower Lane
Birmingham: 2 Edmund Street   Belfast: 80 Chichester Street

LONGMANS, GREEN AND CO LTD
6 and 7 Clifford Street, London. W.1
Boston House, Strand Street, Cape Town
531 Little Collins Street, Melbourne

LONGMANS, GREEN AND CO INC
55 Fifth Avenue, New York, 3

LONGMANS, GREEN AND CO
20 Cranfield Road, Toronto, 16

ORIENT LONGMANS, LTD
Calcutta, Bombay, Madras
Delhi, Vijayawada, Dacca

Price £1 17s. 6d. net

Printed in Great Britain under the authority of H.M. Stationery Office by
The Chiswick Press, New Southgate, N11

CONTENTS

PART II: WAR: 1939–1945

CONTENTS

Page

APPENDICES

MAPS

EDITOR'S NOTE

THE advent of a fourth Service, 'Civil' by designation yet destined in all probability to take permanent place along-side the three Fighting Services, is an historical theme of exceptional importance; but the editor suffered repeated misfortune in his search for an author. Of Mr O'Brien's four predecessors, one died, and two departed to other work before they had produced useful drafts even of a single chapter. The fourth, Mr Francis Wormald (now Professor of Palæography at King's College, London) produced during the latter years of the war a valuable study of Civil Defence manpower; but was then recalled to his duties in the British Museum. When the war ended Mr O'Brien accepted responsibility for the volume, but was unable to work at it full time. His task, which he has now successfully completed, has been arduous and would have been still further protracted had it not been for the aid given by various persons whom he will wish to thank on his own behalf. The editor desires particularly to acknowledge the assistance he has received from the long and valuable studies on the Fire Service measures prepared by Sir Arthur Dixon for departmental use. He desires also to thank Mrs S. M. Ferguson who has been a great aid during the past year in getting some of the later chapters into final shape while Mr O'Brien was working against time.

W. K. HANCOCK

PREFACE

THE subject this volume records was in a state of constant development linked to the growth of threats of aerial attack. It had origins of a kind during 1914–1918, a long period of desultory consideration in the 1920's and 30's, a new practical application after 1935, a more rapid peace-time growth during and after the Munich crisis, and a continuous modification in the long years 1939–1945.

The civil defence of the United Kingdom during the Second World War grew into an affair of great complexity and the area which its history might cover is immense. In order to present an account of manageable proportions the author has been compelled to give his main attention to the preparation and application of 'first-line' passive defences; these comprised what were known for many years as 'A.R.P.' (air raid precautions) and 'Emergency Fire Precautions'. They were the group of functions which were the responsibility of the A.R.P. Department and Fire Service Divisions of the Home Office and (once war began) of the newly established Ministry of Home Security. Many other Government Departments together with voluntary agencies and industrial concerns were also concerned with air raid protection problems. The author has, therefore, tried to give full emphasis to the co-ordinating functions of the Home Office and the Lord Privy Seal before the war and of the Minister of Home Security and his representatives in the country—the Regional Commissioners—during the war. In fact if he were compelled to define British civil defence as organised up to 1945 in one sentence, he would suggest, 'co-ordination (or perhaps co-operation) writ large'.

The most obvious duties of the passive defence organisation were to provide air raid wardens and such specialist branches as the fire-fighting services, first-aid, rescue and decontamination squads and bomb reconnaissance units ready to go into action in air raids. But the functions of civil defence went far beyond the immediate duty of helping to defeat air attacks in detail as they occurred. They included the provision of shelters, arrangements for air raid warnings and the black-out, the supply, maintenance and distribution of many types of special equipment, the recruitment and training of personnel for new and often unpredictable tasks, plans for the best disposition of civil defence's share in the nation's manpower resources and constant readjustment of organisation and methods in readiness for new forms of attack. Civil defence in war-time waxed and waned in size and in variety as the threat it was designed to counter was first postponed, then redoubled and then materialised in an irregular and partly unexpected manner. Although the threat of German air bombardment varied in intensity, it would be wrong not to regard it as continuous. In air attack (even more than in other forms of attack) the enemy possessed the initiative and the civil defence organisation had, therefore, to remain alert and manned throughout the five and a half years of war. There is much truth in the view, expressed to the author by someone who had served for five years as a London warden, that 'civil defence was essentially a waiting game'.

The effort civil defence represented was great and continuing; so great, in fact, that the author has been unable to record all its aspects in the space afforded to him. The reader may be surprised, for instance, at the relatively small proportion of the volume devoted to description of air attacks. The reason is that much more time and effort were spent on preparations for large-scale bombardment than on dealing with the consequences of the bombs themselves. Civil defence planning, administration, training and reorganisation consumed a large share of the nation's war effort; and in the event, the scale of attack was fortunately much smaller than had been expected.

Post-raid activities is another large field of effort that does not receive a great deal of attention in this book. These were not for the most part the executive (as distinct from the co-ordinating) responsibility of the Minister of Home Security; moreover, some of the most important of them are, or will be, recorded in other volumes of this series of histories—for example, the 'care of the homeless' in Professor R. M. Titmuss' *Problems of Social Policy*, feeding problems in R. J. Hammond's *Food*, Vol. II and repairs to housing in C. M. Kohan's *Works and Buildings*.

Slender treatment has been given to the important contribution made to civil defence by certain voluntary organisations. Outstanding among these was the W.V.S. (Women's Voluntary Services for Civil Defence) which after 1938 was closely woven into the Home Security organisation. It has had, however, its own historian; and its manifold functions fell for the most part outside the sphere of 'first-line' passive defence. But the occasional notice accorded to it in this volume must not be read as a failure to recognise the vital services it rendered. It is also regretted that more space could not be given to the prominent contribution in action and in war-time training of the British Red Cross Society (including the Scottish Branch), St John Ambulance Brigade and St Andrew's Ambulance Association. Much of this work comes within the scope of the official *Medical Histories of the War*.

Other gaps of which the author is conscious include fuller treatment of the Home Security organisation's physical communications and the war-time development of industrial air raid precautions, including the policy of dispersing firms. 'Anti-invasion' functions, which bulked so large among the preoccupations of Regional Commissioners and local authorities in some areas, have of necessity been regarded as outside the scope of this history but will no doubt be fully recorded in the official *Military Histories of the War*.

* * *

The rubric printed opposite the title page summarises the conditions under which this book has been written. The practices that have been followed in documentation and the printing of references have been described in the preface to the first volume in this series of histories.[1] The main sources of this volume, like those of the others in this series, have been the official documents. The author tried throughout to base his statements on written evidence, but like his colleagues he found it most necessary and desirable to supplement this evidence where possible by consultation with the active participants in the story.

Unfortunately, apart from three exceptions, time would not permit him to visit and consult local authorities, whose experience would have proved valuable material. Westminster City was the authority within whose boundaries his research was carried on, and Oxford and Dover happened to be the scenes of informal visits; and he would like to thank the officials of these three authorities for their help and kindness.

Officials in the Cabinet Office and the Home Office were unfailing in their kindness and without their help the history could not have been written. In his actual research the author had most valuable help at various times and for varying periods from Miss M. Harrison on air raid shelters, Mr J. C. Sheffield, M.B.E., on the Services' training, warning arrangements and the black-out, Mr A. T. Hardman on the work of the Regional Commissioners and Mr G. N. Seddon, M.C., on fire prevention and air raid operations. More recently Mrs S. M. Ferguson did much to help and encourage the author in the last stages of research and writing. Miss M. M. White of the Home Office gave from beginning to end invaluable and ungrudging clerical help.

T. H. O'B.

Combe,
Oxfordshire,
31st December 1953

---

[1] *British War Economy*, W. K. Hancock and M. M. Gowing, H.M.S.O. 1949.

B

PART I

Preparation: 1924–1939

CHAPTER I

INTRODUCTION

Civil Defence

THE civil defence of the United Kingdom in the war of 1939–45 grew finally into an affair of much complexity. A special Department of State, the Ministry of Home Security, was established at the outbreak of war to administer, with other central authorities and regional and local institutions, the many and changing problems to which it gave rise. Millions of ordinary citizens outside the Armed Forces became involved in its activities, both as victims, in some manner, of enemy aggression and as members of organised bodies giving war service. For the German air offensive against Britain developed, as experience during 1914–18 foreshadowed, into a major item of the enemy's strategy—a campaign in its own right. During certain phases of the six-year struggle the air attack on the people and property of Britain weighed heavily in the balance between victory and defeat.

Though the threat represented by German air bombardment varied much in intensity, it is inaccurate not to regard it as continuous. The enemy, as the attacker, possessed the initiative; and there is evidence to suggest that the initiative is even more valuable in modern air warfare than in land or sea operations. Thus the German Air Force, once overcome by the defences—as in the Battle of Britain of 1940—soon altered its tactics and employed new ruses and weapons. It was not until the main Allied armies had successfully assaulted German territory in March 1945 that the threat to these Islands, then taking the form of long-range rockets, finally ended.[1]

The civil defence organisation had therefore to remain alert and manned during five and a half years. Throughout this period its functions went far beyond the immediate duty of helping to counter air attacks 'on the ground' as these occurred. They included adjusting its operational organisation and methods to new forms of attack, maintaining and supplying special equipment, recruiting and training persons for new and often unpredictable tasks and planning the disposition of its share of manpower resources.

The last item in this list may serve as a reminder that civil

---

[1] Main assault on the Rhine, 23rd/24th March 1945. The last rocket fell on British soil on 27th March 1945.

defence, wide though its activities became, was but one of a number of services defending Britain against air attack. The part of the Royal Air Force in this campaign was, of course, pre-eminent; and that of the Army's Anti-Aircraft Command was of almost equal importance. The Royal Observer Corps, under the control of Fighter Command, was the primary source of intelligence for the whole defence system about the movement over Britain of hostile aircraft.

The part played by these and other services forms a story with which this volume is only indirectly concerned. Attention is drawn to it here owing to the need to recall the wider picture it evokes if certain aspects of civil defence are to be fully understood. Two examples of the type of relationship in mind may suffice. Since during 1939–45 the nation's resources of manpower and materials were strained to an unprecedented degree, competition frequently arose between the claims on these of the more active defences and those of passive defence. Such competition was also evident in the loftier sphere of grand strategy. What, for example, were the respective weights to be attached for the defence of Britain against air attack to the passive method of civil defence and the aggressive counter-action of the Royal Air Force?

An attempt will later be made to notice some of the answers given from time to time to these questions. It will be sufficient to state here that the organisation of passive defence on British soil by civilian forces was given much more weight, both absolutely and relatively to other defence methods, than it had possessed under the German air bombardment of Britain during 1914–18.

It is true that the scale of the enemy's attack in 1939–45 was many times greater than it had been twenty-five years earlier. But this fact, since it is only a statement of quantity, does not destroy the value of all comparison between the air attacks on Britain in the two wars. The quantitative 'progress' which experts measure to estimate the scale of an attack does not, it cannot be too strongly insisted, tell the whole story.

The point is of importance for students of the subject in an era in which marked 'progress' has been made in the technique of air warfare by the invention of the atomic bomb. This invention has given fresh currency to the view that 'nowadays every war is different from the one before'—which, if it were valid, would abolish any need to learn the lessons of past experience.

Clearly, the British authorities planning defence measures between the wars profited from the experience of the air attacks of 1914–18. For this reason, and because of some similarities between the first series of attacks and the later ones, a brief summary of the 1914–18 assault will shortly be attempted.

The study of the planning process which follows will show that the authorities were engaged in marrying the lessons of the past to a future hypothetical experience. Many years before another major war was probable or even possible, they were concerned, as the authorities of every State are bound to do, with preparing for such an event. The process was full of difficulties. For, if the metaphor may be continued, while the first partner brought the solid data of experience to the union the second showed the uncertainties and hesitations of a bride. Against what aggressor or combination of aggressors was Britain preparing to defend herself? What was the capacity of these aggressors in terms of aircraft, explosives and military skill to inflict damage on Great Britain?

The forecasts of the enemy attack, or the experts' answers to the second question, brought some curious results in the sphere of administrative planning. And the difficulties which confronted the planning authorities at the highest level in reaching decisions on the basis of hypotheses were accompanied by difficulties for administrators on a lower, more executive, plane.[1]

Some further observations must be made here on the peace-time planning which forms the topic of the first Part of this volume. This process, extending over most of the twenty-one years of peace, fell into two well-defined phases. In the first, lasting until the spring of 1935, planning for civil defence was the concern predominantly of the top strata of the Government—the Cabinet, the Committee of Imperial Defence and its sub-committees—and was conducted in secret. In the second, which opened with the creation of an A.R.P. Department at the Home Office, plans began to receive concrete application and to involve a much wider circle of central and local officials. They also, it is vital to note, then began to involve the general public, who became aware that practical steps were being taken to defend the nation against future air attack and were asked to co-operate in these preparations.

The forms and degree of this public co-operation during 1935–39 will be examined in the appropriate place. What requires emphasis at the outset is that public opinion, or more precisely the public attitude towards another war, was a cardinal factor in peace-time planning of civil defence, even during the earlier phase when this planning was being conducted in secret.

To state that we are still too close to the epoch now called 'between the wars' to pass lasting judgments upon it is but to repeat a truism. We are, nevertheless, able to distinguish some features of that epoch as pre-eminent. On the material level, for instance, the 'Great War' of 1914–18 had caused an unprecedented drain on the country's economic and financial resources, recovery from which in

---

[1] See R. M. Titmuss, *Problems of Social Policy*, Chapters I and II.

the 1920's and '30's proved slow and difficult. On the moral plane the national exhaustion, though harder to measure, was probably as great. It seems fair to say that a large part of the nation continued right up to the startling international events of 1938 to comfort themselves with the idea that the war which ended in 1918 had been 'a war to end war'.

Both of these features deeply affected preparations for all forms of national defence. Neither the material resources nor the will for re-armament were readily available. To quote an official retrospective judgment, 'the failure to equip our forces on an adequate scale was mainly due to the political and economic circumstances of the decade before 1939, which had the result of postponing until too late the start of an effective programme of re-armament'.[1]

This situation had one unfavourable result on civil defence preparations which deserves to be singled out for mention. Owing to the slowness with which funds were made available for defence, technical experiments of various kinds, urgently needed to provide the planners with information, were long delayed. The formulation of policy regarding air raid shelters, for example, was seriously hampered by lack of data which only up-to-date experiment could provide.

It has been suggested that the public's attitude towards another war was a cardinal factor in planning. The air attacks of 1914–18 had proved that the public attitude *during* a war had attained quite new significance, and this lesson was constantly in the minds of the planning authorities. The first of the many committees to examine the problem of further air attack reported (in 1922) that 'the moral effect of air attack is out of all proportion to the material effect which it can achieve'. It recognised that the problem of morale, hitherto regarded as relevant only to the fighting forces, would apply in another war to the entire domestic population.

Events during 1939–45 were fully to justify this emphasis throughout the planning phase on morale. But it seems, at least on the evidence of recent history, that the temper of the British people does not become warlike until a war has actually started. Still suffering from the exhaustion, material and moral, of the 1914–18 ordeal the people were most reluctant to believe in the probability of another world-wide catastrophe. Planning for air raid precautions thus lacked the public support it might otherwise have received—until the catastrophe was imminent.

It appeared in retrospect to one who had taken a leading official part for thirty years in defence preparations that 'our traditional policy of peace was carried this time to the verge of risk and beyond'.[2]

---

[1] *Central Organization for Defence*, Cmd. 6923, 1946, p. 4.
[2] Lord Hankey, *Government Control in War*, 1945, p. 82.

The War of 1914–1918

The first attack by hostile aircraft on English soil was made on Christmas Eve 1914 when a single German aeroplane dropped a bomb near Dover Castle, which caused no damage except broken glass. London was bombed for the first time on 31st May 1915 by a single German airship which dropped over a ton of bombs, mainly on the East End, killing seven people and injuring thirty-five. From the summer of 1915 until near the end of 1916 *Zeppelin* attacks on Britain by night were fairly frequent, and it was some time before effective means of countering them were devised. The official historian of these attacks reached the conclusion that, even if the *Zeppelins* had been built and maintained solely for the purpose of raiding the United Kingdom, they would from a military standpoint 'have more than justified the money and ingenuity that went to their building'.[1]

Though London was usually the enemy's main objective, navigational difficulties and other factors often resulted in his airships cruising at large over the countryside, dropping their bombs on isolated towns and villages and causing both damage and public alarm. East Anglia, lying on the raiders' normal path to London, received a special share of their attention. In a raid on Hull in June 1915 a single airship dropped high explosive and incendiary bombs which killed twenty-four people, injured forty, destroyed about forty houses and shops and damaged many others. Rioting broke out in the town afterwards, and shops owned (or supposedly owned) by Germans were sacked before order was restored by troops. In the next January the first large-scale deliberate attack on the industrial Midlands caused much public nervousness in that area.

This attack of 31st January 1916, though it was, in fact, to prove the last of the formidable airship raids, led to some important changes in defence arrangements. General responsibility for the air defence of Britain had been vested since September 1914 in the Admiralty, with the War Office playing an important but subsidiary role. This division of responsibility was found unsatisfactory; and in February 1916, when the assumption that the whole country was liable to air attack had been accepted, responsibility for all Home Air Defence was transferred to the Army. The operation of the defence system was in charge of Field-Marshal Lord French, Commander-in-Chief, Home Forces.

Lighting restrictions was the sphere in which the civil authorities, in the person of the Home Secretary, made their first major administrative contribution to the problem of air raid defence. An Order in

---

[1] H. A. Jones, *The War in the Air* (Official History of the War of 1914–1918, Vol. III, 1931, p. 243). The whole of the present section is much indebted to this account.

Council of 12th August 1914, made under Section 1 of the Defence of the Realm Act,[1] which empowered the competent naval or military authority at any defended harbour to order the extinction of all visible lights during specified hours was the first regulation giving power to control lights. About a month later the first general regulation was made authorising the Home Secretary to issue orders for the extinction or dimming of lights in any specified areas. At the request of the Commissioner of Metropolitan Police, whose appeals to the public in the matter had been ineffective, the Home Secretary issued on 1st October 1914 a comprehensive order relating to London which introduced drastic 'dimming' of the metropolis.

Elsewhere in the country lighting restrictions became the subject of some confusion due to the fact that the Home Office, Admiralty, War Office and many local naval and military authorities were all concerned with them. Individual naval and military commanders soon adopted the practice of calling for aid from the civil power, in the shape of the local police, in enforcing their regulations. After many conferences between the three Departments, decisive action was taken to introduce more uniformity. Responsibility for lighting restrictions was concentrated in the Home Office, which issued a series of general orders on the subject on 8th April 1915; all existing orders made by the naval and military authorities were revoked.

A civil Department was thus, in one important sphere of defence and in a spirit of empiricism rather than of logic, given authority overriding that of the two Service Departments. After the big attack on the Midlands already referred to, lighting restrictions were extended to cover the whole of England except six western counties. Many local authorities in these exempted counties asked, however, to be included in the restriction schemes.

The problem of warning proved more difficult of solution. In the first phase of the war distribution of warnings had been entrusted to Chief Constables. Here again the Midlands attack, by causing an epidemic of false reports which in turn caused widespread stoppages of work, brought radical reform. At the urgent request of the Cabinet, Lord French was asked to prepare a new warnings scheme, which came into permanent operation on 25th May 1916.[2] This was based on the division of England, Wales and Southern Scotland into eight 'warning controls', each in charge of a 'warning controller' who represented the Commander-in-Chief, Home Forces. The warning control areas and the many smaller 'warning districts' into which each of these was divided corresponded to the telephone organisation of the country. The military authorities now became responsible for initiating the warnings, which were disseminated by civilian

---

[1] 4 and 5 Geo. 5, Ch. 29.
[2] See H. A. Jones, *op. cit.* Vol. III, pp. 171–178.

telephone operators in accordance with 'warning lists' prepared beforehand by the police.

The warning controllers had various sources of information about the movements of hostile aircraft. The most important, an elaborate system of observer posts, deserves brief mention because in this instance transfer of responsibility took place in the reverse direction. Manned originally by soldiers unfit for more active service, the majority of these posts throughout Britain were taken over by the police in December 1917.

This warning organisation seems to have worked well during the remainder of the war. It was concerned, of course, with operational needs, including the warning of factories on war work, and did not at first include any arrangements for warning the general public.

The controversial issue of public warnings did not become acute until the second chief phase of air bombardment, the daylight attacks by heavier-than-air craft of 1917. During the summer of 1916 the improved technique and organisation of Britain's defences finally got the measure of the *Zeppelins*. The Germans, suffering serious losses, correctly decided that there was no future for this weapon, at least in attacks on Britain. Since bombing attacks by aeroplanes had so far been only 'tip-and-run' affairs the winter of 1916–1917 introduced a welcome lull for the British people and the defences, comparable to the lull of 1943 or the spring of 1944 before the opening of attack by 'V-weapons'.

Lighting restrictions were, as a result, eased and the defences reduced. But in May 1917 the Germans began a series of assaults with twin-engined aircraft, called *Gothas*, which soon became severe. The daylight attack of 13th June on London by fourteen *Gothas* was the worst single attack of the war measured in casualties, which numbered 162 killed and 426 injured; 118 high explosive and incendiary bombs were dropped on the City and the East End. This raid, according to one authority, 'stirred the country'; and it was followed by another on 7th July against roughly the same targets which also caused many casualties as well as material damage estimated at £205,000.

Public feeling was now deeply roused, with indignation against the enemy and irritation at what were regarded, rightly or wrongly, as deficiencies in the defences. After the second big London raid the War Cabinet appointed General Jan C. Smuts as its special adviser on home defence against air raids, as well as on British air organisation in general. The reports he made to the War Cabinet cannot be summarised here[1]; though it must be mentioned that his proposals on air organisation had an important influence on the creation in April 1918 of a separate air service, the Royal Air Force.

The changes which followed mainly concerned the military aspects

---

[1] See H. A. Jones, *op. cit.* Vol. V (1935), Appendices 6 and 7.

of the defence system. What is of more interest to this narrative is the development from the summer of 1917 of greater public nervousness under attack or the threat of attack. The strain of war had by this time been considerable, even for those not on active service. It is not surprising that sections of the public began to demand with some urgency that the Government should institute public warnings and provide public shelters. There was talk, doubtless originating from troops on leave from Flanders, that the enemy would soon employ poison gas against the British people in their homes.

The Government only gave in gradually and reluctantly to demands for public warnings in London. In July 1917 a system was introduced, under the control of the Commissioner of Police, which to those accustomed to the sirens of 1939–45 may appear somewhat primitive. Warnings were distributed partly by maroons (or sound bombs) fired into the air, and partly by policemen on foot, on bicycles or in cars carrying *Take Cover* placards and blowing whistles or sounding horns.[1] By late summer the Germans had abandoned daylight raids and turned to the new tactic of aeroplane attacks by moonlight. In December, after much further discussion, public night warnings for London were introduced, but only with a strict time-limit. It was not until March 1918 that the Home Secretary, on the advice of the Commissioner of Police, authorised the use of maroons at any hour of the day or night.

The problem of providing public shelters began to assume big proportions towards the end of 1917. The daylight attacks of the summer had caused large crowds to seek shelter in the Underground stations; and the moonlight attacks of September had brought a tendency to panic among a section of the people in the East End, well aware of the fragile nature of their dwellings. 'Trekking' into the safer western districts of London became a common practice.

The Commissioner of Police allowed police stations to be used as shelters, and other authorities in charge of public buildings followed suit. After a committee under the chairmanship of the Home Secretary had reported, the Government decided to extend this use of public buildings, and also by an Order-in-Council of October 1917, introduced the requisitioning of premises to serve as shelters. Sandbags were issued at the national expense. The provision of shelters in the provinces continued to be regarded by the Government, in spite of pressure, as a matter for the local authorities. A good deal of work on the provision of shelters, including the adapting of such places as mine workings and caves, was in fact carried on outside London.

By the spring of 1918 the threat was dwindling, though at the time this was by no means obvious even to experts. It is argued by the

[1] See Col. W. T. Reay, *The Specials: the story of the Metropolitan Special Constabulary* (1920).

official historian of the topic that the German High Command's failure to stage a night-bombing campaign against London to coincide with Hindenburg's March offensive was one of its major strategical mistakes. During this period the War Cabinet was engaged in discussing the possibility of large-scale attacks on London by as many as 500 aircraft and of fires being started on a scale beyond the capacity of the fire brigade to handle, as well as the advisability of taking large anti-gas precautions. But the tide was, in fact, already on the turn. The last attack on London which occurred on Whit Sunday, 19th-20th May was also the last serious one of the war on any part of Britain.

Presented as a statistical sum, with the number of enemy raids and aircraft engaged, tonnage of bombs dropped and casualties caused as its components, this experience of air attack on Britain during 1914–18 no longer looks very formidable. There were in all 103 bombing raids (51 by airships and 52 by aeroplanes); and about 300 tons of bombs were dropped causing 4,820 casualties, 1,413 of which were fatal. London bore a large share of the attack, since about one-quarter of the total number of bombs were dropped on the Metropolitan Police District, causing death to 670 persons and injury to some 1,960.

These totals appear small; but when they are broken down into details many different pictures emerge. The two heavy raids on London of June and July 1917, for example, together caused 832 casualties (216 fatal), which amounted to 121 casualties for each ton of bombs dropped; and these casualty figures were to have much significance for the planning authorities of the future. The Midlands attack of January 1916 caused a degree of public nervousness out of all proportion to the total material damage it inflicted. Instances of individual attacks, like that on Odhams Press, Long Acre early in 1918, causing an amount of destruction or alarm which defied the averages could easily be multiplied.

The conclusion, in any case, the authorities reached was that these air attacks on Britain were overwhelmingly justified on military grounds by the results. Men, material and money had been diverted on a large scale from other purposes to Home Air Defence. The output of munitions and other factories had at certain periods been seriously curtailed. The killing and injury of civilians in their homes in a country which had not been invaded was a new feature in war, about the importance of which as an item in the military account there may have been some difference of expert opinion. No doubt, however, was felt that the behaviour of the population under this form of attack had been a most significant factor in the general war effort.

An attempt has been made in these pages to emphasise the main aspects of the experience of 1914-1918 with which the civil authorities were concerned, and to show that the role of these authorities was in most spheres subordinate to that of the Service Departments and local military commanders. The importance of the part performed by what was already being called 'passive defence' did not, however, escape official recognition. An official summary of the matter made after the war was over concluded: "The effective organisation of the 'passive' defence was of great importance from the military point of view".

Epilogue, or Prologue?

The Committee of Imperial Defence, created in 1904 and absorbed into special War Cabinet machinery on the outbreak of war, was re-established in November 1919. The highest organ, under the Cabinet, for planning defence measures from 1904 to August 1914, it was to perform the same function until September 1939, reinforced after 1924 by the creation, as a permanent part of the machinery concerned with defence, of the Chiefs of Staff Committee.

In November 1921 the Committee asked the principal Service experts to report on the problem of possible future air attack on the United Kingdom. This report, which appeared the next year, accepted the conclusions of the Air Staff about future air attack, which were briefly as follows. France was taken as the hypothetical enemy since the French Air Force was the only such force on the Continent in a position to make such an attack—not that the Government in any way anticipated war with France, but this hypothesis gave the military thinkers a basis from which to start diagnosis and planning. France's Air Force could drop an average weight of 1,500 tons of bombs on Britain each month by using only twenty bombing days in the month and only fifty per cent of its aircraft. London, which would be an enemy's chief objective, could be bombed on the scale of about 150 tons in the first 24 hours, 110 tons in the second 24 hours, and 75 tons in each succeeding 24 hours for an indefinite period. It was to be anticipated that an enemy would put forth his maximum strength at the outset. And, as has already been noted, the view was expressed that the moral effect of such attacks would be proportionately much greater than the material damage.[1]

The picture thus presented of the rapid development in air warfare of the superiority of the offensive over the defensive caused some consternation in high quarters. Lord Balfour, then presiding over the Committee of Imperial Defence, drew the attention of the Prime Minister, Mr Lloyd George, to these conclusions in a note which emphasised the serious nature of the potential threat to London. In 1923 a further committee under Lord Salisbury's chairmanship reported that the situation described in this note had become 'slightly

---

[1] p. 6.

worse', since the Air Ministry now calculated that the French Air Force, unless adequately opposed, could (in theory) drop 168 tons on London in the first 24 hours, 126 tons in the second 24 hours, and 84 tons in each succeeding 24 hours for an indefinite period. It will be recalled that the total weight of bombs dropped by the Germans on Britain during 1914–1918 was about 300 tons.

These conclusions had, of course, much bearing on plans for the development of the recently-created Royal Air Force. But there was no longer room for doubt that, however strong the Royal Air Force might eventually become, the menace now presented to Britain by hostile air attack was grave. At a meeting in December 1923 of the Committee on the Co-ordination of Departmental Action on the Outbreak of War, the Air Ministry suggested that the Home Office was the appropriate Department to initiate a scheme of air raid precautions, and the Home Office concurred. In the following month the Committee of Imperial Defence decided to appoint an Air Raid Precautions sub-committee, under the chairmanship of the Permanent Under Secretary of State for the Home Department, and this decision was soon afterwards endorsed by Mr MacDonald's first Labour Government.

CHAPTER II

PLANNING:

(May 1924 – April 1935)

THIS committee met for the first time, under the chairmanship of Sir John Anderson, on 15th May 1924.[1] It met regularly during the first phase of its work which ended in 1929, and continued to function thereafter in somewhat altered form for a further six years. Its chairman, Permanent Under-Secretary of State at the Home Office since 1922, was destined to preside over its deliberations for nearly eight years.

The first year of the committee's work was the most active of the first five-year period; and it produced material for a comprehensive report which must be summarised in some detail. The international background of this year's work was that of transition between post-war disillusionment and differences and a more co-operative era. The differences caused through French occupation of the Ruhr and Germany's default on Reparations had been eased by the summer of 1924 by the fall of Poincaré and acceptance of the Dawes Plan for Reparations. But the pacific policy of M. Briand and the Locarno Agreements still lay somewhat in the future. At home, Mr Mac-Donald's minority Government was decisively rejected at the polls in October 1924 and Mr Baldwin was returned to power with a large Conservative majority.

The A.R.P. Committee was composed, besides its chairman, of six members, representing the Committee of Imperial Defence (in the person of its Secretary, Sir Maurice Hankey),[2] the three Service Departments, the Ministry of Health and the Office of Works. It at once used its power to co-opt additional members to secure representation of the General Post Office. The Air Ministry soon adopted the practice of sending two representatives, and from the autumn of 1925 the Board of Trade usually also sent two. Invitations to other Departments and official bodies (e.g. the Chemical Warfare Research Department) to attend particular discussions were issued fairly often.

The committee's terms of reference were 'to enquire into the

---

[1] The Air Raid Precautions Sub-Committee will usually be called in this chapter the A.R.P. Committee or simply the committee.

[2] Secretary to the Committee of Imperial Defence, 1912; Secretary to the (War) Cabinet, 1916; held both offices until retirement in 1938; member of the War Cabinet, 1939–40.

question of Air Raid Precautions other than Naval, Military, and Air Defences', and to prepare an annual report of progress with such precautions for the consideration of the Committee of Imperial Defence. Even within the bounds of this definition the subject, as the chairman remarked at the outset, was a wide one and presented a problem of much difficulty. The committee's task, in fact, was to examine all means by which the civil authorities could co-operate to make the policy of the Fighting Services effective. The chairman suggested the following seven main topics for discussion—warning, prevention of damage, maintenance of vital services, repair of damage, movement of the seat of Government, legislative powers required, and departmental responsibility for all action recommended. The second of these, the 'prevention of damage', embraced such considerable problems as lighting restrictions, camouflage, shelters, gas masks and evacuation of the civil population.

The Scale of Attack

At its second meeting the committee was given data by the Air Staff on the extent of the danger represented by Continental air attack. The Air Staff had revised its calculations of 1922 and 1923 noticed in the previous chapter, in an upward or less favourable direction.[1]

The scale of attack that might in their opinion be reasonably anticipated was now fixed at about 200 tons of bombs in the first 24 hours, 150 tons in the second 24 hours and 100 tons in each subsequent 24 hours. The conclusions that an enemy would exert his maximum strength at the outset and that London would be his main target were re-affirmed. Allowing for the best that the defence could do, not less than 50 per cent. of the bomb tonnages just mentioned might be expected to fall on some part of London; and the period of attack on a reduced scale after the first 48 hours would probably be at least a month. The Air Staff anticipated that an enemy would concentrate on daylight attacks, which (measured in bomb tonnages) would be three times heavier than night attacks. Both high explosive and incendiary bombs must be expected, though the existing type of French incendiary bomb did not offer serious menace to modern buildings unless these contained inflammable material. Use of poison gas was not considered likely, though the possibility of this could not be ignored.

The serious picture thus presented assumed its darkest tones when the Air Staff proceeded to estimate casualties. The 300 tons of bombs dropped in the 1914–18 attacks, the experts pointed out, had caused 4,820 casualties, or 16 per ton of bombs. The 832 casualties of the two big daylight attacks on London in the summer of 1917, however,

---

[1] pp. 12–13.

C

produced an average of 121 casualties per ton; and sixteen night raids on London in 1917–18 gave an average of 52 casualties per ton.[1] After weighting these figures with various factors, the experts concluded that 50 casualties (one-third of which would be fatal) per ton formed a reasonable estimate of casualties caused by air attacks of the future on densely-populated areas. For other areas this figure should be reduced in proportion to the actual density of population.

By multiplying tonnages which might be dropped on London by this figure of 50, the Air Staff reached the following formidable totals (which they regarded as conservative) of the probable scale of air raid casualties in London at the outset of another war:

	Killed	*Wounded*	*Total*
First 24 hours	1,700	3,300	5,000
Second 24 hours	1,275	2,475	3,750
Every subsequent 24 hours	850	1,650	2,500

Opportunity was again taken to emphasise the probable moral effects of modern air attack. The possibility of chaos in the community, arising from the moral collapse under bombardment of persons employed in vital services such as transport and lighting, was suggested.

These calculations presented the A.R.P. Committee with a formidable problem. To plan adequate precautions against attacks on this scale seemed almost impossible, and they turned to consider whether the most effective precaution and best use of whatever funds would be available might not lie in expanding the active defences. But consultations with the Chief of the Air Staff, Air Chief Marshal Sir Hugh Trenchard, produced neither reduction of the estimates just quoted, nor hope that even largely expanded defence forces would provide much immunity. The only course open to the committee, therefore, was to continue their inquiries 'with a view to mitigating, so far as possible, the evils attendant upon aerial bombardment'. The Air Staff calculations were accepted by the committee as the basis of these inquiries, and included in their first report with the comment that, although they found them alarming, they cast no doubt upon their soundness.

The A.R.P. Committee's First Report

At one of its earliest meetings the committee added a further main heading—education of the general public to realisation of the significance of air attack—to the seven listed earlier. It began examination of the total problem with the aid of memoranda on

---

[1] p. 11.

specific topics by official bodies and discussions in committee with the representatives of various Departments. Early in 1925 the Committee of Imperial Defence gave approval for Departments enquiring into this problem to begin confidential consultations with discreet persons outside Government circles. The committee itself only resorted to this practice on a few occasions, the most important of which in this first year was a discussion with the General Managers of the four chief Railway Groups.

Other action taken this year included submission to the Man-Power Committee (a principal sub-committee of the Committee of Imperial Defence) of a tentative list of the various 'anti-aircraft services' for which men would be required immediately on the outbreak of war, with the comment that an appreciable number of persons would be needed. At the committee's instigation lighting experiments were begun at the Oval cricket ground, and preparatory work was done on the problem of warning. One section of the warning organisation, the 'Observation System', had begun to take practical shape at the circumference of the planning effort. It will be recalled that the duty of manning most of the cordoned system of observation posts of the recent war had been transferred in 1917 from soldiers unfit for active service to the police.[1] The committee was informed in 1925 by the War Office representative (Maj.-Gen. E. B. Ashmore, who had been in command of the London defence system in 1917–18) that the Observation System, manned by unpaid civilian volunteers enrolled as special constables, had been re-established in Kent and Sussex and that practical tests of its efficiency were about to begin.

Though claiming to be no more than a first survey of the problem the report made detailed proposals under each of the eight principal headings of discussion. The summary which follows may seem to the reader of inordinate length, especially in view of the separation in time of these proposals from the outbreak of war. Nevertheless, they reflected the current official thinking on the problem. They represented a comprehensive—and in many respects masterly—effort of administrative planning which contributed much to the future.

The committee's admission, already noticed, of alarm at the Air Staff calculations was due primarily to realisation of the danger which might threaten London. No doubt they were familiar with this prophetic passage in General Smuts' first report of 1917[2]:

London occupies a peculiar position in the Empire of which it is the nerve centre, and we consider, in the circumstances, that its defence

---

[1] See p. 9.
[2] See p. 9.

demands exceptional measures. It is probable that the air raids on London will increase to such an extent in the next twelve months that London might through aerial warfare become part of the battle front.

The attacks of the winter of 1917–18 can hardly, as has been seen, be called the true fulfilment of this prophecy, which still lay in the future. But the emphasis General Smuts had placed on the defence of London acquired deep significance from the increased scale of attack. The committee reported that they had inquired whether, (i) the vital activities normally centred in and round London could be moved to a less exposed part of Britain, and (ii) the life of the nation could be maintained if these activities in the London area should be stopped or seriously curtailed—and had found the answers to both these questions to be a decided negative. They therefore concluded that the hypothesis in regard to London was crucial, and had felt compelled to concentrate their discussions and recommendations on the Metropolis.

Three further general comments on the extent of the menace must be noticed. The Air Staff had given emphatic expression to the view that, whatever defence measures might be adopted, the determining factor in defeating air attack would be the strength of the counter-attack carried out by Britain's bombing aircraft against the enemy in his own country. The committee reported their agreement with this view; and their conclusion that the *Rules of Aerial Warfare*, drafted by a Commission of Jurists at The Hague in the winter of 1922–23 provided no appreciable protection for a civil population against air attack. Apart from the question of how much confidence to place in international agreements, targets recognised as legitimate in these *Rules* would normally be situated so close to populous centres that even a discriminating enemy could not avoid injuring civilians and their property. Finally, the committee put on record that, in view of the seriousness of the menace, their recommendations could only be regarded as palliatives.

The Education of Public Opinion to Realisation of the Menace. The committee showed full agreement with the emphasis of the Air Staff on the serious moral consequences of air attack on the new scale. It was their function to suggest means by which such consequences might be avoided or alleviated; and this, which was to pre-occupy every subsequent committee concerned with air raid protection up to 1939, was far from easy. Part of the difficulty arose from the vagueness of the data offered by past experience. At some times and places during 1914–18 the British public, as this narrative has noticed, had reacted to air bombardment in a mood of indignation; at other times and places it had shown some tendency to panic. It was not surprising that individual members of planning bodies between the wars held various opinions on the vital subject of the probable public reaction to the sustained, heavy, attacks now possible.

Uppermost in the minds of this committee was the prospect of heavy continuous attacks striking the British public, if the phrase may be allowed, 'out of the blue'. They laid emphasis on the fact (undoubtedly true then and for many years to come) that the extent of the danger to which Britain, and especially London, were now exposed was not generally understood. Sudden attacks on a civil population mentally unprepared for anything of this magnitude would entail serious danger of panic on a large scale. The dilemma was posed which had doubtless exercised the highest authorities during 1914–18, and was to become more familiar as the technique of air warfare improved. Should the public be told beforehand in the interests of national safety of a threat that might never materialise? Or should the risk of maintaining secrecy be taken, in the hope that if the worst did happen the necessary courage and steadfastness would be forthcoming?

The remedy proposed by the committee favoured the second of these two courses. They recommended, first, preparation of a Royal Proclamation for issue immediately on the outbreak of war which would outline conditions likely to result from air attack, emphasise the relief a vigorous counter-offensive would afford, stress the absolute necessity of maintaining vital activities, and call on the people loyally to obey any orders and instructions the authorities might make, as well as to exhibit their tried qualities of courage and endurance in danger. But until war actually occurred, the education of the public in this matter should only, the committee concluded, be slow, gradual and deliberate. Consultations had already been authorised between Departments and certain persons outside Government circles. The process of letting responsible persons into the secret should, the committee thought, be expanded. It would be expanded still further if the recommendations made later to train the police, fire brigades and other bodies for special duties in relation to air raid defence were adopted. By such means awareness of the extent and possible consequences of the threat would develop among a portion of the public, and this would be combined with knowledge that steps were being taken to avert or minimise the danger.

The concluding remark of the committee on this topic deserves quotation. 'It has been borne in upon us', they said, 'that in the next war it may well be that that nation, whose people can endure aerial bombardment the longer and with the greater stoicism, will ultimately prove victorious.'

The Warning System. It is important for the future history of this matter to note that the committee's views on it were conditioned by the experts' conclusion that continuity would be an outstanding feature of future air attack. Bombing during 1914–18 had been episodic rather than continuous. Nevertheless, the experience of warnings gained in these attacks, and the successful operation of the system set up in 1916, offered firm data for the committee's examination of this problem.[1]

Experience had proved that interruption of work in factories and elsewhere was a serious by-product of air attack; under continuous bombardment it might well become a major item on the debit side of the account. Instances were not uncommon during 1914–18 of workers refusing to attend factories until they had been given definite promises of early warning of the approach of aircraft; the demand from 1917 onwards for extensions of public warning in London had been insistent. It seemed clear that to accede to demands of this kind by introducing a general warning system immediately on the outbreak of war would be to help the enemy to attain his objects.

The committee proposed that such a system should be worked out in advance, but that it should be left to circumstances after the emergency had arisen to dictate whether this should be put into operation. They outlined in some detail the form which this general system should take. They distinguished between, (i) collection of information by various methods regarding enemy activity which was a Service responsibility, and (ii) distribution of information to the threatened areas and the public, for which the Services and the Home Office shared responsibility. The first function would depend primarily on a system of observation posts which, the last war had proved, could be most efficiently worked through the police. The new network of such posts in Kent and Sussex manned by volunteers enrolled as special constables had successfully passed its first practical tests.

The second function, or warning proper as distinct from observation, was more complicated. The committee first divided air attacks into two main classes on a principle, it is of interest to note, similar to that adopted by Lord Balfour in 1903 for the classification of hostile invasions. Attacks on a scale which might cause much damage and destruction were called 'mass attacks'; those of a less ambitious kind designed mainly to distract and alarm were called 'raids'. A clear demarcation between these two classes should, the committee thought, be established by the Air Staff prior to the outbreak of hostilities. 'Mass attacks', they went on to propose, should alone be considered fit occasions for the issue of warnings to civil organisations; 'raids' should be disregarded for this purpose. After distinguishing between two types of attack, the committee went on to distinguish between two classes of warning. They considered the system should arrange for, (i) a preliminary warning issued only to authoritative bodies such as the police, fire brigades and some industrial concerns

---

[1] See pp. 8–9.

which required time to put their anti-aircraft measures into operation, and (ii) the warning proper to be issued fifteen or twenty minutes later when the attack was imminent. The purpose of this proposal was, of course, to reduce as far as possible the period in which normal activities would be interrupted.

The details of the whole system, it was suggested, should be worked out by the Home Office in consultation with the Air Ministry, War Office and General Post Office. The Home Office should be responsible for compiling lists, to be periodically reviewed, of persons to whom warnings of the two kinds would be sent. Since distribution would be entirely dependent on the public telephone system it was important, from the mechanical point of view, to keep the number of these recipients within strict limits.

The committee held decided views on the advisability of issuing a public warning or 'general alarm'. They deprecated resort to this unless conditions in a particular town or district made it clearly desirable. They advised that discretion in this matter should rest with local authorities, who should be told it was national policy to discourage public warnings. In London it would rest with the Government to determine whether a general alarm was required at the outset of hostilities. This recommendation, it may be remarked, has incidental interest as one of the only three passages in the report in which reference is made to local authorities.

The formidable problem of the *Prevention of Damage* was approached by distinguishing between, (i) measures to increase the difficulties confronting attackers, (ii) measures to protect persons and property and, (iii) what was described as 'evasion'. Protection against poison gas, originally included under this heading, had now been given the status of a separate topic.

The first class of measures comprised, (i) lighting restrictions, and (ii) concealment. The committee frankly confessed themselves somewhat baffled by the divergent views expressed about the efficacy of the lighting restrictions adopted in 1914–18. There had been occasions during the war when in some places, for example the London parks, lighting had been not reduced but increased in order to confuse the enemy. The official historian later expressed the view, strongly held in some official quarters, that 'there is no doubt that the darkening of English cities was overdone' during 1914–18.[1] The degree of success achieved by severe restrictions in misleading the enemy had, according to this school of thought, been outweighed, once efficient warnings had been introduced, by the psychological and material disadvantages.

The committee decided that more practical experiment was required before they could recommend any particular measures of lighting restriction. Experience in 1914–18 pointed clearly to the

[1] H. A. Jones, *op. cit.* Vol. V, p. 3.

necessity for the issue of lighting regulations to be vested in one central authority, which should continue to be the Home Office. The Fighting Services should, in general, be asked to conform with respect to their property with lighting regulations issued by the Home Office.

The question of 'concealment' received only brief treatment. The committee had concluded that the enemy would probably not try to secure high accuracy of bomb-aiming but would be content with indiscriminate bombardment of the capital. To mask the mass of London—Cobbett's 'Great Wen' grown to such further sprawling proportions—did not appear feasible. Smoke screens had not yet been developed to give adequate cover to large areas from the air, and were very costly to operate. The best that could be done was to press on with practical experiment in the hope that means would ultimately be found of concealing restricted areas of vital importance.

Measures of protection included not only the problem of shelters, but the wider subject of protection of public buildings and those of national importance. The committee were not sanguine about the prospect of modern buildings withstanding direct hits from bombs employed in a future war but they thought that adequate protection should be possible against fragments and near misses. What was immediately required was technical data, which could only be obtained by direct experiment, about the damage caused by bombs of 500 lbs. and upwards. The War Office had already been asked to begin experiments on this question, and the Air Ministry and the Office of Works should be taken into consultation. Once the essential information had been obtained, the Office of Works should be asked to prepare plans for provision of public shelters and the protection of national buildings.

The subject of 'evasion', or evacuation as it was alternatively described, is so fully treated elsewhere in this series[1] that only brief attention to the committee's views on it is called for here. Inquiries, it has been noticed, had brought the definite conclusions that, (*a*) no appreciable portion of the activities normally centred on London could be moved to a less exposed area, and (*b*) the life of the nation could not be maintained if these activities in London's area should be stopped or seriously curtailed.[2] The metropolis, the committee had been informed, 'might be taken as representing approximately one-third of the belligerent strength of the nation'. It was clearly necessary to rule out all consideration of its wholesale evacuation, and to concentrate on the opposite policy of bending every effort to maintain its vital functions.

Yet though necessity seemed to demand that the London public should remain at their posts the committee was deeply impressed,

[1] R. M. Titmuss, *op. cit.*
[2] p. 18.

as this narrative has shown, by the moral effects of attack, including the possibility of panic among sections of congested urban populations. They were also fully aware of the limitations imposed, even in grave emergency, on Government regulation in Britain by democratic methods and a democratic outlook, and recorded their belief that the public would not tolerate drastic regulations forbidding all movement. They therefore recommended that, while those concerned with maintaining London's vital activities should be encouraged or even required to stay at work, *les bouches inutiles* (or more politely those, especially women and children, whose functions were dispensable) should be both encouraged and helped to leave. Such help would require much detailed advance planning, especially with regard to transport, accommodation, food and education; and it was proposed that the Ministries of Health and Transport and the Boards of Trade and Education should draw up schemes for these matters. Encouragement of *les bouches inutiles* to put discretion before valour should take the form of full official instructions issued immediately war broke out, either in the Royal Proclamation already proposed[1] or in a special communiqué. These, besides stating official policy, should urge the need to avoid panic and advertise arrangements for transport and accommodation.

The problem of evacuating art treasures and other valuable movable property was more manageable. The Office of Works should be charged with this responsibility and with that of devising means by which important records, such as those in Somerset House, which could not readily be moved might be protected.

The Maintenance of Vital Services, and *Departmental Responsibility for all Action Recommended*. It will be apparent that in the important matter of suggesting allocation of responsibility for the many duties involved to Departments and other bodies the committee had been proceeding in a practical rather than an *a priori* manner. It was not their business, they pointed out, to make concrete proposals regarding matters which were properly the concern of the Departments. They had confined themselves to compiling, after consultations with these, a list of the various schemes which in their view Departments should prepare. This list represented, in effect, an agreed distribution of air raid precautions' functions between the different branches of Government. Twelve Departments and six standing or special committees were involved. For most of these drafting of schemes would entail considerable work, including many inquiries outside official circles, spread over a long time. After Departments had been able to work out schemes and discover the details requiring legislation, they were to take up these points directly with the War Emergency Legislation Committee.

[1] See p. 19.

But this principle of what may be called dispersal of official responsibility was not, the committee well realised, sufficient. The Departments' detailed schemes would need to be dove-tailed and brought within a single plan, for which purpose a standing A.R.P. Committee should be established.

The Committee's remarks on maintaining vital services amounted to little more than enumeration of these (e.g. transport and water supply) with suggestions as to which Department should draft schemes regarding them. But one topic discussed in this context requires fuller notice. It has been mentioned above that early in 1925 the committee had sent the Man-Power Committee a list of the different 'anti-aircraft' services for which men would be required immediately war broke out.[1] The adjective employed is of some historical importance. For it had commonly been used during 1914–18 to indicate all the services, military and civilian, in any way engaged in Home Air Defence; and the committee was still using it in this sense, while careful to disavow its own responsibility for those engaged in military defences. In another war, as the committee envisaged it, all civilians who remained at work in the danger zone would be performing 'anti-aircraft' service. And the list sent to the Man-Power Committee comprised those familiar emergency and utility services—such as ambulance, fire brigade, gas and road transport services—which, being subject to exceptional strain under air attack, would require additional manpower. No conception, that is to say, had yet emerged of specialised A.R.P. services. In so far as duties would arise which could not be regarded (like decontamination after gas attack by municipal street-washers) as an extension of the functions of an existing service these would fall upon the police and special constabulary.

It is also interesting to note that the committee, envisaging all civilians remaining at their posts in the danger zones as performing service merely by so doing, were seriously concerned with the problem of how to keep them 'on the job'. They suggested, first, that the Treasury should draw up schemes for disablement pensions or insurance as an inducement to remain at work. But in case such inducements should be insufficient, advance schemes should be prepared whereby workers would be enrolled in order to secure discipline.

The Form of Control, though one of the last topics to be dealt with, claims attention after the proposals just noticed. Its treatment by the committee must be described as ambiguous, since the type or degree of control envisaged is nowhere defined. It appeared to them that some form of control applicable to the whole population must be in readiness for adoption immediately a war broke out. They discussed the alternatives of military control or some form of civilian

---

[1] p. 17.

control, and decided in favour of the latter. This infant prodigy, still obscure in shape and character, was therefore deposited in the bosom of the Home Office who would be aided in the task of rearing it by the nation's police forces.

The Repair of Damage to persons and property was briefly discussed. Calling attention to the formidable estimate of 2,500 casualties in London every 24 hours (after the first 48 hours, during which the rate would be higher), the planners emphasised the elaborate peacetime arrangements needed to provide an adequate number of doctors, ambulances, hospitals and burial grounds. These problems fell clearly within the jurisdiction of the Ministry of Health. They also pointed out that the fire brigades (like the ambulance services) were responsible to a large number of independent authorities, and lacked adequate reserves of manpower. Being convinced that in future air attack the fire brigades, especially in London, would be faced with abnormal demands they advised that the Home Office should prepare schemes for establishing central control over them, and for expanding them should this prove necessary. They also drew attention to the probable magnitude of the tasks of demolishing half-destroyed buildings and clearing debris from the streets.

The committee gave much attention to the problem of the *Movement of the Seat of Government*, weighing the advantages of safeguarding the central administration by removing it from the capital against the moral depression in the country and throughout the Empire which this exodus would undoubtedly cause. Though recognising that the question could only be settled by the Government in office when the emergency arose, they clearly stated their view that the moral aspects of the matter outweighed the advantages of removal. But they recommended that the Office of Works should make plans for both partial and total evacuation of Whitehall should these courses be dictated by the enemy. Though Departments should stay in their present offices as long as circumstances permitted, plans must in any case be laid for alternative accommodation for isolated 'casualties' within a radius of two miles of Whitehall. Partial removal, should this be necessary, should take the form of first evacuating the Departments least concerned with active prosecution of the war —perhaps *les Ministères les moins utiles*. In the case of complete evacuation becoming necessary Birmingham and Liverpool might be suitable alternative centres for the seat of Government.

Anti-Gas Measures. Poison gas, first used by the Germans near Ypres in April 1915, ranks with aircraft, the submarine and the tank as one of the four chief new weapons of war introduced during 1914–18. Rumours that the Germans would drop gas on the British people from aircraft had been in circulation, particularly in London, during the latter half of the war; by 1918 the War Cabinet had been giving serious consideration to the question of taking large civil anti-gas precautions. The problem, therefore, was not new; and it had acquired a considerable deposit both of battle experience and technical study.

The latest fruits of this study had recently been reported to the Committee of Imperial Defence by the Chemical Warfare Committee in a document called *The Protection of the Civil Population against Gas Attack*. The A.R.P. Committee referred to this report with approval, but recorded that the proposals of the Chemical Warfare Committee had been at variance with their own as regards, (*a*) the form of control to be adopted, and (*b*) issue of warnings to the public. The latter body had emphatically recommended that the central authority which should command the whole scheme of gas protection should be military, and had advised in favour of immediate public warnings. After discussion, however, the A.R.P. Committee had secured the concurrence of the chemical warfare experts with its own, oppo-site, proposals. They disagreed with the arguments for public warn-ings at the outbreak of war since they concluded it was unlikely that gas would be used in the first stages, and that time would therefore be granted to learn from experience whether a general alarm was necessary. They based this conclusion on the facts that France had adopted a formula undertaking to refrain from using gas as a weapon of war provided that her antagonist made a similar undertaking, and that the Washington Convention on this subject had recently been re-affirmed by the League of Nations Conference on Arms Traffic at which most nations of the world, including Germany, had been represented.

Otherwise, the planners confined themselves to advising that four subjects should receive special attention: (i) The service of decon-tamination, which was of the highest importance and should be put into an efficient state as soon as possible; (ii) the problem of gas-proofing buildings which should be investigated by the Office of Works in consultation with the Chemical Warfare Committee; (iii) training, which should begin without delay, of the police in anti-gas measures, the use of gas-masks and protective clothing, and (iv) the spreading as widely as possible of knowledge about the nature of poison gas attacks and the measures which could be taken to guard against them.

Progress, 1926 – 1929

In approving this report the Committee of Imperial Defence agreed that the A.R.P. Committee should become a standing committee and continue its inquiries with the same terms of reference. In addition, they submitted the report to the Cabinet, with particular reference to the topics of education of the public and removal of the seat of government. They authorised Departments to make the preparations just described provided no expenditure was incurred without Treasury authority; and took special note of the Chemical Warfare Committee's report on *The Protection of the Civil Population against Gas Attack* already alluded to, and a Board of Trade report on *The Supply of London in the event of the Port of London being wholly or partially closed.* The Board of Trade was asked to continue its investigations and to examine the best means of maintaining distribution machinery in London and other objectives, and the provision of supplies to areas which might become congested by the influx of refugees. Finally, the Committee asked Departments to give all assistance possible over experiments concerning protection against air bombardment and gas attack. Action of this nature was, of course— and the point requires emphasis—subject to the financial proviso just mentioned.

Before noting the conclusions of Mr Baldwin's Cabinet on the two matters specially referred to it, a few remarks must be made on the political background to the planning of the next four years. By early 1926 what seemed at the time and for some years to come a solid contribution to harmony had been achieved. Austen Chamberlain, Briand and Stresemann had concluded in October 1925 at Locarno agreements which Mr Chamberlain felt able to call 'the real dividing line between the years of war and the years of peace'. The year of the Locarno Treaties, according to an historian of the epoch, 'marks definitely the conclusion of a period of preliminary settlement, and the start of a "policy of fulfilment" which promised at least a temporary stability'.[1] Admission of Germany to the League of Nations and the opening of the League's Preparatory Commission on Disarmament soon followed. Two years later the Briand-Kellogg Pact for 'outlawry of war' was enthusiastically received by world public opinion and signed by almost every State. By 1930, according to the authority just quoted, 'all over the world there appeared at first sight to be solid material for satisfaction'.

Britain shared during 1925–29 in this mood of growing optimism and in the world economic recovery which accompanied and fortified it. The Conservative victory of October 1924 ended minority government and gave Mr Baldwin almost five years of power. Though the General Strike of May 1926 could only be regarded as a domestic disaster, this proved the end of a stormy phase of industrial relations. If the phenomenon of mass unemployment and the condition of Britain's staple industries were causing serious concern to some observers, the annual progress of trade in what was often described as a 'boom period' satisfied the more complacent and the less far-seeing.

Future historians may conclude that relief that Britain was emerging

[1] G. M. Gathorne-Hardy, *Short History of International Affairs* (1938), p. 139.

from the twin horrors of war and economic chaos, satisfaction with the progress being recorded and absence of any desire to look far beneath the surface of events were the main elements of Britain's public temper in the 1920's. The round of matrimonial strife, cocktails and brittle laughter of Mr Coward's characters doubtless portrayed the life of only a fringe of the society of that day. But the chief impresario of the time, Charles Cochran, was later to characterise the attitude of audiences of this period as predominantly one of 'cheerful unconcern'.

Mr Baldwin's Cabinet considered the two matters particularly referred to it by the Committee of Imperial Defence in December 1925.[1] They decided that the question of moving the seat of Government should for the present remain in abeyance; and that the improvement in international conditions caused by the Locarno Agreements made the moment ill-timed for positive steps to educate the public about the threat represented by enemy air attack. The gradual dissemination of knowledge through inquiries of Departments and sub-committees of the Committee of Imperial Defence would be sufficient, though the Committee was asked to keep the problem under review.

When the A.R.P. Committee was reconvened on 1st February 1926 some seven months had elapsed since its previous meeting. The Committee's composition was substantially unaltered by the change of status. At the re-assembly it discussed the method which should regulate its future inquiries, now that its first report had been approved by higher authority and instructions had been issued to Departments to make detailed investigations and draw up schemes. It was practically impossible, it decided, either to draw a picture of conditions likely to result from attack on the scale foreshadowed by the Air Staff or to lay down a set of general working conditions applicable to the very varied problems involved in air raid precautions. It concluded that the best procedure would be to ask Departments concerned with preparation of plans to attend its meetings with the two-fold object of (i) arriving (so far as possible) at a common conception of the conditions which would result from air attack, and (ii) elucidating points presenting difficulties in the drafting of particular schemes for which Departments were responsible.

Discussion of schemes with Departmental representatives had hardly begun before it was clear that much of the detailed planning depended on the answers to two questions. Would London's essential workers need to be prevented from leaving the capital? If so, what form of control should be adopted for this and other purposes? In discussion of a Ministry of Health report on *The Organisation of Medical Services in London* the chairman first expressed the view that a civil general staff

---

[1] pp. 26–27.

capable of organising the civil population would be an essential feature of air raid protection. This suggestion, with a number of other problems, was illuminated soon afterwards by the sensational event of the General Strike.

Depression in the coal industry had caused disputes which, after months of futile negotiation between the Government, owners and miners, ended in complete stoppage of the coalmining industry throughout the country. The day after the stoppage a Royal Proclamation was issued declaring a state of emergency, and the General Council of the Trades Union Congress ordered a general strike to begin forty-eight hours later. The state of feeling may be gauged from the fact that after a debate in Parliament on 3rd May, 'Members separated with a heavy heart, feeling that they were on the eve of a crisis comparable in its gravity to that which had existed at the outbreak of the war.'[1]

At midnight the railway and transport workers, printers, iron and steel and building operatives joined the miners in ceasing work, and the battle was joined. The country on the next day presented an unusual appearance, with practically no trains running, no public transport in the streets and no newspapers. But schemes prepared by the Government long beforehand were quickly put into operation. Under the authority of the Emergency Powers Act of 1920,[2] Britain was divided into eleven areas, each in charge of a Civil Commissioner with special powers for ensuring the maintenance of food supplies and essential services.[3] The Government had also organised Voluntary Service Committees throughout the country for the enrolment of volunteer workers. The response from the public was vigorous; in a short time many thousand volunteers were transporting food supplies by road, running trains and other services and acting as special constables. When first unemployed workers began to enrol freely and then strikers started to drift back in large numbers to work it became clear that the issue would be decided in favour of the Government unless the T.U.C. resorted to more drastic action. But the Council, after a half-hearted attempt to extend the strike, called it off on 12th May eight days after it had begun. The news was heard by Parliament and the public with much relief, and those responsible turned again to attempt to settle the coal industry's problems by negotiation.

The political issues of this strike are of less importance to this narrative than the machinery set up and the relationships established between the Government and the public under such unusual conditions. As an example of the latter factor, it will be recalled that on the second day of the strike the only newspapers procurable were the

---

[1] *Annual Register, 1926*, p. 49.

[2] 10 and 11 Geo. 5, Ch. 55.

[3] These were under the general direction of a co-ordinating Cabinet Committee on which fourteen Departments were represented.

news-sheets of the Government and the Trade Unions (the *British Gazette* and the *British Worker*), and the Paris edition of the *Daily Mail*; later *The Times* and other morning papers appeared in much attenuated form. The Government, in addition, made effective use of a broadcasting system which was just emerging from its experimental stage into the state of adolescence represented by some two million receiving licences. The system was used both to inform the public of the daily course of events, and as a vehicle for the broadcast of important messages by the Prime Minister, Mr Baldwin, in person. It is perhaps not irrelevant to add that sections of the Opposition were severely critical of the use to which the Government put these new broadcasting facilities, and that this criticism had its share in the decision, taken later in 1926, to entrust broadcasting to a public corporation free from direct Ministerial and Parliamentary control.[1]

The A.R.P. Committee gave close attention to the lessons afforded by the Strike. They decided it had effectively demonstrated the need for a civil general staff, and that ways of adapting the machinery recently in use to A.R.P. purposes should be examined. The other main relevant lessons were as follows:—police organisation had worked well, with the numerous police forces of the country showing ability to reinforce one another at need and to operate as a national force. This organisation had shown a capacity for almost indefinite expansion; the 80,000 special constables enrolled before the strike had grown after ten days to 200,000, the 8,000 of these in the Metropolitan area had expanded to 56,000. The country possessed resources of unexpected size in motor transport and personnel with mechanical skill. An efficient telephone system was indispensable in an emergency, and the work of telephone staffs was highly praised by the chairman. Finally, in the absence of newspapers the broadcasting of news to the public was of great importance.

This autumn the committee's discussions with the Ministry of Health led to the conclusion that the questions of provision of accommodation for refugees from London, and of a scheme for treatment of casualties, should be dealt with by *ad hoc* committees. Also, the committee drew the attention of higher authority to the fact that London's Underground Railways depended for power supplies on two generating stations (Lots Road and Neasden) which used a non-standard frequency; in the event of either or both of these being put out of action it would be impossible to draw supplies from elsewhere. They therefore recommended consideration of undertaking the costly process of transforming the stations over a period of years to the standard frequency of 50 cycles.

In March 1927 the committee was faced with two matters which,

---

[1] Royal Charter incorporating the British Broadcasting Corporation, *Wireless Broadcasting*, Cmd. 2756, 1926.

though not intrinsically of great significance, reintroduced important issues. Measures of defence against gas had continued to progress faster than schemes of defence in other spheres. Thus the Home Office had recently appointed an additional Inspector of Constabulary whose duties included making arrangements for police instruction in anti-gas measures. The Admiralty had appointed a special officer to work out anti-gas measures for the Portsmouth dockyards. The Chemical Warfare Research Department had been making experiments to determine how long persons could remain under certain conditions in a 'gas-proof' room; and had prepared a handbook, *The Medical Aspects of Chemical Warfare*, now on sale to the public. The allocation of responsibility for anti-gas measures had been determined. General guidance of the population in this matter fell to the Home Office, acting through the police; the treatment of casualties was the affair of the Ministry of Health, and decontamination must eventually be undertaken by the local authorities' sanitary organisations.

The first of the matters just referred to was a broadcast in February by Professor Noel Baker, on 'Foreign Affairs and How They Affect Us'. This, read in cold print at a distance of twenty years, appears as an attempt to rouse the British public to realisation of the horrors of future war, and to enlist its support for the disarmament negotiations at Geneva. The Professor quoted Mr Baldwin's speech to the Classical Association in the Middle Temple hall, 'Who in Europe does not know that one more war in the West and the civilisation of the ages will fall with as great a shock as that of Rome?' He painted a picture of gas attack from the air in another war and claimed, 'all gas experts are agreed that it would be impossible to devise means to protect the civil population from this form of attack'. The Chemical Warfare Research Department emphatically disputed the accuracy both of the details of the picture and of this general statement. They considered it unfortunate that statements of this nature should have been broadcast to the public, particularly after the Cabinet's decision that the time was not ripe for education of the public in defensive measures.[1]

The committee discussed whether to draw the B.B.C.'s attention to this talk. The Corporation, only a few months old, was then prohibited by the Postmaster-General's instructions from broadcasting 'matter on topics of political, religious or industrial controversy'; but the Post Office representative pointed out this did not mean that his Department was prepared to undertake censoring programmes. The committee, not wishing to incur the obligation to approve in advance all proposed broadcasts relating to their field of study, decided to take no action with respect to the talk in question.

[1] See p. 28.

D

The second matter was a description in a French official publication of the air raid precautions being adopted in the Soviet Union. This country had established an 'Aviation and Chemistry Society' (*Aviokhim*) for training and propaganding their citizens in air raid defence. An important feature of this body was the organisation in different centres of 'chemical detachments' to instruct civilians in methods of gas attack and anti-gas defence. The Chemical Warfare experts made the comment that, even if political reasons precluded instruction of the British population in these matters, steps should be taken to acquaint a wider circle of responsible authorities with the problems involved.

The committee agreed that further progress in many directions was no longer possible without some relaxation of the secrecy rules governing their inquiries. Confidential consultations with a few unofficial persons were no longer enough to cover the measures they wished to pursue. They therefore asked the Committee of Imperial Defence for authority to extend the scope of their consultations outside Government circles. They gave as concrete proposals for the way in which such extension might develop—(i) conferences (which had proved their value in the 1914–18 war) between central and local authorities and chiefs of fire brigades for the preparation of detailed arrangements for co-ordination of fire services in an emergency, (ii) training on a substantial scale of police and fire brigades in anti-gas measures, and (iii) consultations with local authorities about the form decontamination services should take. Such conferences, by involving an ever-widening circle of persons and organisations in the country, would further the aim of a 'slow, gradual and deliberate' education of the public.

These proposals were approved by the Cabinet in July. The committee noted with satisfaction in the autumn that relaxation of secrecy rules would enable Departments to carry preparation of schemes a stage further. They had already taken steps to create inter-departmental committees for various specific inquiries. They now drew the attention of the Committee of Imperial Defence to the growing concentration of industrial and commercial concerns in the London area, and suggested that the Principal Supply Officers Committee (one of the main sub-committees of the Committee of Imperial Defence) in making plans for the development of industrial activity under war conditions should rely as far as possible on undertakings outside the metropolis. The committee resolved to turn in the year ahead to closer examination of the central authority necessary for dovetailing schemes into one general plan.

While the committee was engaged in 1928 in examining this topic higher authority reached a decision of important bearing on the future of its work. It was in the summer of this year that the

Briand-Kellogg Pact, signed by almost every sovereign State, 'served as a magnificent advertisement of the pacific disposition of the world'.[1] The League of Nations Assembly hastened to implement the Pact with a 'General Act for the Pacific Settlement of International Disputes' open for the accession of all States. The Preparatory Disarmament Commission was framing a disarmament convention for consideration of a full-scale Disarmament Conference. In the optimistic atmosphere these events engendered the British Cabinet reaffirmed, for purposes of war preparation, that no major war was likely to occur for ten years.[2] This 'ten-year-rule', as it was called in official circles, had no beginning by the calendar but, like the rising sun, was new every morning. Until such time as the Government decided to revoke it, the possibility of major conflict was to be deemed on any given day as not less than ten years distant. This shifting yardstick (which was subject to annual review) was destined to remain in force for a number of years. It acted, it is hardly necessary to state, as a powerful curb on defence preparations of all kinds and on provision of public funds for defence. After a reference to this rule the chairman of the A.R.P. Committee stated that, as a result of financial stringency, the anti-gas training of the police and others had been postponed and provision for enlarging the Army Gas School was not being made in the 1929 Estimates.

Problem of the Central Organisation

Now that satisfactory, if often slow, progress was being made with Departmental schemes it had become essential, the committee concluded, to define more closely the central A.R.P. authority.

They began by considering the organisation needed in war, and worked back from this problem to determination of what should be established in peace. The main issue lay between adherence to what has been called here earlier 'dispersal of responsibility' and the creation of a special Ministry to deal with all aspects of protection of the civil population and maintenance of vital services. The committee decided readily for the first alternative, favoured in their first report[3] and the basis, in effect, of their inquiries of the past three years. Experience in these had confirmed their view that allocation of specific duties to existing Departments was a better method than creation of an *ad hoc* body to deal with the whole problem. The principle of grafting A.R.P. functions on to existing machinery and resources, hitherto proved satisfactory, should, they considered, be followed in war. Many of the measures which would

---

[1] G. M. Gathorne-Hardy, *op. cit.* p. 172.

[2] This assumption had first been made by the War Cabinet in August 1919, and had in effect governed the Estimates of the Defence Departments since that date.

[3] pp. 23–24.

have to be adopted in war were closely bound up with peace-time functions which would have to be continued whether or not a war existed. To attempt suddenly to divorce the purely war-time responsibilities of many Departments from peace-time ones would lead to much duplication and confusion. In strongly recommending that executive responsibility should rest with appropriate existing Departments, the committee did not overlook the possibility that in the stress of a crisis public demand for an A.R.P. Ministry might arise, and that political considerations might make it expedient to comply. Should such action become inevitable, the reorganisation would they thought be facilitated by their further suggestions.

If decentralisation of action to Departments became the guiding principle, there was clearly need for effective central machinery for the double purpose of co-ordinating policy and consultation over plans. Ultimate decisions on major policy issues would, of course, be taken by the Cabinet. But there would inevitably arise many day to day matters of less importance requiring policy decisions affecting more than one Department. To deal with such matters they proposed a committee of Ministers in charge of Departments most concerned with the problem, presided over in war by a Minister in the War Cabinet.

For the second purpose—consultation and co-ordination of Departmental plans—they found a model in the Chiefs of Staff Committee which had now become a permanent institution.[1] Members of this body, while still responsible as individuals for questions affecting their Service to their Board or Council, had a joint responsibility to advise the Committee of Imperial Defence on matters concerning all three Services and on Imperial defence. The committee suggested that a similar body be set up to examine and advise higher authority on all matters concerning 'what may be described as air raids precautions services'. Composed of officials from Departments directing A.R.P. functions, and presided over by the Permanent Under-Secretary of State at the Home Office, this body would ensure that action proposed by any Department was in harmony with the general scheme. In matters of higher policy they would refer to the Ministerial Committee, but all executive action would continue to be taken by the Departments concerned.

The final principle of this plan was that decentralisation to Departments should be accompanied by centralisation *within* Departments. All functions concerning A.R.P. within any Department should be brought under the immediate direction of one official, preferably the Permanent Head or one of his deputies.

Having proposed this machinery for war, the committee advised it should be set up at once. They continued to be strongly influenced

---

[1] p. 12.

by the conception of a 'knock-out blow'. No time need elapse, they reminded the Committee of Imperial Defence, between the declaration of war and the delivery of the first blow, and, what was more important, this blow might be directed against national interests and activities which in the past had lain comparatively immune from attack behind the shelter of the country's armed forces. It followed that A.R.P. organisation must be ready to function immediately, and should be in active working operation in peace. A definite plan, embracing every aspect of the problem, must be prepared in advance and kept ready. This required that central-isation *within* Departments should include planning sections. The committee's conception of a 'civil general staff' begins to take shape as the body of officials jointly composing these planning sections in the Departments most concerned. If the proposal to set up this machinery at once was approved, transfer from peace to war would be effected with the minimum of dislocation and delay.

There was a further cogent reason for the proposal that Ministers should be included at once in the organisation. The A.R.P. Com-mittee's chairman admitted that he was troubled by the fact that Ministers were not yet in close contact with the problems involved in this wide sphere of inquiry. After over four years' examination by officials and experts, with fair progress in surveying the whole field, collecting information and starting plans, a clear need had arisen for more positive Ministerial support.

It was breaking new ground to expect the Home Secretary, with his varied domestic responsibilities, to pay special attention in peace to foreign policy and defence. Yet his Department was, the committee reiterated, the one most concerned with the now formidable problem of protecting the civil population in war. The Home Secretary at this time, Sir William Joynson-Hicks,[1] it so happened, had developed interest in air warfare during 1914–18 and been a strong advocate of an independent air Service. He had served on the Civil Aerial Transport Committee (which laid the foundations of British civil aviation) and had agitated in Parliament and elsewhere for a stronger Royal Air Force. But it will serve as a reminder of the claims on the Home Secretary's attention to recall four controversies of 1928 with all of which Joynson-Hicks was prominently associated—the Shops (Hours of Closing) Act, 1928 which made certain restrictions of the unpopular war-time 'D.O.R.A.' permanent; the Representation of the People Act, 1928 (the 'Flapper Vote'); an agitation of serious proportions over the Metropolitan Police, and the stormy controversy over the new Prayer Book.[2]

---

[1] Born 1865; Home Secretary, 1924–29; cr. Visct. Brentford, 1929; died 1932.
[2] See H. A. Taylor, *Jix-Viscount Brentford* (1933).

The A.R.P. Committee recognised that Departmental officials would only be able to give 'a residual part' of their time and energy to studying war plans. But this defect in their scheme, they suggested, would be remedied by provision of an active secretariat with responsibility for seeing that progress did not languish, and that the reactions of the parts of the plan on one another were studied.

These recommendations were approved by the Cabinet at the end of January 1929. The new machinery, put into operation in the spring, was to bear responsibility for planning air raid precautions for the next six years. The committee, reconstituted as the 'A.R.P. (Organisation) Committee', with the same chairman and little change in its composition, remained the backbone of the planning organisation.

Before this reorganisation the committee had studied hospital accommodation, the location of lunatic asylums, the problem of shelters, and the enrolment and control of personnel for the various forms of 'anti-aircraft protection services'.

Discussion of the last important matter served to reveal the difficulties encompassing it, and the little progress so far made. Preliminary questions were still unsettled. For example, should some form of conscription be adopted? How were essential workers to be induced to remain at their posts? Was military or quasi-military control essential? The interpretation given to these services was still the wide one of almost everyone in the danger zones engaged in essential work; and the committee again emphasised the difficulty of keeping people 'on the job' and the need for some special degree of discipline. In agreeing that a form of mobile reserve would be needed to supplement and stiffen local labour, particularly at the opening of attacks, they turned for help to the War Office. Would the Army undertake to supply Territorials for this purpose, and to replace them later by special units on the lines of the Transport Workers' Battalions of the Great War? When the answer to this was discouraging, suggestions for forming such a reserve from special constables or from London medical students were considered and discarded. It was then agreed that the forming of a quasi-military organisation on the model of the St. John's Ambulance Brigade should be examined.

Other difficulties were well illustrated by the problem of shelters, responsibility for examining which lay with the Office of Works. This Department had produced various memoranda on the subject, the most recent of which by its Director of Works concluded: (i) it would not be possible to provide adequate protection for London's population in existing buildings, (ii) the cost of constructing special underground shelters on a large scale would be prohibitive, and (iii) the Tubes, though able to offer sound if limited protection, would probably be needed more than ever in war for transport. This report then put forward an elaborate scheme for evacuating thousands of London's citizens by underground railway to the safety which its authors assumed would begin on the city's outskirts where the railways ended.

In this sphere material resources assumed outsize proportions. The amount of bricks, mortar and concrete needed to build adequate shelters and the cost of providing these would, the Office of Works considered, be far too large to be viewed as practical possibilities. The A.R.P. Committee had no alternative but to accept the experts' negative conclusions, while recommending more detailed study and experiment. But the financial aspect appeared a serious impediment not only to any ultimate scheme of construction but to the immediate requirement of conducting essential experiments. It will be recalled that the committee's first report had emphasised the need for these experiments, which the War Office had been asked to initiate.[1] Both experience in this field of inquiry and the funds with which to begin experiments were lacking. The Service Departments alone possessed a measure of these essential ingredients of progress. But the interests of each of these in the effects of air bombardment differed from those of the other two and still more from those of the civil Department, and machinery to co-ordinate experiment and research seems to have been almost lacking. Stalemate over shelters early in 1929 was further aggravated by a clear, and apparently irreconcilable, conflict between the need to send the public underground for protection against high explosive and the need to keep them above ground for protection against gas. Practical experiment in defence against gas could in addition be conducted more cheaply and unobtrusively than experiment into the destructive powers of high explosive missiles.

Publicity, Personnel and Schemes, 1929–1932

The reconstituted or 'A.R.P. (Organisation) Committee' met in late April with terms of reference identical with those of 1924, except that concentration of the inquiry on London now received some formal recognition.[2] It is apparent that this body of officials had much continuity. Its familiarity with the complicated issues involved was of obvious advantage as plans approached nearer some practical application.

The next six years saw the collapse of the optimism prevailing in

---

[1] p. 22.

[2] In the remainder of this chapter the Ministerial (or Policy) Committee will usually be called the Ministerial Committee, and the reorganized Departmental or official Committee will be called the Organisation or simply the A.R.P. Committee. See pp. 34, 39.

1925–29. The United States stock-market 'crash' of October 1929 began an era of world-wide depression; and Mr MacDonald's minority Government soon found itself faced by grave problems, which issued in August 1931 in the formation of a National Government. The general election of that October returned the Conservatives in force, and reduced Labour to a small embittered Opposition. This confusion (as it must be regarded) of domestic politics had its consequences in foreign policy and defence preparations. The reaction of British parties and public to the growth of aggressive nationalism abroad was for long mainly one of bewilderment, and 'its old gift of political relevance appeared to have abandoned the nation.'[1]

A stage had been reached in planning at which progress depended on more relaxation of the secrecy rule. Some schemes could be developed no further without enlisting co-operation of the public. Financial resources for development could not be procured without Parliamentary and public discussion. Also, some awareness among the public of the potential threat to Britain and the steps being taken about it had throughout been regarded by the A.R.P. Committee as an essential precaution against panic. They attached such importance to this aspect of the problem that they made several attempts over the next four years to gain Committee of Imperial Defence approval for the introduction of more publicity. That these met with only moderate success was due to the trends of policy and opinion during the early 'thirties of which mention has just been made.

The Geneva Gas Protocol, aimed at probibiting gas and bacteriological warfare, had been signed by most European countries in 1925 and was about to be ratified by British and Dominion Governments. This instrument referred only to offensive use of poison gas, and did not restrain signatories from defensive preparations and research or from commercial traffic. In considering the situation created by Britain's ratification, the committee recognised that production of poison gas in quantity and secrecy in peacetime was relatively easy. But, while it would be unwise to decrease Britain's research and defensive preparations, the Protocol suggested the course of keeping these within existing bounds, and of reaffirming the original view that use of gas in the first stages of a war was unlikely.[2] The further development of anti-gas schemes would require the publicity now undesirable for reasons of high policy. To halt expansion in this sphere for the time being would enable the committee to concentrate on other problems (notably shelters), the size of which were such as to provide ample work.

---

[1] K. Feiling, *Life of Neville Chamberlain* (1946), p. 198.
[2] See p. 26.

They asked for approval from higher authority to relegate anti-gas measures to a secondary position. When the Committee of Imperial Defence gave consent to this the Prime Minister, Mr MacDonald, made evident the Government's concern with the harm which any misconstruction of the A.R.P. Committee's activities might cause.

The Ministerial (or Policy) Committee was set up in July 1929 and consisted of the Home Secretary (Mr J. R. Clynes), the Secretary of State for Scotland, the President of the Board of Trade and the Ministers of Health (Mr Arthur Greenwood) and Transport (Mr Herbert Morrison). The chairman of the Organisation Committee always attended its meetings.

In the autumn of 1930 the Organisation Committee sought authority both to reverse the policy adopted a year before with regard to gas and to give greater publicity to all A.R.P. schemes. The issue was still one of securing approval for discretion to consult local authorities and other responsible bodies outside the Government, to prepare schemes with their co-operation and to carry out practical tests. How slowly consultation with persons outside the Government had developed since the modification allowed in 1927[1] became more apparent to the planners after studying the practice in this matter of some foreign countries. It seemed that in France, Germany, Czechoslovakia and the U.S.S.R. instruction of the civil population in anti-gas and other air raid defences was regarded in much the same light as the British authorities regarded annual fleet exercises or territorial camps, and given similar publicity. The self-denying ordinance imposed on our preparations a year previously appeared, in view of this, superfluous, and had added to the difficulty of answering questions recently asked in Parliament about British defences.

Early in 1931 higher authority approved some relaxation of secrecy, subject to definite stipulations that consultations should be made with discretion and that every precaution should be taken to avoid misrepresentation. The Preparatory Commission on Disarmament had recently secured adoption of a Draft Convention, and the Disarmament Conference was due to meet before long at Geneva. This Conference, after including discussions of British proposals to abolish bombing from the air and recording a decision to prohibit chemical and bacteriological warfare, adjourned in July 1932. According to Sir Herbert Samuel, by then Home Secretary and a member of the British delegation, its adjournment was accompanied by 'good hopes of further progress'.[2]

The times, therefore, were not very favourable to another request by the A.R.P. Committee in October 1932, in more emphatic terms

[1] pp. 31–32.
[2] Viscount Samuel, *Memoirs* (1945), p. 223.

than on the last occasion, for permission to extend publicity. The relaxation already authorised had enabled the committee's net to be spread a little wider but had not eliminated the need to enjoin persons outside the Government who might be consulted to strict secrecy. Progress was still artificially restricted since, though 'many schemes had reached a stage of theoretical finality', it was proving almost impossible to proceed with practical implementation. In the meantime, Continental countries continued to act with full publicity. The French Government had appointed Marshal Pétain, the venerable hero of Verdun, as Inspector-General of Air Defence. Full-scale exercises had been held in the Pas-de-Calais and elsewhere in France, Königsberg and other Continental cities. Britain's preparations, though perhaps superior to those elsewhere in general design, had been definitely out-distanced in experimental application. Publicity, the committee concluded, was essential to efficiency, and at the best a good many years must elapse before efficiency was achieved. This request, after endorsement by the Ministerial Committee, was approved by the Committee of Imperial Defence, but subject again to the provisos that this action should be gradual and conducted with great caution.

Only slow advance was made in the years under review with the problem of personnel for the 'anti-aircraft emergency services'. The committee, when they returned to the question of the reserve of 5–6,000 disciplined men they regarded as an essential supplement to civilian labour, particularly at the outbreak of attacks, still hoped to persuade the War Office to supply this force.[1] The War Office, however, was still unwilling to do so on the ground that the duties of such a force would not be strictly military in character. The matter was considered in December 1930 by the Cabinet, which referred it back for further investigation. The A.R.P. authorities then re-affirmed their view, which was approved in the following March by the Committee of Imperial Defence.

The rate of progress during 1929–32 with particular schemes varied considerably.[2] Some had early in this period reached that 'theoretical finality' from which no real development could proceed until more consultation was permitted. Others, owing to lack of data, funds or time available to officials, had not reached the stage of rough sketches.

Among subjects well advanced by 1929 were provision for medical treatment of casualties, hospital accommodation, and the evacuation of wounded in the London area. Ministry of Health committees

---

[1] See p. 36.

[2] In the middle of this period the Organisation Committee compiled a Review of the Sub-Committee's Work, 1925-1930, which, by surveying the current position of the forty-five main recommendations of the A.R.P. Committee's First Report of 1925 (see pp. 16–26) demonstrated this inequality of achievement.

had collected a wealth of information on these problems; and the A.R.P. Committee obtained authority to harvest this into a detailed working plan, to include the appointment of persons to 'pivotal posts'. The problem of repairing damage to property had, however, made smaller progress by 1932. Though the Home Office Fire Adviser had supplied much information on fire-fighting organisation and methods, a great deal of preparatory work had still to be done. Investigation by a Ministry of Transport committee into problems of repairing roads and other main services had not yet produced conclusive results. Schemes for the clearance of debris and for decontamination awaited wider consultation with local authorities.

On the problem of maintaining vital services, the G.P.O. had produced a practical scheme for an emergency telephone service; investigations had taken place about maintaining London's gas supply; and, after much discussion, a committee was making progress with a scheme for compensation for personal injury. Regarding the various matters included under prevention of damage the advance by the end of 1932 was, in general, more halting. A plan for protecting London's docks was being completed in detail. But the larger problems of protecting the public by shelters and protecting public buildings were still complicated by lack of information. Aspects of the evacuation problem had been clarified by discussions on use of the Tubes. But by the autumn of 1932 the planners-in-chief were unable to report more than their continued belief in the policy of evacuating as many persons as possible from London, and their intention to reconvene a sub-committee to work out detailed plans.

Most active development of the warning system related to collection of information. Responsibility for this function had been transferred in 1929 from the War Office to the Air Ministry. In that part of England considered within range of hostile bombers the observation system, manned by volunteers of the Observer Corps, was in a sufficiently advanced state to be put into operation at any time.[1] Arrangements, which fell to the Home Office, for distribution of information were still at a preliminary stage.

Defence measures against gas had again made good progress. Designs of a 'Special Service' mask, cheaper to produce than the General Service mask, for the protection of persons required for important services (e.g., employees of some public utility concerns) had gone into preliminary manufacture. The A.R.P. Committee had discussed the question of gas masks for the civil population in general, but had not yet reached a conclusion on this matter. Practical progress had also been made in supply of gas-proof clothing for the police, the supply of bleaching powder and the inclusion of certain anti-gas features in new Tube stations.

---

[1] p. 20.

The Organisation Committee had now made a preliminary draft of an A.R.P. War Book, which they intended to enlarge as circumstances permitted. Early in 1932 Sir John Anderson, who had presided over this committee and its predecessor since 1924, resigned on being appointed Governor of Bengal. He was succeeded by the new Permanent Under-Secretary of State at the Home Office, Sir Russell Scott.

The Air Raids Commandant, and Origins of the National Organisation, 1932–1933

Study of preparations on the Continent also led to the next most positive step in British planning. In 1932 two documents on foreign activities engaged the A.R.P. Committee's special attention. One of these described a scheme by the *Reichsverband der Deutschen Industrie* in co-operation with the German Government for protection of German industry against air attack. The other was a detailed *Practical Instruction on Passive Defence against Air Attack* drawn up by M. Laval, the French Minister of the Interior, and on sale to the public for four francs. This included a complete scheme for organisation at the national, departmental and communal levels of French passive defence. The committee's reaction to this information was expressed by one member as a feeling that they had been 'left sitting on the fence'. Though British planning had started earlier and achieved more in general design, it had now been outstripped in practical application.

The planners turned to remedying this backwardness in organisation. The plan of 1928 under which the two existing committees, with the chairman of the Organisation Committee (i.e., the Permanent Under-Secretary of State for the Home Department) as chief administrative officer, would exercise control in war was seen to be inadequate.[1] Experience had shown that the scope and number of executive responsibilities in war would be much larger than then conceived. Furthermore, the Departmental Committee was finding itself faced with an accumulation of detail which had tended to clog the machine, to slow down the work and, conceivably, to obscure the main issues; some Departments were overburdened with detailed planning and A.R.P. responsibilities. The need for secrecy had played a major part in delaying delegation of much of this detailed work to some other authority who would ultimately be responsible for executing the various plans.

A proposal, arrived at after much discussion, was made to the Ministers about the form this new authority should take. The planners were still concentrating on defence of London, and they

---

[1] pp. 33–34.

dismissed as impracticable suggestions that the Borough Councils or the L.C.C. could perform the functions in question. 'A super local authority' for London, in between the boroughs and the Government, was required; and since no such organ existed it was necessary to invent one. This new A.R.P. authority for the London area might, the committee decided, be put in charge of the Governor of Chelsea Hospital or the Lieutenant of the Tower, with the title of 'Air Raids Commandant'. The senior officers holding these positions only had light duties, and the drawback that they were usually of advanced years could be surmounted by prior consultation with the War Office. The Commandant should have a small staff composed of a Chief of Staff and representatives of the Metropolitan Police, the Ministries of Health and Transport, the Board of Trade and (for advice on anti-gas measures) the War Office. He would be *ex officio* a member of the Organisation Committee which would continue, as heretofore, to supply the main directive force for A.R.P. and to effect co-ordination. But he should possess authority to translate into practical form the general principles given to him for guidance. Experience would show whether his organisation should prepare schemes, or whether this should be left to those who would be responsible for the schemes' detailed execution.

Although the Committee of Imperial Defence approved this plan in the autumn of 1932, it was not until April 1933 that an 'Air Raids Commandant (Designate)' began his duties. After being refused by the Governor of Chelsea Hospital, the appointment was accepted by Major-General H. L. Pritchard.[1]

This addition to the machinery had significance apart from its practical contribution in the next two years. It demonstrated the planners' continued belief that their problem was in large measure military, or at least quasi-military. London would become a battle-field, and special forms of discipline and control would be essential. The problem was a novel one; and search for the types of organisa-tion and leadership to secure this discipline and control was con-tinuous.

After adopting this novel expedient for London the committee turned to consider the organisation of air raid services in the country as a whole. At a meeting in March 1933 they discussed three national organisations which might be used—the police, the Emergency Strike Organisation (proved successful in 1926, and preserved in skeleton form), and the local government organisation. They decided with small hesitation in favour of the local government structure—a decision which, though to meet with many difficulties of application, laid a permanent corner-stone. They were aware that

---

[1] Born 1871; much active service as R.E. officer; former Commandant, School of Military Engineering; Col. Comdt. R.E. at date of this appointment; died 1953.

this might involve overloading central A.R.P. authorities, and agreed that some intermediate organisation would probably be needed. But their immediate concern was to examine the implications of the main decision, and they constituted four of their number into a sub-committee to consider its administrative and financial aspects.

This sub-committee soon produced important amplifications of the plan. Impressed with the need to keep down the number of A.R.P. authorities, they proposed that the administrative organisation should be provided by the County Boroughs within their normal areas and by the County Councils outside these areas; the non-County Boroughs and Urban Districts should only be A.R.P. authorities in exceptional cases. To effect co-ordination between these and relieve pressure on the centre, that part of the country liable to air attack should be divided into Regions, each under the general control of an 'Air Raids Commandant' directly responsible to the central authority. They specified the areas of England and Wales considered most liable to attack; and gave a plan for the siting and equipment of A.R.P. depots. On the cardinal issue of how the cost of this organisation and the bulk of A.R.P. equipment should be met they were unequivocal. The drain on the Government for evacuation and other matters, Continental practice, and the need to increase local awareness of the gravity of the problem together made this a legitimate charge against the local authorities.

Consideration of these proposals by the Ministerial A.R.P. Committee opened an era of greater participation by this body in planning. Ministers accepted readily (though provisionally) the proposals about organisation. But they (and in particular the Minister of Health) could not endorse the view that the main financial burden should be borne by local authorities in the danger areas, and they reserved this issue for later consideration. They also decided that before the proposals were submitted to the Committee of Imperial Defence, the officials should enter into consultations (at which no mention should be made of finance) with selected local authorities about organisation.

A Suggested Programme,
and the Scale of Attack

The Air Raids Commandant (Designate) presented a long *Memorandum on the Preparation of a Scheme for the Passive Defence of London against Aerial Bombardment* to the committee. This summarised all available information on the consequences to London of air attack on the scale accepted in 1924. General Pritchard then offered detailed suggestions, based on the decisions this narrative has been recording, for London's defence. His realistic approach to the nine-year accumulation of schemes was illustrated by his suggestions with regard to enrolment of personnel. After listing the fifteen categories of persons required for A.R.P., he stated that the problem of keeping people on the job was entirely a question of morale. If certain conditions—particularly previous awareness of the job they would be asked to do and some previous training—were fulfilled, 'the people would respond'. He disagreed with schemes for using Transport Workers' Battalions or a reserve supplied by the War Office[1] in terms which forecast the true line of development:

> in organising the whole civilian population to protect themselves they must be organised on a civilian basis in their civilian organisation of the categories named. . . . The A.R.P. Service must create and maintain its own honourable status and prestige and not lean upon some other Service. It would be contrary to the principle of this civilian organisation to resist attack upon civilians if it were to be incorporated in the Territorial Army or any other military organisation.

He then gave a detailed programme which specified sixteen items on which work should begin at once and for which funds should be provided in the next financial year (1934–35) under a consolidated Estimate. These included an establishment for the London Commandant, a full-scale test of destructive powers of the 500-lb. bomb, an A.R.P. exercise in Hackney in 1934, a Press Liaison Officer at the Home Office and the preparation of certain schemes in full detail. He also laid emphasis on the need to create a fire-fighting organisation on a scale never previously contemplated, and suggested that the centralisation (adopted towards the end of the 1914–18 war) of the Greater London fire brigades should be revived for A.R.P. purposes.

After paying tribute to this report, the committee decided they could not recommend to Ministers any programme of works involving expenditure of a good deal of money. Current expenditure on passive defence was about £20,000 a year, most of this being absorbed by the Chemical Defence Research Department. The expenditure General Pritchard recommended—£150,000 in the next financial year—could only, they thought, be justified if the country was under serious possibility of a maximum scale of attack.

The immediate result of this report was re-examination of the scale of attack of 1924—the hypothesis which had governed all subsequent preparations.[2] This hypothesis, with the passage of time, had acquired a somewhat immutable character for the A.R.P. planners. Questions directed on occasion to the Air Staff had shown them not merely unwilling to reduce the maximum scale but

---

[1] See pp. 36, 40.
[2] See pp. 15–16.

inclined to increase it. Continued acceptance of this scale became more difficult for A.R.P. authorities as their plans evolved from theory into application. In 1931 the committee had considered assuming a lesser scale in framing shelter and evacuation schemes; and the programme just mentioned raised this issue with respect to all preparations.

Recollection of some events of the autumn of 1933 may serve to put the committee's views into perspective. In October Germany, now under National Socialism, withdrew from the Disarmament Conference and notified her withdrawal from the League. But the historian's later judgment that 'all hope of disarmament had now vanished'[1] was by no means universally accepted, and the Conference was to re-assemble in the spring. In Britain a by-election at East Fulham in October on the rearmament issue gave a resounding victory to the Labour ('pacifist') candidate. While most sections of the public were still unprepared to think in terms of rearmament, 'the great depression still lay heavy upon the country'.[2]

The committee sought fresh direction from Ministers on the scale of attack which should govern preparations. Their own reconsideration of this started from recognition that the basis of the 1924 calculation—an attack by France with no allies on either side —was obviously a remote contingency. Also, the Cabinet had recently decided that no expenditure should for the present be incurred on defence measures required to provide exclusively against attack by certain countries, including France. Germany, whatever her existing potentialities, would be at a serious disadvantage in air warfare for some years to come. They had concluded that preparations could temporarily proceed without reference to any precise scale of attack. And that, while it should be assumed that the scale of damage might be much below the theoretical maximum which had hitherto been assumed, and which continued to remain as an ultimate possibility, it would probably be very much greater than anything experienced in the last war. They asked authority to devote attention mainly to questions of organisation, and to undertake material preparation only when this did not involve heavy expenditure. This course was approved by the Committee of Imperial Defence at the close of 1933.

Financial Responsibility, and Rearmament, 1934–1935

The committee now reported that tests of the Special Service respirator (the type intended for persons who, while liable to exposure

[1] G. M. Gathorne-Hardy, *op. cit.*, p. 352.
[2] Viscount Samuel, *op. cit.*, p. 245.

to gas, would not require such complete protection as the Fighting Services) had proved highly satisfactory. A committee appointed early in 1934 to examine policy with regard to production and supply of gas masks had made many detailed proposals, forwarded in April to Ministers for guidance on major points of policy. The main question at issue was whether provision was to be made to supply masks to the general public; if so, on what financial basis. The committee were satisfied that the Special Service mask (which could be bulk manufactured for 6–7s. apiece) would be adequate for most persons actively engaged in air raid services and that only a few bodies (e.g., the police and fire brigades) would require the General Service type. They had also concluded that a large section of the population would expect the Government to provide them with some protection against gas, and that a considerable proportion, if not the major proportion, would be unable to provide this out of their own resources. They recommended inquiry into the possibility of designing a cheap respirator (one which could be sold for about 2s.) which could provide a measure of protection for adults and children and could be quickly mass-produced.

Assuming that such masks could be designed, was it probable that many of the public would (even with official encouragement) purchase them in peace-time? Though masks were already on sale in several Continental countries, the committee—either from awareness of the results so obtained, or from knowledge of the reluctance of the British public to spend money on warlike preparations—answered 'no'. It would, nevertheless, be advisable to manufacture in peace and store a sufficient number of these masks to enable the Government to meet a very strong and possibly irresistible demand should an emergency arise; and to arrange in advance for rapid mass production on the outbreak of an emergency.

The financial implications of Government action on these lines were clearly considerable, since the part of England and Wales then regarded as lying within range of attack contained some 20,000,000 persons. While this particular problem had been laid on the Ministers' doorstep, officials found evidence accumulating of need for an early decision about incidence of financial responsibility in general. Following the decisions of the previous summer,[1] they had had confidential talks, at which no mention had been made of finance, with representatives of the County Councils and Municipal Corporations Associations and a few Counties and County Boroughs; and had concluded it was impossible to get down to brass tacks with the local authorities until they were able to say who would pay the piper. Committees on the medical services and on decontamination reported similar inability to make progress until the financial

---

[1] pp. 43–44.

E

issue was decided. The committee therefore decided to re-assemble
their administrative and financial sub-committee with two extra
members (the Air Raids Commandant and a Home Office representative) to consider the broad financial principles which should
govern provision of A.R.P. Services, and to produce what the chairman called 'a speculative estimate' of the cost of these services on the
basis of the peace-time provision of certain essential supplies.

Shortly before this inquiry began Ministers authorised the
Chemical Research Committee to produce designs of a respirator
for general use—though authority was given without prejudice to
'certain questions of large principle' raised in the report on respirators
just mentioned. The administrative and financial committee soon
agreed that planning should now extend beyond preparation of
schemes and questions of organisation to embrace accumulation of
some vital supplies which could not be provided in sufficient time
in an emergency. They regarded respirators, anti-gas clothing,
bleach powder, medical and surgical supplies as the most important
of these; and, on the basis of the first two items alone, reached a
partial estimate of peace-time expenditure of £630,000. Construction of shelters was expressly excluded from this estimate on the
ground of its prohibitive cost; and it was decided that a reasonable
time to allow for the accumulation of these supplies was five years.
These conclusions, a reversal of the programme adopted the previous
December, were accompanied by a recommendation on financial
responsibility which also reversed the view of a year before.[1] It was
now decided that as local authorities, public utilities and other bodies
had no authority to spend money on the purposes in question, and
would (in any event) be extremely reluctant to assume any considerable part of the expenditure contemplated, the bulk of this
expenditure would have to fall on the Government.

In this summer of 1934 the Disarmament Conference reached a
compromise which preserved it in a state of suspended animation.
But by now the hope even of limiting armaments was fading, and
fear of general rearmament and its results was beginning to infect
the world. In Britain, as elsewhere, this infection was gradual,
meeting with resistance among large sections of the public, where
the facts were unknown or there was refusal to interpret these in
pessimistic fashion. The British Government, however, had already
embarked on exploratory steps towards rearmament. In November
1933 they had cancelled the 'Ten-Year Rule',[2] and had appointed
a Defence Requirements Sub-Committee of the Committee of
Imperial Defence, composed of the Chiefs of Staff and representatives
of the Foreign Office and Treasury, to prepare a programme for

---

[1] pp. 43–44.
[2] p. 33.

making good the worst deficiencies in the Defence Services on a five-year basis.[1]

The conclusions early in 1934 of this body of most concern to this narrative were recognition of Germany as the hypothetical enemy for purposes of long-range defence policy, and emphasis on the prime importance of aerial warfare. In its view the threat to Britain now presented by bomb-carrying aircraft had become at least equal to the menace of attack on our sea-communications. Designs and weight-carrying capacity of this weapon had so increased since 1918 that in another war its use against such a concentration of population and activities as London might prove decisive. The Air Staff considered that the best means of defence against this threat lay in attack, or counter-bombing of German air bases and industries. Completion of the programme of Air Force expansion adopted in 1923 but still only partially fulfilled was, therefore, one of this committee's chief recommendations. They proposed enlargements to the slender existing provision for the anti-aircraft defence of London, and that fuller instructions about air raid precautions should be given to the public.

The A.R.P. Committee had the question of publicity again brought to its attention by an incident (similar to that of 1927) in which a former official of the Government establishment at Porton proposed to broadcast about gas attack. They suggested that these broadcasts should be permitted, after scrutiny of the scripts; and that there might be great advantage in a general broadcast on passive defence by a Minister or senior official.[2] They reported growing demand among sections of the public for guidance in matters concerning passive air defence generally, including voluntary attempts at organisation and instruction; and their own conclusion that the time was more than ripe for some more definite statement of Government policy in regard to air raid defence than had hitherto been deemed possible. Discussion of this matter by Ministers showed that the number of persons informed about passive defence was still most restricted; for example, the Home Secretary, Sir John Gilmour, considered that the police had practically no information on this matter at all.

The Cabinet considered this issue at a meeting on 25th July, together with a Chiefs of Staff memorandum emphasising the importance they attached to air raid precautions as a complementary means of defence against air attack. The Cabinet agreed that the

---

[1] The Chiefs of Staff had reported in their annual review for 1933 that the accumulation of deficiencies resulting from the long continuance of the ten year rule was very heavy.

[2] The gentleman who had caused this incident did not deliver the proposed broadcasts, although he contributed two articles on the subject to the *Listener* (27th June and 15th August 1934).

Lord President of the Council, Mr Baldwin, should make a statement about these precautions in a forthcoming speech on air defence policy, and that the Home Secretary should consider following up this statement with a broadcast.

It is evident that the process, so prominent in the recommendations of 1925,[1] of gradually educating the public in A.R.P. by disseminating knowledge among a widening circle of persons had been little developed in practice. The course now chosen of reaching the public through Parliament was entered into with equal caution. During a foreign affairs debate in November 1932 Mr Baldwin had stressed the prevalence of fear in the world, which he attributed largely to 'fear of the air', and stated that 'the bomber will always get through'.[2] After referring to air raid precautions on the Continent, he informed Parliament that the Government was also taking precautions,

> much more quietly and hitherto without any publicity but, considering the years that are required to make your preparations, any Government of this country in the present circumstances of the world would have been guilty of criminal negligence had they neglected to make their preparations.

In March 1934 the Prime Minister stated that the Committee of Imperial Defence had been considering air raid precautions as 'an essential accessory to the arrangement for home defence' ever since 1924.[3]

On 19th July Mr Baldwin announced in the House that the Government had decided on a five-year programme for expansion of the Royal Air Force; and on 30th July in the course of a debate on armaments he referred to air raid precautions in the following terms,

> We feel with regard to the protection of the civilian population that our plans have been carried as far as is possible without wider publicity than has hitherto been deemed to be in the public interest. The next stage involves communications with local authorities, with public utility companies, and so forth, and with all those on whom responsibility for action would fall in the emergency contemplated, and before long, steps will be taken to communicate the necessary instructions to the general public.[4]

An impression was indubitably made upon the nation and the world by the warning with which Mr Baldwin concluded this speech:

> Let us never forget this. Since the day of the air the old frontiers are gone. When you think of the defence of England, you no longer think

---

[1] See pp. 18–19, 26, 28, 38–40.
[2] H. of C. Deb., Vol. 270, Cols. 631–2, 10th November 1932.
[3] H. of C. Deb., Vol. 287, Col. 1240, 21st March 1934.
[4] H. of C. Deb., Vol. 292, Col. 2335–6

of the chalk cliffs of Dover; you think of the Rhine. That is where our frontier lies.

The important proposals of the administrative and financial committee described above,[1] were discussed in November by Ministers now reinforced by the addition of the Financial Secretary to the Treasury, Mr Duff Cooper. Ministers immediately agreed that, (i) some expenditure would have to be incurred in the next financial year if schemes were to be properly completed, and (ii) financial responsibility for certain A.R.P. services should rest with the central Government. The report they forwarded to the Cabinet has claims to be regarded as the birth—after the years of gestation this narrative has been recording—of civil defence. Or alternatively (and perhaps more accurately) as a first pre-natal advance on account of obstetrician's fees, at the onset of what was to prove a difficult period of labour.

This proposed that a sum for A.R.P. Services not above £100,000 should be included in the Estimates for the next year (1935–36) under a new sub-head in the Home Office Vote. The services to be financed in this first year, and their very approximate shares of the Vote, would be as follows:—Central Government administrative services (£7,000); provision for respirators, mainly for training purposes (£40,000); provision for research in the form of a contribution to the Chemical Defence Research Department (£15,000); and certain essential experimental work and training (£30,000). Services for which no provision was made in this estimate, but for which funds might have to be found in future, were medical and surgical supplies, and accumulation of stocks of bleach powder and anti-gas clothing. The A.R.P. Committee refrained from proposing any provision for shelters. They had decided that if local authorities were anxious to build public shelters they ought to bear the cost of this themselves—though they recorded that this decision might have to be reconsidered.

Ministers endorsed the Defence Requirements Committee's view that A.R.P. should be developed *pari passu* with the anti-aircraft defences. They recommended that, now decision had been reached to repair the deficiencies in air defence over a five-year period, the preparations for passive defence should, so far as possible, be completed within five years. They also reminded the Cabinet of the importance attached by the Defence Requirements Committee to publicity in this sphere. The report just quoted had remarked that the German Air Force would derive additional encouragement to attack Britain if they were aware that, unlike the peoples of Continental countries, the British population had no knowledge or

---

[1] p. 48.

warning of the precautions to be observed for the purpose of reducing casualties . . . 'they will count on panic as a powerful ally'. And had urged that, whenever a new defence programme was launched the opportunity should be taken to remove the ban against full publicity that was preventing full benefit being drawn from the years of effort that had been devoted to this matter.

Ministers also referred to Mr Baldwin's statement in Parliament on 30th July that consultations would soon be taking place with local authorities and instructions would be issued to the public. Their inability so far to make any general moves of this kind had been largely due to the need first to obtain decision about the incidence of financial responsibility.

The Cabinet's approval early in 1935 to an expenditure of some £100,000 on certain A.R.P. services registered the birth of civil defence, or—if the alternative suggested above is preferred— counter-signed the first advance payment. But Parliament and the public still knew no more of the matter than the inference, to be drawn from the few statements made since 1932, that the Government was in an interesting condition. The A.R.P. Committee had started six months previously to examine the form in which detailed announcement of the event might be made to the public. They had found that important features of the matter required more clarification before this could be made. They had therefore turned from the problem of publicity to that of organisation, or fuller definition of the division of air raid precautions' functions between central and local authorities.

Drafting the 'First Circular'

They recorded late in 1934 that they had not yet attempted to approach the country as a whole and that this action must await, first a definite decision on the financial question, and secondly enlargement of the administrative staff concerned with A.R.P. They reported a notable growth during the year of requests from unofficial persons for help and advice. In the meantime, foreign activities in this sphere had continued 'with undiminished intensity, especially in Germany'. Progress had, nevertheless, been made in Britain in closer examination of specific problems, including compensation for personal injury, gas-proofing of merchant ships, the possibility of devising a cheap gas-mask, and the evacuation of a limited area of London. A provisional and confidential *Air Raid Precautions Handbook* had been circulated.

The last major preoccupation of these years of planning, the general approach to local authorities, was to take the form of a circular describing the risk air attack represented and the responsibilities the different branches of Government would be expected to assume. Renewed discussion with the Air Staff on the scale and weight of attack confirmed that all England and Wales south of a line drawn from Anglesey to Scarborough was regarded as within the danger zone.

While a circular to local authorities in this area was being prepared, the A.R.P. Committee turned, at the request of the Secretary of the Committee of Imperial Defence, to reconsider the question of the seat of Government in war. As noticed earlier, Mr Baldwin's Cabinet had decided soon after the conclusion of the Locarno Treaties that this question should for the time being remain in abeyance.[1] The temporary character of this decision had been liberally interpreted, for no consideration had since been given to the matter and none of the schemes for partial or total evacuation of Whitehall, first proposed in 1925, had been prepared. Revival of the question caused new discussions with the Air Staff, which proved a forcible reminder of the vulnerability of the metropolis. The Air Staff, now using the German Air Force as the basis of their calculations, produced a darker picture than any hitherto presented. They estimated the capacity of a German Air Force operating from bases in the Low Countries to bomb Britain at 150 tons daily for an unspecified period; and this figure made allowance for all the factors, including the proposed increase of the Royal Air Force and active assistance by France, favourable to Britain's defences. They adhered to the view that London would be a major objective. Its proximity to the coast (or lack of 'depth') added to the difficulties of its defence; and technical developments, including those in bomb-sighting, had increased the probability of specific targets such as the Whitehall area being heavily and accurately bombed.

The A.R.P. Committee's findings on the problem of whether to advise removal of the seat of Government took the form of a series of formidable questions. Final decision in the matter, it was obvious, could only be made by the Government in office in the emergency. But if that decision was in favour of doing what a large part of London's population would be asked to do, or 'staying put', certain action would be advisable in peace. Should plans be made to move *les Ministères moins utiles* (e.g., the Board of Education) for the conduct of the war outside London? Should a nucleus of essential Departments (a war-time Pretoria or Canberra) be retained in Whitehall, and the rest be moved elsewhere in London? If so, should this nucleus be given special bomb- and gas-proof accommodation? To do this would raise the problem of discrimination between officialdom and the public in another form. It would also entail large-scale expenditure in peace, and immediate authorisation of experiments to determine the character of the bomb-proof accommodation required, about which no information was yet available.

---

[1] p. 27.

This problem can, perhaps, best be regarded as a special aspect of the wider problem of shelters, in which the questions of cost and morale were the dominating features. It led, by a long series of irregular steps, from 10 Downing Street, where the major decision would ultimately be taken, through Whitehall and the City of London (for which special measures were proposed) into 'The Bricklayers' Arms'.[1] Ministers recommended immediate confidential inquiry by the Organisation Committee into provision of alternative accommodation both for Government Departments and essential City services in different parts of London. They advocated provision of funds for the experiments just mentioned, details of which had been worked out by a Bombing Test Committee.[2] They favoured continuance of the scheme, already often discussed, for a large new Government building in Whitehall, which would include protection for the most essential parts of the machine of Government. The Committee of Imperial Defence approved these proposals.

Preparation of the circular to local authorities entailed the questions of recruitment and training of persons for the A.R.P. services, and education of the public. Should the first function be delegated to local authorities, to some new civil organisation embracing the whole country or to some existing national organisation? The planners were impressed by the existence ready-to-hand of two national organisations, the British Red Cross Society and the Order of St. John, which already figured prominently in the medical schemes for London. They secured Ministerial approval for investigating the willingness of these societies to undertake much wider A.R.P. duties, including recruitment for various kinds of work, training in first aid and personal anti-gas defence, and 'promulgation of advice to the general public as to behaviour during air raids.' In proposing the education envisaged in the last suggestion the committee were influenced by the method adopted in Germany where a person had been designated in each street, called a Road Warden, whose task it was to act as guide, philosopher and friend to the inhabitants of the street. The problem of educating the general public was, nevertheless, not yet regarded as urgent. The more pressing problem of recruitment received further attention in a request to the Man-Power Committee to take steps to prevent sudden depletion on the outbreak of war of the police and fire brigades, whose assistance was most essential to effective working of the whole air raid precautions scheme.

---

[1] This reference is not necessarily to the well-known public house at the Old Kent Road-Tower Bridge Road crossroads. It is intended to suggest the general body of the public and the factor of morale and the vast quantity of bricks and other materials needed for air raid shelters.

[2] This committee, representing the three Services and certain civil departments, had been formed in 1934 and had reported in February 1935. See p. 83 below.

A shift of emphasis from London to the country as a whole, and preparations to advise local authorities and the public, brought an important change in the central organisation. In March 1935 the committee obtained Ministers' approval for abolition of the post of London Air Raids Commandant, and extension of the central machinery in the form of an Air Raid Precautions Department at the Home Office. The concept of an unorthodox authority for London performing functions of a quasi-military nature was now regarded as mistaken. Furthermore, the planners were unprepared at this stage to elaborate their provisional conclusion about the need for intermediate, or Regional, authorities both in London and the provinces. As a consequence, the Air Raids Commandant (Designate) for London retired.

The positive proposal just mentioned was an extension, not a revision, of existing central organisation. The chief principle of the plan propounded in 1928[1]—dispersal of responsibility among Departments as opposed to creation of an *ad hoc* authority—was not called into question. But in the sphere of function there was definite innovation. The new Department of the Home Office would, first, draw up, on principles laid down by the A.R.P. committees, general instructions and advice to the civil population and, secondly, act as a central clearing house in relation to local authorities concerned with A.R.P. schemes. The second function would include establishing contacts with authorities in London and the provinces, for which an 'out-door' inspectorial staff would be provided. Creation of this Department was announced to the House of Commons by the Home Secretary in reply to a question on 16th April.[2] Wing-Commander E. J. Hodsoll, the secretary of the A.R.P. committees since 1929, was appointed to take charge of it.

On the day of this announcement, Ministers approved the draft circular to local authorities. Certain points in this had still to be submitted to the Cabinet, and its issue was to be postponed until Parliament had debated the matter on the Home Office Vote. But this action by Ministers closed, in effect, the eleven-year period of planning air raid precautions in secret. Plans were now to be given publicity, and the active co-operation of local authorities and the public was to be wooed.

---

[1] pp. 33–34.

[2] Prematurely, from the point of view of the authorities, since the formation of the Department was then still a secret. But a name-plate was put on the Department's premises at 5 Princes Street which was photographed by the wife (Mrs. Mander) of the M.P. who asked the question.

CHAPTER III

THE A.R.P. DEPARTMENT AND ORGANISATION BY PERSUASION (1935 – 1937)

The 'First Circular'

THE first circular on A.R.P. was issued by the Home Office on 9th July 1935 to all local authorities (except parish councils) in England and Wales, and an identical circular was sent by the Scottish Office to local authorities in Scotland; it was also put on sale to the public for 2d. This was the first comprehensive Government statement regarding civil defence. It was an invitation to local authorities, and to private employers, to co-operate with the Government in creating A.R.P. machinery; and to the public to learn the rudiments of protection and to volunteer for A.R.P. duties in their districts. This document was to remain the chart of A.R.P. until the first legislation on the subject of some two and a half years later.

It is evident that there was now a major shift of emphasis. Planning at the centre was, for the time being, secondary in importance to organisation at the circumference. The decision to graft the structure on to normal local government meant that the immediate problem was to persuade local authorities to draw up A.R.P. schemes, and ordinary citizens to give voluntary service. The voluntary character of this arrangement was clearly its principal feature. Though to prove only temporary where the administrative structure was concerned, this was to endure (with some modification in war) as a lasting feature of the relationship between A.R.P. and the ordinary citizen. Its general importance justifies brief attention here to the topic of public reaction to air raid defence.

This problem may best be regarded as that of a challenge to share in a new kind of war service, and the response. Clearly, the ordinary man's response in advance of the event would depend largely on his personal judgment over the probability of war. This judgment (assuming he exercised it) would be formed by events abroad, the statements of political leaders, the Press, the views of authorities on international affairs and many other influences. Certain of these must in this narrative be recalled to the reader's memory; in

56

particular, the main shocks administered to international harmony from the Continent and leading statements by the British Government about defence preparations.

The months before issue of the 'first circular' had produced important examples of these two types of event. Early in March the National Government published a White Paper on Defence which, after declaring that Britain's 'desire to lead the world towards disarmament by our example of unilateral disarmament has not succeeded', began a programme of general rearmament.[1] It would be interesting to speculate whether this programme made a greater impact on British opinion than the action taken soon afterwards by Hitler. On 9th March Germany notified foreign governments that she possessed an air force—an act less important for the information it conveyed than for its character as 'the first open repudiation by Germany of her treaty obligations'.[2] Two weeks later conscription was reintroduced in the Third Reich.

Though the existence of a German air force had been known in Britain, there was difference of official opinion over its size and rate of growth. During a debate in November Mr Baldwin had flatly contradicted Mr Churchill's assertion that Germany's air force was approaching equality with our own. The effect of this reassuring statement, according to one historian, was the direct opposite of the urgent request of the Chiefs of Staff early in 1934 that the people should be roused from 'the state of moral disarmament to which persistent and almost unopposed peace propaganda had reduced them', and that they should be educated to see the need for the financial sacrifices required for defence. In the spring of 1935 the Government became convinced that expansion of Germany's air force was a bigger menace than they had hitherto supposed. On 22nd May Mr Baldwin told the House that he believed his previous statement about the future strength of Germany in the air to have been 'completely wrong'; and said that Hitler had recently told the Foreign Secretary and Mr Eden that Germany had already achieved parity with Britain.[3]

The ordinary citizen was only momentarily alarmed by these revelations. The disease already referred to, fear of another war, was slow in spreading and was being resisted by powerful injections of what the Chiefs of Staff had called peace propaganda. A few weeks after Mr Baldwin's admission, the 'Peace Ballot', a questionnaire initiated by the League of Nations Union, obtained over 11,500,000 signatures. The support for this document, though susceptible to various interpretations, at least showed how strong was the faith

---

[1] *Statement relating to Defence*, Cmd. 4827, 1935.

[2] G. M. Gathorne-Hardy, *op. cit.*, p. 393.

[3] H. of C. Deb., Vol. 302, Cols. 367–8.

still reposed in the League (or in what was called 'the system of collective security') as an instrument for preventing war.

Early in June 1935, Mr MacDonald retired from the Premiership in favour of Mr Baldwin. Reconstruction of the National Government included the exchange by Sir John Simon of the Foreign Office for the Home Office; so that it fell to this Minister to present to Parliament the Estimates for 1935–36 which included the first item (£92,000) on account of A.R.P. The motion for approval of these was made on 16th July, a week after issue of the circular.[1] The Home Secretary, though recalling that he had first borne responsibility for this Department twenty years earlier 'on the day on which the first *Zeppelin* visited London', made no allusion either to the circular or to the new A.R.P. functions of his Department. A good deal of interest in the matter was, nevertheless, expressed in debate. Several Opposition members alleged that issue of the circular was further proof of the inadequacy or insincerity of the Government's efforts for peace, and the problem of incidence of financial responsibility was raised.

More detailed description of the 'first circular' may take the form of elaboration of the three main features mentioned at the opening of this chapter. As a statement of Government policy, the document received an amendment of some significance after leaving the Ministers most concerned. The earlier version had stated, 'it must be assumed that the scale of attack would greatly exceed anything which was experienced in the last war', and that the attack 'would no doubt be directed mainly against the large centres of population and industrial activity, with London as a principal objective'. These passages were replaced by a general assurance that the Government strongly repudiated indiscriminate bombing of civil populations, and would continue to make every effort to avert war. The public was, however, warned that if war came it would be 'impossible to guarantee immunity from attack' by enemy aircraft; and that use of poison gas was a possibility which could not be disregarded.

The Government, the circular continued, would issue general instructions, give technical and administrative advice, provide stocks of certain anti-gas equipment and give some financial assistance over hospital equipment and stores. A straightforward refusal was announced to provide money towards construction of public bomb-proof shelters. Reasons (already familiar to readers) for this decision were stated, and occupiers of premises were told that effective protection could be obtained against blast and bomb-splinters at comparatively small cost. Apart from undertakings to

---

[1] H. of C. Deb., Vol. 304, Cols. 887–1018. The document had not been made available to Members in the Vote Office, with the result that many of them had not read it.

establish a Gas School to train instructors, and to make general arrangements for warnings and lighting restrictions, the foregoing represented the Government's contribution towards the matter. Emphasis was placed on the view that defence of the civil population in this sphere 'must be organised locally', and responsibility was placed squarely on local authorities to arrange for adequate protective measures in their districts.

The vagueness (apart from a few items) of the financial implications was explained by the Parliamentary Under-Secretary to the Home Office, Capt. Euan Wallace, in the debate just mentioned as due to the fact that the Government were asking local authorities to undertake organisation not at present involving 'any appreciable financial outlay'. The organisation was to be based on two leading principles. First, close relationship between A.R.P. responsibilities and the local authorities' normal functions—or 'the full use of all existing machinery, whether of local authorities or of other bodies, which could appropriately provide some needed emergency service'. Secondly, the choice (since 'unified plans for large areas were essential') of the largest local government areas—administrative counties and county boroughs—as the basis of the structure. Emphasis was given to the need for neighbouring authorities of these classes to enter into close co-operation over A.R.P.; but no reference was made to any intermediate or regional authority.

The first step the counties and county boroughs were asked to take was preparation of a general A.R.P. plan. This, it was suggested, could best be entrusted by each authority to a small committee to organise the detailed work of its officers on the matter. Need to include in the plan bodies outside local government machinery, in particular public utilities, was pointed out.

Guidance was given about the general character of local schemes in an outline of the various A.R.P. services required in an emergency. This, since it was mainly a statement for the information of local authorities and the public of those main divisions of the subject the planning authorities had been discussing since 1924, requires no reproduction here. But three items of rather more novelty need mention. It was announced that the Secretary of State would appoint a committee to explore the whole fire brigade problem. Secondly, it was stated that the duty of reporting damage (the fall of bombs, the kind of damage caused, and the presence of gas) was one which must primarily rest on local arrangements. Thirdly, 'rescue parties', or squads of men trained to work in damaged buildings not on fire, were given the status of a separate A.R.P. service.

Local authorities were advised to await receipt of memoranda on the services before starting detailed preparations. Handbooks would also be issued for instruction of the public, in the recruitment and training of whom the Order of St. John, the British Red Cross and the St. Andrew's Ambulance Association would give assistance. The A.R.P. Department, the circular stated, would arrange area conferences of local authorities 'for the purpose of facilitating a start with local schemes'.

Rearmament, and Growth of the Department

The Air Raid Precautions Department began activities on 15th April in a few rooms at 5 Princes Street, Westminster. Its first task, the issue of this circular, bore a close resemblance to one of the first acts of the first Home Secretary one hundred and fifty years before. In 1782, when France and Spain joined in America's war with Britain, Lord Shelburne issued a circular directing mayors of English towns to enrol volunteers for the national defence.

Tradition and convenience, rather than theoretical considerations, dictated choice of the Home Department ('the recognised guardian of the public safety') as the seat of the new agency. Since 1923 the special concern of the Home Secretary with the problems of air raid defence in another war had been recognised, and a close relationship between the police forces and any A.R.P. organisation finally evolved had been assumed. But the new development, it is important to note, made no addition to the Home Secretary's formal responsibility in this sphere beyond the inclusion of a new sub-head in his Department's Vote. The plan of 1925, reaffirmed in 1928, whereby A.R.P. functions were to be grafted on to the normal functions of a dozen or so Departments was still in force.[1] The change now introduced was primarily one of function, not of machinery. The new Department remained under the direction of the two A.R.P. committees of the Committee of Imperial Defence; and its responsibility was defined in the first circular as 'to act on behalf of the various Government Departments concerned' with air raid defence.

The distinction between machinery and function has an important bearing on the developments of the next three years. It is not perhaps fanciful to view A.R.P. when its birth was announced as a foundling. The work of propagation recorded in the last chapter had been carried out in secret, and the infant had now been entrusted to a foster-parent. The true parents, at least for the time being, showed little interest in its upbringing; and the Departments (other than the Home Office) most concerned were to give little evidence of desire to share in this process. For most local authorities, employers and members of the public the infant was a novelty which it was difficult to welcome. Its existence implied the possibility, which still seemed remote, of another and more horrifying general war.

---

[1] pp. 23-24, 33-34.

The A.R.P. Organisation Committee decided soon after issue of the 'first circular' to create a committee to discuss with Departmental Heads the allocation of staffs involved in any scheme for removal of the seat of Government. Having now been informed that mass-production of a cheap gas-mask for general use was practicable, they submitted a series of questions to Ministers. Should gas-masks be available on the outbreak of a war to the public in all parts of the country liable to attack? If so, should stocks of these be accumulated by the Government, and at the national expense? If an emergency arose, should these be issued free of charge? Supply of masks to the public would, of course, involve large expenditure, and production and storage well in advance of the emergency. The decision, therefore, of Ministers in October 1935 that all these questions should be answered in the affirmative, and Cabinet approval of this, rank as events of major importance.

During the next six months the Government added significantly to the scale and tempo of general defence plans. In the General Election of this November they committed themselves to some further measure of rearmament. Later in that month the Defence Requirements Committee proposed large increases to the existing programme. When these revisions were finally approved in February 1936 the introductory period of rearmament was completed (so far as the Government and their chief experts were concerned) and the scale of rearmament had become, in essentials, as plain as it ever was to become before September 1939. Henceforward the main administrative problems were to secure the vastly increased industrial capacity the new scale required, and to plan the division of this among the Fighting Services. Another White Paper[1] acquainted Parliament in March with what Mr Neville Chamberlain called in his Budget speech 'the largest programme of defence ever undertaken by this country in peace time'. The new office was created of Minister for the Co-ordination of Defence, to be filled by the Attorney-General, Sir Thomas Inskip.

In this rearmament programme air raid precautions received only brief recognition.[2] It will be recalled that in 1934 the Defence Requirements Committee had emphasised the threat air attack now presented, and proposed that passive measures should be developed *pari passu* with the five-year programme for active defences. These experts again stressed the danger of this form of attack and the need to awaken the public mind regarding it. They included a short statement of A.R.P. requirements, the largest item of which was a possible total of £4 millions for civilian respirators.

In the summer of 1936 the Home Secretary presented a *Review*

[1] *Statement Relating to Defence*, Cmd. 5107, 1936.
[2] The White Paper made only slight reference to the subject.

of the Work of the A.R.P. Department during its first year to the Committee of Imperial Defence. From the standpoint of the higher direction of A.R.P. this contained one item of special importance. The Department sought definite guidance about whether its programme was considered adequate and in line with the programmes of the three Defence Departments. Recording that it was working to complete its plans by 31st March 1939, it drew attention to the acceleration of the Fighting Services' preparations. If A.R.P. were to keep in step with these, the Department would need larger staff and financial resources, approval for speeding up the proposed production of equipment (especially gas-masks), and a decision about the incidence of financial responsibility.

The Committee of Imperial Defence referred these questions to its sub-committee on Defence Policy and Requirements, and asked the Department to adopt the practice of the Defence Departments of sending monthly reports to this authority. This sub-committee had a status and membership similar to those of its parent body; it met under the chairmanship of the Minister for the Co-ordination of Defence, and included the Home Secretary. As a consequence of its assumption of responsibility for higher direction of air raid precautions the A.R.P. Ministerial and Organisation Committees became extinct.

The Defence Policy and Requirements Committee approved the speeding up of production of civilian respirators. During the next nine months, however, it paid small attention to the A.R.P. Department's activities. In an important memorandum of February 1937 the Chiefs of Staff again expressed the view that the most probable weapon an aggressive Germany would choose against Britain would be immediate large-scale air attack. But it was not until April of that year that the Committee gave earnest attention to passive measures. A memorandum by the Home Secretary on *Financial Aspects of Air Raid Precautions* was then given detailed consideration and laid before the Cabinet. The Cabinet appointed an *ad hoc* committee under the chairmanship of the Permanent Secretary of the Treasury to examine the financial implications of A.R.P. and the distribution of responsibility both between central and local authorities and among the central Departments. This committee's findings implied that arrangements for co-ordination were seriously defective.

This criticism was directed at arrangements for co-ordinating both major policy and Departmental activities. As observed earlier, the allocation of responsibilities to some dozen or so Departments remained (in theory) unaffected by the A.R.P. Department's creation. Practical evolution, however, in the years now in question failed to correspond with the theory. The new Department had been created mainly to be a channel between the Government and local authorities and the public on all A.R.P. matters, and to supervise preparation of local schemes. This shift of emphasis towards the whole country, the preoccupation of other Departments with their peace-time functions, the unpopularity of A.R.P. and apparent remoteness of the threat it was to counter and the factor of personality combined to transform the Department from a channel into a virtual fountainhead. During 1935–37 and beyond it developed in practice a close resemblance to that *ad hoc* authority which, at least as a peace-time measure, had been discarded.

The Ministry of Health, owing to its duties regarding local authorities and medical matters, was the Department whose concern with A.R.P. ranked next to that of the Home Office. Under the 1925 distribution of responsibilities, medical treatment of casualties, provision of hospital accommodation, and evacuation of the wounded had been the first three items allotted to this Ministry. The 'first circular' outlined a scheme for the provision of these services;[1] and in the autumn the A.R.P. Department took over responsibility for the detailed preparation of a casualty scheme for London, and was later granted a medical adviser for this and other purposes. The Department also took up (at the stage where it had been left by a committee in the middle of 1934) the problem of developing a plan for the evacuation of the able-bodied but 'dispensable' citizens of London. Other questions which fell most logically within, or overlapped, the sphere of the Ministry of Health engaged the A.R.P. Department's attention during this phase of practical development. For example, maintenance of water supplies, a variety of services (such as rehousing) for victims of attack and the burial of the dead.

A similar process took place with regard to certain duties originally allotted to the Office of Works. During the planning of 1924–35 this Office had produced several memoranda on shelters, but had possessed neither the funds nor the machinery to undertake practical experiment. It also lacked the power to survey for shelter purposes, or to construct shelters in, buildings which were not Crown property. To supply his Department with data on the effects of high explosive and other bombs and suggest measures of protection, the Home Secretary appointed a Structural Precautions Committee, under the chairmanship of Sir Arnold Wilson and with Office of Works representation, in February 1936.

The A.R.P. 'Department', to the organisation of which brief attention must now be turned, was, though officially so-called, only a small Home Office division. The Home Secretary, the first

---

[1] Paragraph 11 (*g*).

F

of His Majesty's Principal Secretaries of State,[1] was performing his varied functions in 1935 through a Department with a Vote of some £640,000 and a total staff of about 1,100, organised in nine administrative divisions.[2] The A.R.P. agency formed a tenth division. In addition to its use of Home Office machinery for finance and staffing, it had special relations, which were to prove lasting, with two older divisions concerned respectively with preparation of the War Book and other emergency duties and the Home Secretary's functions regarding the police. Some eighteen months later (in October 1936) an eleventh division was created to organise the emergency Fire Brigade Services.[3]

Physical separation of the A.R.P. Department from the Home Office in Whitehall reflected a degree of independence not shared by the older divisions. The novelty of A.R.P., and the lack of enthusiasm with which the topic was regarded in most quarters, combined to give those who composed the embryonic Department a sense of pioneering. They were a small, and in some respects amateur, crew making for deep waters in a ship of light tonnage. Besides the Assistant Under-Secretary in charge, the Department was composed of two Principals, two Inspectors and eight other persons.

Early in 1936 a Civilian Anti-Gas School with a Chief Instructor and three Assistants was formed at Falfield, and a Medical Adviser, later given a staff of Instructors, was added to the Department. The organisation was already finding itself strained and reported, 'a great deal of very important work has come completely to a standstill through sheer lack of physical ability to deal with it'. In April of that year the Treasury sanctioned certain increases of staff; and in the summer a Supply Branch was added to deal with production, storage and distribution of civilian masks and other anti-gas equipment. The Department, having outgrown its accommodation in Princes Street, moved in November further away from Whitehall to Horseferry House, Westminster, where it was destined to remain.

By January 1937 headquarters administrative staff had risen from three persons to eight, the Inspectorate had grown from two to eleven and increases had been made in subordinate staff. But that summer the Department again reported that growth of staff had failed to keep pace with needs and that 'many things have not been

---

[1] The first mention of a Secretary to the Sovereign occurs in 1253, the 37th year of Henry III. Two Principal Secretaries of State, in charge of the Northern and Southern Departments, existed from the sixteenth century until 1782, when the Home Office and Foreign Office became separate Departments. By 1946 the number of Principal Secretaries of State had grown to nine.

[2] See Sir Edward Troup, *The Home Office* (1925) for a general description of the Department between the wars. The author was Permanent Under-Secretary of State, 1908–22.

[3] The emergency fire brigade measures are dealt with separately in Chapter VI.

done which might have been done if more staff had been available'. This view was endorsed by the Warren Fisher Committee[1] which proposed that the Department should be substantially strengthened and arrangements made for regional staffs throughout the country.

During the first two years the only real growth, apart from the training establishment and the technical branches of the Medical Officer and Supply, occurred in the number of Inspectors. Use of Inspectors by the central Government to ensure that the law was observed and standards required for grants-in-aid were maintained had been well-established practice, notably for education, factory management and the police, for over a century. The Department's Inspectors were, however, something of a novelty since air raid precautions still had neither law nor accepted standards. It followed that, unlike Inspectors in other spheres, they were engaged less on control of local initiative and efforts than in stimulating these. In 1933, when it was decided to graft A.R.P. on to local government, the need for machinery to effect co-ordination between local authorities and to relieve pressure on the centre had been recognised and this role had been tentatively assigned (on paper) to regional 'Air Raids Commandants'.[2] Two years later, faced with the practical problem of means to persuade local authorities to begin action, the Government had decided to endow the new agency with an 'outdoor inspectorial staff' to make direct contacts with local authorities both in London and the provinces.[3]

During this first period when much of the Department's work was (to use its own phrase) 'of a missionary character', the Inspectors' role was of great importance. By the autumn of 1936 the two original Inspectors had grown to six, two being Technical Inspectors concerned with structural precautions and securing the co-operation of industrial concerns, two dealing with London and the Home Counties and two with the rest of Britain. Before the end of this year the Treasury had sanctioned a total establishment of a Chief Inspector and ten others. In the meantime, the Department was planning to station some Inspectors permanently in the provinces in order both to enlarge its current activities and provide part of a 'proposed nucleus war organisation' in thirteen provincial areas. This plan was supported by the Warren Fisher Committee in recommending immediate institution of 'a revised administrative organisation which would include not only the existing headquarters staff in London, but the formation of 13 areas outside London, each with its own headquarters staff. This change is necessary in peacetime for the purpose of the effective examination of local authority

---

[1] See p. 98.
[2] pp. 44, 55.
[3] p. 55.

schemes, and in war a regional system of administration will be an essential element in the war-time organisation.'

This recommendation was put into effect early in 1938, after the A.R.P. Act[1] had introduced compulsion into the structure. This attention to the Inspectorate must include notice of the fact that Inspectors were without exception retired officers of one of the Fighting Services. Officers of this type possessed not only detailed knowledge of these Services but also 'the habit of command, which may stand them in good stead in war-time'. Their appointments, being temporary, were unsuitable for civil servants and their receipt of pensions enabled the State to re-employ them at economical rates.

Approach to Local Authorities and the Public; the Anti-Gas School, the Wardens Service

The Department decided at the outset 'to drive ahead on as broad a front as possible'. Its chief purpose of persuading local authorities, employers and the public to begin protective measures had to be combined with definition of many of the forms these were to assume. The 'first circular' was a sketch rather than a blue-print; in particular, it dealt only in outline with the various A.R.P. services local authorities were asked to organise. The Department was also concerned with equipment, with experiments, and the development of schemes for warning, lighting and other matters which fell specially within the central Government's sphere.

The function of education was to be performed by personal contacts, organised training and literature. The Department's publications were to consist of (i) Handbooks, or textbooks and training manuals on particular aspects of A.R.P., and (ii) Memoranda, advising local authorities on the organisation of specific services. Since it was now accepted that most of the British Isles lay within range of aircraft operating from the Continent, the work of organisation was to embrace Scotland and Northern Ireland, being directed respectively by the Scottish Office and the Government of Northern Ireland in collaboration with the Department.

During its first summer the Department issued two handbooks on *Anti-Gas Precautions* and a memorandum on *The Treatment of Casualties*. But the first substantial approach to the country was a series of conferences of local authorities at which the head of the Department explained and (so far as possible) elaborated the first circular. Between September and Christmas this official addressed twenty-one such conferences in Great Britain, and early in 1936 he addressed one in Belfast. These were attended by leading representatives of the City and County of London, the Metropolitan Boroughs,

---

[1] Air Raid Precautions Act, 1937, 1 and 2 Geo. 6, Ch. 6.

all the Counties and nearly all the County Boroughs of England and Wales, and the Counties and Burghs of Southern Scotland.

The outcome was to encourage some authorities to take preliminary steps, and to acquaint the Department with the views of representative persons up and down the country on the Government's proposals, both general and particular. This two-way process, based mainly on the Inspectors' activities, had much importance in the phase with which this narrative is now concerned. Discussion was undertaken, for example, with local authorities over plans for creating two new voluntary local services of 'Gas Detectors' and 'Street Wardens'.

On the general character of the Government's plans it was inevitable that local bodies should show special interest in the topic of the incidence of expenditure. The Department distinguished between expenditure in peace and that required in an emergency or just before an emergency. It assured local representatives that the share of the former falling on them would be comparatively slight, and that should an emergency arise a fair division of the financial burden would be reached. Reactions to such assurances naturally varied. Some authorities were ready to take preliminary steps in spite of the ambiguity of the position. The attitude of the L.C.C., however, was reported by the Department as typical of a large section of opinion, 'which has promised co-operation in so far as it coincides with the normal responsibility of the local authority for the health and well being of their citizens; but subject to the *caveat* that any expenditure incurred must rest on the central Government'.

Readiness of local authorities to take action also hung on their attitude towards the whole rearmament problem, and in that manner they reflected the variety of opinion on this topic still dividing the nation. These conferences had barely begun when Italy, by invading Abyssinia, gave another blow to confidence in the League of Nations. After the General Election of November 1935 Mr Baldwin's National Government had returned to power with a large majority; but the Prime Minister had diluted his promise of rearmament with considerable assuagement of pacifist opinion. The swift public reaction to the Hoare-Laval Peace Plan had shown how many still clung to faith in the 'collective security' they thought was embodied at Geneva. As Edward VIII's reign began, the Cabinet was considering the accelerated programme of rearmament referred to earlier in this volume.[1] But the pattern of events of the previous spring was about to repeat itself. A few days after publication in March of a new White Paper Hitler took advantage of the Italo-Abyssinian war to march into the Rhineland.

Shortly before this event the Government had announced their

---

[1] pp. 57, 61–62.

intention to establish a Civilian Anti-Gas School, and some discussion of gas warfare had ensued.[1] The Opposition, while acknow-
ledging the need for air raid protection, had used the occasion to
criticise the Government's foreign policy as 'one of despair'. On the
larger stage offered by discussion of the defence programme, it
moved rejection of the White Paper, chiefly on the ground that its
policy was 'unworthy and ambiguous' and paid only lip service to
collective security. Criticism at Westminster of the rearmament
proposals as nationalistic and 'war-mongering' found an echo in,
and echoed, many sections of opinion in the country. To the reluctance of many local authorities to embark on A.R.P. plans before the
financial implications were clearer, was added the opposition of
others towards any steps of rearmament.

The Department decided to ask certain authorities to work out
schemes in detail, with a view to finding by trial and error the best
lines of development.[2] The conception, held throughout the previous
phase of planning, of the 'ever-widening net' was now to be applied
in practice. The approach was to be made first to selected bodies
(e.g., some local authorities, police forces and the St. John
Ambulance Brigade) and individuals (e.g., local officials and public
utility managers) in the hope that these would pass on their knowledge to a progressively widening circle. An important share in
promoting this policy was to fall to the Anti-Gas School, which began
to hold courses on 15th April 1936.

Eastwood Park, Falfield, an estate of some 200 acres mid-way
between Bristol and Gloucester, had been bought by the Government
for this school, which was to include practical training in passive
defence. The Chief Instructor, Major F. W. Ollis,[3] had been
responsible for starting the Army Gas School at Winterbourne
Gunner. But training at Falfield 'differed in its emphasis and angle
of approach from military anti-gas training, and the new school
had therefore to evolve a new syllabus and scheme of instruction.'
To the reasons already mentioned for concentration on gas warfare
others had now been added. Gas was the risk most prominently
associated in the public mind with future air attack, as was demonstrated a few weeks before the school opened by British reaction to
Italy's use of mustard and other gases against Abyssinia.[4] In
addition, some supplies of anti-gas equipment, introducing a
realistic element into A.R.P. training, were becoming available.

---

[1] H. of C. Deb., Vol. 309, Cols. 703–731, 27th February 1936.

[2] Nottingham deserves special mention as having acted from an early stage as a field
of practical experiment in organisation.

[3] Remained Chief Instructor until July 1947.

[4] According to the *Annual Register, 1936* (p. 27), 'feeling in England could hardly
contain itself when the Italians were reported to be using poison gas against both
soldiers and civilians'.

The chief purpose of the school was to train instructors who on returning to their homes would train volunteers to the A.R.P. Services and such other members of the public as might show interest. The courses (which were residential) lasted ten days, and first and second-class certificates were granted. The capacity of the school for 30 students at each course would, it was hoped, produce some 600 trained instructors each year. The first five courses were for members of the police and fire brigades of London and elsewhere. In the autumn courses were held for senior local officials, including Chief Constables, Medical Officers of Health, Engineers, the new local 'A.R.P. Organisers' and officials of public utilities. The Department was soon convinced of the value of the school. By January 1937 the capacity of each course had been enlarged to 60 students, and authority had been obtained to establish a similar school, to cater for another 60 students, in the north of England.

In the meantime Inspectors were engaged in visiting local authorities to explain the circular and advise on organisation. After its first year the Department reported that response on the whole had been good, and listed the 23 Metropolitan authorities (out of a total of 30) and the 94 larger provincial authorities in England and Wales (out of 144) which were preparing schemes.[1] At the end of 1936 it abandoned the attempt to summarise local progress statistically since, 'some schemes are advanced, some hardly begun, and the majority are in various intermediate stages'. Some 21 authorities had by then appointed A.R.P. Organisers.

It had for some time been recognised that the St. John Ambulance Brigade, the British Red Cross Society (including its Scottish Branch) and the St. Andrew's Ambulance Association could give valuable help both in spreading knowledge of anti-gas precautions and handling casualties. Early in 1936 the Home Office made specific agreements with these societies, whereby they undertook to train their members in A.R.P. (after sending a number for preliminary training to the Anti-Gas School), to encourage them to volunteer for local A.R.P. services, and to assist local authorities in organising casualty services. The Government promised grants (subject to annual review) to these societies; these for 1936–37 were £2,500 to the St. John Ambulance Brigade, £1,000 to the British Red Cross Society in England, and £250 to the St. Andrew's Ambulance Association and the Scottish Branch of the Red Cross. Other bodies which volunteered to help included the British Legion, which it was thought might undertake to train a projected Wardens Service, and the Boy Scouts Association, which might organise emergency communications.

Local training, since it was mainly to depend on the activities

---

[1] The number which had then actually submitted schemes was only nine.

of 'graduates' from the Falfield school, was only beginning by the end of 1936. But some supplies of Service and Civilian Duty masks and protective clothing were issued during the year, and in the autumn the Home Office distributed some forty motor Gas Vans to the police in various centres. By the end of the year the Department had issued five handbooks and three memoranda; six of these, prepared in conjunction with the Chemical Defence Research Department, dealt with some aspect of anti-gas precautions.

A start was also made in 1936 with a scheme of anti-gas training for members of the medical profession. The Department discovered that the number of doctors in the country familiar with the diagnosis and treatment of gas casualties was very limited. After consultation with the General Medical Council and other bodies, it added to its staff some medical instructors to give anti-gas training to medical, dental and veterinary practitioners and nurses at suitable centres in the country. Ten instructors began courses in the autumn, and the demand for their services proved such that their number was increased after a few months to seventeen.

During these eighteen months the Department made no direct approach to the British public, beyond putting its handbooks and memoranda on sale, and meeting some requests for public lectures.[1] Among other reasons for this, such as the concentration on building local organisation and the need to supply more training equipment, the Department wished 'to avoid creating any sense of panic or alarm, or the impression that war is imminent'. However, it began early to prepare a *Householder's Handbook* designed to tell the ordinary citizen in simple terms how to carry out the basic advice he was being offered, namely to stay indoors in a gas-proof room or refuge.

An announcement that such instructions were being prepared was made in Parliament in June 1936 by the Parliamentary Under-Secretary to the Home Office, Mr Geoffrey Lloyd. Some weeks earlier the Government had told Parliament that 'a simple but effective form of respirator for use by the civil population' had been devised and that, should the need arise, it would issue this free to every citizen liable to air attack.[2] The interest evinced by Parliament in the topic of A.R.P. nevertheless remained slight; the increase of the A.R.P. Department's share of the Home Office Estimate for 1936–37 to £477,500 (mainly on account of anti-gas equipment) occasioned no debate. Warfare, though it ended that summer in Abyssinia with the aggressor's triumph, broke out soon afterwards in Spain. Yet a general war which would involve Britain still seemed a remote contingency. The Labour Party conference

---

[1] Up to the end of 1936 the largest issue of any handbook, including distribution to local authorities, was about 118,000; and the issue of the first circular was 45,000.
[2] H. of C. Deb., Vol. 310, Col. 2799, 8th April 1936.

in the autumn 'showed the Party to be hopelessly divided' on the rearmament issue.[1] Not long afterwards the Prime Minister, in a statement of 'appalling frankness' that was to become historic, admitted delay by the Government in introducing rearmament, and attributed some part of the blame to the electorate and the fact that 'a democracy is always two years behind the dictator'.[2]

As the new year opened the Department took certain steps to publicise its activities more widely among M.P.s and the public. On 12th January the respirator factory at Blackburn, the origins of which will shortly be described, was opened by Mr Geoffrey Lloyd in the presence of photographers and the Press. Later that day Mr Lloyd, in the first official broadcast about A.R.P., described the Government's plans for respirators and appealed for volunteers for A.R.P. duties.[3] Two months later a party of M.P.s visited the Anti-Gas School; at about the same time some 70 supporters of the Government in the Commons formed an A.R.P. Committee to instruct themselves in the subject and pass on their knowledge to the public. To stimulate recruiting the Department began the issue in March of an A.R.P. badge to trained volunteers recommended by their local authorities.

A significant step involving the public was the formation, announced in Parliament on 4th March, of an 'Air Raid Wardens Service'.[4] The idea of forming such a service had been discussed in 1934 by the planners, who had observed the organisation in Nazi Germany of a system of 'House Wardens' (*Luftschutz Hauswarte*).[5] Elaboration of a British version of this system, which would provide 'a link between the local or other authorities responsible for general A.R.P. organisations and the general public' began with a memorandum by the Assistant Under-Secretary of State of July 1935. Discussions with local authorities, who in general approved the idea, and with the Police War Duties Committee followed.[6] The Police Committee did not favour enrolment of wardens as special constables, and secured a limitation of the duties envisaged for wardens which was later to have much significance. The function of fighting, as distinct from reporting, incipient fires was taken away from 'Street Wardens' and assigned to a separate body of 'Fire Wardens', who would form part of an enlarged Auxiliary Fire Service. The general scheme was approved by the Defence Policy and Requirements

---

[1] *Annual Register, 1936*, p. 82.
[2] H. of C. Deb., Vol. 317, Col. 1144, 12th November 1936.
[3] *The Times*, 13th January 1937.
[4] H. of C. Deb., Vol. 321, Cols. 525–8.
[5] During the First World War groups of neighbours in some parts of London had formed voluntary bodies to keep watch at night for raiders and perform other services.
[6] This committee had been appointed by the Home Secretary in April 1935 'to consider and advise on questions relative to the duties of the police in the event of war'.

Committee early in 1937. On the day of the Parliamentary announcement a memorandum was published describing the proposed service in detail;[1] and the Home Secretary, Sir John Simon, made a short broadcast asking for volunteers for 'this very important part of the work of Home Defence'.[2]

The scheme thus launched was, in its essential features, to stand the test of time and to furnish civil defence with perhaps its most distinctive institution. 'The general idea of an air raid warden', the memorandum read, 'is that he should be a responsible member of the public chosen to be a leader and adviser of his neighbours in a small area, a street or a small group of streets, in which he is known and respected'. Endowed with a list of virtues to which many aspire but which relatively few attain, he (or she) was to stand in the front line of the battle performing the important functions of, (i) maintaining morale by setting an example of steadiness, shepherding the public to places of safety, and assisting with casualties and damage after the bombs had fallen, and (ii) reporting the fall of bombs, the damage caused, and the presence of gas or fires to the police, local A.R.P. headquarters and the specialised services. It was proposed that in towns of any size wardens should operate from fixed posts, each responsible for a 'sector' or defined group of streets, containing (in residential areas) some 500 inhabitants; during attacks each post would be manned by two or three wardens. Intimate knowledge of his locality would be an essential part of the warden's qualifications. It was also proposed that before an emergency wardens might help with the fitting, distribution, and replacement of civilian gas-masks.

It was clearly proposed that wardens should 'form a recognised service of their own', or a corps organised locally under a Chief Warden helped by a number of Head Wardens in charge of groups of posts. Men over thirty years of age were to be preferred, and there was no reason why women should be excluded. In such A.R.P. enrolment as had so far taken place, local practice over recruiting women had shown much variation. The Department, while leaving it to local authorities to make their own decisions in this matter, had decided that women should only be excluded from A.R.P. service on grounds of physical weakness and not of danger.

Wardens would require, besides outstanding personal qualities, extensive training of a semi-specialist kind, including anti-gas defence. They would be provided with equipment for personal protection. The number needed throughout the country was stated by the Home Secretary to be no less than 250,000 to 300,000.

It was obvious that wardens' functions would bear close affinities

---

[1] Memorandum No. 4 (1st edn.), *Air Raid Wardens*.

[2] Like Mr Lloyd's broadcast of January, at a relatively unimportant time in the B.B.C's daily programme.

to those of the police. In its recommendations on their local organisation the Department suggested this should take one of three forms: (i) organisation in peace and control in war directly by the Chief Officer of Police, (ii) organisation, independently of the police, under the control of some other local official, and (iii) a hybrid system under which the Chief Warden would bear main responsibility until the outbreak of war, when operational control would be exercised by the Chief Constable. For the Metropolitan Police District, with its many authorities and unwieldy size, the second alternative had been adopted. The preference for decentralisation of the wardens' organisation, which dictated this choice, also led to choice of the borough and district councils as the authorities to be normally responsible outside London for initiating the service.

This plan and the announcement of the Government's plans for the emergency fire brigade services[1] gave the local authorities their immediate recruiting problems. The A.R.P. Inspectors had now completed a first 'cover' of the whole country and reported adequate growth in the number of schemes and in public interest. But evidence had been accumulating of a hardening attitude on the part of many authorities on the financial issue. For some the absolute responsibility of the Government in this matter had, from the outset, been an axiom; others, hitherto more amenable, had reached practical problems involving large expenditure. The previous December the Association of Municipal Corporations had put before the Home Secretary a demand for 100 per cent. Government grant for A.R.P. expenditure. Negotiations on this issue were protracted, and occupied a central place in the A.R.P. story during 1937. An account of them must, however, be deferred until notice has been taken of the approach to industrial organisations and the Government's activities regarding equipment and other matters.

Approach to Industry

The Department defined its work in the summer of 1937 as 'an attempt, for the first time, completely to organise what might be called the Home Front'. If support had been given to this description by addition of the Wardens' Service to the other proposed services, further support was provided by the Department's efforts to extend defence measures to what it described collectively as 'industry'.

In the survey of 1925 the maintenance of vital services had formed an important topic. In a future war, under the accepted scale of attack, damage to water supplies, power, food supplies and communications could present a problem of unprecedented size. During 1925–35 this problem, especially as it concerned London, had figured

---

[1] See Chapter VI.

prominently among the matters engaging the authorities' attention. Under the modest relaxation of the secrecy rule, consultations had begun with London public utilities and some plans had been prepared. Considerable discussion had taken place with the London Passenger Transport Board about the protection and use in war of the underground railways. The G.P.O. had made plans for an emergency system of communications in the Tubes. The Port of London Authority had made an outline scheme for protection of the docks, and the Metropolitan Water Board and the gas companies had begun examination of the problem.

Experience led the planners at an early stage to make two important conclusions. First, that organising passive defence for industry should be regarded as a separate problem from organising this elsewhere; secondly, that much variety of method in organisation of individual branches and units of industry should be allowed for. Managers of undertakings or groups of undertakings would be asked to take measures to protect employees and plant appropriate to their particular business. Action on their part would, like that of local authorities and the private citizen, be voluntary.

Before the A.R.P. Department was formed consultations had been followed by preparation of some confidential instructions, and the drafting of a pamphlet for manufacturers' guidance. With the bringing of A.R.P. into the open consultation with groups of undertakings was to be extended. First consideration was still to be given to water supply, gas, electricity and sewage services and communications. After fuller study of the problems involved for each of these utilities in London, it was hoped to establish principles applicable to utilities of the same type throughout the country.

It was clear that activities in this sphere raised many and varied technical issues; since the only weapon the Department possessed was persuasion, much depended on the goodwill of individual firms. The Department reported in the summer of 1936 that confidential instructions on A.R.P. in gas, electricity, and water undertakings were almost complete, and these were issued, under the titles of *A.R.P. Memoranda, Nos. C1, C2 and C3*, in September. Consideration of the question by the Railway Companies was still rudimentary. But the L.P.T.B. had nearly completed a comprehensive scheme, and the fruits of discussions with it were being used by the Department to frame instructions for all road transport undertakings. With the help of the B.B.C. and Cable and Wireless Ltd., some study had been made of protecting wireless transmission and reception stations, and the G.P.O. had brought its plans to an advanced state. A handbook had been issued on *Anti-Gas Precautions for Merchant Shipping*. Further consultations with the Port of London Authority had produced an outline scheme for protection of the

London Docks area, which was circulated to all other large dock authorities. The Department, in alliance with the Board of Trade, had begun study of the considerable problems of protecting, particularly against gas, goods stored in docks and warehouses and food supplies.

The Department also extended its consultations and advice to industrial and commercial firms of a varied nature. It set out to induce every factory employing more than about 100 persons to prepare a miniature A.R.P. scheme, including plans for first aid to casualties, decontamination of premises and prevention of fire. These concerns were encouraged to make themselves as independent as possible of local authority organisation, without overlooking the need to co-ordinate plans with the local authorities.

Approach to employers took place first through the Federation of British Industries, the Chambers of Commerce and similar bodies. By mid-1936 some 1,500 firms had been made aware of the A.R.P. problem through visits from the Inspectors and other means. Conferences had been held with some large London retail shops, and two London authorities, Westminster and Holborn, had undertaken to circularise every shop in their boroughs on the subject. In November the Department published a handbook on *Air Raid Precautions in Factories and Business Premises*. This and the specialised memoranda on public utilities gave industry basic guides similar to that already furnished to local authorities by the 'first circular'.

While the Department expressed satisfaction with the employers' response, it pointed out that the action these would take would depend in the main on their financial standing. Some large undertakings had shown a readiness to proceed with large plans without questioning their cost which could hardly be expected of less wealthy concerns. The same problem already appeared in more acute form with the utilities. The large London utilities, almost without exception, had adopted the view that any measures unnecessary in peace should be the financial responsibility of the Government. The measures necessary to maintain their services under the scale of attack envisaged would prove most costly. For example, the Central Electricity Board had estimated £500,000 as the cost of a national reserve of switch-gear; the Metropolitan Water Board considered £200,000 would be required for provision of portable plant and another £200,000 to improve the Board's system at a number of points where supplies were considered inadequate for fire fighting.

In the memorandum on the *Financial Aspects of Air Raid Precautions* submitted to the Defence Policy and Requirements Committee early in 1937 the Department produced a gross estimate of the total cost of safeguarding electricity, water, domestic gas, railways, docks and oil supplies over the whole country of not less than £10 millions. It proposed that the maximum Government contribution under this heading should be £5 millions distributed among these services. The Committee decided to refer the problem to a special sub-committee on the protection of vital services.[1]

The Department's approach to industry had followed much the same course as that to local authorities. General presentation of the problem had been followed by specialised study and advice with respect to industrial groups or individual concerns. Concrete application of the principles established, though it had made progress, began after a time to meet the stumbling-block of cost. For industry this difficulty was aggravated by the fact that structural alterations, included among the recommendations made in the relevant handbook, were treated for income tax purposes as capital expenditure and therefore did not earn relief.[2]

During 1937, nevertheless, further general advances were made. A beginning was made in March with the formation, in the electricity supply industry, of the first of a number of national A.R.P. Committees, designed to work out schemes in more detail and to extend the series of confidential memoranda. Some utilities (e.g., the L.M.S. Railway) and private firms (e.g., Messrs. Boots) appointed A.R.P. organisers. The Department enlisted the support of the Factory Inspectors of the Home Office, and extended its educational efforts to the coal mines and the shipbuilding and brickmaking industries. Increasing provision was made for public utility and other officials at the Anti-Gas School.

The decision to ask industry to organise A.R.P. independently of the main (local government) structure created the problem which even at this stage caused some concern, of devising means for co-operation between the two spheres. In a few centres (e.g. Sheffield) joint A.R.P. Committees of local government and industry had been established. In May 1937 the Home Office emphasised to local authorities the need for co-ordination of plans with those of industry and suggested the creation, where possible, of joint committees. An appeal of a similar kind was made by the national employers' organisations to industrialists.

Special Problems, Equipment and Experiments

The emphasis placed by the planners on the danger of poison-gas was, it may be remarked, by no means confined to British authorities. It had caused the British authorities, like those of various Continental countries, to devote early attention to improving and

---

[1] See p. 62.
[2] H. of C. Deb., Vol. 323, Col. 526, 29th April 1937.

extending the protective equipment used during 1914–18. It will be recalled that by 1935 the Committee of Imperial Defence had reached certain decisions in this sphere.[1] Two types of gas-mask, the General Service and Special Service, and protective clothing would be supplied to persons whose duties might require them to enter and remain in gassed areas. Provision for respirators and a contribution to research by the Chemical Defence Research Department had accounted for more than half the original total of £100,000 authorised for A.R.P. expenditure. Some months after the A.R.P. Department's formation an adequate preliminary design for a respirator which could be mass-produced at a cost of about 2s. apiece had been evolved, and the Government had undertaken to issue this free to all citizens in the danger areas.[2]

The obligation was novel, since in no previous war had a Government had to contemplate the possible death or injury of so large a proportion of the civil population, and damage to so much civilian property, by one weapon. The memorandum on A.R.P. requirements which the Department had sent to the Defence Requirements Committee in October 1935 contained these items—respirators, a device for protection against gas of children under five, protective clothing, bleach powder and hospital equipment. Of the estimated cost of providing these during 1936–39 of £5,540,000, the three types of respirator accounted for £4,520,000. Requirements of the General Service and Special Service masks were estimated at 400,000 in each case and would cost some £520,000. For the civilian mask, the figure of 30 million, arrived at by excluding only areas in the extreme west, south-west and north-west of Britain in which the risk was most remote, was proposed as a minimum. If the population of these areas was included, the requirement would be 40 million and the cost £4 millions.

After authority had been given to proceed on the basis of 30 million of the civilian masks and 400,000 of each of the others, a sub-committee of the Committee of Imperial Defence examined the production problem. The General Service mask was produced under War Office arrangements which included an assembly factory at Leyland in Lancashire, and it was agreed that A.R.P. requirements could be met from this source. The War Office undertook to supply the Department's demand for the Special Service type, but only until such time as an emergency arose. The Home Office had therefore to solve the problems of producing its war-time requirements of this second type and the 30 million civilian masks needed by March 1939, and providing for replacement of these and their continued supply in war.

---

[1] pp. 47–48, 51.
[2] pp. 61, 70.

The designers, the Chemical Defence Research Department, secured provisional Home Office agreement that they should aim at perfecting design of the civilian mask by the end of 1936.[1] In addition to other technical problems involved, this design had to allow for resistance to deterioration during long periods of storage. During the summer of 1936, however, the Home Office expressed its satisfaction with the design and approval was given by the Defence Policy and Requirements Committee to a speeding up of the programme, by which 5 million civilian masks would be produced by the end of that year and the balance by the end of 1937.

The solution to the problem of an assembly factory for these masks was found in a disused cotton mill at Blackburn, not far from the War Office factory at Leyland. This choice was mainly due to the fact that the Home Office had obtained authority to employ the firm managing the War Office establishment, the only one in the country with this type of experience, as its agents in the new undertaking.[2] The mills passed into Government ownership on 13th July, and the work of dismantling weaving machinery and installing the new equipment proceeded. The factory began assembly of the civilian mask (in three sizes) on 30th November. By the next February it had assembled three quarters of a million, and achieved a weekly production rate of a quarter of a million. Authority was obtained in that month to raise the programme to a total of 40 million masks to be produced by the early summer of 1938. Mention has been made earlier of the formal opening of the Blackburn factory on 12th January 1937 by Mr Geoffrey Lloyd.

The new mask consisted of a facepiece, a container which held the two filtering media, an india rubber band to connect these two parts, and an india rubber non-return valve for the inner end of the container. The variety of components involved was considerable, and the total numbers of some items required were astronomical. The facepiece, for example, included vulcanised sheet rubber, cellulose acetate eyepieces, cotton webbing, slides, buckles, safety pins and other materials. Ninety million safety pins and the same number of slides were needed and thirty million of the other items. The complete container included canister bodies and ends, wire diaphragms, cotton pads, muslin diaphragms, filter pads, springs and activated charcoal. From ninety to thirty millions of these individual items were necessary, and 4,000 tons of activated charcoal.[3] Contracts for the facepieces were placed with a number of private firms for delivery of the article complete. The components of the

---

[1] Some General Service respirators had been sent to Malta and Aden for protection of the civil populations during the winter of 1935–36.

[2] J. E. Baxter & Co Ltd, of Leyland.

[3] For a fuller description of respirators and other anti-gas equipment see A.R.P. Handbook No. 1, *Personal Protection against Gas.*

container were contracted for separately and then assembled at Blackburn. Delays naturally occurred through the reorganisation and additional plant required by these orders, and for some time the total supplies in the country of activated charcoal were far below the Blackburn factory's needs.

Before this factory began operations the Department had started to examine 'the very big question' of storage of respirators and anti-gas clothing. No issue of this equipment except for training purposes, either to the A.R.P. Services or the public, was proposed until an emergency arose. But plans were based on the assumption that if an emergency did occur distribution might have to be completed in a matter of hours rather than days. The problem of preserving the rubber in the facepiece had been overcome through the development of a method of storing this part in nitrogen; it was therefore decided to store containers separately, and to leave the work of fitting the two pieces together to the final distributor (e.g., the warden).

In June 1936 the Department had appointed a Director of Supply and begun to form a Supply Branch, composed mainly of officials on loan from the Admiralty, to arrange manufacture of the civilian mask and provision of other equipment. By the end of 1937 this Branch had expanded considerably and included officers in charge of Regional Stores and an inspecting staff. Further measure of the scale of these activities was given by the Estimates. For the second year of operations (1936–37) the Department's Estimate rose to £477,500 of which £390,000 was on account of anti-gas equipment and materials. For the third year (1937–38) the total increased nearly tenfold to £4,617,500. Almost £4,000,000 of this sum was needed for respirators and other equipment; another £191,000 was estimated for the respirator factory, and for equipment inspection, storage and distribution.[1] The Home Office contribution to research in this sphere by the War Office rose from £16,500 in 1936–37 to £60,000 in the next year.

It had been decided to store masks and other equipment in a number of Regional Stores, situated if possible in relatively non-vulnerable areas. The first of these was opened in October 1936 at Manchester; the facepieces were sent by contractors to this store, which included plant for vacuumising and recharging with nitrogen the cans in which they were packed. By the end of 1937 seven (out of an intended total of thirteen) Regional Stores had been opened; these contained 18¼ million civilian masks, and a further 3 million such masks were in storage lent by the Admiralty.

In the meantime, production had been further speeded up. During February 1937 the Blackburn factory, by introducing double shifts,

---

[1] Civil Estimates and Estimates for Revenue Departments for the year ending 31st March 1938. H.C. 58.

had attained an assembly of civilian masks of half-a-million per week. On 1st April the Home Office, by agreement with the War Office, had taken responsibility for assembling all Special Service masks, now renamed 'Civilian Duty' masks. By December 1937, with some help from Boots Drug Company in assembling the civilian mask containers, 23 million of these and 25 million facepieces had been produced.

Once design of the civilian mask was undertaken it was realised that a special device would have to be evolved to protect children under five. The Chemical Defence Research Department and the Porton Experimental Station worked on various devices which, for one reason or another, had to be discarded. These included a cardboard box, fitted with a hand pump to which the container was attached; a portable tent, to be erected inside a room by some such means as suspension from picture rails, and a hood to be fitted to perambulators. By the end of 1937 a device, described as an 'anti-gas helmet', for babies up to about two had been evolved and provisionally accepted by the A.R.P. Department. The question of how to protect infants too large to wear this but unable to wear the small-size normal respirator presented difficulties still to be overcome.

Another technical problem deserves bare mention, as it illustrates the novelty of equipping the whole civil population. Wearers of the General Service mask would not be expected to include large numbers who used spectacles; but with civilian users of the other two types the situation was otherwise. It was found that while flat-sided spectacles could be worn with the Civilian Duty mask this was not so with the normal civilian type, and at the end of 1937 experts were still working on this problem.

Two other matters relating to masks require some notice. At an early stage the authorities had given thought to protecting the public against commercial sale of masks and other anti-gas equipment of inferior quality. During its first year the Department published a certification mark system for masks. A standard specification, roughly equivalent to that of the Civilian Duty mask, was available to any firm wishing to manufacture this article. After submitting its mask for inspection and passing this test, the manufacturer could stamp each specimen with a national mark, registered by the Home Office at the Patent Office. The buyer would have the assurance that the article would give him protection of a certain minimum officially-approved standard. A similar system was contemplated for air filtration units to ventilate large shelters and similar places.

The announcement in April 1936 of the Government's plans for civilian masks virtually eliminated commercial production for the home market. Some firms, however, later undertook production of the Civilian Duty type, mainly for sale to industrial concerns, and with respect to these the certification mark system filled a useful purpose.

A final matter which concerned gas-masks belongs perhaps more properly to the topic of public reactions to A.R.P. Early in 1937 some scientific workers at Cambridge University, who described themselves as the 'Cambridge Scientists' Anti-War Group' and their function as that of acting as 'a technical and advisory body to national and international peace movements', published a book attacking the Government's A.R.P. plans.[1] This body had studied the official advice about the 'gas-proofing' of rooms, the civilian mask, and extinguishing incendiary bombs, and then conducted some experiments. It claimed to have shown that the measures officially proposed were ineffective or inadequate, and implied that these constituted deception of the public. The mask they had put to various tests was of a 'civilian type' bought on the open market, and not the official article. And their book's declared aim of offering a critical examination of A.R.P. measures was faithfully followed, to the exclusion of any positive counter-suggestions.

It has been noticed that as 1937 opened the Government was taking steps to make A.R.P. plans more widely known to the public;[2] and this deliberate challenge found a sympathetic echo in various quarters, and caused it some concern. Questions about the Cambridge experiments were asked in Parliament, for example on the occasion of the announcement of the new Wardens' Service; sections of the Press began a critical campaign, and questions were put to officials trying to build up A.R.P. services over the country. The Government's reply was that the experiments were academic (in the sense of removed from reality), and based on fallacious assumptions about the conditions likely to be met in actual warfare.[3] In spite of pressure the authorities refused to engage in technical controversy with the scientists in question and within a few months the agitation subsided. At the close of the year, however, a report on the official experiments (in supervision of which the Chemical Defence Committee had been helped by eminent scientists not in Government employment) was circulated to local authorities and otherwise made public.

While it can be argued that the scientific details and administrative repercussions of this affair have only small historical significance, interest attaches to the attitude of this group of scientists and their supporters to rearmament. The Group, in spite of its title, did not in their book attack general preparations for war, but only these

[1] *The Protection of the Public from Aerial Attack* (Left Book Club Topical Book, Victor Gollancz Ltd, 1937.)

[2] p. 71.

[3] H. of C. Deb., Vol. 320, Col. 1348, 18th February 1937.

particular preparations—an ambiguous position which was perhaps not uncommon in 1937.

After the mask, the main item of personal anti-gas equipment was clothing to protect the body against mustard and other blister gases. By the end of 1936 the A.R.P. Department had obtained from the War Office and issued on loan for training some 6,000 suits of protective clothing of the kind then designed for the Fighting Services. This pattern, however, suffered from two serious defects— it was too cumbersome to be worn except for a very short time by anyone engaged in heavy work, and it deteriorated in storage. The Chemical Defence Research Department was undertaking research into the impregnation of uniforms, which might provide the solution for the 250,000 sets of clothing required for A.R.P. Services. This method, in turn, met with difficulties. During 1937 the possibility was being examined of producing suits of anti-gas clothing by proofing various fabrics with linseed oil.

The last of the main items concerned with gas defence, large supplies of which had to be arranged for well in advance, was bleach powder for cleansing and decontamination. The Department's estimate for its war-time need of this article was 1,500 tons a week, and when the requirements of the Service Departments were added the total much exceeded existing British production. There was also the complication that commercial bleaching powder deteriorated rapidly in storage. In 1937, however, the War Office decided to erect a factory to produce chlorine and agreed to furnish the supplies of bleach required for A.R.P. purposes.

In the Department's memorandum to the Cabinet on *Financial Aspects of Air Raid Precautions* of March 1937 authority was sought to buy the most elementary means of protection against high explosive bombs—namely, sandbags. A rough calculation had estimated the number of sandbags for which demand might arise on the outbreak of a war as one thousand million. On the assumption that sandbags or paper bags could be mass-produced at a flat rate of 1d. each, the total cost would be about £4¼ millions; and the Department asked permission to proceed to buy over a number of years half the quantity just mentioned, or five hundred million. By the time this matter was discussed by the Defence Policy and Requirements Committee the estimated cost of supplying this article had risen considerably, and it was clear that provision of the quantity suggested would put some strain on the jute or paper industries. The Committee therefore instructed the Department to make a preliminary purchase over six months of about forty-two million bags, and to investigate the possibility of obtaining further supplies made from paper.

Production of these different types of anti-gas equipment owed much to continuous research and experiment. These activities possessed a deposit of practical experience, dating at least from the introduction of gas into war by the Germans in 1915, and their own organisation and funds. About the modern use and effects of the two other main ingredients of air attack—high explosive and incendiary bombs—much less was known. The A.R.P. Department reported in the summer of 1937 its work to be seriously handicapped by 'the absence of practical experience of the effect of modern weapons of air attack, and the lack of reliable data from which to deduce their probable effects'.

Before the Department's formation the Bombing Test Committee had made plans for three groups of tests into penetrative and other effects of high explosive bombs, and the designs of concrete structures to resist such bombs.[1] When some funds had been made available for experiments, this committee was reconstituted under the chairmanship of H.M. Chief Inspector of Explosives. Since no special facilities for A.R.P. purposes existed, these experiments were carried out under authority of the Ordnance Committee at Woolwich Arsenal, Shoeburyness and other places where the Service Departments' needs enjoyed priority.

For some years after 1935 progress in establishing the special data required for A.R.P. purposes was slow. It has been noted that in February 1936 the Home Secretary appointed a strong technical committee under the chairmanship of Sir Arnold Wilson on Structural Precautions against Air Attack. This was asked to recommend, in the light of the information available on damage caused by the main types of bomb, protective measures to be incorporated in new or existing buildings. It appointed various sub-committees, including a Data Committee to collate the available material, and a Shelters Committee. Though these made some advance, the main committee found it necessary in November 1937, when the A.R.P. Bill was in preparation, to examine the causes of a general lack of progress. It concluded there was still a serious lack of data on which to base any recommendations, including lack of information about some of the trials carried out under the Bombing Tests Committee's auspices. And it recorded its considered opinion that structural precautions were of such importance that it was in the highest degree desirable that the Home Office should have an independent research department.

Delays in establishing this data did not prevent a growing number of requests to the Department for information and advice. The Government had stated that effective blast and splinter protection could be obtained at comparatively small cost, and promised advice to occupiers of premises and others. Also, local authorities had been

---

[1] p. 54.

asked to earmark places which might be used as shelters, and to plan to make these proof both against gas and high explosive blast and splinters.

The official distinction between 'bomb-proof' shelters and those to give only blast and splinter protection was important, and centred on issues not only of cost but of the safety likely to be obtained and of morale. In 1917 a Cabinet Committee had reported in favour of a shelter policy of 'dispersal', or encouraging the public to rely in general on the protection offered by their homes rather than to gather in crowds in any public place. This view had, on the whole, persisted; and the shelters which, as just stated, local authorities were asked to earmark were intended for citizens caught unawares in the open streets.

At an early stage, however, the A.R.P. Department, though stating that it strongly deprecated the congregation of large numbers of persons in one place, was forced to admit some exceptions to this policy. The Dover caves and the Mersey Tunnel, for example, offered obvious attractions as air raid refuges; since to deny their use for this purpose 'would probably appear highly illogical', it assisted in projects to make this use safe. But its main preoccupation in this sphere before 1938 was with giving advice to industrialists and other private enquirers (e.g., builders of blocks of flats) and to those responsible for erection of buildings such as police and fire stations.

There was similar need for experiment to establish data on which defence against the incendiary bomb might be based. The planning of defence against the element of fire in air attack (to which small reference has so far been made) was distinguished from planning against high explosive and gas attack by one essential feature. Fire was not a calamity which occurred only in war, or owed much to the invention of bomb-carrying aircraft. London, for example, was nearly destroyed by fire in the year 798; and methods of defeating fire, which doubtless existed even then, had been maintained ever since.[1] Nevertheless, the development of aircraft and the light incendiary bomb introduced problems that were new in scale if not in kind and called for fresh planning on two complementary lines: first to expand and equip the fire brigades to deal with the serious fires in number and in scale that must be anticipated from incendiary attack from the air, and second, to discover means whereby the public could co-operate in protecting their own homes and business places against this new menace.

---

[1] The Royal Commission of 1921 recorded that at Rome under the Caesars, 'there was a large body of Imperial Firemen and some kind of hose, commanded by a Siphonarius or Firemaster'. *Report of the Royal Commission on Fire Brigades and Fire Prevention*, Cmd. 1945, 1923.

At the end of the First World War English fire-fighting services were in a stage of transition from the era of the horse-drawn steam fire engine to that of the self-propelled motor-driven pump. But if use of mechanical equipment was becoming more general, the organisation may fairly be described as archaic. The fire brigade powers were spread over a great number of separate authorities,[1] most of whom were responsible for very small areas and had slender resources. No authority except the L.C.C. was under any statutory obligation to maintain fire services of any kind: no standards of efficiency had been laid down and such arrangements as there were for mutual support were generally on a small scale and inadequate. The Royal Commission on Fire Brigades and Fire Prevention which had reported in 1923,[2] had made recommendations for improving fire brigade organisation, but so far the Government had been unable to find time for legislation.

The Home Office was the Department concerned with problems of fire prevention in general; and it possessed a Fire Adviser who, as noted earlier, had furnished the A.R.P. Committees with information in the years before 1935. The first A.R.P. circular of July 1935 had referred to a forthcoming inquiry into the fire brigade services of England and Wales, and the report of this (Riverdale) Committee was published a year later.[3] The Committee dealt with both peacetime and emergency problems. On the former, it supported in the main the recommendations of the Royal Commission, though legislation did not follow until 1938. The work of preparing both the new legislation and the emergency measures was entrusted in October 1936 to a new Home Office division, in charge of the Assistant Under-Secretary of State who directed the work of the Police Division, Mr Arthur Dixon.[4] The circulars laying the foundations of the emergency measures were issued in February, 1937. These, it must be noted here, were more liberal than the A.R.P. circular regarding financial assistance to local authorities.

On the question of how the public might co-operate with fire brigades, experience of fire attacks on London and elsewhere during 1914–18 was no longer of much technical relevance, owing not only to aircraft development but to evolution of the incendiary bomb, and particularly of the so-called 'kilo magnesium (elektron)' type. In the summer of 1935 H.M. Chief Inspector of Explosives,

---

[1] In England and Wales, they were the London County Council, the Town and Urban District Councils and the Parish Councils and Parish Meetings, and in Scotland the County Councils and Town Councils.

[2] Cmd. 1945.

[3] *Report of the Departmental Committee on Fire Brigade Services*, Cmd. 5224, 1936.

[4] This work is fully discussed in Chapter VI.

Lt.-Col. R. A. Thomas, and the Home Office Fire Adviser, Lt.-Col. G. Symonds, had begun experiments with the Research Department at Woolwich into the effects of and defence against this type of bomb. It is important to note that from the outset these experiments embraced investigation of methods (including appliances) by which householders and factory staffs, as well as trained fire brigades, might extinguish or remove such missiles.

Early in 1936 two sub-committees were formed, under the chairmanship of H.M. Chief Inspector of Explosives and including representatives of the Service Departments, one being concerned with the incendiary bomb and the other with the problem of fires in oil depots. Trials were continued under their supervision at Shoeburyness, Woolwich Arsenal and elsewhere. Later that year these trials became more realistic as a result of use of incendiary and other bombs by German and Italian aircraft supporting General Franco in the Spanish Civil War. Specimens of these weapons, as well as a detailed report on *The Effects of Aerial Bombardment and Emergency Measures taken by the Municipal Authorities in Madrid*,[1] were furnished by an A.R.P. Department Inspector who visited Spain in the winter of 1936–37.

A demonstration of how to deal with the light incendiary bomb had been included in the Anti-Gas School curriculum in November 1936; and in February 1937 the Home Office Fire Adviser staged a demonstration at Barnes at which bombs were successfully controlled and fires extinguished by teams of girls with only short training. At an exercise held later at Southampton a group of air raid wardens carried out this function with such success that the Department concluded it must aim to train all householders in the handling of incendiary bombs. Various ways of doing this were being discussed during the latter months of the year.

Experiments relating to modern weapons of attack were accompanied during 1935–37 by others relating to different problems, notably warning and lighting systems. Attention to these must, however, be deferred until some miscellaneous topics have been mentioned.

The Defence Requirements Committee had emphasised in November 1935 the dangers to which Britain's vital industries were liable under air attack. The next March the Committee of Imperial Defence approved the appointment of a sub-committee of the Home Defence Committee to investigate and co-ordinate all methods of protecting 'vital points'. These comprised factories and other places of special war importance; and the protection to be examined covered not only passive defence but active defence and the problem of location in relation to defence. The specialised and prolonged

---

[1] Prepared by the Home Office (March 1937).

inquiries necessary were conducted by a few inspecting officers, working in conjunction with the A.R.P. Department.

Problems of smoke screens and camouflage were similar to some of those just discussed, in combining some experience acquired in 1914–18 with considerable technical novelty (in which all the Service Departments felt interest) for potential use in a future war. Use of smoke screens for air raid defence had been considered in 1925, and with the formation of the A.R.P. Department this matter was revived. In the spring of 1936 a sub-committee on this subject, under the chairmanship of the head of the Department and with representatives of the Service Departments and of chemical and oil concerns, was formed. Thereafter tests showed the need for further research, and provision of a new type of generator, before a full-scale trial for A.R.P. purposes could be staged. Research and experiment regarding camouflage as it might serve the purposes of A.R.P. were met during 1937 by provision of facilities at the Royal Aircraft Establishment at Farnborough.

Examination was being continued by a Committee of Imperial Defence sub-committee, presided over by the Permanent Secretary to the Treasury, into the question of the location of the seat of Government in war.[1]

The A.R.P. Department's assumption of responsibility for planning certain medical services entailed collection of data and research in this sphere.[2] The medical arrangements proposed in the 'first circular' were to rest on the three institutions of the first aid post, the 'casualty clearing station' and the 'base hospital' situated beyond a 15-mile radius from the centre of London or other main target; and in May 1936 the Department asked local authorities to provide information to enable it to compile a national survey of bed accommodation in hospitals. The next November the Minister for Co-ordination of Defence appointed a committee to consider the co-ordination of medical arrangements in war. This, on which the Home Office, the Health Departments and the Service Departments were represented, was later reconstituted under the Chairmanship of the Chief Medical Officer of the Ministry of Health, Sir Arthur S. MacNalty. Its proposal that organisation of base hospitals should be the responsibility of the Minister of Health and the Secretary of State for Scotland was approved by the Committee of Imperial Defence in December 1937.

In the meantime, the A.R.P. Department had been holding conferences with the L.C.C., the Voluntary Hospitals and the St. John and Red Cross Societies to work out a detailed scheme for a network of casualty clearing stations in the London area. It had

---

[1] Appointed February 1936, pp. 53–54.
[2] p. 63.

also been examining the layout, staffing and equipment of first aid posts, and what it called 'the vast ambulance scheme' which would be required. This problem embraced designs for a stretcher more suitable for civilian use than the accepted military article, and for a fitment to enable normal commercial vehicles to be used as ambulances.

In the autumn of 1936 the Department appointed an Intelligence Officer. The survey in the last chapter of planning from 1924–35 should have indicated the attention the British authorities had paid to foreign passive defence activities. An A.R.P. intelligence section was to continue this study, on information obtained through Service channels, from foreign literature and other sources; and was to act as an intelligence agency on passive defence for the Service Departments. The Intelligence Officer and others of the Department made visits in this phase to A.R.P. exercises in Berlin and Vienna, to Paris to inspect French arrangements for shelters and to Spain.

On the outbreak of the Italo-Abyssinian war in the autumn of 1935 an officer of the Department and an officer of the Chemical Defence Research Department visited Malta and drew up a scheme of passive defence for the Island's civil population. The Department already sent its publications and gave information to the Dominion, Indian and Colonial Governments. Officials from the Colonies and from Egypt attended the Anti-Gas School in this early period, and delegations from Sweden and Yugo-Slavia were given facilities to study British A.R.P. methods.

Warning and Lighting

The warning and lighting arrangements, like most of the problems just described, were still mainly a matter of discussion and experiment rather than of practical organisation. They had certain common features which set them apart from the problems discussed in previous sections of this chapter. The first circular placed them at the head of the list of subjects on which action was to be taken by the Government, and political, administrative and technical reasons made them the special concern of the central authorities. Experience regarding them in the First World War still had considerable relevance, notwithstanding increases in the speed and range of aircraft. And divisions of official opinion then manifest on such important issues as whether warnings should be extended to the general public, and whether lighting restrictions were on balance an asset or a liability, had persisted.[1]

---

[1] See pp. 7–8, 21–22.

The report of 1925 had defined the sub-divisions of a future warning scheme, the most basic of which was that between collection of information and its distribution, or 'warning' proper.[1] It will be recalled that the first task had been performed in the First World War mainly through an elaborate system of observer posts, and that this system had been kept in being in a small area as an 'Observer Corps', composed of volunteers enrolled as special constables and placed early in 1929 under the Air Ministry's control.[2]

This Corps had since proved its efficiency in annual R.A.F. exercises; and it would form an important source of intelligence (for both active and passive defence) of the movements during another war of friendly as well as hostile aircraft, notwithstanding the secret development after 1935 of R.D.F. (Radio Direction and Finding) later to be known as 'radar'. By the beginning of 1935 the Observer Corps had only been developed for parts of the southern and eastern English coasts and the counties bordering London; though its expansion, *pari passu* with the general expansion of the R.A.F., had been recommended. The Home Office, as the authority responsible for distribution of air raid warnings, was eager for this expansion to be accelerated and consulted the Air Ministry. After much discussion, these Departments submitted a joint proposal to the Committee of Imperial Defence for extension of the Observer Corps to cover virtually all England and Wales and Eastern Scotland; and the Committee gave its approval in July 1937. Certain new Groups of the Corps in the West Country, Wales and Scotland would be created (it may be noted) solely to meet Home Office needs for rapid and adequate civilian air raid warning.

Italy's attack on Abyssinia in the autumn of 1935 made it conceivable that Britain would be involved in war, and necessitated action over air raid warnings which was somewhat impromptu in character. The Home Office sent in January 1936 a secret circular to Chief Constables in the south-easterly zone then covered by the Observer Corps organisation. This outlined the principles of a warning system, including its sub-division into 'preliminary' and 'action' warnings, and asked Chief Constables to compile (without consulting either local authorities or occupiers of premises) and send to the Home Office lists of persons who should receive each class of warning.

Subsidence of this particular threat gave the A.R.P. Department opportunity to develop further and in consultation with others concerned a scheme for warnings. In September 1936 it sent a circular and memorandum, similar in content to the one just mentioned but

---

[1] The word 'warning' had already become a technical term of A.R.P., just as 'intelligence' had, at a far earlier date, become a military technical term. The words 'shelter' and 'warden' were in process of acquiring the same status.

[2] pp. 20, 41.

now confidential instead of secret, to all larger local authorities and Chief Constables of England and Wales. The warning scheme proposed bore close affinities to the system evolved in the First World War. Britain would be divided into a number of warning districts (based not on local government boundaries, but on telephone areas) which would be the primary units of the system. Normally, warnings would be issued to those districts a certain distance ahead of the place over which enemy aircraft were reported; and it was hoped to supply them to inland districts from 7-10 minutes before the enemy's arrival. In advance of the main warning, a 'preliminary caution' would be distributed over a larger area to a strictly limited number of recipients such as the police, fire brigades, headquarters of A.R.P. organisations and some industrial establishments. The messages of both types would be passed over the telephone system to prearranged lists of telephone subscribers. Local authorities as well as Chief Constables were now asked to prepare these 'warning lists', which would be finally settled by the Home Office in consultation with the General Post Office.

The foregoing part of the warning scheme concerned only persons or institutions (numerous as these would be) with some operational interest in the movements of enemy aircraft. The question of warning the general public was (logically at least) a separate issue, and the reader will recall that the report of 1925 had advised a policy of discouraging 'general alarms'. The central authorities, though still leaving to local discretion the decision as to whether public warnings should be issued, now suggested that this should normally be done in all urban areas; and they were investigating the problem of apparatus for this purpose. The operational core of the scheme was further complicated by the necessity to arrange for local gas alarms.

In the spring of 1937 the Home Defence Committee appointed a sub-committee on the Co-ordination of Active and Passive Air Defence, which gave first priority in its work to co-ordination of warning and lighting arrangements. This body made good progress in establishing the principles (especially the division of responsibilities between Fighter Command and the civil authorities) and examining the technicalities of the warning scheme;[1] its conclusions belong to a later stage of this narrative. Tests at which warnings were passed from H.Q., Fighter Command over the G.P.O. trunk system to telephone subscribers were held during 1937.

In the previous year the Home Office had formed a committee to make detailed plans for a centralised London warning system— and this had appointed two technical committees on 'Loud Noise Warnings' and the 'Remote Control of Signals'. These carried out experiments with a variety of possible devices for warning the

---

[1] The A.O.C.-in-C. Fighter Command attended a number of meetings.

public. By the end of 1937 they had decided to rule out maroons for this purpose and to concentrate on evolving a satisfactory type of siren.[1]

The speed and adequacy of warnings bore a close relationship to lighting restrictions. During the years before 1935 A.R.P. Committees had discussed the lighting problem on various occasions without reaching any very definite conclusions. But by the time the A.R.P. Department was formed the planning authorities had adopted the view that drastic lighting restriction, or an almost complete darkening of towns and other places, should be attempted. The success (from the point of view of the defences) which had attended this policy in some large English towns (e.g., Norwich) during the First World War, and more topically during a recent exercise in Berlin, lent support to this conclusion.

In the next few years the A.R.P. Department concentrated its efforts on attempts to evolve a system of public lighting which would give the lowest degree of visibility to hostile aircraft while providing for the safety and movement of citizens and traffic. Experiments hitherto carried out had related mainly to visibility of direct lighting, or of lights at sea, and had been little concerned with shaded (or indirect) lighting and reflection of artificial lights. In April 1936 the Home Office appointed a committee on lighting experiments, under the chairmanship of the Chief Inspector of Factories, which proceeded to arrange trials. Organisation of these was complicated by the fact that local authorities (though not, outside London, legally required to provide street lighting) could be held responsible in law for accidents caused by such experiments, and motorists involved in accidents would be liable to both civil and criminal proceedings.

Nevertheless, trials were held in 1936 and 1937, in co-operation with the Royal Air Force, at Henlow, Bedford, Marlborough and (as part of the Coast Defence Exercise of 1937) in the Southampton area. No attempt can be made in a general history to describe the technical problems these were trying to resolve, or the various methods, fittings and devices which were used. But two general conclusions appear to have emerged. First, the Air Force continued to insist on a standard of lighting (or a degree of invisibility) which the civil authorities with their pre-occupation with what might happen on the ground found impracticably 'low'. Secondly, the A.R.P. Department began to abandon the conception of shaded lighting for one of 'aids to movement', or methods such as guide lights and white-painted kerbstones.

During 1936 the Department prepared a Draft Order on lighting

---

[1] Following their use for air raid warning in the First World War, maroons had been employed to mark the beginning and end of the silence on Armistice Days.

restrictions which would require (among other things) the 'extinguishment' of exterior shop and advertisement lighting, the extinction or screening of all internal lights in houses and factories, and the disuse of vehicle headlights. It divided Britain into three zones (later reduced to two) in which these restrictions might differ in severity.

Early in 1937 the Home Office sent the Air Defence Research Committee a memorandum which described the experiments so far made and sought further advice on lighting restrictions.[1] Discussion by this and other bodies led to important decisions in November by the Committee of Imperial Defence. These endorsed the view that a policy of the severest lighting restrictions practicable in war should be adopted.

In the meantime the lighting experiments committee had been paying attention to problems presented by the introduction of severe lighting restrictions in factories, shipbuilding yards, railways and other places in which uninterrupted work would be of obvious importance to the nation's conduct of a war.

The Financial Issue, New Scale of Attack (1937), and the Warren Fisher Committee

Allusion has already been made to two important developments taking place in the winter of 1936–37. A hardening of the attitude of numbers of local authorities on the question of expenditure; and the effort of the central authorities to make the public more widely aware of their A.R.P. plans.

As already observed, a deputation from the Association of Municipal Corporations in December 1936 had presented the Home Secretary with a demand for 100 per cent. Government grant for A.R.P. expenditure.[2] As the new year opened, the Home Secretary told the Defence Policy and Requirements Committe that the issue of financial responsibility for A.R.P. was becoming prominent; and the A.R.P. Department began to prepare detailed estimates of expenditure.

Preparation of these was necessarily influenced by the production of a new estimated scale of attack by the Air Staff. The Air Staff had now, as the fruit of continuous study of Germany's air force, raised the weight of bombs which might be dropped daily on Britain during the earliest stages of another war from 150 tons to no less than 600 tons. The Chiefs of Staff discussed this figure and

---

[1] This sub-committee of the Committee of Imperial Defence had been formed early in 1935.

[2] The system, originated by Mr Gladstone, of consultation with affected interests before bringing a Bill before the House played an important part in A.R.P. planning.

referred the matter to the Home Defence Committee. It will be recalled that in a memorandum of February 1937 on *Planning for a War with Germany* the Chiefs of Staff re-emphasised the threat represented by immediate large-scale German air attack on Britain.

The hardening of the local authorities' attitude on the financial issue was carried further at a conference of the L.C.C. and the local authority associations at County Hall on 18th March, which ended with dispatch of a letter to the Home Secretary arguing that 'the whole financial responsibility for the measures to be taken, which are as national in character as are the defence services, should rest with His Majesty's Government'. In addition to the question of the incidence of financial responsibility, some authorities were beginning to feel concern over the lack of specific authority for any A.R.P. expenditure they might be prepared to make. The Home Secretary drew the attention of the Cabinet to this aspect of the situation, and sought authority to prepare A.R.P. legislation. The Cabinet gave this authority; and concrete proposals on the wider issue were made to the Defence Policy and Requirements Committee in a comprehensive Home Office memorandum on the *Financial Aspects of Air Raid Precautions*.

This endeavoured to forecast all expenditure required for an adequate national scheme of A.R.P., including emergency fire measures; though some of its figures were of a provisional character. It began presentation of its case with certain presuppositions of wider historical interest, which may be summarised as follows: (1) civil air raid precautions could not be expected to reach the same state of readiness in peace-time as the Defence Services, since they involved interference of various kinds with the normal life of the community (this was well illustrated by the case of first aid posts, for which buildings in everyday use as schools were especially suitable.) (2) Such precautions, being of a purely passive character, might properly be initiated during a period of tension without prejudice to a peaceful settlement of any negotiations that might be in progress. (3) Local authorities and others should work out their preparations on the assumption that 4 days would be available before the outbreak of war in which to complete them; the degree of preparation necessary before this 4 days' warning period would depend to some extent on the particular service involved and the liability of the particular area to attack. (4) Plans for, (a) the emergency fire brigade system of London and other main targets, and (b) distribution of civilian gas-masks should be excluded from this programme of partial postponement.

A distinction between peace-time expenditure and 'immediately pre-war expenditure' (that necessary in the 4-day period) formed the starting point of the financial proposals. With respect to the former, it was suggested that the Government should make early announcement of their willingness to assist local authorities and that this assistance should normally be 60 per cent. of approved expenditure. The Government should also announce their intention to give larger Exchequer assistance towards completing preparations in the 4-day period, and to pay compensation to members of A.R.P. services and of the Auxiliary Fire Service injured on duty in war.

The memorandum estimated the local authorities' expenditure (including that on the fire brigade services) as £1,300,000 annually; £15,325,000 capital expenditure (non-recurrent) before the 4-day period, and £2,315,000 similar expenditure during this period. The second of these figures included an item of £2,600,000, frankly stated to be of a very speculative nature, to make good the estimated national deficiency of hospital accommodation. The contributions which (it was proposed) the Government should make were £780,000 of the annual expenditure and £17,640,000 of the preliminary capital outlay.

In addition, proposals, noticed earlier in this narrative, were made for Exchequer expenditures of £5 million towards measures for safeguarding vital industries, and £2 million for purchase of sandbags. The amount already spent or authorised on the central Government's A.R.P. measures (including anti-gas equipment) was some £5½ million, which was expected to rise to £8 million by the time the current programme was completed. The total Government contribution on these various items before the 4-day period was some £26 million; the local authorities' suggested contribution was £4 million, and that of industry £5 million. By adding the (undivided) £2 million required for capital expenditure during the 4-day period, the memorandum concluded with a grand total (apart from the £1.3 million per annum) of some £37½ million.

These proposals, when they were considered by the Defence Policy and Requirements Committee, were described by the Chancellor of the Exchequer as implying a very alarming addition to our financial liabilities. The committee considered both that an effort should be made to reduce the figures by more elaborate grading of areas in accordance with liability to attack, and that resistance by the local authorities to contributing so much as 40 per cent. of the cost was likely to be strong. The Minister of Health, Sir Kingsley Wood, emphatically agreed with the second point, and expressed scepticism over the adequacy of the figure of £2.6 million for making good the estimated deficiency of half-a-million hospital beds.

The committee, nevertheless, after re-affirming the local authorities' responsibility to take effective measures on their own account, endorsed the four presuppositions summarised above. But, while accepting the distinction between 'peace-time' and a warning period, they eliminated definitions as to how long this warning period would last. They proposed the Home Secretary should be authorised to open negotiations with the local authorities on the general basis of a Government contribution of 60 per cent. of approved expenditure, but that no public announcement of the Government's intentions should be made until after these negotiations. The question of compensation for injury was reserved for consideration elsewhere, and that of war-time expenditure was left for further discussion. The proposals regarding vital industries and the purchase of sandbags were referred elsewhere.[1]

The issues these conclusions raised were considered soon afterwards by the Cabinet, which decided that negotiations with local authorities should be suspended while re-examination was made of Departmental responsibility for air raid precautions. A sub-committee of the Committee of Imperial Defence was accordingly formed, under the chairmanship of the Permanent Secretary to the Treasury, Sir Warren Fisher,[2] with wide terms of reference. This was to examine existing proposals about the nature, scale and distribution of A.R.P. services, including hospital and fire brigade services; to report upon distribution of responsibility between the central and local authorities and (if desirable) voluntary organisations, and on any necessary adjustments of Departmental responsibility and organisation.

The findings of the Warren Fisher Committee, submitted to the Cabinet at the end of June, formed one of those surveys of the essentials of the problem which constitute a landmark, at least for the historian. The committee began by defining the aims of air raid precautions services as follows: (a) to maintain the morale of the people, (b) to ensure continued functioning of the activities vital to the effective prosecution of the war and the life of the community, (c) to reduce to a minimum the destruction of life and property likely to be produced by air raids. They pointed out that translation of these principles into administrative action necessarily involved some apportionment between the claims of the passive and active defences. They suggested that it should be recognised from the outset that it was impossible to secure anything approaching 100 per cent. security by passive defence, and that, in spite of this fact, it was essential to ensure a reasonable degree of protection in the light of the weight of attack likely to be encountered.

The committee re-examined the hypothesis—the scale of attack— which underlay all their deliberations. As already observed, the

---

[1] See pp. 62, 76, 82.

[2] Born 1879; Permanent Secretary to the Treasury and first 'Head of the Civil Service' 1919–38; subsequently C.D. Regional Commissioner for the North-West and Special Commissioner for London; died 1948.

H

Air Staff had raised their estimate of the weight of bombs which an enemy (now Germany) might drop on Britain during the first stages of an attack from 150 tons *per diem* to no less than 600 tons. The committee proceeded, as their predecessor of 1924 had done, to question the experts and then to accept their hypothesis.[1] The estimate of over 600 tons of bombs *per diem* during the first few weeks (which took account of Britain's various potential forms of counter-offensive) also embraced the possibility of a special bombing effort on the part of the enemy in the first 24 hours which might amount to 3,500 tons. Consideration had to be taken not only of this greatly increased weight of attack but of new methods of attack for which past experience afforded no precedents. The measure offered by the accepted air raid casualty figure of 1914–18 (50 per ton of bombs, 17 of which were killed and 33 wounded) was subject to the *caveat* that modern bombs were more effective. The committee pointed out that an arithmetical computation on this basis for the scale of attack at 600 tons *per diem* would indicate casualties of the order of 200,000 a week, of which 66,000 would be killed. The possibility of very heavy attack in the first weeks of a war led them to the question of evacuation. This had not, owing to the uncertainty of its financial implications, been included in the Home Secretary's memorandum.

Air raid precautions, the committee stated, were designed to meet two distinct but concurrent sets of conditions—physical damage to life and property, and panic and disorganisation. To this second (mainly psychological) danger they attached the same high importance as their predecessors. Maintaining the people's morale would, they considered, be best achieved by frank explanation of the risks, combined with making the people realise, through participation in measures designed to meet these risks, that the problem had been thought out by the Government with the aim of providing all the protection reasonably possible.

As regards the scale and distribution of A.R.P. services, the committee concluded that no attempt should be made to apply the 4-day warning period rigidly but that measures should be carried far enough to be completed within a relatively short time. They, nevertheless, attached much importance to the grading of the country into areas based on their presumed liability to attack.[2] They concluded that the most basic financial proposals of the Home Secretary's memorandum should be accepted in principle

---

[1] The new estimated scale of attack had been referred to the Home Defence Committee, and was not approved by the Committee of Imperial Defence until 28th October 1937.

[2] The A.R.P. Department had now divided Britain into five grades 'tapered' in such a way that a district in grade 5 might only receive one-seventh of the protection afforded to a district in grade 1.

as representing the deficiency programme of the A.R.P. Department. These were the annual expenditure of £1.3 million, and the capital expenditure of £12,725,000 (which represented the £15,325,000 allotted to the 'peace-time' phase, less the item of £2.6 million for hospitals).

Accommodation for civil casualties in base hospitals was a question, the committee concluded, which needed reconsideration in the light of the new scale of attack. Their attention had been drawn to a proposal for the structural alteration of new houses. The estimated cost of this for subsidised housing schemes would mean such an extra burden on the social services that they proposed it should not be adopted, though this should not hinder giving information about structural precautions.

The committee had been informed that the manpower requirements for A.R.P. had been estimated at 1,398,500, about half of which would only be required on a part-time basis, and only 200,000 of which need be males under the age of 40.

In reporting on the second major issue presented to them—distribution of responsibility between the central and local government—the committee re-affirmed the position outlined in the first A.R.P. circular and since developed in practice. The division of functions set forth in the circular only needed modification where it concerned emergency fire brigade measures. After endorsing the system whereby a network of local schemes, varying in accordance with the particular conditions and vulnerability of the area, would be subject to central examination and approval, they expressed the hope that in the bargaining process which must soon take place any payment in excess of a half-and-half basis would be conceded only on the clearest proof that it was indispensable to get the work done.

The final major issue—the responsibility and organisation for A.R.P. of the central government—is one to which a good deal of attention has been given in this volume. While the theory of the matter (it has been suggested) had remained constant, the practice had for various reasons developed somewhat independently of it.[1] In one important respect the Warren Fisher Committee confirmed the practical development. After stating they had been impressed by 'the variety of the interests involved and the consequent interlocking of Departments', they concluded that the novel problem of A.R.P. needed unified and separate treatment and that on this account responsibility for it should rest with a single authority; and that in peace this authority should continue to be the Home Secretary, as the Minister responsible (in England and Wales) for services such as police and fire protection which had the most bearing on the public safety.

[1] pp. 60–63.

Regarding the institutional superstructure they made two proposals which implied defects in existing methods of effecting co-ordination.[1] Namely, that questions of major policy and appeals on policy resulting from Departmental differences should be referred to the Defence Policy and Requirements Committee; and that normal methods of consultation should be supplemented by a Joint Standing Inter-Departmental Committee, composed of members of adequate rank of all the Departments concerned with A.R.P.

The A.R.P. Department should be substantially strengthened, not only for current developments but also because in war it would be necessary for the central authority to assume greater control, and perhaps for the Department to be put under a special Minister. The organisation immediately necessary should include 13 administrative areas outside London, or the beginnings of the regional system which would be essential in the war organisation.[2]

Finally, the committee made conclusions about the special case of Scotland. The circular of July 1935 had also been issued by the Scottish Office, and as it became less certain that enemy aircraft would confine their attention to English and Welsh cities, the A.R.P. Department had begun extending its activities north of the Border. The main proposals now advanced were: that the Secretary of State for Scotland, acting through the Scottish Office, should continue to be responsible for all Scottish fire brigade matters; that the A.R.P. Department should deal direct with Scottish local authorities on all A.R.P. matters other than fire brigade measures or existing grant-aided services; that financial provision for A.R.P., including emergency fire brigade services but excluding those relating to existing grant-aided services (e.g., police), should be borne on the Home Office Vote; and that co-ordination in respect of Scotland should be achieved by normal consultation between the Home Office and Scottish Office, and by membership of the Secretary of State for Scotland and of Scottish officials on the co-ordinating committees previously mentioned.

While this committee had been making its survey changes had occurred in the composition of the Government. Soon after the Coronation on 12th May of King George VI Mr Baldwin retired from the first office in the State in favour of Mr Neville Chamberlain, who for some time had held undisputed claim (in the Conservative Party) to the succession. Sir John Simon became Chancellor of the Exchequer and Sir Samuel Hoare, who had returned to office by way of the Admiralty, became Home Secretary. Mr Duff Cooper was appointed First Lord of the Admiralty, and Mr Hore Belisha

---

[1] pp. 62–63.

[2] p. 65.

became Secretary of State for War. Mr Eden, Lord Swinton and Sir Kingsley Wood remained in the offices, respectively, of Foreign Secretary, Secretary of State for Air and Minister of Health.

The new Cabinet considered the conclusions of the Warren Fisher Committee early in July. They decided, first, that the Home Secretary should enter at once into negotiations with the local authorities and propose an equal sharing of financial responsibility between central and local government. He should not go beyond a proposal for a 60:40 partition of the cost without further reference to the Cabinet, and he should avoid giving indications of any figure of total expenditure contemplated by the Government. Secondly, the Home Secretary should at the appropriate moment make an unostentatious announcement in the House of Commons that he was in touch with the local authorities on the subject.

The A.R.P. Bill

On 7th July the Home Secretary told Parliament that he was arranging to begin consultations with local authorities. On 19th July he and the Secretary of State for Scotland, Mr Walter Elliot, met the local authority associations, who were led by Mr Herbert Morrison, the Leader of the L.C.C.[1] After describing A.R.P. as one of the most complex defence problems he had encountered during his public career, the Home Secretary reminded his audience of the financial contribution in this sphere, for gas-masks and other purposes, being made by the Government. He proposed that the main items still to be provided—e.g., local staff and office accommodation, first aid posts, storage depots and fire-fighting equipment —should be an equal charge between the central and local authorities. This in effect meant that the central Government was undertaking to bear some 70 per cent. of the total cost. Mr Morrison contended for the local authorities that A.R.P. was similar in nature to the other Defence Services and should be the undivided financial responsibility of the Government, to which local authorities should only stand in this matter in the relationship of agents. The 'united front' of local authorities, formed the previous March and consolidated during the subsequent months, remained unimpaired and the conference was adjourned. The position was made public the following day by a Parliamentary statement and a communiqué to the Press.[2]

Soon afterwards the Home Secretary proposed to the Cabinet that a new offer should be made to local authorities which, while

---

[1] Born 1888; Minister of Transport, 1929–31; Labour M.P. for S. Hackney, and Secretary to the London Labour Party. The Labour Party had gained control of the L.C.C. for the first time in 1934.

[2] H. of C. Deb., Vol. 326, Col. 1984, 20th July 1937.

not relieving them of the whole burden of expenditure, would be substantially more favourable to them than the one already made. He put forward the following three possibilities: (*a*) payment of Exchequer grants at the rate of 75 per cent. of approved expenditure for the principal items, instead of 50 per cent.; (*b*) payment by the central Government of the whole of the capital cost of new buildings, conversion of existing buildings, and certain items of equipment; (*c*) payment of these capital costs, plus grants to a maximum of 50 per cent. in aid of the administrative expenses and maintenance charges falling on the local authorities.

The Cabinet considered these proposals late in July, but decided that no immediate decision of principle should be taken.

They authorised the Home Secretary to announce in Parliament that an A.R.P. Bill would be necessary in the autumn, that this would be discussed beforehand with local authorities, and that authorities which had incurred expenditure over their approved schemes would be reimbursed as from 1st January 1937; and to take advantage (in consultation with the Chancellor of the Exchequer and other Ministers) of any opportunity to conclude a favourable financial arrangement with the local authorities. The Home Secretary made this announcement in the Commons on 29th July.[1] The arrival of the holiday season brought a halt, destined to last for a number of weeks, in negotiations between the Government and local authorities.

At the end of 1936 the A.R.P. Department had reported to the Committee of Imperial Defence that future progress must largely depend on, (*a*) the availability of instructors in anti-gas measures, and (*b*) the readiness of the public to volunteer for the various A.R.P. Services. And it had stated that the general public knew very little about A.R.P., and proposed that a more general appeal should be made on the subject.

The deliberate attempts, already recorded, in the early months of 1937 to cast the A.R.P. net wider coincided closely with the formation of the 'united front' of local authorities on the financial issue. Local authorities were reported by the Department in April as showing a distinct tendency to 'go slow' with A.R.P. measures. By June the situation had deteriorated to the extent that while some authorities were getting on with training or recruiting, generally in a small way, the majority of schemes were almost at a standstill.

The casting of the net wider continued, therefore, to depend mainly on the activities of the Department and the Anti-Gas School, and those of a limited number of local authorities, organisations and individuals with interest in the topic which was above the average. The Falfield School had trained some 1,200 students by 30th June 1937, and close on 2,000 by the end of the year. Of this

---

[1] H. of C. Deb., Vol. 326, Cols. 3294-6.

last total some 360 were senior officials and medical officers of health; and about 1,400 had qualified as anti-gas instructors (first and second class) and were given the title of 'Instructors, C.A.G.S.' This figure was approaching half the estimated minimum (3,000) of instructors needed throughout the country. During 1937 the difficulties encountered in finding a suitable property in the north of England for a second Anti-Gas School were finally overcome. The Hawkhills, Easingwold, some twelve miles from the city of York, was bought by the Government, and began its first course (for Metropolitan Police Officers) on 27th December.

The main classes of persons who attended courses at Falfield during these early years have already been mentioned.[1] In addition, two courses were held in the spring of 1937 for over a hundred persons from the London, Liverpool, and Birmingham areas who were described as 'Gas Detectors'. These were persons with scientific training who were invited to acquire more specialised knowledge of what became known as 'gas identification'.

The extent to which the one thousand or more 'Instructors, C.A.G.S.' carried out local training in their districts in this early phase naturally varied. In April the Department reported that anti-gas training of the regular police (including police firemen) of the whole country was almost complete, and that training of special constables was beginning. The St. John Ambulance and the Red Cross which, like the police, sent representatives to Falfield had given a considerable amount of training to their members by the end of 1936. A third specialised section of the populace, the medical profession, embracing dentists, veterinary surgeons and students, was being catered for by the scheme under which the Department had established Medical Instructors in anti-gas defence at a dozen or so of the largest centres in Britain. By the end of 1937 some 10,000 doctors, 16,000 nurses, and smaller numbers of the other branches of the medical profession had received A.R.P. anti-gas training.

These specialised bodies apart, anti-gas training of a locally-inspired, organised character was still in a rudimentary stage. In March 1937 the first municipal anti-gas school in the country was opened at Leeds, and soon afterwards an anti-gas training centre was established in Surrey. By the close of the year, as the Parliamentary Under-Secretary told the Commons, between 30 and 40 local schools had been formed and about 100,000 local authority employees (apart from the police) had been trained in anti-gas and general A.R.P. duties. The Under-Secretary added that A.R.P. training had 'a long way to go yet'.[2]

---

[1] pp. 68–69.

[2] H. of C. Deb., Vol. 329, Cols. 1389, 1514–5, 25th November 1937.

General training of a more realistic kind began during the Coast Defence exercises held by the Services in the Portsmouth Naval Area on the night of 15th–16th July. Now opportunity offered, the A.R.P. Department arranged to try out the A.R.P. Services, including the embryonic Wardens' Service, in parts of Portsmouth and Southampton, and to test the schemes for warning and lighting. The exercise, which the Home Secretary visited, was thought to have proved of much value. The black-out, the Department reported, was most successful and showed that the population was prepared to co-operate in an exercise of this kind to the fullest extent. Valuable lessons were also learnt about organisation of the services, methods of dealing with the light incendiary bomb and the warning system, and these were incorporated in a report sent to the larger local authorities. Several smaller exercises attended, like the one just described, by officials from outside the area involved were held elsewhere in the south during the remainder of 1937.

In September the Home Office issued an A.R.P. memorandum on *Anti-Gas Training*, which described in a comprehensive way the system and methods already proposed, and was destined to remain (in later editions) the chief manual for instructors. In spite of relatively slow progress in recruitment and local training certain training problems of much future significance were already exercising the A.R.P. Department. These included the questions: What qualifications should be prescribed for local instructors who had not 'graduated' at one of the Anti-Gas Schools or been trained in one of the voluntary aid societies? How should training for wardens in matters other than anti-gas be provided? What system should be adopted for local training in ways of defeating the light incendiary bomb? Should any payment be made to local authority employees who volunteered for training?

The slowing down after the spring of 1937 of organising A.R.P. in the country inevitably delayed the public's further education in the matter. The *Householder's Handbook*, designed as the basic guide for the ordinary citizen, had been completed by the Department and approved by the Cabinet. But its public issue was deferred until the autumn. As the holiday season approached, the Department was considering other methods of appealing to the public, such as posters, A.R.P. cigarette cards and exhibitions, including some form of display at the Ideal Homes Exhibition and the British Industries Fair.

It is perhaps doubtful whether many of the British public were as yet prepared to include a gas-proof room in their conception of an ideal home. Alongside discouragement in some quarters of greater publicity for A.R.P. must be set a degree of unreadiness which defies precise measurement by British citizens to devote effort (and expenditure) to defence against another war. Two conclusions on this subject, one contemporary and one retrospective, may give at least a partial answer. In August, H.M. Chargé d'Affaires in Berlin sent a despatch to the Foreign Office which compared the state of air raid precautions ('the third line of air defence') in Germany with that of these precautions in Britain, to the marked disadvantage of the latter. This contended that while in Germany the whole nation was already rendered 'air protection minded', in Britain public opinion was apathetic, sceptical and largely uninstructed; in addition to the automatic discipline a totalitarian State exacted, the Third Reich had spared no expense in building up this part of its defences. Secondly, the Kent County Council, responsible for an obviously vulnerable area, expressed the view in an official publication after the war that 'the period between 1935 and 1938 was in many cases, owing to public opinion, one of frustration of endeavour in that it was difficult to interest the public and that efforts in that direction were generally criticised as "war-mongering".'[1]

Of the two wars actually proceeding at this time one, in the Far East, was too remote to arouse much interest in the average British citizen but the other, the civil war in Spain, was nearer home. In July 1937 the Spanish War reached its first anniversary and there was no obvious reason (at least to the layman) why it should not continue indefinitely. Through the Non-Intervention Committee Britain and France were continuing efforts to circumscribe a conflict which the non-democratic powers of Germany, Italy and Russia saw as a suitable arena for ideological warfare and the testing of their military weapons. While all Parties and most of the people in Britain supported the main lines of Government policy, the ideological issues caused lively controversy and some confusion. 'The British "War of the Spanish Obsession", which played its "ideological" accompaniment to the grimmer warfare in Spain itself, was fought on diverse fields: in the Houses of Parliament at Westminster; on platforms all over the country; in the organs of the British Press; and even in the rear of the two contending armies in the Peninsula, where a continual stream of British visitors circulated behind the front on either side.'[2] The clouds of British witnesses in either camp were, however, probably smaller than contemporary controversy suggested; and the attitude of 'a plague o' both your houses' was probably widespread among the larger, less vocal, sections of Britain's population. Though the fighting in Spain, including bombardment of civilians from the air, undoubtedly caused the British public anxiety, Hitler appeared for the time being less aggressively inclined.

---

[1] *Kent: the County Administration in War*, 1946, p. 67.
[2] A. J. Toynbee, *Survey of International Affairs, 1937*, Vol. II, p. 153.

Operations in Spain and the air raid defence adopted by each side were studied by the A.R.P. Department. In addition, shelter policy in France, Switzerland and elsewhere was observed. Perhaps of greater importance was the attention paid to developments in Nazi Germany. In May of this year the Germans published three decrees in application of the A.R.P. law (*Luftschutzgesetz*) of 26th June 1935, which disclosed in some detail the structure of their system. These and other German ideas on the problem, including those about lighting restrictions and camouflage, were examined and made available to the British authorities concerned.

In September, an official of the Ministry of Health joined the Department as an Assistant Secretary with the special function of piloting the proposed legislation through the shoals which still lay in front of its voyage to the statute book. Some progress was made in the latter half of the year with increasing the financial status and numbers of the Inspectorate. Treasury sanction was obtained for creation of two grades of Inspector, and for the principle of forming thirteen Regional Inspectorates. On 1st November a Regional Office in charge of an Inspector was opened at Leeds, and in the middle of that month a second such Office was opened at Birmingham.

Revival of negotiations between the Government and local authorities took place with the issue by the Government of a memorandum on 13th October, and reassembly of the conference between the Home Secretary and the Local Authority Associations two weeks later. This development was preceded by considerable interdepartmental and other discussion concerning the concessions the Government were now clearly compelled to offer. New proposals by the Home Secretary had been referred to a Cabinet Committee, consisting of the Prime Minister, the Chancellor of the Exchequer and the three other Ministers most concerned, which approved the memorandum (i.e., the public announcement of the Government's revised views on the matter) of 13th October.

This stated that the Government looked to the local authorities to prepare and execute A.R.P. schemes, and that many of the services required were 'so closely interlocked with existing local government services' that they could only be effectively conducted by 'extensions and developments of existing local machinery'. For the Government to treat local authorities merely as agents would tend to deprive them of responsibility for the efficiency and economy of local services. The Government intended to lighten local financial burdens by asking Parliament's consent for the Exchequer to provide the following additional major items—emegency fire-fighting appliances, stretchers, blankets, decontamination and rescue equipment, and stores for first aid posts and parties and new casualty clearing hospitals. The local authorities must provide for —'structural precautions in public buildings, public refuges and the organisation of local services and the recruitment and, if necessary, training of personnel for decontamination, emergency fire fighting, rescue and repair work and the provision of first aid'. The Government would ask Parliament to classify local authorities in four groups and provide grants ranging from 60 per cent. to 75 per cent. with intermediate rates of 65 per cent. and 70 per cent. The burden of expenditure to be borne by local authorities in any year did not at present appear 'at all likely to exceed on the average the product of a 1d. rate'.

At the resumed meeting between the Home Secretary and the Associations on 26th October Mr Morrison (on behalf of the English and Welsh local authorities), though accepting this memorandum as a basis of discussion, in general condemned its proposals, including the adoption of the 'block grant' formula[1] and the fixing of the minimum grant-in-aid as low as 60 per cent. The Associations suggested, among other things, that the standard rate should be from 70–80 per cent.; and that to any approved expenditure costing the authorities more than the product of a 1d. rate the State should contribute 90 per cent., and to such expenditure over a 2d. rate 100 per cent. The Scottish representatives were even more intransigent, declining to consider anything but full reimbursement. Since the Home Secretary stated that the Government were not prepared to alter the main outlines of their scheme, the scene of the discussion necessarily shifted to the House of Commons.

The new Parliamentary session was opened by the King on the day of this conference; and the King's Speech included the statement, 'My Ministers are anxious that energetic steps shall be taken to complete the measures for the protection of the civilian population against air raids', and gave first place to this matter in the legislative programme. The A.R.P. Bill was presented by the Home Secretary to the House on 4th November.

The Cabinet Committee previously mentioned had in the meantime held fresh meetings, in an atmosphere of some urgency, to attempt to make some further concession which might transform the Bill from a controversial into an agreed one. Discussion centred on the question of giving more assistance to authorities whose expenditure on A.R.P. might exceed the product of a 1d. rate. It was decided that, if this contingency arose, an authority in one of the two lower categories (i.e., normally entitled to 60 or 65 per cent. grant-in-aid) would receive 75 per cent. on all approved expenditure in excess of the amount which a 1d. rate would produce, while an

---

[1] Instituted by the Local Government Act, 1929, as a method of measuring the capacity to meet their expenditure of different local authorities.

authority in one of the higher categories (i.e., entitled to 70 or 75 per cent.) would receive 85 per cent. on such expenditure.

The Bill's Second Reading took place on 15th November, and the debate which followed was the first in which the still unpalatable subject of A.R.P. was extensively discussed by Parliament.[1] The Home Secretary announced the final concession by the Government on the financial issue, namely that they were prepared to consider the possibility of putting a time limit on the Bill. Mr Morrison, as spokesman of the Opposition, moved the rejection of the measure. After stating the request of the local authority associations that the full cost of A.R.P. should be borne by the State had never been withdrawn, and blaming the Government for an 'unfortunate loss of time' in the whole matter, he concluded 'this is a regretted Bill, but it is a necessary Bill'. The Opposition, however, divided the House on the Second Reading, which was carried by 324 votes to 135. The promise to include a time limit was fulfilled by the introduction of a new clause during Committee stage.[2] Apart from this, the financial provisions remained those which have already been described.

During the debates the Under-Secretary of State to the Home Office, after a tribute to the work done by the A.R.P. Department since 1935, said, 'this (air raid precautions) is an enormous and a new problem. It is new, technically, new administratively and, above all, it is new psychologically to our people'. The general nature of the discussion suggested that the problem was one to which the majority of Members had not so far devoted much attention.

The Second Reading of the Bill in the Lords was moved by the Secretary of State for Air, Lord Swinton, with the words, 'This, I think, is a Bill which all your Lordships will welcome and will wish to advance'.[3] The Bill was reported back to the House of Commons without amendment, and received the Royal Assent on 22nd December.

The Air Raid Precautions Act 1937[4] came into force on the following 1st January. It brought to a close the two and a half years of voluntary effort on the part of local authorities by imposing on the larger authorities the duty to submit A.R.P. schemes to the Secretary of State. It did not, however, enter into details about the nature of these schemes. During the debates the Home Secretary, Sir Samuel Hoare, had remarked that, 'as soon as this Bill has passed we have to start a new chapter in which the Government and the local authorities and the citizens in this country will all co-operate to make a much more comprehensive plan of air raid precautions than anything that we have contemplated during the last few years'.[5]

---

[1] H. of C. Deb., Vol. 329, Cols. 41–165, 243–312; 15th, 16th November 1937.
[2] H. of C. Deb., Vol. 329, Cols. 1437–1563, 1905–2035; 25th and 30th November 1937.
[3] H. of L. Deb., Vol. 107, Cols. 423–462; 13th December 1937.
[4] 1 and 2 Geo. 6, Ch. 6.
[5] H. of C. Deb., Vol. 329, Col. 43.

CHAPTER IV

A.R.P. SERVICES IN FORMATION, AND A DRESS REHEARSAL

(January 1938 – 'The September Crisis')

LOCAL authorities throughout Britain were now compelled to prepare measures of defence, and could proceed with the assurance that a substantial part of the cost of these would be met from national funds. The 'staff' in Whitehall responsible for planning and directing A.R.P. during the past two and a half years had now been formally provided with 'subordinate' staffs to perform the same functions in every area of the field of operations. Some six months after the Act's passage the Home Secretary felt able to announce that 'there was growing up a complete new public service'. This development was given impetus during 1938 by a number of international crises.

The A.R.P. Act, 1937, and the Regulations

The 1937 Act[1] imposed on local authorities the duty to take precautions for 'the protection of persons and property from injury or damage in the event of hostile attack from the air', or, more specifically, of drawing up 'air raid general precautions' schemes. General precautions schemes, which are the main concern of this chapter, were normally to be prepared and submitted to the Secretary of State by the larger authorities—i.e., the county councils (including Scottish joint county councils), county borough councils and, in Scotland, councils of large burghs—henceforward to be known as 'the scheme-making authorities'. Provision was, however, made for the Secretary of State, after consulting the appropriate county, to direct municipal boroughs, urban districts or small burghs which might apply for the privilege to prepare schemes. Allocation of this responsibility between the chief London authorities was to be the subject of a special Order. Counties were obliged to consult districts or small burghs before preparing schemes, and it was the duty of these smaller authorities to assist the counties. The Act empowered the Secretary of State to prescribe by regulation the matters to be included in schemes, as well as to relieve councils

---

[1] 1 and 2 Geo. 6, Ch. 6.

of any of the obligations which these regulations might prescribe. Although schemes were to be submitted as soon as practicable after passage of the Act, separate schemes might be submitted either as parts of the comprehensive scheme or in respect of parts of a county area. Any authority might make provision for certain functions to be exercised by another scheme-making body acting as its agent. Mutual assistance was made a statutory duty; but the extensive provisions of the Local Government Acts for combination of authorities, the appointment of joint committees and the delegation of functions were not to be exercised without prior approval of the Secretary of State.

Under the financial provisions local authorities were empowered to incur expenditure on A.R.P. (whether forming part of a scheme or not), and such expenditure since 9th July 1935 was legalised. The Secretary of State was empowered to pay grants at the standard rates of 60–75 per cent. of approved expenditure. As observed, a clause had been inserted in the Bill in Committee Stage requiring the Secretary of State to conduct, within three years of passage of the Act, an inquiry into the working of these financial provisions 'with particular reference to the expense falling to be borne by local rates'.[1] Other sections of the Act dealt with details of its application to Scotland, and removed the possible constitutional restriction on action by the Government of Northern Ireland.

Most of the foregoing provisions applied equally to 'fire precautions schemes'. These, however, were to be prepared and submitted to the Home Secretary for the administrative county of London by the L.C.C., for the rest of England and Wales by the borough (county and municipal) and urban district councils, and permissively by the rural district councils; and to the Secretary of State for Scotland by county and town councils in Scotland.

At the end of January 1938 the Home Office sent local authorities a summary of the Act's provisions and draft Regulations for both types of A.R.P. scheme. It drew attention to the wide latitude given to counties over the organisation adopted in preparing general schemes; and emphasised the need for consultation between all parties concerned in preparation of any particular scheme, as well as for the inclusion in schemes of arrangements for mutual assistance. The two main sets of Regulations became substantive some six weeks later.[2] Those concerning general schemes require summary in some detail, since they replaced the 'first circular' as the leading scriptural authority for local bodies, with the important difference that, unlike the earlier document, they were compulsory reading.

---

[1] p. 106.
[2] S.R. & O. 1938, Nos. 251 (General Schemes), 252, 220/S.12 (Fire Schemes), 10th March. The latter are dealt with in Chapter VI.

Matters for which provision had to be made in schemes, or (less formally stated) the functions or groups of functions which the authorities had to arrange to perform, either immediately or once hostilities and air attacks had started, numbered seventeen. Listed in the order they appeared in the regulations, and condensed into the headings used in a 'model' scheme issued by the Home Office in March, they were as follows: instruction and advice to the public; information and warnings of air raids; information and reports of casualties and damage; air raid wardens; casualty services (first aid parties and posts, casualty clearing stations and ambulance services); rescue parties, demolition and clearance of debris; gas detection; decontamination services (of streets and public buildings); repair services (for the same); recruitment and training of personnel; protection of premises which would be used by A.R.P. services in war; provision of shelters for the protection of the public; lighting in highways, streets and public places; distribution of civilian respirators; the storage and maintenance of equipment and material; transfer of the civil population; and arrangements for the control and co-ordination of general precautions services in war.

Shortly after the issue of these regulations the Air Raid Precautions (London) (Allocation of Duties) Order 1938[1] determined the distribution of responsibilities between the main London authorities. The City and the Metropolitan Boroughs became scheme-making authorities charged with performance of the functions just listed, modified by (*a*) allocation of the duty of providing casualty clearing stations and ambulance services to the L.C.C. and (*b*) more limited responsibilities for the repair of streets, etc. and lighting arrangements. The L.C.C. became responsible for these functions, and five others out of the remaining fourteen, namely—arrangements for receipt of information about raids (but not for giving warnings), protection of premises, storage and maintenance of equipment and material, transfer of the civil population and arrangements for control and co-ordination. Further matters which might arise regarding 'general' arrangements might be allocated by the Secretary of State to these various London authorities after consultation with them.

The main foundation of legislation and regulation on which the developments soon to be described were built was completed later in 1938 by regulations for the approval of expenditure. The framing of these proved difficult, involving much consultation between the A.R.P. Department, the Treasury and the Local Authority Associations. The Home Secretary, being responsible to Parliament for monies voted for this purpose, had a constitutional obligation to exercise strict control over local expenditure, which in extreme cases

---

[1] S.R. & O. 1938, No. 253, 21st March.

might claim an Exchequer contribution of 85 per cent.[1] The local authorities, on the other hand, tended to be critical of central control, and to emphasise the delays likely to be caused by requirements that prior Home Office approval should be obtained to individual items of expenditure. Provisional Regulations issued at the end of July, which applied both to general and fire precautions, represented a compromise to which recognition on both sides of the urgent need for pressing forward with schemes made its contribution. Adoption of the provisional form meant, first, that the regulations came into force at once and local authorities could obtain grant for expenditure incurred in the fifteen months after 1st January 1937 and also on account of the first six months of 1938–39; and secondly that a way was left open for revision in the light of experience.[2] Owing to differences of Scottish procedure separate, though similar, regulations on this subject were issued for Scotland;[3] and it was possible to make these substantive at once.

The Regulations, after laying down that expenditure to qualify for grant must represent an additional liability on the authority 'incurred specifically for the purposes of air raid precautions', dealt mainly with matters of procedure. They were accompanied by a long memorandum which indicated in detail the principles on which administrative decisions as to items of expenditure would be based.[4] 'Arrangements for the organisation of air raid precautions services', this stated, 'are still to some extent in an experimental stage, and it is of great value to the Secretary of State to know what is proposed in various areas, and, where appropriate, to have an opportunity of prior discussion of the proposals with the local authority'. The orthodox practice of prior approval was, nevertheless, dispensed with in certain matters, including appointments to subordinate staff and minor constructional works; and the aim was expressed to draw up more general standards in consultation with local authorities as soon as enough information was available for this to be done.

Reorganisation of the Department, and the Inspectorate

During debate on the A.R.P. Bill the Home Secretary had said the time had come for 'greatly strengthening' the A.R.P. organisation at the Home Office.[5] He stated frankly that he had come 'very

---

[1] When the approved expenditure of certain authorities for any year was greater than the grant payable at the standard rate by an amount in excess of 1d. rate (Schedule to the Act).

[2] Provisional Regulations, though operating at once, have to lie on the table of the House and are challengeable within 28 sitting days; there is no limit on the period they may run before they are made substantive.

[3] Air Raid Precautions (Approval of Expenditure) (Scotland) Regulations, 1938, S.R. & O. No. 699/S.45.

[4] Issued with the Provisional Regulations and a circular of 29th July 1938.

[5] H. of C. Deb., Vol. 330, Cols. 281–3, 7th December 1937.

reluctantly' to the conclusion that A.R.P. must be a Home Office responsibility, and that search for some other department, for example the Ministry of Health, to which 'these very onerous obligations' might be transferred had been finally baulked by the fact that the new measures were so closely connected with police and fire brigade administration, traditionally the Home Secretary's responsibilities. He was, however, 'convinced that the A.R.P. Department, so different from the other sections of the Home Office administration, must be organised upon distinctive lines' and, though it was a civil and not a military department, 'upon what I should describe generally as a service basis'. He distinguished between 'staff duties and administrative duties', and said he proposed to differentiate between these two sides of the organisation. Wing-Commander Hodsoll would be appointed 'Chief of the A.R.P. Staff with the post of Inspector-General' and the special functions of advising local authorities on schemes and controlling research, and Mr Eady, Secretary of the Unemployment Assistance Board, would join the Home Office as a Deputy Under-Secretary of State to supervise the administrative side of A.R.P. work.

These proposals were given effect in January 1938 when the retirement of the Permanent Under-Secretary of State at the Home Office, Sir Russell Scott, and the promotion to this position of Sir Alexander Maxwell[1] caused changes in the hierarchy of what must be called 'the Home Office proper '.The rock, if such a term may be applied to this venerable institution, had acquired a limpet of some proportions, which was destined to grow steadily in size. Of a total staff of some 1,600 employed by the Home Office in April 1938, about 360 were occupied in the A.R.P. Department.[2] The Home Office Vote had risen from £640,000 for 1935–36 to some £830,000 for 1938–39. The latter sum included £116,000 for the salaries and expenses of the A.R.P. Department headquarters staff; but this item apart, expenditure on A.R.P. Services now figured, with that on Emergency Fire Brigade Services, as a separate Vote (Class III, 2) in the Civil Estimates. The item on account of A.R.P. Services for 1938–39 reached more than £6,381,000, most of which was attributable to provision and maintenance of gas-masks and other equipment.[3] As the A.R.P. Department grew, some expansion of the Home Office 'general service' divisions and branches on which it relied became necessary. Establishment matters were entrusted early in 1938 to the Home Office Finance Branch, and after the Munich

---

[1] The office of Deputy Under-Secretary of State had been created in 1922 and Sir A. Maxwell had become its second holder in 1932.

[2] The total excludes some 600 industrial staff, the majority of whom were employed at A.R.P. Regional Stores.

[3] Civil Estimates and Estimates for Revenue Departments for the year ending 31st March 1939. H.C. 57.

crisis to a new Establishment Division. The Finance Branch acquired a section concerned exclusively with A.R.P. and Fire Service grants. And the staff of the Press Liaison Officer, first appointed to the Home Office in 1936, was enlarged.

In the early months of 1938 substantial enlargement and re-organisation of the A.R.P. Department was effected. By the beginning of March the organisation had achieved a size and degree of specialisation that justified its title of a 'Department' within a department in the more traditional sense. Supervised by the Deputy Under-Secretary of State assisted by the Inspector-General, it now consisted of three administrative Divisions in charge of Assistant Secretaries; the Inspectorate, in charge of a Chief Inspector; a Technical Adviser, concerned with a wide range of matters and especially structural precautions; Intelligence, Medical, and Supply Branches; the two Anti-Gas Schools and a smaller General Training School recently opened in London; and a section concerned with domestic administration. The headquarters staff amounted to some 120 persons of all grades earning salaries which totalled £101,000, or double the figure of the previous year. The remaining 240 persons worked outside London, mainly at the Anti-Gas Schools, the Regional Stores and the Blackburn Respirator Factory.

Of the three divisions which formed the Department's core, one was concerned with examining and approving the local schemes, another with general problems of local organisation, policy with respect to equipment, warning and lighting and other matters, and the third with war organisation, aspects of training and liaison functions. At the outset of the new phase a 'Heads of Divisions Council' was formed to co-ordinate the work of these various divisions and branches.

In the months which followed expansion continued, though at first on a modest scale, and some further re-organisation was made. A new division was created to administer the grant to public utilities and to organise general precautions in London, and the war organisation staff was strengthened. By August the peace-time financial curb on additions to departmental staffs appears (in this case at least) to have appreciably relaxed, and another reorganisation, to include three new officials to deal with evacuation schemes, was in prospect. Growth of work during the months now in question continued, nevertheless, to outpace increases of staff. At the close of the Parliamentary session the Home Secretary stated the organisation had been 'working under great pressure', and Sir John Anderson spoke of 'conditions of prolonged and severe over-work' in the Department.[1]

The description already given of the Department as hybrid

---

[1] H. of C. Deb., Vol. 338, Cols. 3279–81, 28th July 1938.

requires some explanation. The distinction the Home Secretary had made between 'staff and administrative duties' was not easily translated into practice in a branch of a civil department immediately concerned with administration of an Act by customary civilian methods. Orthodox methods of administration co-existed from the earliest stage with less orthodox outlook and procedure, which stressed the 'operational' purposes for which the structure was in the last analysis designed. The machinery and the impulses which drove it were both civil and military in origin. Three main elements composed the staff, namely permanent civil servants (both from other Home Office divisions and from other departments), former officials of the Indian and Colonial Civil Services and retired members of the Armed Forces.

Reference has been made to the beginning in the autumn of 1937 of the planting out of Inspectors in thirteen Regional areas.[1] The cities chosen as headquarters and the boundaries of areas closely followed those chosen for the Civil Emergency Organisation, except in the case of London and certain Home Counties. By the end of January 1938 the Department had opened Regional Offices at Leeds, Birmingham, Edinburgh, Liverpool, Newcastle-on-Tyne and Nottingham; another was opened soon afterwards at Reading. Some delay followed while eleven new Inspectors were appointed to complete the authorised total of twenty-one. During the course of the summer Offices were opened at Bristol, Glasgow, Cambridge and Cardiff. The embryonic Regions of London and certain Home Counties were administered at this stage from the headquarters of the Department.

These Offices consisted during most of the period up to the Munich crisis of only one Inspector with a small clerical staff. They represented, nevertheless, an important development which was to acquire permanence. The Inspectors' functions of assisting local authorities on the spot with preparation of schemes and reporting to the centre on both general and local difficulties grew steadily in significance.

Co-ordination, and Plans for War Organisation

The A.R.P. Department was an organism extending its activities on four levels—the Minister for Co-ordination of Defence and the Committee of Imperial Defence (which continued to co-ordinate all defence measures), other central departments, the local authorities and the public. It will be convenient now to record its activities regarding the first and second of these.

At the end of 1937 the Cabinet had approved a report by the

---

[1] pp. 65–66.

Minister for Co-ordination of Defence which proposed as the objectives of British defence policy, in this order of priority—the protection of the United Kingdom, the preservation of our trade routes, the defence of British territories overseas and co-operation in the defence of any allies we might have in war. The report contained the statement:

> It is clear that . . . if the survival of Great Britain is accepted as the primary condition of success, the greatest danger against which we have to provide protection is attack from the air on the United Kingdom, designed to inflict a knock-out blow at the initial stage of the war, and that our first endeavour must be to provide adequate defence against this threat.

Home Defence continued to be the first aim of the rearmament programme, and within this sphere emphasis on air attack gathered strength throughout the period which remained for preparation. Expansion of the Air Force continued to make first claim on rearmament resources, and contribution to the Air Defence of Great Britain (A.D.G.B.) was conceived as the primary role of the Army until, after the Munich crisis, Continental commitments were again undertaken.

Details of the plans to develop individual Fighting Services are no concern of this narrative. It must, however, be noted that the priority given to Air Force expansion was as a rule the work of the Cabinet; the Chiefs of Staff normally produced what they considered to be more balanced schemes, in which the claims of the three Services were more evenly apportioned. The importance public opinion attached to the air menace continued, that is to say, to have much influence with Cabinet decisions on defence. Secondly, the character of Air Force expansion was finally determined by further Cabinet emphasis on the defensive, in the form of unwillingness to attach as much importance as the Air Staff to the counter-offensive and decisions to give priority to 'active close defence' (i.e., fighter aircraft) in the series of programmes produced up to the outbreak of war.

In November 1937 the Defence Policy and Requirements Committee had ceased to exist, and the detailed progress of the A.R.P. Department was thenceforward considered by the Committee of Imperial Defence itself. This body had recently, after considering the Foreign Office despatch previously mentioned[1] and a report by the Department, recorded anxiety at the serious disadvantage in which Britain stood by comparison with Germany in this sphere, and concluded that, in view of the close and increasing inter-relation between the Fighting and the A.R.P. Services, the necessary co-ordination in matters of principle and policy should be brought into

---

[1] p 103.

the orbit of the Chiefs of Staff Sub-Committee, the head of the
A.R.P. Department being called into consultation as necessary.
They approved in December a proposal by the Minister for Co-
ordination of Defence for the appointment of a committee of one
officer from each of the Services and one from the A.R.P. Department
to draw up a Home Defence Scheme for the purpose of knitting
together all Home Defence arrangements. This body would work
in the orbit of the Deputy Chiefs of Staff Committee, and would
need about a year for its task.[1]

In the White Paper on Defence which, for the fourth successive
year, was presented to Parliament in March, A.R.P. was for the
first time the subject of more than brief allusion.[2] When asking for
the approval of the House for this programme Mr Chamberlain re-
affirmed his double policy of rearmament combined with what he had
called not long before his exploration for the basis 'on which we
might build up a general scheme of appeasement'; and he spoke
optimistically about the progress of the former.[3] A few days later,
however, Hitler took action which formed a far more serious threat
to peace than the breaches of agreement which had closely followed
the White Papers of 1935 and 1936. The German leader's 'uncanny
manipulation of the Austrian body politic from his wizard's cave
at Berchtesgaden'[4] was followed by seizure of this independent
State.

A broadcast appeal by the Home Secretary for one million
A.R.P. volunteers made three days after this event had been
arranged some time beforehand. The immediate consequences of
Germany's aggression on Britain's defence plans were cancellation of
the principle so far underlying the rearmament programme that
the course of normal trade should not be impeded by the recon-
ditioning of the Services, and new steps of acceleration announced
by Mr Chamberlain on 24th March.[5]

The Minister for Co-ordination of Defence reported to the Cabinet
that A.R.P. plans were already in an advanced stage of development,
and good progress was being made. But that even in this region,
acceleration might be practicable; and he drew attention to some
responsibilities of the Board of Trade and the Ministries of Health
and Transport which needed definite acceleration.[6] His suggestions
that war preparations by these Departments should have equal

---

[1] The members of this sub-committee were a Captain, R.N., and others of equivalent
rank.
[2] *Statement relating to Defence*, Cmd. 5682, 1938.
[3] H. of C. Deb., Vol. 332, Cols. 1555–1567, 7th March 1938.
[4] A. J. Toynbee, *Survey of International Affairs, 1938, Vol. 1*, p. 194.
[5] H. of C. Deb., Vol. 333, Cols. 1399-1413.
[6] The C.I.D. had recently agreed that the A.R.P. Department's Progress Reports
should be rendered at bi-monthly instead of monthly intervals. Three months, in fact,
elapsed between the 17th (February) and 18th (May) reports.

priority to civil work and should be completed as early as possible received Cabinet approval. The Committee of Imperial Defence soon afterwards received fresh reports of the state of passive defence in Germany and France which caused them some anxiety about the progress, and especially the co-ordination, of British measures. The Home Secretary considered that a gradual tendency towards unified control was making itself felt.

A less optimistic view of Britain's preparedness in this sphere had, however, just been presented by the Chiefs of Staff in a general appreciation. Our A.R.P. Organisation, this stated, was only just emerging from the embryonic stage, and there was no centralised control and co-ordination. Shelters and fire-fighting requirements were especially deficient; and the organisation had not yet reached a stage when air attacks could be faced with any confidence, although much valuable preparatory work had been done. France's passive defences were far more advanced than our own, though probably less complete than those of Germany. Subsequently, the Deputy Chiefs of Staff reported on the co-ordination and control of defence operations. While noting that plans for warnings and lighting were well advanced, they expressed anxiety about the adequacy of existing and projected measures for co-ordination of 'civil passive defence' throughout the country.

When the Committee of Imperial Defence considered this report on 5th May, German designs against Czechoslovakia were assuming an alarming nature. The Home Secretary acknowledged the need for reaching decisions as to, first, which central department should be the co-ordinating department for the various civil organisations concerned with defence measures, and secondly, since there was 'no tradition and no chain of command' among the civil authorities, the form which 'the executive command' in the field of passive defence should take. The committee invited the Secretary to the Treasury to consult with their own Secretary on these two problems. The two weeks which followed were a period of mounting crisis over German intentions towards Czechoslovakia, at the pinnacle of which 'Europe believed herself to be very near war'.[1] At the conclusion of this crisis Sir Warren Fisher and Colonel Hankey proposed to the committee that in war two institutional novelties should be created for passive defence—a 'Minister of Home Security', and an over-riding Regional Organisation.

The Fisher-Hankey proposals represented a decisive return under the pressure of events to matters which, though present to the minds of the authorities in the years before 1935, had received scant attention during the subsequent phase of development. They again extended the problem, both in depth and breadth. The situation

---

[1] J. W. Wheeler-Bennett, *Munich* (1948), p. 58.

to be catered for was one of intensive air attacks sweeping simultaneously over many parts of the country, and creating 'a real
danger, especially at the outset of war, that the national will to resist
might be broken, if the situation in the devastated areas could not be
got under control at once'. This re-emphasis on morale found one
expression in the title suggested for the war-time Ministry.[1] Also, a
number of civil departments, responsible not only for air raid
precautions but for law and order, food, transport and so on would
be 'literally "in the front line" from the very outset'. The widening
of the enquiry is indicated by the emergence at this time of the term
'civil defence' to embrace almost all the exceptional war-time measures
to be undertaken by civil departments.

The Minister of Home Security, it was proposed, should combine
in war responsibility for the passive defence services currently
administered by the Home Secretary (air raid and fire precautions
and police) and the function of co-ordinating the war-time services
of all other civil departments. He should be a member of the organ
of supreme control (e.g., a War Cabinet), and preside over a
'standing council' of Ministers of the departments most concerned.

The proposals for Regional Organisation owed much to the
Civil Emergency Organisation formed soon after the First World
War for supervising, co-ordinating and if necessary controlling the
activities throughout the country of the civil departments concerned
in dealing with an emergency. This had been used in the General
Strike of 1926, and kept in being in skeleton form ever since.
The Fisher-Hankey proposals embraced a considerable measure of
executive responsibility delegated to Regional authorities, at least in
the critical period immediately after the outbreak of a war. Britain
should be formed into a number of 'divisions', each in charge of a
person of outstanding ability and experience responsible to the Minister of Home Security. These 'divisional commanders' would co-
ordinate the activities in their divisions of officials administering
services on behalf of central departments; and these activities would,
if necessary, be subject to their over-riding orders. The officials made
clear that these proposals were only broad principles on which future
plans might be worked out; and concluded with the suggestion that if
an emergency arose before such plans could be prepared the Civil
Emergency Organisation should be brought into operation. The
Committee of Imperial Defence gave the main scheme provisional
approval, and also sanctioned the final suggestion.

This story of planning war-time control must be briefly interrupted
to note certain developments of this early summer. Since Hitler's
seizure of Austria the interest shown by Parliament in the passive

---

[1] Choice of this term seems to have been due to the expectation of the many-sided
threat which another war would offer to domestic security in its widest possible sense.

defences had perceptibly increased, and the measures contemplated both for evacuation and for treatment of civil casualties had figured increasingly in Questions. On 26th May the Home Secretary announced the appointment of a committee under the chairmanship of Sir John Anderson to review the problem of evacuation.[1] Shortly afterwards, in debate on the Vote for A.R.P. Services, the Minister announced decisions to abolish 'the old distinction that we attempted to draw between casualty hospitals and base hospitals', and to transfer responsibility for a national hospital service for victims of air attack from his department to the Ministry of Health.[2] Recent Cabinet changes had caused Mr Walter Elliot (who as Secretary of State for Scotland had been concerned with A.R.P.) to become Minister of Health, and to be replaced in the former office by Colonel Colville.[3] Parliament's growing interest in the topic had included some pressure on the Government to delegate A.R.P. duties to a special Minister, or at least to ask the Under-Secretary of State to the Home Office to devote all his time to this work. The Prime Minister resisted these proposals until 23rd June, when he stated his intention to adopt the second course.[4]

Planning of war organisation was advanced a stage further by the Prime Minister's appointment on the day of this statement of a committee of Permanent Heads of the chief civil departments, under the chairmanship of the Secretary to the Treasury, on the Co-ordination and Control of Civil Authorities for Passive Defence Purposes in War. As the international situation continued to deteriorate, the Prime Minister instructed this body to pay first attention to adapting the Civil Emergency Organisation to the purposes of civil defence in war.

During the next three months tension rose steadily to a point, in the final week of September, at which war seemed inevitable; and this committee was engaged in planning the essential civil defence mechanism through which the Government might function immediately before and after the outbreak of a war. Before Parliament rose at the end of July it presented the Committee of Imperial Defence with provisional suggestions. The Civil Commissioners should if appointed in war be known as 'Regional Commissioners', and a list was submitted of persons provisionally earmarked for these offices. The Commissioners' powers, the appointment of additional officers to their staffs, the progress in reaching departmental agreement

---

[1] H. of C. Deb., Vol. 336, Col. 1380. Sir John Anderson had entered Parliament as Member for the Scottish Universities in the previous February.

[2] H. of C. Deb., Vol. 336, Col. 2091, 1st June 1938.

[3] Following the resignation of Lord Swinton, Secretary of State for Air, on 16th May and his replacement by Sir Kingsley Wood.

[4] H. of C. Deb., Vol. 337, Col. 1271.

on boundaries,[1] and other matters were briefly set out. The committee expressed the view that the Civil Emergency Organisation so modified could, by the end of the first week in August, be embodied at a few hours' notice.

The committee next reviewed a Home Office passive defence plan, from which it became clear that improvisation would be needed over large areas of the problem, and that the function assigned to the Home Office of co-ordinating action in this sphere had received little detailed attention. Inter-departmental discussions were intensified to give the plan for Regional Authorities immediate practical shape; and by the middle of August the essential instructions to Regional Commissioners and others were completed in the form of a supplement to the Government War Book, known as 'Civil Defence Emergency Scheme "Y" '.[2]

Building the National Structure

Attention must turn back from these high-level activities up to the brink of Munich, concerned with the superstructure, to the efforts being made by local authorities and the public to provide the substance of air raid precautions. Neither local authorities nor the public, it is necessary to recall, were aware of the high-level plans just described, or of the full seriousness of the international crises of these months. Rearmament was now accepted as necessary among most sections of the nation, and events were offering a clearer challenge to the individual to participate in defence. Yet optimistic statements by the Prime Minister and others in the Government about the progress of rearmament and the success of 'appeasement'[3] encouraged belief in the inevitability, so far as Britain was concerned, of peace.

The term 'the A.R.P. Service' and analogies with military organisation, though now in greater use by the central authorities, still had most limited truth as descriptions of the facts. For local authorities and the public neither the unitary or the quasi-military aspect of the A.R.P. problem was conspicuous. The Act had made some 230 local authorities the primary 'scheme-making authorities'. These presented great variety in historical antecedents, number and character of inhabitants, area and working structure. Large differences prevailed in their financial resources, administrative

---

[1] A considerable amount of discussion was still proceeding on the problem of adapting the areas of the C.E.O. to serve the purposes of all Departments in war.

[2] It may be mentioned in this context that on Sir Maurice Hankey's retirement at the end of July 1938, Mr Edward Bridges was appointed Secretary to the Cabinet and the Cabinet Office, and Col. Ismay Secretary to the Committee of Imperial Defence.

[3] e.g., the Prime Minister's statement at the close of the Parliamentary session that there was 'a relaxation of that sense of tension which six months ago was present' (H. of C. Deb., Vol. 338, Col. 2963, 26th July 1938).

efficiency and local estimates of the danger future air attack presented to their areas. If diversity was the most obvious feature of the pattern, one common characteristic, also of permanent importance to the topic of this volume, needs mention: the traditional spirit of local independence *vis-à-vis* both the central Government and other local authorities.

The problem of organisation which A.R.P. presented was stated by Sir John Anderson in Parliament later this year to be so vast and complex as almost to induce despair, and to be soluble under democratic processes only by a great enlargement of 'free collaboration'.[1] The Act had made evident that collaboration between local official bodies (to mention only one form) would be needed on a novel scale. The measures of units composing administrative counties would have to be combined into a single scheme. Arrangements would have to be made for mutual assistance between neighbouring authorities. Within individual authorities, even of the so-called 'compendious' type, the A.R.P. scheme would require exceptional co-ordination of the functions of officials and departments.

When the A.R.P. Department issued the Draft Regulations at the end of January it was preparing to deal with local schemes of a much more formal and elaborate kind than those made under the previous voluntary system; and these, it expected, would soon be submitted in large numbers.[2] Now that local A.R.P. planning was a statutory duty and the Government's grants-in-aid had been decided, formal procedure for central examination and approval of all local proposals would be required. Local scheme-making would be accompanied by the Department's elaboration of the organisation appropriate to different matters, and by its help with recruitment, publicity and training.

The Home Secretary began the fresh campaign for volunteers with a broadcast on 14th March which, as already stated, had been arranged before Hitler's seizure (on 11th March) of Austria.[3] After stressing A.R.P.'s value as a deterrent to an enemy contemplating the strategy of an aerial knock-out blow, the Home Secretary appealed for at least one million active workers in the Service, though without mentioning any date by which it was hoped this total might be reached. He first asked for large numbers of male and female Air Raid Wardens, and then outlined the other local organisations for which volunteers were required. The needs and conditions of the A.R.P. Services and Fire Services for the first time received extensive

---

[1] H. of C. Deb., Vol. 336, Cols. 2109–2115, 1st June 1938.

[2] p. 108.

[3] *The Times*, 15th March 1938. Unlike the last broadcast on A.R.P. by the Home Secretary (Sir John Simon) a year before, this appeal was made at the peak hour following the 9.0 p.m. news.

notice in the national Press. These were also the subject of a widely-distributed official pamphlet called *What You Can Do*, which told the public that the minimum age for men in the General Services was normally thirty; that most of the service in war would be part-time but those employed whole-time would be paid, and that peace-time training would be free and covered by compensation for injury. The immediate public response to this appeal was encouraging.[1] To whatever contribution Hitler's act made to this must be added the impetus of a series of fresh and exceptionally heavy air raids by Spanish insurgent forces on Barcelona in mid-March.[2]

It soon became apparent that the A.R.P. Department had been over-sanguine in expecting many complete local schemes to be submitted at an early date for formal approval. Many authorities which had ceased or deferred preparations during 1937 were proving slow in resuming action. Delay in reaching agreement on the Regulations for approval of expenditure offered a reason (though not, the Home Office insisted, a valid one) for postponement. Numbers of authorities were still engaged on the preliminary task of creating an administrative A.R.P. structure by adjusting their organisation or by appointment of special officials. And it had soon become clear that numerous 'subordinate' authorities (boroughs, and urban and rural districts) wanted to take advantage of the provision of the Act which empowered the Secretary of State to permit them to prepare their own schemes.

The Department, like the local authorities, was learning by trial and error to administer an Act new both in character and purpose. The volume of requests sent to it since the opening of the year for advice about schemes had been putting a big strain on its resources. Delays in answering requests caused criticism at the periphery and gave further grounds for postponement of local action.[3] The Department sought to hasten the procedure by issuing at the end of March a 'model' for schemes. These, it suggested, should be confined to essentials and to the main framework of local proposals; details of equipment, appliances and works raising questions of grant should be submitted independently of the formal documents.

With four of the seventeen functions outlined in the Regulations —the warning and reporting systems, gas detection and evacuation —local action had to await fuller Home Office advice. But the

---

[1] e.g., in the Metropolitan area in the first 10 days about 7,000 volunteers enrolled and a similar number took preliminary steps towards enrolment.

[2] Strong British feeling had been aroused for some time past by the use of the air weapon against defenceless civilians in the Spanish War. See, for example, H. of C. Deb., Vol. 331, Cols. 305-334, 2nd February 1938.

[3] Congestion of work at one stage caused a delay of three weeks before letters received by the Department began to be dealt with by the appropriate official.

circular accompanying this 'model' scheme urged that this should not be used as grounds of delay, and that advantage should be taken of the procedure of submission of separate schemes relating to separate subjects as well as to separate areas. The Government's shelter policy of 'dispersal' was restated, and the new proposal made that authorities should make surveys of possible public shelters. The most urgent local tasks, after creation of proper administrative arrangements, were enrolment and training of persons for the A.R.P. services, decisions about the number and distribution of these services, and selection of buildings for A.R.P. headquarters, respirator stores, wardens' and first aid posts.

Some weeks later the Home Secretary and the local authority Associations discussed means by which general progress might be given more momentum. The main obstacle to the development of local scheme-making, the Associations insisted, was the need to obtain central approval for all items of expenditure ranking for grant, and the Home Secretary expressed the hope that the forth-coming financial regulations would give alleviation in this matter.[1] In Parliament criticisms of the Government for procrastination aroused the retort that the 'united front' of local authorities in the previous year had been the main impediment to progress. Criticisms of over-centralisation were met to the extent that the strengthening of the Department was continued, and the Department now relegated to a more remote future its expectation of receiving complete schemes. Experience had convinced it that the best procedure was to continue to sanction particular local proposals—for example the appointment of area A.R.P. officers in a county or the adaptation of a building for a respirator store—which could ultimately be embodied into a full scheme.

Recruitment for A.R.P. was now, in many areas, falling below the Government's expectations; and the local authorities, a number of whom had as yet made no appeal for volunteers, accepted the Home Secretary's offer of a greater assistance from the centre with this. As the summer of 1938 opened the Department arranged for widespread distribution of posters and more A.R.P. exercises and exhibitions, including a display in the Glasgow Empire Exhibition. More fundamental, however, to maintaining satisfactory recruitment was the provision throughout Britain of local training. If experience that 'the number of volunteers dwindled appreciably by the time training started' reflected some lack of enthusiasm by the public, it also reflected serious delay in many places in providing local training.

The Department followed the Home Secretary's March appeal with a request to local authorities 'to make every effort to organise

---

[1] pp. 109–110.

courses of instruction as quickly as possible'.[1] But it was soon compelled to recognise that a dearth of qualified instructors often rendered this a counsel of perfection. By May 1938 some 2,000 persons had qualified as instructors at the two Anti-Gas Schools, which had established high training standards and instilled much enthusiasm in those from all over the country who attended them. But in addition to the fact that some authorities sent unsuitable persons to these schools, many of those who qualified became, for many reasons, unavailable for local training. The question for the Department became one of providing many more local instructors without lowering the standards it had so far maintained. A solution was sought by what was called 'second-hand training', or the authorisation to a proportion of 'graduates' of the two Schools of the right to train local instructors. A circular and a new edition of the memorandum on 'Anti-Gas Training' notified scheme-making authorities in mid-May that individuals belonging to a new grade called 'Instructors, C.A.G.S.—Special' (i.e., those who had graduated with marks of over 85 per cent. at Falfield or Easingwold) might give courses on a prescribed syllabus for persons to qualify as local instructors in all anti-gas measures other than decontamination; those so qualified would be known as 'Instructors, L.A.G.C.' (Local Anti-Gas Course).[2] A month later it was decided that this scheme was too restricted and authority to train local instructors was extended to the larger class of 'Instructors, C.A.G.S.' holding first-class certificates.[3]

Suggestions in Parliament that additional A.R.P. Schools were needed, particularly in Scotland, did not find favour with the Government. But the Department's direct contribution to training had been enlarged in March by the creation of a third institution, an A.R.P. General Training School in London. This was to give officials entrusted by local authorities with preparation of schemes courses concerned mainly with administrative aspects of the problem, and lasting three weeks. It was also designed as 'a focal point for the accumulation and dissemination of the knowledge acquired by A.R.P. Officers' in applying in their areas the principles the Department laid down.[4]

The fresh international crisis over the Sudetenland in May was the occasion of a second broadcast by the Home Secretary asking men and women, and particularly the latter, to volunteer for 'this

---

[1] H.O. Circular of 18th March 1938.

[2] H.O. Circular of 19th May 1938; the Memorandum (No. 5) contained detailed syllabuses for this training.

[3] H.O. Circular of 21st June 1938. At the end of June about 550 persons had qualified as Special Instructors and 1,800 as First Class Instructors.

[4] H.O. Circular of 22nd August 1938. The school opened in Whitehall Gardens on 14th March 1938 and moved to Cromwell Road, South Kensington in September. It had a capacity for about thirty-five students at each course.

citizen's job' of air raid protection.[1] The number already enrolled, the Home Secretary said, was about 400,000; and the Government wanted to complete the total of one million 'before the summer holidays'.[2] The fact that preparation of complete local schemes would take time was 'no reason why we should not get great parts of them into operation with little or no delay'. The new training scheme would soon provide many more local instructors, and personal contact, hitherto lacking, between A.R.P. and the individual citizen was being introduced in some areas through house-to-house wardens' visits. The Home Secretary's total of 400,000 existing volunteers (it should be added) was an estimate, since no system of regular returns by local authorities was yet in operation. It included both the nucleus who had shown interest in A.R.P. over the past three years, and a much larger number whose activity had been confined to the act of enrolment.

In Parliament, which fully debated the topic of A.R.P. soon afterwards on the first separate A.R.P. Vote, general apathy had now been replaced by greater interest.[3] A number of Members, some with first-hand knowledge of air bombardment in Spain, had begun special study of the subject. Fresh evidence was offered that provision of shelters and arrangements for evacuation from the most vulnerable areas were widely regarded as outweighing in importance all other measures; and that the Government's proposals regarding these were thought inadequate. The Government replied that progress in accumulating information on these subjects was satisfactory, and emphasised the responsibility now resting on local authorities.

Criticism was repeated that the Government had neglected to provide ordinary citizens with any A.R.P. instruction. The main instrument designed for this purpose, the reader will recall, was a *Householder's Handbook*, in gestation since the early days of the Department. A version of this manual had been completed during 1937, when the Cabinet had decided that the financial negotiations then proceeding made its publication inopportune.[4] After the Act's passage the Home Secretary had decided that the local authorities, now formally responsible for A.R.P. instruction of the public, should be asked to comment on the booklet before its publication. A new edition, *The Protection of Your Home Against Air Raids*, had been circulated in February for this purpose and for the use of volunteers in the A.R.P. Services.[5] It was not, however, until shortly after the

---

[1] 23rd May 1938, again after the 9.0 p.m. news.

[2] By way of comparison, the Territorial Army at this date had a strength of 170,000 and an establishment of 204,000.

[3] H. of C. Deb., Vol. 336, Cols. 2079-2196, 1st June 1938.

[4] pp. 70, 102.

[5] H.O. Circular of 25th February 1938. By the end of March some 700,000 copies had been issued.

debate just mentioned that the Department asked the local bodies to forward their views on the manual's suitability.[1] After these had proved strongly in favour of the booklet's issue at the earliest date, the Department arranged for an edition to be published in the autumn.

More importance was attached by the central authorities at this stage to the more personal method of approaching ordinary citizens of the house-to-house visit by wardens. The Wardens' Service had been instituted more than a year before as a corps of citizens which would form a link between the official machinery, including the more specialised services, and the average citizen.[2] The general idea of this service and character of its functions had been determined some time before, and announced at the time of its formation.[3] A handbook now issued on *The Duties of Air Raid Wardens* was to give wider currency to the service and help to train the men and women who volunteered for it.[4] It restated the warden's chief peace-time duties as to advise the inhabitants of his sector on precautions in their homes, to fit gas-masks and help prepare the local scheme for distributing these in a crisis, to persuade his friends to enrol in A.R.P. and to train himself for his war functions. The local council, it was suggested, should provide the trained warden with evidence of his position in the form of a card of appointment. The warden's equipment would be an armlet, a steel helmet and a Civilian Duty respirator, and some simple equipment for wardens' posts was now proposed. Wardens' war functions would now include patrolling the streets and calling the occupiers' attention to unobscured lights in buildings.

Though in some places wardens' house-to-house visits were beginning, much had still to be done in recruiting sufficient persons for this service and training those who had joined it. Special emphasis, for example, had been laid by the Department earlier in 1938 on the help which wardens who had completed the approved anti-gas training might give by fitting gas-masks and making a census of the number and sizes of these needed in their areas.[5] It was announced towards the end of June that some 200,000 men and women (or one-half the total now required) had volunteered for this service; of these only 50,000 were described as trained, although a further 58,000 were 'under training'.[6] Local training, which naturally

---

[1] H.O. Circular of 9th June 1938.
[2] pp. 71–73.
[3] Including Memorandum No. 4, *Air Raid Wardens*, issued in March 1937 primarily for the information of local authorities.
[4] Handbook No. 8, issued 11th June 1938.
[5] H.O. Circulars of 4th April and 6th July 1938.
[6] H. of C. Deb., Vol. 337, Col. 1735, 28th June 1938. The figure was compiled from returns by 216 out of 236 scheme-making authorities.

varied in intensity and efficiency, was still almost confined to anti-gas precautions. The handbook just mentioned had outlined a much wider field for a warden's training, and given an undertaking that the Department would supply a syllabus for this purpose.

A review of training by the Inspector General had emphasised that little had so far been done to extend this to topics other than gas defence. During the early months of 1938 the Department had issued revised editions of its handbooks or memoranda on *Personal Protection against Gas, First Aid and Nursing of Gas Casualties, The Organisation of Decontamination Services,* and *Anti-Gas Training.*[1] Training of wardens and others in protection against high explosive bombs and means of dealing with incendiary bombs, and the broadening of first aid instruction, now demanded urgent attention.

Of the A.R.P. General Services, the Wardens' was the only one with functions which could truly be described as general and which were peculiar to the needs of A.R.P.[2] The others were designed for tasks in greater or less degree specialised, and carried on in some form as services in peace. Thus the Casualty Services—First Aid Parties, First Aid Posts, Casualty Clearing Stations and an Ambulance Service —would be doing work, the basic training and experience for which were provided in peace by the 'voluntary aid societies' such as the Red Cross. Notice has been taken of the arrangements of 1936 whereby these societies, assisted by Government grants, had agreed to encourage their members to volunteer for A.R.P. and to train them without charge in anti-gas measures, as well as to help local authorities in forming A.R.P. Casualty Services and in training recruits from outside their own organisations.[3] These arrangements were now, for various reasons, proving inadequate. A tendency for local authorities to leave the initiative in the whole matter to the societies was now at variance with the statutory position. Difficulties had arisen in reconciling the societies' practices with the Government's undertaking to provide all A.R.P. volunteers with free training. No adequate means had been found for training in 'pure first aid' (i.e. matters other than treatment of gas injuries) the A.R.P. recruits who did not belong to one of the societies and who, in the aggregate, would much exceed the combined membership of these bodies. Consultations held in May and July 1938 resulted in clear assumption by scheme-making authorities of responsibility for organising Casualty Services and precise definition of the way in

---

[1] Handbooks Nos. 1, 2 and Memoranda Nos. 3, 5. Handbooks were intended mainly as textbooks for members of the services, and Memoranda as descriptions of organisation for local officials.

[2] The term 'General Services', which endured, had its origin in the necessity to distinguish in the 1937 Act between 'air raid fire precautions' and all other kinds of air raid precautions.

[3] pp. 69, 101.

which parts of this work might be delegated to the 'uniformed first-aid organisations'.

A Home Office circular at the end of August formed the new charter in this matter, and defined for the first time stages in the formation of a local Casualty Service, now in most cases the responsibility of the Medical Officer of Health.[1] Enrolment of all persons (whether a member of one of the societies or not) would be followed by instruction in first aid and anti-gas treatment, and then by allocation to a Casualty Service unit. 'Post-instructional training' in A.R.P. would be carried on within the unit, and thereafter combined training would be given to units. The societies (it was anticipated) would continue to give much help, as sources of volunteers already trained in first aid and as training and examining bodies for local authorities under conditions now clearly laid down. In addition to fees paid to them for local training, Exchequer grants would be continued.

The other projected General Services were Decontamination Squads, Rescue Parties, Report Services, Messengers, and Clerks and Storekeepers. Members of Decontamination Squads would in the main be recruited from employees of the local authorities' cleansing departments. The emphasis since 1935 on defence against gas had brought adequate progress in recruitment and training of this service; though departures had sometimes been made from the voluntary principle in the form of payment for training outside working hours. The state of the Rescue Service was much less advanced. While a nucleus of men with the skill essential for this might be found among employees of the larger authorities, the majority would have to be drawn from the building and similar trades. The A.R.P. Department's tendency to assume that enrolment of skilled men from these sources and (where necessary) their local training would not present much difficulty was now being corrected. In negotiations with building trades representatives this summer the issue of payment for training assumed prominence and, apart from sanction for payment of travelling expenses, was left unsettled.

The need was becoming urgent to provide A.R.P. volunteers and the public with training in dealing with incendiary bombs. Though a start had been made in 1937 with some training in this subject,[2] none of the schemes to make this general had approached the stage of application. Now that A.R.P. training was a local authority responsibility, it seemed logical that the local experts in fire-fighting, the fire brigades, should give the elementary instruction in 'incendiary bomb control' required for wardens and others, and a proposal to this effect was made by the A.R.P. Department to the Fire Brigades

[1] 26th August 1938.
[2] pp. 85–86, 126.

K

Division. But the fire brigades, now occupied with creating the emergency fire organisation and training recruits to the Auxiliary Fire Service, were unwilling to undertake this task. The Department then decided that the curricula of the Anti-Gas Schools must be extended to include instruction in this subject. Scheme-making authorities were told that this innovation would be made in the early autumn.[1]

Since the passing of the Act training in the form of A.R.P. exercises had been given in some areas in which the volunteers' individual and collective training was sufficiently advanced. A proposal early in 1938 that a large exercise should be held in the London area in the summer had been found impracticable; and the central authorities' efforts in this sphere had been devoted to assisting local exercises of a general kind and staging exercises with the limited aims of testing plans for communications, warning and lighting. The most ambitious performances of the first kind, in which in addition to all A.R.P. services aircraft and anti-aircraft units took part, occurred at Nottingham and Leeds; and a night exercise on a similar scale was conducted with naval co-operation in the area of the Nore Command. A communications test was held in the Southampton area, and limited tests of lighting arrangements were made in the Wolverhampton area and in northern and eastern counties during the Home Defence Exercises in July.

Recruitment for the A.R.P. Services became a matter more of knowledge and less of estimate at the end of June, when the first regular returns about this had been sent in by local authorities. The persons enrolled, two-thirds of whom were men, numbered 488,659. About 140,000 of this total were described as fully trained for a particular service, and a rather smaller number were reported to be 'undergoing training'.[2] In the London area, where somewhat over 100,000 volunteers were needed, 40,000 had enrolled and 26,000 of these had been trained or were receiving training. Although in most areas enrolment was officially described as 'proceeding satisfactorily', there was obvious need to speed up public response. Plans were laid to hold a new recruiting drive on a larger scale than any so far undertaken after the holiday season. The months of July–September 1938 were to prove (though this could not be foreseen) the last for a considerable time in which either officials or ordinary citizens could look forward to holidays on a generous scale.

An important part in stimulating recruitment was to be taken by a new civilian body, 'The Women's Voluntary Services for Air Raid Precautions'. At a meeting of the chief women's organisations of the country at the Home Office during the Sudetenland crisis it

---

[1] H.O. Circular of 18th August 1938.

[2] These figures excluded recruits to the Auxiliary Fire Service.

was agreed to form this organisation, in charge of the Dowager Marchioness of Reading.[1] Its aims were said in a letter from the Home Secretary to Lady Reading to be, 'the enrolment of women for the A.R.P. Services of the local authorities, to help to bring home to every household in the country what air attack may mean, and to make known to every household what it can do to protect itself and help the community'.[2] Preparations for this new embodiment of women, announced to the country on 18th June, were energetically undertaken.[3] Its headquarters staff was provided with accommodation in Horseferry House, and the Government undertook to defray its general administrative expenses. A beginning was made with appointment of W.V.S. representatives in each of the thirteen A.R.P. Regional areas and creation of local W.V.S. branches, known as 'centres', throughout the country.[4]

The autumn campaign for the second half-million volunteers was being planned, with the help of a special director of 'publicity, in lavish manner. A sense of urgency transmitted from high levels was presumably responsible for mid-August being chosen to tell local authorities of these plans and seek their support[5]. The Home Secretary had enlisted the sympathy of the Churches, the Press and various other bodies. It was hoped that references to the 'civic duty' of actively supporting A.R.P. might be made from pulpits on the first Sunday in October, and the Home Secretary was to address an Albert Hall rally of London volunteers on the next day. Local authorities were asked to exhibit posters, arrange for appeals in theatres and cinemas, stage A.R.P. displays and make special efforts to gain the interest of business firms.

These measures to extend training and speed up recruitment had been accompanied by additions to the Department's plans for organisation. Earlier in the year guidance had been given to local authorities in memoranda on *Personnel Requirements* for the different services, *Local Communications and the Reporting of Air Raid Damage*, and *The Air Raid Warning System*.[6] Circulars had been issued in April describing new arrangements for the staffing and lay-out of First Aid Posts,[7] and plans for local storage and emergency distribution to the public of civilian masks.[8]

---

[1] Widow of Rufus Isaacs, 1st Marquis of Reading (died 1935) former Viceroy of India.

[2] 20th May 1938.

[3] The announcement was made to local authorities in a circular of 24th June which described the primary purpose of the W.V.S. as assistance in the enrolment of women for A.R.P. services and for emergency hospital services.

[4] See Charles Graves, *Women in Green: the story of the W.V.S* (1948).

[5] H.O. Circular of 18th August 1938. Further details of the campaign, including a suggested programme for each day of the first week, were announced in a circular of 16th September.

[6] Memoranda Nos. 6, 7, 8, issued March, April, June 1938.

[7] 26th April, supplemented by circular of 19th August 1938.

[8] 4th April 1938.

The latter formed a notable example of plans begun long before-hand at the centre now awaiting local application. Some 30 million masks of this type now available in Home Office Regional Stores were to be distributed to 'local respirator stores', which had to be suitable both for the masks' preservation and for the functions of final assembly and further distribution. From these masks were to be issued to 'respirator distributing depots', where wardens or others would make final distribution to the public.[1] In the months following publication of this plan progress with choosing and adapting build-ings for local stores proved slow, and the Home Office appealed to scheme-making bodies to make every effort to prepare at least parts of this plan and accept delivery of civilian masks by the end of August.[2] For training and fitting the public (as distinct from ultimate distribution) about 800,000 masks of all types had been issued to local authorities and others by the middle of 1938.

The preparation and submission to the centre of local schemes had, in the meantime, been proceeding by the piecemeal method.[3] The procedure of submitting parts of schemes for formal approval had been welcomed by local authorities; and since grant became payable on the parts approved, this enabled local endeavour on particular items to proceed from planning to execution. It had become even more clear, however, that the date by which most authorities might be expected to complete their schemes lay far ahead; and that examination and approval of instalments of schemes were putting a large strain on the A.R.P. Department's resources. In addition to the 230 or more normal scheme-making bodies, 'subordinate' authorities throughout the country, numbering many hundreds more, were seeking the help of Regional Inspectors and referring directly for advice to the fountain-head in London. The instalments of local plans, therefore, amounted in the aggregate to many thousand.[4] The Department's correspondence over schemes was 'voluminous'. Its practice of holding interviews with local officials who had brought plans to a certain stage, though found to be fruitful, did not decrease the demands on its time and energy.[5]

Fresh efforts had therefore become necessary to simplify the scheme-making process. A circular of early August defined precisely to local authorities the stages they might adopt in preparing items of the 'model' scheme already issued.[6] New emphasis was placed

---

[1] The proposed normal capacity for a local store was 30,000 masks, and for a dis-tributing depot 4,000 masks.

[2] H.O. Circular of 6th July 1938.

[3] See pp. 121–122

[4] A senior officer of the Department estimated in July that plans (i.e., parts of total schemes) either in existence or likely to mature would number at least 20,000.

[5] A good illustration of this practice was provided by the scheme for the County of Salop.

[6] H.O. Circular of 9th August 1938; definition of the stages was contained in an accompanying memorandum.

on central examination and approval of instalments by informal means, and some more responsibility in this matter was given to the Inspectorate. The Provisional Regulations for approval of expenditure had finally been issued a short time before this announcement, and had dispensed with prior approval in respect of certain minor items.[1] Regional Inspectors were empowered to agree plans with scheme-making bodies on constructional works (such as depots of various kinds) costing less than stipulated sums.[2] They were not, however, empowered to give approval of expenditure, which had ultimately to be obtained from the Department.

The Department, hitherto reluctant to ask scheme-making bodies to make many returns, now asked each authority to report on the state of its whole A.R.P. scheme. Until these reports had been received, few generalisations about national progress could be accurate or profitable. Apart from expressing their aim to enrol one million volunteers by the end of the year, the Government (it must be noted) had given no indication to local authorities of any date by which the need for air raid precautions might arise. The appointment throughout the country by midsummer of an estimated 264 A.R.P. Officers (or Organisers) provided one measure of general achievement. 'All local authorities', the Department reported, 'are now co-operating, but progress is uneven'. Only one authority, the city of Manchester, had completed a scheme within the limits of the 'model' introduced in March and obtained formal approval for this.[3] Other industrial cities in the North and Midlands were among the minority of authorities which had made conspicuous progress. On the part of the majority progress was satisfactory; and a small number had failed to begin preparations. London, however, was described at this stage as 'deplorably behind-hand'. Though a number of Metropolitan Boroughs were taking effective measures, in others progress was almost at a standstill; and the allocation of duties between Boroughs and the L.C.C. agreed in March had not proved generally acceptable. The Department expressed an intention of making special efforts in the autumn to improve the position throughout the London area.

Industry and the Financial Issue

In the large sphere of protecting essential services and extending A.R.P. to industry in general, as in that for which local authorities were responsible, progress from planning to execution had been seriously delayed in 1937 by financial uncertainty.[4] Home Office

---

[1] pp. 109–110.
[2] The biggest sum concerned was £500, in respect of a large First Aid Post.
[3] This (the first) formal approval of a complete scheme was dated 16th August 1938.
[4] pp. 75–76.

proposals about the most essential services had been referred by the Defence Policy and Requirements Committee to an interdepartmental committee on protection of vital services. This produced in the final month of 1937 some general conclusions and also detailed findings regarding gas and electricity, which were considered by the Cabinet. Soon afterwards the Home Secretary announced that to ensure the continued functioning in war of certain utilities the Government would contribute towards the expenditure of these on precautions 'additional to those falling on industry generally'.[1]

This statement gave notice to industry of the Government's views that 'good employers' would be expected to provide from their own resources adequate standard protection for their employees and plant, and that the Exchequer's liability should be confined to part of the cost of special measures needed for certain services. No compulsion on utilities or employers in general to furnish air raid protection was yet contemplated, and the Government expressed no immediate intention of giving the principle of their limited *ad hoc* contributions legislative form.

The interdepartmental committee just mentioned proposed that grants of 40–60 per cent. should be paid towards special measures needed for gas and electricity supplies, at maximum costs to the Exchequer of £1 million for gas and £1½ million for electricity. Early in 1938 negotiations with the industries were opened on this basis by the appropriate Departments (the Board of Trade and Ministry of Transport) and the A.R.P. Department; but in spite of the groundwork already laid of information and consultation, including A.R.P. Committees for each industry, these proved protracted. Important sections of the industries regarded the proposal that 'a grant from the Exchequer should be dependent upon the expenditure by the undertaking of an equivalent amount' as altogether too stringent. The number and variety of units within each industry were considerable,[2] and the official suggestion for limiting help to units in the most vulnerable areas added a further factor of complexity. The London Gas Companies produced an estimate of nearly £2 million for maintenance of supplies in war; and the Electricity Commission estimated that £5½ million would be needed for special precautions in the electricity supply industry.

As regards the country's water undertakings, railway and dock services fact-finding was still continuing. The first of these was the subject of the interdepartmental committee's next report which included the view that plans for supply of water for fire-fighting in

---

[1] H. of C. Deb., Vol. 330, Cols. 2138–40, 23rd December 1937.

[2] Many gas and electricity undertakings were owned by local authorities relying on standard grants of 60–75 per cent. for their other or non-industrial A.R.P. measures.

London and other big centres were 'profoundly unsatisfactory'.[1] For measures to provide supplementary supplies for London and ten big cities they proposed an exceptional Exchequer contribution of 80-100 per cent. at a maximum cost of £1 million, and the principle of 100 per cent. contribution in this case was approved by the Chancellor of the Exchequer.

In referring in the 1st June debate to the very urgent question of public utilities the Home Secretary announced the Government's decision to maintain the principle of 50 per cent. as their normal contribution towards special measures of protection.[2] The Metropolitan Water Board, which in common with other concerns accepted this partition with much reluctance, agreed with the Government upon a scheme to cost some £395,000. An agreement was also concluded in mid-summer with the National Gas Council.

Discussions with electricity, railway and dock undertakings had reached no conclusive stages before the summer holidays. The A.R.P. Department, in the meantime, had extended its advisory activities by the issue of memoranda on A.R.P. in collieries, and for 'canals, navigable rivers, land drainage channels and tidal embankments'.[3] Two other developments of these months, outside the immediate framework of the negotiations just described, need mention. Consideration of the important matter of protecting oil supplies had been postponed by the interdepartmental committee until proposals had issued from the wider investigations of a committee on Petroleum Products Reserves. The oil companies, it was now apparent, were taking active measures at their own expense to reduce the danger of fires caused by air attack; but small progress had been made with provision for protected storage for oil supplies. Secondly, positive progress was made in fact-finding with the completion in June of the national survey of the protection needed against air attacks by 'points of importance'. This classified such points (which included industrial establishments of many types) in accordance with anticipated risk, drew attention to cases of special weakness, and made proposals for strengthening the active and passive defences of individual installations.[4]

As regards industry other than public utilities, it had been fully demonstrated in 1937 that the fact that the structural precautions recommended in the official handbook ranked for tax purposes as capital expenditure, and therefore did not earn relief, was proving an obstacle to action; and the Government's statement on this

---

[1] From three-fifths to four-fifths of public water supplies were provided by local authorities. Their legal responsibility was limited to providing supplies for domestic purposes.
[2] H. of C. Deb., Vol. 336, Cols. 2090-1.
[3] Memoranda Nos. C6 and C7, July 1938.
[4] pp. 86-87.

matter during passage of the A.R.P. Bill had offered no alleviation.[1] Discussions carried out late in 1937 between the Treasury and other Departments foreshadowed the possibility of a Government offer to pay a share of industry's expenditure; and in an announcement on 18th March 1938 the Chancellor of the Exchequer clarified the position and offered some concession. Expenditure on respirators and protective clothing, training, protection of glass with wire netting, black-out, and first aid and decontamination equipment would, he said, be admissible as deductions; and a wear and tear allowance would be permitted in respect of machinery and plant such as fire appliances and air filtration units. 'No deduction', however, 'would be allowable in respect of expenditure of a capital nature, for example, expenditure which results in the physical alteration of, or in the incorporation of additions to, the structure of the trading premises', though items not forming part of the permanent structure would in most cases be allowed.[2] The Chancellor later announced the Government's intention to introduce legislation to prevent annual values of property being increased for tax or rating purposes by expenditure upon 'structural alterations, additions or improvements made solely for the purpose of protection in the event of air raids'; this promise was given effect at the close of the Session.[3]

Some commercial undertakings in the country, principally Government contractors and firms with large resources,[4] were, like some utility concerns, proceeding with A.R.P. schemes and training without waiting for clarification of the financial issue. The Anti-Gas Schools continued to provide courses for representatives of industry, and in some large cities courses on A.R.P. in industry were being held. By the middle of 1938 some 50,000 employees of the railways and other utilities had been trained in anti-gas measures or were undergoing training. The A.R.P. Department had for some time past lent anti-gas equipment to utilities for training, and this practice was now extended to other large concerns, though on the basis that this equipment would form part of the mobilisation stocks of the relevant local authority. The first large practical exercise by an industrial concern was held by Imperial Chemical Industries at Buxton in the summer. An important contribution was also being made by certain railway companies, iron and steel works and other concerns to official experiments, to be shortly described, with lighting restrictions.

The branch of the Chief Technical Adviser to the A.R.P. Department had been created early in 1938 to advise local authorities and others on structural precautions and all other technical matters, and

---

[1] H. of C. Deb., Vol. 330, Col. 316, 7th December 1937.
[2] H. of C. Deb., Vol. 333, Cols. 748–9.
[3] Rating and Valuation (Air Raid Works) Act, 1938, 1 and 2 Geo. 6, Ch. 65.
[4] e.g., Boots, Vickers, I.C.I., Imperial Tobacco Coy., Coats, Unilevers and the London Brick Company appear to have made conspicuous progress.

to be generally responsible for technical experiments. Consisting of only a few officials, this was unable to advise individual industrial concerns. Its advice was given to industry by publications and conferences with the Royal Institute of British Architects and other professional bodies and employers' and labour associations.[1] The introduction of A.R.P. into industry was much helped by the creation in some places of joint A.R.P. Committees of the local authorities and business, though examples of co-operation in this form were still rare.

Progress at the Centre: (i) Warning, and the Black-Out

In the first eight months of 1938 plans for warnings and for wartime lighting restrictions were substantially advanced. The memorandum of the A.R.P. Department on warnings of September 1936 had provided the basis for detailed examination by an inter-Service committee;[2] and this body made proposals which were accepted by the Committee of Imperial Defence at the onset of the Sudetenland crisis. Approval was given for announcement of the main features of the warning system, effected soon afterwards by a Home Office circular and memorandum.[3]

The important matter of whether responsibility for initiating air raid warnings should lie with the A.O.C.-in-C., Fighter Command or with Home Office representatives stationed at his headquarters had been decided in favour of the former system. The essential features of the plan outlined eighteen months earlier were retained. The inter-Service committee made the general suggestion that in order to build up public confidence in the warning system it would be advisable in the early stages of a war 'to err on the side of over-insurance as regards both the area warned and the length of warning given'. They abandoned as impracticable an earlier proposal to distinguish between 'massed aerial attacks' and 'raids', and confine warnings to the former.[4] The separate warning districts were now defined in detail and numbered over a hundred. The confidential 'preliminary caution' was to be restricted to as few recipients as possible, with the Home Office having the final word in settlement of the lists both of these recipients and of the larger class who would be sent the main or 'action warning'. The action warning would be timed to give at least five minutes' notice of the enemy's arrival, and the preliminary caution would be distributed ten minutes in advance of this. A large-scale test of distributing messages over the G.P.O.

---

[1] On the eve of the holidays consideration was being given to the appointment of architects to Regional Offices.

[2] pp. 89–90.

[3] H.O. Circular of 4th May 1938, Memorandum No. 8, *The Air Raid Warning System*, issued to local authorities 14th June 1938.

[4] The proposal was included in the A.R.P. Committee's First Report of 1925, which in general made a substantial contribution to the scheme now adopted. See pp. 19–21.

telephone system made in the previous November had produced satisfactory results, and the committee had decided this was the best distribution method available. The elaborate technical arrangements of the system would culminate in simple spoken messages, as follows:

The Preliminary Caution	'Air Raid Message—Yellow'.
The Action Warning	'Air Raid Warning—Red'.
Raiders Passed	'Air Raid Message—Green'.
Cancel Caution	'Air Raid Message—White'.

Aside from improvement in technical methods and facilities, this operational part of the system needed only the preparation of two sets of warning lists for each district for its completion. Experience since the Home Office had asked certain local authorities and Chief Constables to take action of this kind in September 1936 showed that compilation and co-ordination of these lists consumed much time. The request was repeated early in June in somewhat altered form.[1] All scheme-making authorities were asked to supply the telephone numbers of defined categories of persons to Chief Constables, on whom responsibility for preparing the lists, in consultation with local telephone managers, would now rest. It was proposed that this work should be completed by the end of September.

Hesitation by the planning authorities over the question of public warnings had been abandoned, and the main problem in this sphere was to devise technical means of transmitting the action warning to the public. Early in May the urban scheme-making bodies were told that their discretion about this matter had been changed into an obligation, and were offered advice about instruments which might be used for this purpose.[2] After tests had been made with local instruments, such as hooters and factory sirens, a detailed local scheme was to be submitted to the Home Office. The idea of associating public warnings with some peculiar sound had been officially discarded in favour of a distinctive 'code of blasts', to be as follows:

For the 'Warning'.—A signal of 2 minutes' duration consisting of either a fluctuating or warbling signal of varying pitch, or a succession of intermittent blasts.

For the 'Raiders Passed' message.—A continuous signal of 2 minutes' duration at a steady pitch.

The more primitive methods used in the First World War were to be brought into use for 'shorter range' warnings and local gas alarms. Policemen and wardens, it was proposed, should repeat the siren's warning by blasts on whistles. After much experiment with

[1] H.O. Circular of 14th June 1938, and Memorandum No. 8.
[2] H.O. Circular of 4th May 1938, on *Air Raid Warning Signals*.

instruments with which persons wearing anti-gas clothing and masks might give the gas alarm, choice fell on the hand rattle. The 'all clear' signal for raids of all types would be repeated by ringing hand bells.

Continuing experiment under direction of the Loud Noise Warnings committee to discover the best type of siren resulted in the selection in August of an electrically-driven type, particulars of which were notified to local authorities and a number of which were ordered for installation in London.[1] The committee on Remote Control of Signals was examining the possibilities of using wireless for this purpose.[2]

Though the plan for lighting restrictions was also substantially settled, much had still to be done about its application. Final approval had been given by the Committee of Imperial Defence in November to the policy of the 'black-out' or the severest lighting restrictions practicable in time of war.[3] Some officials and members of the public up and down the country had become familiar with this feature of A.R.P. on such occasions as the Southampton exercises; and the Government's decision in the matter had been announced during progress of the A.R.P. Bill.[4] All local authorities were told in February 1938 the nature of the drastic lighting restrictions which 'would impose general darkening as a permanent condition from the outbreak of war'.[5]

The obligation, as later became clear in the event, spared no citizen or section of the nation. The householder and occupier of premises would be required to make all lights in his building invisible to an outside observer for the duration of a war. Illuminated advertisements and signs would be forbidden. Street lighting would be extinguished, and pedestrians and traffic forced to rely on white markings and other 'aids to movement'. Motor vehicles would be required to mask their headlamps, and public carriers to screen interior lighting. Essential services such as fire brigades, factories, railway systems and shipping would have to conform as closely as possible to the black-out principle. The earlier proposal for dividing the country into zones in which restrictions would differ in severity was now being abandoned.

An extensive experiment in Leicester late in January into the movement of traffic in unlighted streets formed the climax of experiments of this type conducted for some two years past by the

---

[1] p. 90.

[2] p. 90.

[3] The term 'black-out' had been in use by the limited number of officials concerned with the matter for a number of years.

[4] H. of C. Deb., Vol. 329, Col. 1949, 30th November 1937.

[5] H.O. Circular of 14th February 1938. A separate circular to Chief Constables promised amendment of Police War Instructions to conform with the plans now adopted.

Lighting Experiments Committee.[1] A headlamp mask used on this occasion was accepted by the Home Office as satisfactory, though modifications and the Service Departments' concurrence were still required.[2] Before the promise of the February circular to give local authorities more precise particulars of 'aids to movement' could be redeemed, a good deal more experiment was necessary and arrangements for this were being made by the Ministry of Transport. In the meantime, some local authorities continued to stage practice blackouts, and a large-scale test was made of lighting arrangements during the Home Defence Exercises in July.

Much more research was needed into means of achieving the formidable aim of blacking-out all factories and industrial premises. Direct and reflected light from factory buildings would, the Home Office stated, 'normally be prevented by the screening of all windows and skylights with dark blinds or paint', and 'external lighting would normally be prohibited'. Undertakings engaged on vital national work might be granted exemption by the police from these restrictions, on condition that their lighting was as far as possible screened and could be immediately extinguished on receipt of a warning.[3] The cost to factories, particularly modern ones with large areas of glass, of complying with these restrictions promised to be considerable;[4] and one of the Factory Inspectors was engaged in investigating ways in which this might be brought to reasonable proportions. A majority of factory owners were hoping, at this stage, to avoid the cost and inconvenience of complete darkening of their premises, and optimistically assuming that their obligations would be limited to extinction of lights on receipt of the warning.

Investigations begun in the previous summer by a lighting committee of the main-line railways into means of eliminating the 'arcing' of electric trains, of 'hooding' steam locomotives and reducing signal and train-lighting were being carried forward. Tests made in marshalling and goods yards and with station and train-lighting during the first half of 1938 helped to establish the practical limits of lighting restrictions in this general sphere. Conferences between the A.R.P. Department, Factory Inspectorate and owners of iron and steel works, coke ovens and brickwords laid foundations for study of the problem of glare. Repeated questions in Parliament in this phase about progress regarding glare gave evidence that the policy of the

---

[1] pp. 91–92.

[2] This mask was evolved by the Metropolitan Police largely from the design of one used on the North West Frontier of India.

[3] Handbook No. 6, *A.R.P. in Factories and Business Premises* (November 1936), had foreshadowed these restrictions.

[4] e.g., the H.M.V. Coy., Hayes, Middlesex, estimated at this time the cost of installing blinds as £12,000.

black-out, whatever the difficulties of its individual application, had much general support.[1]

Progress at the Centre:
(ii) Anti-Gas Equipment, and other Supplies

The 25 million civilian gas-masks accumulated by the opening of 1938 were, from various points of view, one of the most tangible assets of the A.R.P. Service. The assembly of containers at the Blackburn factory (still working double shifts) and contractors' deliveries at Regional Stores of facepieces, then 'canned' in nitrogen for long-term storage, were fulfilling the programme for completion of 40 million masks by the coming summer.[2] In view of official recognition that no part of Britain could be regarded as completely immune from attack, and the delicacy of attempting discrimination between areas in this matter, the promise to supply a mask to every citizen in danger areas now involved supplying the whole population of some 44 million souls. Owing to the difficulty of estimating the numbers required of the three different sizes, the need to allow for population shifts during holidays and other factors a reserve of 20 per cent. (8.8 million masks) was decided on. While informing the Committee of Imperial Defence that 52.8 million masks would be needed, the Department confined its immediate request to approval for production of 45 million masks by the end of 1938.

Early in April the Department gave local authorities a detailed account of its plans for Local Respirator Stores, Respirator Distributing Depots, the preliminary wardens' census of numbers and sizes of masks, and the final assembly and distribution to citizens.[3] The Government, the reader will recall, had been working on the assumption that final distribution might have to be carried out in hours rather than in days; and the Department considered that this necessity for speed called for elaborate physical arrangements. For most scheme-making bodies, however, preparations on the scale suggested were far from simple. For example, a town of 150,000 persons, such as Southampton, was asked to provide 5 Local Respirator Stores, conforming to various requirements of space, lay-out and temperature and evenly spaced over its area, and 35 to 40 Distributing Depots; and the siting, and financial arrangements for adapting or acquiring these buildings, would need central approval.

During the Sudetenland crisis the possibility of immediately

---

[1] e.g., H. of C. Deb., Vol. 337, Col. 383, 16th June 1938.
[2] pp. 77–80.
[3] H.O. Circular and Memorandum of 4th April 1938; p. 130.

issuing civilian masks from Regional Stores to the local authorities was considered and discarded. The gas-mask (it was clear) was a defensive weapon with a double moral edge; if its existence gave citizens confidence in the effectiveness of the Government's preparations, its general distribution might be interpreted as meaning the hour for its use had struck. The course taken, once this particular threat had subsided, was to emphasize anew to local bodies the need for rapid completion of plans and to express earnest hope that the larger authorities at least would be able to take delivery of civilian masks by the end of August.[1] The central scheme issued in April was to be regarded as an ideal arrangement, modifications of which would be sympathetically considered. Arrangements made by some authorities with industrial concerns for help in the task of final assembly were quoted for emulation, and instructions and tools for this work were soon to be issued.

Effective response to this request, and to the scheme for wardens' census of numbers and sizes, was likely to take time. The census was only to be made by wardens who had 'undergone the approved anti-gas training', of whom by the middle of 1938 there were some 140,000 unevenly spread throughout the country. It is not surprising that, as the holiday season opened, few scheme-making bodies had made much progress in this sphere.[2] The A.R.P. Department, in the meantime, had been forced to conclude, after various experiments, that its calculations of the proportions in which the three different sizes of mask would be needed were most approximate. More satisfaction was obtained from the evidence afforded by trials at Bristol in this summer that the civilian mask could be worn for half-an-hour 'without discomfort' by persons carrying on a variety of normal tasks. By the middle of the year some 360,000 civilian masks had been issued to local authorities for use in the census, and 160,000 had been distributed for training.

Among reasons for the decision not to issue civilian masks to local authorities in May was the fact that means of protecting small children and babies against gas attack were still in the experimental stage. The provisional design for a 'baby bag', or anti-gas helmet, evolved by the end of 1937 was subjected to numerous later tests, which caused modifications and acceptance of an improved device in August.[3] The problem, presenting much smaller technical difficulty, of evolving a 'small child's respirator' for children between two and five had by this date only reached the stage of a tentative design.

---

[1] H.O. Circular of 6th July 1938.

[2] By the end of July the City of Westminster had received and stored all their respirators and opened an experimental fitting centre. Many London Boroughs, on the other hand, still had few wardens either enrolled or trained.

[3] p. 80.

Now that supplies of the civilian mask were assured the Department's Supply Branch paid chief attention to the various items of anti-gas equipment needed for the General Services, Police and Fire Brigades. The appointment in January 1938 of a new Director of Supply was the occasion for the Branch, which had borrowed most of its chief officials from the Admiralty, to be given an establishment and made an integral part of the Home Office. As with other branches in the period from the Act to the 'September crisis', the expansion in its staff was much outpaced by growth in the volume of its work. This included decisions with the Chemical Defence Research Department and other expert bodies on designs for the novel requirements of A.R.P. equipment, and arrangements for provision, usually on an unprecedented scale, of a large variety of materials and components. Contracts for anti-gas clothing were placed through the Admiralty contracting department, and those for most other supplies through the Directorate of Army Contracts of the War Office.

The question of mobilisation equipment for the Services just mentioned was brought by the A.R.P. Department before the Treasury Inter-Service Committee in May. With the exception of steel helmets, all the items involved were anti-gas equipment, namely—Service and Civilian Duty respirators, heavy and light anti-gas suits, anti-gas hoods, curtains and gloves, gum boots and eyeshields. Provision of this equipment for the 1,400,000 volunteers (including police and fire brigades) hoped for by the end of 1938 would cost over £2.5 million, £1.5 million of which had already been approved with respect to various items. The Committee was sceptical about some features of this programme, including the provision of anti-gas equipment to all wardens, and authorised an additional £$\frac{3}{4}$ million instead of the £1 million requested. On being approached again in August it sanctioned some enlargement and acceleration of the programme.

By midsummer the programme for 900,000 Civilian Duty masks was approaching completion. The Department's responsibility for producing these through assembly of containers at Blackburn and arrangements with contractors for facepieces extended to the final act of assembly, carried out at the Regional Stores at Alperton, Middlesex. Some 160,000 of these respirators had been issued by this date to local authorities for training, and satisfactory means, in the form of a microphone attachment, had been found for enabling persons wearing them to use the telephone. The certification mark scheme was brought into use with two firms manufacturing masks of this pattern, and was now to be extended to the civilian mask.[1]

The position regarding anti-gas suits, the main item of protective

---

[1] pp. 80–81.

clothing, was far less satisfactory. The productive capacity of the country's oilskin manufacturers had proved inadequate to meet the Department's requirements of heavy anti-gas suits, even for training; and a decision had been taken in the spring to rely much more on light suits, which could be proofed in large quantities by linoleum manufacturers.[1] Though by the middle of 1938 manufacture of light suits was proceeding steadily and some improvement over heavy suits had taken place, the number of both types issued for training was less than 50,000.

The Department's requirement for 1 million Service masks was to be met by the War Office, but by mid-August no deliveries of these had been made. Anti-gas equipment of these various types, though still the supply officials' first preoccupation, was losing its monopoly of their attention. The Government's promise to help with provision of war-time hospital supplies included stretchers, bulk purchase of which had still to be arranged. The proposal for some standard equipment for wardens' posts entailed the free issue of stirrup pumps and armlets, and the grant-aided issue of hand rattles. For this and other equipment the processes of settling final designs, obtaining Treasury authority, and arranging for payment, large-scale manufacture and distribution were being carried on within the framework of the five-year programme, ending in March 1939, which governed all the Department's preparations. Since the Home Office was not a contracting Department, a large share of this work fell on H.M. Office of Works.

Steel helmets for the General Services, Police and Fire Brigades would be forthcoming at some date in the autumn. At the opening of the year delivery of the 42 million sandbags authorised had been nearing completion,[2] and the Home Secretary had asked for authority to purchase an additional 275 million bags (20 million for Government buildings, and 255 million for 'vital points') over the next three years.

The Scale of Attack, and Scales of Preparation

In his report to Parliament on 1st June the Home Secretary again subdivided the A.R.P. problem into defence against high explosive bombs, defence against incendiaries and defence against gas. Before noticing the steps taken in this phase to deal with the problems of fire, shelters and evacuation, brief attention must again be paid to the hypothesis of Germany's scale of attack.

It will be recalled that early in 1937 the Air Staff had produced a revised scale of attack, which estimated that in two years Germany's Air Force would be capable of attacking Britain (from bases in

---

[1] p. 82.
[2] p. 82. The Department's request in the previous year had been for 500 million, which was twice the annual output of the Scottish industry.

Germany, and against French opposition) on the scales of, (i) over 600 tons of bombs *per diem* sustained for some weeks or, (ii) a much larger weight, attaining a possible maximum of 3,500 tons in the first twenty-four hours, delivered in the opening days of a war. These figures had been subjected to much scrutiny including that (which specially concerns this narrative) of the Warren Fisher Committee,[1] and it was not until almost the end of 1937 that they received formal approval from the Committee of Imperial Defence.[2] This approval included agreement with two observations made with emphasis by the Home Defence Committee and endorsed by the Chiefs of Staff. First, that the weight of attack to be anticipated was so great that not even unlimited financial and other resources could prevent heavy injury to life and property. Secondly, a *caveat* that the estimates composing the scale of attack, like other estimates expressed in terms of averages, were of theoretical rather than practical value, since any attempt to translate them into terms of the effects likely to result in any particular locality or set of circumstances might be very misleading.

The first of these conclusions had been familiar to the planning authorities for the past thirteen years. The scale and intensity air attack might attain in another war had, since the start of their inquiries, been overwhelming; and the practical problem had always been one of furnishing mitigation of the consequences from whatever manpower, money and materials might be available for this purpose. From one important aspect the fact that the maximum attack of which Germany would soon be capable was now to be expressed in the revised formula of 600 tons a day brought no essential change to the problem.

The *caveat* mentioned above was of small assistance to those planning passive defence, since translation of the scale of attack into certain probable effects was essential to their activities. Manpower, money and materials for rebuilding defence were all limited; and A.R.P., as the newest and most passive arm of defence, had the lowest priority in competition for these. Three broad translations—geographical distribution of the attack, types of attack, and rate of casualties—had been employed by the A.R.P. authorities for some years past. These admittedly contained much speculation, and their influence on practical preparations had so far been 'long range'. The Warren Fisher Committee had attached great importance to attempts to limit the financial implications of the problem by grading the country into areas of differing vulnerability.[3]

---

[1] pp. 95–96.

[2] Ibid. The Committee reduced the actual Air Staff figure of 644 tons *per diem* to the round figure of 600 tons. Variations were made in the scales to meet other conditions (e.g., a single-handed British war), but these are irrelevant to this narrative.

[3] p. 96.

L

During 1937 the A.R.P. Department had obtained from the Air Staff fresh hypotheses on the geographical distribution of attack, which employed the new formula of 600 tons a day. The features of the knock-out blow, of centres of government and industrial production, communications and power stations as the most likely civil targets, and of bomb-aiming of high precision still governed these. The parts of Britain considered liable to severe continuous attack were still, nevertheless, only those lying broadly in the eastern half of the island.

After the 1937 Act had placed new emphasis on organisation throughout the country, the Department's most advanced essay in translation of 'scale of attack' into 'scale of risk' took the form of elaborate differential scales of local preparation. Using a grading of Britain into areas of differing vulnerability, it computed the numbers of persons in the various A.R.P. services, and hence the main items of equipment, needed by individual scheme-making authorities. It decided that publication of these scales would be politically and financially inexpedient; and during the course of 1938 discrimination between areas in the two important matters of civilian masks and restricted lighting was being abandoned.[1] Scales of local preparation became henceforward an important guide in weighing the needs in manpower and material resources of individual areas.

The broad hypotheses of casualties and types of attack were still, for the most part, long-range in their bearing on practical preparations. The formula that each ton of bombs dropped on a densely-populated area would cause 50 casualties (17 killed and 33 injured) had with the passage of time acquired much standing as a forecast of the future.[2] This was now used by the Department in estimating the number of First Aid Parties and Posts and Rescue Parties at which local authorities were asked to aim. The order of importance of types of attack employed by the Home Secretary was now expressed by the Department in a rough formula for its guidance. It was anticipated that the German Air Force would devote 50 per cent. of its bomb-carrying capacity to high explosive, 25 per cent. to incendiary bombs, and 25 per cent. to gas; but the use of gas, the formula continued, 'remains problematical', and should it not be used this load would probably be replaced by high explosive.

The Fire Problem, the Shelter Problem, and the Question of Evacuation

Practical development of defence against these different threats, it is hoped the reader will already be aware, had by no means

---

[1] pp. 137, 139.
[2] See R. M. Titmuss, *op. cit.*, pp. 12–14; and this volume pp. 11, 15–16, 96.

followed this order of importance. The main factors governing this had been financial provision, the information available about the effects each threat might produce and the relevant administrative machinery in existence. British preference for entrusting new functions to existing institutions, or grafting new branches of effort on to some well-established tree, received an important application in measures to deal with one part of the fire problem.

The fire brigades were a local authority service, similar in important respects to the police forces, with which they often had close historical affinities. They, to an even greater extent than the police, performed in peace functions identical in kind (if far from identical in degree) to those they might be expected to perform in another war. Brief notice has already been paid to the nation's fire brigade 'system'.[1] The foundation of the emergency fire brigade measures had been laid with the issue in February 1937 of circulars to Britain's local fire authorities. From this date onwards, the development of emergency fire brigade measures proceeded in the main independently of that of 'general' air raid precautions by the A.R.P. Department. This administrative bifurcation (which was to continue) was rooted in the fact that the fire brigades had traditions, an administrative framework and technical processes and apparatus different from those of the A.R.P. General Services. It forms the justification for deferring to a later chapter the account of emergency fire brigade measures undertaken before the war.[2]

The emergency plans of the Home Office Fire Brigades Division were formally reported for the first time to the Committee of Imperial Defence at the opening of 1938. A full survey of the problem included remarks on the nature and scale of the 'air raid fire risk'. These, it is important to note, contained the conclusion that 'the explosive bomb can be virtually disregarded as a fire-raising agent as compared with light incendiary bombs', and gave calculations of the formidable numbers of fires which aircraft carrying this missile might cause.[3]

Questions of broad policy affecting both the A.R.P. Department and the Fire Brigades Division related, in this phase, mainly to manpower and conditions of service in the various emergency bodies now in process of formation.

Brief allusion is also necessary here to the legislative framework within which reform of the peace-time organisation and emergency fire brigade measures were proceeding. The A.R.P. Act of 1937 obliged the L.C.C., the boroughs, urban district councils and

---

[1] pp. 84–85. Students of the Report of the Royal Commission of 1923 (Cmd 1945), which deals exhaustively with the fire-fighting institutions and methods in existence at the time, may conclude that the word 'system' is misplaced.

[2] Chapter VI below.

[3] e.g., a single bomber carrying 1,000 such bombs might cause 150 fires in a congested area.

(permissively) rural district councils of England and Wales, and the county and town councils of Scotland, to prepare and submit to the Secretary of State fire precautions schemes.[1] The main Regulations, under which approved expenditure on the schemes ranked for grant on the same basis as expenditure on general precautions schemes, entered into force on 10th March 1938. The Fire Brigades Division was, therefore, like the A.R.P. Department, engaged at this time in advising upon, examining and approving a large number of local schemes. And these processes were accompanied in this phase by special attention to recruitment and training for the Auxiliary Fire Service. In the middle of this year the proposals for peace-time reorganisation made by the Riverdale Committee two years earlier bore fruit in the Fire Brigades Act 1938.[2]

But the fire problem of a future war, the reader will recall, was not exhausted by the measures being taken or in prospect to improve the fire brigade organisation. For some years past the Home Office Fire Adviser and others had been examining the question of how ordinary householders, staffs of factories and members of the A.R.P. Services might be helped to defeat the novel and formidable threat of widely-scattered small incendiary bombs.[3] The Incendiary Bombs Committee, under the chairmanship of H.M. Chief Inspector of Explosives, was continuing throughout the months with which this chapter deals both to acquire knowledge about the performance (e.g., penetrative power) of various fire-raising missiles, and to investigate substances, methods and appliances by which the 'amateur' in fire-fighting matters might be helped to protect himself and his property against this threat.

This small body of experts had early concluded that nothing the householder or other amateur could do would actually extinguish the light magnesium bomb, and that their search must concentrate on means of enabling him to 'control' this weapon and extinguish the fires it would almost inevitably cause. Among these means they had always assigned a predominant place to simple substances and appliances which were, or might be made, generally available. The tests at Barnes early in 1937 with teams of girls acting as fire-fighters had proved, from several points of view, a landmark in their investigations.[4] They had shown that women with simple equipment and little previous training could deal with the menace of the incendiary bomb promptly and with success.[5]

The chief appliances used in these tests were a simple hand pump

---

[1] pp. 108–109.

[2] 1 and 2 Geo. 6, Ch. 72 (29th July 1938).

[3] pp. 85–86. The novelty, as already suggested, was the outcome of the technical development of aircraft since 1918 multiplied by the development as a practical weapon of the light magnesium bomb.

[4] p. 86.

[5] A genuine problem confronted the A.R.P. authorities over the capacity of women to take part in the various A.R.P. and fire-fighting services.

(the 'Mark 2 Bantam') and the 'Redhill sand container', a metal receptacle accompanied by a long-handled scoop and a hoe. The former instrument, which operated by means of a jet of water, was used to control and extinguish the fire; and the second appliance was used, at a later stage of the proceedings, to control and eventually remove the incendiary bomb. The Bantam hand pump, however, though it gave satisfaction in these trials, was weighty and cumbrous for the purpose and had the drawback of costing some £3–4, which was too much for the average householder. The Incendiary Bombs Committee had therefore examined the possibility of adapting the type of hand pump commonly used for washing motor-cars or white-washing outhouses. By August 1937 they were satisfied with the design of a pump of this kind which cost 12s. 6d.; as it was fitted with a foot support it was called a 'stirrup pump'.

The birth, in a complete scientific sense, of this celebrated pump must, however, be dated nearly a year later, for its development had to go through many stages before, largely through the efforts of the Home Office Fire Adviser, a more satisfactory design was obtained.[1]

The Incendiary Bombs Committee undertook a series of experiments in using a spray, instead of a jet, of water to attack burning magnesium, and in June 1938 these achieved success. They then substituted for the nozzle of the stirrup pump as already designed a 'dual purpose' nozzle, the spray of which could be used to control the incendiary bomb and the jet to extinguish the accompanying fires. By the onset of the Munich crisis, the stirrup pump of this improved design had—in the realm of scientific discovery— superseded the 'Redhill sand container' as the amateur's main fire-fighting appliance. And it remained throughout the war the house-holders' chief implement against incendiary bomb attack.

For the historical student, the stirrup pump must rank with the civilian gas-mask as one of the chief protective instruments evolved for the use of British civilians in the Second World War. But this similarity, which was apparent at the date with which this volume is now concerned only to a limited number of officials, raised some difficult problems of supply and distribution. The A.R.P. Department decided to supply stirrup pumps, in the first instance, free of charge to one-half the anticipated number (100,000) of wardens' posts required in the country. In March 1938, it obtained Treasury approval for the purchase of 50,000 pumps; and it began to make arrangements with the Office of Works for supply of this first instalment. It should be mentioned that much difficulty was being experienced at this stage in obtaining light magnesium bombs in any quantity for training.

---

[1] A British Standards Institute specification was issued in June 1940 and an amended specification in the following October.

Training of the A.R.P. services in incendiary bomb control had not, as noticed earlier, begun by the date of the crisis.[1] A popular account of precautions against fire which every householder was advised to take and of methods and appliances for fighting fires was issued, for the first time, in the draft handbook *The Protection of your Home against Air Raids* circulated to local authorities in February 1938.[2] In a revised edition of this distributed to every home in the country when the Munich crisis occurred, the chief means by which, it was suggested, amateurs should attack incendiary bombs was to spray them with water from stirrup pumps.

But for a variety of reasons, which included familiarity with fires in peace-time and knowledge that organisation to deal with them was in existence, the fire risk involved in future air attack appeared less grave to most citizens than the high explosive and gas risks. In the debates on the A.R.P. Bill, Parliament had shown itself chiefly concerned over the two most radical solutions to these risks—the large-scale provision of air raid shelters, and arrangements for wholesale evacuation from London and other congested areas of citizens taking no vital part in the war.[3]

When moving the Bill's Second Reading the Home Secretary had dealt first with defence against the high explosive bomb and had stated, 'neither this Government nor, so far as I know, any Government in Europe, can protect a building, short of an overwhelming expense, from a direct hit by a high explosive bomb'. He had then announced the Government's intention to provide public shelters giving protection against blast and splinters for, (*a*) persons caught during an air raid in the streets and, (*b*) those whose houses were in such a condition that the creation of 'makeshift refuges under their own roofs' would be impracticable. As part of this policy of 'dispersal', the Government proposed to furnish each householder with detailed advice on ways of improvising a refuge room against blast and splinters.[4]

The new feature in this statement was that provision of public shelters for these limited purposes would be an obligation on local authorities under the Act, and would, like other items of general schemes, normally attract a grant-in-aid of 60–75 per cent. During the debate some Members on both sides of the House expressed strong dissatisfaction with the 'unambitious' nature of this shelter policy, as well as doubts about the technical presuppositions on which it was based.[5] After replying to such criticisms the Under-

---

[1] p. 126.

[2] pp. 124–125.

[3] p. 106.

[4] H. of C. Deb., Vol. 329, Cols. 45–46, 15th November 1937.

[5] H. of C. Deb., Vol. 329, Cols. 55–165, 243–315; 15th and 16th November 1937.

Secretary to the Home Office announced that the Government would provide local authorities free of charge with sandbags, 'to meet approved requirements for the purpose of public shelters'.

Lack of knowledge about the effects high explosive bombs produced continued to be a restraint even on this modest programme. The Structural Precautions Committee had found on the eve of the Act's passage that data available for their purposes was far from adequate, and had stressed the need for an independent Home Office research establishment. In the spring of 1938 they were unable to record much improvement.[1] Though the Bombing Test Committee was making progress with three specific groups of tests, the conditions under which it was working led to serious delays.[2] Preparation of full-scale trials and assessment of the results required, in general, much time; and the Service Departments had prior claim on the limited physical facilities for carrying out these trials. In addition, a good deal of this committee's effort up to early in 1938 had been given to testing various anti-gas devices at the expense of concentration on the damage caused by high explosive blast and splinters.

The regulations issued in March included arrangements both for protection of premises such as headquarters and first aid posts needed by A.R.P. services in war, and provision of such shelters for the public as might be necessary.[3] These two obligations were among the subjects more fully dealt with in the important circular issued with the 'model' scheme later this month.[4] This document, after restating that 'the wisest policy is to aim at the dispersal of the population', expressed the assumptions that householders, helped by advice from local officials, would 'generally do what they can to increase the natural protection of their homes', and that employers would take steps to protect their premises and instruct employees about the action to be taken in air raids.

It then asked all scheme-making authorities to make a careful survey of accommodation distributed through their areas, particularly in relation to shopping thoroughfares, which might be used as public shelters. The experience of some authorities which had done this during the past few years suggested that in most towns there existed 'a large amount of accommodation which by adaptation and strengthening and by the use of sandbags, could be made to give reasonable protection'.

---

[1] In January the Department's Chief Technical Adviser had replaced Sir Arnold Wilson as chairman of this Committee.

[2] p. 83.

[3] Schedules 11, 12 of S.R. & O. 1938, No. 251. The Act contained a section (No. 9) conferring 'blanket powers' regarding expenditure on the Secretary of State, which was at this date intended to apply mainly to emergency fire appliances, but which later became important with respect to shelter provision.

[4] Paragraphs 8–10 of circular of 28th March 1938; pp. 121–122.

At his meeting a month later with the Local Authority Associations the Home Secretary called the shelter problem, 'probably the most difficult of all the questions with which they were confronted'.[1] He asked the authorities to treat the surveys just mentioned as a matter of great urgency. He also suggested, for the first time, that the principal cities, besides making surveys of buildings, should make plans for construction of an organised system of trenches in parks or other open spaces.

In his report to Parliament on 1st June the Home Secretary re-affirmed the dispersal policy, and repeated this request to local authorities to survey buildings and open spaces without delay. The central Government had taken urgent recent action to survey both shelter accommodation in the three 'typical' London boroughs of Holborn, Stepney and Wandsworth, and the opportunities for digging trenches and dug-outs in London's open spaces. But after expressing some satisfaction with progress he acknowledged that 'so far as shelters are concerned, we have only begun to touch the fringe of the problem'.[2] During a debate largely dominated by this problem Members again strongly criticised the inadequacy of the Government's plans.[3]

By the onset of the holiday season local surveys—or the fact-finding on the ground—seem to have made fair progress. The A.R.P. Department reported that on the whole, and with the exception of sections of London and other cities, 'reasonable shelter accommodation would be available for a considerable proportion of the persons for whom it is intended', though it added that 'in many cases preparations will have to be made for strengthening the accommodation to withstand the collapse of the buildings and blast and splinters from explosions'. As regards trenches, the Government thought it undesirable 'to immobilise open spaces during peace-time by turning them into a trench system'; but local authorities were advised to have materials for the prompt construction of trenches ready to hand.

The promise to give all householders detailed advice about ways of improvising a 'refuge-room' was fulfilled in the booklet, *The Protection of your Home against Air Raids*.[4] For householders and persons in charge of a business, shop, hotel, lodging house or tenements the first action this recommended (under the heading 'Things to do now') was choice of a refuge-room, to be protected against gas and furnished for habitation during a raid. This room would be the householder's or shopkeeper's 'first line of defence because a respirator cannot protect the other parts of your body from dangerous

---

[1] 25th April 1938; p. 122.
[2] H. of C. Deb., Vol. 336, Cols. 2079–2096.
[3] Ibid., Cols. 2096–2196.
[4] pp. 124–125, 148.

liquids, such as "mustard gas" '. It should be in the cellar or basement, if this could be made reasonably gas-proof and secure against
flooding; otherwise it might be any room on any floor below the top
floor. 'Any room within solid walls', the handbook urged, 'is safer
than being out in the open'. If war broke out and air raids took
place, the head of the household's first duty after hearing the
warning would be to send all under his care, with their respirators,
to the refuge-room; and he should keep them there until he heard
the 'raiders passed' and had satisfied himself that the neighbourhood
was free from gas.

Brief notice must again be paid to the problem, regarded in earlier
chapters as a special aspect of the shelter problem, of the war-time
location of the seat of Government. The committee appointed in
1936 to investigate this matter had recommended 'the principle of
dispersion' of the Government machine, which included earmarking
in peace alternative accommodation in the London suburbs for
the most essential Departments.[1] After these principles had been
approved by the Cabinet, a further committee began to elaborate
them into a detailed scheme.[2] As the shadows of war grew longer this
was further developed with particular secrecy.

Late in 1937 the Office of Works began to survey existing Government buildings, and to make proposals for structural protection of
new ones. The new buildings, including the proposed Whitehall
building,[3] would be given extra protection against air attack such as
strengthening of roofs and floors and shelter accommodation which,
while not bomb-proof, would protect the staffs against splinters,
blast and gas. By mid-summer 1938 the Office of Works had completed a survey of all the main Government offices in London and
surveyed some such establishments in the provinces; and had
estimated that at the current rate of progress it would take several
years to complete this work. In July it began specific inquiry into
methods and cost of strutting the official shelter accommodation
already earmarked.

The shelter problem was clearly linked in logic with evacuation.
The reader will recall that the first A.R.P. Committee had reached
these important conclusions in 1925—no appreciable part of the
vital activities of Greater London could be moved elsewhere in war;
the 'dispensable' part of London's population (also called the
'useless mouths') should, nevertheless, be officially encouraged and
helped to leave the capital; and an exodus of this scale and kind

---

[1] p. 87.

[2] Known as the 'Rae Scheme'.

[3] In the previous July the Cabinet had authorised beginning of the scheme for a new
Government building on the Whitehall Gardens—Montagu House site, which would
include a gas and splinter-proof basement.

would need much detailed planning in advance of the possibility of its becoming necessary.[1]

These conclusions had been accepted by the authorities during the ten years which followed and exerted an important, if catalytic, influence on their varied inquiries. In 1931 a committee had begun close examination of the problem of evacuating some 3½ million citizens from a certain area of London.[2] Its findings, reported three years later, had, however, been submerged for practical purposes by the enlargement in 1934–35 of the scope of the A.R.P. inquiry from London to the country as a whole and by the passage from the phase of secret planning to that of nation-wide organisation.

The Warren Fisher Committee had noted that the Home Secretary's financial recommendations contained no reference to evacuation owing to this question's uncertain financial implications, but added that the topic was under the A.R.P. Department's intensive consideration.[3] The A.R.P. Bill, as introduced in the next November, likewise contained no reference to evacuation; and Members, now conscious of the inevitability of passive defence, showed special concern over this omission. After resisting an amendment to make local authorities responsible for framing evacuation schemes, the Government had introduced a clause requiring these authorities to furnish the Secretary of State with any information he might request which might help the Government to prepare 'plans for any necessary transference of the civil population' in the event of air attack.[4]

In spite of optimistic statements by the Home Secretary in these debates and later, the Government's plans for large-scale evacuation from the most vulnerable areas 'were still in a rudimentary state early in 1938'.[5] The important circular of 28th March instructed scheme-making bodies to take no action in this matter until specific directions had been furnished by the Home Office.[6] Genuine planning of what was undeniably a major series of operations began with the Home Secretary's announcement on 26th May that he had appointed a committee of four Members of Parliament, under the chairmanship of Sir John Anderson, to review the question.[7]

The Anderson Committee pursued their inquiries with vigour and reported to the Home Secretary before Parliament rose at the end of

---

[1] pp. 18, 22–23.

[2] p. 41.

[3] p. 96.

[4] H. of C. Deb., Vol. 329, Cols. 1437–1486, and Vol. 330, Cols. 229–258, 25th November, 7th December 1937.

[5] R. M. Titmuss, *op. cit.*, p. 27.

[6] p. 121.

[7] p. 118. Sir John Anderson had presided over the first A.R.P. Committee and its successor the A.R.P. (Organisation) Committee from 1924–32.

July.[1] They concluded that 'the whole issue in any future war may well turn on the manner in which the problem of evacuation from densely populated industrial areas is handled'. For reasons both of humanity and expediency arrangements must be made for removing non-essential persons—possibly one third of the inhabitants—from these areas. There would in any case probably be large-scale exodus from those areas under repeated air attack. Schemes should, in all but exceptional circumstances, be based on voluntary evacuation. Arrangements for reception of 'refugees' should rest primarily on accommodation in private houses under compulsory billeting powers, with the initial cost being borne by the Government though refugees able to do so should later be required to make some contribution. Detailed plans should be laid to evacuate schoolchildren, with the consent of their parents, school by school in charge of teachers and at Government expense. The committee considered that a scheme of this nature could be organised for the whole country in a few months. They emphasised the importance both of establishing at an early date central and local machinery to execute the large amount of detailed planning needed, and of undertaking large-scale education of the public about the scheme.

When presenting this report to Parliament the Home Secretary promised to arrange its publication without delay, and to start work on the lines of its recommendations.[2] Some additions were soon afterwards made to the A.R.P. Department's staff for work on a London evacuation scheme. But it was not until seven weeks later, when the Munich crisis was entering an acute phase, that the major questions of policy the Anderson Report raised were presented to the Committee of Imperial Defence.[3] The Committee accepted the recommendations, but decided that the time was inopportune for their publication. As the crisis developed, the ordinary citizen lacked any official instructions on the matter other than a brief injunction to town-dwellers in the *Householders' Handbook* to consider sending children, elderly persons and pets to some place of greater safety.

The Munich Crisis

The crisis over the Sudetenland in May had caused the Committee of Imperial Defence to examine A.R.P. measures in the searching light of their ability to stand the test of imminent war.[4] There were two considerable gaps, it had been clear, in the structure needed for war—first, means to co-ordinate the miscellaneous functions of the

---

[1] Report of Committee on Evacuation, Cmd. 5837, 27th October 1938. For reasons stated below publication of this report was postponed for some three months.

[2] H. of C. Deb., Vol. 338, Cols. 3283-4, 28th July 1938.

[3] p. 156.

[4] pp. 116-119.

various Departments involved; secondly, absence of a civil 'chain of command' or machinery for the Government to exercise its authority over passive defence throughout the country. A plan to meet the first need by creating a Ministry of Home Security had been provisonally accepted, but laid aside in favour of detailed attention to the problem of control.

This problem, it has been seen, had held a conspicuous place since the outset in the minds of the planning authorities. Future air attacks, on the hypotheses which faced them, could create moral and physical dislocation on a scale far exceeding all past experience. Warfare of this character, they had long been convinced, would demand exceptional means of conveying the central Government's instructions and exerting its authority throughout the country. These means, though broadly conceived as resting on some system of regional bodies, had not been studied in detail when events in the summer of 1938 became most menacing. In the Civil Emergency Organisation a scheme of regional control which had stood the test of brief application lay ready to hand. The urgency now prevailing allowed of no more than modernisation of the chief features of this scheme and their incorporation, under the title 'Civil Defence Emergency Scheme "Y"', in the intricate mechanism of official action to be taken in transforming the nation from a state of peace into a state of war.

This scheme was completed in mid-August and designated a number of Regional Commissioners.[1] It was, its compilers took pains to stress, essentially provisional, and primarily concerned with procedure; it was also strictly secret. In order to avoid precipitating the crisis it was essential that war preparations should be confined as long as possible to action which could be taken in secret. But reconciliation of this need for secrecy with adequate preparation against large-scale air attack raised new and formidable problems. The speed with which such attack could be delivered implied the need for a high degree of previous preparation; and this in turn demanded widespread consultation and organisation. 'Scheme "Y"', concerned with setting up an unpopular form of central control, made no concessions over secrecy. But it included provision for the Regional system to be set up in advance of general mobilisation and other war preparations.[2]

The powers to be conferred on Regional Commissioners and others responsible for passive defence if war broke out were only defined by the scheme in brief general terms. The Commissioners

---

[1] The Commissioners were mainly persons provisionally chosen as Divisional Commissioners of a future Ministry of National Service. They were figures of wide local, rather than of national, eminence.

[2] By the device of introducing a 'preparatory stage' before the 'precautionary stage' of the Government's secret war preparations.

would act as the representatives of His Majesty's Government in their Regions with the responsibility of seeing that effect was given to the Government's 'measures for civilian defence'. Their powers would normally derive from the appointment to their Regions of representatives of central Departments invested with powers by their respective Ministers; and their function would thus be to act as chairmen of Regional committees, with responsibility mainly for co-ordination. But circumstances might arise which would necessitate the Commissioners taking emergency action on the Government's behalf beyond the powers entrusted to Departmental representatives, and without consultation with the Ministers concerned. They would then assume a personal executive responsibility and their action would subsequently be supported by the Government.

The most important of the Departmental representatives at Regions would be a Ministry of Health official, to be described as 'Principal Officer' and to bear responsibility for all matters within the Region concerning his Ministry. A Hospitals and a Finance Officer from this Department, and representatives of the Ministry of Transport, Food (Defence Plans) Department of the Board of Trade, Office of Works and General Post Office were among others to be appointed.

After the delegation in certain undefined circumstances of special powers to the Commissioners, the most drastic feature of the plan was the appointment of Chief Constables throughout the country (with the exception of London) as Chief Air Raid Precautions Officers for their police districts. Since no scheme had been worked out by which local authorities might exercise executive or operational control of the A.R.P. Services they were engaged in forming, recourse was had to the police, who were used to taking executive responsibility and to whom certain duties in passive defence had long since been assigned. For the London area different arrangements were made. The Commissioner, Metropolitan Police was designated Chief Executive Officer with the function of co-ordinating police action, including maintenance of order, within the whole London and Home Counties Region; the Clerk of the L.C.C. was appointed Chief A.R.P. Officer for the Metropolitan Police District, and the clerks of boroughs and other councils in this District were to act under his authority as A.R.P. Officers for their respective local government areas.

Instructions to Regional Commissioners to be issued under this plan laid emphasis on arrangements for police reinforcements within and between Regions, for the employment of military forces 'to sustain public morale', and for communications and schemes for mutual reinforcement between fire brigades.

'Scheme "Y".' had barely been completed when German manoeuvres on an unprecedented peace-time scale gave new tension to the situation. August, however, formed the height of Britain's holiday season, when Ministers, officials and the public were accustomed to taking as much relief as possible from business. Mr Chamberlain's confidence in his policy of appeasement continued to infuse a sense of security; and his feeling that war would be so appalling a calamity that it was inconceivable it could actually occur seems to have been widely shared by the public. As the month proceeded, however, an 'inner cabinet' of four principal Ministers, including the Home Secretary, met to give daily attention to the alarming deterioration of events. By the end of the first week of September it had become necessary for the Prime Minister to delegate authority to an informal conference of Ministers to decide what stages of war preparation should be put immediately into force. In the course of the next few days proceedings at the Nuremberg Rally and strenuous diplomatic activities, culminating in the sensational news of Mr Chamberlain's intention to visit Hitler at Berchtesgaden, revealed to the public the rapidity with which Britain was approaching war.

On the eve of the Prime Minister's flight to Berchtesgaden on 15th September the Passive Defence Committee of officials again reviewed 'Scheme "Y" '. They concluded, though with misgiving, that it could be put into operation at once, provided that higher authority sanctioned immediate consultations, particularly about evacuation, with local officials and others outside the central Government. The Committee of Imperial Defence now, for the first time, considered the Anderson Committee's proposals for a national evacuation scheme, and gave these approval.[1] But events, it was clear, had overtaken the possibility of preparing a genuine scheme on this matter; and the Committee decided that the Anderson Report should not for the present be published, and that departments should use its main features as a basis for improvising short-term measures. They supported the view that the crux of the problem presented by air attack on London was the maintenance of public order, and felt concern over lack of concrete arrangements for allocating Army units to assist in this. They authorised confidential disclosure of the outlines of 'Scheme "Y" ' to a strictly limited number of persons outside the central Government.

The view of the Minister for Co-ordination of Defence at this time that evacuation schemes might be required in three weeks or a month was quickly to prove out-of-date. During the week which followed, the Prime Minister was paying a second visit to Hitler at Godesberg; and the Home Office instructed Regional Commissioners

---

[1] p. 153.

to begin the secret consultations which formed the first phase of 'Scheme "Y" ', and sent sealed instructions to borough and district clerks in the London area. The return of Mr Chamberlain, baffled in his efforts to deter Hitler, on Saturday, 24th caused immediate intensification of defence measures, including both secret and widely public passive defence arrangements. Local authorities throughout Britain were asked by the Home Office during the week-end to begin to assemble and distribute gas-masks to the public, dig trenches and prepare first aid posts.[1] The beginning all over London on Sunday of gas-mask fitting and trench-digging gave citizens their first visible, personal, proof of the threat which overhung them. On the next day the conference of Ministers instituted the preparatory stage of the Government's war measures, requiring Regional Commissioners to establish their headquarters in secret.

The description applied by one Regional Commissioner to himself as 'the head of a breakdown gang ready to ensure the smooth working of the administrative machine during abnormal conditions' reflected accurately enough the spirit in which the organisation was set up. Under conditions of secrecy which added greatly to the difficulty of their undertaking, and sometimes bordered on the bizarre,[2] the eleven Commissioners and certain District Commissioners[3] proceeded to the places chosen as their headquarters and began consultations. In the majority of cases the buildings chosen as headquarters, which ranged from a small suburban villa to a prison, proved quite unsuitable; and the tasks of finding better accommodation, office organisation, billeting, and establishing essential communications absorbed much of the attention of Commissioners and their staffs. Consultations with Army authorities over military aid, arrangements about police reserves and Chief Constables' jurisdictions and subdivision of Regional areas into 'groups' were energetically pressed forward in most Regions. But these processes, as they advanced, laid bare the improvised nature of the structure and a host of undefined relationships. The extent of the Regional Commissioners' authority over Chief Constables, particularly their power to replace those they considered inefficient, gave rise to doubt. Fundamental questions arose over the relationship of the Chief Constables to the local authorities. The former, though amply provided with instructions about their police functions in emergency, had often had small previous connection with A.R.P. They were in the anomalous position of being asked to take executive control (as agents of the central Government) of A.R.P. machinery while being

---

[1] H.O. Circular of 24th September 1938.

[2] e.g., when the Leeds City Council grew suspicious of the concealed activities of the Regional Commissioner and resolved to send a deputation to the Home Secretary.

[3] Appointed to act under the Regional Commissioners in London and the Home Counties, Scotland and Wales.

prevented by secrecy requirements from consulting the local officials and A.R.P. Organisers who had hitherto been in charge of this machinery.[1] Their areas of jurisdiction, the police districts, often failed to correspond with existing arrangements for co-ordination and mutual support.[2]

The hasty assembly of representatives of Whitehall Departments to function, without the knowledge of local authorities, as Regional staffs offered in general a scene of strenuous individual endeavour struggling amid administrative confusion. These officials had been instructed, so far as the immature nature of many central plans allowed, by their own Departments but were usually unaware of the duties of their Regional colleagues. The relationship of 'Principal Officers' to the representatives of other Departments was undetermined. The duties of A.R.P. Inspectors and Ministry of Health officials as Personal Assistants to Regional Commissioners were little defined, and the former had been taken away from their normal activities when these were most needed. No provision had been made for essential technical advice, in particular from medical officers and engineering inspectors, or for liaison with the Admiralty and Air Ministry.

London had received special attention from the planning authorities, and its Regional Organisation was in charge of persons of much administrative experience.[3] Good progress was made with arrangements for military aid, police reinforcements, and the unified command of fire brigades; and, at a later stage, with gathering data on the state of A.R.P. arrangements in the London Boroughs and other parts of the Region. But the task of evolving a Regional Headquarters met with difficulties similar to those experienced in the provinces. Departmental representatives remained, in this case, in their parent offices in Whitehall or elsewhere; and most Departments regarded them more as liaison officers than as members of a Regional staff. The functions of Personal Assistants and the Regional Finance Officer, here as elsewhere, were ill-defined. Accommodation, staff and arrangements for transmission of intelligence proved quite inadequate.[4] It soon became the view of those in charge that the secrecy with which 'Scheme "Y"' had been prepared constituted,

---

[1] The secrecy was modified after a few days to the extent of allowing Regional Commissioners to inform County and Borough Clerks confidentially about the organisation.

[2] Notably in the Home Counties.

[3] The London and Home Counties (No. 5) Region comprised the Metropolitan Police District, the City, and the remainder (organised in two Districts) of the counties of Herts, Essex, Surrey and Kent. Sir John Anderson was Regional Commissioner, with headquarters at New Scotland Yard, and Sir George Gater was Chief A.R.P. Officer for the Metropolitan Police District and the City.

[4] By the end of the crisis a War Room for the Metropolitan Police District had been installed at County Hall, but this was still lacking at Regional Headquarters.

even in the preparatory period, a serious obstacle to the establishment of the organisation.

While Regional Commissioners were forming headquarters, arrangements for control and co-ordination at the centre were being hastily improvised. The proposal that a Minister of Home Security, presiding over a Standing Council of the Ministers most concerned, might act as the supreme co-ordinating agency in war had not been given any detailed examination.[1] On 26th September the Prime Minister gave instructions for this Home Security organisation to be set up. The Secretary to the Treasury was appointed Principal Officer to the Minister and the Council 'with functions akin to those of a Chief of Staff', and the head of the A.R.P. Department and the Inspector-General would act as his deputies. Departments were instructed to continue to perform their respective functions, but in matters—which remained undefined—involving co-ordination to have recourse to the new organisation. Home Security headquarters, to which Departments would attach liaison officers, would be a special War Room in the Home Office basement. Communications linking this War Room with Regional Commissioners' headquarters were being installed.

On the day this organisation was set up the Observer Corps and the anti-aircraft units of the Territorial Army were called out, and the warning system for eastern parts of the country was brought to a state of readiness. Chief Constables had continued to find much difficulty in compiling warning lists of practicable size, so that resort was now necessary to provisional lists of the most essential recipients.[2] On the day before Mr Chamberlain went to Berchtesgaden the general public had heard for the first time, through a B.B.C. broadcast, the wailing despondent notes of the siren which was to warn them of air attack. The Home Office then instructed the police to set up immediately systems of public warnings; since not many electrically-driven sirens were available, use was to be made of factory sirens and hooters.[3]

In protecting the principal Government offices in London there had been small progress. By the onset of the crisis the Office of Works had completed its survey of the main London buildings.[4] But no structural alterations had begun either for refuges or first aid rooms, supplies of medical stores, blinds and fire-fighting appliances were everywhere inadequate, and the training of departmental fire-squads had made little headway.[5] Efforts were hastily made to

---

[1] pp. 116–117, 154.
[2] H.O. Circular of 13th September 1938; p. 135.
[3] H.O. Circular of 26th September 1938.
[4] p. 151.
[5] e.g., the Air Ministry War Room, Adastral House, and the Ministry of Health in Whitehall had most inadequate protection.

M

protect Government buildings with sandbags, select some shelter accommodation, screen windows with brown paper and build up stocks of war equipment.

A scheme for dispersal at some stage after the outbreak of war of the principal parts of the Government machine to the London suburbs and evacuation of other parts to the provinces was, it has been noted, being prepared with particular secrecy.[1] Departmental officials found that practical organisation of these possible moves, including division of staffs and offices, choice of alternative accommodation and supply of communications, presented almost insuperable difficulties.

The public, used to hearing their leaders speak confidently about appeasement and desperately hoping they would not be called on to fight again, were far from being psychologically prepared for war. Organisation of A.R.P. had been confronted by general reluctance to think of war as a possibility; progress had been hampered by local refusal or inability to incur expenditure and a central procedure geared to an ample period of preparation. The news of Mr Chamberlain's flight to Berchtesgaden gave the public the first indication that peace was gravely threatened, and air attack much more than a remote disaster. During the rising tension of the following week most local authorities began to review their A.R.P. arrangements. The Home Office instructions of 24th–26th September began a phase of strenuous nation-wide effort to supply the first-line defences of gas-masks, trenches and essential arrangements for treatment of the injured.[2]

The Government had, for both political and technical reasons, postponed issue of gas-masks to the public until the latest practicable stage.[3] The decision that issue should now take place imposed a concrete task on all local bodies, and gave every citizen a personal stake in preparations. Scheme-making bodies had in general made slow progress with the census of sizes of masks needed in their areas, and with arrangements for storage, assembly and distribution.[4] The 40 million civilian masks accumulated by the Government had, for the most part, to be issued directly from Regional Stores; and the considerable operations of fitting the public, assembly and distribution had now to be carried out by various methods hurriedly devised. In the City of Westminster fourteen fitting centres were opened on Friday, 23rd; and the public all over London was exhorted during the week-end by posters, loudspeakers on cars, and announcements at football matches, on cinema screens and from pulpits to go to town halls or schools to be fitted for masks. In the new week these appeals

---

[1] p. 151.
[2] p. 157.
[3] There was a considerable chance that the facepieces would deteriorate once they had been taken out of their cans.
[4] pp. 139–140.

and activities were repeated in towns and villages up and down Britain. Since there were seldom enough wardens to fit and distribute masks, large numbers of volunteers from all walks of life came forward to help. The assembling of masks, by attaching the facepieces to the metal containers, took time and a good deal of dexterity. Some councils were helped by factory staffs; but the untrained volunteers who did most of this work found in general that the assembly tools promised by the Government were defective or not available.[1] As the week advanced, public issue made rapid progress, though there was general shortage of cardboard boxes or other containers. It was found that the Home Office had over-estimated the need for large masks, so that medium and small sizes were often short of requirements. More serious was the Government's failure, which in places caused open discontent, as yet to provide means of protecting babies and small children against gas attack.[2]

Most adult citizens, nevertheless, were now acquiring a gas-mask, and with it some sense of their personal stake in the grim prospect of air attack. For those already enrolled or now volunteering in large numbers for the A.R.P. Services supplies of special masks, steel helmets and anti-gas clothing were quite inadequate. The discouragement of wardens and others who found themselves equipped with ordinary masks, and with no badges of authority, protective clothing, tin hats or whistles was reported from many areas.[3]

The mixture of reassurance and anxiety with which citizens received their gas-masks was stimulated further by the sight of trench-digging going on day and night in the parks and open spaces of London and many provincial towns. Before the crisis the Government had discouraged this measure as an undesirable disturbance to the amenities of peace.[4] In mid-September the A.R.P. Department enlisted the help of the Federation of Civil Engineering Contractors in making co-ordinated plans for trench-digging all over London, based on estimates and maps hastily supplied by the boroughs.[5] On 24th September the Home Office asked local authorities in all densely-populated areas to begin to dig immediately, and if possible complete in three days, trenches for 10 per cent. of their populations; though open spaces which were not the authorities' property could only be used with the owner's consent. A

---

[1] The facepieces were packed in cans of 50 weighing 11 lb., and the containers in cartons of 50 weighing 40 lb. Complete respirators for 100,000 persons weighed, without packing, about 50 tons.

[2] Some Chief Constables restricted the general issue of masks on this account, and more than one London Borough reported 'deep public concern' over this omission.

[3] e.g., in Hackney, one of the London Boroughs most advanced in its general A.R.P. measures.

[4] p. 150.

[5] It was found that the amount of mechanical equipment available was small and that most of the digging would have to be manual.

detailed 'model' of a block-system of trenches was circulated.[1] In London, with its centralised plan, fair progress was made in those boroughs with open spaces; though it soon became clear that little of the work would be finished in three days. And a number of authorities in southern counties, the industrial midlands and the north began to exert much energy in digging up open spaces.

These trenches were intended only for those caught in the open, or to be complementary to the protection afforded by houses and any places available as public shelters; though there was evidence that the public, especially in London, frequently failed to appreciate this fact.[2] In conformity with the official policy of dispersal, individual householders were exhorted to prepare, in addition to 'refuge rooms', simple trenches in their gardens, an official design for which was put on sale and given wide notice in the Press. The Government's request to local bodies to 'arrange simple shelters where necessary with the use of improvised material' was one which could now produce only meagre results. The authorities' inability to use buildings as shelters except with the occupier's consent, lack of technical information from the centre, and shortage of sandbags, timber and other materials restricted most councils to hurried completion of their surveys and earmarking of some basements and cellars as public shelters. Progress was made by a limited number with the shoring up of basements.[3] But the majority of London Boroughs still reported, after the crisis had passed, that they had no public shelters.

Most local authorities were making vigorous efforts to adapt their normal machinery to the needs of the Casualty and other A.R.P. Services. Events, once again, had forestalled the arrangements for a large-scale appeal to the public to join these services.[4] Large numbers of men and women began in almost every area to volunteer for A.R.P.; and stimulated by local appeals and the sight of anti-aircraft guns and searchlights being mounted, trench-digging and sandbagging of buildings this flow showed no signs of slackening. But though, 'at the last moment, leadership sprang up all over the place'[5] to support the efforts of hardworked officials, the greater part of this volunteer army was untrained. A week after the start of active preparations, the number of wardens in many districts had reached or was approaching estimated needs; but only a small proportion of these had undergone training.

---

[1] H.O. Circular of 24th September 1938.

[2] e.g., the Commissioner, Metropolitan Police anticipated a serious problem arising from a general rush out of houses into trenches.

[3] e.g., Birmingham, where basements for 10,000 persons were selected and shored up in 48 hours.

[4] pp. 128–129.

[5] W. G. Eady, 'The Progress of Air Raid Precautions', *Journal of the Royal United Service Institution* (February 1939).

The most conspicuous feature in the mosaic of local A.R.P. was the shortage of trained staffs and equipment. But some parts of the structure essential for war were beginning to take shape. The selection and preparation of First Aid Posts and formation of First Aid Parties were making progress; though the Voluntary Societies, who formed the backbone of these operations, appealed urgently for more recruits and local improvisation could only provide a small part of the necessary medical supplies, stretchers and ambulances. Most councils were able to mobilise trained Decontamination Squads, and a number were forming 'scratch teams' for rescue, road repair and demolition. Some were selecting and equipping Control Centres, and making arrangements for co-ordination of services and transmission of intelligence. The police, everywhere taking a major part in preparations, were organising a public warning system,[1] and under their instructions some councils were trying out dimmed traffic lights, painting pavement-edges and introducing other 'aids to movement' in a black-out.

The public in general remained calm as, but five or six days from the start of intensive preparations, the country approached the edge of the abyss. When on Wednesday, 28th September the Fleet was mobilised and Parliament met by the Speaker's special summons, war within a few days seemed inevitable. The news, announced by the Prime Minister in the House that afternoon, that an avenue of escape had opened caused a state of high tension to change instantly to one of profound universal relief.

The Home Security organisation at the centre thus never came into being, apart from some exercise by the Secretary to the Treasury of his co-ordinating functions and the brief manning of the Home Office War Room.[2] But the Home Secretary asked local authorities and the public to complete the chief precautionary measures, and the momentum of preparations continued until some days after Mr Chamberlain had returned from Munich. On the day after the sensational change in the outlook, the delivery was begun to every householder in the country of the booklet *The Protection of Your Home against Air Raids*.[3] To take advantage of the public mood, the plans laid some time before for an 'A.R.P. Week' at the beginning of October were widely publicised. The A.R.P. Department issued instructions for lighting restrictions in industrial establishments, railways and dockyards and stated arrangements for central purchase of picks and shovels for wardens' posts.[4] On Thursday, 29th the

---

[1] H.O. Circulars of 26th and 27th September 1938.

[2] This was first manned on 30th September to give the Regional Commissioners their 'standstill' instructions.

[3] Fourteen million copies had been ordered by the Department in August from the Stationery Office, which had undertaken to fulfil the order in mid-November.

[4] H.O. Circulars of 27th, 28th and 29th September 1938.

Government published plans for the voluntary assisted evacuation from London of 2 million persons, including 500,000 schoolchildren.

The forecast that if war threatened large numbers in the chief cities would move of their own accord to places of greater safety had proved accurate. An exodus of large proportions from London and other centres had been proceeding, the railways had been handling traffic of Bank Holiday proportions and parts of Wales and the West Country were already crowded with refugees. To the many unable to move without help, or uncertain where their duty lay, the Government's failure to indicate its intentions had been causing much disquiet. But it was now too late for official help in this matter to amount to more than some improvised partial schemes. The A.R.P. Department, with some temporary help from officials of the Ministry of Health, produced a scheme to move a considerable number of 'useless mouths' out of London. This was timed to begin with the evacuation of schoolchildren on Friday, 30th and was cancelled at the eleventh hour.[1] Some local authorities, including the London County Council, had similar plans in readiness.[2] Arrangements for reception and billeting of official evacuees were everywhere in the most rudimentary state; and a Regional Commissioner's conclusion that if the crisis had continued 'evacuation was where our greatest trouble would have arisen' was emphatically endorsed by his colleagues.[3]

The conference of Ministers began on the morning the Munich Agreement was signed at once to cancel or suspend war preparations. Regional Commissioners, less than a week after they had begun to set up their headquarters, found the need for their activities abruptly over, though the Regional Organisation remained formally in being. Their last effective act was to transmit to local authorities the Government's decisions that assembly and public distribution of gas-masks and arrangements for first aid posts should be completed; and that while trenches already dug should remain and be put in order, the digging of new ones should stop.

When Mr Chamberlain, flying home from Munich, felt deep thankfulness that London's sprawling East End had been spared the disaster of air bombardment he again reflected the prevailing emotion of his countrymen.[4] The high tension of this short dress-rehearsal gave way to universal relief that the horrors of large-scale air assault had been averted, springing from new realisation that the

---

[1] Mr Eady concluded that this would 'just about have stood up to the requirements of getting refugees out of London and bedding them down that night while we tried to sort out what was going to happen afterwards' (W.G. Eady, *op. cit.*, pp. 12–13).

[2] The L.C.C. actually moved a few thousand schoolchildren to the country.

[3] See also R. M. Titmuss, *op. cit.*, pp. 29–30.

[4] See Keith Feiling, *op. cit.*, p. 321.

nation was still 'lamentably unprepared' to meet this type of warfare.[1] The secrecy in which most of the Government's preparations had been shrouded, it was apparent, had been a serious obstacle to rapid mobilisation for passive defence. Improvisation had been everywhere, at the centre of affairs as well as at the circumference, the keynote of activities; inadequate co-ordination of plans, at every level, had been a conspicuous weakness. The most concrete, visible, measures of defence—the distribution of 38 million civilian gas-masks, the digging of a million feet of trenches, and fresh thousands of volunteers for A.R.P. service—had reflected much credit on the energy of officials and the readiness of ordinary citizens to give voluntary service once danger clearly threatened. But these, it was widely felt, were 'amateur' inadequate achievements when measured against the size of the menace. Preparations in peace against air attack must henceforth be on a scale and of a pervasiveness far exceeding previous efforts.

The Prime Minister's frank admission that Britain's passive defences were 'far from complete'[2] was echoed by other members of the Government and by responsible officials[3]; and official stock-taking of all war preparations was now thoroughly undertaken. From this it was soon to be confirmed that the crisis had made two real contributions to the future. It had provided a valuable, if brief, practical test of the machinery designed for passive defence, and especially for the system of Regional authorities. And it had trans-formed the spirit of reluctance with which, for the most part, the Government, officials and the public had so far approached the problem of defence against air raids into one of more determined co-operative effort.

---

[1] The phrase represents Mr Churchill's conclusion (W.S. Churchill, *The Second World War*, Vol.1, p. 265).

[2] H. of C. Deb., Vol. 340, Cols. 83–85, 1st November 1938.

[3] Notably by the Home Secretary in a speech at Clacton (*The Times*, 21st October 1938), and by Mr Eady in a talk to the Royal United Service Institution on 26th October which was destined to receive much publicity (see p. 162).

CHAPTER V

THE NEW ARM OF CIVIL DEFENCE

(October 1938 – September 1939)

New Machinery and New Urgency

THE scepticism prevailing before the crisis about the possibility of war had been replaced by a feeling, to grow steadily in force, that the country had obtained no more than a breathing space. Though the merits of the Munich Settlement roused bitter argument for months to come, opinion was now almost unanimous on the need for rapid completion of rearmament. In this 'strong forward surge for invigorated rearmament'[1] both active and passive defence against air attack were given much emphasis. The Labour Party decided that 'air raid precautions must be regarded as of equal importance with the other three Defence Departments and made thoroughly efficient',[2] and chose to censure the Government on their 'unpreparedness to protect the civil population when the country was brought to the brink of war'.[3] Fatalism about providing effective protection against air attack was being replaced by a feeling that this could be done, if the authorities showed enough will and energy. The Government reacted promptly to this new perspective by creating machinery to hasten defence measures on the whole 'home front' and to extend direct air raid protection.

After the Committee of Imperial Defence had decided that the country's passive defences were substantially behind military preparations and were especially weak in co-ordination, the Government decided to establish at once some features of the Home Security plan. A Cabinet Minister would be given responsibility for the work of the A.R.P. Department of the Home Office, together with the duty of planning a system of national voluntary service. He would preside over a committee of Ministers whose Departments were 'specially concerned with the Home Front' which was to plan and co-ordinate all civil defence measures, and over a committee of Permanent Heads of these Departments. The Home Secretary would still act as

---

[1] W. S. Churchill, *The Second World War*, Vol. 1, p. 296.
[2] Labour Party Manifesto of 29th October 1938, *A Supreme National Effort for Peace*.
[3] H. of C. Deb., Vol. 340, Cols. 411–535, 3rd November 1938.

Minister of Home Security in the event of war, when the new Ministerial committee would be merged in a 'Standing Council of Home Security'. The Prime Minister told the Cabinet that he had asked Sir John Anderson, who had just been appointed Lord Privy Seal, to undertake these far-reaching duties.

When explaining these arrangements to Parliament Mr Chamberlain said that A.R.P. had 'assumed such gigantic proportions and developed such complexity' that it was now too great a burden for the Home Office, and he called the new Minister the 'Minister of Civilian Defence.'[1] In fact, the arrangements returned to the principle, largely ignored in practice for some years but never in theory abandoned, of spreading the burden of A.R.P. duties among all relevant Departments; and they revived, in much strengthened form, the machinery used for co-ordination in the earlier years of planning.[2] But in spite of past planning and the foundations the A.R.P. Department had laid, the task of applying this principle was of such magnitude as to seem almost new.

Sir John Anderson told the committee of officials that his duties, though somewhat vaguely defined, were clearly very wide. His executive responsibility for action to counter immediate effects of air attack included, in addition to the A.R.P. Department's work, ultimate responsibility for matters such as evacuation plans now being transferred or developed elsewhere. His functions to plan and co-ordinate embraced the 'large ill-defined field' now called 'civil defence'.[3] To carry out these double functions he would employ two separate administrative staffs. The A.R.P. Department would henceforth be confined to current administration of A.R.P. measures, which were expanding in complexity and number.[4] Planning and co-ordination of civil defence would be carried out by the Lord Privy Seal's Department acting as the 'civil general staff' proposed in the earlier phase of planning,[5] in charge (as 'Chief of Staff') of the Director General of the Post Office, Sir Thomas Gardiner.

An interdepartmental post-mortem into the experiences of Munich decided that the A.R.P. policies so far pursued needed, in general, no drastic alteration, and indicated the way in which the burden of civil defence duties would henceforth be spread. The Food (Defence Plans) Department of the Board of Trade, for example, would prepare schemes for the supply, distribution and protection

---

[1] H. of C. Deb., Vol. 340, Cols. 83–85, 1st November 1938.

[2] pp. 60, 62–63, 97–98.

[3] The expanding contours of the problem were reflected in the confusion of terms which now arose. 'C.D.' and 'A.R.P.' were sometimes used synonymously, sometimes to distinguish between the more remote and more immediate types of counter-measure.

[4] The legal transfer of responsibility to the Lord Privy Seal was not made until the passage of the Civil Defence Act some nine months later (Civil Defence (Transfer of Functions) Order, 1939, S.R. & O. No. 862, 25th July 1939).

[5] p. 34–35.

in war of every important commodity or group of commodities.[1] The Ministry of Transport would be responsible for the A.R.P. measures of the railways and certain other public utilities, and for general war transport arrangements. The Ministry of Labour would make the plans for National Service. Air raid precautions in schools (apart from evacuation) would be dealt with by the Board of Education and Scottish Education Department. Of more immediate concern to this narrative was the transfer now made of responsibility to the Ministry of Health and Department of Health for Scotland for evacuation plans and for certain of the A.R.P. Casualty Services.[2]

The evacuation measures in readiness when the crisis ended formed but small instalments of the plan which the Anderson Report had regarded as essential.[3] This report was now made public, and, in the new atmosphere of urgency strong pressure was exerted on the Government to press on with turning its principles into detailed schemes. Preparations by the Health Departments and local authorities had to embrace short-range and long-range schemes for dispersing throughout Britain, on the voluntary principle, some 4 million persons from the most congested areas. The manner in which this considerable task was undertaken is recorded in another volume of this series.[4] It may, nevertheless, be stressed here that schemes drawn up at Munich had envisaged the removal from London and other cities of many types of 'useless mouths', but had failed to take fully into account the insufficiency of billets in the safer areas.[5] The main difficulty with evacuation plans, it became clear after the crisis, lay in this and other problems arising in the reception areas. The Ministry of Health, with its housing and health responsibilities, was clearly better equipped than the Home Office to deal with reception area problems.

The transfer of responsibility to the Health Departments, effected in stages before the crisis, for a national hospital service for air raid victims was now logically extended to the two Casualty Services of First Aid Posts and Points and Ambulances.[6] Central responsibility for these services was therefore to be divided, since the Home Office retained control of First Aid Parties, of recruitment to all the Casualty Services and of some phases of Casualty training. Divided responsibility gave rise to problems, which were to prove persistent, of reconciling departmental views on the role of these services, and

---

[1] See R. J. Hammond, *Food*, Vol. I. in this series.

[2] A new Division of the Ministry of Health created for this purpose was partially staffed by officers of the Board of Education.

[3] pp. 152–153, 155, 164.

[4] R. M. Titmuss, *op. cit.*

[5] See p. 164.

[6] p. 118; H.O. Circular of 23rd December 1938.

the centralising claims of the emergency hospital scheme with the local diffused character of A.R.P. organisation.

The Ministry of Health also now took charge of plans for maintaining water supplies in war, and the large-scale arrangements needed for burial of victims of air attack and registration of their graves. It followed from the grim nature of the scale of attack hypothesis, and from concentration of effort in past years in a single Department, that measures for dealing with the dead and the injured still preceded comprehensive inquiry into the help which might be needed by those who suffered in less drastic a fashion. Progress had indeed been made in settling the terms on which financial help might be given to certain classes of the community. A scheme to give partial compensation at the end of a war to owners of damaged property had been settled and approved by the Cabinet; and the basic principles of compensation to civilians injured or killed in air attacks had been worked out. A plan was maturing for relief by cash payments through the Assistance Board to persons in distress due to industrial dislocation and evacuation. Serious attention was now turned by the Ministry of Health to action which might be necessary to re-house, clothe, feed and otherwise help persons made homeless by air raids[1].

This spreading of duties among Departments was to be accompanied by more determined devolution of central functions to regional bodies. The system of Regional Commissioners set up in the crisis was regarded more firmly than before as the linchpin of the structure—the chief agency in extremity of central authority, and the method in circumstances short of this of co-ordinating local efforts. But 'Scheme "Y" ', though regarded as sound in conception, contained many defects for the remedying of which much work would be needed. Chief attention in the development of plans would now be given to strengthening the A.R.P. Department's Inspectorate and to much fuller definition of the powers and organisation to be at the Regional Commissioners' disposal.

The scheme for Regional Commissioners lay at the heart of the one substantial criticism of A.R.P. plans seen in the light of their dress-rehearsal—the very high degree of secrecy so far enforced. Preparation of civil resources against the swift, perhaps catastrophic, knock-out blow needed organisation well in advance of the event, and such organisation spelt consultation with officials and enlistment of public support on an ever-widening scale. Planning at the centre, this narrative has tried to show, had already had substantial results, notably in delivery of a gas-mask to almost every adult citizen. But plans at high levels must now, it was clear, be translated more quickly into plans and execution at lower levels, and mobilisation of

---

[1] See R. M. Titmuss, *op. cit.*, Chapter IV.

civilians in peace-time must be carried to new lengths. Some further lifting of the veil of secrecy had now, the Committee of Imperial Defence decided, become essential; though the scheme for Regional Commissioners was still only to be disclosed gradually.

Because they commanded general assent, and also because the time-factor now counted for much, the essential A.R.P. structure and policies were, with one important exception, to be unchanged. Preparation in future was to mean, above all, more positive development of plans and spheres of action already well marked out; though the Government, being ready to give more vigorous financial and other leadership, would seek new statutory powers including more measures of compulsion. The principal task now resting on local authorities was rapid completion of schemes, and especially the training of A.R.P. Services and better arrangements for co-ordination in peace and war. The Government was, however, faced with the important problem of reconciling the full responsibilities resting on local authorities in peace with the system of placing executive control in other hands when war arose. The ordinary citizen volunteering to train in peace to perform part-time duties in war remained the most essential single feature of the structure, though the authorities were now convinced that in war a larger nucleus of whole-time personnel would be needed. Industry, which the crisis had proved to be generally most backward in preparations, would still be treated as a separate problem to which the 'good employer' relying on his own resources would make the main contribution; though the Government was now prepared to give employers greater help in return for obliging them to provide workpeople with basic standards of A.R.P. training and protection.

The one important exception to continuity of plans was the discovery of new practical means of supplying large numbers of the public with air raid shelter, and the Government's decision to shoulder the financial burden this would involve. Experience in the crisis had done nothing to alter the long-standing policy of 'dispersal', with its corollary that the chief protection available to most citizens would be that afforded by their homes. But public demand that the Government should take steps, regardless of cost, to provide some form of universal protection had become emphatic, and brought admission from the Home Secretary that 'a more comprehensive policy was needed'.[1] The Government decided, first, to make the trenches dug in the crisis a permanent feature, and secondly to give more help, including new statutory powers, to local authorities over strengthening existing buildings for use as shelters. Soon after his appointment, the Lord Privy Seal sought technical advice about helping the householder to protect himself by supplying him with a steel structure,

---

[1] H. of C. Deb., Vol. 340, Cols. 411-535, 3rd November 1938.

capable of mass production, which he could erect in his home. The conclusion, rapidly arrived at, was announced by the Minister to Parliament on 21st December.[1] The Government had designed a domestic steel shelter, giving protection against splinters, blast and debris, which they intended to supply free to the poorer inhabitants (estimated at about 10 million persons) of vulnerable areas. The cost of these shelters, together with new steel fittings for strengthening private basements, of about £20 million would be borne wholly by the Exchequer. These new domestic appliances, measures soon to be introduced for compulsory protection of employees, and public shelters would provide fair protection for some 20 million persons. Addition of the domestic air raid shelter to the civilian gas-mask and the stirrup pump as a third basic item of personal equipment to be furnished to large numbers at the national expense must be regarded by the student as revolutionary.[2] The household shelter was to remain, notwithstanding provision of many other forms of shelter, the foundation of shelter arrangements throughout the war.

By the end of 1938 the Government had decided on fresh practical steps for applying these policies. A phase of review and consolidation at the centre was to be followed by new public appeals, consultation and Parliamentary discussion. But before these could be fully set in motion the balance between peace and war had, for the Government and their chief advisers, become still more precarious. The Committee of Imperial Defence asked the Lord Privy Seal and Service Ministers to give urgent attention to means of speeding up defence preparations, and instructed all departments to give higher priority to war planning.

The White Paper on Defence of 1939 stated the need for large increases in the scale and tempo of war measures, and further advanced recognition of civil defence as a 'fourth arm'.[3] Expenditure on the three Defence Departments of £262 million for 1937 and £388 million in the year just ending was to grow to £523 million for 1939. This 'enormous rise', as the Chancellor of the Exchequer described it, was, in conformity with the guiding principles of defence policy, due mainly to expansion of active defences against air attack.[4] But passive defence was put on a formal footing of equality with the Defence Services when the Chancellor asked Parliament for new borrowing powers for defence.[5] Expenditure on Air Raid Precautions would amount in the current year to £9¼ million. It was

---

[1] H. of C. Deb., Vol. 342, Cols. 2880–2892.

[2] The accent is here on the word 'personal'. Each of these items (though remaining Government property) was for personal use and relied for its efficacy on a definite measure of skill and attention on the part of its possessor.

[3] Cmd. 5944, February 1939.

[4] See p. 114.

[5] H. of C. Deb., Vol. 344, Col. 47, 20th February 1939.

estimated for 1939 at £42 million, including the £20 million to be spent on the new shelter programme but excluding the 'civil defence' items of help to public utilities, and emergency food, water and hospital arrangements.[1]

The scale of attack, as the reader is aware, had been revised in April 1937 in an upward direction.[2] Now, nearly two years later, the Air Staff had to present a still more forbidding picture. No part of Britain would be beyond the reach of long-range bombers based in Germany, though the intensity of attack could be expected to diminish as the enemy penetrated to the west. Northern Ireland would represent about the extreme operational range.

Though, in the absence of experience, the hypothesis contained large elements of conjecture, the Air Staff now estimated the possible scale of attack in April 1939 at a daily average of 700 tons of bombs (dropped by some 650 German aircraft) as a maximum effort during the first week or fortnight of a war. The comparable figures for April 1940 would be 950 tons of bombs dropped by some 800 aircraft. Naturally, attack on this scale could not be maintained for long; but after a substantial reduction it might from time to time be revived. As an alternative to an attack of this kind over a week or more, the Germans might choose to deliver as much as 3,500 tons on London or elsewhere in the first twenty-four hours of a war. A still higher degree of accuracy in bomb-aiming was now, the experts considered, probable.

The experience of air bombardment in the Spanish Civil War, though closely studied, had not offered much useful general data applicable to the British hypothesis.[3] Barcelona, a capital and a port, was in some respects and on a smaller scale comparable to London as a target. The 230 or so raids against this city had been mainly directed against the coastal area and the port. But many of these had been made by Italian squadrons and others by one or two German seaplanes; and though much general destruction had been caused, the marksmanship of the attackers was often indifferent. Some 2,500 persons had been killed in the city, and a rather higher number seriously injured. One of the chief deductions from Barcelona's experience was that in the indiscriminate attacks of March 1938 a total of 44 tons of bombs had caused 3,000 casualties, about 1,000 of which were fatal. This tended to confirm the British experts' long-established estimate that each ton of high explosive dropped on a congested area might cause 50 casualties.

---

[1] These, less hospital arrangements, were estimated at another £14 million.

[2] pp. 96, 142–143.

[3] pp. 103–104.

Further Growth at the Centre

The development of machinery at the centre into the instrument to be used in war must now be further described. 'We have to create our machine', Sir John Anderson told Parliament after four months of office, 'and we have simultaneously to make it work. That is, indeed, a formidable task'.[1] The scale and novelty, the historian may add, of this organising process gave the factor of personality, at all levels, much significance. What now took place at the centre of affairs owed a debt which cannot be measured to the Lord Privy Seal's intimate connection with the earlier phase of planning and to the wide confidence and respect his abilities commanded.

In spite of periodic complaints of 'diffusion of responsibility' and demands for concentration of powers over all civil defence matters in one Minister,[2] the Government held firmly to the peace-time separation of co-ordination and planning from current A.R.P. administration. The instrument performing the first functions was comparable, in some respects, to the general staff of a commander in the field gathering intelligence and co-ordinating the plans of a number of allied commanders.[3] The Lord Privy Seal established his headquarters in the Home Office. His staff consisted of a few administrative officers, drawn mainly from this department, to whom were later added the Controller of Publicity seconded from the Post Office and an adviser on industrial affairs.[4] His 'Chief of Staff', being free from departmental ties, was able to promote increasingly close co-operation between the various departments and agencies involved. This staff derived further authority in Whitehall from its duty to remodel and institute the scheme for Regional Commissioners.

As a succession of crises made it essential to speed up preparations, formal machinery for co-ordination gave way increasingly to informal consultation and liaison. The committee of Permanent Heads of Departments fell into disuse.[5] Ministers concerned began to take much larger personal share in interdepartmental planning, especially after the turn of events for the worse in March 1939. The Committee of Imperial Defence had become, as a consequence of the new arrangements after Munich, more exclusively concerned with military preparations, though many of its committees remained of much importance to civil planning. The directing authority of the new arm, the Ministerial committee presided over by the Lord Privy Seal, began steadily to assume the character of the 'Standing

---

[1] H. of C. Deb., Vol. 344, Col. 1291, 1st March 1939.
[2] H. of C. Deb., Vol. 346, Cols. 805–826, 24th April 1939.
[3] p. 167.
[4] Of a total staff of 33 in May 1939, 11 were administrative or specialist staff.
[5] p. 166.

Council of Home Security' designed for co-ordination and rapid decision in war.[1]

From the standpoint of the 'general staff' the A.R.P. Department was but one of a number of executive instruments for civil defence. The 'Chief of Staff' maintained a relationship with the head of this department broadly similar to his relationship with the heads of the other departments concerned. The A.R.P. Department, nevertheless, was the instrument employed in building the 'first-line' defences against air attack, now much enlarged by the new shelter plans. Early in 1939 it began a rapid further growth in size and specialisation.[2] In January a fourth main administrative division was formed, under a Principal Assistant Secretary, to prepare shelter legislation and deal with general policy over structural precautions. After a few months of existence this had expanded, like the two original divisions, into the responsibility of an Assistant Under-Secretary and been subdivided into three branches. The proposal made by the Structural Precautions Committee in 1937 that the Home Office should have its own research establishment was given effect by the appointment of a Chief Adviser on Research and Experiments, Dr Reginald Stradling.[3] The Research Branch he began to form, with the help of the Department of Scientific and Industrial Research, was to take responsibility for all experimental work, involving each type of weapon and such matters as camouflage and lighting, needed by the Department. It would provide data to the Chief Technical Adviser, now renamed the Chief Engineering Adviser, who would henceforth concentrate on the application of structural and shelter programmes. The varied functions the Department was required to perform and the hybrid nature of its staff became increasingly apparent. The Inspector-General's Department was engaged in an important strengthening of the size and authority of the Regional Inspectorate. The division concerned with operations and staffed by former officers of the Fighting Services was transferred early in the summer to the Lord Privy Seal's Office. A Supply Policy Division, embracing the existing Supply Branch, and a separate Communications Section had been added after Munich and an A.R.P. Grants Section had been formed in the Home Office Finance Division. Co-ordination of these divisions' and branches' activities continued up to the war to be effected by the Heads of Divisions Council.

Six months after taking office the Lord Privy Seal described the staff of the Department to Parliament as 'very substantial'. Its headquarters staff, together with the Minister's personal staff and the Fire Brigades Division, had grown in this period from 321 persons

---

[1] p. 166.

[2] pp. 111–113.

[3] p. 83.

of all grades to 688; and the total staff, including administrative and industrial staff employed in the provinces, to over 2,000. Compared with the situation a year or so before, the limpet had assumed still larger proportions in relation to its rock.[1] Of a total non-industrial staff of some 2,400 persons employed by the Home Office in April 1939 about 600 were occupied in the A.R.P. Department. The Home Office Vote, raised to £1,100,000 for 1939–40, included £266,000 for salaries and expenses of the headquarters staff of this Department.[2] The main expenditure on A.R.P. and Emergency Fire Brigade Services formed a separate Vote in the Estimates.

By the middle of 1939 these developments at the centre had produced the essential features of the instrument with which the war was to be fought. The decision had been made to appoint Sir John Anderson immediately war broke out to the double office of Home Secretary and Minister of Home Security. As Minister of Home Security he would continue to perform the two functions of co-ordinating all civil defence activities at the seat of Government and through Regional Commissioners, and controlling A.R.P. operations. His small general staff and the rapidly expanding A.R.P. Department would be fused into the single instrument of a Ministry of Home Security.

Regional Organisation

The experience of the crisis had convinced the Home Office and other departments that the scheme for Regional Commissioners was right in conception; what was now required was its fuller preparation in advance of any need arising for its use.[3] The Permanent Secretary designate of the Ministry of Home Security, Sir Thomas Gardiner, had been closely concerned with the regionalisation being carried out by the Post Office, and made proposals for giving 'Scheme "Y" ' fuller administrative form. The central idea behind the scheme, it must be emphasised afresh, remained unchanged and took on permanent significance. The Regional Commissioners were to employ two types of authority, appropriate to two different sets of war conditions. In what was now defined, without attempt at precision, as 'normal war conditions' their authority would be limited to personal persuasion and their task to co-ordination of the actions of departmental agents. In extremity, now defined as the more or less complete disruption of their communications with Home Security headquarters, they would add to the co-ordinating function that of executive control and exercise 'full powers of civil government'.

---

[1] pp. 111–113.

[2] Civil Estimates and Estimates for Revenue Departments for the year ending 31st March 1940, H.C. 70.

[3] p. 169.

Official action now concentrated, not on fuller definition of Commissioners' powers in extremity, but on the task of erecting in peace the essentials of the structure designed for 'normal war conditions'. The Commissioners, it was proposed, should be appointed in peace and should be 'men of national standing' and assisted by Deputy Commissioners. After appointment they should be asked, first, to familiarise themselves with departmental war plans and meet members of their future staffs, and then to get into touch with local authorities and stimulate interest in civil defence in their Regions. Their war staffs should, in the meantime, be built up both in Whitehall and in the Regions. These should be put in charge of Principal Officers, chosen at once from serving civil servants of Principal Assistant Secretary rank, who would act in Regions in a capacity like that of Permanent Heads of Departments. A strengthened A.R.P. Inspectorate should be preparing accommodation for Commissioners' headquarters, and the scheme for grouping local authority areas in certain Regions should be actively pursued.

When the civil defence committees approved these plans they added two features of importance. One of these proposed arrangements to be set up at once for London Region, shortly to be noticed more fully. The other concerned the crucial matter of the relation in war between the Home Security Organisation and the local authorities. The plan adopted in the crisis of giving Chief Constables executive control of A.R.P. operations was an improvisation which, viewed merely as a matter of machinery, had one substantial defect —the divorce of authority in war from responsibility in peace. The Home Office had therefore proposed that persons, whether Chief Constables or others, to be given executive control in war should be designated in peace and should, if possible, be the officials responsible for peace-time co-ordination. When Ministers considered the remodelled Regional scheme its publication was imminent, and they were less concerned with the mechanical defects of this divorce than with its political and financial implications. They decided that the emergency scheme must provide without any shadow of doubt an effective and clearly defined chain of executive control deriving ultimately from 'the Home Security Minister of Government'. But the problem remained of maintaining peace-time collaboration and responsibility by local authorities who were to be superseded when the emergency arose. Ministers reached a solution which derived from their developing conception of different sets of war conditions or degrees of immediacy in war. They proposed that local authorities should delegate powers in war to small Emergency Committees which would act as what may be called half-links in the chain of Home Security command. If conditions in any area became extreme, the A.R.P. Controller or other local officials would act at once on

Home Security instructions, reporting afterwards to these committees. Under conditions falling short of this, they would report their instructions to the committees before taking action.

The publication at the opening of February of this plan for Regional Organisation formed an important landmark.[1] The secrecy enshrouding the Regional Commissioners' activities in the crisis had, once the danger had passed, been a good deal diluted; and the procedure, including the functions conferred on Chief Constables, had caused much resentment among local authorities. Subsequently, consultations between the Government and local authorities had, on account of urgency, been considerably restricted. Proposals of this nature, bringing memories to some of Cromwell's Major-Generals or Hitler's Gauleiters and suggesting the insidious approach of 'dictatorship' and 'militarisation' were bound to arouse certain public misgivings.[2] The Prime Minister reassuringly described the plan as but an 'incident in the general scheme of policy',[3] and Government statements stressed the peace-time A.R.P. regional development and minimised the plan's more drastic features. The Regional Commissioners, the public announcement stated, would have no function in peace except that of keeping in touch with local authorities to promote co-ordination; and Regional Councils of representatives of local authorities and central departments would be set up. The Commissioners would not proceed to their headquarters before a threat of war, and 'the degree of control exercised by a Regional Commissioner in time of war on his own responsibility would depend on the extent to which communications had been affected'.

It was a measure of the gravity with which air attack was now regarded that suspicions of this plan as sinister and dictatorial were few and, for the time being, short-lived.[4] Parliament had been expressing satisfaction with the vigour implanted into civil defence by the Lord Privy Seal's direction, combined with demands that the scope and pace of preparations should be still further enlarged. The Regional plan was generally welcomed as evidence of the Government's foresight, and as furnishing a much-needed means of speeding up local measures.[5]

---

[1] A.R.P. Dept. Circular 20, 2nd February 1939. From the start of 1939 the Department's circulars were numbered serially. The description Home Security Circular was not adopted until January, 1940.

[2] It was later discovered that, by a freak of history, the name of the Newcastle Regional Commissioner was the same as that of Cromwell's Major-General for the North District of 1655; and that the boundaries of this and other Regions bore similarities to those of Cromwell's eleven Districts.

[3] H. of C. Deb., Vol. 343, Col. 744, 7th February 1939.

[4] As one exception, see report of a meeting held by the Lord Privy Seal in Glasgow, *The Times*, 15th February 1939.

[5] H. of C. Deb., Vol. 344, Cols. 1287-1292, 1st March 1939.

Publication of the Regional scheme was soon followed by announcement of the way this would now be linked in war with local government machinery.[1] The Government, it was emphasised, must be able in war to send information 'and, when necessary, instructions to some one person who is empowered to take immediate executive action' over any aspect of A.R.P. in his area. Scheme-making authorities were asked to appoint such war-time 'A.R.P. Controllers' without delay. They should be chosen on personal grounds as being 'likely to inspire confidence under conditions of severe strain and as capable of ensuring harmonious co-operation of all persons concerned in civil defence'. They might be one of the authority's chief officers or the chief police officer or some other person, and peace-time A.R.P. Officers would normally serve under them. Authorities were also asked to nominate Emergency Committees of not more than three members of their councils, to whom Controllers would report all communications received from the Home Security Organisation. The important matter of whether Controllers reported before or after taking action would depend on the urgency of the particular local situation.

Soon afterwards the names of Regional Commissioners and their Deputies,[2] and the headquarters and boundaries of Regions, were published. The areas chosen remained, with only one important exception, those of 'Scheme "Y" ', which in turn had closely followed those of the Civil Emergency Organisation. Grouping of counties into units of convenient character and size for emergency administration was the guiding principle, and the Boundaries Committee reaffirmed the precedence of civil 'operational' needs and made no attempt to embark on a general redrawing of boundaries.[3] The London and Home Counties Region of the crisis, however, was thought too great a complex of authorities and too large a burden in war for one Commissioner.[4] London Region was henceforth to coincide with the Metropolitan Police District. Kent, outside this District, and Sussex were to form a new twelfth Region, with headquarters at Tunbridge Wells; the remaining parts of the Home Counties were to be added to the Eastern and Southern Regions. Scotland, as in the crisis, was to be one Region with headquarters at Edinburgh, subdivided into five Districts. The ideal plan for Wales remained a perplexing and controversial question; it was decided that it should continue as one Region, with a District Commissioner and a special grouping for economic purposes in North Wales. The

---

[1] A.R.P. Dept. Circular 57, 21st March 1939.

[2] *The Times*, 19th April; A.R.P. Dept. Circulars 93 and 94, 28th April 1939.

[3] p. 169.

[4] p. 158, footnote 3.

Peak district of Derbyshire, as an exceptional arrangement, was to be included in North Midland Region in peace and in North Western Region in war. The areas so determined were to continue unaltered, except for some changes concerning Surrey and Dorset, throughout the war.

In the choice of Regional Commissioners 'national standing', or removal from intimate association with local affairs, was generally emphasised. Only one of the Munich Commissioners was re-appointed;[1] though a number who had served in this capacity were now, with their special local knowledge and ties, to be Deputy Commissioners. London Region was to be in charge of a Senior Regional Commissioner and two Regional Commissioners, but since special machinery was already in being for London appoint-ment of the Senior Commissioner was deferred. For similar reasons, the Commissioner for Scotland was not to be appointed until an emergency arose.[2] When the appointments were made public little disagreement was expressed with the view that they formed 'a good list' dictated only by the consideration of first-class qualifications.[3]

CIVIL DEFENCE REGIONS

on their institution, April 1939

Region	H.Q.	Regional Commissioner and Deputy Commissioner
1. Northern	Newcastle	Sir Arthur Lambert Appointment deferred
2. North Eastern	Leeds	Lord Harlech Sir Charles McGrath
3. North Midland	Nottingham	Lord Trent Mr H. A. S. Wortley
4. Eastern	Cambridge	Sir Will Spens Lord Eltisley
5. London	London	Appointment of Senior R.C. deferred Two Regional Commissioners: Sir Ernest Gowers Admiral Sir Edward Evans
6. Southern	Reading	Mr Harold Butler Mr W. M. Goodenough
7. South Western	Bristol	General Sir Hugh Elles Mr Geoffrey Peto

[1] Lord Trent, North Midland Region.

[2] Mr Thomas Johnston, M.P. and the Lord Advocate for Scotland were announced as planning the Scottish organisation; the former was appointed Commissioner in September 1939.

[3] *The Times*, 19th April 1939.

CIVIL DEFENCE REGIONS

on their institution, April 1939 (*contd.*)

Region	H.Q.	Regional Commissioner and Deputy Commissioner
8. Wales	Cardiff	Lord Portal Captain G. Crawshay
9. Midland	Birmingham	Earl of Dudley Mr S. J. Grey
10. North Western	Manchester	Sir Warren Fisher Mr J. R. Hobhouse
11. Scotland	Edinburgh	Appointment deferred Earl of Airlie
12. South Eastern	Tunbridge Wells	Sir Auckland Geddes Viscount Knollys

The Regional areas are shown as a map facing page 309 below.[1]

The Regional Organisation was now evolving in a two-fold manner—through elaboration at the centre in shadow form of this Regional Commissioner apparatus and through development of the A.R.P. Inspectorate. The Inspectorate was being transformed after four years from a few 'missionaries' in the field into a series of more substantial administrative staffs.[2] Inspectors were to be raised in status and trebled in number. The title Inspector, except in the case of the Inspector-General, was to be abandoned and 'Regional Officers' of three grades would be appointed. A Chief Regional Officer was to serve under the Inspector-General at headquarters, and a Senior Regional Officer and two Regional Officers would be posted to each Region. This reconstruction was quickly effected. By the end of January some forty Regional Officers had been chosen, and after some training at headquarters they took up their duties in Regions.[3] In view of the permanence this system of A.R.P. Regional Officers was to acquire, it is of interest to record that an effort to base it on officers from the Civil Service and Local Government Service met with small success.[4] Members of the existing Inspectorate, who were almost all retired officers of the Fighting Services, and

---

[1] They were formally defined in detail in the Civil Defence Regions Order 1942. (S.R.& O. No. 17.) The changes made during the war among Regional Commissioners and Deputy Commissioners, and the District Commissioners for Scotland are shown at Appendix I of this volume.

[2] pp. 65–66, 113.

[3] A.R.P. Dept. Circular 20, 2nd February 1939.

[4] The maximum salary of a Grade I Regional Officer was £1,050 p.a.

others with like experience secured a large share of the appointments. A tradition and methods which had already given their distinctive character to the A.R.P. Department's 'outdoor' work were thus maintained.

Regional Officers, consolidating their position with new authority, were the vanguard of a military penetration of significance to the topic of this volume. Persons of military training and experience were to contribute substantially, as Regional Commissioners and at many lower levels in the structure, to civil defence in peace and war. If their conceptions of administration were sometimes in conflict with civilian views and methods, this result was unavoidable; for civil defence was both civil and military. Though Civil Servants formed the leaven of the organism, there were quite inadequate numbers of these available to administer the new arm;[1] and the conditions deplored by Milton three hundred years before had perhaps not greatly altered:

> For Britain (to speak a truth not often spoken) as it is a land fruitful enough of men stout and courageous in war, so it is naturally not over-fertile of men able to govern justly and prudently in peace, trusting only in their mother-wit.

When the Regional Officers took up their duties early in March local preparations were reported by the Department to be proceeding more smoothly and rapidly than at any former time. Yet, despite the great impetus the crisis had furnished, much remained to be done. The action local authorities had taken in the crisis had been largely the anticipation of schemes still far from complete and unapproved; and thereafter central examination and approval by instalments of the sixteen chief measures to be included in each local scheme had been resumed. The attitude of the two major parties involved had been defined afresh when the Lord Privy Seal met the Local Authority Associations in December. The Minister acknowledged the considerable strain which air raid defence imposed on local machinery; but the Government felt it necessary that the authorities should abandon the view that A.R.P. was 'something extraneous and apart from their normal functions', and increase the tempo of preparations by spreading the burden more effectively among their officials. The authorities, for their part, re-emphasised the delays and difficulties caused by the need to submit all items of schemes for detailed approval to Whitehall.

Regional Officers were provided with an elaborate Code of Instructions which defined their main duties as follows: to further good relations between the A.R.P. Department and the public, approve expenditure and other matters, advise authorities on the

---

[1] In 1939 the Administrative Class of the Home Civil Service numbered about 1,500.

details of schemes, stimulate public interest in A.R.P. and watch the authorities' performance of their duties under the 1937 Act. They were asked to be in frequent touch with the chief officers of each scheme-making authority and representatives of all central departments concerned with civil defence in their Regions, with the principal bodies, such as the Red Cross, co-operating in civil defence and with leading industrial firms. Stress was laid on informal contacts, and on the fact that A.RP. was 'essentially dependent upon voluntary effort and the goodwill of the people'.

Regional Officers outside London were predominantly engaged in liaison, and they were only entrusted at this stage with limited powers to approve expenditure on schemes. Communications about schemes were to be sent in the first place (as hitherto) to the A.R.P. Department or its new Scottish Office in Edinburgh.[1] In what the Department called 'a transitional period of devolution' the Senior Regional Officers' authority to approve expenditure did not extend beyond the following main items: appointment of A.R.P. Officers and certain other persons earning up to £450 per annum, the renting of premises to a rental of £250 per annum, structural alterations to a maximum of £500 and the erection of certain buildings such as respirator stores. No authority was delegated to them regarding the purchase of property, evacuation, or fire brigades and police organisation and expenditure.

The staffs of Regional Offices were increased in March by appointment of Regional Technical Advisers, who were engineers by profession and took technical instructions from the Chief Engineering Adviser.[2] They were mainly concerned with helping local authorities over the new public shelter and structural precautions plans; advice about A.R.P. buildings was still furnished at the centre. The emphasis now placed on shelters caused admission a few months later of the principle of direct communication between Technical Advisers and scheme-making authorities.[3]

Administrative devolution to Regional Officers was not much further enlarged until war was imminent. The annual meeting in May of the Municipal Corporations Association repeated the familiar charges of excessive centralisation and the difficulties of dealing with officials in Whitehall; and the Home Office maintained that decentralisation was proceeding and pleaded the difficulties of establishing general standards of A.R.P. administration and expenditure. But in August more delegation was introduced. Correspondence about general schemes was henceforth to be sent by authorities

---

[1] A.R.P. Dept. Circular 62, 25th March 1939.

[2] A.R.P. Dept. Circulars 62 and 91, 25th March and 25th April 1939.

[3] A.R.P. Dept. Circular 110, 22nd May 1939.

direct to Regional Offices.[1] Senior Regional Officers were given more financial authority over public shelters, report centres and other matters, and supervision of Regional training. Immediately before the war Regional Technical Advisers' staffs were enlarged and Works Advisers appointed to each Region.

London, the Lord Privy Seal reminded Parliament, had lost nothing of its 'very special position' in civil defence. It was pre-eminent as a target; and application of the principle that A.R.P. was a local responsibility to the sprawling area of Greater London, with its hundred or so authorities, presented a large problem of co-ordination. After consultations with the L.C.C., the City, the Boroughs and others the Government set up in February 1939 an executive authority for the whole Metropolitan Police District to which local authorities would have direct access.[2] This took the form of a separate division of the A.R.P. Department, in charge of Mr Harold Scott, then Chairman of the Prison Commission, with the title of Chief Administrative Officer.

This arrangement represented devolution to a Region or a fusion of peace-time preparations with war organisation much in advance of the development in the other eleven Regions. The Chief Administrative Officer would become Principal Officer to the Commissioner in war and was now, with his main war-time staff, 'in post'. His responsibility for administration of the Act and approval of the schemes of about forty scheme-making authorities (except as regards the shelter programme which was still to be wholly administered for London by the A.R.P. Department) will receive some notice later. But administration of this kind was progressively merged with concentration on methods for 'the effective control and employment of regional services in war'.

The London Civil Defence Region, as the authority was soon known, received valuable lessons from the Munich dress-rehearsal.[3] It was helped in its tasks by a small co-ordinating committee, composed of the two Regional Commissioners, the Chief Administrative Officer, the Commissioner, Metropolitan Police and representative County and Town Clerks. The larger Regional Council, provided for in the main regional plan and representing all authorities in the area, met occasionally for general discussion. By the early summer the Region had made a big advance in developing its war structure. For the A.R.P. Services, the special arrangement was made of placing all the Region's wardens under the control of Sir Philip Game

---

[1] A.R.P. Dept. Circular 167, 3rd August 1939.

[2] The Metropolitan Police District had a population of nearly 9 million in 1939. The scheme-making authorities, in addition to those mentioned, were the five bordering Counties and three County Boroughs.

[3] pp. 158–159; Mr Scott had then acted as Personal Assistant to the London Regional Commissioner.

(though not in his capacity as Metropolitan Police Commissioner) assisted by a Principal Air Raid Warden,[1] and good progress had been made with selecting and equipping wardens' posts. The Ambulance Service throughout the Region was being organised by the peace-time head of the London Ambulance Service, who would also control operations of mobile First Aid Units. Responsibility for Rescue and Demolition Parties in the County of London should, it had now been decided, also reside with the L.C.C., and agreement had been reached with the building trades over recruitment, composition and terms of service of these. The L.C.C. was co-ordinating, in collaboration with public utility undertakings, the organisation of Repair Parties in the County. 'Stretcher Parties', as First Aid Parties were to be permanently known in London Region, remained the Boroughs' responsibility; but a County scheme for their collective training by the St. John Ambulance Brigade under the supervision of a London Region medical officer was now in force. All local authorities in the Region had now appointed A.R.P. Controllers, and a scheme had been prepared for mobilisation of the services at short notice.

The important matter, advocated in the general Regional plan, of grouping local authority areas for war-time control and mutual support had been organised in detail by the middle of 1939. The twenty-nine scheme-making authorities of the County had been divided into five Groups, three north and two south of the Thames; and buildings for Group Centres had been chosen and were being strengthened and equipped. Outside the County, four other Groups had been formed, to serve Middlesex and Hertfordshire in combination and the areas within the Region of the other three bordering counties. Direct telephone lines had been installed from war-time Regional Headquarters to Group Centres, and from these to local Control Centres; and exercises were in progress over this network in reporting and the control and movement of reserves. Close links had been established for war between this new system of control and the Army and police authorities, including appointment of military and police liaison officers to Regional Headquarters. A plan by the Chief Officer of the London Fire Brigade, who would become Regional Fire Officer in war, for organisation and mutual aid had been agreed with the seventy or so fire authorities in the Region.

The Region's war headquarters was to be the Geological Museum, Exhibition Road, South Kensington, and by June this building had been adapted and essential communications installed.[2] The equipment, staffing arrangements and operational procedure of the

---

[1] H. of C. Deb., Vol. 345, Cols. 2039-2041, 29th March 1939.

[2] The Region's headquarters remained in Tufton Street, Westminster until the end of August 1939.

Regional War Room were then worked out in detail; and these provided a model on which other Regions began to make such arrangements in the weeks immediately before the war.

This development of London Region towards its war-time stature was, as already observed, unique. In other Regions the civil defence war structure, as distinct from the A.R.P. Department's Regional Organisation, was only being established in shadow form. Principal Officers and Regional Treasury Officers had been chosen before publication of the plan and allotted on paper to Regions at the end of March. But being senior civil servants in various departments these could give only limited attention to war duties. They helped the Lord Privy Seal's Department in planning the Commissioners' war staffs and such matters as the functions of Regional Councils and relations between the Commissioners and the Press. In the nature of the case they remained largely detached from the development being made 'on the ground' by the A.R.P. Department's Regional staffs.

At the opening of May the Lord Privy Seal gave Regional Commissioners a description of their functions. Their office in war he called a 'dormant commission' from the Government which would become active under circumstances of which they themselves would be the judges. If communications between the Region and Home Security headquarters were seriously interrupted they would, at their own discretion, take over full powers of civil government and be held indemnified for everything done in good faith. Each departmental representative would be instructed to look under these conditions to the Regional Commissioner as his source of authority 'for any action that he does not feel able to take on his own responsibility when he cannot get covering authority from his own departmental chief'. The Minister stressed the probability of long periods in war during which 'more or less normal working' could proceed in large areas of the country. During these the Commissioners, while refraining from active intervention, should 'keep in touch with events and be in constant readiness, to assume effective control'. Their detachment from departmental ties would enable them to play an important part in resolving departmental claims and interests. So long as peace lasted, the Regional Commissioners would have no executive powers and normal processes of administration would go on as if they did not exist. He advised them to make the keynote of their peace-time activities 'a maximum of contact and a minimum of interference', and to base approach to their Regions on Regional Councils. Both the letters nominating Commissioners and their Deputies from 1st April (for a term of three years), and the subsequent Regional Emergency Instructions, defined the Commissioners' powers in similarly broad terms.

The Regional Councils were designed to establish formal contact and to give opportunities for mutual discussion between the Commissioners and local authorities.[1] They had no executive functions, and were not concerned with the details of A.R.P. scheme making. They were large bodies composed, besides the Commissioner and his Deputy, of the senior regional representative of every department concerned with civil defence, representatives of the counties and county boroughs (though not in their capacity as scheme-making bodies) and usually also of the Army command, industry, public utilities and other interests.[2] These Councils met in all Regions for the first time in May, when Commissioners explained their powers and duties, and in the following months they met at least once more. They fulfilled an important function in beginning to dispel distrust of the Regional Commissioner idea; and in giving opportunity for Commissioners and departmental representatives to supply information, especially about shelter and evacuation plans and ways of educating the public, and for local authorities to voice their main problems such as that of finding enough whole-time volunteers. The Midland Regional Council paid special attention to the problem, which had so far only made progress in London, of grouping local authority areas.

These Councils apart, the Commissioners only made informal contacts with local authorities and strictly observed the principle of 'non-interference'. They also made some study of departmental war plans and met departmental officers nominated to their war staffs. The Lord Privy Seal met them again late in May when it was decided that Commissioners should meet in future to discuss common problems in three geographical groups. Only one such formal meeting, of the Southern Group to study the problem of unofficial evacuation from London, was held before war supervened.

By the middle of 1939 the nerve-centre of Home Security, the War Room in the Home Office basement, had been protected and equipped, and most of the staff required to man it had been recruited and trained. A duplicate War Room had been established in Cornwall House, near Waterloo Station. From the end of July Regions outside London were improvising War Rooms and recruiting and training the staffs, mainly of volunteers, who might be needed to man them.

Shelters, and the Civil Defence Act, 1939

The shelter programme the Lord Privy Seal had announced at the end of 1938 did not depart from the long-held policy of

---

[1] A.R.P. Dept. Circular 65, 30th March 1939.

[2] A District Council was also formed for each of the five Scottish Districts.

'dispersal'.[1] Its outstanding feature was the Government's decision to give substantial help to citizens dispersed in their own homes. The invention of a practical household shelter—to be quickly known as the 'Anderson'—had transformed the possibilities hitherto envisaged for protection of homes against air attack. The Government had undertaken to supply these shelters, as well as steel fittings for strengthening basements, free to some 2½ million families. They would also give more positive help over the provision, as a subsidiary means of protection, of public shelters. This programme was welcomed by Parliament and the public as evidence of the Government's determination to press on with a method of defence which they regarded, with the complementary method of evacuation, as over-shadowing all others in importance.

The 'Anderson' had originally been conceived as a shelter to be erected inside the average small working-class home. But the experts soon discarded this idea as open to various objections, including the probability that occupants would be trapped by the fall of their house and killed by fire or escaping coal-gas.[2] During Munich householders had been advised to dig trenches in their yards or gardens, and now, by an extension of this plan, the 'Anderson' was designed as an outdoor or surface shelter. It consisted of fourteen corrugated steel sheets weighing, with other components, about 8 cwt. A corrugated steel hood, curved for greater strength, would be sunk some two feet in the ground and covered with earth or sandbags. The structure would be 6 ft. high, 4 ft. 6 in. wide, and 6 ft. long and provided with two exits. It was intended to accommodate four, or at a pinch six, persons. It could be erected fairly quickly by unskilled labour and would not take up much space. It would not, as the authorities made plain from the outset, be 'bomb-proof', i.e. protect its occupants against a direct hit. But it would offer a good measure of protection against bomb-splinters, blast and falling debris.[3]

The shelter would cost about £5, which was less than the cost per head of trenching or providing concrete structures, and had the additional advantage from the Government's point of view of some 'residual' or peace-time value. The steel industry set up an organisation to handle the contract arranged by H.M. Office of Works for the Government and allocate orders for components to individual firms; productive capacity was estimated at two million shelters within nine months. Distribution presented a new and intricate problem. As it would not be practicable for local authorities to store

---

[1] pp. 170–171

[2] *Air Raid Shelter Policy*, Cmd. 5932, December 1938.

[3] For a fuller description see *Sectional Steel Shelters*, Cmd. 6055, July 1939. Dr. David Anderson had taken a large part in the designing of this shelter.

the shelters, the railway companies agreed to collect the components from manufacturers, sort them into shelter units and deliver these to householders at addresses supplied by local authorities. These arrangements would be synchronised by the A.R.P. Department, helped by a committee of representatives of the British Iron and Steel Corporation and the railway companies; and an elaborate system of demand notes, consignment notes, despatch notes and address lists had to be devised by the Department's new Shelters Supply Branch. The railways, though not agreeing to a flat-rate charge, made some reduction of normal freight charges.[1]

These details give one illustration of the degree in which A.R.P. now involved execution, or the diversion it already represented of civil administrative effort into war preparations. The new shelter programme, of which the 'Anderson' formed only one feature, was to absorb an important share of the attention of officials concerned with A.R.P. in the remaining months of peace. In the earlier part of 1939, as already observed, development was taking place at the centre and in Regions of machinery to administer shelter matters.[2] At the opening of February local authorities were told of the arrangements just described.[3] Distribution of 'Andersons' was to be limited, for the time being, to large towns in the most vulnerable areas. Those entitled to free issue were householders compulsorily insured under the National Health Insurance Acts[4] (i.e., the majority of manual workers) and those not in this class with, broadly speaking, an income of not over £250 a year. Others would be given the chance to buy these shelters once free distribution had been substantially completed. The delivery of 'Andersons' started at the end of February, or but two months after the Lord Privy Seal had announced their invention.

In what the Government claimed was a 'balanced programme of reasonable protection' public shelters would take the form of trenches and some existing buildings, where necessary strengthened. The decision that the trenches dug in the Munich crisis should (if suitably sited) be made permanent by lining and strengthening was the beginning of the more positive approach to the whole shelter question.[5] After much public criticism of delay, the A.R.P. Department issued local authorities with a standard design and general

---

[1] They also charged the high delivery rate of 6s. 6d. in London because shelters had to be delivered to the site of erection—normally the back-garden or yard. In at least one instance a shelter had to be taken upstairs and dropped through a first-floor window because the ground-floor tenant refused access.

[2] pp. 174, 182.

[3] A.R.P. Dept. Circular 28, 8th February 1939.

[4] 26 Geo. 5 and 1 Edw, 8, Ch. 32.

[5] H. of C. Deb., Vol. 340, Col. 425–428, 3rd November 1938; p. 162.

specifications for permanent trenches eligible for grant.[1] Authorities were asked to provide shelter for up to 10 per cent. of their populations by making permanent trenches already dug to a depth of at least four feet. These were to be lined and covered with concrete or steel; but their entrances were to be closed, and they were not at present to be fitted with duck-boards, seats or sanitary equipment. The Department subsequently received and approved a large number of designs for reconstructing trenches submitted by private firms. Towards the end of 1938 the decision was made to retain most of the trenches dug in the crisis in London's Royal Parks.

The Government resisted suggestions that they should pay the whole cost of trench-digging in the crisis. But they agreed to pay the sum of something under £1 million incurred by authorities for timber, steel and other materials not delivered by the time the crisis ended or no longer appropriate to the standards recommended.[2] During early 1939 the Department tried, without much success, to dispose of surplus material of this kind to the War Office and other departments.

Although trenches may seem to the reader a primitive method of protection, such an attitude was foreign to the prevailing views at this time. Concern was felt at the opening of 1939 both by the Government and the public over slow progress with trench reconstruction, especially in London. A decision was taken by the Government to introduce twenty-four hour working. By the end of March the information (which was far from complete) sent to the Department suggested that, while most unwanted trenches throughout the country had been filled in, many authorities had taken no more than first steps to reconstruct trenches they intended to preserve. The Department asked Metropolitan Boroughs to complete this work with all speed and explain the reasons for delay.[3] It was clear that administrative and technical difficulties bulked large; though some Boroughs were stalling while awaiting the Government's decision on certain elaborate shelter schemes. A month or so later, however, the Department viewed the situation as 'convalescent if not healthy'.

Trench-reconstruction had, for the time, diverted energy from provision of shelter in existing buildings. The Government had decided in November that local authorities might strengthen these buildings in peace or else collect suitable materials for the purpose.[4] During and for some months after Munich supplies of sandbags

---

[1] H.O. Circular of 25th November 1938. Within a fortnight the Department found that its design did not comply with its specification and a revised version of both were produced in January (A.R.P. Dept. Circular 2, 9th January 1939).

[2] H. of C. Deb., Vol. 342, Col. 2196, 15th December 1938.

[3] A.R.P. Dept. Circular 66, 30th March 1939.

[4] p. 170.

had been quite inadequate, but by the spring of 1939 this situation was improving.[1] Progress was, nevertheless, much restricted until legislation had given the authorities power to enter private buildings. At the end of April authorities in the more vulnerable areas were urged to aim at providing some form of public shelter for about 10 per cent. of their populations in mainly residential areas and about 15 per cent. of the day-populations in business areas.[2]

When launching the new programme Sir John Anderson had said the Government did not consider it practicable to provide 'bomb-proof shelters', at least as a short-term policy, though they were ready to give this question more consideration. He was meeting a challenge, growing in force before the crisis and now assuming much larger dimensions, to the whole dispersal policy, with its corollary of partial protection. Those making this challenge believed it was one of the Government's first duties to furnish protection by 'deep shelters' of some kind for the public in the principal danger zones. Experience in the Spanish war, where Barcelona and other cities had offered good protection in simple tunnels underneath streets and pavements, seemed to reinforce this argument.[3] For some time past proposals for making deep shelters with some peace-time value —e.g., underground garages, warehouses, shops and cinemas—had been presented to the Government.

In August 1938 the 'A.R.P. Co-ordinating Committee', an unofficial body of architects, surveyors and engineers, had submitted a detailed scheme for a system of tunnel shelters in St. Pancras. They claimed this would give bomb-proof protection at a smaller cost per head than any other type of shelter, and would mean that those in the densely-populated parts of this borough would have to walk at most two hundred yards to shelter. Soon afterwards a book by Professor J. B. S. Haldane called *A.R.P.* gave details of a shelter scheme on these lines, and strongly attacked the dispersal principle.[4] This publication was accompanied by meetings which began a deep-shelter campaign by Communist and other left-wing forces which was to prove a serious source of embarrassment to the Government.

As a consequence of Munich the demand for some form of deep shelters grew more general and was supported as a long-term policy

---

[1] A.R.P. Dept. Circular 55, 22nd March 1939.

[2] A.R.P. Dept· Circular 91, 25th April 1939.

[3] pp. 86, 124.

[4] In an article in *Nature* for October 1938 Professor Haldane demonstrated mathematically that there were no grounds for assuming that bombs dropped at random would cause fewer casualties if people were dispersed than if they were concentrated. This, though correct, was not relevant to the Government's policy of avoiding the expected effect on morale and strain on the A.R.P. services of mass casualties in one spot.

by both the Labour and Liberal Parties.[1] Ministers felt concern at the opening of 1939 at a growing feeling of restlessness on the part of the public over this question. Apart from questions of morale and of technique, a comprehensive deep shelter plan would make stupendous demands on money, materials and labour. After agreeing it would be necessary to devote some resources to deep shelters for certain types of work in the vulnerable areas, they set up an independent body under the chairmanship of Lord Hailey in February to survey the whole problem.

While this inquiry was in progress new substance was added to the deep shelter agitation by a much-publicised scheme for underground shelters put forward by the Finsbury Borough Council.[2] During debate on the Civil Defence Bill early in April satisfaction was expressed that nearly 300,000 'Andersons', representing protection for some 1½ million people, had already been delivered. But the Opposition's claim that the Government had still failed to announce a 'comprehensive shelter policy', and that 'very strong feeling existed throughout the country' in favour of deep shelters of some kind, was supported from various parts of the House.[3]

The Hailey Conference findings, reported to the Government soon after this debate, were to exert much influence on future developments.[4] The Conference returned to fundamental problems, examining the scale and character of attack, length of air raid warning, evacuation and the relative weights to be given to active and passive defence. They viewed the problem as one of devising the degree of protection most appropriate to the probable type and weight of attack. 'Bomb-proof shelters' they defined as those which would give much protection against a direct hit by a 500 lb. bomb. The still limited technical data at their disposal suggested that, if they were to rely on depth, these would have to be 60–80 feet underground; alternatively, they would have to be covered with a concrete canopy of at least 3 feet, with an expansion chamber below this and a concrete roof about 2½ feet thick, preferably supported by a steel lining. After exhaustive analysis of practical and technical issues the Conference recommended that no attempt should be made to provide such shelters for the general public, either in parks and open spaces or as tunnels beneath the streets. In reaching this conclusion they gave less weight to the factor of cost, which they viewed as of only relative importance, than to the vast diversion of labour and

---

[1] Labour Party Manifesto, 19th December 1938; Liberal Party request to A.R.P. Department.

[2] These were designed with a continuous spiral ramp turning about a central column to overcome the problem of access.

[3] H. of C. Deb., Vol. 345, Cols. 2633–2751, 4th April, and Cols. 2811–2958, 5th April 1939.

[4] The Conference consisted, besides the chairman, of a prominent trade unionist, two industrialists, a lady doctor, an accountant, an engineer and a scientist.

materials from other war preparations which a deep shelter programme would involve. Moreover, the time-factor now loomed large; experience, for example, in constructing London's Underground suggested it would take at least two years to build sixteen miles of tunnel to protect some 160,000 persons.

The Conference emphasised that shelter protection depended not only on strength but on accessibility. Since warning of attack would be only about seven minutes, those seeking shelter would only have time to travel some three hundred yards along congested streets by day, or half this distance by night. Even in the most thickly populated parts of London the number of people sleeping within one hundred and fifty yards of one spot would be much fewer than 6–7,000, which was the capacity of the proposed deep shelters. Such shelters would also need long ramps or stairs, thus adding a serious danger of confusion or panic. And if a deep shelter failed to resist a bomb of exceptional weight, mass casualties would occur. Most of these objections applied with equal force to such places as underground car parks, designed to combine shelter protection with a peace-time use. The London Tubes, the Conference assumed, would continue to be used in war for traffic and could in any case make only a small contribution to the problem.

Such practical considerations, and the view that a deep shelter system might create a 'shelter mentality' which would interfere with essential war-production, caused the Conference to confirm the Government's general policy. They regarded it as of much importance for morale that there should normally be an equal standard of protection in areas exposed to equal danger. Nevertheless, they recommended that more strongly protected shelters should be furnished for some vital industrial undertakings such as engineering works, port and dock installations and hospitals.

The Government accepted the Hailey report, though with some apprehension lest this last proposal should occasion widespread demands for action of this kind; and the report was published as a White Paper.[1] On 20th April the Lord Privy Seal told Parliament that the Government saw no grounds for departing from their general policy; though they would select some establishments to be given heavier than normal protection.[2]

While this deep shelter controversy was mounting, the Government introduced a Civil Defence Bill to give effect to their shelter policy, extend A.R.P. obligations to industry and deal with miscellaneous matters. It was a long and complicated measure, absorbing much time in preparation and in Parliamentary discussions during

---

[1] *Air Raid Shelters*, Cmd. 6006, 6th April 1939.
[2] H. of C. Deb., Vol. 346, Cols. 471–476.

the first half of 1939.[1] As a direct result of Hitler's seizure of Czecho-slovakia the time for consultation between publication and Second Reading was severely curtailed. It conferred large new peace-time powers both on the Government and local authorities.

It empowered local authorities to designate buildings or parts of buildings for use as public shelters or other A.R.P. needs, such as first aid posts and ambulance stations, and it enabled them to enter such buildings to do necessary preliminary work. Limited right of appeal to the Minister against a local authority's decision to designate premises was granted. Provision was made to prevent owners inter-fering with work on adapting buildings, and for compensation. Local authorities were given wide powers to construct shelters underground and on highways. If an emergency became imminent they might requisition any designated premises, as well as vehicles.

Among clauses relating to domestic shelters one new specific obligation was laid on local authorities. In addition to 'Andersons'—officially called 'standard steel shelters'—material for strutting private basements was being supplied free to the same categories of house-holders, and local authorities were given the duty of installing this. This part of the Bill also gave the Minister power to make regulations requiring inclusion of structural precautions in new buildings.

Of comparable importance to these provisions about shelters was the introduction for the first time of a legal obligation on employers to organise A.R.P. services in their firms or factories, and to provide shelters for their workpeople. These obligations had long existed in moral form, in accordance with the conception of A.R.P. as a sharing of responsibility between the Government, local authorities, industry and the ordinary citizen. But the Government was now to give financial help to employers in return for compelling them to take certain action. They proposed to pay grants equivalent to the standard rate of income tax (7s. in the £) on capital expenditure on shelter provision if this work was completed or effectively begun before the following September. This shelter obligation was placed on occupiers of factories and owners of mines and commercial buildings employing more than fifty persons and situated in 'specified areas'—which embraced nearly every industrial centre of any size over most of Britain, as well as some isolated likely targets.[2] Small establishments in these areas who chose to provide shelters would be given financial help on the same terms, but employers outside these areas would not normally be so helped. To assist employers the Government was about to issue a 'Code of Protection'

---

[1] After a good deal of discussion on the point, Ministers chose 'Civil Defence' in preference to 'A.R.P.' for the Bill's title, owing to its better psychological value.

[2] These 'specified areas' were provisionally defined at the end of April, and more finally on 14th August (Civil Defence (Specified Areas) Order, 1939, S.R. & O. No. 893). See also p. 196.

giving detailed advice on standards and types of industrial shelters. The standard contemplated for most employers was that of 'a really good type of splinter and blast-proof protection'.[1] After issue of this Code employers would be required to report what action they had taken, if they were factory or mine owners to the Factory or Mines Inspectors, and otherwise to their local authority. The feature of compulsion was introduced here by provision for Inspectors or local authorities to require employers who had taken no action to do so within a specified time.

The obligation to organise A.R.P. services and train employees was not limited to the vulnerable areas but embraced employers throughout Britain with a staff of at least thirty persons.[2] Detailed guidance was later to be given in this matter. The Government suggested that firms employing a few hundred persons should train about 10 per cent. of their staff in fire-fighting, first aid and anti-gas measures; in larger establishments a smaller proportion of trained employees would suffice. Procedure for reporting action of this kind was similar to that for shelters. It was expected that most employers would ask local authorities to help them with training. The Government, though not undertaking to find supplies of A.R.P. equipment for industry, would do their best to help over this.

The duties laid on public utilities were in general the same as those for the rest of industry, but these would be given additional help to ensure continuance of their services in war. The grant was increased to 50 per cent. for utilities in general, and to 85 per cent. for some undertakings which might be required to take A.R.P. measures which would bring them no returns in peace.

The Bill, though concerned more with shelters than any other subject, gave the Government and local authorities new powers over a large miscellaneous group of other matters. In particular, it obliged industry (other than commercial concerns) to take advance action to comply with the drastic lighting restrictions to be introduced immediately a war broke out, to deal at once with the problem of glare from blast furnaces and so on and, if requested, to make camouflage arrangements. It added to the duties of the Health Departments and local councils regarding the treatment of casualties and evacuation. It authorised grants at rates up to 90 per cent. towards the cost of providing emergency water supplies for fire-fighting in areas of special risk. It established that equipment such as gas-masks and shelter materials issued free by the Government would remain the property of the Crown. An important clause contained the scheme, already announced in general terms, for

---

[1] H. of C. Deb., Vol. 345, Col. 2641, 4th April 1939.

[2] The obligation was widened at Committee Stage of the Bill from the original limitation to employers with a staff of at least 50.

compensation for injuries incurred in peace-time A.R.P. training. Finally, the Government took powers to deal by a transfer of functions with a defaulting local authority.

The new financial burdens the Bill imposed, especially on the shoulders of the general taxpayer, were large. Grants to employers for shelters would cost the Exchequer about £8 million, which represented over one-quarter of the expenditure, based on the assumption of an average cost of £4 per employee, which industry was expected to incur in meeting this obligation. Assistance to public utilities was now to cost the Government £9 million. The new Government expenditure contemplated under the Bill was £25 million, which was additional to the £20 million to be spent on free 'Andersons' and basement fittings.

This Act, with that of 1937, gave civil defence an extensive legislative code. Its principles, in the main, had been decided on for some time past, and its primary effect was the creation of much new machinery for applying these in time of peace. It sought, the Lord Privy Seal said, 'to capitalise the great volume of good will and readiness to collaborate which exists in all sections of the community'; its penal sanctions would be held in reserve since the Government believed they were 'putting the yoke on a willing horse'. Debates on the Second Reading proved, in fact, what strong support now existed for more vigorous and all-embracing passive defence.[1] The view prevailed that in the lengthening shadow of another war, compared with which 'the last one would look like a picnic', the Government was moving neither fast nor far enough and the Bill was criticised not for its principles but for its omissions. The Labour Opposition forcibly repeated the view that civil defence, as the 'fourth arm', should be an entirely national charge and complained of the 'enormous financial liabilities' now imposed on local authorities. Its chief spokesman, Mr Morrison, called the shelter provisions 'a collection of odds and ends' falling far short of a comprehensive policy; and feeling that the Government should do more to provide deep shelters at least in the chief danger zones was widely expressed.[2]

Though the Bill was regarded by various critics as 'no more than a foundation', it imposed so complex a system of peace-time duties that its passage through Parliament consumed much time. Discussion at Committee stage continued until mid-June,[3] and the Bill did not reach the statute book until the middle of July.[4]

Attention must return to the practical progress over shelters during

---

[1] H. of C. Deb., Vol. 345, Cols. 2633–2751, 2811–2958, 4th and 5th April 1939.
[2] p. 190–191.
[3] H. of C. Deb., Vols. 347 and 348; 9th, 23rd, 24th May, 12th and 13th June 1939.
[4] 2 and 3 Geo. 6, Ch. 31, 13th July 1939. A summary of the Act's main provisions was issued by the A.R.P. Department to local authorities as A.R.P. Dept. Circular 158, 3rd August 1939.

these months. So far as the public at large was concerned this still chiefly took the form of domestic shelters. The programme for manufacture and distribution by the end of 1939–40 of 2½ million 'Andersons' to protect about 10 million citizens was being steadily carried through.[1] The specified areas to which this supply was for the time being restricted had been provisionally defined at the end of April, and comprised industrial centres of some size and other probable targets containing a population of about 27 million.[2] A good many protests by local authorities at their exclusion caused additions to a revised list of these areas issued in August.[3] House-holders could either store the parts of 'Andersons' or erect them with the advice of local authorities, who, however, were not obliged to help in the work of erection.

The difficulty still experienced in establishing data about high explosive attack was illustrated by the fact that distribution of 'Andersons' had begun before their testing had been completed. At the opening of 1939 'load tests' had shown that 'Andersons' were strong enough to bear the weight of any debris falling on them from the type of house for which they were intended. But it was not until some months later that a series of 'explosion tests' proved conclusively that their fabric could withstand without damage a 500 lb. high explosive bomb falling at least fifty feet away; and it seemed probable that this represented the minimum degree of protection they would afford.[4] It was established at the same time that they would protect their occupants against blast from a bomb of this size bursting in the open at a distance of thirty feet or more. But this soundness of the 'Andersons' from a structural standpoint, it soon became clear, was counterbalanced by an important practical defect, namely liability to flooding. Soon after delivery began, local authorities in some areas were being asked by householders to remove shelters which had become waterlogged, and in mid-summer the A.R.P. Department issued the first of many circulars suggesting remedies for this problem.[5]

It was obvious, in addition, that 'Andersons' and steel basement fittings would not be suitable for every type of dwelling. During May the Department gave local authorities information about a third form of domestic shelter, a surface shelter of brick and concrete.[6] This, in its standard design, had the same floor space as the 'Anderson' and could also provide shelter for up to six people. It

---

[1] p. 193.

[2] A.R.P. Dept. Circular 91, 25th April 1939; p. 192.

[3] Civil Defence (Specified Areas) Order, 1939, S.R. & O. No. 893, 14th August. This twofold division of the country for domestic and industrial shelter purposes was distinct from the more elaborate grading of (mainly eastern) areas for the A.R.P. Services.

[4] *Sectional Steel Shelters*, Cmd. 6055, July 1939.

[5] A.R.P. Dept. Circular 136, 11th July 1939.

[6] A.R.P. Dept. Circulars 91 and 102, 25th April and 5th May 1939.

could be built as a separate unit or grouped with several others to give some mutual protection. It was, however, only to be supplied free, and with the sanction of the Regional Technical Adviser, to houses for which 'Andersons' and basement fittings were unsuitable. The material for shelters of this type would be a charge on the Exchequer: but erection, like the installation of free basement fittings, was a new obligation on local authorities.[1]

The emphasis the Government had placed on domestic shelters led to various difficulties when tenements and blocks of flats were considered. Buildings of this kind in the occupation of working-class families could often only be furnished with basement shelters by the eviction of tenants; and if there was ground available outside, this, especially in Scotland, was in the joint use of all the occupiers. The Government decided that when a majority of householders living in a building of this type were entitled to free shelters, the full cost of materials for some form of communal shelter should be borne by the Exchequer.[2] The Act provided that neighbouring ground might be used for this purpose if more than half the occupiers agreed; and it compelled owners of blocks of flats the majority of whose occupants were not entitled to free shelters to provide shelter at the request of more than half the residents, recovering the cost by making an all-round addition to rents.

When war broke out provision of domestic shelter, the core of the Government's programme, was only beginning to assume large proportions. Delivery had been made of nearly 1,500,000 free 'Andersons' which were estimated (optimistically) to offer shelter to 6,000,000 persons, and rate of production of these had reached 50,000 a week. But this, representing under two-thirds of the programme, had not fully met the needs of even the main danger zones. Many 'Andersons' had not yet been installed, or installed so badly as to be almost worthless. Only a small number of basement fittings had been distributed, and the contribution this method could make was limited.[3] Not much headway had been made with construction of domestic surface shelters of brick and concrete. No 'Andersons' were yet on sale to the general public; and though the Act empowered local authorities to help the public by loans to provide their own shelters, the official programme had absorbed most of the available materials and labour.

Public shelters were meant only for those whose homes could not be protected by one of these methods and those caught in the streets during raids; and provision of these was to be undertaken by

---

[1] The Civil Defence Act placed responsibility for domestic shelters on the county boroughs and county districts.

[2] A.R.P. Dept. Circular 158, 3rd August 1939.

[3] At the end of July 500 units had been distributed, although 10,000 had been manufactured.

counties and county boroughs over the whole country.[1] Good
progress had been made since early in 1939 with trench reconstruction; as war approached, about three quarters of London's Munich
trenches and a fair proportion of these elsewhere had been made
'permanent' by lining. Choice of buildings for public shelters was
also well advanced. The City of London and a number of London
Boroughs had completed this task by early June, and two months
later most authorities were using their powers of designation.
Progress with strengthening buildings, however, was in many places
still negligible.

Towards the end of August the Government and local authorities
made strenuous efforts to complete and extend public shelters. The
Home Office asked the authorities to provide simple forms of lighting, seating and sanitation for trenches and also to dig more
trenches where these could be revetted either by timber locally
procured or (since steel would not be available) by pre-cast concrete
linings which the Government would attempt to supply.[2] It urged
authorities to press on with designation of buildings, and gave
permission for materials intended for strengthening private basements to be used for public shelters. The Defence Regulations empowered authorities to requisition buildings for A.R.P. purposes,
including use as public shelters.[3] In the few days before war, authorities in London and most other cities took over and labelled as
'Public Shelters' a large number of extra buildings, as well as such
places as vaults and cellars under pavements.

The effectiveness of such action depended, in general, on the
existence of modern steel-framed buildings, and the Government
was now forced to recognise that in many areas trenches and
existing buildings would not give sufficient public shelter. They
therefore asked authorities, for the first time, to build structures
specially designed as public shelters.[4] These were to be 'brick and
concrete surface shelters', similar to the domestic surface shelters
already authorised but large enough to hold up to fifty persons.
These could, the Home Office considered, be built 'at considerable
speed' with local supplies of labour, bricks and reinforced concrete.

Progress with shelters of these types had failed appreciably to
reduce the demand from various quarters for 'deep shelters'.[5] The
Government, however, stood firm on their plan only to provide
what they preferred to call 'strong' or 'heavily protected' shelters

---

[1] H. of C. Deb., Vol. 348, Cols. 620–621, 8th June 1939.

[2] A.R.P. Dept. Circular 204, 28th August 1939.

[3] Defence Regulations 23, 38 and 51. These powers were now extended to boroughs
and urban districts.

[4] A.R.P. Dept. Circular 204, 28th August 1939.

[5] e.g., H. of C. Deb., Vol. 348, Cols. 941–1070, 12th June 1939.

in exceptional cases.[1] They had allowed a few local authorities to convert natural features into shelters where this could be done easily and fairly cheaply. Ramsgate, for example, had been authorised to improve access to a disused railway tunnel and to the caves in its chalk cliffs (used as shelters in the First World War) and to bore new tunnels. The history of various similar schemes was foreshadowed in the fact that by late in June the estimated cost of these tunnels had risen from £17,000 to £30,000 per mile. Dover was authorised to protect the entrances to its caves which the council had begun two years earlier to rent and adapt as shelters, and to bore special tunnels. Other exceptional arrangements included tunnels beneath the streets in the built-up area of Luton, adaptation of the Ouseburn Culvert and the Victoria Tunnel at Newcastle, and a tunnelling scheme at Runcorn where storage of chlorine gas presented a special danger.

In the spring the Government had reaffirmed their long-held conclusions that London's Tubes would be needed in war to handle evacuation of casualties and other abnormal traffic and that the stations should not be available as public shelters, and they proposed to include a statement to this effect among the broadcast announcements to be made on the outbreak of a war. They recognised, however, that it would be impossible in practice for railway officials to distinguish between *bona fide* travellers and members of the public who might disregard these instructions. They therefore agreed to the London Passenger Transport Board's plan that all but twenty of the most vulnerable stations should stay open for traffic in raids until they became reasonably full. Makeshift measures taken by the Board during Munich to prevent flooding of the Tubes by the Thames were being followed by installation of floodgates to shut off sections under the river during raids, and protection of some stations against flooding from water-mains and sewers. The Board was continuing to adapt ventilation arrangements in defence against gas.

The Government had announced their intention to confine 'strong' protection for the time being to Government and Regional 'command headquarters', Control Centres, and some industrial concerns; but their selection of individual cases proceeded slowly. By early August advance had been made in giving such protection to certain generating stations, docks, and railway establishments in the most threatened towns. Various important firms, including aircraft and munitions factories, were by this date making progress with shelters of the standards recommended in the official Code, and conversion of these into shelters of a stronger type was found to offer difficulties. The Government therefore decided that existing factories should continue the arrangements they were making, and that extra protection should in general be confined to important new ones.

---

[1] p. 192.

Stronger protection for local Control Centres was, in the meanwhile, being sanctioned piecemeal, and the authorities had as yet no intention to make such action compulsory. By the outbreak of war schemes had been approved for some fifteen specially protected control rooms in London, but no control room of this type in London or elsewhere had, so far as the A.R.P. Department was aware, been completed. Nor had any general decision yet been taken about special protection for first aid posts and other A.R.P. buildings.

Though it had long been assumed that the most vital parts of the Government machine would need special protection, practical steps in this matter had awaited maturing of plans for the location of the Government in war.[1] In the months after Munich these plans, in the shape of elaborate alternative arrangements for moves of both 'essential' and 'non-essential' official staffs, had been given much fresh consideration; and emphasis had been laid both on the removal of 'non-essential' staffs from London in peace-time, and on relaxation of secrecy over the whole question.[2] In January 1939 the Committee of Imperial Defence reaffirmed the assumptions that the seat of Government would be in Whitehall at the outbreak of a war, and would remain there as long as physically possible. And recommended that, if evacuation became essential, this should be carried out not (as hitherto proposed) first to the London suburbs and then (if necessary) to the Western counties, but in one move direct to the Western counties.

The Cabinet gave authority soon afterwards for special protection to be furnished in Whitehall for the Central War Room and the War Rooms of the Service Departments and Ministry of Home Security. By the outbreak of war strong, though not 'bomb-proof', accommodation had been provided for the Central and AirMinistry War Rooms in the block of Whitehall buildings known as the New Public Offices and for Home Security headquarters in the Home Office basement; and some strongly protected alternative War Rooms were being built in London's suburbs.

The Office of Works, in the meantime, had adopted the standards of the 'Code' issued for industry's guidance in arranging shelter for Government staffs in general in London and the other main danger zones. Strengthened basements, and occasionally trenches, were the usual forms of this protection. By September 1939, though much remained to be done, this work was making fair progress.[3]

. It was clear from the record of the first eight months of 1939 that

---

[1] p. 151.

[2] The Rae Committee was reconstituted and reported in January 1939; pp. 151, 160.

[3] pp. 151, 159.

much time and effort were needed before the complex machinery
required to carry out the shelter programme could produce more
substantial results. It was not until early in this year that creation
of an independent Home Office Research and Experiments Branch
offered means to overcome the long-standing scarcity of data about
the effects of high explosive attack.[1] In May the Lord Privy Seal
asked some prominent scientists to form a Civil Defence Research
Committee to advise this branch; and the Bombing Tests Committee,
which was continuing to supervise trials at Shoeburyness, and the
Incendiary Bombs and Oil Depots Committees became parts of this
organisation.[2] Elaborate machinery was formed for liaison between
the 'R. and E. Branch' and building, electrical and other professional bodies, and the British Standards Institution undertook to
prepare specifications for A.R.P. needs.[3]

The new committee approved a programme of research covering
a wide range of problems—e.g., structural, anti-gas, lighting, camouflage, warning, steel helmets and the stirrup pump; and they were
told this work would no longer be hampered by lack of funds. For
most subjects two kinds of inquiries were needed—general research,
and *ad hoc* experiments to find quick solutions to urgent practical
problems. Most of the committee's attention at this stage had to be
given to what a member called 'brainwaves to get over immediate
difficulties which will not wait'. By the outbreak of war three full-
scale bombing trials had been made, on a brick basement, an
underground reinforced concrete structure, and a brick surface
building, as well as a blast and splinter trial. The 'Anderson' shelter
had also been fully tested. Full-scale trials were, however, still
delayed by difficulty in obtaining use of suitable sites. When the
new branch was formed the Home Office decided to try to find a
testing ground of its own. Though a site for this purpose was
eventually chosen in Cumberland and work was begun on roads and
buildings, this project was abandoned after the outbreak of war.

In June 1939 the long-awaited handbook of technical information
about shelters and structural precautions for local authorities and the
public was published under the title *Structural Defence*.[4]

The A.R.P. Services: (i) Recruitment

Though civil defence was described as a 'fourth arm' it was, as the
Government took pains to emphasise, essentially different from the

---

[1] pp. 149, 174.

[2] See pp. 146, 149.

[3] The Structural Precautions Committee was dissolved in April 1939.

[4] A.R.P. Handbook No. 5, which was supplemented by No. 5A, *Bomb Resisting Shelters*,
issued in August.

Fighting Services. The Lord Privy Seal reminded Parliament that it was not really service to the Government, but service to the community in which there was a part for all to play.[1] It was a local authority service to be formed by moulding normal functions to the needs of war. Procedure by this method necessarily produced much variation in the pace and quality of civil defence performance.

In the phase of fresh appeal which began early in 1939 the Government urged local authorities to abandon the view that A.R.P. was 'a matter extraneous to the ordinary functions of local government'.[2] They asked that responsibility should be spread more actively among local officials and that some chief officer should be appointed 'general co-ordinating officer' for local schemes. Though A.R.P. Officers had done much useful work, a tendency to leave too much responsibility to them was not uncommon. The Government stood firm on the principle that counties should normally be responsible for scheme making, and that districts would only be granted leave to make schemes in exceptional cases.[3] In spite of the impetus of Munich 'much remained to be done' before local A.R.P. could be regarded as satisfactory.

Though the gearing of local machinery to A.R.P. needs now proceeded more rapidly than heretofore the large adjustments this represented were still often dominated, in the last resort, by financial issues. The Government's attitude that effective partnership could only be attained by a sharing of the financial burden continued to be opposed or accepted with reluctance by many authorities. The large new obligations the Exchequer had undertaken, notably over shelters, offered from their point of view little compensation for the fact that the burden A.R.P. imposed on their resources was being 'constantly added to little by little' until it had become 'a very grievous one'.[4] The claim that this burden was the major factor in delaying local preparations was consistently maintained.

Considerations of finance still dominated the procedure, resumed after Munich, of approving instalments of some 250 local schemes. Most councils remained unwilling to act on any instalment which involved large expenditure before securing 'chapter and verse', or specific central approval. The A.R.P. Department was still severely taxed by the task of examining a rising flood of instalments. Attempts to relieve this pressure and hasten preparations by establishing universal standards—e.g., for wardens' posts or protected control centres—were usually frustrated by the formidable cost to the

---

[1] H. of C. Deb., Vol. 344, Col. 1314, 1st March 1939.

[2] pp. 171, 181; A.R.P. Dept. Circular 9, 26th January 1939.

[3] At the end of 1938 only fourteen such applications from county districts had been granted.

[4] Annual Meeting of Municipal Corporations Association, May 1939.

Exchequer this would involve. Although as 1939 advanced the Department established more such standards, its normal procedure continued to be piecemeal decision on particular proposals.

After Hitler's seizure of Czechoslovakia the Government addressed a further appeal to the authorities to hasten preparations, asking them to arrange during the next three months to give priority to civil defence over all other business, to appoint adequate staff for A.R.P. and not to await the Civil Defence Bill's passage into law before taking the action this contemplated.[1]

Differences between the 'fourth arm' and the older Services were nowhere more pronounced than in the character of the A.R.P. 'army'. Munich had produced the second half-million A.R.P. volunteers; and by the end of 1938 total strength was estimated at some 1,140,000, which was only about 300,000 short of the proposed establishment.[2] This large force, more than twice the combined strength at this time of the three Fighting Services, consisted of men and women prepared to give some part of their leisure to defence of their homes. But they were under no obligation to serve for longer than they found convenient, organisation and equipment were still rudimentary, training (where they had had this) had been mainly confined to anti-gas measures, no system of local command had been invented (except partially for the wardens' service) and no traditions and little discipline as yet existed. Moreover, enthusiasm in the individual was not always matched by adequate ability or physical fitness; and enthusiasm among volunteers in general had been proved a fluctuating factor.

Attainment of the total strength required no longer appeared to the Government to be a serious problem. What had now to be done was, first, to make good the deficiencies local returns might later reveal both in particular A.R.P. services and in particular areas; secondly, to provide more thorough organisation, training and equipment without which, experience had shown, volunteers were apt to lose heart and melt away. The Government had also been convinced by the Munich experience of the need to stiffen this 'army' by enlisting in the main danger areas a substantial nucleus of volunteers prepared to serve in war on a whole-time paid basis.

The Lord Privy Seal's responsibility for inaugurating national voluntary service was somewhat anomalous in that, in his capacity as 'Minister for Civilian Defence', he was himself in competition with other Departments for manpower.[3] He had decided to deal with the problem through an existing agency in a neutral position,

---

[1] A.R.P. Dept. Circular 88, 18th April 1939.

[2] In addition about 100,000 men and women had enrolled in the Auxiliary Fire Service.

[3] pp. 166–167.

the Ministry of Labour. Arrangements for recruitment already set up by local authorities and many other agencies were to continue, but to be co-ordinated by National Service Committees in towns and counties throughout Britain. Decisions in the Manpower Committee, in spite of War Office concern over competition with the Territorial Army and Ministry of Labour concern over needs of war-time industry, had favoured a lowering of age groups for A.R.P. volunteers. On 1st December 1938 the Lord Privy Seal announced the intention to start a National Voluntary Register.[1] The new recruiting campaign was launched on 23rd January with a broadcast by the Prime Minister.

The *National Service Guide*, distributed at the same time to every household in the country, lent support to Mr Herbert Morrison's contention that the new term 'national service' was 'really A.R.P. writ large on a co-ordinated basis'.[2] The A.R.P. Services headed the list in this handbook, followed by the Police, the Fire Services, the Nursing Services, the Women's Land Army, the Mercantile Marine and the Fighting Services. The minimum age for men had been fixed at 25 years for Rescue and Demolition Squads, First Aid Parties and Decontamination Squads and at 30 years for Wardens, the Ambulance Service and the First Aid Post Service. Men between 25 and 30 might join as Wardens if not required for military service. Those volunteering for Report Centres and miscellaneous duties had to be over 45, and the Communications Service was only open to men over 40 and boys under 18.

A striking feature was that one-third of the whole A.R.P. force was to consist of women. Women were not to serve in Rescue, First Aid Party or Decontamination Services; but it was hoped they would provide one-fifth of the Wardens, two-thirds of Report Centre staffs, the great proportion of the First Aid Post service and all the Ambulance drivers and attendants. The W.V.S., re-named in February the 'Women's Voluntary Services for Civil Defence', had by now much outgrown its original function as an A.R.P. recruiting agency.[3] Though continuing to enrol volunteers for the Casualty and Nursing services,[4] it was now, as its new title implied, occupied with many matters beyond the sphere of A.R.P., notably organisation of hospital supply depots and help to local authorites in planning evacuation.[5]

Shortly before the recruiting campaign opened the A.R.P.

---

[1] H. of C. Deb., Vol. 342, Cols. 597–604, 1st December 1938.

[2] H. of C. Deb., Vol. 344, Col. 1324, 1st March 1939.

[3] pp. 128–129

[4] At the end of 1938 the Health Departments had created a Civilian Nursing Reserve to provide 100,000 nursing auxiliaries.

[5] A.R.P. Dept. Circular 13a, 3rd February 1939.

Department had told every scheme-making authority its maximum war establishment for each A.R.P. service.[1] Some time before, the reader will recall, the Department, using an Air Staff grading of Britain into four or five areas of differing vulnerability, had compiled 'scales of local preparation' or figures for personnel and equipment of each authority weighted according to a local 'scale of risk'.[2] These scales had not, for obvious reasons, been published and authorities were now merely told their individual ceilings. For example, the least vulnerable ('D') areas were to provide 20 First Aid Parties for each 100,000 inhabitants, 'C' areas 26 parties, 'B' areas 33 parties; while the most vulnerable ('A') areas—which contained over 27 million of the population—were to double bank these parties with two reliefs of thirty-three. They were asked to enrol reserves in each service, for example a reserve of at least 50 per cent. for First Aid Parties, and to make fortnightly recruitment returns to Regional Officers and National Service offices.

Though whole-timers would not be employed before a war mobilisation, the authorities were asked to make returns of volunteers ready to give whole-time paid service. Rates of pay, announced in Parliament in February, would be £3 per week for men and £2 per week for women.[3] These would be universal, taking no account of different duties to be performed, with the one exception of foremen and skilled men in Rescue Parties. This standard pay was intended to be broadly equivalent to the pay, allowances and estimated cost of maintenance of a married infantry soldier with one child.

The immediate public response to the campaign was good; and Hitler's new aggression in March caused 'a steady, and last week almost spectacular, increase in the numbers volunteering for A.R.P. services'.[4] Agencies of Government publicity, including the Public Relations Branch of the Lord Privy Seal's Office, increased their efforts to spread information about all forms of national service. More reliable local returns, however, had now revealed that there was still a considerable A.R.P. recruiting problem. Total strength of the services at the end of March was calculated as still under 1,200,000, or about 400,000 short of the proposed establishment.[5]

Surpluses in some areas and services had, in the past, masked serious deficiencies in others. Figures for counties had often failed to show deficiencies in districts, local returns had included Munich volunteers who had drifted away, and even persons who had undertaken no more than assembling gas-masks. Many authorities had

---

[1] A.R.P. Dept. Circular 1, 4th January 1939.

[2] pp. 143–144.

[3] H. of C. Deb., Vol. 343, Col. 1923, 16th February 1939.

[4] *The Times*, 31st March 1939.

[5] p. 203.

no one available to compile accurate statistics, a task of special difficulty in areas such as some London boroughs with large floating populations.[1]

The picture, now more clearly defined, revealed shortages of some size in all the A.R.P. services in some important areas, and in the Casualty services throughout much of Britain. Rural areas, with retired or otherwise leisured persons, traditions of local leadership and absence of rival spare-time attractions had, as a rule, produced volunteers in plenty.[2] The problem was predominantly one of the towns and industrial centres—i.e., the most vulnerable areas. London had failed to reach its war establishment, and London Region was brought to address an urgent appeal to the Boroughs in May to complete their establishments in two months. Deficiencies of some size existed in Bristol, Manchester, Glasgow, Leeds, Sheffield, Liverpool, Newcastle, Dundee and several other centres. In a few places, notably Glasgow and parts of London, repercussions of the controversy over national service were seriously impeding A.R.P. recruitment.[3] But, in the main, poor public response reflected local backwardness in organisation and training, or unfavourable local publicity arising from such matters as shortage of equipment. By mid-May the figure of national enrolment was approaching 1,400,000 (some 900,000 men and 500,000 women), and a further 160,000 men and women had joined the Auxiliary Fire Service. But though this position was considered generally satisfactory by the Home Office, there were still large shortages in many urban areas.

The Government was not prepared to accede to demands, growing in some quarters since Munich, for introduction of a formal contract of service for A.R.P. volunteers or for the professionalising of the Service by adoption of a hierarchy of ranks (except to a limited degree for wardens) and some stricter form of discipline. They wished to maintain strong emphasis on A.R.P. as a local voluntary service, rooted in local leadership and enthusiasm and adapting plans evolved at the centre to local differences. Experience was proving, for example in Birmingham, that when general organisation and training improved arrears of enrolment were soon made up. The number of local instructors was increasing, and exercises were making the public more aware of A.R.P. The Lord Privy Seal's announcement on 10th July that all volunteers would be supplied with a uniform of an overall suit of dark blue cotton cloth with chrome buttons

---

[1] e.g., Islington recorded 40 per cent. removals annually.

[2] e.g., in East Anglia, the West Country and the West Riding enrolment was particularly high.

[3] The Prime Minister's announcement on 26th April of the decision to introduce compulsory military training had aroused strong protest from both sections of the Opposition.

and a scarlet badge would, it was hoped, stimulate enlistment.[1]

What now gave the Government most concern, apart from the shortage of volunteers in certain areas and the state of the Casualty services, was the position about whole-time volunteers. When the campaign was launched they had contemplated a stiffening of such volunteers which might grow to some 250,000 men and 100,000 women, or about one-quarter the whole A.R.P. force. In January they had told authorities in all but the least vulnerable areas the proportion of whole-timers they should try to recruit.[2] They had urged those in the main target areas to aim at enrolling one-fifth of their wardens on a whole-time basis. Report Centres in these areas would be manned by day, so far as possible, by the authorities' staffs; but that these might be manned day and night in war, 50 per cent. of the extra men required and 75 per cent. of the women should be whole-timers. In 'A' areas all the men in First Aid Parties and three-quarters of those in Rescue Parties, and in 'B' areas one-half and one-third of these Parties, should serve on the same basis.

The Government, though aware that readiness to offer whole-time service was falling far short of their hopes, lacked, as late as the middle of 1939, comprehensive data on this matter. Local authorities, subjected (as the Minister of Health acknowledged) to 'enormous floods of paper' from above, were finding much difficulty in furnishing Whitehall with up-to-date information on recruitment or any other aspect of A.R.P. The A.R.P. Department therefore decided in June to ask its Regional Officers to attempt, for the first time, systematic surveys of local preparations.

The result, presenting a broad picture of local preparedness late in July, was regarded by the Department as in general distinctly encouraging. Though only a handful of authorities had completed A.R.P. schemes, a large proportion had made good progress by the piecemeal method. Local authority machinery, though slow, had been proving thorough, and response to the request that civil defence should be given three months' priority had been good.[3] Progress on the physical foundations—buildings, communications and warning arrangements—was satisfactory; in a few more months most authorities would have finished their building programmes (excluding measures of heavy protection). Almost all Regional Officers reported that 'a reasonably effective organisation could be brought into being if a sudden emergency arose'.

Anxiety was not, however, removed about human resources.

---

[1] H. of C. Deb., Vol. 349, Col. 1827; A.R.P. Dept. Circular 149, 18th July 1939.

[2] A.R.P. Dept. Circular 14, 27th January 1939; p. 205.

[3] p. 203.

P

National strength had reached a total not far short of the establishment of some 1,600,000; but maldistribution between areas and services still meant the need for about 250,000 more men and 160,000 more women.[1] Casualty services in London and other chief danger zones were still far below war establishment. The state of affairs regarding whole-timers was serious. Local authorities had still made little progress with recruiting such volunteers, and the reasons were now more apparent. In many industrial areas the £3 basic pay was considered too low, especially in comparison with anticipated war-time wage rates. Failure of the Government to announce precise terms of compensation for injury or death in war was a deterrent. Prospective volunteers wanted more information about whether whole-time duty would protect them from military conscription, how long it would last and whether it would mean service away from their homes, whether different rates of pay and ranks would be introduced and what type of discipline they would encounter.

As the holiday season began the Government decided it had become essential to define conditions of whole-time service more fully, and take steps to pull the separate services together and give the large A.R.P. army more definite form. The beginnings of a corporate existence had been made a fortnight earlier when for the first time representatives of the A.R.P. and Auxiliary Fire Services from all over Britain paraded in Hyde Park before the King and Queen. Few of these 20,000 men and women were used to marching, and except for the Auxiliary Fire Service and some members of the Casualty Services they wore civilian clothes, with mackintoshes (since the weather was uncertain) carried over their arms. All except the nurses had steel helmets, and the painting of these in bright colours to indicate the various services produced a motley effect. If this force had obvious weaknesses judged by military standards, it also expressed a certain strength. A large crowd of spectators sensed the determination it represented to resist aggression in new forms.

The A.R.P. Services:
(ii) Organisation, Training, Equipment

The A.R.P. Department had throughout been attempting the double task of establishing a new 'A.R.P. Service' and creating within this five main branches or specialised services. By Munich it had made genuine progress in planning and publicising the organisation and functions both of the 'Service' and the separate

---

[1] The actual figures were: establishment, 1,022,000 men and 549,000 women; strength, 915,000 men and 569,000 women. By this date about 240,000 men had been recruited for the auxiliary police forces, and 190,000 for the A.F.S.

services, as well as in building a national training system.[1] It was a striking fact that in the crisis several hundred thousand men and women up and down Britain were enrolled as air raid wardens with fairly clear ideas what to do if air bombardment suddenly began.

But the crisis had also revealed how much remained to be done before central designs were translated into effective nation-wide organisations. Training had been largely confined to anti-gas measures. Over 2,000 instructors trained in the Home Office Schools and several times this number of locally-trained instructors fell far short of the numbers required if local training was to be universal. Barely one-third of those in the Wardens' Service were trained. The Department had overestimated the possibilities of training and organising the Casualty and Rescue Services from existing resources.

It now set out to broaden general training,[2] arrange more specialist training for particular services and ensure that better use was made of local instructors. Heavy investment in defence against gas had provided, and was to continue to provide, both the stimulus to volunteers of various concrete tasks and general confidence in the Service's ability to meet this particular threat effectively. The level of protection against gas achieved by early in 1939 had already, the Government considered, 'rendered the risk of gas attack less likely'.[3] But little had been done to provide training in incendiary bomb control or in simple protection against high explosive attack. At the end of 1938 the courses at the Home Office Schools had been enlarged to include these subjects, and the schools re-named 'Air Raid Precautions Schools'. The school in London concerned mainly with administration was re-named the 'A.R.P. Staff School'.[4]

One of the chief difficulties of A.R.P. in the view of the Inspector General was still 'the feeling amongst the volunteers that the blind are leading the blind. The moment we can get our technique home to them, not only will it enhance the prestige of the leaders of the various services, but it will give them much greater confidence in tackling any problems with which they are confronted'. The Falfield and Easingwold schools had proved successful over several years in rousing enthusiasm and winning the loyalty of those who went to them. They acted as clearing houses of ideas and kept in touch with former students, helping them to keep up-to-date. By early 1939 they had trained nearly 4,000 'Instructors, C.A.G.S.', who formed the backbone of the national training system. The best qualified of these had, under the 'second-hand training system',

---

[1] See pp. 119–131 ('Building the National Structure').

[2] pp. 126-127.

[3] H. of C. Deb., Vol. 346, Col. 931, 24th April 1939.

[4] p. 123.

now passed on their knowledge of anti-gas measures to about 11,000 'Instructors, L.A.G.C.'.[1] But though these figures were impressive, wastage of local instructors owing to other calls on their services or failure by authorities to employ them was still considerable. Of the 1 million or more volunteers at the end of March 1939 only about one-half had been fully trained in anti-gas, about 190,000 in first aid and some 91,000 in other subjects. Though many more were then under training, reports were still common of discouragement caused by lack of training opportunities.

It was not until mid-1939 that facilities for training instructors in incendiary bomb control and in dealing with high explosive bombs were introduced. In April the first manual for the Services on *Incendiary Bombs and Fire Precautions* was issued.[2] During the next two months ten temporary schools were set up in various parts of the country to train 'graduates' from Falfield and Easingwold in the two extra subjects. Once qualified, these changed their title from 'Instructors, C.A.G.S.', to 'Instructors, A.R.P.S.' and then began to train the 12,000 or so local instructors to teach these subjects.[3] The Department reconsidered in May the question of giving training in incendiary bomb control to the public; but decided, owing mainly to the scarcity and high cost of practice incendiary bombs and stirrup pumps, to restrict this for the time being to a short lecture and demonstration by local instructors.[4]

The Home Office Schools considered that 'training can never be finished and should not, as far as possible, be allowed to become stereotyped'. At the opening of 1939 the Department had urged authorities to plan training in three definite stages—'individual training', in which each volunteer would learn the work of his particular service; 'collective training', to practice trained persons of one service to act as a team, and 'combined training' in which all local services, and perhaps Army and Air Force units, would take part.[5] It proposed that authorities with war establishments of over 1,000 should form 'Training Centres' with lecture rooms, a gas chamber, office and storage accommodation and facilities for re-creation.[6] Few authorities, in fact, had been able to establish centres of this ambitious kind by the time war broke out.

The number and scale of exercises, however, grew steadily as 1939 advanced. Many authorities were now staging tests of their black-out

---

[1] Local Anti-Gas Course; p. 123.

[2] A.R.P. Handbook No. 9.

[3] A.R.P. Dept. Circular 99, 3rd May 1939.

[4] The cost of incendiary bombs needed to give widespread practice to the public was estimated at £86,000. Stirrup pumps on sale to the public cost at this time 24s. 6d.

[5] Memorandum No. 9, *Notes on Training and Exercises*, February 1939.

[6] A.R.P. Dept. Circular 9, 26th January 1939.

and communications arrangements, and some of the more enterprising held surprise mobilisation exercises for all their A.R.P.
services. During April and May, 34 combined training exercises
were held in different parts of Britain. A full-scale daylight exercise
in Chelsea in June, at which wardens appeared for the first time in
uniforms (of local design), was the first test in London of the effects
of the warning sirens on the public and traffic. Three R.A.F. Home
Defence exercises in July and August gave an opportunity for tests
of A.R.P. arrangements to be made in many places. These ranged
from simple exercises in which only wardens and report centres took
part, to a large exercise in Tunbridge Wells Region which embraced
all authorities and services in Kent and East and West Sussex. They
included the first experiment, as the result of much previous planning,
in blacking-out London and large areas in the eastern half of Britain
on the night of 9th-10th August. The Department's survey of local
preparedness in July stated, 'the last three months have witnessed
very real activity in training. Individual training has made great
progress and many authorities have begun collective training
. . . in many areas a real corporate spirit is beginning to be
evident'.

Training efficiency and the maintenance of enthusiasm depended
in no small degree on equipment, and by early in 1939 the increase
of volunteers had overtaken supplies of most items of personal
equipment.[1] While some 50 million civilian masks with containers
had been issued by this date, supplies of steel helmets and Service
and Civilian Duty masks were still far short of requirements. By the
middle of June, though the situation had improved, more than half
the number of these items needed, amounting in each case to some
two million, had still to be distributed. Supplies of 'tin hats' were
improving fast, but all the Service masks would not be delivered
before September and the Civilian Duty masks until even later.
Enough light anti-gas clothing would not be available until the end of
1939. Badges and brooches had been distributed in large numbers
to trained volunteers, but the first deliveries of A.R.P. uniforms
would not be made until September. A proposal that wardens
might, in the meantime, be supplied with webbing belts from which
to hang torches and other equipment was found to be too expensive.

The Wardens' Service, embracing some 500,000 men and women
or about one-third of the whole A.R.P. force, had continued to prove
the most attractive to volunteers.[2] The promised syllabus to enlarge
wardens' training was issued early in 1939, and included a large
variety of matters (for example 'relations with the police and the

---

[1] H. of C. Deb., Vol. 344, Cols. 1287-1408, 1st March 1939.
[2] See pp. 125–126, 162, 209.

public') besides anti-gas measures.[1] The organisation was now being given its final, and more elaborate, form.[2] The plan for a post for each 'sector' of 500 inhabitants had been dropped, as liable to cause undue strain on the telephone service in urban areas. Sectors were still to be the basic A.R.P. areas, manned by 3–6 wardens according to the density of population, but a number of these were now to be worked from one post and posts were nowhere to exceed ten to the square mile. Sectors were to be in charge of 'Senior Wardens', any one of whom might, according to local arrangements, be put in charge of the post; though in London, 'Post Wardens' were appointed at an early stage. Posts were to be formed into 'Groups' (called 'Districts' in London), each serving a population of 6–10,000 and in charge of a 'Head' (or 'District') Warden. In cities of over 400,000 inhabitants Groups were to be formed into 'Divisions' in charge of 'Divisional Wardens' directly responsible to the Chief Warden.

The Home Office now proposed that authorities with more than four Wardens' Groups should appoint a paid officer to supervise peace-time organisation and training. Chief, Divisional and Head Wardens would, like most other members of the service, continue to be unpaid. It was now finally determined that (outside the Metropolitan Police District) Chief Constables would normally be responsible for peace-time organisation as well as for control over the service in war; though this arrangement might be deferred in places where the service had been successfully organised hitherto independently of the police.[3] In March 1939 the expedient was adopted of placing the Commissioner, Metropolitan Police, in his personal and not his official capacity, in charge of the 'practical' (as distinct from the 'preliminary') training of London's wardens in peace as well as of their operations in war; and the Commissioner appointed the Chief Warden of Westminster to act under him as Principal Warden for London Region.[4]

The wardens' chain of control just described was for administrative purposes only, and was not to be a chain of command and reporting in operations. During raids each wardens' post would be a separate unit under the A.R.P. Controller, reporting 'incidents' direct to him and obtaining from him instructions and the help of the other services.

Posts, with a telephone and protected against blast and splinters, were to be large enough to store wardens' protective clothing and other gear and in a position easily found by the public. Post equip-

---

[1] Memorandum No. 4 (2nd ed.) _Organisation of the A.R. Wardens' Service_, February 1939.
[2] A.R.P. Dept. Circular 25, 9th February 1939.
[3] Memorandum No. 4, February 1939; pp. 72-73.
[4] Hon. Arthur Howard, M.P.; H. of C. Deb., Vol. 345, Col. 2040, 29th March 1939.

ment was to consist of torches, whistles, hand rattles and bells, a first-aid box and a log, most of which items were now being supplied in adequate quantities from the centre.[1] Though as early as March 1938 the Treasury had approved free issue of 50,000 stirrup pumps to wardens' posts (a scale of one to each 1,000 of the population) delivery of this important item was long delayed. In April 1939 local authorities were warned that only 10 per cent. of these pumps would be available in the near future;[2] in June first deliveries were made and the Department obtained authority to double the free issue to 100,000. Yet three weeks before war only 8,500 pumps had been received at wardens' posts; and it appeared that large supplies were being diverted for sale to the public and industry at higher prices.

Though the number of posts was increasing by early in 1939, many authorities found difficulty in obtaining suitable buildings.[3] During March and April the Department approved the construction of some new protected posts, and in May it told all authorities that if suitable accommodation was still lacking they might build new posts at maximum costs of £50 for the smaller and £75 for the larger ones.[4] Many posts built under these arrangements were small surface structures, not unlike protected telephone kiosks. Though they could serve as reporting centres and rallying points, they could for the most part give protection against blast, splinters and the weather to only a small proportion of the wardens concerned.

The only service more completely developed than the Wardens' Service early in 1939 was the Decontamination Service, the smallest and most limited in its functions.[5] Decontamination Squads of seven men including a driver had been formed for some time past without much difficulty from borough cleansing staffs and county highway employees. They were only concerned with one matter, the decontamination of streets, buildings and vehicles from liquid gases; their training was well advanced, and most of their equipment was used in their normal work. Their needs, however, for Service masks had not been fully met, provision of heavy anti-gas suits still presented great difficulties, and bleach powder supplies were only improving slowly.

The Rescue and Demolition Service was the third of the services in size, with a 'paper' strength at the opening of 1939 of some 125,000 men. Its effective organisation, however, still awaited decisions on the extent to which it was to rely on skilled men from the building

---

[1] Memorandum No. 4, February 1939; pp. 125, 142.

[2] A.R.P. Dept. Circular 85, 17th April 1939.

[3] A.R.P. Dept. Circular 25, 9th February 1939.

[4] A.R.P. Dept. Circular 101, 4th May 1939.

[5] pp. 127, 163.

and similar trades, and the terms on which such men would be employed.[1] The chief advance was now made in London Region where, after much discussion, arrangements quite different from those hitherto laid down at the centre were introduced. The L.C.C., working through contractors, was to take over responsibility for demolition and road clearance, and the Rescue Parties' function would be predominantly rescue of trapped persons, including only such debris clearance and demolition as was needed for this task. The composition of parties was also changed. 'Heavy Parties' (those with the heavier articles of equipment) would still consist of eight men and a driver. But 'Light Parties' were enlarged to ten men and a driver, four of whom would be trained in first aid.

In spite of this limitation of functions, the Home Office was convinced that rescue required a high proportion of skilled men drawn from local authorities' works departments or from the building trades. The main difficulty arose over pay. The L.C.C. took the view that skilled men should be paid normal trade rates both under peace-time training and in war. The Lord Privy Seal, in reply, was inclined to agree that these men might be paid for specialised training if this was given on employers' premises, and added, as regards service in war, 'I agree that men asked to undertake whole-time service in A.R.P. because of their industrial skill should receive an allowance, over and above the basic allowance of all A.R.P. whole-time volunteers, which would make their weekly allowance broadly equivalent to their industrial remuneration'. He was, however, uncertain whether skilled men in Light Parties could be regarded as carrying out their normal trade duties. The Treasury recommended that skilled men to receive rates above the basic £3 allowance should be reduced to one in each party. The National Federation of Building Trade Operatives, however, maintained that there must be three skilled men besides the foreman in each type of Rescue Party; and after prolonged conversations this was agreed upon. The Home Office told all authorities in July that the form of organisation adopted in London, with four skilled men in every party, was to be applied throughout the country.[2] Men obtained through local building trade organisations were normally to be trained by their employers in paid time, though the authorities were to reimburse employers for wages paid on unremunerative work.[3] If the local authority itself recruited men for this service, it would have to arrange for their technical training. All members of Rescue Parties were to be trained in anti-gas measures, and four of

---

[1] p. 127.

[2] A.R.P. Dept. Circular 142, 13th July 1939; Memorandum No. 2 (3rd ed.), *Rescue Parties and Clearance of Debris*.

[3] Memorandum No. 2.

the six unskilled members of Light Parties in first aid, including special methods of handling casualties trapped under debris.[1]

Equipment for Rescue Parties, designed from experience gained in the 1931 Tokyo earthquake, consisted mainly of levers, crowbars, ropes, jacks and other instruments in common use. As every party would need a complete set of these for instant turn-out in war, the Government decided in March on the principle of central supply. It proved difficult, as usual, to procure the large quantities required, and in June orders were placed for two of the most important items, lifting tackle and ratchet jacks, in the United States. By early August good progress was being made with the delivery of most of these articles to local authorities.

While the Home Office remained responsible for First Aid Parties and for recruitment and some training of all three Casualty Services, responsibility in other respects for the First Aid Post and Ambulance Services had been transferred in the autumn of 1938 to the Ministry of Health and Department of Health for Scotland.[2] Recruitment and training of these services presented serious difficulties, arising mainly from the fact that in the years before Munich it had been too readily assumed that these could be performed by the Voluntary Organisations, whose members were in fact too few and too unevenly distributed.[3] The War Office had the first claim in war on members of the Red Cross and did not release even 'immobiles' from their military obligation until May 1939; many members of the St. John Ambulance Brigade, despite its civilian character, were joining the R.A.M.C. In addition, the work of First Aid Parties was regarded by many A.R.P. volunteers as either a soft or an unpleasant job. The degree in which this service had become 'nobody's child' is suggested by the fact that as late as August 1939 a Bournemouth staff instructor could write to the A.R.P. Department saying his authority had decided to form First Aid Parties and asking which central Department was responsible for the service.

By August 1939 the service still needed 78,000 volunteers, equivalent to 44 per cent. of its establishment. The position, in view of the heavy air raid casualties expected, was so serious that the A.R.P. Department asked the War Office to enlarge the Territorial Army medical service to provide war reinforcement for A.R.P. needs. The War Office agreed on condition that the Home Office provided

---

[1] H.M. Office of Works was also organising Rescue and Demolition Squads which were eventually integrated with the general rescue organisation.

[2] pp. 168–169.

[3] pp. 126–129; e.g., in October 1938 the County of London Branch of the British Red Cross Society had 1,593 members, of whom seven-eighths were women and more than one-quarter lived in Chelsea or Westminster (see H. S. Reid, *Story of the County of London Branch of the B.R.C.S.*).

instructors and equipment; but when the Home Office found they were to provide these to train the whole British Expeditionary Force in stretcher bearers' duties they allowed the proposal to drop.

Training for this service had been causing much difficulty. The syllabus and manuals of the Voluntary Societies, though sound for their own purposes, were in various ways unsuited to A.R.P. volunteers.[1] The Department took two steps to remedy the situation. First, courses were given at the Staff School to qualify organisers both to train instructors for First Aid Parties and to perform administrative duties concerning these parties. Secondly, a handbook was produced on training and organisation which tried to relate principles of 'pure first aid' to A.R.P. needs, dealt with team training, and stressed combined training with (in particular) the Rescue and Ambulance services.[2] After some disagreement with the Ministry of Health over its contents, this was sent to local authorities three days before the outbreak of war.

By May 1939 only 30,000 persons, out of a total estimated need of 130,000, had joined the Ambulance Service. The L.C.C. had obtained under 5,000 drivers and attendants (about one-quarter part-time) for an establishment of over 17,000; and Birmingham, Leeds, Manchester and other areas were in equal difficulties. Only slow improvement was made in the following months. It was estimated in mid-summer that only about 40 per cent. of those in the service were trained. In London and most other towns vehicles available for use as ambulances were still far short of needs. Stretchers and stretcher-carrying fitments had been made generally available by the Government. Stretchers were of a standard size, all-metal and easily decontaminated, though not being collapsible they were difficult to store.

Recruitment for First Aid Posts and Mobile Aid Posts (cars or vans to carry doctors, nurses and equipment to an incident) had proved much more satisfactory.[3] First Aid Posts were normally to be at hospitals or other medical establishments, and by mid-summer a large number of these had been chosen. But a Ministry of Health survey in July of sixteen important areas showed that in other respects progress in this service was fairly slow. Not much had been done to adapt or give blast protection to posts, arrangements for personal decontamination were backward, some areas had not appointed doctors or nurses to posts, and less than half had made messing and sleeping arrangements for whole-time staff. About half those in the service had been fully trained. Fair progress was being

---

[1] A.R.P. Dept. Circular 16, 26th January 1939.

[2] A.R.P. Handbook No. 10, *Training and Work of First Aid Parties*, August 1939.

[3] By June 1939 about 122,000 volunteers had been recruited for an establishment of 160,000.

made with distribution of drugs and dressings, though supplies of surgical instruments were inadequate. In the weeks before the war the Ministry of Health was examining ways of improving organisation of the service; on 9th September it asked local authorities to make large increases in the proportion of whole-time staff for both fixed and mobile posts.[1]

The Report and Control Service was the slowest to develop of the main A.R.P. services. Its organisation and training could not proceed far until other services had reached a fairly advanced state, arrangements for local co-ordination had been determined and the precise role which local authorities were to play in war had been defined. Since the service was to be composed mainly of local authorities' staffs, recruitment presented no special problem. In April 1938 the A.R.P. Department had sent authorities detailed guidance on the lay-out, staffing arrangements and operational functions of Report Centres;[2] and when Munich was at its height it had hurriedly issued more instructions about reporting.[3] Control, it will be recalled, was to be exercised in every area by Chief Constables, acting on central instructions; but since this arrangement was secret local authorities had been in a state of some bewilderment about the functions they were expected to exercise in war. Only a handful had succeeded by the end of the crisis in equipping Report or Control centres or making more than the simplest arrangements for co-ordination of services and transmission of intelligence.[4]

The effective beginning of this service dated from the Government's announcement in March 1939 that every scheme-making authority was to appoint an A.R.P. Controller, who would act in war under instructions either from Home Security or his authority's Emergency Committee.[5] The authorities acted promptly over these appointments. About 120, or roughly one-half, appointed their County or Town Clerks as Controllers, 70 appointed Chief Constables, and most of the remainder one of their aldermen or councillors.[6] Though Controllers were to have no executive functions in peace, they were to co-ordinate the current preparations of the Medical Officer of Health, Borough Surveyor, Chief Warden and other Heads of A.R.P. Services.

Impetus had been given these preparations by the issue, at the same time as the announcement about Controllers, of full (provisional) 'Local War Instructions', which set out in detail the

---

[1] Ministry of Health Circular 1869, 9th September 1939.
[2] Memorandum No. 6, *Local Communications and the Reporting of Air Raid Damage*, April 1938.
[3] H.O. Circular of 20th September 1938, and revised Memorandum No. 6, September 1939.
[4] pp. 162–163.
[5] A.R.P. Dept. Circular 57, 21st March 1939; p. 178.
[6] Nine A.R.P. Organisers were appointed Controllers.

stages by which (if need arose) the Home Office would require authorities to put particular features of their A.R.P. schemes on a war basis—for example, by the reduction of street lighting, call-up of paid volunteers and opening of trench shelters.[1] Arrangements for Controllers' headquarters and local communications were now pressed forward, helped by further Home Office advice.[2] The individual warden's report of attack, casualties and damage in his sector was to be the basis of the A.R.P. intelligence system. A chain of simple Report Posts in rural areas, or more elaborate Report Centres (one for each 100,000 of the population) in the larger towns, was to lead to the Control Centre of each scheme-making authority, thence (in certain districts) to the Group Centre and on to Regional Headquarters.[3]

In creating an intelligence network of this kind and putting it to practical tests London Region, as noticed already, had been making good progress.[4] During the summer an increasing number of authorities held trials of communications and reporting systems, and during the R.A.F. exercises in July and August civil defence reporting arrangements were tested over areas covering several Regions.[5] The Home Office concluded in mid-July that development of the Report and Control service was generally satisfactory; physical accommodation was well advanced, and training was making good progress.

At the same date the Government defined fully, for the first time, the war functions of A.R.P. Controllers.[6] Their responsibility would be limited to the strictly A.R.P. services just described and would not extend, for example, to the fire brigades or the police. Since each A.R.P. service would be in charge of its own officer (e.g. the Chief Warden or Borough Engineer) Controllers would confine themselves in active operations to giving, should the necessity arise, 'broad general decisions' on the manner in which local resources were employed. Co-ordination both of the services under their ultimate control and of these with other local services, and ensuring co-operation with neighbouring authorities, would be their main functions. Though normally responsible to a war-time Emergency Committee, they would carry out any instructions issued to them by the Regional Commissioner or the Government.

---

[1] A.R.P. Dept. Circular 59, 22nd March 1939. The Home Office telegrams were to be sent out to local authorities under the code name LOWIN.

[2] A.R.P. Dept. Circular 45, 6th March 1939.

[3] Smaller towns were establishing combined 'Report and Control Centres'; and some counties were forming 'Sub-Control Centres'.

[4] p. 184.

[5] pp. 210–211.

[6] A.R.P. Dept. Circular 144, 19th July 1939.

Industrial A.R.P.

By Munich industry, with certain notable exceptions such as Boots and Imperial Chemical Industries, had made only slow progress with A.R.P.[1] General backwardness had been due to uncertainty over the Government's financial plans, lack of precise technical advice and lack of concerted action within industry itself. Negotiations between the Government and public utilities had only produced agreements with the gas industry and the Metropolitan Water Board.[2] The Minister of Transport reported at the end of 1938 complete deadlock in financial negotiations with the railway companies, though these were going ahead with preparations. Of 700 firms engaged in some aspect of aircraft production no more than seven or eight had, at this date, taken active A.R.P. measures.

Before the end of 1938 Ministers had approved draft legislation to oblige employers both to organise A.R.P. services and to provide workpeople with some type of shelter. Soon afterwards, problems of the application of A.R.P. to industry were, for the first time, comprehensively studied by the Advisory Panel of Industrialists appointed to advise the Prime Minister on defence measures in general. This Panel approved, in the main, the proposed legislation; but showed much heart-burning on financial issues. Besides complaining that the 'good employer' doctrine was nullified by financial uncertainty, it strongly criticised the Government's failure to give industry clearer indication of what was meant by 'reasonable shelter protection' for employees.

Early in March 1939 the Lord Privy Seal obtained Cabinet approval for a concession to industry for shelter provision equivalent in value to income tax concession, with an upper limit of £4 per employee. This, it was estimated, would cost the Exchequer £7–£8 million. The Minister also proposed that assistance to a maximum of 50 per cent. of the agreed cost should be given to firms required to undertake structural work and other types of capital expenditure for obscuring lights from blast furnaces and similar processes. This would put the 'anti-glare' problem on the same financial footing as the special precautions to be taken by utilities, and would cost the Exchequer an additional £3 million. The Lord Privy Seal's announcement of these proposals on 16th March brought financial uncertainty to an end and opened a phase of more positive action.[3]

---

[1] pp. 131–135.

[2] pp. 132–133

[3] H. of C. Deb., Vol. 345, Cols. 603–612.

The Minister described the obligations to be placed on industry and urged employers not to await translation of these into law before taking action. The shelters grant, he explained, would be subject to two limitations—an overriding limit on expenditure by reference to the ascertained cost of providing certain 'standard protection', and restriction to employers in the most vulnerable areas, shortly to be defined in detail. A Code of Protection prescribing standards and giving technical guidance was about to be issued. When he introduced the Civil Defence Bill a fortnight later, he said that, though this laid a specific legal duty on employers, 'we propose to rely in the main, on good will'.[1] During Second Reading debate the Bill's industrial clauses aroused no significant opposition.[2]

The three broad obligations the Bill imposed on employers have been noticed earlier in this narrative.[3] That to organise A.R.P. services and train employees applied to firms (classified into factories, mines and commercial buildings) throughout Britain employing at least 30 persons. The more substantial obligation to provide shelters applied only to firms in the most vulnerable areas or those elsewhere considered high on the list of likely targets employing at least 50 persons. The duty to take immediate action (especially the screening of flames or glare) to comply with a drastic war-time black-out applied to factories, mines and public utilities (but not to commercial concerns) in all parts of Britain. Employers were to report within specified periods what measures they had taken to the Factory or Mines Inspectorate or the local authority, who were empowered to compel recalcitrant employers to act. During the Bill's committee stage its industrial clauses were little amended, though much criticism was expressed of the intention to limit grants-in-aid to shelters in areas classed by order as vulnerable.[4] The extension to all employers with a staff of 30 of the obligation to provide training brought complaints that no obligation was placed on employees to undergo training and caused the Lord Privy Seal to rejoin, 'in this, as in many other matters arising under the Bill, good will and good sense will go much further in the direction in which we desire to see progress than compulsory provision'.[5] To this reaffirmation of the voluntary principle must be added the reason the Minister gave for refusing to guarantee that the Code of Protection would not be unnecessarily altered—'the whole science of

[1] H. of C. Deb., Vol. 345, Cols 2634-2751 and 2811-2958, 4th and 5th April 1939.
[2] Parts III, V and VI of the Bill.
[3] pp. 193–194.
[4] H. of C. Deb., Vol. 346, Cols. 806–932, 24th April 1939.
[5] H. of C. Deb., Vol. 347, Col. 2211, 23rd May 1939; p. 194. The voluntary principle was not departed from in this matter until the Fire Guard Orders of 1943.

civil defence', he said, 'is in an experimental and developing stage'.[1] After the Bill had finally become law the Lord Privy Seal's Office issued a memorandum on its complex industrial provisions.[2]

The shelter Code had been issued in provisional form at the end of April; it was then subject to much revision and re-issued shortly before war broke out.[3] It dealt only with shelters to protect work-people, and was not concerned with protection of plant and equipment. It gave detailed information regarding both general shelter standards and the way in which these might be applied to various types of factories and business buildings. The general standard to be aimed at was 'a really good type of splinter and blast-proof protection'.[4] In accordance with the dispersal principle, shelters were to be limited when possible to fifty persons, be accessible within seven minutes and be spaced at least twenty-five feet apart. Soon after the first issue of this Code the list (also provisional) of the 'specified areas' to which the industrial obligation applied was published.[5] These included industrial centres of some size over most of Britain, which contained some 12,000 factories, employing $2\frac{1}{2}$ million persons, and mines and other establishments employing a further $1\frac{1}{2}$ million.

The basic information employers needed was completed by the issue in June of guidance on organisation and training of A.R.P. services.[6] Local authorities were again asked to help employers by training factory workers to act as instructors and other means.[7] Factories and firms employing less than 500 persons were to train 10 per cent. of their staffs in anti-gas measures, first aid and fire-fighting. Larger firms were provided with special scales for trained personnel, and were to establish control and internal warning systems, first aid posts and more elaborate fire-fighting arrangements. An industrial Wardens' Service was to be formed, on the basis of one warden for fifty employees or for each shelter. Equipment for factory squads was to be steel helmets and civilian duty masks,[8] both of which the Government had now undertaken to supply on payment, and anti-gas clothing, which employers would have to buy on the open market. The cost of training and equipping A.R.P.

---

[1] H. of C. Deb., Vol. 346, Col. 923, 24th April 1939.

[2] *A.R.P. in Industry*, July 1939.

[3] *Air Raid Shelters for Persons working in Factories and Commercial Buildings;* Civil Defence (Approval and Revision of Code) Order, 1939, S.R.& O. No. 920, August 1939.

[4] H. of C. Deb., Vol. 345, Col. 2641, 4th April 1939.

[5] p. 193. This list was also issued in revised form as Civil Defence (Specified Areas) Order, 1939, S.R. & O. No. 893, on 14th August 1939.

[6] 'Preliminary Memorandum on the Organisation of A.R.P. Services in Industrial etc. Undertakings and the Training and Equipment of Personnel', June 1939.

[7] A.R.P. Dept. Circular 133, 4th July 1939.

[8] For a proportion of industry civilian respirators were considered adequate; a few utilities and other firms were to be equipped with Service respirators.

squads might be deducted when computing profits for income-tax purposes.[1]

Public utilities were obliged, like the rest of industry, to perform the three broad duties just described, reporting the action they had taken to the appropriate department, in most cases the Ministry of Transport or Board of Trade. The Government had now decided to make a contribution of 50 per cent., which might rise in certain cases to 85 per cent., towards the cost of special measures utilities might have to take to secure 'the due functioning of their undertakings in time of war'.[2] Negotiations with the railways, docks and harbours, canals, and other utilities on the details of these measures had been speeded up since the end of 1938 by transfer of the main responsibility in this matter to the relevant departments.[3] A survey in mid-1939 showed that, though much remained to be done, most utilities had made progress training employees, providing shelters, and taking steps to protect plant and ensure supplies of reserve plant and repair materials.[4]

If the Government had had to give first attention to protecting essential services, it was clear that Government factories and firms working on Government contracts also needed special consideration. At the end of 1936 the Committee of Imperial Defence had suggested that departments should emphasise the importance of A.R.P. to firms with whom they were placing orders. In Government and shadow factories the cost of these would be borne by the Exchequer; but contractors, it was decided at the end of 1938, would be on the same footing as the rest of industry. In May 1939 it was decided to pay contractors grant equivalent to the standard rate of income tax for protecting vital plant. Provision for this was regarded as inappropriate to the Civil Defence Bill and was later included in the Ministry of Supply Act, which gave the Minister power to direct firms on Government work.[5] A proposal that contracting Departments should enlist special staffs to advise contractors on A.R.P. and make inspections resulted in the creation of Passive Air Defence Departments first at the Air Ministry and later at the Admiralty and Ministries of Supply and Aircraft Production. It was thought in May 1939 that only two or three thousand firms would be involved. When industry turned over in earnest to war production this number began rapidly to increase; and in course of time much of the responsibility for industrial A.R.P. devolved upon these two Service and two war-time civil Departments.

---

[1] p. 134.

[2] Civil Defence Act 1939, Part V.

[3] H. of C. Deb., Vol. 345, Cols. 2747–2751, 4th April 1939.

[4] Important exceptions were the vulnerable state of L.P.T.B. electricity supplies, and the state of railway lighting.

[5] 2 and 3 Geo. 6, Ch. 38, Section 13, July 1939.

'The knowledge', the Lord Privy Seal said in April, 'that our preparations cannot be completed for some considerable time to come weighs very heavily, on all of us'.[1] Once the Bill and the shelter Code had been published, employers in general began effectively to respond to the Government's request that A.R.P. should henceforth be treated as an essential function of management. A good deal of preliminary work was done on shelters, especially in factories, before the Act came into force, though it was found that some of the earliest plans needed much revision to conform with the Code. The date by which employers had to take preparatory steps in this matter to earn grant had been fixed at 30th September 1939; and adequate general information of employers' progress with this and other A.R.P. measures did not become available until many months later. By the outbreak of war most factories had made a good beginning with blast and splinter-proof shelters, and by 30th September 90 per cent. of the 12,000 or so establishments concerned had submitted shelter schemes.[2] It was not, however, until the end of 1939, after four months of war, that a substantial proportion of factory owners had completed their shelters. Progress with shelters in offices and shops proved much slower.

In organising and training A.R.P. services industry, though with many exceptions especially among the larger firms, adopted a more leisurely attitude.[3] The Home Office Schools and the Staff School continued to devote certain courses to representatives of industry, and the latter was planning a big extension of this training once the Civil Defence Bill became law.[4] But only a few hundred industrial organisers had passed through these schools by the outbreak of war. Smaller firms relied for the most part on local authorities for training, and during this summer most authorities were fully occupied organising their own services. These difficulties were only beginning to be overcome by formation of training centres at factories, and arrangements for sharing instructors. Backwardness in training was also due to what the Department called in February the 'profoundly unsatisfactory state' of the supply of A.R.P. equipment to industry. Proposals that employers should borrow equipment from local authorities' mobilisation stocks for training had not proved popular with the authorities, and could only offer a most partial solution. The Government had therefore undertaken in April to supply employers with steel helmets (at 8s. 6d. each) and Civilian Duty

---

[1] H. of C. Deb., Vol. 345, Col. 2923, 5th April 1939.

[2] *Annual Report of the Chief Inspector of Factories for the year 1939*, Cmd. 6251, 1941.

[3] Ibid., p. 42; pp. 134, 194.

[4] Nominees, in addition to those from public utilities and manufacturing concerns, from the Stock Exchange, Lloyd's, banks and insurance companies had already attended the Staff School.

Q

masks (costing 7s. 6d. to 8s. od.), but deliveries of these and of anti-gas clothing to employers had not taken place on any large scale before war broke out.[1]

In their operational arrangements factories paid most attention to means for prompt relaying of the warning (for example by signals and lights) and for quick evacuation of employees to shelters. The policy officially laid down was that on sounding of the 'alert' all but key men (who should be given special protection at their posts) were to go to shelter and stay there until the 'all clear', and factories were advised to divide workpeople into small parties in charge of wardens who would act as shelter marshals.[2] Factories were experiencing small difficulty at this stage with recruitment for A.R.P. services, with the exception of the fire parties which, consisting of the younger and more active men, became subject to much change as the military call-up gathered pace.

As war drew near the problem of obscuring ordinary industrial lighting still defied easy solution, and was causing employers in general much anxiety.[3] Good progress had been made jointly by the Government and industry in working out means of obviating glare, though no easy means had yet been evolved for dealing with burning slag heaps.[4] Camouflage possibilities were still mainly at the theoretical stage, though some Air Ministry factories had begun practical work of this kind. After passage of the new Act responsibility in this matter had been transferred to the Lord Privy Seal, who began to form a central organisation to administer it and a camouflage establishment.[5]

The Government decided early in 1939 that evacuation of firms in danger zones which were not immediately concerned with war production should be a question for employers themselves to decide. But they adopted the policy of encouraging 'permanent' evacuation by such firms to neutral or reception areas while peace still obtained, provided this would not interfere with their efficiency. Responsibility for advising employers on this matter lay with the Health Departments.

Warning and Lighting

The warning system in its operational aspect had reached an advanced state of preparation by Munich.[6] When the crisis became

---

[1] pp. 221, 236.

[2] 'Preliminary Memorandum on the Organisation of A.R.P. Services in Industrial etc. Undertakings and the Training and Equipment of Personnel', June 1939.

[3] pp. 138–139.

[4] p. 194.

[5] p. 194.

[6] pp. 135–137, 159.

acute on 15th September the system had been brought to full working order in London, and a week or so later it had been effectively established over much of the country. Once the crisis had subsided the chief tasks were the further improvement of the telephone and other technical facilities, and preparation by Chief Constables of shorter and more final warning lists. A national test at the end of October satisfied the authorities that the system would function in war with 'reasonable efficiency', and more tests were held early in the New Year. Teleprinter apparatus in the chief War Rooms would enable Home Security headquarters to send warning messages simultaneously to all Regional Commissioners.[1] Good progress was made with revising the lists and instructing A.R.P. Control Centres, industrial concerns and other recipients of messages on the procedure to be followed. Before the end of June 1939 the G.P.O. reported that the operational system was complete and available for use.

This, which was put into readiness ten days before war broke out, was in outline to operate as follows. Responsibility for initiating all air raid messages would rest with the A.O.C.-in-C., Fighter Command who would be told of the approach and course of enemy aircraft by radar, the Observer Corps and other means. This officer would be given the widest measure of discretion in deciding whether or not on any given occasion to send out warnings. By the outbreak of war Fighter Command Headquarters Operations Room had been heavily protected, and an alternative Operations Room and Warning Centre established at Leighton Buzzard. The country had been divided into 111 warning districts and, in pursuit of the primary aim of reducing interruption of essential work, messages would be directed to one district at a time. Districts receiving a given message would be defined by the use of a protractor, with the centre of its base at the invaders' reported position. The 'preliminary' (or 'yellow') message, representing twenty-two minutes' flying time, would be transmitted as the outer lines of the protractor touched a warning district, and the 'action' (or 'red') warning, representing twelve minutes' flying time, as the inner lines touched it.[2] The 'raiders passed' (or 'green') message would be sent when the enemy had passed out of a district, and the 'cancel caution' (or 'white') when all precautions could be relaxed. The messages would be sent by direct telephone lines to three trunk exchanges at London, Liverpool and Glasgow, each of which had been linked with about six group exchanges, connected in turn with the local exchanges which would pass the messages to those for whom they were intended. The 'yellow' would be sent on a strict order of

---

[1] Investigation of control of warning messages by wireless had produced no useful result by the outbreak of war; p. 137.
[2] See p. 136.

priority to those on the warning lists—Government departments, military establishments, A.R.P., police and fire brigade headquarters and a large number of industrial concerns. It would be confidential, in the sense that recipients were to take the necessary precautions in as unobtrusive a manner as possible. The 'red' lists followed the same order of priority, but contained a larger number of recipients. Receipt of this 'action' warning would be the signal for sounding the public sirens, for all industrial activities to stop and for everyone to seek shelter.

The detailed plans worked out at the centre before the crisis for relaying the 'red' warning to the general public in all urban areas had, in the meantime, been taking practical shape.[1] The Government, the reader will recall, had decided to aim at creating public confidence in the system by erring, at least at the outset of a war, on the side of over-insurance as regards both length of warnings and the size of the areas to be warned. By early in 1939 several types of electrically-driven siren approved by the Home Office were becoming generally available, and good progress was being made with their installation. Responsibility for operating public warnings rested on the police; but the physical arrangements, outside central London, consisted of only a small proportion of sirens under direct police control linked up with sirens and hooters in factories and elsewhere.

Manning this extensive public system in war now constituted a major problem. By the crisis of March 1939 London was fairly well covered over a radius of eight miles from its centre by sirens at police stations which could be sounded at very short notice; but no other sirens could be sounded at night unless factory and shop owners had been warned to keep their telephones permanently manned. In May the Lord Privy Seal told the Committee of Imperial Defence that in planning the rapid mobilisation of civil resources in an emergency the problems both of warning and lighting were most difficult to solve. Permanent manning of sirens under private control in advance of declaration of an emergency would not only be most expensive, but would clearly give rise to great public alarm. There was also difficulty in reconciling this desire to avoid causing alarm with public education in the nature of the signals. By the early summer a few exercises which included the sounding of sirens had been held in the provinces. But the exercise held in Chelsea in June was the first in London to include the public warning.[2] In spite of occasional broadcasts and written explanations, the vast majority of the public, in London or elsewhere, had only vague knowledge of the signals when the 'red' warning ushered in war on Sunday morning, 3rd September.

---

[1] pp. 136–137.
[2] p. 211.

Efforts to prepare for a universal war-time black-out were a more formidable and complex matter. Control of internal domestic lighting was mainly a matter of educating the public, and was not thought by the Government at this stage to offer any special problems. But in spite of much planning and experiment, effective control of external lighting—in the streets, on vehicles, and in use by the railways and industry—still raised immense technical and practical difficulties.[1]

Experience during Munich had proved that the quick extinction of street lighting was no easy matter; lighting concerns had had to employ large staffs on continuous stand-by for telephone instructions and prepared, since central disconnection would usually interfere with household lighting, to go round the streets removing the bulbs. A meeting early in 1939 between representatives of the Home Office, the Metropolitan Police, the Electricity Commissioners and the gas industry concluded that 5 to 6 hours was the minimum time required for effective reduction of street-lighting, and agreed that the Home Office should compile lists of all local lighting undertakings and prepare with the G.P.O. some centralised system of sending these undertakings confidential warnings.[2] By June 1939 plans had been completed for the Home Office to send a series of code messages in an emergency directly to about 3,000 electricity and gas concerns. 'Street Lights Message Grey' would be the signal for these to assemble staffs and take other preparatory steps. If the Government decided to introduce the precautionary stage of war preparations partial street-lighting was to be attempted, but if total extinction was necessary the message 'Street Lights Message Black' would be sent.

During the March crisis the Chiefs of Staff noted that nothing could immediately be done to reduce the six hours needed to black-out London's streets, but proposed that the feasibility of central disconnection should be more fully examined. Shortly afterwards the Committee of Imperial Defence asked the Lord Privy Seal to report on the whole problem of the black-out in the event (then assuming growing prominence in their minds) of a 'bolt from the blue', or sudden unheralded air attack. The Minister replied that under such circumstances the police would take immediate steps to enforce the extinction or screening of all lights, and the public would be further instructed by broadcast announcements. Street lighting could be extinguished in six hours, and all other lighting effectively reduced within twenty-four hours. He considered existing arrangements preferable, on grounds of general policy and expense, to more drastic measures involving central disconnection or the continuous

---

[1] See pp. 137–139.

[2] A.R.P. Dept. Circular 19, 2nd February 1939. Many local authorities took a considerable time to provide information about their lighting undertakings.

stand-by of lighting staffs. A 'bolt from the blue' would find large congregations of people in the streets and other public places and inevitably cause much panic, which would be much aggravated if whole towns or districts were plunged into darkness. The Committee agreed with these conclusions.

The considerable research concerning 'aids to movement' of pedestrians and traffic in the black-out was beginning to bear fruit.[1] In January 1939 a large test was held in the Nottingham area in which sixty vehicles, including buses, fire engines and A.R.P. cars, equipped with headlamp masks, travelled over six miles of road furnished with 'aids' in the form of reflectors, painted kerbstones, illuminated direction signs and pedestrian crossings and even ultra-violet light shining on to luminous paint on the clothing of a policeman on point duty. The Home Office considered the results encouraging, and in June supplied full information on these methods to all local authorities.[2]

Disagreement between the A.R.P. Department and Service Departments on the nature of the headlamp mask which would be compulsory under the Lighting Order for almost all vehicles continued up to the eve of war. While the Department had designed a hood covering a mask which only emitted light through a narrow horizontal slit and pressed for this to be generally adopted, the Services favoured a simpler device.[3] Trials, spread over several months, were held of the efficiency of these rival designs from the point of view of aerial observation, convenience to drivers and danger to road users. It was decided in July that the Department's design should be adopted for all vehicles except those of the Services, and arrangements for its commercial production were put in hand.

Although some large firms, such as the General Electric Company, Imperial Chemical Industries and some railway companies, had cooperated actively with the Government over experiments, industry as a whole had made little progress by early in 1939 with arrangements for the black-out.[4] Many employers still hoped they would earn exemption under the general authority given to Chief Constables, and the Home Office had not yet issued guidance on how lighting restrictions might be applied in practice. Much difficulty was being experienced by the Home Office in convincing the Service Departments, particularly the Admiralty, that screening of all lighting in their establishments—as distinct from the simpler

---

[1] pp. 137–138, 163.

[2] A.R.P. Dept. Circular 121, 15th June 1939. Some steps had been taken by the trade association to restrain undue rises in the price of white paint. Birmingham City alone had painted kerbstones etc. over 100 miles of road in the Munich crisis.

[3] Consisting only of a mask over the headlamps containing a semi-circular hole.

[4] p. 138.

processes of shading or power reduction on receipt of a warning—
would be essential.

But publication of the Civil Defence Bill in March removed all
doubts about the seriousness and universality of this obligation.[1]
Factories, mines and public utilities throughout Britain would be
compelled as soon as the Bill became law to take immediate steps to
ensure that, in the event of sudden air attack, they could immediately
obscure their lights without interruption of their work. No external
lighting would be allowed, except for work of special national
importance and under rigorous control arrangements, and special
attention was to be paid to elimination of glare.[2] Detailed guidance
was issued to employers in May in a handbook *War Time Lighting
Restrictions for Industrial and Commercial Premises*, which re-emphasised
the drastic nature of the proposed arrangements. Employers must
be able to complete arrangements to extinguish or obscure lights
within a few hours from the onset of an emergency. They were
told the best methods of screening windows, doorways and roof
lighting and the most suitable materials for blinds and mixtures
for painting glass.

Though this guidance stimulated effort, the black-out problem
was, as war approached, causing employers in most sections of industry real anxiety. In many factories the only practicable means
of achieving this aim was to cover all windows with paint or other
permanent material, which would involve continuous work in
artificial light with results on production that could not be foreseen.
Much discussion and experiment had been devoted since the
beginning of 1939 to defining standards of external lighting in railway marshalling yards, dockyards and other places where this would
be allowed; but the practical application of such standards had not
yet proceeded far. Satisfactory means had been evolved for dealing
with glare in the clay pottery and glass industries.[3] But the steel
industry decided in May that screening of blast furnaces and coke
ovens would take up to three years to complete, and that most of the
material for this work would have to be imported.[4] No simple means
had been found by the outbreak of war of eliminating glare from
slag heaps.

In June arrangements for continuous research into means of
achieving a full black-out in industry, and into problems of street
lighting, illuminated signs, lighting of shop windows and vehicles
and many other matters, had been strengthened by the formation of a
joint committee on A.R.P. Lighting Problems, on which the Home

---

[1] p. 194.
[2] Civil Defence Act, 1939, Part VI.
[3] pp. 138, 224.
[4] The screening of coke ovens alone was estimated to cost about £300,000.

Office, the Ministry of Transport and numerous societies and firms concerned with lighting were represented.[1]

During the summer more exercises which included a black-out were held up and down the country. These caused some improvement in municipal arrangements, and spread experience of the conditions to be introduced in war. In July areas embracing several civil defence Regions were partially blacked out, and during Home Defence exercises over much of eastern Britain on 9th-10th August the attempt was made, for the first time, to black-out London.[2] Most London authorities took advantage of this occasion to practise their A.R.P. arrangements, and the Home Office reported that the results, viewed as a first experiment and with the exception of lighting on the railways, were encouraging.

Supplies and Transport

Decisions to supply the whole civil population with gas-masks and to provide some 2,000,000 members of the A.R.P. Services, Police and Fire Brigades with more elaborate personal protection against gas attack had, it has been seen, set the Home Office new and large problems of design, manufacture and administrative action.[3] By the onset of the crisis the A.R.P. Department's five-year programme of supplies concerned predominantly with anti-gas equipment was, on the whole, being fulfilled on time, but the only item actually delivered to the public or the Services on a scale approaching the aims of the programme was the adult civilian gas mask.[4] Much improvisation had been necessary in dealing with the problem of supplies, which lay far outside normal Home Office responsibilities. After the Lord Privy Seal's assumption of responsibility for civil defence a large development of the A.R.P. Department's supply machinery was undertaken.[5] A Supply Policy Division was formed to conduct negotiations with the Treasury and determine the nature and scales of A.R.P. equipment, with the assistance of H.M. Office of Works, and the Supply Branch was expanded.[6]

A considerable new task had been set by the decision to begin the supply early in 1939 of 2,500,000 Anderson shelters and certain steel fittings free of charge to families in the main target areas.[7] Apart

---

[1] This committee first met in July 1939 and continued its activities until 1941.

[2] Provision had been made for this by the Civil Defence Act, 1939 (Sec. 49).

[3] pp. 139–142.

[4] pp. 160–165.

[5] Lord Privy Seal, H. of C. Deb., Vol. 344, Cols. 1287–1316, 1st March 1939.

[6] pp. 141, 174. By the outbreak of war the staff of this Branch numbered over 1,200, including an inspectorate at the works of over 200 contractors.

[7] pp. 186–188. Shelter supplies were administered by the Department's Shelters Division.

from this, the Department's energies in the supply sphere were still primarily concerned with anti-gas equipment, sandbags and medical stores. The problem's scale may be gauged from the fact that by the early months of 1939 it was engaged in arrangements for purchase and distribution throughout Britain of the following :

for the civil population in general :
    2,500,000 'Andersons', and basement fittings.
    50,000,000 Civilian respirators.
    1,500,000 Children's respirators.
    1,400,000 Babies' anti-gas helmets.
for other Departments, the Services, etc.
    475,000,000 sandbags.
for the A.R.P. Services, Police and Fire Brigades, etc.
    1,300,000 Civilian Duty respirators (to include supplies to other Departments, the Services, Governments overseas and industry).
    1,400,000 Service respirators (to be obtained from the War Office).
    1,800,000 steel helmets (to include supplies for industry).
    150,000 heavy anti-gas suits.
    1,700,000 light anti-gas suits, and several million curtains, pairs of gloves, pairs of gumboots and eyeshields.
    20,000 tons of bleach powder.
    50 tons of gas detector paint.
    £200,000 worth of medical stores (for First Aid Parties and Wardens' first aid boxes).
    An unknown quantity of jacks, chain tackle and other equipment for Rescue Parties and Decontamination Squads.
    50,000 stirrup hand pumps (for Wardens' Posts).
    Whistles, rattles, hand bells and log-books (for Wardens' Posts).
    Electric torches (for all the A.R.P. Services).
    Several thousand badges, brooches and armlets.

Once Munich had subsided, the Government had decided to leave civilian masks already distributed in the hands of the public for a trial period of six months, to issue cartons for their protection and to institute an inspection system.[1] The normal life of the mask, when assembled and distributed, was estimated by the experts as at least two years. The Government asked all local authorities to furnish more accurate estimates of their requirements, to continue with assembly and public distribution and to arrange for the regular inspection of masks by wardens.[2] By March 1939 both masks and carton boxes had been distributed to local authorities in most parts of the country, but it had also become apparent that the Government would have to build up a substantial reserve. The numbers

---

[1] About 38 million masks had been distributed to local authorities in the crisis, and 35 million assembled and issued to the public; pp. 160–165.

[2] H.O. Circulars 7th and 28th October 1938.

required by the authorities to complete public distribution were proving much greater than the recorded populations of their areas, and damage to masks during assembly and in the hands of the public was proving considerable, in spite of much official exhortation on this matter. Although the Chemical Defence Research Department was evolving an improved type of civilian mask, the decision was taken to proceed with the design already in use, and in April the Treasury approved the increase of total supplies for Britain to $57\frac{1}{2}$ million.[1]

Introduction of the 'Anderson' shelter had, from the standpoint of official doctrine, increased the importance of the civilian gas-mask. For large numbers of citizens who would now leave their houses during a raid to enter 'Andersons' the gas-mask had superseded the gas-proof room as the first line of defence against this form of attack. The existence of an adequate supply of masks was now, however, taken for granted by Parliament and the public who, for the time being, showed little interest in this topic.[2]

By May the Government had accumulated a reserve of about 3 million masks, and a month later they decided, in view of rising international tension, to complete distribution to local authorities throughout the country.[3] Many authorities had still failed to follow the request of the previous autumn to continue issuing masks to the public, and the Home Office was not satisfied that arrangements for this were, in general, adequate. At the end of July they asked all authorities to furnish more up-to-date returns and to complete issue to the public at once.[4] The position was now complicated by the fact that thousands of people were on holiday, and the Home Office had to rearrange stocks in Regional Stores so as to supply holiday resorts in the event of sudden attack. As small children's masks were not yet available, the Home Office also decided to increase stocks of small size respirators by 15 per cent. in the more vulnerable areas. Throughout August the issue proceeded of masks to the public, though in some areas this was not completed until after the opening of war.

Supply of masks for small children and babies continued to present many difficulties. The 'baby-bag' had been finally designed just before the crisis.[5] It consisted of a hood of rubberised fabric to be fitted over the baby's head, shoulders and arms and closed at the waist by a tape; a metal frame surrounding this gave support to the baby's back and was fitted with a window, and air was supplied by means of a bellows pump and respirator container. The device cost

---

[1] About $2\frac{1}{2}$ million had already been sent to N. Ireland, Malta and elsewhere.

[2] H. of C. Deb., Vol. 344, Col. 1296, 1st March 1939.

[3] H. of C. Deb., Vol. 347, Col. 721.

[4] A.R.P. Dept. Circular 157, 27th July 1939.

[5] pp. 140, 161.

about £1, and the Treasury gave approval in January 1939 to the purchase of 1,400,000 with the stipulation that these should not be issued until war was imminent. Assembly of these helmets at Blackburn from components supplied by many contractors proved a considerable task, and met with unexpected difficulties. The same proved true of the 'small child's respirator', a modification of the normal civilian type costing about 3s. 6d.[1] This included harness to make displacement difficult, and—with the idea of making it more palatable to children—a red rubber facepiece, blue container and bright eye-piece rims, and it became known as the 'Mickey Mouse'. At the end of 1938 the Treasury approved the purchase of 1,300,000 and some months later raised this to 2,000,000. Experience during and since Munich had proved that the question of protecting children against gas roused strong feelings in the country. Concern was therefore caused to the Government by the fact that in August babies' helmets and children's respirators were still only being manufactured in small quantities.[2]

Until the invention of the Anderson shelter the only item for universal use against high explosive attack was the sandbag, and at the end of 1938 sandbags still presented a large supply problem.[3] Two hundred and seventy-five million had been ordered. But this colossal total, though absorbing the entire production of the Scottish jute industry, would suffice to protect only Government buildings, vital points and the most essential A.R.P. buildings. In December the Committee of Imperial Defence agreed to an order for a further 200 million bags from India, with delivery to be completed by August. By the following March the combined production of Dundee and India had reached 12 million a week, and the Home Office began distribution to local authorities for vital points and the sale of bags to public uilities at the price of £10 per thousand. Supplies henceforward came in steadily, and as the Home Office decided not to attempt to supply bags to the public or industry in general it became possible to offer them on sale to local authorities for their own buildings and to begin to build up a national reserve. Though development of the shelter programme somewhat reduced local authorities' demands, the needs of Departments and the Services proved so great that the total order was raised shortly before war broke out to 525 million.

At the end of 1938 the Treasury agreed to large increases in the scales of anti-gas equipment and steel helmets to be provided for the A.R.P. Services, Fire Services and Police.[4] Expenditure of about

---

[1] p. 140,

[2] H. of C. Deb., Vol. 350, Col. 2316, 1st August 1939.

[3] pp. 142, 162.

[4] pp. 141–142, 161–163.

£5 million on these was approved; this, together with £5 million being spent on civilian masks and £2 million on children's devices, meant that nearly £12 million would be spent on anti-gas equipment. In spite of some public criticism that anti-gas precautions were being overdone, the experts were not prepared to advise the Home Office that there had been a substantial decrease of this risk.[1] At the opening of 1939 the Home Office told scheme-making authorities the scales on which this equipment would be furnished to each service, and urged them to provide local storage without delay.[2]

When the March crisis brought the need to speed up production and delivery of all A.R.P. supplies, three items—Service respirators, steel helmets and anti-gas clothing—were still far short of requirements. The Home Office was dependent for supplies of Service masks on the War Office, which could not undertake delivery before three months. Only a fraction of the nearly 2,000,000 steel helmets needed for civil defence had been received, and inquiry was made into the possibility of manufacturing these from mild steel. Trials were also being made into the manufacture of anti-gas clothing from rubberised fabric instead of oilskin.

By mid-summer supplies both of Service masks and steel helmets were steadily improving.[3] Deliveries of the former were approaching 1,000,000, though there was a serious shortage of haversacks; it was expected that local authorities' needs would be met by September, and the balance needed for a national reserve by March 1940. The position regarding steel helmets had been completely changed by the discovery of new methods of large-scale manufacture from manganese; the Department's own stocks would be delivered by the end of July and the 750,000 required for industry by the end of September. The problem of anti-gas clothing, however, was still proving most difficult.[4] Trials with rubberised fabric had not met with success, and no improvement in supplies of oilskin was in sight; only 65,000 heavy suits and less than one half the 1,700,000 light suits needed had been provided. The requirements of the A.R.P. services for suits of either type would not be adequately met until well into 1940; and even items such as anti-gas gloves and eye shields, the rate of production of which was most rapid, would not be fully delivered until the end of 1939. Hoods, essential for those who might have to work in heavy concentrations of gas, would not be available until a year later.

Among other items needed in substantial amounts for A.R.P. services, medical stores for First Aid Parties and wardens' posts

---

[1] p. 209.

[2] A.R.P. Dept. Circular 4, 17th January 1939; 205.

[3] p. 211.

[4] pp. 141–142.

had, by this date, been delivered in quantities approaching estimated needs.[1] Provision of bleach powder was improving; the requirement for 20,000 tons was now regarded as excessive, and satisfactory supplies were being delivered direct from the works to local authorities. Supply of special detector paint for the quick detection of gas had also proved difficult, owing to the secrecy of the manufacturing processes involved; but as war approached enough of the total order of 50 tons was being delivered to satisfy first local requirements. In March the Treasury had approved the central provision of all main items of Rescue Party equipment. Obtaining some of these items proved difficult and orders for jacks and lifting tackle had to be placed in the United States. But by August delivery of most of the other items to local authorities was proceeding well.[2]

The large-scale problem of supplying hose and appliances for the emergency fire services is described later in this volume.[3] The stirrup pump for fire-fighting by wardens and others had, it will be recalled, been designed in final form some months before Munich, and the Treasury had authorised its purchase on the modest scale of 50,000 for the equipment of wardens' posts.[4] It was not until April 1939 that the A.R.P. Department informed local authorities that delivery of 10 per cent. of this number was due to begin shortly.[5] In July the Department obtained approval for purchase of a further 50,000 pumps, and soon afterwards it told the authorities that these need not be restricted to wardens' posts but might be used for fire-protection of A.R.P. buildings.[6] By the middle of August, however, only 8,500 pumps had been delivered to local authorities.

Central purchase had been arranged during and after Munich for a standard all-metal stretcher which could easily be decontaminated after exposure to gas, whistles, rattles, hand bells and log-books for wardens' posts and for certain equipment for Decontamination Squads; and by midsummer fair quantities of these articles were being delivered to local authorities.[7] The problems of ingenuity and scale which equipment of the A.R.P. services presented may be illustrated by the case of hand torches. A variation of the standard bicycle lamp, fitted with a special hood for use in the black-out and able to take the standard small battery, was designed, and authority obtained for the free issue of 250,000 of these to local authorities.

---

[1] pp. 142, 163.

[2] p. 215.

[3] Chapter VI, 'Emergency Fire Brigade Measures'.

[4] pp. 146–147.

[5] A.R.P. Dept. Circular 85, 17th April 1939; p. 213.

[6] A.R.P. Dept. Circular 168, 10th August 1939.

[7] p. 213.

The decision was taken in May to supply more than 1 million members of the A.R.P. services with a 'uniform' not merely to promote *esprit de corps* but also because volunteers were wearing anti-gas suits during training to protect their own clothing. The announcement was made in Parliament on 10th July that an overall suit of dark blue cotton cloth with a simple badge on the left breast and chrome buttons would be supplied to men, and a long coat of similar material to women.[1] The man's overall would cost (with gas-proofing) 6s. 9d., and as war approached the G.P.O. was arranging on behalf of the A.R.P. Department for the purchase of over 1 million of these garments.

Industry, in the meantime, had been experiencing much difficulty in acquiring basic articles of A.R.P. equipment. Arrangements entered into after Munich whereby local authorities lent employers equipment for training had not, since this equipment formed part of their mobilisation stocks, proved popular with authorities, and the Civil Defence Act made provision by employers of certain items in war an obligation. Supplies of Service masks were, until midsummer, far short of official needs, and the certification marks scheme for Civilian Duty masks had not made much progress.[2] It was therefore decided in April that the Home Office should supply employers affected by the Bill with Civilian Duty masks and steel helmets on payment, though employers would have to continue to buy anti-gas clothing on the open market.[3] Deliveries of these three items had not been made to employers on any significant scale by the time war broke out.

In spite of much interdepartmental discussion on the use of civilian transport in an emergency, the Home Office had been unable to give local authorities any guidance regarding the earmarking of vehicles for A.R.P. purposes until Munich was at its peak.[4] The procedure for acquiring the 60,000 or more vans, lorries and private cars required for A.R.P. services was a complicated one, and the view still prevailed that vehicles would only need to be taken into use during periods of actual attack. After the crisis the Ministry of Transport had become responsible for allotment and co-ordination of all civilian transport to be used in war; and early in 1939 it published a proposal that goods vehicle operators should form voluntary working groups for war purposes, and began to prepare a voluntary register of goods vehicles.[5] New instructions

---

[1] H. of C. Deb., Vol. 349, Col. 1827; A.R.P. Dept. Circular 149, 18th July 1939; p. 207.
[2] pp. 80–81, 141.
[3] pp. 223–224.
[4] H.O. Circular of 20th September 1938; Ministry of Health Circular 1764, 10th January 1939.
[5] This voluntary grouping sometimes afforded an excuse for not offering vehicles for A.R.P.

issued by the A.R.P. Department to scheme-making authorities in March laid down that vehicles earmarked for A.R.P. use must be approved by the Chairman of the Traffic Commissioners of the area; but the duty of finding these vehicles and making arrangements with their owners rested with the authorities, and financial principles were still undefined.[1] The 'local war instructions' issued at this date envisaged that when an emergency arose authorities would collect the vehicles so reserved by stages corresponding to the call-up of volunteers, and then proceed to carry out any adaptation or special fitting required.[2]

Progress by this method through the summer proved slow, on account of the demands of the Army and other Services for transport, the exclusion of various classes of goods vehicles from A.R.P. use and the small number of private cars available in many urban areas. Many authorities found difficulty in obtaining even a small proportion of their needs by voluntary agreements with private owners, but the Ministry of Transport showed reluctance to resort to the requisitioning of vehicles for A.R.P. needs provided for in the Civil Defence Act. During active mobilisation in the last days of August requisitioning powers were first conferred on local authorities, subject to the Traffic Commissioners' consent, and then transferred to the new Regional Transport Commissioners and District Transport Officers.[3] And though shortage of vehicles for ambulances and other A.R.P. needs was almost everywhere acute, the authorities were still urged to rely as far as possible on voluntary arrangements. Methods of insuring cars used for A.R.P. training had been laid down some time previously. But when war broke out neither the terms of compensation for requisitioned vehicles nor the scales of payment for vehicles obtained under voluntary agreements had been determined.[4]

---

[1] A.R.P. Dept. Circular 60, 27th March 1939.

[2] A.R.P. Dept. Circular 59, 22nd March 1939; pp. 217-218.

[3] A.R.P. Dept. Circulars 193 and 199, 25th and 29th August 1939. By a change of procedure from an Order under the Civil Defence Act to an Order under Defence Regulation 53.

[4] A.R.P. Dept. Circular 236, 9th September 1939.

CHAPTER VI

EMERGENCY FIRE BRIGADE
MEASURES

(February 1937 – September 1939)

UNLIKE most of the other civil defence services that were organised after 1935, the Auxiliary Fire Service was not a complete innovation demanding new techniques to meet new situations. Instead it was a service that could be built up on a corpus of knowledge, experience and skill that already existed among long-established fire brigades, and its problems were those of scale rather than of the unknown. And, as has been mentioned earlier,[1] the fire services differed from the general A.R.P. services in other ways. They had a traditional relationship with the police services, both locally and centrally. They were, moreover, an essentially combatant service; unlike most A.R.P. services, whose main work would come after the raid, the fire brigades could take active measures to check the destruction the incendiary bombs might cause while air attack was in progress; their main task was indeed to *fight* fires. These were among the reasons that caused the emergency fire services to be organised in a separate Division of the Home Office and to remain with the Home Office when the A.R.P. Department was transformed into the Ministry of Home Security.[2] For these same reasons the progress of the Auxiliary Fire Service becomes a separate issue and needs to be told as a separate story in the development of civil defence.

The effective organisation of emergency fire-fighting measures dates from the beginning of 1937. Increased fire risks in a future war had, of course, been among the issues considered since the 1920's by the various committees concerned in civil defence planning, but speculation and proposals had remained largely academic. In 1932–33, however, memoranda by the Home Office Fire Adviser and the Air Raids Commandant designate for London drew attention to the need to create a fire-fighting organisation on a scale never before contemplated. Two elements had revolutionised war-time

---

[1] See p. 145.

[2] In Scotland also this work was organised in a separate Division located in London, and later much of the work was transferred to the headquarters of the Scottish Home Department in Edinburgh.

fire hazards—the new light incendiary bomb and the constantly increasing range and capacity of aircraft. But despite the serious views held on fire dangers, the 'First Circular' on air raid precautions of July 1935 contained little mention of air raid fire-fighting. At this stage the Home Office believed that the development of air raid fire precautions was inextricably bound up with the long-term reform of the peace-time organisation, which had to wait until there was an opportunity for legislation. The circular foreshadowed, however, the appointment of a Committee— the Riverdale Committee— to investigate the fire brigade problem as a whole.

By this time a fairly clear picture was beginning to emerge in the Home Office of the sort of fire situations which might arise if light incendiary bombs were to be scattered in built-up areas, and detailed plans were being made to meet the situation. Schemes were worked out for the mutual reinforcement of brigades, based on Home Office schemes that had been given a trial during the First World War. But it had also been realised that the size of the problem would involve considerable expansion of the fire brigades and that it would be necessary to organise help from the A.R.P. Services and the public in fighting incipient fires.

The Riverdale Committee report, presented in May 1936,[1] dealt with the two main aspects of the fire problem—the improvement of the peace-time organisation, including the development of fire research, and the planning of emergency measures. The recommendations of this committee, together with the results of much Home Office study, took effect in two lines of development: firstly, in the comprehensive and detailed memorandum on Emergency Fire Brigade Organisation of February 1937, which inaugurated the planning of the local air raid fire schemes, and, secondly, in the preparation of legislation to reform the peace-time services which became the Fire Brigades Act, 1938. The Riverdale Committee report had been quickly followed by the establishment of the separate Fire Brigades Division of the Home Office and by the appointment of two technical committees to investigate aspects of the emergency fire problem.[2] By the beginning of 1937, therefore, much preliminary work had been done and the general pattern of the future emergency fire-fighting organisation had taken definite shape. The memorandum on the emergency organisation became a major land-mark in the pre-war Fire Service story; it marked the end of a long period of planning and the beginning of the phase of action. The antiquated organisation of the nation's fire services in the

---

[1] *Report of the Departmental Committee on Fire Brigade Services*, Cmd. 5224, 1936.

[2] The Committee on Fire Brigade Reserves and Auxiliary Firemen and the Committee on Light Fire Brigade Appliances.

R

inter-war years has been mentioned earlier in this book,[1] but it is perhaps worth making this point again in order to show on what foundations the emergency services had to begin to be built. In 1937, when this story begins, local authorities, with the exception of the London County Council, were under no statutory obligation to maintain a fire brigade or fire services of any kind; there was no central supervision of whatever fire services the local authorities chose to provide, and in consequence no standards of efficiency, organisation, manning or equipment had been laid down. A medley of local authorities possessed permissive powers to organise fire brigades; outside the boroughs and urban districts the normal fire brigade area in England and Wales was the parish, rural district councils becoming fire authorities only in particular areas where they had obtained special powers. There were, therefore, some hundreds of independent local fire brigades ranging from the meanest 'parish pump' to the large and efficient London Fire Brigade.[2] While the brigades protecting London and some of the larger cities were well equipped and highly trained, and even some of the smaller brigades manned largely by part-time firemen were adequate enough for the districts they served, large areas of the country had little or no efficient fire protection, and there were only very limited arrangements between the brigades for mutual support. It was on this heterogeneous collection of brigades that the emergency organisation would have to be built. The need for thorough-going reform had been recognised for many years; the Royal Commission already mentioned had made extensive proposals in 1923,[3] but it was not until 1938, when the anxieties of an impending war had highlighted the serious deficiencies of the situation, that the Government could see their way to introduce the necessary legislation.[4] When, therefore, the Home Office prepared their emergency plans, they had to be based on the fire brigade system as it stood.

The 'First Circular' on Fire Schemes

The important circular and memorandum on Emergency Fire Brigade Organisation which were issued by the Home Office and the

---

[1] See pp. 84–85.

[2] A story told by a Member of Parliament during the Debate on the Fire Brigades Bill illustrates the sort of situation that could arise. Recently '. . . a fire broke out in the parish. Upon the wall in the shed which housed the pre-war manual, there was a nominal strength of 14 men. Only 2 old men answered the call on this occasion. It was later discovered that the remaining 12 had been dead for several years'. (H. of C. Deb., Vol. 335, Col. 1450, 10th May 1938.)

[3] *Report of the Royal Commission Fire on Brigades and Fire Prevention*, Cmd. 1945, 1923. See pp. 84–85.

[4] See p. 249.

Scottish Office to the principal fire authorities[1] on 23rd February 1937, may be regarded as the foundation of the emergency fire brigade measures which followed. They stated the Departments' plans in detail and asked the country's more than a thousand fire brigade authorities to consider the problem of war-time fire risks for their districts and to draw up individual fire precautions schemes.

The authorities were to plan their schemes under a series of heads, including: (a) the organisation of auxiliary fire stations; (b) the augmentation of heavy fire-fighting appliances; (c) the organisation of a system of fire patrols,[2] equipped with light trailer pumps; (d) the provision of vehicles for towing trailer pumps; (e) the recruitment and training of fire brigade reserves and auxiliary firemen; (f) the augmentation of water supplies, especially the preparation of natural and static supplies, and (g) the provision of emergency means of communication. On the question of equipment, especially of the main types of pump, it was explained that the only way to produce enough appliances, hose and other equipment for the vast expansion needed was to set up a central purchasing and supply organisation. The Departments were prepared to undertake this responsibility and the memorandum specified the principal types of equipment that would be lent as soon as supplies were available. Advice on recruitment included a model syllabus for training auxiliary firemen and information on conditions of service for both auxiliary firemen and reservists.[3] The problem of emergency water supplies was explored at some length. The use of all forms of natural and static water supplies and the need for appliances and hose for water relaying were strongly emphasised.[4]

The circulars that accompanied the Emergency Fire Brigades memorandum contained important provisions on the financing of the

---

[1] The circulars were addressed to the London County Council and the Councils of the Boroughs and Urban Districts in England and Wales, and to Town and County Councils in Scotland. They were also sent to Rural District Councils in England and Wales 'for information'. (H.O. Circular 23rd February 1937, and Scottish Office Circular No. 3207, of the same date.)

[2] This was a rather novel suggestion that a large proportion of fire appliances should be dispersed among a series of patrol units with patrol 'beats' keeping every street under frequent observation. The aim was to ensure that fires would be quickly observed and attacked if fire calls could not get through to the stations. A good many authorities included this system in their early plans and some followed it out in operations later, but most fire brigade officers preferred to deploy their appliances from fire stations as calls came in, and in the most intensive attacks the system became inapplicable.

[4] Reservists were retired members of brigades who undertook to rejoin for duty in an emergency or beforehand, if required. They could be paid a 'retaining fee' (up to £5 annually). They did valuable work in training, especially during the early stages of the emergency, but their numbers were relatively small.

[4] Air raid fire precautions got their first public mention in the Government's Statement on Defence Expenditure of February 1937. 'The fire risks from incendiary bombs dropped from aeroplanes present a problem which is beyond the capacity of normal peace-time fire brigade organisations. Arrangements are being planned to accumulate the additional fire-fighting appliances required to meet the risk and to train reserve personnel.' (Cmd. 5374, February 1937.)

measures that the local authorities were being urged to take. Financial issues, it will be remembered, were still causing major difficulties in connection with general air raid precautions schemes.[1] But during 1936 the Home Office had been able to convince the Treasury[2] of the special claims of the fire brigades, that the production of most of the emergency fire-fighting equipment that would be required would have to be directed centrally and that, whatever might be the outcome of the discussions on A.R.P. finance generally, a substantial proportion of such equipment should be lent to the local authorities at the expense of the Exchequer. The circulars, therefore, told the local authorities that, pending a settlement on the issue of the cost of air raid precautions generally, they could rely on receiving on loan, from central sources, emergency appliances and hose for approved schemes up to a substantial proportion of the whole quantity they would require. Grants would also be made on a *per capita* basis towards the cost of recruiting and training auxiliary firemen and providing them with uniforms and towards the fire authorities' incidental expenses. These special grant arrangements were superseded at the end of the year by the provisions in the Air Raid Precautions Act of December 1937, under which all save a few special items of the emergency equipment were to be lent free of cost and other expenditure on approved measures would rank for grant on the same basis as for the other A.R.P. services.[3] The advance announcement of these special financial arrangements was, however, of some importance at the time since it gave the fire authorities an interim assurance of substantial Exchequer assistance.[4]

Although the memorandum gave the authorities the general pattern of the measures to be organised it left many particulars to be filled in, especially as to the scale on which auxiliary firemen should be recruited, auxiliary stations organised and water supplies provided. It would not be enough to leave it to local authorities to plan the degree of protection they should provide with only a general indication of the conditions to expect. The vital consideration was the wholly novel scale on which the Home Office believed the measures would be needed. It was not a question of, say, doubling the number of firemen and appliances but of achieving perhaps a tenfold expansion, and the fire authorities would probably find it

---

[1] See pp. 92–99.

[2] A preliminary announcement about these arrangements had been made by the Parliamentary Under-Secretary of State for The Home Department on 30th July 1936 (H. of C. Deb., Vol. 315, Cols. 1852–3.)

[3] In the year 1938–39 local authorities' expenditure on fire precautions schemes in England and Wales came to just under £600,000; for the year 1939–40 it had risen to £3,400,000, the latter including, of course, some war-time expenditure.

[4] Such assurances were not, however, sufficient for all authorities. See pp. 244–245.

impossible to conceive of circumstances in which such quantities of men and equipment could be required. What was wanted, therefore, was a yardstick which could be applied, area by area, to determine the appropriate scale of local measures on the basis of some measurable local factor.

The Home Office, in the course of their study of the potentialities of the light incendiary bombs of the 1 kilogram magnesium type,[1] had formed decided opinions about the destruction missiles of this sort might cause, especially in a 'high density' area where fires would be only too likely to spread and get out of control. Many dangerous factors would combine against the fire brigades—the large number of fires which might break out simultaneously, the speed with which they might spread, the difficulty of manoeuvring large numbers of fire appliances in narrow streets and the serious problem, if not the impossibility, of bringing up sufficient supplies of water if water mains were smashed. So serious would be these factors that, however much the brigades might be expanded and however well trained and led, they might well be unable to hold the fires in check. Areas presenting particularly formidable risks included the City of London, the dock and warehouse districts of the big ports. In such circumstances, to attempt to provide fire services on a scale to match the risk would have been impossible. All that could be aimed at, as in most other civil defence planning, was to arrive at the best possible estimate of the situation that might arise and devise measures to mitigate the consequences. The Departments were now ready to tell fire authorities the scale of preparations on which, in their opinion, it would be advisable to work.

The yardstick which the Home Office decided to adopt was based on street mileage 'weighted' by an assessment of fire risks. Working on the one hand on the fires that might be caused in a distributed attack (i.e., assuming no great degree of concentration), and on the other hand on the street mileage of high, medium and low fire risk,[2] the Departments thought an estimate could be made of the vulnerability of each area. Accordingly, the fire authorities were

---

[1] These were designed by the Germans before the end of the 1914–18 war, and were much smaller and lighter than the rather clumsy incendiary bomb weighing 20–30 lb. that the enemy had been using previously. They could be carried by aircraft in much greater numbers than the earlier types and were a much more efficient incendiary weapon and difficult to extinguish. The Home Office appear to have rated the incendiary weapon much higher than did the Air Ministry at this time.

[2] The classification was as follows:

Class A Risks—Large business premises, warehouses, large retail shops and stores, large works, munition stores and factories, aeroplane stores, docks, timberyards, railway depots, oil and petrol depots, refineries and similar risks.

Class B Risks—Small factories, medium sized shops, warehouses not exceeding three storeys, store yards (except timber yards), public garages, small oil depots and similar risks.

Class C Risks—Residential and small shop properties.

asked to calculate the street mileages in their areas under the classification provided, so that a 'weighted street mileage' could be worked out and used to estimate the equipment, firemen and auxiliary fire stations that would be needed. Local adjustments would also have to be made in the general assessments to take into account such circumstances as convenience of town configurations and presence of natural water supplies. By use of these formulae, consistency in handling local schemes at the centre could be secured, together with a speedy appreciation of total national demands for equipment.

By the end of the year the general principles embodied in the memorandum of February 1937 had been worked out in a 'Sketch of an emergency fire brigade organisation for a hypothetical town of medium size' and a corresponding scheme for a Scottish town.[1] The radical nature of the Departments' view on the possible scale of fire-fighting is illustrated by the fact that the hypothetical town with a population of 80,000, adequately provided for in peace-time by a fire brigade of nine whole-time and 15 part-time firemen manning two fire engines (with a trailer pump in reserve) was now assumed to need 30 emergency power appliances and 'not less than 300' auxiliary firemen.

So far the information supplied to local authorities had been of a purely advisory character—fire authorities could act on these lines, or not, at their own discretion. Some authorities set about preparing schemes without delay; others, including the London County Council and some other important authorities, refused as a matter of principle to take any kind of action involving expenditure until the terms of the Exchequer grant towards the cost of A.R.P. generally had been settled.[2] However, when the settlement on A.R.P. expenditure was eventually reached and embodied in the A.R.P. Act, 1937,[3] it became obligatory for the London County Council and every fire authority of a borough or urban district in England and Wales or of a burgh or county in Scotland to prepare an emergency fire precautions scheme along the lines of the measures recommended in the February memorandum.[4] Under the Air Raid Precautions (Fire Schemes) Regulations made by the Secretary of State in the following March[5] each scheme was to cover: the

---

[1] H.O. Circular 15th December 1937, and Scottish Office Circular No. 3333, of the same date.

[2] The London County Council, for instance, told the Home Office categorically that they would do nothing that would involve specific expenditure from County funds until the financial issues were out of the way, and for nearly a year after the issue of the memorandum the Council still had no emergency fire brigade organisation.

[3] pp. 107–109, 145–146 and 242.

[4] H.O. Circular 28th January 1938, and Scottish Office Circular No. 3331, of the same date.

[5] S.R. & O. 1938, No. 252 and for Scotland No. 220/S.12.

organisation of an emergency fire brigade service, including such provision as was necessary of auxiliary fire stations, fire patrols and fire posts; arrangements for making use of natural and static supplies of water; the storage and maintenance of equipment and material; the recruitment and training of auxiliary firemen and other personnel; and arrangements for securing the use of vehicles. Rural District Councils in England and Wales were empowered but not compelled to submit schemes.[1]

By the beginning of 1938, therefore, the development of emergency fire brigade measures had begun in earnest. Urban authorities, and in Scotland, counties, were under an obligation to prepare A.R.P. emergency fire precautions schemes; they had been shown the general pattern these schemes should follow in the 'First Memorandum' and had subsequently been advised on the scale of preparation needed for different areas; the financial issues had been settled and responsibility for the provision of equipment had been assumed by the central Departments. The Auxiliary Fire Service should now be able to expand and prosper.

But for the Home Office and the Scottish Office, and indeed for each fire authority, the growth of the Auxiliary Fire Service was inevitably a lengthy and detailed administrative task. Each of the more than one thousand fire authorities[2] in Great Britain was required to set out its scheme on a standard set of forms. It had to give particulars of street mileage of high, medium and low risk, of the principal fire risks, of the water supplies and of the regular fire brigade strength and equipment. This information had to be supported by maps and details of the emergency organisation proposed, including auxiliary fire stations, emergency water supplies, auxiliary firemen enrolled or expected to be enrolled, and the arrangements for training them, and the appliances and equipment required. Each scheme had to be examined in detail by the central Departments, who commented on the scheme as a whole, raised questions where points were not clear and suggested improvements or modifications where desirable. The opportunity was also taken to review the strength, organisation and equipment of the regular fire brigades. It was, indeed, one of the conditions of the loan of emergency equipment (insisted on by the Treasury) that authorities should have provided an efficient service for ordinary peace-time purposes, or, if the current services were defective, should have at least undertaken to remedy the defects.

The great volume of work involved in all this had, however, uses

---

[1] pp. 247–248.

[2] To begin with schemes were asked for from 1,193 fire authorities, but after the Fire Brigades Act, 1938, had made rural district councils fire authorites, another 475 authorities were added. In some cases, however, authorities combined and submitted joint schemes.

beyond the immediate emergency purposes in view. In the study of local schemes and consultations with the fire authorities and their offices, the Departments gained a detailed knowledge of the fire risks and fire-fighting arrangements throughout the country that was to prove invaluable in the expansion of the Service and changes in organisation that followed. And in the country districts in particular, work on the schemes led to marked improvements in the arrangements for fighting peace-time fires.

When each scheme had been scrutinised and passed as satisfactory, the Departments gave each authority a preliminary estimate of the number of auxiliary fire stations, patrol units and firemen they would approve for purposes of the Exchequer grant and the number of appliances they would provide on loan. So that training could proceed, an initial allocation of pumps was usually made— normally of the order of one or two pumps and ancillary equipment in the case of the smaller brigades, or 10 per cent. of the total estimated requirements in the case of larger schemes. However, where local emergency schemes were well advanced and a large number of auxiliary firemen had been recruited, an allocation of pumps up to as much as 40 per cent. of total requirements might be made. As each authority's scheme was passed, a running total of pumps and equipment that would be needed was being built up and became the basis on which contracts for appliances were placed with manufacturers by H.M. Office of Works.

By the spring of 1938 only about 130 schemes had reached the Home Office out of the 965 required from boroughs and urban districts (allowing for joint schemes); about 30,000 firemen had been recruited and 360 emergency pumps supplied. Progress was still very patchy—good progress had been made in some areas but hardly a beginning in others, including some of the important cities and towns.[1] During the following months, however, much progress was made. By June 1939, nearly 900 schemes had been received and most of them had been approved; the Auxiliary Fire Service now numbered 120,000, with 18,000 watch-room attendants and a number of women and youths, and the brigades had 4,350 emergency appliances, 470 miles of hose and a considerable quantity of other equipment. In Scotland progress was rather slower; by June 1939, only 115 schemes had been received from the 228 fire authorities and only 61 of these had been settled.

The special case of London calls for separate mention. Although

---

[1] Departmental inquiries made in May 1938 showed that areas where arrangements were going ahead well included: Birkenhead, Birmingham, Bristol, Cardiff, Coventry, Croydon, Derby, Edinburgh, Leeds, Newcastle, Portsmouth and Southampton. Areas that appeared to be backward included Glasgow, Hull, Plymouth, Reading, Sheffield, Stoke-on-Trent and Warrington, as well as several places in the London area, notably East Ham and West Ham.

the submission of emergency fire schemes on standard forms was effective in the case of a single city or town, it was not applicable to the most important fire brigade area of all—the City and County of London. In this case the main elements of the scheme were worked out in consultation between the Home Office, the London County Council and the Fire Brigade. Soon after the financial issues had been settled by the passing of the Air Raid Precautions Act,[1] the London County Council submitted tentative proposals for their scheme; this involved not only the provision of 2,500 trailer pumps and the recruitment of 30,000 auxiliary firemen but also the immediate recruitment of 120 regular firemen to act as instructors to Auxiliary Fire Service recruits and of a larger number of regular firemen to strengthen the brigade for its emergency duties and to improve the current hours of duty of the brigade. The provision of 120 instructors and of a small staff to assist the Chief Officer with emergency measures was approved, but the further augmentation was rejected as being outside the scope of the emergency measures. On the scale of the provision to be made, based on 'weighted street mileage', and on points of organisation many proposals and counter-proposals were discussed. They were indeed still being discussed when war broke out, and it was not until January 1940 that a scheme officially came before the County Council's Fire Brigade Committee. By then the Home Office had agreed to provide over 2,800 pumps, with other equipment in proportion, and the approved establishment of personnel came to just under 20,000.

It has been mentioned earlier that the memorandum of February 1937 was sent to rural district councils for their general information,[2] though at this stage they were not asked, nor even authorised, to draw up fire precautions schemes. Later in the year the Air Raid Precautions Act, 1937, empowered but did not require rural district councils to prepare and submit such schemes.[3] This was intended as a stop-gap measure pending the new Fire Brigades Bill, under which, it was assumed, all rural district councils would be made fire authorities. Some rural districts, which might quite easily have more important fire risks than many of the smaller towns and urban districts, promptly went ahead and worked out emergency schemes under these temporary and permissive arrangements. Later, when the Fire Brigades Act, 1938, had been passed and all rural district councils were required to establish an efficient peace-time fire brigade, the Home Office sent them a detailed 'Memorandum on Emergency Fire Brigade Measures in Rural Districts'

---

[1] p. 244.

[2] p. 245.

[3] This was held to carry with it the power to provide a regular as well as an emergency fire service, where the council did not already possess this power.

and forms for the submission of schemes.[1] The Treasury, not unnaturally, wished to guard against rural district councils evading their new responsibilities by relying wholly or mainly on auxiliary fire stations established and auxiliary firemen trained and equipped with Exchequer aid; it stipulated, therefore, that no appliances must be lent, even for training purposes, unless the area was specially vulnerable, until the Department was satisfied that efficient fire protection for peace-time purposes had been provided.[2]

Schemes from the 475 rural districts came in fairly slowly: by the end of 1938, 33 had been received; by June 1939 the number had reached 125 and by May 1940, 300. These schemes took a somewhat different shape from those for urban areas, for the conception of 'weighted street mileage' bore little relevance to country problems. In some cases a borough or urban district fire brigade provided the primary protection for an adjoining rural area and organised the emergency measures; in other cases a joint scheme was submitted by a rural district council and another authority, but in most cases the councils organised their own schemes for their own districts. Once again, as schemes were approved the Home Office told the authority what equipment would be allocated to them, made an initial allotment for training and informed them of the amount of Exchequer grant that would be payable.

While these varied and complex administrative problems had been developing the Fire Brigades Division itself had been gradually expanded, and by the spring of 1939 had been organised in three Branches, each under an Assistant Secretary or officer of equivalent rank, one dealing with matters of peace-time legislation and general policy and the others with the emergency schemes and the equipment programme; and by the end of the year it had been further expanded and reorganised into five Branches. In the meantime an Inspectorate, initiated in March 1937, had been gradually built up. By November 1939, there was an Inspector and an Assistant Inspector at each Regional Commissioner's Headquarters, with a Chief Inspector and two Engineering Inspectors at the Home Office. The Division remained under the general direction of the Assistant Under-Secretary of State who also had charge of the Police Division.

The Riverdale Committee had recommended the recruitment of a corps of fire wardens, separate from the fire brigades. The Fire Brigades Division did not favour this scheme, though in the

---

[1] The Memorandum was sent out in August 1938 and a parallel 'Memorandum on Emergency Fire Brigade Measures in Landward Areas' was issued by the Scottish Office in October 1938.

[2] Standards of efficiency of a fire brigade organisation for a rural area were therefore laid down in the Memorandum on Local Fire Services in Rural Districts issued by the Home Office on 31st July 1939. A similar document was issued in Scotland.

instructions of February 1937 they had advised fire authorities to provide for the formation of fire posts, manned by 'fire pickets', whose training might be combined with the training of householders and others in dealing with incendiary bombs. In fact, responsibility for training the A.R.P. Services and the public in incendiary bomb control had been left with the A.R.P. Department, which had made small progress with this by the outbreak of war.[1] The invention of the stirrup-pump for amateur fire-fighting and the slow progress with supplies of this have already been recorded.[2]

The Fire Brigades Act, 1938

Concurrently with the work on emergency schemes the Home Office and the Scottish Office had been engaged in preparing the legislation to reform the peace-time service. In many respects the legislation followed the recommendations of the Riverdale Committee, but in other respects it took a different line, in particular in the matter of Exchequer grants. Eventually on 28th July 1938 the Fire Brigades Act received the Royal Assent,[3] two years after the Committee had reported and fifteen years after a Royal Commission had made very similar proposals.[4] As the Home Secretary remarked on the Second Reading of the Bill, 'Perhaps the feature' (of the history of fire protection in this country) 'that is most constant is the fact that we have seldom taken action in the development of fire protection unless we have been stimulated by some calamity or the threat of some calamity'.[5]

The Fire Brigades Act laid down that the fire brigade authorities in England and Wales, outside London, should be the councils of the boroughs, urban districts, and rural districts (to the exclusion of the parishes) and, in Scotland, county and town councils, and that they should be obliged to provide or arrange for the establishment of an efficient fire brigade service. The Act introduced machinery for securing mutual assistance between fire brigades and for providing an efficient brigade in case of default by any fire authority. Central Advisory Councils for Fire Services were to be appointed for England and Wales and for Scotland, for the purpose of advising the Secretary of State on any question which he might refer to them in connection with the working of the Act. The Secretary of State was to be empowered to set up Fire Service Training Centres and to appoint Fire Brigade Inspectors to report on the manner in which the

---

[1] pp. 71, 127, 209.

[2] pp. 146–147, 235.

[3] 1 and 2 Geo. 6, Ch. 72.

[4] Cmd. 1945, 1923.

[5] H. of C. Deb., Vol. 335, Col. 1429, 10th May 1938.

Act was being carried out. But there was to be no Exchequer grant to the fire authorities to help them meet these peace-time obligations.

The Act laid the foundation on which a comprehensive service with high standards of efficiency and measures for mutual co-operation could be developed. But even when the functions of the parish councils had been taken over by the rural district councils, the Act still left the administration of the fire brigades in the hands of no less than 1,440 separate fire authorities in England and Wales and 228 authorities in Scotland.[1] The aggregate strength of the regular fire brigades at this time was only about 6,600 whole-time and 13,800 part-time firemen (and nearly one-third of the whole-time men were in the London Fire Brigade); it can readily be seen therefore that the service was broken up into a great number of very small units, most of which could command only very limited resources. Such fragmentation at the foundations was a serious element of weakness, which under the stress of war-time conditions was ultimately to lead to the supersession of the fire authorities and the transfer of their brigades to a unified National Fire Service.[2]

Problems of the Auxiliary Fire Service

Important though the Fire Brigades Act is to the story of the pre-war Fire Service, the resources of the regular fire brigades, however much improved by the new legislation, were soon to be over-shadowed by those of the expanding Auxiliary Fire Service. Fire risks in war-time presented a problem of such alarming dimensions that the peace-time conception of adequate protection was not in the same realm of discussion as the emergency planning. Early in 1938, for instance, the Home Office, in its report to the Committee of Imperial Defence, calculated that in an attack by a single bomber over a fairly closely populated area (15 per cent. built-over), something like 75 fires might break out over a distance of 3 miles along the track of the aircraft, or in a congested area (30 per cent. built-over) as many as 150 fires; a single formation of 10 bombers might cause 750 and 1,500 fires respectively. It was recognised that on grounds of cost and manpower alone it would be quite out of the question to set up a fire brigade organisation capable of giving complete protection everywhere at every time. The aim was, however, to provide every important centre (i.e.,

---

[1] These consisted of: (a) in England and Wales, the London County Council, the Councils of 83 County Boroughs and 309 Non-County Boroughs, 572 Urban District Councils and 475 Rural District Councils, and (b) in Sco'land, 33 County Councils and 195 Town Councils.

[2] This is described in Chapter XI of this book.

towns of 20,000 and more inhabitants, areas around important industrial establishments and railway junctions, etc.) with an emergency organisation capable of dealing with fires that might result from fairly intensive bombing by a single aircraft; for the rest of the community, provision should be on similar lines but on a reduced scale.

In accordance with the general policy for all the arms of civil defence, emergency fire services were to be locally provided, although there would be central direction and Exchequer participation in the costs. In particular, nearly all the essential fire-fighting appliances and equipment would be provided on loan at Exchequer expense. Although all areas were drawing up their schemes to conform to the same general plan, the essential nature of local government meant that there were inevitably great variations in the effectiveness of the local measures taken. Different degrees of enthusiasm, administrative ability and initiative brought different results in the finding of accommodation, the recruitment and training of volunteers, the organisation of communications systems, and in the relations between auxiliary firemen and the regular fire brigades. The practical problems for each authority and for the co-ordinators at the centre were manifold and it would be impossible to explore them all. Instead it is proposed to select some of the main issues that arose. First, the problems associated with the three essential components of fire-fighting—men, equipment and water. Then the framework of accommodation, communications and command within which these tactical weapons were to be handled.

(i) Manning the Service

The earliest step to safeguard the strength of the fire services was an arrangement made in April 1936 with the Committee of Imperial Defence whereby regular firemen with reserve obligations in the Armed Forces would not be lost to the brigades immediately war broke out. The London Fire Brigade and other professional brigades had been in the habit of recruiting naval reservists, and their immediate loss would be a serious matter if, as was expected, a future war opened with heavy air attacks. Every regular fireman would be needed to lead whatever auxiliaries had been recruited and generally to stiffen the expanded emergency organisation. The Service Departments therefore agreed that reservists (with certain exceptions) who were members of public fire brigades would not be mobilised until at least three months after a war had broken out.[1]

---

[1] In July 1936 the total number of reservists serving with the fire brigades was 485, 331 of whom were in the London Fire Brigade.

At a later stage, the position of other regular firemen was also made secure, though in this case they were to be protected for a longer period than merely the opening months of war. Whole-time members of fire brigades serving on 3rd June 1939 were exempted from the call-up under the Military Training Act, 1939,[1] and from the age of 18 members of public fire brigades were included among the reserved categories in the Ministry of Labour schedule of reserved occupations.

These two measures protected the hard core of the Service—the peace-time brigades. But most of the manpower problems that were to arise were concerned with the recruitment and training of the great body of men and women needed to supplement the regular firemen.

Until the memorandum of February 1937 no specific invitation had been given to the public to volunteer for emergency fire brigade work. The 'First Circular' on A.R.P. of July 1935 had, it is true, mentioned that the fire brigade service would need to be strengthened, but little had been said on practical measures to obtain recruits. A few local authorities acted on this general exhortation or as a result of 'missionary' work by the A.R.P. Department, but in most areas nothing was done until 1937 to recruit volunteers.

The memorandum of February 1937 inaugurated serious recruiting for the Auxiliary Fire Service, laying down the principles on which auxiliary firemen—those without previous fire brigade experience who volunteered for duty in an emergency—should be recruited. The specified ages for enlistment were between 25 and 50, and the memorandum gave guidance on such administrative details as conditions of service and forms of application for enrolment. All recruits were to be medically examined to ensure their fitness for strenuous physical duties,[2] and each man enrolled had to undertake to come forward in an emergency for part-time, or if willing and selected by the Chief Officer, for whole-time service.

As soon as new volunteers were recruited, it was vital to maintain their enthusiasm and train them quickly. Auxiliary firemen would have to be able to handle power appliances, to enter a burning building and withstand punishing heat and smoke, and to carry an insensible person down a ladder; they might at any time have to cope with a situation where the safety of members of the public or their comrades depended on their strength, their endurance and

---

[1] F.B. Circular No. 20/1939, 31st May 1939.

[2] Most authorities took advantage of an insurance scheme negotiated by the Home Office with the Insurance Companies, under which compensation was paid to a fireman who was incapacitated or who died as a result of injury on duty. These compensation arrangements were later superseded by the Personal Injuries (Civilians) Scheme which took effect from the outbreak of war. (H.O. Circular, 30th April 1937 and subsequent circulars.)

their skill and judgment. The memorandum set out a model syllabus for the guidance of brigades in organising their local training, and courses extending over a total period of 60 hours were sketched out. It was emphasised that initial training should be followed by refresher courses at regular intervals and that auxiliaries should be given every possible opportunity to gain practical experience in actual fire-fighting in peace-time.

Most fire authorities now proceeded to train their auxiliaries in accordance with the official syllabus, although a shortened version had sometimes to be used when a rapid intake of recruits led to congestion at a training centre. At first most of the work necessarily fell on members of the regular fire brigades and their reservists,[1] but gradually more and more trained auxiliaries were able to help. Accommodation was a serious problem. As in other A.R.P. measures, improvisation was the order of the day, and training centres had to be set up in shops, garages and all sorts of makeshift premises, and, in the nature of things, most of the work had to be done in the evenings with some of the volunteers attending only irregularly. However, by the autumn of 1938 much had been achieved: about 2,250 training classes were being held weekly; 13,000 auxiliary firemen had completed the prescribed course, 50,000 more were under training out of the 82,000 then enrolled, and exercises to accustom pump crews and staffs of control rooms to fire-fighting procedure had been held by some local authorities.

Although the basic principle of civil defence service was that of unpaid voluntary work, it was clear that conditions of service and pay would have to be fixed for those volunteers who, in an emergency, would become whole-time workers. This was particularly true of the Auxiliary Fire Service, for the Home Office believed that this Service would require a higher proportion of whole-time members than would the other civil defence services. The special characteristic of efficient fire-fighting—that of speed—demanded a strong contingent of whole-time men in all important centres with high fire risks. It was important, therefore, that the pay of men and women who volunteered for possible whole-time service should be announced in good time, so that those who might be able to serve would know exactly how they would stand. The Government decision on this subject was announced in February 1939.[2] The basic pay of £3 a week for men and £2 a week for women,[3] and the general conditions of service were to be the same for the A.F.S. as for the other civil defence services, subject to the important qualification that the

---

[1] pp. 242–243.

[2] H. of C. Deb., Vol. 343, Col. 1923, 16th February 1939.

[3] The basic pay also applied to part-time regular firemen who undertook whole-time duty.

A.F.S. would have officer ranks with differential rates of pay.[1] It was not, of course, easy in peace-time to discover with any degree of certainty which auxiliaries could be relied upon to take up whole-time duty, but gradually Chief Officers of the fire brigades began to form some idea of what the numbers might be. In May 1939 for instance, they estimated that about 65,000 auxiliaries out of the 140,000 then recruited would be available for whole-time duty if required. Women auxiliaries were already making their mark as telephonists, watch room workers and drivers in London and some of the large cities. By this time some 4,500 had been enrolled.

Another condition of service (apart from officer pay) that differed in the A.F.S. from the other civil defence services was the policy on uniforms, sometimes viewed by the other services as putting the auxiliary firemen in a privileged position. From the beginning the Auxiliary Fire Service was planned as a uniformed service. The fire brigades, it was successfully argued, were by tradition uniformed, and a fireman needed his uniform to give him some measure of protection from heat and water, and to save his own clothing from excessive wear and tear.

The original memorandum of February 1937 had given advice on the items of uniform and equipment to be supplied to auxiliary firemen, but each authority could adopt whatever patterns of uniform or types of equipment it thought fit. In the following year, however, the question of standard designs was taken up and detailed specifications were circulated to fire authorities.[2] Recruits were to be supplied with the authorised complement of uniform in two stages—overalls, rubber boots, cap, belt, axe and pouch during preliminary training; and tunic, trousers, and oil-skin leggings when the recruit needed them for 'wet' drills.   Later, a waterproof coat could also be supplied.[3] Provision was also made for women in the Service. The A.F.S. cap badge, buttons and breast badges which became the distinguishing marks of the Service, were centrally produced (through the Post Office Stores Department) and distributed

---

[1] On this question of senior ranks and rates of pay the A.R.P. Department feared 'repercussions' on the other services, but eventually the Fire Brigades Division, which regarded some such provision as essential, got their way and pay scales for A.F.S. officers were announced on 2nd September 1939:
  Patrol Officers: normal rate £4 a week.
  Section Officers: normal rate £5 a week.
  Divisional Officers: between that for Section Officers and £400 per annum.
  Commandant and Deputy or Assistant Commandant: to be determined in each case individually.
  An addition to the basic rate was added later for Leading Firemen.

[2] H.O. Circular 15th June 1938 and Scottish Office Circular 3617, 23rd August 1938.

[3] F.B. Circular No. 76/1939, 12th October 1939 and Scottish Home Department Circular No. L88/1939, 21st October 1939.

to all authorities. The A.F.S. also had a distinctive button-hole badge for its members to wear when out of uniform.[1]

The existence of the regular fire brigades on which the emergency structure could be built brought great benefits but also some problems. Relations between the A.F.S. and the regular brigades developed very differently in different areas. In particular there were considerable variations in the extent to which officer ranks were created in the new service, and the extent to which auxiliary officers were given responsibility for the development and control of the emergency services and were able to take part in active peace-time operations. In some areas the A.F.S. was organised with a cadre of volunteer officers exercising a large measure of initiative and responsibility in matters of organisation and supervision; in others, among them the London Fire Brigade, the few auxiliary officers appointed were allowed little voice in the organisation or in the control of auxiliary firemen.

In the main, appeals for fire service recruits were made along with the general propaganda for volunteers for the other civil defence services, though these were also supplemented by more specific appeals for firemen through such media as broadcasts, posters and press notices, either nationally or locally organised. In one respect the fire brigades were at a disadvantage with the other services in recruiting volunteers—they needed a large proportion of young and active men, and were therefore more in competition with the Armed Forces. (This element of competition for younger men naturally became more acute after the war had broken out.) On the other hand the fire brigades had some advantages—their work was more obviously dramatic than other forms of civil defence, and the fact that the A.F.S. was a uniformed service was said to attract potential recruits.

Recruiting, which started fairly slowly, speeded up after the passing of the Air Raid Precautions Act in December 1937, and particularly after March 1938, when the Home Secretary launched the national recruiting campaign for the A.R.P. Services generally. The increasing tension of the international situation after the German occupation of Austria brought in more volunteers, and in the autumn of 1938 recruitment was still further stimulated by the Munich Crisis. In April 1938, it was announced that auxiliary firemen over the age of 25 who had been recruited and trained, and were available for duty with the public fire brigades, would not be called up for other duties in the first stages of an emergency.[2] In

---

[1] H.O. Circular of 24th August 1938, Scottish Office Circular No. 3376.

[2] H. of C. Deb., Vol. 335, Col. 286, 28th April 1938, quoted in memoranda issued by the Home Office and Scottish Office on 24th October and in December 1938 respectively.

S

March 1939, local fire authorities put their requirements at about 175,000 auxiliary firemen (as against the Home Office estimate of nearly double that number) towards which, as has already been mentioned, about 140,000 had been recruited. About 65,000 of these, as it was understood, would be prepared to serve whole-time in case of emergency. The proportion of recruits to the numbers required, however, varied a great deal from one area to another. Already, therefore, the A.F.S. was many times greater numerically than the fire brigades on which it was based, though still far short of the number estimated as necessary if emergency measures on the scale then being planned were to be fully implemented.

(ii) Equipping the Service

This narrative has already recorded the decision that the main items of equipment needed for the new schemes would be purchased centrally and that at any rate a substantial proportion of the quantities required would be lent out to the local authorities.[1] The main reason for this decision was that no manufacturing capacity existed capable of producing appliances in the quantities needed. The large and heterogeneous collection of fire authorities had in the past each bought their engines and other items of equipment in one's and two's according to their individual specifications. If manufacturers were to turn out large amounts of apparatus at speed, it was clearly important for them to have bulk orders on a scale sufficient to make it worth their while to embark on the high capital outlay or expensive re-organisation needed for the setting up of 'production lines', with special tools, jigs, testing gear, etc.[2]

From the beginning, pumps were the most important single item in the manufacturing programme. They were not only the most vital fire-fighting appliance but they were used as the measuring rod against which the whole plan was set, since it was on the basis of their numbers that the needs for other equipment were assessed. The equipment problem was not, however, simply one of settling designs and finding enough manufacturing capacity for the pumps—there were also the many and varied items of ancillary equipment without which pumps were useless. Any breakdown in the supply of many of these items would have been just as fatal as a breakdown in the supply of pumps. Even before the war the production programme included over 120 separate categories of

---

[1] pp. 241-242.

[2] Not only would the provision of equipment 'on the basis of selected types and capacity specification . . . purchased in bulk . . . effect large savings as against purchase by the local authorities', said the Home Office in their memorandum to the Treasury, but 'it would be possible to lay down specific conditions and ensure a full measure of control over the use and maintenance of the equipment'.

pieces of equipment, including by way of example (in round figures), 50,000 suction hose couplings, 200,000 delivery hose couplings, 20,000 suction delivery heads, 50,000 branch pipes, 100,000 nozzles, 45,000 ladders (30 feet or less), 30,000 (each) axes, picks and spades and 170,000 canvas buckets.

In addition there were such questions as the supply of vehicles for towing trailer pumps and the provision of suction and delivery hose, turntable-ladders, escape units, hose-laying lorries, water tenders, water tanks and canvas 'dams'.

At the outset, before the fire authorities had been able to prepare their emergency schemes, and before any very definite ideas had been formed on the scale of expansion needed, the number of pumps required could only be vaguely guessed. It was, however, abundantly clear that in comparison with the number of fire engines already in the hands of the brigades and in the context of the manufacturing capacity available, equipment would be needed in quantities that by ordinary standards were colossal. Another important considera-tion was the need for at least some of the appliances to be supplied quickly, so that local authorities could train their new recruits. It was, indeed soon evident that the scale of production required, coupled with the time factor, was going to set the Home Office a very considerable manufacturing problem.

Since the Home Office was not a contracting Department, it was decided that H.M. Office of Works should act as agents for the Home Office and the Scottish Office; the Office of Works was familiar with many of the engineering problems likely to arise and experienced in buying a wide range of supplies for government use. The Home Office laid down the type, performance and quantities of the various items of equipment required, the period within which they should be supplied and where they should be delivered; the Office of Works translated these requirements into drawings and specifications, enlisted the interest of suitable firms, advertised for tenders and, together with the Home Office, selected tenders, placed contracts, tested samples and gave delivery instructions.

One issue that proved difficult to settle at this time was the question of the condition under which emergency fire appliances were to be lent to local authorities. The Air Raid Precautions Act empowered the Secretary of State to acquire equipment 'for the purpose of affording protection to persons and property from injury or damage in the event of hostile attack from the air' and to make Regulations providing for the loan, gift or sale of such equipment.[1] But the Act did not cover the use of the appliances for any save emergency purposes, whereas it was important for auxiliary firemen to gain experience in their use at peace-time fires. To remedy this

---

[1] Sections 9 and 11 of the Air Raid Precautions Act, 1937.

deficiency, therefore, a clause was inserted in the Fire Brigades Act, 1938.[1] The Treasury were, however, anxious to ensure that authorities should not rely on loaned emergency appliances manned by auxiliary firemen to fill any gaps in their ordinary peace-time services and thus evade their obligations under the Fire Brigades Act, 1938. Towards the end of 1938, therefore, a set of rules were laid down specifying the conditions under which emergency appliances were supplied to authorities on loan.[2]

The administrative complications involved in organising such a large and speedy expansion in the production of so many items were innumerable and there is no space in this volume to explore in any detail these labyrinths of official endeavour. Three policy decisions taken during this period must, however, be examined briefly, for they were important in determining the pattern of the emergency pump production programme. The decisions were: first, to concentrate mainly on trailer pumps; secondly, to depart from previous practice in the design of the heavy pump, and thirdly, to buy pumps of several different designs in each range (heavy, large, medium and light) instead of placing orders for a single standard design.[3]

The decision to adopt trailer pumps for all emergency power-driven machines except the heavy pumps was important, and trailer pumps, in their battleship grey (the colour used for all emergency appliances as opposed to the red of the regular fire brigades) towed by a miscellaneous collection of vehicles, were to become familiar objects in the war-time streets. Trailer appliances were not completely new; while most of the peace-time fire engines were self-propelled, many brigades kept a trailer pump for occasional use. It was, however, quite a new departure for self-propelled machines to be greatly outnumbered by the trailer type. The main reason for

---

[1] Section 21, Fire Brigades Act, 1938.

[2] The appliances might be used in peace-time for maintenance purposes, for training and for extinguishing fires in exceptional circumstances when necessary to save life and property, and when local equipment was insufficient or not readily available; the local authority must keep the appliances in good working order and might be held responsible for repairing any damage or replacing any loss (the cost would, however be reimbursed if the peace-time fire was being used as a training fire); it must keep records of the use of the equipment and allow it to be inspected as required. The local authority must carry out its functions under its air raid precautions scheme, maintain proper services for peace-time purposes and make no alteration in the emergency equipment without the Department's consent. (Air Raid Precautions (Loan of Appliances) Provisional Regulations, 10th December 1938; H.O. Circular of 20th December 1938 and Scottish Office Circular No. 3449, 20th December 1938.

[3] The pump production programme included: 1. Heavy pump: capacity 700/900 gallons per minute at 100 lb. pressure, mounted on a frame, which could be carried on a motor vehicle chassis or mounted on a fire boat etc. 2. Large trailer pumps: capacity 350/500 gallons per minute at 100 lb. pressure. 3. Medium trailer pumps: capacity 250/350 gallons per minute at 100 lb. pressure. (At a later stage this type was dropped out.) 4. Light trailer pumps: capacity 120/150 gallons per minute at 80 lb. pressure. 5. Manual pumps which could be operated by two men and hand pumps that could be operated by a single person. At a later stage an 'Extra Heavy' pump, capacity 1,100/1,400 gallons a minute, similarly mounted to the heavy pumps, was introduced.

this policy was the belief that by concentrating on these smaller machines the large number of pumps needed for tackling air raid fires could be provided in the shortest possible time and at the lowest possible cost. These pumps were particularly suitable for emergency work; the light trailer pumps were of smaller capacity than the regular brigade machines, but could be man-handled over debris or (in later designs) detached from the trailer chassis and carried on a lorry. In addition, they were simpler and quicker to manufacture. They were, however, dependent on a towing vehicle. As in the case of other A.R.P. vehicles[1] the Treasury hoped, to begin with, that local authorities could borrow the necessary vehicles or, when war came, requisition them, but as war became imminent it was clear that these optimistic 'arrangements' were not working out[2] and fire authorities had to be authorised to buy second-hand high powered motor cars thrown on the market by their owners on the outbreak of war and a limited number of lorries as towing vehicles.[3] These 'arrangements' in turn broke down later, largely on account of the unsuitability of motor cars for the heavy work and, during the war, it became necessary to purchase centrally towing vehicles specially built for the purpose and to lend them to local authorities.[4]

The second decision on pump production concerned the design of heavy pumps and involved a radical departure from the current practice whereby a heavy pump was operated by a power 'take-off' from the same engine that propelled the vehicle. The essential feature of this new plan consisted in coupling the pump direct to an engine of a type best adapted to driving the pump and mounting both together on a frame, thus providing a self-contained pumping unit but one which was itself immobile and had to be mounted on a motor vehicle chassis or a fire boat, etc. It did, in fact involve the need for two engines, one for propulsion and one to drive the pump itself. Nevertheless the Departments believed that great advantages would spring from the simplification of the pump mounting. It would be possible to use mass produced engines which would result in both a great saving in cost, and, even more important at this stage, a better rate of production. Moreover such a standard type of unit could be used in several ways—it could be mounted on a chassis to form a mobile land appliance, on a river or sea-going craft to form an emergency fire boat or on a pier or dockside to provide a

---

[1] See p. 237.

[2] For example, at the time of the Munich Crisis it was claimed in the House of Commons that the London Fire Brigade had no vehicles at all except the cars of the volunteers themselves and 60 vans that had been bought by the Council for training work. (H. of C. Deb., Vol. 340, Cols. 422–423, 3rd November 1938).

[3] For example, F.B. Circular No. 41/1939 of 24th August 1939, Scottish Office Circular No. L.83/1939. These authorities were extended in subsequent circulars.

[4] See Chapter XI below.

fixed pumping station. After some experiment on the most suitable vehicles on which to mount these heavy pumps, it was decided about the end of 1937 to provide a special self-propelled chassis with a built-up body providing seats for the crews and lockers for the hose. In the course of the next three years some 1,360 heavy pumps, mounted on the special chassis to form complete self-propelled units, were delivered to the fire brigades—a production figure that could not have been approached under the manufacturing conditions that prevailed if the Departments had adhered to the conventional type of unit.

The third feature of the production programme which calls for special comment was the decision to purchase different designs within each type of pump instead of demanding a standard design for each type. Naturally enough the Home Office would have preferred to adopt standard designs and obtain them in bulk at reasonable prices, but when the programme was put in hand this policy did not seem practicable. Each fire brigade had its own views on the design of equipment, and to work out the best possible designs for standard types would have required long experiment and research at a stage when time was all-important. It seemed wiser, therefore, to give the manufacturers some latitude and to allow each of them to incorporate their own specialities and ideas in the machines they produced. In this way good features appearing in one design could often be incorporated in others. Most of the national production came from eleven manufacturers; three produced all the heavy and extra heavy machines, three most of the large trailer pumps and five nearly all the light trailer pumps.

In addition to deciding what types were most suitable for the emergency production programme, the Home Office had also to try to reach some conclusions on the number of appliances that would be needed to complete the programme or at any rate to carry it well on its way. While the Departments were convinced from their study of the light incendiary bomb that fire brigades would need large quantities of emergency appliances in comparison with peacetime standards, they had at the start no basis on which to make any very precise estimates. Working on a study of a few sample areas, they soon found that the figures were assuming immense proportions in comparison with the equipment already in the hands of the brigades. The first serious estimate based on the examination of local authority schemes was made in the autumn of 1937 and was reported to the Committee of Imperial Defence in January 1938.[1] It put the number of pumps of all types likely to be required at between 17,000 and 21,000. Ancillary equipment needed in proportion included, for example, 3,000 miles of delivery hose, and the total

---

[1] pp. 145, 250.

cost was put at £5 million. This first estimate was prepared from very scanty data when only a small proportion of local schemes had been received, but it proved reasonably near to the amounts that were in fact provided to equip the Auxiliary Fire Service in time for their great tests of 1940–41.

Once the arrangements for central purchase had been agreed, the first objective was to find sufficient manufacturing capacity. At first the tenders received were disappointing—there were relatively few firms who were interested, deliveries were too slow and prices too high. Gradually, however, prospects improved, especially after the beginning of 1938, when the Departments considered that the types of pump then being offered would justify the placing of orders for as many as 1,000 pumps at a time. At this time the Treasury was rather concerned lest the programme should be pressed too rapidly—the orders the Home Office now proposed to place would cover one-quarter of the total estimated requirements. The Home Office was, however, able to convince the Treasury that large orders were essential if the firms concerned were to lay down plant and organise their works for rapid production. By May 1938, orders had been placed for about 4,500 pumps and for most of the equipment to go with them, to a total cost of about £1 million.

Although fairly substantial orders had now been placed, actual delivery was still very slow. In May 1938 only 425 pumps out of the 20,000 or so that the brigades were estimated eventually to require had actually been delivered and the bulk of the equipment had still to be ordered. During that summer deliveries were extremely slow, especially of the light trailer pumps that were needed in such large numbers. Already many of the fire brigades had recruited auxiliaries sufficient to man many more pumps than they had received, and some of the appliances that had been delivered were immobilised through lack of ancillary gear.[1] And by now the tension of international events focused public attention on these deficiencies. In the course of proposing a motion of censure on the Government for their 'unpreparedness to protect the civil population when the country was brought to the brink of war', Mr Herbert Morrison, who as Leader of the London County Council had been personally concerned in London's air raid precautions measures, severely criticised the arrangements made to equip the fire brigades. In London, he said, it had been agreed that 3,000 emergency fire appliances were needed, but the number supplied to the time of the Munich Crisis was 99. The professional fire brigade could have used all these appliances itself, leaving none for the 4,000 auxiliaries then in training, who could have manned at least another 300 pumps. By November 1938, said Mr Morrison, the London Fire

[1] p. 263.

Brigade had recruited 13,500 auxiliaries but still had only 145 auxiliary appliances. With this personnel London could easily use 1,300 pumps. 'It is shameful,' he declared, 'that these volunteers who have come forward to do a very dangerous job should be short of the essential appliances.'[1]

Although the Auxiliary Fire Service had certainly been inadequately equipped at the time of Munich, appearances were to some extent deceptive. A considerable manufacturing capacity had now been built up, especially for the light trailer pumps that had caused such difficulties in the past. By the time of this Parliamentary criticism, orders for pumps had been increased from 4,500 to 7,000 and the Departments were able to look ahead to the completion of this programme within a measurable time. But now there were added demands for fire-fighting appliances for the Service Departments, whose requirements were pooled with those of the brigades, and early in November 1938, an extended production programme was approved and further orders placed for over 11,000 pumps.[2] This programme would provide about 80 per cent. of the total number likely to be required under the latest revised estimates.[3]

As late as November 1938 the target for the completion of this production programme was the spring of 1941; a target that had been settled on the basis of an Air Ministry appreciation in 1937. In December 1938, however, the Departments took fresh steps to accelerate deliveries and advanced their target date to the spring of 1940. Later in the month the Committee of Imperial Defence gave instructions that all possible progress should be made with preparations of every kind during the early months of 1939. In March and April 1939, the Committee on Defence Programmes and their Acceleration and the Prime Minister's Advisory Panel of Industrialists both urged strong measures to complete the programme. And, after some demur on the part of the Treasury, orders were placed to cover the balance of the calculated requirements plus a 5 per cent. reserve, bringing the total orders up to 26,900 machines.

By the middle of 1939 the fresh orders placed in 1938 were beginning to take effect and deliveries rose from about 300 a week in May, to 400 in June, 600 a week by the end of July and 500 a week throughout August. Some Fire Brigade officers, unable to conceive of circumstances in which these streams of appliances could be put to any practical use, viewed them with astonishment. Storage presented quite a problem; but there is no record of any brigade

---

[1] H. of C. Deb., Vol. 340, Cols. 421–422, 3rd November 1938.

[2] This brought the total orders placed up to 19,000 units (including 1,500 pumps for the Service Departments), split up as follows: 100 extra heavy, 750 heavy, 6,450 large trailer and 11,810 light trailer pumps. The total cost of the new orders and the necessary ancillary equipment was about £3,250,000.

[3] F.B. Circular No. 4/1939, 23rd March 1939.

declining to accept any of the pumps supplied. Thus, whereas the crisis of September 1938 had found the fire brigades with a total of less than 2,000 emergency pumps, about 14,000, or 60 per cent. of estimated requirements, were in the hands of the brigades at the outbreak of war a year later.[1]

As yet this consideration of the pre-war problems involved in equipping the Auxiliary Fire Service has concentrated on the basic issue of pump supplies. But many difficulties also arose over the production of other vital items of equipment, including such special apparatus as suction and delivery hose and other ancillary equipment for use with pumps, turntable ladders, steel tanks, canvas 'dams', and steel piping. Some of these items were, in fact, not provided on any scale until after the outbreak of war. In particular, there was considerable difficulty and much criticism of the failure during 1938–39 to arrange for the distribution of ancillary equipment to tally with the distribution of pumps.[2] In order to save the cost of storage and handling, the Departments arranged that deliveries of the various items should be made from the manufacturers direct to local authorities. This would have served very well if deliveries of the different items had synchronised, but they did not. Consequently, until the programme was well advanced it often happened that a brigade had pumps but not the essential equipment to enable the pumps to work, while others were receiving ancillary apparatus for which they had no immediate use.

The Prime Minister's Advisory Panel of Industrialists investigated the whole programme early in 1939. They found that the progress made in pump production was a considerable achievement but were dissatisfied with the mobilisation of production capacity for other essential gear. In particular, they urged the Office of Works, in placing their contracts for the items still required, to subordinate price considerations more to the acceleration of deliveries.

Individual practice and prejudices of the brigades were among the factors that could complicate central planning. One example which can be quoted related to hose couplings, i.e., the device that joins one length of hose to another or to a pump. The Home Office decided at an early stage in their production planning to disregard the many variations in types of coupling in use throughout the country and to adopt a standard pattern—2½-inch instantaneous coupling—for all emergency hose that the Department would provide

---

[1] Of the total number delivered, 2,018 had been allocated to the London Fire Brigade, 10,716 to the provinces, including the Greater London area and Scotland, and 865 to the various Departments.

[2] See for instance the criticism by Mr Herbert Morrison in the House of Commons, November 1938. Most of the pumps delivered to the London Fire Brigade, he claimed, had been sent without the necessary equipment, which had to be supplied out of the Brigade stores. (H. of C. Deb., Vol 340, Cols. 421–422, 3rd November 1938.)

on loan. The London Fire Brigade, however, resisted this proposal and made strong representations to be allowed to retain the particular type in use in the County area—a round thread coupling—claiming that they had no experience of and little confidence in instantaneous couplings. The Home Office conceded London's point, but this made it necessary to provide them with adaptors of various types to enable them to work with other brigades using the standard coupling. More serious was the fact that screw couplings could not be made on mass production lines, and it was not long before both couplings and adaptors fell far short of the number required. Eventually, in 1939, the London Fire Brigade agreed to accept instantaneous couplings, though it was not until after the heavy raids that 'round thread' complications were entirely eradicated.

Similar but less easily soluble difficulties came from the great diversity of hydrant equipment throughout the country. A report prepared in 1939 by the London Regional Fire Officer indicates the scale of the problem: there were six types of hydrant outlet in the London Region, only half of the 95,000 being of the 2½-inch round thread screw type used by the London Fire Brigade, the rest being of five different types. As long as each brigade was operating only in its own area these differences were not important, but if called to reinforce neighbouring services a brigade might well find that the standpipes it carried would not fit the local hydrants. Standardisation of hydrants seemed impracticable, however, as it would have involved the conversion of about 800,000 hydrants in England and Wales, and all attempts to devise a universal hydrant adaptor proved, unfortunately, unsuccessful. The best that the Home Office could do, therefore, was to urge all authorities to provide sufficient spare standpipes for their own hydrants for the use of any reinforcing crews that might arrive from other areas, and to try and provide standard standpipe heads to match the 2½-inch instantaneous couplings on the delivery hose that the Department was supplying.

Another supply problem to prove most difficult and stubborn was that of delivery hose. Three main categories of hose were required: (a) hose for general fire-fighting purposes based on a quota for each type of pump; (b) additional supplies, including larger diameter and rubber-lined hose, for water relaying; (c) reserve stocks to be brought into use to supplement local supplies during heavy air raid fire fighting and to replace hose that had been destroyed or damaged. Total hose requirements were always based in a general way on the number of pumps the Departments proposed to supply, so that hose estimates had to be revised and increased to keep in step with each successive revision in the pump manufacturing programme. Unfortunately, and here was the crux of the problem, hose manufacturers were quite unable to keep pace with pump deliveries, especially with the vastly increased pump manufacturing capacity that was eventually achieved.

Delays in placing the initial contracts aggravated an already difficult situation. To begin with the Departments were unwilling to place orders with any of the principal manufacturers, who were organised into a price-fixing ring, and whose tenders seemed unreasonably high; and it was not until November 1937 that any considerable order was placed. Fresh difficulties arose in 1938 owing to the manufacturers' unwillingness to disclose particulars of their manufacturing costs, when the Departments wished to place contracts for much larger quantities of hose. The House of Commons Select Committee on Estimates, after investigating the emergency fire equipment production programme, commented on the hose manufacturers' formation of a cartel, within which firms quoted uniform prices and pooled the orders they received: 'We cannot but deprecate', said the Committee, 'any action calculated to enhance or unduly maintain the cost of supply at a time when greatly increased quantites of hose are required in a vital national interest.'[1] This expression of disapproval of 'rings', particularly in relation to hose supplies, received considerable press publicity. In October 1938, the Hose Makers Association offered terms which the Departments could accept, and fresh contracts were placed for about 570 miles of hose, making a supply of nearly 1,000 miles in all.

The next problem in connection with hose was the supply of flax, which, towards the end of 1938, was running low. And, in any case, it was becoming clear that there were not enough skilled workers nor sufficient manufacturing capacity to keep pace with the increasing production of pumps. Even if delivery promises were kept and much overtime worked, there seemed no chance of obtaining from home sources more than half of the 3,000 miles of hose needed to match the pumps to be provided during the next twelve months. None of the various expedients considered seemed likely to bridge this formidable production gap and the only alternative was supplies from abroad. Early in 1939, therefore, the first foreign contract was placed in France for 1 million feet of hose, and this was later revised to 2½ million feet. But even these supplies were uncertain— the French themselves needed hose and were in an exposed geographical position *vis-à-vis* the potential enemy. In any case the order was not enough to bridge the gap completely, and in May 1939 the Departments approached the Treasury for authority to purchase hose in America.

The decision to buy hose from America was on quite a different technical footing from the decision to buy supplies in France, for it

---

[1] Report of the Select Committee on Estimates, 11th July 1938. H.C. 158.

involved the introduction of a new type. British fire brigades used almost exclusively unlined flax hose, and the lockers for carrying hose in the new trailer pumps had been designed on the assumption that this type of hose would be used. In America, however, cotton jacketed rubber hose was in general use, and was the only type of hose that American manufacturers could supply in quantity. The American hose had some technical advantages over unlined hose, but it was much heavier and more cumbrous to handle, and would be awkward to stow in the pump lockers. Moreover, the fire brigades might not take very kindly to this unfamiliar and heavy hose. Yet another complication was that it would be impossible to rely on the home supplies for the great number of hose couplings that would be required, and the 'instantaneous' type, which was now standard, was not in production in America. But the situation was serious, and in March 1939 the Home Office placed a trial order with American manufacturers for 250,000 feet of 2½-inch hose. Before this order had been completed, the whole matter came before the Committee of Imperial Defence. On the urgent request of the Lord Privy Seal, the Chancellor of the Exchequer agreed to hose purchases in the United States up to 3 million feet, all of which was to be fitted with instantaneous couplings manufactured in America to British speci-fications. Altogether, even before the outbreak of war, the orders for delivery hose came to over 3,400 miles and 1,500 miles had been delivered.[1]

Another attempt at overseas purchase—in this case of turntable ladders—did not work out so satisfactorily. Turntable ladders are important appliances and, especially where tall buildings are involved, are invaluable for rescue work and for providing positions from which to bring fire-fighting jets to bear. They are, however, very expensive; even in 1938 a ladder cost over £3,000 and there were only about 100 of them in the country, owned by 80 brigades. In March 1938, the Chief Officer of the London Fire Brigade proposed that a further ten of these ladders should be added to the thirteen London already possessed. The proposition was not accepted as it stood, but after the Munich crisis the Home Office obtained Treasury consent to buy 20 machines. These were not to be lent to local authorities but could be bought by them on a grant basis, making a valuable addition to their peace-time fire apparatus. There was, however, only one maker of these machines in Britain, and the capacity of this firm was limited. Most of the machines already owned by the brigades had ladders of German manu-facture mounted on an English chassis. Part of the order was,

---

[1] A year later, at the opening of the 'blitz', the orders had reached nearly 6,000 miles and the brigades had received 3,500 miles, including 1,000 miles from Canada and the United States (Chapter XI).

therefore, placed with two German firms, but war broke out before any of the ladders had been delivered. The brigades had to manage, therefore, with the production achieved by the single British manufacturer, though a smaller type of hand-operated machine designed by the Home Office engineers was later brought into use as a stop-gap expedient.

The problems connected with water supplies for emergency fire-fighting will be considered shortly. But two aspects of the production programme specially related to water supply need mention here— the supply of water tanks and 'dams' and of 'fire boats'.

Water tanks and 'dams' fall roughly into two categories—fixed and mobile. Fixed tanks were required for the storage of small but distributed supplies of water and as discharge points for relaying lines, while mobile tanks were needed for carrying water from a major source to points where it was needed or for taking a supply of water along with a pumping unit. The first supplies of fixed tanks were distributed to local authorities during 1939 and were 5,000 gallon steel tanks built up with flanged steel sheets.[1] They possessed the great advantage that the components were quick and easy to manufacture, could be easily assembled on almost any ground that was not too uneven, and with small modifications could be used to construct tanks of almost any capacity. As for the mobile tanks and 'dams', there were several types and sizes, including those with folding steel frames which when erected supported a canvas container of 500 to 1,000 gallons capacity (the Sparshatt type);[2] the 'Sportapool' type made in various sizes from 20,000 gallons downwards;[3] and the type which consisted of a canvas container of 5,000 gallons capacity slung on a steel framework built up from lengths of tubular scaffolding.[4] From the 500 or 1,000 gallon mobile types it was also possible to construct a 'mobile dam unit', which was a tank or 'dam' carried on a lorry, which either towed a pump or carried a light pump detached from its trailer.[5]

Fire boats are, of course, restricted in their movements but possess the great advantage that they have ample supplies of water

---

[1] The use of water basins in the basements of houses was also recommended but little was done along these lines until the war, when there was much development of basins in the basements of bombed buildings and tanks built up at ground level. (See Chapter XI below.)

[2] This very useful type was invented by the late Mr Sparshatt, who also designed the fixed rectangular tanks made from flanged steel sheets.

[3] This consisted of a self-supporting canvas container without steel supports.

[4] Produced from a design suggested by Mr B. A. Westbrook, Chief Fire Brigades Inspector, and especially useful because of its large capacity and the speed with which it could be dismantled and reassembled where needed.

[5] This type of appliance proved so useful in many forms of fire-fighting, especially in country districts where even a limited supply of water may be invaluable if it is available directly the brigade arrive at a fire, that it has won a permanent place in fire brigade equipment. Since the war a more elaborate descendant has become one of the most useful machines to many brigades.

to hand wherever they can go, and, unlike appliances that have to be manoeuvred in the streets, they need not be so restricted in size and can carry exceptionally powerful pumping equipment. Where suitable water-ways existed, therefore, fire boats would be invaluable in fighting fires on the water side or supplying relay lines to other fires. Two types of fire boat were included in the 1938–39 production programme; one to dimensions suitable for use on canals (8 of these being supplied to the Birmingham Fire Brigade on a grant basis) and one of a larger type for use on the Thames (10 being supplied to London as part of the special scheme to augment London water supplies).[1] Each boat had mounted on it from one to four standard heavy or extra-heavy pumps. Many local fire brigades also improvised craft of various kinds. In 1939, for instance, some of the lifeboats of the *Berengaria*, then being scrapped, were turned into fire boats. By the outbreak of war at least 75 fire boats (including 36 on the Thames) were ready for action and 25 more were under construction or planned.

In addition to the problems of production and supply there were the related questions of repair and maintenance. The Government not only provided the pumps, but also made themselves responsible for the cost of repairs to those which developed defects or were damaged (except, of course, where the damage was due to negligence), although it left the organisation of the repair work to the fire authorities, who also had to provide storage for any pumps they had in reserve. But the Home Office maintained a general reserve of pumps and equipment to make good the wastage which might be expected if and when air raid fire-fighting began, and provided three main Storage Depots for this purpose, at Greenford, Swindon and Wakefield. It was intended that when these depots had served their primary purpose as pump storages they should take on the role of workshops, where the Home Office Engineers could provide for major overhauls and conversions and develop new and experimental types of apparatus.

The pumps, moreover, needed not only to be kept in repair but also to be assured of adequate petrol supplies—a problem in which the fire brigades had a double concern, as they needed petrol not only to keep their appliances mobile but also to drive the pumps, and in the event of large scale fire-fighting the quantities required for the second of these purposes would greatly exceed those required for the first. These quantities might be very large indeed—a single city might need 40,000 gallons in a single raid. The plan worked out with the Petroleum Department was to earmark selected petrol

---

[1] See pp. 270–272. Later, a further 10 fire boats of a sturdier type were provided for the lower reaches of the Thames and the cost was substantially borne by the Exchequer.

filling stations for use as emergency fire brigade depots, to be kept
supplied by the pool petrol organisations which would be set up in
war, and to have local storages on fire brigade premises and vehicles
for transporting petrol in bulk or cans to these or to the fire.[1]

(iii) Water

The third component in the organisation of emergency fire-
fighting measures was that of adequate water supplies. Fire-fighting,
whether in peace or war, consists primarily of getting a sufficient
supply of water to a fire and applying it in the best way to prevent
the spread of the fire, and eventually to extinguish it. Other extinguishing materials are occasionally of use for special types of fires, but in the
great majority of cases water is the vital factor—the ammunition
of fire-fighting without which equipment and men are useless. It was
therefore of fundamental importance that the water problem should
be given close attention in the planning of fire precautionary
measures. If, as was expected, large numbers of fires were to break
out at one time, it was improbable that normal water supplies would
be enough, even in the unlikely event of the mains remaining intact.

An early appreciation of the need for large emergency water
supplies had been given by the Fire Adviser to the Home Office in
1932. He reviewed the principal natural (unpiped) water supplies
in the London area such as the Thames, the Docks, the canals and the
Serpentine, and discussed the possibility of using light portable steel
piping to construct emergency surface mains for bringing up supplies
from such sources—an idea implemented on a large scale after the
formation of the National Fire Service in 1941.

During the next three years more detailed consideration was given
to the question of probable water requirements and methods of
meeting them, and in the Memorandum on Emergency Fire Brigade
Organisation, issued in February 1937, a prominent place was given
to the water problem. Recommendations included: (*a*) the survey of
alternative supplies such as canals, rivers, streams, swimming baths
etc., and the clearing of the approaches to suitable supplies; (*b*) the
installation of pumps on barges or other craft so as to make use of such
supplies in fighting fires on the banks and for feeding relaying lines
to fires farther away; (*c*) the installation of underground tanks or the
preparation of cellars and basements for flooding as emergency
tanks; (*d*) the organisation of mobile supplies of water in road tank
waggons, etc.; (*e*) the preparation of measures for relaying water
over distances, including the use of light steel piping and large
diameter hose. These were expanded in various supplementary
instructions, in particular in a detailed memorandum sent to local

---

[1] F.B. Circular No. 9/1939 of 14th April 1939; Scottish Office Circular No. L.A.3.

authorities in April 1939.[1] Among the new measures advocated were the installation of special hydrants on trunk water mains (which for technical reasons, do not as a rule have hydrants fitted) and the use of emergency water tanks in the roadways—measures which were to take an important place in schemes later on. The memorandum announced that an initial supply of 5,000 gallon steel tanks was being sent out to local authorities, and discussed in detail the use of water-carrying 'mobile dam units'.[2] Brigades were also to train their fire crews in the intricate and difficult art of relaying water by means of a series of pumps and long hose lines.

It was clearly important that measures for augmenting water supplies should take a major place in every local authority scheme. But the scale on which water might be required was so far beyond anything the brigades had previously experienced that requirements were not always fully realised or, if realised, were regarded as impossible to attain. One important city, for instance, which later on suffered severely from incendiary bomb attacks, refused to install the 5,000 gallon steel tanks provided by the Home Office because the tanks 'would disturb the amenities of the city'.

The water problem was particularly difficult in the London area, and from the end of 1936 a series of conferences were held with representatives of the London County Council, the Fire Brigade and the Metropolitan Water Board to try and assess the scale of the problem and arrive at some sort of solution. The first need was to find out the quantities of water that might be available from the mains (assuming they remained intact) as compared to the quantities that might be needed. A memorandum of 1938 put water requirements at 4,000 gallons per minute to hold a single large fire, such as a large warehouse well alight, and 10,000 gallons per minute to hold a fire which was threatening to spread. It might be necessary in an emergency, urged the memorandum, to have sufficient fire-fighting units and water to deal with at least 20 simultaneous fires of this size in the City of London area. Another estimate thought that the London Fire Brigade might have calls to as many as 1,500 fires in a raid.[3] On these assumptions the London Fire Brigade might need water in the City alone at the rate of 80,000–100,000 gallons per minute. But the tests carried out by the Metropolitan Water Board showed that the aggregate water supply available in London would be only a fraction of what might be required, even if mains and pumping stations remained intact. As a result of these joint

---

[1] Memorandum on 'Emergency Water Supplies for Fire Fighting'. F.B. Circular No. 13/1939, 21st April 1939. Scottish Office Circular No. 3520.

[2] Originally referred to in the earlier circulars F.B. Circular No. 10/1939 and Scottish Office Circular No. 3520.

[3] This estimate was in fact a remarkably accurate forecast, as the 1,500 figure was reached and passed on two occasions, and two only, during the raids of 1940–41.

consultations, a skeleton scheme for the London area was drawn up. It included such measures as laying emergency 24-inch mains, installing hydrants on trunk mains, installing pumping stations on the river side or on the bridges, providing light steel 6-inch piping for surface emergency mains and providing additional fire boats on the Thames. But all this work would cost about £1 million and the controversial issue of who was to pay was to cause some delay.

Similar water problems, though in less acute forms, were bound to exist in other large cities and, as major works of this kind would take a long time to complete, it was clearly urgent to put these matters in hand without delay. The Home Office feared, however, that the cost might well be regarded by local authorities as prohibitive under the ordinary rate of grant of the Air Raid Precautions Act. In March 1938, therefore, it proposed to the Treasury that the Exchequer should bear the whole cost of such works. But as the Treasury were at first unwilling to pay more than half and the L.C.C. felt strongly that this was too little, some months were spent in haggling about the amount of grant to be payable.[1] Eventually in August 1938, it was agreed that the L.C.C. and ten other large cities that were to be included in the scheme should bear 10 per cent. of the cost of the emergency works and 20 per cent. of the cost of the hydrants on trunk mains, the Treasury finding the balance. The total expenditure was not to exceed £500,000 for London and £500,000 for the ten cities.[2]

While these financial negotiations had been going on the technical plans for improving London's water supplies had been in abeyance, and it was not until late in 1938 that the way was clear to go ahead. Even then differences of opinion on the relative value of different measures held up progress, so that not until the middle of 1939 had installation work begun in earnest. The scheme adopted by the L.C.C. and the London Fire Brigade, acting in consultation with the Home Office and the Metropolitan Water Board, included:

(1) Three 24-inch mains through high risk areas—
    (*a*) The City Main, connecting the Thames near Cannon Street Station and the Grand Junction Canal near City Road,

---

[1] On the 15th June 1938 the Chancellor of the Exchequer wrote to the Home Secretary that in the last resort he would be prepared to accept the whole charge, if it could then be guaranteed that the L.C.C. would proceed swiftly with their air raid precautions as a whole—'You have represented very strongly', said the Chancellor, 'the political difficulty you expect to meet in forcing this conclusion (i.e., that the L.C.C. should share the cost) upon the L.C.C. and the delay which the dispute may entail in the execution of essential Air Raid Precautions work, now much behindhand in London. I am bound to recognise that we are not altogether our own masters in the matter'.

[2] There was the understanding that the charge on L.C.C. funds should not exceed £75,000. The scheme for the ten cities was not announced until February 1939. See p. 272.

with pumping stations at each end and giving a combined capacity of 20,000 gallons a minute.

(*b*) The West End Main, from the Grand Union Canal at Regent's Park to Shaftesbury Avenue, with a pumping station at the Regent's Park end, and capacity of 10,000 gallons a minute.[1]

(*c*) The City-East End Main, from St. Katherine's Dock to join the City main, with a pumping station at the dock and a pumping capacity of 10,000 gallons a minute.

(2) Five 8-inch pipe lines from the Serpentine and the Round Pond in Kensington Gardens to different points on the roads around the park.

(3) A considerable number of hydrants on trunk mains.

(4) Two riverside pumping stations, one at Blackfriars and the other at Charing Cross (capacity 5,000 gallons per minute), the latter connected by a short main to Trafalgar Square.

(5) A number of underground water tanks, and

(6) Additional fire boats and barges with pumps.

Only a little of this installation work had actually been carried out when war broke out.

Progress in the provision of large water tanks was also slow. Sites for water tanks were difficult to find: in congested areas where they were most needed there was little room for surface tanks of any considerable size, and in the case of underground tanks the uncertainties of shelter policy added to the problem, since suitable sites might be needed for shelters. (This site problem was, of course, later to be mainly solved by using spaces where buildings had been destroyed or by converting the basements of bombed buildings into water tanks.) In July 1939, however, some progress was made when a scheme was adopted for the construction of 5 tanks each of about 200,000 gallons capacity, built up from the components of the 5,000 gallon tanks with slight modifications. Later, these large tanks were increased to 20 and were set up in London squares and gardens, providing a total capacity of some $2\frac{3}{4}$ million gallons.[2]

In February 1939 it was announced that the special grant conditions agreed to for the London water scheme also applied to approved installations of a similar kind in ten big cities—Birmingham, Bristol, Leeds, Liverpool, Manchester, Newcastle-on-Tyne, Nottingham, Sheffield, Bradford and Coventry—subject to an aggregate cost of not more than £500,000. The Treasury insisted that this grant would be available only for specifically emergency projects and that any improvements to the mains supplies should be carried out under local authorities' normal powers. But none of the ten

---

[1] This was later connected up with the emergency pumping station at Charing Cross.

[2] See also pp. 465, 492.

authorities proposed measures of any magnitude and their aggregate expenditure on purposes for which the special grant had been made available amounted to only £80,000 out of the £500,000 authorised.[1]

Home Office fears that shortage of water might prove the greatest handicap that the fire brigades would encounter were to prove all too well founded.[2] No measures that would have been practicable before the war could have given sufficient supplies of water to make good the losses of the ordinary supplies when mains were fractured to the extent they often were during heavy raids. Nevertheless more could have been done during this pre-war period if more money had been made available sooner for the major schemes in London and the ten large cities, and still more could have been done in the country as a whole if the systematic measures described in Chapter XI had been started earlier.

(iv) Organisation and Communications

The three essentials of fire-fighting—men, equipment and water—had to be welded together and directed by organisation and communications, both central and local. Once again the issues involved were innumerable, and it is only possible to touch on a few of the more important of them.

For both men and equipment, accommodation was a primary need—for auxiliary fire stations, for recruiting and training, for new or expanded control rooms, for storage, and for administration and recreation. Regular fire brigade premises varied from those of the larger authorities with modern headquarters buildings, control rooms and staff accommodation to those of the hundreds of small part-time brigades which could often do little more than house a single engine and gear. Although in many cases accommodation was good enough for normal purposes, and the Fire Brigades Act, 1938 would stimulate further construction, it was clear, as the emergency organisation developed, that auxiliary stations would greatly outnumber the regular stations and new premises would have to be found in large numbers.

At first the main emphasis was laid on improvisation. In pursuance of the general policy at this time, accommodation for the hundreds of trailer pumps and the men to man them was to be found in premises already available to local authorities, or in other premises adapted at small cost. New building, purchase or hiring would only be approved if there were no cheaper alternative, and sheds

---

[1] Including a scheme for drawing water from the River Trent at Nottingham (£25,000) and the construction of sluice gates on the River Sherborne to improve the water supplies at Coventry.

[2] See pp. 460–461.

or buildings of light construction should then be used where possible.[1] Suitable garages should be earmarked for future possible use as auxiliary fire stations, and authorities were warned that in an emergency it might be necessary to improvise sleeping and messing arrangements for the crews of patrol units.

No more definite lead on accommodation problems was given to local authorities until the end of August 1939, when they were advised on the procedure for requisitioning the buildings they would need and on the measures necessary to protect stations against blast and splinters, fire and gas.[2]

A vital element in the organisation of emergency fire-fighting measures was that of communications. Although a certain amount of advice was given to fire authorities, there was no general plan and it was left to each authority to organise supplementary communications.

One of the chief difficulties was to reach agreement on the best method of 'meshing in' with the incident reporting arrangements of the other A.R.P. Services. The fire brigades, the police and the various air raid precautions services were to some extent autonomous, often based on different local government areas and controlled from different stations. Should reports from wardens on outbreaks of fire go to the A.R.P. Report Centre or direct to the fire station? To what extent would A.R.P. Controllers have any general direction of the fire brigade resources in their areas? At the centre there was some controversy. The Air Raid Precautions Department thought that the central A.R.P. Control for each area should be the pivot of all operations; there, all information should be collected, the local resources deployed in the light of the situation as a whole and reinforcements obtained from other areas if required. The Fire Brigades Division, on the other hand, wanted a separate system of fire communications, with fire calls going direct to the nearest local station and with co-ordination and reinforcement from fire brigade headquarters. Some of these questions took a long time to settle, but in the end the Fire Brigades Division got their way. In July 1939 it was laid down that A.R.P. Controllers would not exercise any control over the fire brigades and that calls for fire brigade assistance made to the A.R.P. Control were to be passed on at once to the brigade.[3] On the question of reporting fires by wardens no final decision had been taken when war broke out. After much discussion and experiment it was decided early in 1940 that wardens should

---

[1] Memorandum on Special Points arising under Fire Precautions, Schemes, September 1938, (i.e. in relation to the A.R.P. (Approval of Expenditure) Provisional Regulations, 1938)·

[2] F.B. Circulars Nos. 35, 39 and 44/1939; Scottish Office Circulars Nos. 3643 and 3624.

[3] F.B. Circular No. 33/1939, 28th July 1939. Scottish Office Circular No. 3620, and A.R.P. Dept. Circular 144, 19th July 1939. See pp. 217–218.

report direct to the fire station and not through the A.R.P. organisation.[1]

The first and most obvious need in communications was to provide each station with one or more exchange telephone lines, to link each station with its headquarters and to expand the main controls at each headquarters. These mechanical measures were to be supplemented by messengers or fire patrols.[2] Lads recruited as cyclist messengers had a part in the emergency organisation of most brigades; they were later to render invaluable and gallant service in many a raid. Observation posts, though established by some brigades at an early stage, did not assume their full importance until after the outbreak of war. The expansion of the main controls in each locality was a formidable operation calling for additional lines, switchboards and accommodation, and the evolution of specialised techniques to handle a great volume of message work. Again the crux of the problem was the expected scale of operations. Fire stations, it was believed, would have to be ready to handle scores or hundreds of messages where they would normally have handled two or three. In June 1939 local authorities were given guidance on the scale of the communications systems they should provide and a 'tariff' was laid down specifying the number of additional telephone lines that should be installed.[3] Shortly before the war, measures were worked out to ease the situation if telephone services were overtaxed or broke down under air attack. These included cutting off telephone services from non-essential users and organising a despatchrider service. In one Region these measures were supplemented by a pigeon service. Other methods of communication included field telephones and, after the outbreak of war, wireless installations were introduced in some areas.

Before August 1941 and the institution of the National Fire Service, there was no special system of communication between the Home Office and the fire authorities. As soon as war broke out the Home Office would, of course, be linked by telephone and teleprinter with the Regional Offices and so could obtain information on any major fire situation and transmit any general operational instructions. To handle this message work, the Home Office established its own Fire Control Room, which, though remaining independent, was later linked with the Home Security War Room.

Mobility of fire-fighting resources was another vital consideration. Arrangements for inter-brigade reinforcement in the case of exceptional fires were required under the Fire Brigades Act, 1938, but

---

[1] F.B. Circular No. 29/1940 of 8th April 1940, Scottish Home Dept. Circular No. L40/1940, Home Security Circular No. 60/1940.

[2] See p. 241.

[3] F.B. Circular No. 22/1939, 14th June and Scottish Office Circular No. 3576 of 26th June 1939.

mutual assistance in peace-time did not have to be much more than the provision of appliances and men for a single serious fire and therefore hardly touched the air raid problem. The provision of inter-brigade reinforcement on a wider scale for air raid fire-fighting had been the first of the emergency measures to be considered in the planning of the war-time fire services. Indeed, the scheme which was eventually adopted had its origins in the regional schemes worked out by the Home Office and the Fire Adviser towards the end of the First World War, when the disaster at the Morecombe Filling Factory exposed the weaknesses of the fire brigade organisation for dealing with fires on any great scale. A tentative scheme which was drawn up in 1927,[1] and revised from time to time to take account of changes in fire brigade organisation and equipment, was circulated to the brigades at the time of the Munich crisis and, after further revision, reissued shortly before the outbreak of war. There was a corresponding scheme for Scotland.

Under this plan Regions were to be divided into Districts, each with its District Officer, and specified brigades could be called on in three stages to send assistance. The first and second stage units could be called upon through the District Officer, and all three stages could be called upon through the Regional Commissioner. If all the resources under a Regional Scheme proved insufficient the Regional Commissioner would apply to the Home Office Fire Control for the additional pumps and fire crews needed, and these would be obtained from other Regions through the medium of the appropriate Regional Scheme. These schemes became operative and compulsory on 1st September 1939, under Defence Regulation 29, and in a revised form[2] they became an essential element in fire brigade organisation and operations until superseded by the institution of the National Fire Service in 1941.

London was, of course, a special case. In the autumn of 1938 it was decided that in the event of war the London problem would be dealt with under a Defence Regulation placing the Chief Officer of the London Fire Brigade in general control of the fire-fighting resources of the area that was to become London Region. In January 1939 the Chief Officer and a small staff were temporarily attached to the Home Office as a preparatory measure, to work out a regional emergency fire brigade organisation. Details of the London scheme were circulated in July 1939 and the Order was made on

---

[1] See p. 32.

[2] The original schemes for England and Wales, S.R. & O. 1939, Nos. 1256–9, 1261–5 and 1267. (The original London Order was not published in this series.) The revised schemes S.R. & O. 1940, Nos. 507–19. The revised London Orders (S.R. & O. Nos. 508 and 513) were amended by later Orders Nos. (1940) 1279, 1280 and 2191. The Scottish Orders were issued as S.R. & O. 1939, No. 1266/S.89 and (1940) 151/S.2.

the 1st September 1939. London Region with its 67 fire brigades (the London Fire Brigade with 61 fire stations and 66 other fire brigades, mainly with one station apiece) was divided into 11 Districts, 6 in the Administrative County and 5 outside, and the Chief Officer of one of the Brigades was designated Assistant Regional Officer in each District. Assistance would be available to each brigade in three successive stages: (*a*) *first stage*—they could call on adjoining brigades, working on a pre-arranged schedule specifying the units that could be called: (*b*) *second stage*—they could notify the Assistant Regional Fire Officer who could order pumps up to a scheduled maximum from specified brigades: and (*c*) *third stage*—if more reinforcements were needed the Assistant Regional Fire Officer could notify the Regional Fire Officer who could, if practicable, send help from such resources as were still available in the Region or obtain assistance from other Regions. To assure fire authorities that their own areas would not be too depleted under this scheme, it was laid down that a fire brigade would not be required to send more than one-third of its total pump strength outside its own area.[1]

Thus, in September 1939, the formal outbreak of war found the fire-fighting services only partially ready. Real progress had been made in the supply of fire-fighting equipment; the pump production programme was in top gear and the brigades already possessed much of their vital equipment. Men had been found and trained in considerable numbers, although total strengths were still well below the planned ideals of the Home Office. And at least the beginnings of an administrative organisation and chain of command had been established. On the other hand there were some serious gaps. There were shortages and makeshifts in important ancillary equipment, transport and accommodation, and above all, adequate water supplies were not yet assured.

---

[1] Later amended to half the major appliances or a quarter of the whole number.

PART II

War: 1939–1945

CHAPTER VII

RESPITE

(September 1939 – April 1940)

AT 11.15 on the morning of Sunday, 3rd September, a clear and invigorating day, the Prime Minister broadcast to the nation, 'this country is at war with Germany'. Great numbers of his audience had already abandoned hope and been occupied for the past ten days in eleventh-hour preparations to meet a new catastrophe. But Mr Chamberlain's announcement that the gulf separating peace from war had at last been crossed was followed by an impressive silence, a hush which fell over the manifold activities of a national mobilisation. A few minutes later the strange fluctuating notes of the air raid warning signal broke out over London, and other places in Britain including Scotland.[1]

The form of attack most closely associated with new war in the minds both of the best-informed and the least-informed in the land—devastating assault from the air—seemed about to be promptly delivered. Cabinet Ministers and officials in Whitehall engaged in the most urgent matters took up their papers and their gas-masks and went underground to basements.[2] Civilians on their lawful occasions in the streets were shepherded without ceremony by police and steel-helmeted wardens into the nearest shelters. All traffic stopped. Casualty and rescue squads stood ready in depots to rush to the scenes of attack; and officials waited in town halls to hear where the first bombs had fallen. After about half-an-hour the sirens wailed again, this time in the steady note of the 'all clear'. The shelterers emerged; the traffic in the streets restarted; and amid a mingled sense of relief and anti-climax national mobilisation proceeded.

In the middle of the following night (or, more precisely, at 2.46 a.m. in the London area) the warning was repeated. After many persons had left their beds and spent an uncomfortable hour or so in basements the 'all clear' again sounded.[3] On 6th September

---

[1] The sirens sounded in the London area at 11.28 a.m.

[2] For an account of this process in the War Office see Dudley Clarke, *Seven Assignments* (1948), pp. 19–21.

[3] The length of the warning in London was about half-an-hour, but many citizens were still either unable to distinguish between the 'alarm' and the 'all clear' or to hear the signals clearly.

early risers in London and the south-east on their way to work were greeted with a third warning not followed by any attack. The warnings of 3rd–4th September had been 'false', in the sense that units of Fighter Command had not accurately identified aircraft which proved innocuous.[1] But that of 6th September was genuine or due to German aircraft approaching the eastern coast.

Mobilisation against a Knock-Out Blow

Britain, again at war, was confronted with a threat more deadly than any in her long experience. Germany could use the air weapon to attack her people and cities with a speed and force capable of causing widespread heavy destruction of life and property, grave dislocation of industrial processes, and disintegration of morale to the point, possibly, of extinguishing the people's will to carry on the struggle. The logic by which wars had hitherto been fought might easily be reversed by conversion of civilians and civil occupations into the 'front-line'. Direct onslaught against the nation's vitals— the Government and higher apparatus directing the war, factories, businesses and communications, the families and homes of those on active service—might paralyse all military operations and cause defeat.

The fact that this threat did not materialise at the time or in the form in which it was expected may too easily obscure its historical reality. It is in human nature both to forget—especially, perhaps, a catastrophe averted—and also to be wise after the event or to claim prescience that events which did not happen could not have happened. These remarks are intended to reach further into the narrative that follows than the immediate topic of the nation's mobilisation late in the summer of 1939 against an aerial knock-out blow. It was to be proved, in the event, that large quantities of manpower, materials and money were spent in preparations against attacks from the air which either were not made at the time and in the form in which they were expected, or were not made at all.

Mobilisation, in the broad sense intended here, may be dated from nearly two weeks before Mr Chamberlain announced the state of war and the first air raid warning was sounded. Before attempting a summary of its course some brief recapitulation of certain features of the situation seems advisable. For some years past the British Chiefs of Staff, assessing Germany's likely course of action, had regarded as highly probable her choice of all-out lightning air attack on Britain immediately after, or perhaps before,

---

[1] On the Sunday morning a single light aircraft returning from France had failed to report its movements to the authorities and had therefore been presumed hostile.

a declaration of war.[1] The character of this attack could, in the nature of the case, only be conceived in general terms. Its clearest and starkest feature was its scale—the enormous weight of bombs which Germany's air force, operating from its home bases and in spite of the best efforts of the Allied defences, could drop on these islands.

Limitations of range would restrict the heaviest and most sustained attacks to the eastern half of Britain. For the rest, British experts could only make broad assumptions, deduced from German tactics and temperament and what was known to them of German armaments, that the enemy would concentrate his attempt in a series of raids of great violence but fairly short duration and mainly, though not exclusively, by day; that he might choose as his immediate objective the dislocation of Britain's war industry, and in particular the destruction of the Government offices, business organisations, communications, docks and factories of Greater London; and that the tonnage of bombs he delivered might be in the rough proportions of one-half high explosive, one quarter incendiary and one quarter gas bombs.

The consequences of this assault could, likewise, only be measured in broad terms. Use of the air weapon against China, Abyssinia and Republican Spain had been too limited in scope to furnish much useful data. But Spanish experience had reinforced the most important conjecture—suggested by the bombing of London in the First World War—that high explosive attack on this scale, apart from any use of gas, would cause an extremely large number of casualties. Material damage, especially—since high accuracy of bomb-aiming was assumed—to essential services and war factories, would also be of large proportions. The effects on Britain's morale could be measured with even less exactness. But the authorities considered it certain that the strain on the people's endurance would be of the severest order and that this might well, on particular occasions and in particular places, cause panic and serious disintegration.

The size of this threat—its merely quantitative aspect—had, from the outset, shaped the character of Britain's counter-measures. The active defences of the Army and Royal Air Force had been given chief emphasis in the total rearmament programme. And the role of the passive defences against such assault had been conceived as necessarily limited to mitigation of its consequences. Heavy loss of life and material damage were, by the terms of the hypothesis, inescapable. But precautions of a definite character could be taken which, it was confidently hoped, would minimise the scale of these disasters. From this conception successive Governments had evolved

---

[1] pp. 142–143, 172.

a strategy of passive defence which, though most complicated in practical application, was based on a few guiding principles. The danger, seen in the framework of limited resources of manpower, money and materials, had led to a policy of spreading the A.R.P. burden as widely as possible. Passive defence had been predominantly regarded as an additional service to be grafted on to familiar institutions—civil Departments, the normal organs of local government, industrial employers, and citizens enrolled as members of the A.R.P. services and taking personal action to defend their own homes.

'Total war' would be met, in the first instance, by democratic self-help, with responsibility placed squarely on each local community and factory to take the major part in organising its own defences. Service in A.R.P. was to be looked upon by the individual citizen less as a new form of national service than as service to the particular community in which he lived or carried on his business. These diffused responsibilities, finally, were to be welded together by reliance on 'free collaboration', with the Government introducing the element of compulsion only as a last resort.[1]

For over four years these principles had been used to forge certain weapons of defence. Mobilisation of civilian resources against this threat—the superimposing of A.R.P. duties on the pattern of normal life—had been proceeding since early 1935. Its pace had depended, primarily, on the judgment of the Government, officials, employers and private citizens as to whether, and how soon, the hypothesis of war would become fact. British Governments had been set the new problem of arousing the whole nation to the need for taking defensive action, while avoiding causing alarm and the dislocation of normal activities by suggesting that war was either inevitable or imminent. Their preference for cautiousness had been overborne by the Munich crisis, which by making the nearness of danger apparent to all had greatly stimulated preparations. Thenceforward, with new machinery and vigour at the centre, progress had been more rapid. The further crisis of March 1939 had caused most local authorities and employers to make strong efforts to press on with A.R.P. By the end of August, when the Government began to put passive defence on a war footing, a large part of the nation had reached a state of mental preparedness for large-scale assault from the air. And much had been done in constructing five principal weapons, or methods of protection.

An air raid warning system, the first weapon of defence, had been extended beyond its primary operational role to give warning of impending attack, first to a considerable number of civil establishments and factories and then to the public at large. Its purpose to

---

[1] Sir J. Anderson, H. of C. Deb., Vol. 336, Col. 2113, 1st June 1938.

save life by giving individuals the time to seek shelter and take other measures had, by elaborate organisation, been blended with the second strategic aim of reducing industrial and general dislocation to a minimum. Secondly, severe restrictions on all forms of lighting, aiming at an almost total nation-wide black-out, would attempt defence against air attack by the method of concealment. Industrial and other essential activities would, it was hoped, be continued without serious interruption in spite of the grave handicaps this method would clearly impose. Much responsibility in this sphere rested with individuals, particularly employers; and many technical difficulties remained to be overcome. Other methods of attempting concealment, for example by camouflage or the use of smoke, had not yet reached much practical development.

The two, as it seemed to the ordinary person, most certain methods of defence—evacuation from the danger zones, and protection in the form of shelters—had raised grave strategic implications. Each, to be organised in peace on a large scale, would require much diversion of effort, materials or money; and each, if resorted to on such a scale in war, might spell submission to the enemy's main aim of causing wholesale dislocation. The provision of each had, in the result, been built on a series of compromises. All those who would be engaged on essential war work had been asked to refrain from evacuation and to stay on the job. Plans of a secret nature had, however, been made for the Government machine to move out of London should attacks develop to the point of threatening its physical existence. Others, private citizens, businesses of all kinds and some Government staffs had been exhorted either to move from the danger zones in peace, or to have plans in readiness to move immediately a war began. The private migration of these 'non' or less-essential persons would, it was hoped, besides saving their lives, reduce the proportions of the problem in the threatened cities. Fairly large-scale movement from London and other cities of families, business firms, schools and other institutions had, in fact, been taking place since about the end of June. Elaborate plans, to be put into force when war was imminent, had been made for the official but voluntary evacuation from the danger zones of about 4,000,000 children, mothers and invalids.

Belief that dispersal would save lives, shortages of time, materials and labour, and apprehension about the psychological results of prolonged sheltering had caused a policy of widespread official provision of shelters offering only moderate, or blast and splinter, protection.[1] Citizens had been assured that the basements and ground floors of their homes, or trenches in their gardens, would give

---

[1] The basic standard, it will be recalled, was safety from the blast and splinters of a 500 lb. bomb bursting 50 feet away.

good protection against anything short of a direct hit. While the majority were expected to rely on their own resources in protecting their homes, some 1,500,000 of the poorest householders (to be increased, it was hoped, to 2,500,000) in the danger zones had been given free 'Anderson' shelters; and several thousand others had been helped to strengthen their basements. Employers of some size in all industrial centres had been compelled to provide their work-people with blast and splinter-proof shelters; though this compulsion, not introduced until July 1939, was only beginning to produce positive results. For those caught in the streets and other public places during attacks—roughly estimated at a maximum of 10–15 per cent. of the populations of the most congested areas—public shelters of various kinds had been planned. Trenches of a permanent kind, sufficient throughout the country for about 500,000 persons, were the main form of such shelter so far provided. But in addition many buildings had been earmarked by local authorities, and a small proportion of these strengthened, for use as public shelters.

Personal protection had, for reasons familiar to the reader, been carried furthest with respect to the menace of gas. Every adult had been furnished by the Government with a mask, believed to be quite efficient against all gases the enemy might use; and special masks for babies were being distributed by the outbreak of war in London and other cities. Personal anti-gas equipment in the form of more durable masks and protective clothing was being issued to the A.R.P. services, the fire brigades and the police. Various methods had been devised for gas-proofing householders' refuge rooms and other forms of shelter; extensive arrangements had been made for the cleansing of casualties caused by liquid gases, and for the decontamination of streets, buildings and vehicles; and special methods had been set up to detect gas attack and give public warnings of this.

The fifth and most active major weapon of defence was the organised formations charged with the duty of repelling the onslaught on the ground by ensuring that the public took proper defensive action, reporting the attacks when they came and thereafter saving lives and property. The heterogeneous, locally organised, voluntary A.R.P. services had grown to over 1,500,000 men and women whose training and equipment, though still far from complete, had made substantial progress. In addition, an unknown number of persons employed in factories and offices had been in some degree trained and equipped to defend their fellow-workers and places of employment. And the regular police forces and fire brigades had been given substantial war-time reinforcements.

The German-Soviet non-agression pact, announced to the world on 21st August, caused the Government to take the first steps to make these defensive weapons ready for immediate action. The 'bolt from the blue', or a German air assault before any declaration of war, had so far not been delivered; and the state described by the Home Secretary as 'a twilight between peace and war', which had prevailed in Britain at least since early summer had given further valuable time for preparation. But the speed with which air attack could be launched had, as the Munich experience proved, made the problem confronting the Government of timing the final preparations most delicate.[1]

Secrecy was essential in order to avoid action which might precipitate war and give negotiation the utmost chance. But bringing civil defence to a state of final readiness—carrying out official evacuation, and manning the air raid warning and lighting arrangements—would require widespread publicity and organisation. On 22nd August 1939 the Cabinet took the first major step by deciding to call up the active defences against air attack—the R.A.F. fighter squadrons, anti-aircraft guns and searchlights, balloon barrage and operational warning system. It also gave the Lord Privy Seal, Sir John Anderson, wide discretion to take parallel action in mobilising passive defence.

At the centre of affairs the main change was in the high pressure of events and the new atmosphere of urgency. The Lord Privy Seal had been responsible for over nine months for co-ordinating the measures of the various Departments most concerned and also directing the activities of the A.R.P. Department.[2] He had been asked to continue to perform this double function in war while holding the two offices of Home Secretary and Minister of Home Security. He had already established the practice of relying, to an extent unknown under normal conditions, on informal methods for achieving co-ordination. A group of Ministers had formed the habit of meeting under his chairmanship frequently for informal consultation; and his Office, using personal informal methods of liaison, had become the main instrument for co-ordinating departmental action. This machinery now began to assume a character similar to that of a supreme military headquarters, with Ministers meeting daily to take major decisions and officials transmitting instructions for instant action to local authorities and the public. The Lord Privy Seal's Office now began to direct local authorities to act on particular items of the full local war instructions which had been issued to them five months before;[3] and the A.R.P. Department began to issue a large number of circulars amplifying its previous instructions.[4] The operational warning system had been brought to a state of

---

[1] p. 154.

[2] pp. 166–167, 173–174.

[3] pp. 217–218.

[4] A.R.P. Dept. Circulars 175–228, 23rd August–3rd September 1939.

V

readiness without attracting public notice, and no question as yet arose of manning the public warnings.[1] The first major step which local authorities were asked to take was to complete their arrangements to extinguish street lighting as soon as police instructions to this effect were received, and to begin installing 'aids to movement' for pedestrians and traffic.[2]

Parliament, recalled from recess on 24th August, was told by Mr Chamberlain that Germany was now 'in a condition of complete readiness for war'. Its immediate passage of the Emergency Powers (Defence) Act followed the precedent set in the First World War, though with two important differences.[3] The speed with which air and other forms of attack could be delivered compelled the Government, on this occasion, to ask for emergency powers before war broke out; and these powers were, as the Home Secretary admitted, 'very wide, very drastic and very comprehensive'.[4] In the course of the following week the Government issued a large number of Defence Regulations, which empowered it to exercise general control over industry and prices and, among other matters concerning civil defence, to order evacuation from specific areas; requisition premises, hospital accommodation and vehicles; restrict lighting; and coordinate the war activities of the nation's police forces.[5] On the day after Parliament's recall the Home Security War Room in the basement of the Home Office was fully manned, and the Lord Privy Seal instructed Regional Commissioners to proceed with their war staffs to their headquarters. The Commissioners, in strong contrast to the secrecy which had enshrouded them at Munich, were now, in the main, familiar figures in their Regions with functions to perform which were roughly understood. London Region had existed in almost its war-form for some months, and had brought its operational arrangements, including a grouping of local authorities, to an advanced state.[6] Elsewhere the regional organisation for A.R.P. had been strengthened, and some progress made in establishing Regional War Rooms.

Local authorities up and down the country turned urgently to acquiring, equipping and protecting battle headquarters and other war premises.[7] Control and report centres had, in general, already

---

[1] pp. 224–226; A.R.P. Dept. Circular 184, 23rd August 1939.

[2] pp. 227–228; A.R.P. Dept. Circular 183, 23rd August 1939.

[3] 2 and 3 Geo. 6, Ch. 62.

[4] H. of C. Deb., Vol. 351, Cols. 63–109. The powers the Government had taken in 1914 were probably just as wide. But general preparations, including the regulations to be applied in the civil defence sphere, were then, by comparison with 1939, much less advanced.

[5] Defence Regulations 1–104 were issued on 25th August 1939.

[6] pp. 183–185.

[7] A.R.P. Dept. Circular 203, 28th August 1939.

been set up in the basements or ground floors of county and town halls. For wardens' and first aid posts and depots for other services many additional buildings, including private houses, shops, warehouses and schools, were now taken over under new requisitioning powers or by voluntary arrangements.[1] The face of London and other cities began to be transformed by the boarding up of windows, the erection of sandbag walls and the strutting of buildings. Sandbags, now available in large quantities for Government offices and A.R.P. buildings, were still the most universal method of protection.[2] Mechanical excavators digging up earth in the parks were reinforced by teams of voluntary diggers. In the background of these visible preparations local officials were feverishly reviewing arrangements for operations, enrolling a fresh stream of volunteers and wrestling with innumerable problems of organisation and supply. The greater number, thanks to the Munich dress-rehearsal, had completed the assembly, fitting and distribution of gas-masks to the public.[3] But some authorities had still to perform these tasks; and in holiday resorts thousands of visitors who had not been issued with masks, or had forgotten to take them away, had to be hurriedly fitted and supplied. The Home Office felt much concern over the facts that 'babies' helmets' were only beginning to be distributed, and no respirators for small children were yet available.[4] It told local authorities that production of helmets had now reached several thousand a day and their issue to the main danger zones was being urgently undertaken; that supplies of small children's masks would soon be forthcoming and that, in the meanwhile, children between two and a half and four years old could be well protected by the ordinary small size mask.[5]

The local authorities, in common with the Government and employers, were making strenuous efforts to furnish more shelters.[6] Nearly 1,500,000 'Andersons' had been delivered to homes in the most threatened areas, and large deliveries of these were now being made weekly.[7] But their erection—involving the digging of foundations, the fixing of fourteen or more steel sheets weighing at least eight hundredweight, and the protection of sides and top with earth or sandbags—had proved a difficult matter for many householders.

---

[1] A high proportion of elementary and secondary schools in evacuation and reception areas were taken over for civil defence.

[2] p. 233.

[3] pp. 231–233.

[4] A.R.P. Dept. Circular 164 of 1st August 1939 had promised the early issue of samples, and been accompanied by the public sale of pamphlets describing these masks.

[5] A.R.P. Dept. Circular 219, 1st September 1939.

[6] pp. 195–200.

[7] The Home Office assertion that 1,680,000 had been delivered by the outbreak of war later proved to be an overstatement.

Pressing demands were made on local councils for help in this task; and the success of the Government's efforts to build up confidence in the 'Anderson' was reflected in urgent requests from householders for distribution to be completed and in many new applications. For shelters for people caught unawares in the streets and elsewhere there was still great official reliance upon trenches. Sufficient of the trenches dug hastily at Munich to accommodate about 500,000 people had now been reconstructed. The Government asked local authorities to provide these with ramps or stairs and some forms of lighting, seating and sanitation; and also to begin immediately to dig more trenches, where they could arrange to line these with local timber or (since no steel would be available) with pre-cast concrete linings which it would attempt to supply.[1] Digging by day and night in the parks and other open spaces was resumed, with appeals to the tenants of L.C.C. flats and others for help in this operation; and the authorities informed the Government that they hoped to construct new trenches for a further 1,000,000 people. Simultaneously, the local councils began to make wide use of their new powers to earmark buildings suitable for sheltering the public.[2] Notices of 'Public Shelters' appeared outside town halls and other civic buildings, railway stations, offices, shops and, in parts of London, the entrances to vaults and cellars. Structural adaptation of these miscellaneous buildings had not, however, proceeded far; and even modern steel-framed buildings would, it was thought by the Home Office experts at this time, require reinforcement. Help to local authorities was increased by the further enlargement of Regional Technical Advisers' staffs and the appointment of a Works Adviser to each Region;[3] and efforts were made to strengthen buildings in the time still available by use of the steel fittings supplied by the Government for private basements, sandbags and local timber. The London public had not yet been told that they would be debarred from using the Tubes as shelters; though, as the days passed, a number of stations in central London were closed so that work against flooding could proceed. The Government now began to fear that trenches and existing building would provide insufficient public shelters; and they asked local authorities, for the first time, to build structures specifically for this purpose. These were to be brick and concrete surface shelters for the protection of fifty persons similar in design to the domestic surface shelters authorised in the summer; and might, the Government thought, be built 'at considerable speed'.[4]

In Government offices the provision of shelters in the form of

---

[1] A.R.P. Dept. Circular 204, 28th August and addendum 1st September 1939.

[2] Defence Regulations 23, 38, 51.

[3] A.R.P. Dept. Circular 221, 1st September 1939; pp. 182-183.

[4] A.R.P. Dept. Circular 204, 28th August 1939; pp. 196-198.

strengthened basements, and occasionally trenches, was now pressed forward. But apart from the principal Whitehall War Rooms and a few alternative War Rooms being built in the suburbs, no stronger or bomb-proof protection was yet available. Employers had only been compelled for some two months past to provide their work-people with shelters, and the time allowed to them for reporting action in this matter had recently been extended to November.[1] But considerable numbers of factory-employers now sent in schemes to the Government and began, without waiting for formal approval, to strengthen basements and build trenches and surface shelters.[2] Apart from a handful of big establishments in London and other cities, not much effective shelter was as yet being furnished in offices and shops.

In matters other than shelters, the application of A.R.P. to industry had been advanced by the powers given to the Minister under the Ministry of Supply Act to direct essential undertakings to carry out such 'P.A.D.' measures as the structural protection of vital plants, and the provision of alternative supplies of water, electricity and gas.

The general public, forced to recognise the approach of catas-trophe, hurried on with various personal preparations. The author-ities, as the summer proceeded, had greatly increased the volume of their advice on A.R.P., without minimising the possible proportions of the danger.[3] War, if it came, would be an 'all-in war'. Air raids, the public had been told, would be affairs of extreme violence, punctuated by lulls, and immensely noisy. It would be one of the enemy's main objects to spread panic; and gas attack might be a powerful instrument to this end. It was the duty of every citizen, like a soldier entering battle, to make a will. For thousands who cut short their holidays and were faced with some large but obscure upheaval in their lives, the general uncertainty was made more bearable by the need to perform a number of concrete A.R.P. tasks. Large numbers were engulfed in plans to evacuate their families, to move with their businesses to safer areas or in practical steps for the protection of their homes. Blinds, curtains and paint had to be bought to carry out the Government's first injunction to prepare for the black-out; windows and fanlights screened with cardboard and brown paper and protected against splintering; gas-masks unearthed from cupboards or collected from the authorities and rooms gas-proofed with cellulose sheets and tape; 'Andersons' installed with the help of neighbours, or refuge-rooms, with first aid kit, a wireless

---

[1] pp. 220-223.

[2] The grant regulations were hurriedly issued on 29th August 1939.

[3] e.g., in a number of officially-inspired broadcasts and a new series of Public Information Leaflets distributed to every householder in the country.

set and toys for the children, prepared in basements; a shovel and bucket and some garden hose placed in readiness for fighting fires; the nature of the air raid warning signals studied from pamphlets; the name of the local warden discovered, and attention paid to the news and the latest broadcast official instructions.

The Government now made what proved to be their last bid for peace by appealing to Hitler to open direct negotiations with Poland. Mr Chamberlain, outlining the military and civil preparations to Parliament on 29th August, described the mood of the nation as a 'general absence of fear, or, indeed, of any violent emotion'.[1] Knowledge of the extent of the Government's civil defence preparations, particularly for the evacuation of women and children, had produced much public confidence and, amidst all the disturbance and activity, a prevailing atmosphere, remarked on by many observers, of calm. A review in *The Times* of the 30th August of 'A.R.P. in being' claimed, without undue exaggeration, that the nation had been brought to a state of organisation against air attack which had eliminated the factor of surprise.

Some further days were granted before the chasm, as it seemed at this time, still separating peace from war was crossed. The key to the Government's timing of the last steps of mobilisation was official evacuation—the mass movement from London and other cities which would be taken by the British public and the world at large as evidence of hope abandoned, and would interfere seriously for some days with military use of the nation's traffic. The Government, striving to give negotiation its final chance and resisting strong pressure by the Opposition in the matter,[2] finally gave the order on 31st August for evacuation to begin on the following day. That night Germany broadcast her terms to Poland, as if they had been rejected; and the next morning the public woke to the news that Hitler's troops and aircraft were attacking Poland.

As thousands of schoolchildren carrying gas-masks and packages of clothing were shepherded by their teachers into railway trains, the Government gave orders for the general mobilisation of Britain's armed forces. While, Britain still not being at war, suspense continued, the transformation of the civil structure into a 'home front' proceeded fast. Arrangements were completed to set up a censorship, to disperse foodstocks from threatened areas, to protect vulnerable points all over the country from sabotage and to bring passive defence into a state of final readiness for action. During 1st and 2nd September the Home Office sent out instructions to local authorities to appoint their Emergency Committees, invest A.R.P. Controllers

---

[1] H. of C. Deb., Vol. 351, Cols. 111–116.

[2] e.g., H. of C. Deb., Vol. 351, Cols.111–116, 29th August 1939, and a deputation on this day to the Prime Minister from the National Council of Labour.

with executive powers, call up the members of the A.R.P. services, and take all other steps to put A.R.P. schemes fully into force.[1] As the newspapers reported the heavy bombing of Polish towns and President Roosevelt's appeal to governments to refrain from bombing civilians,[2] wardens and members of the casualty and rescue services reported in thousands for duty, received equipment and took up stations at posts and depots on a twenty-four hour basis. Hospital beds were cleared, fresh medical equipment issued and extensive mortuary services made ready. Vehicles were taken into service and their conversion into ambulances, trailers and rescue party lorries pressed forward.[3] Further gas-masks were distributed, and instruments for gas warnings and gas detector paint installed. The sandbagging and strutting of innumerable buildings continued. Trenches and other public shelters were opened up, furnished with illuminated signs and put under the supervision of police or wardens. The public warning system was fully manned and the use of factory sirens and hooters forbidden except for the purposes of warning.[4]

The strange public silence this introduced was, from the individual's standpoint, but one feature of a general closing-in of life. If protection against the knock-out blow offered new forms of public service and many new responsibilities its overwhelming effect was contraction, a circumscribing of private and social habits, on a scale hitherto unknown. At sunset on Friday, 1st September the black-out was brought into force and transformed—perhaps more than any other one feature of the whole range of war restrictions—the life of the individual and the nation.[5] The statement of Britain's Foreign Secretary when the First World War broke out that 'the lamps are going out all over Europe' was, in a way he could not have imagined, being fulfilled. A pall of darkness descended upon Britain's streets and cities. Royal Air Force observers flying over Britain on the night of 3rd September reported that this drastic accompaniment of total war had, on the whole, been effectively brought into being. On the same night the B.B.C., synchronising its transmitters as a vital feature of air raid defence, reduced its public output to a single programme broadcast on two wave-lengths. The Government, owing to the speed with which air attack could be launched, had attached great importance to the wireless as the means of public instruction

---

[1] i.e., following the Government's institution of the 'precautionary stage' on 1st September 1939, it instructed the authorities by a succession of telegrams to bring the remaining items of LOWIN into force; pp. 217–218.

[2] 2nd September 1939.

[3] pp. 236-237.

[4] Control of Noise (Defence) Order, 1939, S.R. & O. No. 1169; A.R.P. Dept. Circular 225, 1st September 1939.

[5] Lighting (Restrictions) Order, 1939, S.R. & O. No. 1098; A.R.P. Dept. Circulars 223, 224, 226, 1st and 2nd September 1939.

and given considerable effort to the preparation in advance of full broadcast announcements. Though the time granted for mobilisation had allowed them to use other methods,[1] the one B.B.C. programme was now filled with official instructions and advice. And this stream of positive information was already, if unavoidably, corrupted by a further feature of contraction, the voluntary censorship of news introduced as a measure of national security.[2]

Mr Chamberlain, as he finished his broadcast on the Sunday morning, asked the nation to give close attention to the Government announcements that were to follow. These stated that all cinemas, theatres and other places of entertainment were immediately to be closed, and that football matches and similar gatherings involving large crowds were henceforth forbidden. They announced that London's Tubes would be needed for traffic and would not be available as air raid shelters. And they repeated the primary A.R.P. duties expected of every citizen—to observe the black-out from dusk till dawn; to listen regularly to news bulletins; to carry a gas-mask everywhere; to make sure that his name and address were carried on his own and his children's persons; and, when he heard the air raid warning, to go immediately to shelter and stay there until the 'all clear' sounded.

'Stand-by', and the Factor of Morale

After the outbreak of war and the first air raid warning on 3rd September Germany waited six weeks before dropping the first bomb of the Second World War on British soil, and over eight months before beginning attack on the civil population.[3] Throughout this period of 'twilight war' her capacity to deliver a blow from the air which might knock Britain out remained unchanged. Her restraint gave this country further valuable time in which to prepare and test her passive as well as her other defences. And the civilian 'stand-to' of the earliest days of the war was transformed into a continuous 'stand-by'. Before describing the growth of the physical defences in this phase some attention must be paid to the effects of Germany's abstention on Britain's morale.

On entering the tangled undergrowth of this topic the historian may be permitted some general observations. He is discussing a factor which had assumed new, and some would say supreme,

---

[1] e.g., the new series of Public Information Leaflets being distributed by the G.P.O. to every householder.

[2] Defence Regulation 3 made it an offence to publish, without authority, anything which might be useful to the enemy, and the Press and the B.B.C. were advised of the particular matters which it was desired they should voluntarily submit to censorship before publication.

[3] p. 280.

importance in war; but which was an imponderable, not susceptible to genuine scientific measurement. From the outset of the war reports on the state of public feeling began to pile up on the desks of those in authority; and as time proceeded the simpler methods of assessing this matter were supplemented by various new 'techniques' and elaborate special organisation. These reports, however compiled, were influenced to a peculiar degree by individual judgments. Regional Commissioners, police authorities and Ministry of Information officials reporting on morale in a particular area frequently took different views about the elements to be included in their compound, and reached different results. Likewise, the Ministers and officials to whom these reports were presented inevitably brought a strong personal element into their interpretations of them. Some, for example, took a consistently hopeful, and others a consistently pessimistic, view of the ability of the public to withstand serious air attack.

The historian's selection of evidence about the state of civilian morale at any stage of the war must, therefore, to an unusual degree be arbitrary. It behoves him to emphasise that he is only offering suggestions on this subject and not recording conclusions; and also to establish at the outset certain definitions. Morale, in its accepted sense of the state of mind or spirit of the 'troops', will be regarded here as only one aspect of public opinion on Britain's home front. Public opinion at any given time was, of course, formed by innumerable factors, including food supplies, prices and other domestic conditions, and the progress of the war at sea, on land and in the air on other fronts.[1] The continuous influence of these on the fighting spirit of the mass of civilians who stayed at home in Britain can, of course, be given no more than glancing reference in this narrative. The novelty of the situation in September 1939 was that all civilians stood for the first time in the front line and could, irrespective of age or sex, properly be called 'troops'. But the civilian, it is important to remember, was distinguishable from the member of the traditional Fighting Services in two fundamental ways. He had, in the first place, the advantage that he was fighting to defend his own home and soil; and he had the disadvantage of being unarmed and without a weapon with which to fight back.

The function of civil defence was, speaking strictly, by no means passive.[2] The civil defender could act both before and after the assault. He could do a number of things beforehand to reduce its violence—or possibly to prevent the enemy from making it at all.

[1] See other volumes in this series of Histories. Ample material exists for a volume devoted to public opinion in the war on Britain's home front.

[2] Though the term 'passive defence' will of course have to be retained throughout this narrative.

And he could do other things afterwards to repair any destruction of or damage to human life and property it might have caused. His or her appointed role was not, therefore, inaction but continuous action. The unforeseen character of the first eight months of total war was about to demonstrate that action in the form of preparation for attack was often the hardest to undertake. And that good morale, both in the individual and the nation, was often harder to sustain under the threat of attack than under the bombardment itself.

Mention has already been made of the atmosphere of calm prevailing in London and elsewhere during the days leading up to the outbreak of war.[1] Many who had experienced the onset of the First World War twenty-five years earlier remarked the complete contrast in the nation's mood on this occasion. Instead of the unconcealed emotion, sometimes reaching hysteria, of August 1914[2] there was an absence of visible feeling which included much bewilderment. But the Prime Minister of Southern Rhodesia, to quote one observer, noticed in addition to the peoples' 'extreme calmness' a unanimity behind the Government's decision to enter war which had been absent in 1914.[3] A Regional Commissioner in the north reported that although there was 'no enthusiasm for war, there was a patient acceptance of it as a grim necessity'.[4] The British people, in fact, were fed up with a succession of crises and in a mood of, 'as it's got to come, let's get on with it!'

Only a few of the reasons for this mood can be suggested here. Air attack of the size and character expected transcended any former experience, and was believed in the highest quarters and in the lowest to be imminent. Hitler's propaganda abroad and stories of barbarities in concentration camps and elsewhere had spread knowledge of a sinister revival of German ruthlessness. The Munich crisis, on the other hand, with all its tension and drama had produced a stiffening effect.[5] Progress with the passive defences— most notably the invention and distribution of the Anderson shelter —during the past twelve months had engendered much public confidence. Finally, almost every British citizen was occupied in September 1939 with some personal preparation for war.

When days passed and no blow from the air was delivered the nation's mood changed with great rapidity from calm and resignation to one of complacency and scepticism about this threat. Barely two weeks from the outbreak of war Ministers concluded that 'the

---

[1] p. 292.

[2] Expressed at one level in Rupert Brooke's poem *Peace*, and in C.E. Montague's *Disenchantment* (1922).

[3] Senator Godfrey Huggins, *The Times*, 8th September 1939.

[4] Lord Harlech.

[5] Chapter IV.

general mood of the country in the present disturbed conditions was almost one of disappointment and anti-climax, owing to the fact that the dangers against which precautions had been taken had not materialised'. The bracing of effort to meet the onslaught had produced a correspondingly sharp reaction. The Home Secretary had to take steps to remind the public that Britain was engaged in 'a struggle for life' in which 'the home front is a vital front', and that 'a state of war readiness must be maintained'; and to answer rising public complaints that the Government had recruited an unnecessary number of persons for the A.R.P. services; had introduced restrictions on lighting and amusements which were unnecessarily severe; and had withdrawn normal facilities such as hospital treatment from the public in too drastic a fashion.[1]

During the next three months public criticism that the nation's civil defence measures represented over-insurance grew in scope and volume. It is difficult, with a knowledge of later events, to appreciate the strength attained in these weeks by the feeling expressed in the slogan 'turn on the lights and turn out the A.R.P. workers!' In a condition described by the Prime Minister as 'this strangest of wars, a sort of siege'[2] A.R.P. represented burdens and discomforts which were heavy, novel and impossible for the public to relate to any actual experience. The War Cabinet's announcement early in September of its intention to base its policies on the expectation of a three years' war had suggested to many that the air threat had been overrated.[3] And this scepticism was nourished by a growing confidence, due in part to official statements, in the capacity of the active defences to ward off any blow.[4]

The Government, confronted with this criticism, promised no more than amelioration of restrictions and adjustments in the light of experience of civil defence arrangements. But by December the Civil Defence Committee had become so disturbed by the nation's 'mood of easy optimism' and its effect on their preparations that they concluded that urgent action was required. In a review of the situation to the War Cabinet, which deserves fuller summary than this narrative can afford, they pointed out that complaints against one or other form of evacuation had now crystallised into general criticism of the whole policy of dispersal. Criticism of the black-out, of the size of the A.R.P. services and of the emergency hospital scheme all reflected a growing tendency for the public to question the need for precautions on the scale adopted. Fresh consultation

---

[1] The Times, 22nd September 1939.

[2] Guildhall luncheon, 9th November 1939.

[3] The Times, 11th September 1939.

[4] e.g., the Secretary of State for Air's review, H. of C. Deb., Vol. 355, Cols. 1067–74, 12th December 1939.

with the Air Staff had confirmed that these were, in fact, in no way excessive for their purpose. Nothing, that is to say, had occurred to prevent the German Air Force from delivering 2,000 to 3,000 tons of bombs for several days, or 700 tons a day for a period of weeks, on London and other cities.[1] If public opinion was allowed to maintain its present course the whole structure of civil defence might be 'so seriously impaired' that it would be impossible to rebuild it when attack became imminent.

The action requested by the Ministers was an early and clear pronouncement to the nation by a member of the War Cabinet, and preferably by the Prime Minister, of these facts. The situation, it must be emphasised, was a repetition in graver circumstances of one that had pervaded the pre-war years of preparation. The menace from the air, it has already been argued, had confronted British statesmen with a new dilemma or, if the reader prefers, with an old one in a new form. To warn the public constantly of the threat and reiterate its dangers might cause undue alarm, divert effort from normal activities including essential production and bring disagreeable political repercussions. Defence against it, however, meant civil organisation on a novel scale, based on the readiness to appreciate the risk and act accordingly of thousands of officials and ordinary citizens. A difficult balance had therefore to be maintained by those in authority between over and under-emphasis to the public of the danger or, to put the issue in other terms, between political and administrative needs.

Mr Chamberlain, in this vital matter, had always chosen the course of under-emphasis. And his difficulty, before the catastrophe, in understanding the character of Hitler's Germany persisted in the form of declining belief in the enemy's intention to undertake large-scale air assault on Britain.[2] But he agreed on the need for steps to bolster up the nation's morale and made a speech with this intention at the Mansion House on 9th January of the new year. In a brief reference to air attack he told his audience that he did not consider that this risk was over 'or even that it has diminished'; and he asked parents to leave their children in safe areas. He also warned the nation that it 'would have to face a phase of the war much grimmer than anything it had yet seen'.

This reminder, with other factors, helped to check the immediate danger to the civil defences, and to establish an equilibrium in the state of Britain's morale. The war remained in what Mr Churchill has called its 'sinister trance'; and boredom and apathy continued to be widespread. The Government and people were still 'out of tune with each other, the nation was divided within itself, men and women

---

[1] pp. 282-284.
[2] See also K. Feiling, *op. cit.*, pp. 425, 445.

were divided within their own minds'.[1] But for A.R.P. in general a dangerous corner had been turned. The achievement so far attained had not been thrown away, resources had not been seriously dissipated and the work of preparation went on. Large numbers in the civil defence services and among the public were learning that passive defence was more than an affair of unpleasant duties to be performed under the stimulus of bombardment and included waiting in a state of readiness to counter a distant threat.

In March the Civil Defence Committee, in spite of strands of pacifist feeling and the absence of any deep feeling of hostility towards the enemy, had ceased to be perturbed about declining morale. But one factor, not yet mentioned, had proved of unexpected importance. The genuine lack of news in the first months of war, combined with the claims of security, had caused a 'black-out of information' which contributed powerfully to depressing the spirits of the public.[2] The public appetite for military and other information, it was becoming apparent, would be in continuing conflict with the need, more stringent than in any former war, for withholding intelligence from the enemy. The physical and information black-outs had already, for example, caused considerable listening-in to German broadcasts and particularly those of 'Lord Haw-Haw'. The Ministry of Information, however, now reported itself ready to go fully into action on the home front, with an effective regional organisation to report on public morale and disseminate news of the Government's policies.

The Structure in War

Morale was the mortar of a structure which embraced almost every civil organisation. Seen in this complex of official and unofficial bodies civil defence appears, not as a special war-time institution, but as an additional war service. It had, nevertheless, certain machinery in its own right, which must again occupy attention. This had been performing the three broad functions of evolving the technique of passive defence, administering the A.R.P. services and co-ordinating the plans for countering air attack of all other civil agencies. It had now the fourth function of control, or the ultimate conduct of operations in face of the enemy.

The expectation of immediate attack had caused the Home Security organisation in Whitehall and in the Regions to be brought to a state of readiness in the last days of August.[3] The inactivity on the part of the enemy which followed, it must be noted, astounded

---

[1] W. K. Hancock and M. M. Gowing, *op. cit.*, p. 150.

[2] S. King-Hall, *History of the War*, Vol. 2 (1939).

[3] pp. 287-288.

everyone, including those in the highest places.[1] But war, though it might soon appear to some of the public little different from the preceding peace, had put official machinery into a new gear. Ministers and officials engaged in civil defence were at war stations. A faster tempo and more informal methods of conducting business immediately prevailed. The need was felt at all levels to take the opportunity of whatever further respite might be granted to complete or extend preparations.

The chief components of the civil defence machinery were in existence by September 1939 and remained so until the end of the war. It will therefore be convenient here to carry the story of their development somewhat beyond the summer of 1940, and to include some general observations. The reader should set these specialised organs in the framework of a rapid, continuous, expansion of Government business and the Government structure.[2] The small War Cabinet, it is necessary to remember, was concerned day by day with a huge range of domestic and strategic issues; and it delegated wide functions to Cabinet Committees. The Defence Committee, advised by the Chiefs of Staff Committee, became after May 1940 pre-eminent among these. Five main committees, of which the Civil Defence Committee was one, directed domestic business; and each of these was served by a network of Ministerial and official sub-committees. After May 1940 the work of these five was co-ordinated by the Lord President's Committee, which was almost equal to the Defence Committee in authority and status.[3]

The Civil Defence Committee was, for all but the largest issues, the peak of the structure which concerns this narrative. This was, as the reader is aware, the continuation of established machinery under new forms. Sir John Anderson had been appointed on the outbreak of war both Home Secretary and Minister of Home Security. The Ministry of Home Security Order of 4th September gave the new Minister the powers hitherto exercised by the Lord Privy Seal; and also gave the Lord Privy Seal's Office and the A.R.P. Department of the Home Office in combination the status of a separate Ministry.[4] Whether this represented a triumph of British flexibility it will be left to the reader to judge. The Home Secretary (as for convenience the Minister of Home Security must often be called in this narrative) presided over the Civil Defence Committee throughout the war with a double authority and a double function. He was not, until several years had elapsed, a

---

[1] W. S. Churchill, *op. cit.*, Vol. I, p. 330.

[2] See W.K. Hancock and M. M. Gowing, *op. cit.*, Chapter III.

[3] i.e., the committee under the chairmanship of the Lord President of the Council.

[4] S.R. & O. 1939, No. 1142 under the Ministers of the Crown (Emergency Appointments) Act, 1939, 2 and 3 Geo. 6, Ch. 77.

member of the War Cabinet; though Sir John Anderson in fact attended most War Cabinet meetings during his tenure of this office.

The Home Secretary's double role as (*a*) co-ordinator in chief of 'civil defence' and (*b*) administrator of certain services familiarly known as 'A.R.P.' requires emphasis, since it was reproduced at most lower levels of the structure. Difficulties of language afflicted those concerned at the time (as well as the historian later), and are significant of the degree in which the problem was still a developing one.[1] Briefly, as the reader is aware, 'A.R.P.' signified the services developed in peace-time by the Home Office and now the responsibility of the Ministry of Home Security, and 'civil defence' a much wider and less well defined sphere. During the phase this narrative has now reached the term 'A.R.P.' was beginning to decline in popularity in favour of 'civil defence' used as its equivalent, or in a relatively narrow sense.[2] In spite of any confusion for which the writer must take the blame, the reader should constantly bear in mind the two meanings of 'civil defence'. In its restricted sense it indicated those defences to counter the immediate effects of attack, most of which were already in being. In its broader sense it indicated new services or functions in process (throughout the war) of being planned or developed. Thus the Civil Defence Committee was composed of no less than sixteen Ministers whose departments were actually or potentially involved in the problem.

This Committee was clearly too large a body for rapid consultation and decision; and it became in practice a forum for discussion by Ministers not in the War Cabinet of many topics, some of which had little connection with civil defence.[3] The effective direction of civil defence continued to be exercised by daily or frequent meetings between the Home Secretary and the six other Ministers most concerned—the Secretary of State for Scotland and the Ministers of Health, Transport, Education,[4] Works and Food—and their chief officials. This machinery was, in marked degree, informal; and has already been compared to a supreme military headquarters. Decisions, that is to say, were taken rapidly and with a minimum of written records; and Ministers delegated much authority to their Permanent Secretaries, who in turn delegated much to their chief Departmental subordinates. The historian, it may be interpolated, is faced with the grave handicap that in the higher levels of the structure written records were drastically

---

[1] pp. 167, 193 (footnote 1).

[2] Although the A.R.P. General Services were not renamed 'Civil Defence General Services' until September 1941, and the title 'A.R.P. Controller' was retained throughout the war.

[3] Its original title of 'Home Security Committee' was changed to avoid confusion with the Home Policy Committee.

[4] p. 287. The President of the Board of Education and the First Commissioner of Works did not in fact become Ministers until 1944 and 1942 respectively.

reduced, while at lower levels these began to accumulate more thickly than leaves on the brooks in Vallombrosa.[1] The decisions reached at the Home Secretary's informal meetings were reported weekly to the Civil Defence Committee. But these meetings were not recorded until September 1940, when they were put on the more formal basis of an 'Executive Sub-Committee' of the larger body.

As an instrument for co-ordination the Ministry of Home Security relied extensively on informal contacts with the senior officials of other Departments. Once war had broken out this function became, and remained, its crucial one. Though the seven Departments just mentioned constituted the 'inner ring', co-ordination also became necessary of the relevant activities of an increasing number of peace-time Departments, new Departments and other agencies. Functions regarding the police and the security of the nation remained, where they had always been, in the Home Departments; and the title of the new Ministry, it may be observed in this context, had turned out to be misleading. The civil defence reports submitted regularly by the Ministry to the War Cabinet now included, in addition to progress in A.R.P. and the Fire Service, the plans or activities of the two Health Departments with regard to evacuation, the emergency hospital scheme, the casualty services, water supplies and repairs to houses and buildings; of the Ministry of Transport regarding roads, railways, docks and harbours; the Office of Works regarding Government evacuation and other matters; the Scottish Home Department regarding fire brigades; the Ministry of Pensions regarding compensation and activities of the Unemployment Assistance Board; and the Board of Education regarding the billeting of evacuated schoolchildren. Co-ordination had also to be achieved of the activities of the Service Departments, Ministry of Supply and other civil Departments concerning the passive defence of war factories under their control.

Since co-ordination formed so much of civil defence, to under-rate its difficulties, either in or outside Whitehall, would be seriously to falsify the story. British independence and respect for established methods and the preference of British institutions, official and unofficial, for ploughing their own furrow are as relevant to the matter as British capacity for improvisation and, under certain circumstances, for co-operation. The new Ministry, despite four years' apprenticeship, was a war-time Department. And it would be foolish to pretend that its parent office and other old-established Departments regarded it as their equal in experience and ability, or that newer institutions invariably smoothed its path.[2] A sub-

---

[1] And often, it must be added, with the same obscuring effect.

[2] Ten new Ministries were created in the war, apart from substantial accretions to existing ones. It was perhaps due to the inherent difficulties of co-ordination that the sobriquets earned by the Ministry of Home Security included 'Ministry of Some Obscurity'.

ordinate status and a relative lack of administrative skill remained continuing handicaps. But these were in varying degree offset by the facts that the Minister was also the Home Secretary; that he had in the persons of the Regional Commissioners eminent representatives in the country; that the Home Security and Regional War Rooms provided an excellent intelligence network and centre for interdepartmental liaison in day and night operation throughout the war; and that this machinery had a function of ultimate control which, under certain circumstances, might greatly increase.

The organism had in its pre-war existence settled the main features of its domestic structure and also attained a respectable size.[1] In its new status it was reinforced by a Parliamentary Secretary in charge of its A.R.P. functions; which office was held during the earlier years of the war by Mr William Mabane.[2] After heavy attacks on London had started a Joint Parliamentary Secretary, Miss Ellen Wilkinson, was appointed to take charge of shelter matters.[3] The Lord Privy Seal's 'Chief of Staff' became the Ministry's first permanent head;[4] and it is a measure of the gravity of the danger in September 1939 that it was considered desirable to 'double-bank' this office by the appointment of a Joint Secretary. Sir George Gater, Clerk of the London County Council, who had been Chief A.R.P. Officer for the Metropolitan Police District and the City during Munich, was appointed to this office. Although he left after the danger had temporarily receded, he returned to serve as Secretary soon after the opening of the Blitz.[5]

Though the Ministry's main domestic structure had been settled, important additions were made in the first year or so of war to the duties of most divisions and several new branches were formed. The division responsible for general co-ordination and the Regional Commissioners' affairs became concerned after nine months with a wide range of problems connected with invasion. The Shelters Division had to administer a sphere of growing complexity which included new central supplies and examination of industrial shelter grants. The Warnings and Lighting Division acquired a branch to experiment with smoke production. A Principal Priorities Officer was appointed to the Ministry on the outbreak of war.[6] The Supply

---

[1] pp. 174-175.

[2] Born 1895; Nat. Lib. M.P. Huddersfield 1931-1945; Assistant P.M.G. 1939; Parl. Sec., M.H.S. Oct. 1939–June 1942, M. of Food 1942-1945.

[3] Lab. M.P. Middlesbrough E. 1924–31, Jarrow 1935–47; trade union official; Parl. Sec. M. of Pensions, 1940, M.H.S., Oct. 1940–May 1945; Minister of Education 1945 to death in 1947.

[4] p. 173.

[5] He remained Secretary until April 1942. Mr Harold Scott (to November 1943) and Sir W. Brown (to October 1945) were the Ministry's subsequent permanent heads.

[6] To co-ordinate the Ministry's demands and represent it in the Ministry of Supply's Priorities hierarchy.

w

Policy Division and its adjuncts became concerned with the design, manufacture and distribution of many articles besides anti-gas devices and with guidance on the care and maintenance of these.[1] The Intelligence Branch undertook the dissemination within the Ministry of the information which flooded into the War Room and of foreign intelligence gathered from the Service and other Departments.

The Research and Experiments Branch, in accordance with general policy, was evacuated to Princes Risborough, Bucks, on the eve of war.[2] Its responsibilities then rapidly increased and acquired an importance to which most inadequate attention can be paid in this narrative. Under the Chief Adviser, a network of expert committees and officials carried on the functions suggested by this title over a huge range of matters—e.g., armaments, the effects of bombs of all kinds on buildings, shelters and fire. In time this information, intended for passive defence, became of considerable value to British offensive air operations; and then to other British and United States' Fighting Services. Shortly before the war the Ministry had acquired from the Air Ministry two agencies of importance. A Camouflage Establishment set up in September at Leamington was still occupied during the twilight war and later with experiment rather than with application. But by 1941 its work was bearing practical fruit both for civil defence and the Fighting Services. And a Key Points Intelligence Branch was occupied in compiling information, which when the enemy struck included intelligence of damage, about vital factories, public utilities, railway centres and other places.

Although the limpet (if this metaphor may be revived) had gained new status it would be wrong to regard it as separated from its rock. The Ministry continued to rely on Home Office divisions for the important matters of legal advice, establishments, finance and public relations.[3] A proportion, though a fast diminishing one, of its staff of most grades was provided by the Home Office. Its headquarters were in the Home Office in Whitehall, and it shared Home Office buildings elsewhere in London.

Viewed as an employer of administrative and other staff the limpet now rapidly outstripped its host. In 1940 it was employing some 1,500 persons at a cost of about £890,000. By 1942 these figures had reached some 5,700 persons and about £1.7 million, where they remained during the next two years. Home Office expenditure, by contrast, on salaries for general administration

---

[1] pp. 230–237.

[2] pp. 174, 201.

[3] The public relations work was strengthened in the autumn of 1940 by the appointment of a Director concerned with both institutions.

during these years averaged about £612,000. The preponderant part of these totals consisted of non-industrial staff working at the Ministry and its twelve Regional Offices. It is of interest to record that in 1941 the total employed at the Regional Offices of some 2,250 overtook the total employed at headquarters. The headquarters figure reached its peak of about 2,335 in 1942; and the regional figure its peak of some 2,945 in 1943. These totals include the paid staff in London and the Regions of the W.V.S., which reached a maximum of nearly 500 towards the end of the war.[1]

While these figures are significant, some less tangible factors must be suggested. Departments of State, it is important to remember, 'are staffed by human beings, and a department or a division has as real and individual an existence as any other human community'.[2] The Ministry's headquarters seems never to have developed a strong sense of unity; and corporate personality was to be found less in the whole than in the parts or the divisions, swollen by 1941 into departments and directorates, just enumerated. This comment, it may be necessary to add, is made solely to underline the internal problem of co-ordination presented to the institution by reason of its size, physical dispersal, temporary character and variety of work. When the Ministry is considered in relation to its Regional Offices the diversity of the picture becomes even more apparent. It was to some extent intended that these Offices, under the Regional Commissioners, should evolve an independent existence. And under the conditions that actually developed it was probably inevitable that in most Regions the centrifugal forces should gain strength over the centripetal ones.

Though the attempt, if it were possible, to characterise the Ministry and its Regions in human terms belongs to the novelist rather than the historian, these further factors need mention. Both at headquarters and in the Regions the proportion of professional (i.e., established) trained civil servants was small. In the organisation as a whole this amounted, at the peak, to less than one quarter of the non-industrial staff.[3] This nucleus of professionals was drawn from a variety of central Departments and, in the case of London Region, also from the L.C.C. The temporary civil servants naturally followed many peace-time callings. And emphasis must again be laid on the fact that these included many retired members of the Fighting Forces in a variety of important positions.[4]

---

[1] On the outbreak of war the Home Secretary had agreed to pay salaries or expenses of some members of this body.

[2] W. J. Mackenzie, 'The Structure of Central Administration' in *British Government Since 1918* (1950).

[3] The national ratio at the peak of Civil Service expansion in 1943 was about one-third established.

[4] i.e., professional soldiers, etc. A much larger number of civil servants and others had, of course, served in these Forces during 1914–18; p. 181.

The Ministry's communications, in the technical sense, were in full readiness by the outbreak of war. These consisted of land lines (i.e., telephones and teleprinters) rented from and maintained by the General Post Office connecting the Home Security and Regional War Rooms (including alternative War Rooms). The communications' staff, as previously mentioned, was also for the most part recruited from the General Post Office. The technical system could thus, from the layman's standpoint, be described as super-imposed upon the country's normal civil facilities.

Communications in the non-technical sense of all exchanges of information were, of course, vital to the co-ordinating function; and these increased rapidly in volume and variety from the moment the war began. It is only possible here to indicate some of the forms they assumed and some of the problems they presented. The in-formality which war had introduced into dealings between Ministers and Heads of Departments regarding civil defence, also prevailed in the Ministry of Home Security's upper levels and in many of its dealings with its Regions.[1] Personal interchange—for example by Regional Commissioners' telephone conversations or visits to head-quarters, the visits of the Inspector-General and other central officials to Regions, and conferences in London of Principal or Regional Officers—assumed much importance. Yet in spite of this, and to an extent no one could have foreseen, written communications of many kinds developed on a scale far exceeding that of any previous war.

The War Room network, designed to transmit news of attack in the shortest time to the centre, began at once to serve a wider purpose. Many matters—for example war-time interruptions on the railways or the breaking adrift of barrage balloons—which might affect the civil population over wide areas needed instant reporting. Events which were already operational combined with administrative matters of all sorts to establish the system; and time was granted to recruit further staffs, elaborate the procedure and improve the physical arrangements.[2] When attacks began in earnest the War Rooms in general proved highly efficient; though this is not to say that they failed to present various problems. What is most relevant here is that under heavy attack the work of issuing instructions to many authorities, receiving or extracting intelligence from these and filtering it for transmission upwards to London could severely tax the resources of any Regional War Room.[3] Also that on a night, for

---

[1] No equivalent seems to have been established at any stage of the war to the A.R.P. Department's useful informal 'Heads of Divisions Council' (see Chapter V).

[2] e.g., Reading Region H.Q. was situated in Reading Gaol, which was structurally inconvenient and uncomfortably close to the main railway line, prior to April 1940.

[3] Not excluding the highly-organised War Room of London Region during the Big Blitz.

example, of heavy raiding on several Regions the task of the Home Security War Room in rapidly presenting those concerned with a balanced summary of events was no light one.

The speed of attack, it must be concluded, here presented (apart from the warning system) the principal challenge to the intelligence resources, human and technical, of the defences. The chief contrast to this type of communication, in terms of speed combined with importance, was the circulars which the Ministry issued throughout the war both to Regions and to local authorities in numbers much in excess of those issued during peace. Most matters of administrative and operational importance were, usually after discussion between the Ministry and Regions, embodied in this form as instructions of a relatively long-term nature. These, whether addressed to Regions or to local authorities, might be only for information, or permissive or mandatory.[1] They might, for instance, supply Regions with information which they could at their discretion reproduce; or explain to Regions in advance an instruction about to be issued to some or all local authorities.

When to these is added the many other types of written communication—e.g., periodical reports and returns, minutes of meetings, semi-official correspondence, training pamphlets and memoranda—it is not surprising to learn of a Regional Commissioner complaining before the onset of serious attack that there was too much 'paper' in this war.[2] This complaint, though echoed in most other spheres of war activity, expressed a problem which, it is possibly true to say, bore with particular weight upon civil defence. The operational-plus-intelligence functions of instructing the defences and reporting the consequences of attack over the whole of Britain were, as this narrative has suggested, exceptional; and to these was added a function of what can only be called normal civil administration under peculiar pressure.

It will be apparent to the reader what types of problem the Ministry's abundant flow of written communications presented. There was a natural, and often unavoidable, tendency to record too little on paper during periods of high activity and too much once the enemy had offered a breathing-space. There was also a tendency for a proportion of officials of lower grades, and irrespective of this time-division, to write instructions and so on at inordinate length. A third tendency, connected with both of these, was perhaps of greater importance—namely the failure of Regions to furnish the Ministry with periodical reports on essential matters. For example, the Ministry received no systematic reports from its Regional

---

[1] They were known after 1st January 1940 as 'H.S.Rs.' and 'H.S.Cs.' respectively.
[2] Gen. Sir Hugh Elles.

Officers until March 1940; and long after that date this particular problem persisted.[1]

Communications, it may perhaps be concluded, illustrate better than any other function the Home Security structure's quasi-military character. The reader must be left to contrast the ramifying civil organisation under discussion here with any of the Fighting Services. And to recall that in this matter of communications a Fighting Service has already in peace-time (a) well-established rules, (b) trained staffs and (c) sanctions, or the power to impose penalties on those who fail to comply with any orders to report.

The Regional Commissioners and their Deputies, soon after assuming office late in August, had been furnished with Royal Warrants of Appointment. These charged them individually with the duty of 'securing the proper co-ordination of all such measures (of civil defence) and the exercise of such authority and control as may be necessary for their due and efficient execution' within their Regions.[2] The Regional Commissioners Act, 1939[3] passed on 1st September merely provided for the payment to Commissioners and their Deputies, and to District Commissioners and their Deputies in Scotland, of salaries and expenses, and protected them from Parliamentary disqualification. Since a number of Commissioners had asked to serve without payment the Act did not specify actual salaries. But the Home Secretary told Parliament that maximum salaries would be £2,500 per annum for Commissioners and £1,000 for their Deputies and for Scottish District Commissioners.[4]

The Commissioners, though without legal powers, had both moral authority and political responsibility of an unusual kind. It will be apparent that under these circumstances their personalities, past experience and individual approach to the problem counted for much. The thirteen Commissioners who took office on the eve of war can be summarily labelled as follows: three past holders of high political office, a former Permanent Secretary to the Treasury and another retired civil servant, a retired admiral, a retired general, a past Director of the International Labour Office, the Master of a Cambridge College and four industrialists.[5] The appointment of a Commissioner for Scotland, Mr Thomas Johnston, was made at the beginning of September; but that of a 'Senior Commissioner' for London was deferred until May 1940, when Captain Euan Wallace

---

[1] H.S.R. 53/40, 21st March 1940.

[2] The use of the phrase 'civil defence', as distinct from 'civil government', later gave rise to important official discussions.

[3] 2 and 3 Geo. 6, Ch. 76.

[4] H. of C. Deb., Vol. 351, Cols. 209-12.

[5] See List, pp. 179-180. The number includes the two London 'Joint Commissioners'.

assumed this office. Only five Regions were destined to have the same Commissioner throughout the war.[1] But continuity was greater than this figure might suggest since (*a*) Sir Ernest Gowers was in charge of London Region for all but about eight months, and (*b*) only one Region (Manchester) had more than one change of Commissioner.[2] In all, twenty-three persons held this appointment.

Though the headquarters town is preferred in this narrative to the geographical name to describe particular Regions, neither label in most cases conveys very much. The reader must be left to consult the map and to draw upon his own knowledge of the group of counties and towns in question. Emphasis, however, must be laid on the obvious variety in character of these twelve areas. London Region, as a target and in almost every other respect, was *sui generis*. 'Manchester' and 'Leeds' were highly industrialised, 'Cambridge' mainly rural and 'Nottingham' a mixture of the two. 'Birmingham', like 'London', was compact; while 'Bristol' was a sprawling area, and 'Reading' stretched to Portsmouth and Southampton. Much variety also prevailed in the local authority structure which the individual Regions contained, and in their presumed attractiveness to the enemy as targets.

The Regional Commissioners' war staffs, as the reader is aware, had been planned in detail after Munich; and the A.R.P. Regional Organisation had been built up during these months to some size.[3] On the outbreak of war, elsewhere than in London, the task of fusing the Regional Commissioners' Headquarters with the Ministry's Regional Offices, or new personalities and functions with those already established, had begun. It seems better to err by exaggerating, rather than by minimising, the real difficulties and continuing nature of this process. Functions changed in accordance with the changing character of the threat or the incidence of attack; and domestic re-organisation became a recurring phenomenon. Personalities, from Principal Officers to junior staff, came and went.[4] Though some Regions enjoyed more stability than others, the majority, viewed over five years and in comparison with peace-time official organisations, can fairly be described as fluid.

Though detailed description of the structure of Regional Headquarters is impossible in this narrative, some further elaboration is essential. The Principal Officers had been clearly designated the Permanent Heads (in the Whitehall sense) of their respective

---

[1] The Commissioner for Bristol (Sir Hugh Elles) held an appointment at the Ministry of Home Security for six months in 1940.

[2] On the death of Captain E. Wallace in January 1941, Sir E. Gowers became Senior Commissioner. For the war-time changes among Commissioners see Appendix 1.

[3] Chapter V.

[4] e.g., when the knock-out blow was deferred most of the original Principal Officers returned to London and were replaced by officials of lesser rank and experience.

institutions or alternatively the Chiefs of Staff to their Commissioners.[1] As such, they became primarily occupied with assisting Commissioners with their co-ordinating functions, and delegated large responsibility in all A.R.P. matters to Senior Regional Officers. For a number of reasons, including changes of Principal Officers, this dichotomy tended to persist, causing, especially in the earlier stages of the war, some serious mistakes of administration. The devolution in practice of administrative, including financial, responsibilities to 'S.R.O.'s' much increased after the outbreak of war.[2] And some time elapsed before the formal situation, and in particular the Principal Officers' overriding financial responsibility, was clearly established.

It was found by the Ministry in the autumn of 1939 that the standard organisation proposed for Regions had been generally adopted; though there was considerable variety, then and thereafter, in the duties actually performed in Regions by officers with the same title and general function. The London staff, under its Chief Administrative Officer, was inevitably more elaborate and also, it would appear, more firmly organised than those elsewhere.[3] Senior Regional Officers were in administrative charge of most of the War Rooms, assisted by Operations Officers, Intelligence Officers and others whose functions varied from Region to Region. Of the senior officials the Regional Technical and Works Advisers have already been noticed as installed by the outbreak of war. The preoccupation of Home Security with structural questions also caused the appointment early in the war of Regional Technical Intelligence Officers as representatives 'in the field' of the central Research and Experiments Department.

As a consequence of stand-by conditions the functions of two members of Regional Commissioners' staffs, Treasury Officers and Ministry of Health General Inspectors, declined in importance. But these same conditions caused the general addition early in 1940 of Training Officers; and the redoubling of the threat in May caused the appointment of Deputy Principal Officers. Of comparable importance to those already mentioned were the Police and Fire representatives (called by various titles) and the Military and Air Force Liaison Officers. All Regions had a varying number of other liaison officers who (except in London) were not normally accommodated at Regional headquarters. The most important of these was the Ministry of Health Liaison Officer.

The size of Regional staffs was somewhat increased in the spring of 1940. But it is true to say that those under attack in the Blitz of the

---

[1] p. 176.

[2] pp. 181–182, 331.

[3] pp. 183–184.

following autumn were hard-pressed; in London and other Regions, for example, administrative staff took regular turns in manning the Control or War Rooms. Real expansion, due in large part to the creation of the National Fire Service and to Fire Prevention arrangements, did not begin until late in 1941.[1] London Region reached its peak of over 800 persons and Birmingham (to take a provincial example) its peak of some 280 persons about the middle of 1942. Both the variety of peace-time occupations and the turnover of members of these staffs need re-emphasis. Reading War Room, for example, was manned for a time by volunteers from Huntley and Palmers' factory, and University dons acted as Operations and Intelligence Officers throughout the war at Cambridge. Though 'regulars' drawn from various Departments occupied many of the offices just listed, they were assisted in positions too numerous to specify by military men, colonial civil servants, lawyers, business men, landed gentry and the youth of both sexes awaiting their military call-up.[2]

The Commissioners' and their Deputies' activities during the twilight war were manifold and can be described, according to the reader's preference, as planning, organisation or liaison. Owing to the novelty of their position they were peculiarly exposed to the type of outside criticism which regards activities of this kind as the equivalent of doing nothing. Though the Home Secretary had clearly restated their position to Parliament in September, a decided ground-swell of mistrust about their role and usefulness was maintained in various quarters;[3] and this factor doubtless contributed to Lord Harlech's statement in June 1940 that the Commissioners' activities up to that date had in the main been 'diplomatic rather than executive'. Varying in accordance with the character of the Region concerned, these included establishing close relations with adjoining Regions, concerting plans with the local Army commanders and effecting liaison with the police and fire authorities. Certain Commissioners took early steps to hold meetings with Members of Parliament and with the local Press.[4] One later recorded that almost from the onset of war Commissioners became 'the receptacle for enquiries and complaints upon a very large number of questions not strictly appertaining to the Ministry of Home Security'.

The Commissioners' tasks of co-ordination were, of course, assisted by the knowledge among officials, central and local, that if communications between any particular Region and the Government were seriously interrupted the Commissioner could (at his own

---

[1] p. 305.

[2] The staff of one Region was described by one of its Intelligence Officers to the author as a *macédoine*.

[3] H. of C. Deb., Vol. 351, Col. 644–5, 13th September 1939.

[4] The Ministry of Information was experiencing large teething troubles and its original regional organisation had been curtailed in October 1939.

discretion) assume considerable powers. This commission, however, remained dormant until such time (if any) when this hypothesis became fact. The unexpected restraint shown by the enemy meant that the Commissioners, in general, were still guided by the principle of 'a maximum of contact and a minimum of interference'.[1] And it would be an error to emphasise the prestige which their position conferred on them while neglecting the particularism (already referred to in another context) of central departments and local authorities.[2] In official quarters the Commissioners were exposed, especially in the first phase of the war, to the opposite criticism to the one just mentioned, or to that of doing too much.[3]

They made progress, nevertheless, in improving co-ordination between Departmental Representatives in their Regions, most of whom, in the experience of one Commissioner, 'had previously worked in watertight compartments'. The idea, it is necessary to emphasise, of interdepartmental co-operation on this scale within regions was novel; and while the practical boundaries of civil defence were still indefinite, the regional representation of many departments actually or potentially concerned with the matter was still rudimentary.[4] Questions which particularly involved this type of co-ordinating activity on the part of Commissioners during the twilight war included morale, the Ministry of Health's arrangements for evacuation and future casualties, the Office of Work's requisitioning of buildings for evacuated Government staffs, and the Board of Education's arrangements for the protection and (later) the re-opening of schools.

Co-ordination of the local authorities' 'operations' had from the start been envisaged as one of the Regional Commissioners' main functions. Centring in a physical sense on the War Rooms, this included arrangements for mutual aid between authorities in each Region, progress with which after the outbreak of war will be described in a later chapter.[5] The strange character of the twilight war had also endowed the Commissioners with the role, largely unforeseen, of agents of the Ministry of Home Security during a further respite. Their activities, by delegation from the Ministry, in what one of them called 'helping the authorities to fulfil their statutory obligations' will be referred to below. It is only possible here to point out the usefulness and variety of the Commissioners' task of

---

[1] p. 185.
[2] p. 302.
[3] e.g. the Ministry of Labour's protests against some Commissioners issuing what it regarded as instructions to its officers.
[4] As time advanced the Regional War Rooms became an important means of effecting and strengthening interdepartmental liaison.
[5] Chapter XIV below.

administration and operations of the local structure. At the time of their appointment in the spring of 1939 nearly one-half of them were County or Town Clerks, over one-quarter were Chief Constables and most of the remainder Aldermen or Councillors; and these general proportions prevailed throughout the war.[1] The variations of local organisation adopted in practice can only be hinted at here. Many County or Town Clerks assumed a commanding role from the start; and it is relevant to add that numbers of these had been members of the Fighting Forces in the previous World War. Others in this category delegated most of their civil defence responsibilities to Deputy Controllers. Chief Constables who were Controllers often injected a valuable drive and discipline into the local organisation; but, it must be added, sometimes introduced a rigidity which was far from finding universal favour.

It will, it is hoped, already be apparent to the reader that at all levels of the civil defence structure the factor of personality was of particular importance. And on the local level the personality of the Controller or his Deputy was usually the decisive factor. His task was the difficult one of co-ordinating first his own, or the A.R.P., services and secondly these with the police, fire and other civil defence authorities. The novelty of this is illustrated by the fact that, in spite of the instructions issued before the war, the Ministry concluded in March 1940 that there was still much uncertainty about the scope of Controllers' duties and a widespread misconception that Controllers had no operational responsibilities.[2]

Attention must be drawn to the variety of ways in which the local police might be woven into the structure. In those authorities, for example, where Controllers were not Chief Constables, police officers often acted as Deputy Controllers. And the Wardens' Service was in general charge of Chief Constables in about 200 of the 250 scheme-making areas. This summary of what, in effect, was the 'staff' of civil defence must end with a reference to the Heads of Services, i.e., the Medical Officer of Health, Borough Surveyor or Engineer and others. Although normal development of local services had largely ceased on the outbreak of war, these officials, it should be recalled, had many preoccupations outside civil defence. Secondly, the persons employed by local authorities in England and Wales in 1939 have been estimated at some 125,000, of whom only about 9,000 had 'higher qualifications of a professional, technical or academic character'.[3] A considerable exodus of younger local government officials took place as the war proceeded, thereby increasing the burden carried by those in responsible positions.

[1] pp. 217–218.
[2] pp. 176–177, 218, 274.
[3] J. H. Warren, *The English Local Government System* (1946), p. 19.

CHAPTER VIII

RESPITE (Continued)

The Warning System Tested, and the Black-Out Modified

HIS MAJESTY'S ships in their home bases had the honour, fittingly enough, of being the first target for air attack on the British Isles since 1918. On 16th October about twelve German aircraft dropped bombs on warships lying in the Firth of Forth, killing or wounding twenty-five officers and sailors and damaging several ships. Two of the attackers were brought down by British fighters. The next morning a smaller attack was made on H.M. ships at Scapa Flow, and two high explosive bombs which dropped harmlessly on the Orkney Island of Hoy were the first bombs of the Second World War to fall on British soil.

The Firth of Forth attack provided the civil defence authorities with an incident of importance. Although no bombs fell on land, a good many splinters from anti-aircraft guns descended on Edinburgh and Dunfermline. And while the naval authorities in the area exercised the discretion they possessed to sound their own sirens, no public civilian warning was sounded and confusion and indignation resulted. Similar trouble, it may here be said, was later to arise in other naval co-ordinated areas such as Portsmouth; and to cause prolonged discussion between the Admiralty and the Ministry of Home Security before various local compromises were arranged.

More important was the evidence this attack afforded of the intense dislike of the public of being bombed—or nearly bombed—without a warning. In fact, some defect had developed in the local radar station; and the A.O.C.-in-C., Fighter Command, not being satisfied that an attack would be made on the mainland, had decided against issuing a 'red' warning. But the more general explanation which the Prime Minister had necessarily, for security reasons, to give Parliament was described by *The Scotsman* in a scathing article as 'particularly inept'.[1] Experience during the preceding six weeks had also shown that the public disliked (though less intensely) the opposite situation of being warned without being bombed; and that the system needed time and practice for its perfection. Peace-time exercises had been mainly confined to the passage of messages over the telephone, and had offered little practice to those responsible for

---

[1] H. of C. Deb., Vol. 352, Cols. 691–3 and 904, 17th and 18th October 1939.

operating the public signals. In war, nervous tension had caused police, firemen and factory employees to sound the sirens. Mechanical defects (mainly short circuits) both at this stage and throughout the war caused a number of false warnings. And the transmission of bogus alarms over the telephone by unbalanced or malicious individuals was responsible for others.

The Government, after reaffirming their intention to err on the side of safety in issuing public warnings, had asked for tolerance while the system continued to be tested and improved. Following the Firth of Forth attack the Home Secretary reported to the War Cabinet that some difficulty had so far been found in distinguishing between friendly and hostile aircraft, although new equipment would soon, it was hoped, reduce this. The A.O.C.-in-C., Fighter Command had also to distinguish between German reconnaissance flights and bombing attacks; and between the likelihood of attack on some general objective, such as an industrial area, and on some limited target within that area. Unless he was automatically to release the warning system, with its consequent dislocation of production and disturbance to morale, every time a raider approached the coast, he must 'make the best judgment possible of the probable intentions of hostile aircraft'. Though it was inevitable that he would 'on occasion make what will be described as a mistake and either withhold a warning or give warning of an attack which does not develop', he alone was in a position to make the study of enemy tactics on which the sensible operation of the warning system depended. The Minister and his colleagues also concluded that the A.O.C.-in-C.'s monopoly as the originator of warnings needed guarding more strictly. A tendency on the part of police and A.R.P. officers—who might be able to see an attack developing but were incapable of judging accurately when the raiders had passed—to sound the sirens on their own initiative had already caused complications. It was essential that once the A.O.C.-in-C. had made his personal decision 'the rest of the process should be as automatic as possible and interfered with at no stage by any personal judgments'. These principles were announced soon afterwards by the Secretary for Air, Sir Kingsley Wood, to Parliament.[1] They have been quoted here at length because they governed the warning system throughout the war.

As the weeks advanced the calls on the active defences grew steadily, and the warning system in its primary or military aspect came into full action. German aircraft were engaged almost every day and night in attacking shipping, laying mines[2] or penetrating

---

[1] H. of C. Deb., Vol. 352, Cols. 1404–7, 25th October 1939.

[2] Minelaying by enemy aircraft began, in fact, on 20th November 1939. Mines had been laid in our coastal waters since the outbreak of war by enemy submarines and surface craft.

Britain for reconnaissance or to test our defences. Though they were paying main attention to Scotland and the north-east coast, there was growing activity over East Anglia, the Thames Estuary and elsewhere in the south-east.The first specimen of a magnetic mine was captured by a naval party near Shoeburyness on 23rd November.[1] Twice in November and again in January the Germans dropped bombs ineffectively on the Shetlands. But on 16th March 1940 they attacked the Orkneys' base on a much larger scale, dropping about 120 high explosive and several hundred incendiary bombs. These did no damage to naval establishments. But, besides injuring seven civilians and damaging houses and roads, they caused the first fatal civilian air raid casualty of the war, at the Bridge of Waith.

Experience was thus accumulating of the manifold problems presented by civil warnings. During November some part of Britain was under the preliminary or 'yellow' warning almost daily; and a single enemy aircraft caused a 'yellow' on one night in nine Regions. Thus the Regional War Rooms and many local report centres, police and members of the A.R.P. Services were gaining experience of passing genuine messages and bringing their local arrangements to a further state of readiness for action. Though genuine action or 'red' warnings were infrequent, the public sirens continued to be sounded in error fairly often in some part or other of the country; and caused, for example, serious interruption of work in a northern factory, more outspoken complaints from Scotland and wrath in Poplar over unnecessary early-morning sheltering.[2] The Home Office, it will be recalled, had decided to restrict public warnings to towns on the ground that there was no action which those in rural areas 'can reasonably be expected to take, in advance of bombs being dropped, merely on an intimation that hostile raiders are somewhere in the vicinity'.[3] Experience had quickly shown that this view did not commend itself to many who lived in the country. Villages had raised public subscriptions to provide themselves with sirens, and rural police had shown energy in relaying the warning by bicycle and other means. Uneasiness in East Anglia and elsewhere was not allayed by the Ministry's reaffirmation of its view on this matter at the close of the year.

The technical apparatus was at the same time being improved. The mechanical defects to which the sirens had shown themselves liable made it necessary to introduce regular testing. But the Ministry, when authorising authorities to take this step, asked that tests should

---

[1] This threat was rapidly met by a method, known as 'degaussing', of passive defence for shipping.

[2] *The Scotsman*, 31st October 1939; H. of C. Deb., Vol. 353, Cols. 1381–2, 23rd November 1939.

[3] A.R.P. Dept. Circular 10, 26th January 1939.

be given the fullest publicity and should not be more frequent than once in four weeks.[1] Of greater importance was the discovery in the earliest days of war that the sirens interfered with the sound locators which were, at this time, the chief means by which A.A. search-lights and guns detected the enemy. In London it was possible to reduce this trouble fairly quickly by eliminating the 'pick-up' sirens, or those sounded by operators in factories and elsewhere when they heard the wail of neighbouring instruments. But else-where such sirens, with the considerable time-spread they often involved, formed the majority, much outnumbering those under direct control of the police. Serious difficulty was also experienced by many authorities as the war proceeded in finding sufficient volunteers to man the sirens throughout the twenty-four hours.

The Ministry therefore re-examined the practicability of 'remote-control', or systems of directly controlling a large group of public signals from some central point. In February 1940 they introduced grant-aid and gave the authorities more detailed descriptions of these systems.[2] The increase of enemy activity in the spring (to carry the story forward) gave this problem much extra urgency. In June the Ministry instructed its Regions that (i) all 'pick-up' sirens should be eliminated as soon as possible, (ii) all sirens must start promptly and last for two minutes only and (iii) remote control schemes should be worked out over as wide areas as possible without reference to local authority boundaries.

The black-out had some close affinities with the warning system. It was, as the Home Secretary reminded Parliament in November, 'fundamentally strategic' or designed in the first place to serve the active defences.[3] It had large-scale technical and other implications of which the public was little aware; and it constituted, for these reasons, a special concern of the central authorities. In their practical application, however, these two methods of defence had many obvious differences of which the principal was that warnings were occasional or intermittent and the black-out was continuous or permanent.

It is probably not too much to say that the black-out, imposed on the whole country on 1st September, transformed conditions of life more thoroughly than any other single feature of the war. The historian, incapable of describing it, may be allowed recourse to the statement that it had to be seen (or experienced) to be believed. It made all movement by pedestrians or vehicles on the roads after dark a matter at least of difficulty and frequently of danger; subjected

---

[1] A.R.P. Dept. Circular 310, 21st November 1939. This prefix was given to the Ministry of Home Security's circulars until the end of 1939.

[2] H.S.C. 23/40, 8th February 1940; also A.R.P. Dept. Circular 179, 23rd August 1939.

[3] H. of C. Deb., Vol. 352, Col. 2269, 2nd November 1939.

all work in factories, offices and shops to new physical and mental strains; seriously hampered all railway and dock operations; conferred on each citizen an additional responsibility for the public safety, and gave him in his own home a new and often unwelcome sense of isolation. It clearly (as had long been foreseen) set the authorities difficult problems in balancing strategical advantages with disadvantages.

What could not have been foreseen were many of the actual difficulties and hardships it would introduce, or the amount of public complaint which, under static conditions of war, it would occasion. A contemporary observer stated in November that the topic of the black-out had already provided enough material for a 500-page volume.[1] Its immediate consequences had included, as specific examples of the conditions just mentioned, serious delay in postal deliveries in London and elsewhere, special difficulties for baking and other trades carried on by night, stagnation in the evening trade of urban shops, excessive strain on the drivers of buses and other public vehicles and innumerable problems of ventilation. The impact of these restrictions on the ordinary citizen was not made easier by excessive zeal on the part of police or wardens in some places over their enforcement.

When the war was little more than a week old Ministers were urgently considering ways in which these difficulties and hardships might be reduced. At the end of September the War Cabinet, concerned over the handicap which the lighting restrictions were placing on industry, appointed a Ministerial Committee, which included the Home Secretary and Secretaries for War and Air, to review them. The Air Staff informed this body that any substantial change in existing arrangements would (until experience had been acquired to prove otherwise) seriously hamper the Royal Air Force in its task of defence. In their first report the committee agreed that the existing situation should in general be maintained; and this view was based in large part on their belief that public opinion had become so impressed with the necessity of the black-out as a method of defence that it would be seriously puzzled if substantial relaxations were made before even one night of bombing had occurred. The committee later considered the arguments of the First Lord of the Admiralty, Mr Churchill, in favour of substantial relaxations.[2] But they preferred a policy of cautious modification.

The chief action taken by the Ministers was the appointment of an interdepartmental Lighting Committee, including representatives of the Ministries of Home Security, Air, Transport, Supply, Shipping and the T.U.C., to examine the problems of the many industrial

---

[1] S. King-Hall, *op. cit.*
[2] See W. S. Churchill, *op. cit.*, Vol. I, Appendix L.

establishments (and notably docks) which had been failing to use the full standards of lighting allowed them. Chief Constables had been instructed in the first week of war to be more liberal in granting exemptions to industry, particularly steel works, important new factories and military establishments.[1] But difficult problems of practical adaptation of theoretical standards remained to be solved; for example, many factories were showing isolated points of light far above the maxima permitted, while their total distribution of light was insufficient for their needs. Few industrial concerns, apart from the railway companies, had staffs trained to deal with technical lighting matters. The committee engaged experts who proceeded late in the year to visit ports and shipyards, giving advice, approving adjustments and submitting detailed proposals to the centre. While many unforeseen difficulties had arisen, the problem of glare, which had caused such concern before the war, had proved more tractable than had been expected.[2] By the end of the year over half the coke ovens in the country had been screened, and good progress had been made in dealing with slag heaps and iron and steel works. Some time before attacks began in earnest the Home Secretary reported that the danger from glare had been largely eliminated.[3]

Certain steps, in the meantime, had been taken by the Government to make the situation more tolerable for the general public. Summer time, due to end early in October, had been extended to mid-November. The hours of shop-closing in London and elsewhere had been put forward; though this gave rise for some time to come to numerous complaints of hardship to the 'small man'.[4] In mid-October two bolder concessions, as they seemed at this time, were made. Members of the public were allowed to use hand-torches in the streets, provided these were dimmed in the manner officially prescribed. And the severe limitations on car-lighting were slightly eased by permission to civilian drivers to use the simple type of headlamp mask employed by the Fighting Services until enough supplies of the more elaborate Home Office 'A.R.P. mask' had come on to the market.[5] Public vehicles were permitted to use a special headlamp mask on the near side which illuminated passengers waiting on the pavement.

Early in November the Government decided, in response to requests from employers and organised labour, that the period of the black-out should be reduced by one hour—or should henceforth

---

[1] A.R.P. Dept. Circulars 235 and 262, 7th September and 3rd October 1939.

[2] p. 229.

[3] H. of C. Deb., Vol. 358, Cols. 1354 and 1356-7, 14th March 1940.

[4] Order in Council adding Regulation 60A to the Defence (General) Regulations, 1939, S. R. & O. No. 1464, 19th October 1939.

[5] A.R.P. Dept. Circular 257, 27th September 1939 gave a detailed description of the tandards permitted to road vehicles.

begin half-an-hour after sunset and end half-an-hour before sunrise.[1] Shortly before Christmas some further relief was introduced. Churches, markets and stalls in the streets could be partially illuminated during black-out hours; a small measure of light was allowed, as an experiment, in shop-windows by the use of special fittings; restaurants and places of amusement could use illuminated signs in their windows and doorways.[2] All these had, however, to be extinguished immediately an air raid warning sounded. Many complaints were still voiced about prosecutions of householders in various parts of the country for minor black-out offences.[3] But instructions to the police to use reasonable discretion, and the greater efficiency of householders in blacking-out their homes, had begun to reduce this source of irritation.

The concern which had been rising throughout the winter over the high rate of accidents on the roads was forcibly expressed in Parliament early in the new year.[4] During the first four months of war 2,657 pedestrians had died as the result of road accidents, or more than double the number for the corresponding months of 1938. In December deaths from this cause had risen to no less than 1,200, some 900 of which had been due to accidents in black-out hours; and a further 30,000 persons had been injured. The Government, after some disinclination (on practical grounds) to do so, yielded to a public demand for the imposition of a 20 m.p.h. speed-limit in all built-up areas during black-out hours.[5] During the debate when this step was announced the Home Secretary stated firmly that the military aim of the black-out must remain 'the dominant consideration'. He stated the Government's conviction that it was depriving the enemy of 'the means of launching an attack unexpectedly on this country the consequences of which would be little short of disastrous'. The evidence, he added, in the Government's possession suggested that Germany had adopted a black-out which was even more stringent than our own.[6]

The Government had announced before Christmas that their experiments with a form of street lighting of such low intensity (.00025 feet candles on the ground) that it could remain alight while air raids were in progress had been successful. It would be quite impracticable, they repeated, to restore anything like peace-time street lighting, or to arrange to extinguish these lights when the

---

[1] A.R.P. Dept. Circular 294, 3rd November 1939.

[2] A.R.P. Dept. Circulars 318, 319 and 343, December 1939.

[3] e.g., 40 prosecutions were made in Oxford City in one week of October.

[4] H. of C. Deb., Vol. 356, Cols. 473–548, 23rd January 1940.

[5] There was already a peace-time 30 m.p.h. limit throughout the 24 hours in these areas.

[6] H. of C. Deb., Vol. 356, Cols. 539–548, 23rd January 1940.

warning sounded. But this new 'diffused lighting' (later to be also known as 'glimmer' or 'pin-prick' lighting), though much below the standards permitted in the First World War, would increase the safety of pedestrians and help movement in the streets without reducing the effectiveness of such lighting as was permitted to vehicle-drivers.[1]

This innovation, it soon became apparent, would require time to produce much alleviation. The manufacture of special lamps and fittings had to be undertaken. Many local authorities took the view that the cost of installing the system outweighed its advantages; and others gave new proof of public faith in the black-out by deciding, in spite of the Ministry's assurances to the contrary, that the system would increase danger to their towns. But in the new year the A.R.P. headlamp mask was available at the price of a few shillings to the public, and was made compulsory on all civilian vehicles.[2] A new Lighting (Restrictions) Order of January gave authority for the various modifications already mentioned and remained, without much amendment of significance, the code governing the complex requirements of this matter for the next five and a half years.[3]

The Government also took the unprecedented step of beginning Summer Time for the new year at the end of February. The later employment of this device, which originated in the First World War, may conveniently be included here. Summer Time was retained in 1940 up to the last day of the year. It was reintroduced on the 1st or 2nd January and retained until 31st December in each subsequent year of the war.[4] Double Summer Time was introduced in May 1941, ending in August; and again in April of each of the next four years, ending between July and September.

The overriding need, as it appeared to the Government, for dispersal had caused the closing on the first day of war throughout Britain of all theatres, cinemas and other places of amusement to which the public paid for admittance.[5] But relaxation followed fairly quickly by means of a series of Public Entertainments (Restriction) Orders, which gave Chief Constables considerable discretion in this matter.[6] By 14th September all such places were allowed to open except between the hours of 10 p.m. and 8 a.m. and in Central

---

[1] H. of C. Deb., Vol. 355, Cols. 1244–5, 14th December 1939; A.R.P. Dept. Circular 344, 23rd December 1939.

[2] This only emitted light through a narrow horizontal slit and included a hood to confine the beam to the ground in front of the vehicle.

[3] S. R. & O. No. 74, 19th January 1940. This contained 53 sections and occupied 26 pages.

[4] In 1945 it ended on 7th October.

[5] Prohibition of Public Entertainments (Defence) Order, 1939, S. R. & O. No. 1241, 3rd September 1939.

[6] Seven such Orders were made before the end of the year.

London 6 p.m. and 8 a.m. As a consequence of strong representations by various interests a proportion of theatres and cinemas in the heart of London were next allowed to remain open until 11 or 11.15; and on 1st December this permission (though on a staggered basis) was made general. The normal closing hour elsewhere had, in the meantime, been altered to 11. Dancing in public halls, after this hour, had been generally introduced (subject to the discretion of Chief Officers of Police) before Christmas. The owners of theatres and so on had been asked to take various A.R.P. measures on behalf of their patrons and staffs. And after much discussion it was decided that when a warning was received managers should personally announce the fact, permitting those who wished to leave to do so, but 'the show would go on'.

Football matches, 'the dogs' and horse racing in a total war, like theatre-going, set the authorities some novel problems. The Government reached agreement with the Football and Greyhound Racing Associations over arrangements which included severe limitation in evacuation areas of the number and times of matches and meetings and of the spectators permitted to attend.[1] The horse-racing programme, through voluntary action by the Stewards of the Jockey Club, was severely curtailed. As the winter began to pass with attack on the population still deferred, demands grew for the raising of the level (the lowest in their history) to which these sports had fallen. Considerations of safety began to assume less prominence, and those of morale and of hardship to different commercial interests to be strongly emphasised.

Early in the new year a limited reopening of museums and galleries was permitted, although their most valuable contents had been sent away to places of safety. Churches had, of course, exceptional difficulty in obscuring their lights; and mainly for this reason most of them throughout the country had ceased to hold their customary evening services and substituted services in the early afternoon.

Evacuation of the Government

Evacuation and sheltering, it should be re-emphasised, were the two most drastic methods of defence, in terms alike of their potentialities for social and industrial dislocation, relationships with morale, administrative complexity and cost to the State. Evacuation, whether as a plan or an historical event, affected four main groups of citizens: (1) the nearly 4,000,000 children, mothers and invalids living in London and other cities whom the Government had arranged to remove, if they wished, at its expense to safer areas;

---

[1] *The Times*, 22nd September 1939.

(2) other individuals who chose to leave under their own arrangements; (3) business firms, schools and other private institutions, and (4) the Government, or Ministers, M.P.s and all employed as civil servants.

The dramatic exodus between 1st and 3rd September of nearly 1,500,000 official evacuees, their subsequent experiences in the reception areas and speedy return in large numbers to their homes have been recorded in detail in another volume of this series.[1] The novelty of this situation, in one aspect, is illustrated by the fact that some time elapsed before the Government was aware that it had not moved nearly 4,000,000 persons but less than half this number. The scale of private evacuation was unknown to the Government or to anyone else. But Mr Titmuss concludes that between June and early September 1939 this involved about 2,000,000 persons in England and Wales. He further concludes that these various large migrations 'directly affected the daily lives of from one-quarter to one-third of the people'.[2] The official exodus, it is important to note, was carried out in an orderly manner and without a single casualty or accident. And the unofficial one occurred in a steady flow spread over several weeks, and without panic.

Though the public, for obvious reasons, was little aware of the fact, the evacuation of the Government itself presented intricate administrative and political issues. By the outbreak of war the Office of Works had detailed plans in readiness to move the entire headquarters machine of Government, then consisting of some 60,000 persons, from London at short notice over a period of three or four days.[3] This machine was for this purpose carved up into two unequal parts. The seat of Government—the Cabinet, Parliament and the most essential officials to the number of some 16,000—would, if need arose, be evacuated in what was officially called the 'black move'. Less essential staffs of Departments, or some 44,000 officials, would be evacuated under a 'yellow move'. A few days after the country's entry into war the Government gave instructions for the accommodation for both these moves to be requisitioned, and for the 'yellow move' to be put into immediate operation. The Office of Works took over some 220 hotels, 30 public and other schools and various other buildings in the provinces; and branches of some Departments, for example the Admiralty and the Air Ministry, began to move out of London.

Experience showed after barely a fortnight the many practical difficulties to which these moves, projected or actual, gave rise. The

---

[1] R. M. Titmuss, *op cit.*, Chapters VII–X.

[2] Ibid., p. 137.

[3] p. 200. The Civil Service (non-industrial staff) was then approaching 400,000, about one half of this being G.P.O. staff.

transportation of only a few thousand civil servants, drawn from several Departments, had shown striking weaknesses of co-ordination. There had been serious muddles over billeting, and officials had been sometimes compelled to sleep in offices or share a double-bed. For other reasons, including separation from their families, they had already begun to voice protests. Departments in London had been, in various degrees, disorganised by the removal of their branches. And the owners of hotels, schools and other places which had been requisitioned but not yet occupied were beginning to lodge strong complaints.

A special inquiry into these problems suggested that there was much to be said for putting an immediate stop to the 'yellow move'. Administrative convenience, it was clear, prompted this course; and opposition by the staffs concerned had grown stronger. If, however, this action were taken, pressure on the part of owners of empty premises to take them back into use might become irresistible and many billets earmarked for official staffs might be lost. What perhaps weighed still more with the Civil Defence Committee was the picture presented to them of what might occur if the mass evacuation of the Government from London were attempted after heavy attack had begun. The exodus of thousands of officials, with even the most essential papers and records, would offer many practical difficulties; and its effect on public morale would probably be grave. This move, in fact, was one more necessary insurance. Though causing some current dislocation, it was providing valuable experience and might prevent possible future chaos. The War Cabinet decided in mid-October that it should be gradually continued, though subject to the decision of individual Ministers that their Departments would not lose seriously in efficiency.

Ministers then turned to earnest consideration of the practicability of the 'black move'. This, though in part still a plan, had already involved considerable official action and brought concrete political repercussions. Rising public complaints about hotels, buildings and billets standing empty over a considerable area of the Western Midlands could not, owing to the need for strict secrecy, be effectively answered. Certain Ministers and officials were losing faith in the policy of evacuation. Some Departments were pressing for larger representation in the seat of Government, and new ones with obvious claims in this matter were being formed. The Civil Defence Committee sought to discover whether the problem could be simplified by confining the move to one Midlands or Northern town. But strong insistence by the Air Staff on dispersal, and difficulties of accommodation, billeting and communications ruled out this alternative.[1]

---

[1] The G.P.O. had been occupied for two years in installing communications in the 'black area' which, nevertheless, were very restricted compared with those normally available in London.

They made detailed adjustments in the plan; and modified security to the extent of permitting notices to be served on householders in the areas concerned, warning them that they might be required to accommodate Government staffs at twenty-four hours' notice. They reported to the War Cabinet that this move, though bound to involve 'very serious difficulties and loss of efficiency' was nevertheless a practicable operation. But they strongly urged that orders for its execution should not be issued until heavy persistent air attack had rendered the conduct of the nation's business in London quite impossible.

The 'yellow move', in the meantime, was continuing to prove a source of difficulties and embarrassment. The Minister of Labour and National Service, Mr Ernest Brown, visited some 1,300 members of his Department evacuated to Southport to investigate complaints about muddles over billeting, inadequate canteens and lack of provision for recreation and medical care. Weeks, it was alleged, had been spent in controversy with other Departments about whether official accommodation might be used for recreations. 'No one', Mr Brown reported, 'who has seen evacuation at first hand can have any doubt about the need for the appointment of sufficient welfare officers', and added 'one of the most burning questions is the matter of visits home'. The Minister of Health (with his wider responsibilities in this matter) concluded that Government staffs in general deeply disliked the policy of evacuation. Most of those already evacuated were low-paid workers and many were women or young girls, who were unable to live anything like their normal lives. He feared that the efficiency of the Government machine would be prejudiced by further moves, and proposed that abandonment of the whole process, at least until attack on London had begun, should be considered.

This problem, important in itself, was related to the almost spectacular return of the officially-evacuated mothers and children to their homes in London and other cities. This strong, human, ebb-tide must be regarded as the main expression of the public scepticism about the danger to which attention has already been drawn.[1] By Christmas more than one-half of the 1,500,000 mothers and children concerned had returned home; in the London and Liverpool areas about two-thirds of the evacuated children had returned.[2] It had been apparent for some time past to the Government that this evacuation scheme had, as Mr Titmuss says, 'largely failed to achieve its object of removing for the duration of the war most of the mothers and children in the target areas'.[3] But being

---

[1] pp. 296-299.

[2] The first count taken in January 1940 disclosed that about 900,000 had returned.

[3] R. M. Titmuss, op. cit., p. 172.

convinced that this scheme should rest on a voluntary basis, they had been unable to hinder the steady drift back. The whole policy of evacuation had, in consequence, begun to seem inconsistent and confusing to the other sections of the community involved. For example, many business firms had been returning their headquarters' staffs to London, and the business community in general was agitating for firmer official guidance in this matter.[1]

This wholesale criticism, it has already been noted, led the responsible Ministers to remind the War Cabinet that evacuation was an integral part of civil defence policy; and to suggest a clear statement by the Prime Minister to the nation that the danger remained as grave as ever.[2] Mr Chamberlain's Mansion House speech of early January succeeded in restoring a certain equilibrium. The ebb-tide of mothers and children continued, but at a slower rate.[3] The Government announced in February that they proposed to maintain a voluntary scheme of this nature, but that this would in future be confined to a limited number of schoolchildren and would not be brought into operation until serious attacks had developed.[4] Business firms were left, as before, to decide for themselves between the claims of safety and efficiency; but many, though impatient over the difficulties of carrying on 'somewhere in the country', showed less inclination to return to the cities.

The Government staffs already sent to the provinces had received public assurance that the hardships they were undergoing were still the outcome of strategic need. Ministers were satisfied in February that their living and working conditions had genuinely improved. Welfare officers had been appointed, medical care at reasonable cost made generally available, more canteens provided and visits home at reduced fares arranged. And Ministers asked the Treasury to continue pressing Departments to speed up the evacuation of their less-essential staffs. Yet it was characteristic of this phase of the war that inconveniences which, seen from a later perspective, appear trivial caused much dissatisfaction. Soon afterwards the Staff side of the National Whitley Council complained vigorously about the conditions of evacuated staffs—still only numbering 20-25,000— and maintained that these had no confidence in the general scheme. A few weeks later, when a new phase of the war was starting to transform the issue, the first substantial financial concessions to these staffs, which included help with the movement of their families to reception areas, were introduced.

---

[1] *Annual Register, 1939,* p. 127.

[2] p. 298.

[3] The unaccompanied schoolchildren in the reception areas fell from 420,000 at the beginning of January to 347,000 on 31st March and about 254,000 in May.

[4] Ministry of Health Circular, 15th February 1940.

Anti-Gas Defence, and Shelters

Mention has already been made of the Government's statement in April 1939 that the degree of protection by then attained against this danger had 'rendered the risk of gas attack less likely'.[1] It can be asserted with confidence that in the following September Britain's defences in this sphere much surpassed those of any other nation, including Germany. The data available to experts had suggested that a high degree of protection could only be reached by equipping every civilian with a gas-mask. In Germany the gas training of the civil defence forces, arrangements for treating gas casualties and the gas-proofing of shelters and other places had proceeded far. But on the outbreak of war only about 12,000,000 respirators had been issued to civilians, and progress in adding to this total proved slow. Priority for the *Wehrmacht*, difficulties over rubber supplies, and official reliance on gas-proof shelters combined to deprive German civilians, including many in the principal cities, of the personal protection of a mask throughout the five and more years of war.

Gas, in the general sense of the term understood in this volume, was clearly an imponderable factor. The reader is aware that it was never, happily, used against civilians. The historian may therefore here anticipate events by putting two questions, the first of which lies somewhat outside his proper province. How far did Britain's defence on the outbreak of war and later deter Germany from using this weapon against her? It will be assumed throughout this volume that Hitler and Goering's restraint in using any weapon cannot be attributed to motives of humanity, but solely to fear of reprisals or calculation that the aircraft and crews available could be used to better advantage in some other way. On this assumption, and taking into account Allied investigations after the war, it would seem that the deterrent effect was considerable to the point, perhaps, of being decisive.

What, secondly, was the impact of Britain's defence of this kind on British morale? The individual's possession of a mask and his knowledge of widespread anti-gas preparations could, of course, arouse in him the opposite emotions of despondency or hope. Yet there appears to be good evidence for concluding that the Government's early investment in this sphere contributed powerfully to sustaining morale both during the Munich crisis and again on the outbreak of war a year later.[2] As the twilight war proceeded the authorities were concerned first to correct the too close identification by the public of aerial attack with gas, and then to maintain this type of defence at an adequate level.

---

[1] p. 209.
[2] pp. 161-165.

Every British adult civilian, for the first time in history, entered war with an article of personal defensive equipment. The distribution of gas-masks begun at Munich to all citizens over about five years old had been virtually completed by mid-September 1939; and embraced the inmates, for example, of casual wards, prisons and Borstal institutions. The total distribution of this civilian mask, in three sizes, had reached about 44,000,000; and the Ministry and local authorities were adding to and storing reserve supplies.

On the outbreak of war issue of the baby's anti-gas helmet was only beginning; and that of the respirator, known as the 'Mickey Mouse', for infants of two to about four-and-a-half years had not started.[1] But in the following months the issue of both these articles made rapid progress. By late October a large proportion of helmets had been issued, and a special distribution was under way to mothers who had brought their evacuated children back to the cities. The Ministry advised local authorities to ask women wardens to arrange, whenever possible, the exchange of helmets for children's masks.[2] This, the mothers should be told, would make their task much easier by relieving them of the need to supply their babies encased in helmets with air by pumping this through bellows. By the end of January 1940, the essential issue of helmets, to a total of some 1,400,000, had been completed; and enough children's masks, or about 2,000,000, had been distributed to cities and towns.

Possession of masks (which remained the property of the Government) endowed citizens with some positive duties. The Government, though they had taken no steps to introduce compulsion in this matter, had made it plain that they expected every citizen to carry his mask wherever he went. With Cabinet Ministers and others in high places setting an example, and most employers adopting a firm attitude over this matter to their staffs, the buff cardboard container became almost overnight the accepted appendage of the British citizen in war.

Inevitably, individual habits, including the habit of carelessness with public property, soon began to assert themselves. Women quickly replaced the drab official container with a large assortment of more decorative receptacles. Members of both sexes left their gas-masks at home and carried other articles in their haversacks or containers. Complaints arose that police and wardens in safe areas were unduly pestering small children and others caught separated from their masks. The Home Secretary announced in October that the Government no longer regarded the carrying of masks in reception areas as essential, but still strongly advised everyone

---

[1] pp. 232-233.
[2] A.R.P. Dept. Circulars 271 and 280, 10th October and 9th December 1939.

elsewhere to continue this practice.[1] Instructions, in the meantime, were multiplying about the citizens' duties over care and maintenance. Early in 1940 the Ministry proposed an immediate inspection by wardens of all civilian masks, and asked that such inspection should develop into a monthly routine. They introduced a charge to the citizen for the replacement or repair of a mask lost or damaged through his negligence.[2] In February they consolidated the guidance to local authorities and the public about care and repair in a new memorandum; and asked every scheme-making authority to establish a local depot, in charge of a qualified instructor, to repair masks and oilskin clothing.[3]

Precautions against gas and other forms of attack were not restricted to *homo sapiens*. Before the war the Home Office had published full advice about A.R.P. for animals.[4] This recommended, among other things, that all animals in the danger zones should be evacuated; that stables and similar places should be gas-proofed, indoor pets be given gas-proof boxes, and the legs of contaminated animals treated with anti-gas ointment. The People's Dispensary for Sick Animals had formed an 'Animal A.R.P. Service', and evolved a gas-proof kennel fitted with bellows to be operated by its dumb occupant. Clearly, however, there were practical limits to solicitude of this kind. The London Zoo, for example, had been temporarily closed on the outbreak of war; and the newspapers reported its keepers to be 'visibly affected' by the destruction of poisonous snakes.[5]

The distribution of other supplies besides civilian masks and anti-gas training still occupied much of the authorities' attention. Supplies of Service and Civilian Duty masks, though improving, were still far from adequate. The special modification of the latter type for the use of switchboard operators, evolved in 1938 and now called the 'telephone respirator', was being issued.[6] Equipment such as metal triangles, rattles and the yellow detector paint to detect blister gases had still to be distributed in some areas. Further supplies of bleach powder and anti-gas ointment had to be issued.[7] In most areas much had still to be done to adapt and equip rooms as public cleansing stations. Wardens were continuing to instruct themselves and the public about gas matters. The Rescue and Decontamination

---

[1] H. of C. Deb., Vol. 352, Cols. 501–2, 12th October 1939.

[2] H.S.C.s 40, 47/40, 6th, 14th March. The citizen was already liable under the Civil Defence Act to a fine of £5 for failing to use reasonable care in preserving his mask.

[3] Memorandum No. 13; H.S.C. 24/40, 22nd February.

[4] Memorandum No. 12, August 1939.

[5] *The Times*, 9th September 1939.

[6] p. 141; A.R.P. Dept. Circular 320, 6th December 1939.

[7] H.S.C.s 1 and 7, 2nd and 10th January 1940; p. 235.

Services were practising in anti-gas clothing, and the casualty services preparing for large-scale gas casualties.

Further steps were taken in September to enlist persons in what was called the Gas Identification Service. The Government appointed a Senior Gas Adviser to each Region, and asked all scheme-making authorities to act immediately on the proposal, first made about two years earlier, that they should appoint Gas Identification Officers.[1] It was hoped by this means to form a small corps of 1,400 experts, drawn from universities and elsewhere and serving part-time without pay, continuously available to identify known or detect strange gases. These were to receive A.R.P. training, and be supplied with full protective clothing and various kinds of special equipment.[2]

Early in 1940 the Government received reports that the Germans had found a method of using arsine gas (arseniuretted hydrogen) in the aerial bombardment of civilians. Since only the Service masks offered full protection against this gas, the Government ordered the supply of 70,000,000 filters of an improved type for Civilian Duty, civilian and children's masks.[3] In May the first of these—known as 'contex' since they formed small extensions to existing containers —were distributed to local authorities, and wardens began the considerable task of fitting them to the millions of masks in the possession of the public.[4]

While the problem of anti-gas defence was becoming in large part one of maintenance, it was far otherwise with shelters. Certain Regional Officers had reported something like panic by authorities over this problem in the last days of August 1939. The spur of war greatly increased activity in this sphere; and it was said in Parliament in November that London had been provided 'with thousands of shelters since the outbreak of war, shelters which there were all sorts of difficulties in providing in the weeks before'.[5] Yet the large diversified shelter programme was far from complete; and it soon began to seem, as another Regional Officer expressed it, that shelter construction might go on for ever.[6]

No activity in civil defence—since the Government had asked all engaged on any kind of essential work to 'stay put'—was now probably more important. And none better illustrated in practice the Government's leading principle that the burden of civil defence must be shared. The Home Secretary reaffirmed in September the

---

[1] A.R.P. Dept. Circular 252, 21st September 1939.

[2] Memorandum No. 11, October 1939; A.R.P. Dept. Circulars 273 and 316, 12th October and 13th November 1939.

[3] A contract had previously been placed for 50 millions at an estimated cost of £403,000.

[4] H.S.C.s 84, 94, 11th, 18th May 1940.

[5] H. of C. Deb., Vol. 352, Col. 2170, 2nd November 1939.

[6] pp. 289-291.

basic policy of providing moderate protection to as large a number as possible in what, at this time, amounted to a liberal interpretation of the threatened areas. Though the central authorities still played the leading role by establishing standard designs and prices, allocating materials and supplying a proportion of the shelters, the burden of practical effort now lay with the local authorities, employers of all kinds and the public.

Since the matter was essentially technical and relatively new its administrative problems loomed large. The Ministry still nominally examined and approved all London's shelter schemes, all those for the other Regions costing more than a limited sum, and a large number of special cases such as the project (which aroused much public interest) for using Southwark Tunnel as a shelter. In practice it was compelled to delegate substantial responsibility in this sphere to Senior Regional Officers, who possessed limited powers of financial approval, and Regional Technical and Works Advisers. The Regional Commissioners soon confirmed the impression that shelter activities had much increased, but expressed anxiety over administrative obstacles. Many local authorities had inadequate or insufficiently trained staffs for this work. The county boroughs had, naturally, made most progress, but numbers of these preferred their own designs and arrangements to those centrally prescribed. A steel-producing town on Tees-side, for example, insisted on cast-iron shelters and using sandbags instead of brickwork from the conviction that the war could not last for three years.[1]

Many difficulties were arising through the varied manner, alluded to earlier, in which counties delegated powers to districts. In Leeds Region, for example, one of the two counties delegated powers over domestic shelters to districts while retaining control over public shelter construction; the other first delegated powers over both and later recalled them. For this and other reasons much controversy over the division of financial responsibilities was accumulating for the future. Regional Officers, under considerable pressure at this time and sometimes inexperienced, were later to discover that many authorities had spent 'alarming sums' over shelters during this phase by misunderstanding official instructions or without, they alleged, seeking Regional sanction.

The provision of enough 'Andersons' to give at least 12,000,000 of the poorest inhabitants of the target areas shelter in their own homes was still the Government's first aim; and the 1,500,000 or so delivered by the outbreak of war fulfilled under two-thirds of this plan.[2] New applications from the public for 'Andersons' had, once war began,

---

[1] Middlesbrough which, it so happened, was the first industrial centre to be bombed (on 25th May 1940).

[2] These figures were theoretical in the sense that it was improbable in fact that the shelters would be filled to capacity.

flowed in to the authorities and been transmitted by these to Whitehall. The Home Secretary said that deliveries to local authorities had been fairly consistent at 50,000 a week for some weeks;[1] but he could not forecast any date for completion of these or agree to extend free distribution to persons with incomes of over £250 a year.[2] At the end of October the Government fulfilled their promise to put a limited number on sale to the public of London and about fifty other towns. These cost from £6 14s. od. to £10 18s. od. and could be bought on the instalment system.[3]

Not only had the time factor now become more than ever important. With the nation at war the priorities for labour and materials formerly accorded to shelters of all types no longer obtained, and prices as well as supplies of essential materials began to show large fluctuations. Demands for steel for other civil defence needs, such as the galvanised sheets used to black-out factories, compelled the Ministry to reduce the size of some 'Andersons'. The type so far produced (henceforth to be known as the 'standard') was 6 ft. high, 4 ft. 6 in. wide and 6 ft. 6 in. long and included six curved steel sheets. It was now regarded as adequate for six persons and could be enlarged by adding more sheets to hold ten persons. The Government also began to issue a number which were only 4 ft. 5 in. long, with a capacity of four persons.[4] This reduction had important consequences when, contrary to official expectations, raids took the form of all-night attack and the occupiers of 'Andersons' wanted to lie down in them to sleep.

By early 1940 the competition for steel for different purposes was becoming acute, and the rate of production of 'Andersons', already reduced, had to be halved. The Joint Production and Materials Committee began to exert strong pressure on the Ministry of Home Security to reduce the amount of steel being used for shelters of all types.[5] They proposed that the allocation of steel for 1940 to the Home Office and its offspring Ministry for all building and A.R.P. purposes should be reduced from their requested 670,000 tons to 100,000 tons; and delivered what the Home Secretary called a bolt from the blue by suggesting that the manufacture of all 'Andersons' should cease. The Ministerial Priority Committee, in reviewing the problem, granted an allocation of 334,000 tons; but they also considered that the manufacture of 'Andersons' should stop. In the middle of April the production of 'Andersons' of all sizes, and of basement fittings, was therefore suspended.

---

[1] H. of C. Deb., Vol. 352, Col. 2263, 2nd November 1939.

[2] H. of C. Deb., Vol. 351, Col. 1195, 26th September 1939.

[3] A.R.P. Dept. Circular 287, 28th October 1939.

[4] A.R.P. Dept. Circular 281, 21st October 1939.

[5] The chairman even questioned the need for more shelters of any kind.

A considerable share of this part of the programme was, nevertheless, fulfilled. In the course of the next few months the total number of 'Andersons' sent to the danger areas reached over 2,300,000, which could shelter a maximum of 12,500,000 persons. The majority were the 'standard' six-person shelters, about 500,000 were of the smaller four-person type, and 100,000 or so of the larger type.[1] The general public, it is of interest to record, had not shown much interest in the scheme for buying 'Andersons', since when production stopped they had bought somewhat under 1,000 of these.

The 'Anderson' could provide no solution for working-class homes which had no kind of yard or garden. Though in target areas as a whole such homes formed a small proportion, in some districts of London and other cities they were numerous. The satisfaction with shelter progress voiced in Parliament in the previous November was qualified by criticism that not enough had been done to protect the working-class flats of London.[2] Westminster, for example, being unable to use many 'Andersons', had provided domestic shelters in the vaults and cellars underneath the pavements of Pimlico and elsewhere.[3] Leeds, Huddersfield and other cities contained many rows of terraced houses which could only be protected by strengthening cellars. But no general solution had so far been found for the protection of these miscellaneous types of buildings. This need, combined with cessation of the production of 'Andersons' and basement fittings, now compelled the Government to place the main emphasis in the sphere of domestic shelter on brick and concrete surface structures.

Before the war the Government had recommended provision of shelters of this type for individual homes or a few adjoining homes, and had undertaken to reimburse the costs of materials needed for these.[4] For various practical reasons few such shelters had in fact been built. In March 1940, by an extension of this idea, they introduced what they called by the cumbrous name of 'communal domestic surface shelters', sometimes shortened to 'communal shelters'. These, though similar in design to the former type, were to be built to protect forty-eight persons living in groups of adjoining houses and to stand in the middle of the street.[5] They became, in course of time, a significant example of the Government's basic plan to provide the fullest possible amount of domestic shelter and avoid the congregation of large numbers of shelterers in one place.

---

[1] The exact total distributed before the heavy raiding of September was 2,300,878; of these 1,661,275 were 'standard', 507,688 small, and 131,915 large.

[2] H. of C. Deb., Vol. 352, Cols. 2160–2278, 2nd November 1939.

[3] W. Sansom, *Westminster in War* (1947).

[4] A.R.P. Dept. Circular 102, 5th May 1939; pp. 196-197.

[5] H.S.C. 38, 4th March 1940. They were also sometimes given the less misleading official name of 'multiple unit domestic shelters'.

Though tremendous activity was reported from most of the country over public shelters, a great deal had still to be done to achieve the aim of providing these for some 10-15 per cent. of the inhabitants of the most threatened cities.[1] It was considered by officers of Birmingham Region 'that the quickest way to perform this most urgent task was to adapt every available basement, or to construct trenches and line them with timber, steel or concrete. Obviously all shelters had to conform to certain standards, and all proposals had therefore to be submitted to Regional Headquarters to check these details and consider whether the costs were reasonable. It was a time of innumerable meetings, visits, inspections and telephone calls, when quick decisions were asked for and given, although perhaps not always carefully recorded in writing. On the whole, good relations were established with local authorities, a number of which proceeded with energy, some with discretion, and a few with apathy'.

No complete picture could be formed in Whitehall for a long time to come of the results of these complex activities being carried on in twelve Regions. In November, however, the Ministry considered the rate of progress to be unsatisfactory. Public shelter had perhaps been provided for nearly 2,000,000 of the 27,500,000 persons in the specified areas, though work was in hand to protect 1,300,000 more. In the County of London such shelter was ready for 520,000 persons, and work still proceeding represented provision for a further 300,000. The pace and the quality of local performance showed infinite variation. The city of Birmingham, for example, had public shelters in readiness for about 5 per cent. of its population, an important East Anglian town had made slight progress, and the authorities in Cambridge (among other places) had taken no action whatever. Severe winter conditions later caused many delays, and in many areas supplies of bricks, timber and concrete proved very short. By the spring, nevertheless, certain Regional Officers reported that 80 per cent. of their public shelters had been completed. Though the calculation of Birmingham Region that 50 per cent. of these shelters were ready was probably nearer the truth as regards most of the danger zones.

By telling the Government in the first days of war that they hoped to build trenches for 1,000,000 more persons the local authorities had shown their continued reliance on this type of shelter. Trenches could be speedily built, and the public showed preference for shelters which were both underground and in the open. The Government then began an attempt to make good their promise to supply pre-cast concrete trench linings, and this move is of historical interest as an example of the administrative difficulties to which the

---

[1] p. 200.

shelter programme gave rise. In October the Ministry made a contract with the British Concrete Corporation for the supply of 8,000 standard linings for trenches to hold fifty persons; these were to be mass produced by some eighty-five firms all over the country and to cost £63 apiece.[1] A month or so later, when delivery of these had become due, only twenty-seven had in fact been produced. Many local authorities, in the meantime, had made their own arrangements for linings; and bad weather had shown that the pre-cast concrete variety often let in water. The Ministry, after appeals by Regional staffs to the authorities to use standard linings had been ineffective, was compelled to close the contract. Though over 2,000 linings had by then been supplied, the authorities had only asked for about 700; and the Ministry found difficulty in disposing of the surplus for other shelter purposes and to other Departments. In the new conditions of the summer of 1940 a further order was placed for these linings. But when a short experience of raids had proved that they buckled easily, their manufacture was finally abandoned.[2]

'Permanent' trenches had nevertheless been provided throughout the country by early 1940 for perhaps 1,000,000 to 1,500,000 persons; and in the matter of public shelters authorities had already been paying more attention to strengthening any available buildings.[3] Sandbags had been distributed in huge numbers for this (among other) purposes, and their preservation had begun to present a large-scale problem. The Ministry had issued advice on this matter in October, and some weeks later they warned the authorities that supplies of bags were becoming exhausted and asked them to substitute brickwork, concrete blocks or other materials for shelters whenever possible. Timber supplies, though inadequate, were proving less scarce than had been feared. By March the Ministry was satisfied that substantial progress had been made in adapting existing buildings as public shelters in many areas. Also the experiments carried on by the Research and Experiments Department through the winter, besides introducing better methods of strengthening old buildings, had led to the conclusion that modern steel-framed buildings which had not been strengthened would offer adequate protection.

By the end of the first month of war some 90 per cent. of the 12,000 factories in the specified areas upon which the Civil Defence Act imposed a shelter obligation had submitted schemes. The

---

[1] The design consisted of interchangeable concrete units the moulds for which could be produced quickly in large quantities.

[2] H.S.C. 290, 11th December 1940.

[3] The cellars of public houses, it had been decided, were not suitable as public shelters and customers on the premises in a raid who lived or worked nearby were to be asked by publicans to leave. (A.R.P. Dept. Circular 284, 27th October 1939.)

Home Secretary told Parliament in November that two-thirds of the factory schemes had already been sanctioned and that a high proportion of employers had started to build shelters without awaiting official approval of their plans.[1] At the end of 1939 the Factory Inspectors reported that a large proportion of factory shelters had been completed, and that only a handful of employers had still failed to submit schemes.[2] A considerable number of factory shelters had at first taken the form of trenches. But as the owners had realised the liability of these to flooding, they had turned to greater reliance on underground rooms and various surface buildings.

The owners of offices and shops were making much slower progress, though no reliable information was available to the Government on this matter for a long time to come.[3] The majority of these were restricted to the method of strutting basements, and were therefore dependent on adequate steel and timber supplies. The local authorities, though responsible for seeing that commercial firms took some action in this sphere, were reluctant to press them at a time when materials were scarce and the Government was encouraging evacuation. As the year ended Regional Officers roughly estimated that shelters in shops and offices in the danger zones were only sufficient to protect about 10 per cent. of those who worked in these places; though there was reason to think that this was too pessimistic a figure. The period allowed to employers to begin shelter work which would qualify for grant had been extended before war broke out and was then again extended to the end of March 1940.[4] As this date approached the Government, though admitting that industrial shelter provision on the scales laid down in the Act had not been reached, described its general progress as very satisfactory.[5]

The application of A.R.P., other than shelters, to industry once war had started cannot, for reasons already explained, be adequately noticed in this volume. But it must be interpolated that the powers conferred on the Ministry of Supply to direct factories on the 'vital list' to protect plant, furnish alternative water and electricity supplies and take other steps were already producing effective response.[6] In addition, the planning of new capacity was taking account of 'Passive Air Defence' (P.A.D.)—to use the title adopted by the Ministry of Supply and Service Departments. For example,

---

[1] H. of C. Deb., Vol. 352, Col. 2265, 2nd November 1940.

[2] *Annual Report of the Chief Inspector of Factories for the year 1939*, Cmd. 6251 of 1941, pp. 40–41.

[3] The authorities were not required to furnish returns to the Government on the subject of shelters in 'commercial buildings'.

[4] A.R.P. Dept. Circular 158, 3rd August 1939.

[5] H. of C. Deb., Vol. 358, Col. 2142, 21st March 1940.

[6] See p. 291.

new plant was being sited or constructed, when possible, with reference to visibility from the air, alternative power supplies available, the restrictions of the black-out and problems of camouflage. Grants were made by the Ministry of Supply towards the cost of P.A.D. measures taken under direction by industrial concerns.

The many-sided shelter programme included the Government's responsibility in this respect towards its own employees. The shelters ready in Government offices on 3rd September were, like those for the general public and for office and factory workers, far short of the estimated needs. But the scale of the Government's problem when compared with that confronting private employers was quite small. Its headquarters staff in London, as previously mentioned, numbered about 60,000 officials. A large proportion of these worked in buildings in Whitehall or elsewhere of solid construction, and as Departments expanded or new ones were formed the Office of Works was able to take over a number of steel-framed buildings left empty by business firms.

Serious difficulties, however, arose in deciding how far the general principle that shelters in Government offices should not be above the standards which private employers had been asked to adopt should still obtain; and in relating this to the problem, discussed earlier in this volume, of Government evacuation.[1] The Chiefs of Staff had proposed in September that all Government Offices, whether in London or sent away to the provinces, should be protected against air attack 'on the same lines as those of military headquarters in the field in static warfare', i.e., with thorough systems of slit trenches, sandbag emplacements and other forms of shelter. When it became apparent that the knock-out blow was being deferred, Ministers had to decide whether to continue with plans for the large-scale protection of the Government in London, and what shelters should be built both in the areas where accommodation for the seat of Government had been reserved and those to which a number of less-essential staffs had already been moved. Shortages of building materials dictated, in large part, the answers to all these questions. The scheme for a system of underground chambers in Whitehall for the core of the Government was reconsidered by Ministers in October and abandoned; besides needing huge quantities of steel and cement this might well, it was thought, take two years to complete. Either the Government would survive in Whitehall for this period, and by doing so prove that such protection was unnecessary, or—as seemed probable at this time— heavy attacks would be followed by its attempted evacuation.[2] Special, though not bomb-proof, protection in London for Ministers

---

[1] pp. 324–328.
[2] p. 200.

and their principal officials was therefore still confined to one or two War Rooms in Whitehall, and a few alternative War Rooms still under construction in the suburbs. It was not until after some months of heavy raiding that new schemes for the stronger protection of the Government were brought forward and given effect.[1]

To adopt the Chiefs of Staff proposals in any of the evacuation areas would, besides consuming large supplies of materials, introduce a shelter standard far above that being provided for the general public and perhaps create an acute air raid consciousness among the local communities. Some towns, such as Bath and Harrogate, were already regarded by their residents as more vulnerable on account of the presence of official staffs. Ministers decided on a series of compromises which, in general, offered much more modest protection to Government officials than that suggested by the Chiefs of Staff. In 'black areas' and a few other places the Office of Works was to proceed unobtrusively with bricking up buildings and other special shelter measures; but elsewhere the standard for Government staffs was to be assimilated to the standard provided for the local citizens. Practical progress in this matter, nevertheless, proved very slow.

The A.R.P. Services Reviewed

The citizens, male and female, who had reported in thousands for A.R.P. duty in the days leading up to war formed, it can safely be said, as motley a force as had ever been called to arms in Britain.[2] The only generalisations it seems possible to make are that they were predominantly middle-aged or more, and were ready to give national service near their own homes. They were not, since no medical examination was involved, necessarily able-bodied. They came from every class of society and civil occupation. Though some were persons of exceptional public spirit, others had joined from a variety of motives. A proportion (of unknown size) had been enrolled and trained, mainly in anti-gas defence, for several years past. But numbers of those whose activities have been described in earlier chapters had, as war approached, left A.R.P. for other services or duties. They owed a double loyalty, the proportions of which varied from individual to individual, to the nation and to their own locality. They belonged to a national service in a sense which was perhaps mainly mystical, for they were enrolled and administered by their local government officials.

The Ministry reported laconically to the War Cabinet on 8th September that this unprecedented mobilisation of civilians had been 'quite satisfactory'. The total of some 1,500,000 men and

---

[1] See Chapter XII.

[2] The metaphor should not be allowed to obscure the important fact, stressed at the outset, that the A.R.P. Services had no offensive weapons.

women needed for the General Services had about been achieved. The difficulty which some main danger areas had experienced in peace-time in enrolling enough volunteers appeared to have been solved. Most important, the reluctance of the public to commit themselves before war to whole-time service had vanished and large numbers were now enrolled on this basis.[1]

The enemy's unexpected tactics of holding his hand quickly set the problem of the A.R.P. Services, both for the Government and the thousands of individuals concerned, in new terms. A period of adjustment began which was to prove both difficult and slow. The Government had announced shortly before the war their intention to reimburse to local authorities the pay of all whole-time volunteers (up to the limit of the authorised local establishments).[2] They were now faced with the need to reduce continuous manning of the whole civil defence structure in the interests both of other forms of war effort and of the public purse. The total of whole-time volunteers in the General Services, so far as they knew, had now reached about 320,000, and such volunteers in the A.F.S. about 70,000.

The volunteers themselves, male and female, had found themselves confronted, not with the stimulus of action and danger but with tasks of further preparation and organisation. They met the frictions and frustrations inevitable among such mixed collections of citizens, many of whom were new to their tasks. Though leadership, as a Home Office official had remarked at Munich, sprang up all over the place, there were many units and areas in which this only emerged slowly. In general, hours of duty by day or night were long and arrangements for sleeping, feeding and sanitation were so inadequate as to be summarised by the Inspector-General as 'most acute discomfort'.

The experience of changing from stand-to to stand-by conditions was not made easier for the volunteers by a chill wind of public criticism which—with what, in retrospect, seems astonishing speed—began to blow upon them. The growing public scepticism over the danger and criticism of the Government for over-insurance, emphasised above, found in the 1,500,000 or so A.R.P. workers a convenient and visible target for complaint.[3] Explanations by the Prime Minister and the Home Secretary that considerable numbers had still to be kept at action stations did not allay mounting criticism of the thousands of A.R.P. and A.F.S. members and auxiliary police alleged to be standing about and doing nothing.[4] Regional Commissioners, for example in Scotland, Birmingham and Wales,

---

[1] pp. 205–208.
[2] p. 205; A.R.P. Dept. Circular 197, 31st August 1939.
[3] p. 297.
[4] H. of C. Deb., Vol. 351, Col. 677, 13th September 1939.

promptly reported rising complaints by local authorities, employers and the public over lavish expenditure on A.R.P. wages. The agitation reflected the fact that this form of war service touched almost every national interest. Individuals wrote indignant letters to the Ministry of Home Security, in the capacity both of unsuccessful candidates for paid work and outraged taxpayers. Members of Parliament complained that A.R.P. workers were better paid than those in the Fighting Forces, and that unemployed miners were being debarred from this work.

Employers in areas where the A.R.P. flat rate was higher than the general level of wages expressed a special grievance.[1] Allegations began to grow that the officials of one city were giving the paid positions to their relatives; that the prosperous citizens of a well-known spa were drawing £3 a week as full-time wardens; and, more generally, that 'there were too many people in A.R.P. simply for what they could get out of it'.[2] Inevitably, the fact that the majority of the A.R.P. force was composed of part-time unpaid volunteers was soon obscured in this vortex of criticism.

Eight days after the outbreak of war the Government had, in fact, taken the first steps to reverse the aim formerly pursued and begin the process of scaling down the paid A.R.P. establishments. On 19th October the Home Secretary explained fully to Parliament the Government's proposals in this matter.[3] He stressed the impossibility of undertaking any wholesale demobilisation of civil defence workers; the structure had to be kept continuously manned and ready for action, which could not be done without a substantial element of whole-time paid staff. He was, however, trying to devise a system whereby the organisation might be manned by a minimum number of volunteers always ready for action and yet also be capable of rapid expansion to deal with repeated and intensive attack. First-line units would be supported by a much larger second-line, for which relatively few paid members would be needed. He energetically defended the volunteers against the charges that they were 'slackers' and 'parasites', and deplored the failure of the public to recognise more generously the vast volume of purely voluntary effort being given to the A.R.P. Service.

A review of establishments initiated by the Government two days later consumed so much administrative effort, central, regional and local, during the next six months that it must be recorded here in some detail.[4] The reader should perhaps be reminded that the A.R.P.

---

[1] Many unskilled workers in major industries were at this date earning less than £3 per week.

[2] e.g., *Edinburgh Evening News, Daily Express,* 12th, 13th September 1939.

[3] H. of C. Deb., Vol. 352, Cols. 1026–33.

[4] A.R.P. Dept. Circular 275, 20th October 1939.

Services under discussion in this chapter are the seven so-called 'General Services' and do not include the Auxiliary Fire Service (which will be considered in a later chapter) or the Police War Reserve, neither of which was the responsibility of the A.R.P. Controllers. It must also be emphasised that the authorities in Whitehall in their continuous efforts, now and later, to introduce more common standards into the A.R.P. Service were in large measure dealing with an abstraction. All central or vertical planning was, it may be said, cut across horizontally in a two-fold manner. First, by the fact that every volunteer enrolled in a separate branch of the Service. Secondly, by the fact that the interpretation and execution of all conditions of service lay with hundreds of local authorities.

The circular setting the review in motion asked all scheme-making authorities to submit plans as soon as possible for re-organisation of each of their seven services to Regional Commissioners, who would give them fuller guidance about proposals for paid staffs and had been empowered to approve local adjustments. Though it was mainly permissive, the circular introduced some important new standards. The large number of volunteers who worked on their normal jobs during the day and gave A.R.P. service three or more times a week should not be asked to do more than 4-hour shifts or more than occasional night-duty. Paid staffs' weekly hours under stand-by conditions should not be less than 72 for men (normally a 12-hour shift on six days) and 48 for women; and every effort should be made to provide sleeping accommodation in or near posts and depots.

The proposals for reducing the 'first line' and increasing the number 'at call' in the different services were drastic. Wardens' regular patrolling in day-time should stop, and only posts in the most vulnerable areas be continuously manned. Paid staff in the Rescue and First Aid Parties in these areas might be halved by suspending 'double-banking', and building trade members of the former needed for urgent work should be temporarily released.[1] The proportion of ambulances on stand-by duty might be reduced from one-half to one-third; and Decontamination Squads need not stand-by. The wholetimers who might be released by applying these principles were not being demobilised but should be asked to remain on their local establishments as a form of reserve. The Ministry tried to clear up a recurring difficulty by defining an 'effective', paid or otherwise, in this diversified force as a person who was trained or in training and 'attended his agreed duty shifts with reasonable regularity'. Finally—and most important in immediate effect—no further enrolment of paid workers was to be made until the general review had been completed.

[1] pp. 205–216.

The Government was now spending over £3 millions a month on paid A.R.P. staff; and pressure by public opinion for reductions was vigorously maintained.[1] Yet the Regional Commissioners encountered much resistance by individual authorities to any cuts. The London authorities had recruited about up to their war establishments. By December the Boroughs had over 9,000 paid wardens (more than 9 per post) and over 10,000 whole-timers in Stretcher Parties; while the County had a well-organised Rescue Service of 12,000 paid members. But the Ministry's proposals that paid wardens should be reduced to 5 or 6 per post, that 1,500 members of Stretcher Parties should be released, and the Rescue Service be cut to 8,000 were, for the time being, successfully resisted. Elsewhere resistance was strong, though generally less effective. Some authorities in Newcastle Region took the attitude that their Commissioner was imposing reductions which would increase the threat to their areas and threatened to make this public. In Cambridge Region two county councils and some important boroughs were still resisting cuts in the following February. Leeds, Sheffield and other cities raised particular objection to applying the standard of 12-hour shifts.

As information accumulated at the centre, it began to appear not merely that the original estimate of total paid strength was quite out-of-date but that the real strength of this kind might even be below that at which the new arrangements were aiming. The drive for economy, based on inadequate information, was threatening to become too effective. Some local authorities had been dismissing paid staff without central approval; and the public agitation, combined with the superior attractions of other war work, had been causing considerable wastage. By December the national strength of paid A.R.P. staff was estimated at under 200,000, and the maldistribution of this total had again become a significant problem. Some authorities were seriously below operational strength, and were pressing for the ban on enrolment of whole-timers to be lifted.

By the end of January 1940 the review had only been half-completed with results described by the Ministry as unreal and unsatisfactory. 'Some of the services', they decided, 'are seriously under strength; the relation between stand-by strength and strength at short call is incoherent; there is wastage which will increase as the withdrawal of two million men for the Forces and the increasing need for munitions production and export trade put pressure upon the labour market, and in some areas there is evidence of a partial disintegration of the service under the stand-by and uninformed criticism'. The Inspector-General was alarmed over 'the large amount of unsettlement in the services'.

---

[1] e.g., H. of C. Deb., Vol. 352, Cols. 2160–2262, 2nd November 1939.

Recourse was therefore had to review of a more substantial kind. A Departmental Committee under the chairmanship of Mr William Mabane and including a number of Regional Principal Officers began in January to examine the system of responsibility, structure and conditions of the civil defence services. Its conclusions, reported two months later, must be summarised here at some length since many of them were to prove of lasting importance.

It is significant that these officials, in the light of six months' practical experience, still weighed the possibility of removing these services from local to central control; but decided that the case for so radical a change was not proven. Local control, in spite of its obvious drawbacks, had made local patriotism and material resources of all kinds available to the Government, and averted the need to create a large new administrative machine. The Ministry and other Departments should, these officials nevertheless concluded, present their proposals in future in more mandatory a form, and exercise closer supervision by means of inspection and returns.

The central problem, it was now clear, was that of maintaining a state of readiness in many services in vulnerable areas for an indefinite period. The stand-by presented difficult issues not only of finance but of numbers, efficiency and morale. For long-term reasons, the committee decided, there was an urgent necessity for the Government to stress publicly the importance of part-time A.R.P. service. But at present any further reduction of paid staffs would involve an unwarranted risk. The committee also reaffirmed the voluntary principle, not only on political grounds but also on account of the large administrative difficulties which compulsion, particularly of part-timers, would create.

Pay for these volunteers, they continued, should be governed by the doctrine that 'civil defence is a service and not an employment'. The principle of paying a uniform rate roughly similar to the wartime pay and allowances of a married private soldier with one child should be maintained.[1] The committee agreed with the view, gathering strength in various quarters, that new A.R.P. volunteers should give some more definite undertaking of service, though they rejected any sanctions 'of a military or penal character'. They also proposed, inter alia, regular central inspection of local training; machinery by which volunteers could express their views on conditions of service; and the training of members of certain services in the duties of others—a principle which, under the label of 'interchangeability', was soon to be much emphasised.

The committee defined in detail the manner in which the first and second line conceptions could be applied to the separate services, and in doing so made an important contribution to what must still be

---

[1] p. 205.

called the theory of passive defence operations. These proposals were, in the main, adopted in a new circular on 'Organisation of A.R.P. Services' issued by the Ministry on 18th April 1940 which embodied the fruits of six months' negotiation.[1] New maxima, which were mandatory, were prescribed for both paid and unpaid staffs; these, it was hoped, would cause a further overall reduction by June of some 35,000 whole-timers.[2] Even in the chief target areas, for example, paid wardens were to be reduced to two per post. Grant-aid was introduced for Wardens' Group Centres where wardens from a number of posts might train, eat and sleep. The larger authorities were again urged to appoint special officers to help Chief Wardens with organisation and training.

The 'double-banking' of Rescue and First Aid Parties, and the distinction between Heavy and Light Rescue Parties (except in London) were both abolished.[3] All Rescue Parties were henceforth to consist of eleven men, with seven standing by, and the practice of using municipal employees for this service was commended. The new instructions gave much emphasis both to the importance of specialised rescue training, and to the need to train Rescue and First Aid Parties and Decontamination Squads in the work of the others. Paid staff in Report and Control Centres were to be further reduced. None of these new instructions, it is important to note, applied to London Region; though the Senior Commissioner agreed that, if the enemy continued to show restraint, large reductions in this Region, especially of paid wardens, would be necessary.

This decision on reduction of paid workers evoked a request by the Parliamentary A.R.P. Committee to the Ministry for an assurance that further reductions would be made in six months' time; and also much enthusiasm from the Press. The ban on enrolment of new paid staff by those authorities which were under establishment in this respect was lifted. Simultaneously with publication of the new circular the Home Secretary launched an appeal for a further 250,000 part-time A.R.P. volunteers.

For the staffs of civil defence, or the Regional and local officials, these months had been fully occupied. Local organisation had to be completed, responsibilities defined and liaison with other areas extended. Much had still to be done in establishing local communications, protecting control centres and posts and now making these habitable for permanent occupation. Vehicles had to be adapted or acquired, and supplies of many kinds distributed. The shelter programme, as recorded earlier, still presented formidable problems.

The troops, or the rank and file of the services, had also for a time

---

[1] H.S.C. 58, 18th April 1940.

[2] Local authorities were asked to complete reductions by 18th June 1940.

[3] pp. 205, 214–215.

been fully occupied with unit organisation, protection and equipment of their depots or posts and—largely through improvisation and self-help—making these habitable for twenty-four hours occupation. Wardens, perhaps numbering 500,000 up and down the country, had been advising their neighbours, practising reporting, patrolling their sectors by day and night and enforcing (sometimes with more zeal than discretion) the black-out. But once a short period had passed even the Wardens—and to a greater extent those in the Rescue, Casualty and Decontamination Services—were beginning to find time hanging heavily on their hands. Even the most enthusiastic units were finding that training on duty, in such forms as inventing a sudden gas attack or staging an incident in the streets, had practical limits.

The King and Queen, by visiting numbers of civil defence units in London in the first few days of war, had conferred distinction on their activities.[1] But the volunteers' many difficulties were soon aggravated, to an extent which it is difficult to measure, by the chill wind of public criticism already referred to. Though the fact had quickly become obscured, the large proportion were part-timers carrying on their normal occupations by day or night; and so, as a Chief of the Imperial General Staff has said of volunteers in the Territorial Army, 'were twice citizens'.[2] They not unnaturally felt surprise, and sometimes resentment, at finding themselves regarded in the spirit of 'Chuck him out, the brute! But its "Saviour of 'is country" when the guns begin to shoot'.

Boredom, flavoured with unpopularity, had taken the place of bombardment. And the opinion of a Group Officer in the East End of London that these 'weary months of waiting inactivity' were the hardest of his service was probably shared by all who stayed on and served for the following five years.[3] It is hardly surprising that many volunteers, under the influence of discouragement or frustration, left the service.[4] Or that the responsible authorities, as Christmas approached, were seriously perturbed about the possible disintegration of the structure.[5]

A nucleus of volunteers—of the size of which there is no evidence —more stout-hearted, or sometimes less ambitious, than the rest carried on. These had, at least, the reward of a gradual improvement in their conditions of service. The Ministry, it must be said, was still without systematic reports from its Regional Officers on this essential

---

[1] *The Times*, 6th September 1939.

[2] Field-Marshal Sir W. Slim, *The Listener*, 6th November 1952.

[3] R. Bell, *The Bull's Eye* (1943).

[4] Many, it must be added, had not even signed the vague 'honourable undertaking' of service which was all that was then required of them.

[5] pp. 297–299.

matter.[1] But it seems that its October circular led to widespread, though by no means universal, reduction of the part-timers' long hours of duty; and (though this proved more difficult) to fairly general introduction of the whole-timers' 72-hour week. The measures, hurriedly authorised on the eve of war, for some central supply of folding beds, for limited grant-aid for sleeping accommodation and billeting and for one free meal at a maximum cost of 1s. for a volunteer on duty for at least twelve hours were beginning to have effect.[2] Local ingenuity and purchase brought further improvements. The suggestion of a Member of Parliament that the B.B.C. should broadcast music throughout the night for A.R.P. workers was not pursued. But in October the Government offered grant-aid for recreational equipment and asked the public to present books and wireless sets to A.R.P. depots and posts.[3]

Loss of wages by part-timers had, early in the war, become a serious issue, and the Government's attitude that employers should shoulder this responsibility had aroused strong opposition. In October the Government admitted a change of front on this matter, and some weeks later they empowered local authorities to make up wages to maxima of 10s. a day for men and 7s. for women.[4] Part-timers were reminded of the fact, over which there was much misunderstanding, that the Personal Injuries (Civilians) Scheme announced at the outbreak of war entitled them to compensation for injuries received on A.R.P. duty which was roughly equivalent to that paid to the private soldier.[5] By the end of the year whole-time staffs had been granted paid annual leave of twelve days, and paid sick leave for a maximum of three weeks.[6] In the following April payment of part-timers' travelling expenses was introduced.

The needs of the services up and down the country for buildings, vehicles and different kinds of supplies were considerable. Special construction for A.R.P. purposes continued during these months to be mainly confined to shelters, and local officials were still engaged in adapting existing buildings or in searching for more suitable ones. Many of the schools they had occupied in target areas in September had, as the ebb-tide of evacuation began to run, to be given up. Work continued on giving special protection to control centres and some wardens' posts.[7] These apart, the services' premises, it was officially considered, needed no more than the normal blast and

---

[1] pp. 307–308.

[2] A.R.P. Dept. Circulars 200, 203, 228, 28th, 29th August and 3rd September 1939.

[3] A.R.P. Dept. Circular 275, 20th October 1939.

[4] A.R.P. Dept. Circular 317, 2nd December 1939.

[5] A.R.P. Dept. Circular 313, 25th November 1939; S. R. & O. 1939, No. 1143.

[6] A.R.P. Dept. Circulars 313, 336, 25th November, 11th December 1939.

[7] H.S.C. 16, 13th January 1941.

splinter protection. Since attacks were expected to be violent and short most volunteers would be on duty in the open.[1]

The large programme of anti-gas and other supplies for the services was by no means complete on the outbreak of war. Volunteers outside the main target areas who reported for duty in September were frequently, if sometimes unreasonably, annoyed at the scarcity of equipment. The distribution from Regional stores, or under central instructions to contractors, of many articles to hundreds of local authorities was inevitably accompanied by confusions and delays. The Home Secretary reminded Parliament in November that the A.R.P. supplies programme had been designed for completion at the end of 1941, and that his Department had forgone its full share of some important items to help the Fighting Services; and stated, 'broadly speaking, the equipment position is wholly satisfactory'.[2] In February 1940 the Ministry reported to the War Cabinet that the issue of personal equipment to the services had reached the final stage.[3] By about May steel helmets had been issued to the whole force, and service and civilian duty masks and anti-gas clothing to a substantial proportion of those for whom they were intended.

Steel helmets, superior gas-masks and various types of armlet were still, as serious attacks began to develop, the only signs distinguishing most A.R.P. volunteers from their fellow-citizens. In October the Ministry had announced that the first issues of the A.R.P. uniform, or overall suit of blue cotton, would soon be made; but this proved too sanguine.[4] The public criticism, incidentally, of the services in this phase was illustrated by recurring complaints in Parliament that the issue of this garment (now costing 11s.) to over one million persons was 'a scandalous waste of money'.[5] By April 1940 the overalls had still only been issued to a small proportion of volunteers, and three months later the Ministry was proposing to restrict them to certain services and furnish a standard civil defence armlet to the remainder.[6] Its further proposal that overalls issued to male wardens should be withdrawn was successfully resisted. A.R.P. 'tin helmets', in the meantime, had been painted in a uniform black with white lettering to indicate the branch of the Service. Police helmets were blue, and those of the Fire Service grey.

This progress was the fruit of the early emphasis on defence against gas, and equipment for other purposes was far less developed.

---

[1] A.R.P. Dept. Circulars 101, 134, 4th May, 7th July 1939.

[2] H. of C. Deb., Vol. 352, Cols. 2267–9, 2nd November 1939.

[3] Steel helmets and respirators were the only strictly 'personal issues'.

[4] A.R.P. Dept. Circular 274, 13th October 1939; p. 236.

[5] H. of C. Deb., Vol. 352, Col. 1025, 19th October 1939.

[6] H.S.C. 155, 3rd July 1940.

Fewer than 9,000 stirrup pumps had been delivered to local authorities by the outbreak of war.[1] In April 1940 the loan of pumps to fire authorities for training the public was begun;[2] and two months later the deliveries of pumps to these and to A.R.P. authorities still totalled under 100,000. Much had still to be done in supplying over 6,000 Rescue Parties with special equipment—a problem made more complicated by free local purchase on the outbreak of war.[3] As experience from training began to accumulate new standard items of rescue equipment were added.

The scale reached by the equipment problem is illustrated by the fact that the Ministry began the issue in October of periodical 'A.R.P. Equipment Bulletins'. In February 1940 they issued Equipment Regulations prescribing the manner in which the authorities were to conserve and account for the considerable stocks they were now accumulating.[4] This was followed by detailed guidance on the 'Care and Custody of Equipment'.[5]

The many thousands of vehicles required by the services were, it will be recalled, to be obtained mainly by voluntary arrangements with private owners.[6] Though large numbers were secured in this way during mobilisation, numerous difficulties soon arose. Competition between the Service and other Departments for transport grew intense and many towns, for example Birmingham and Leeds, were unable to obtain nearly enough A.R.P. vehicles. Many of those which were hired and adapted proved unsatisfactory, and after a few weeks the total expenditure on hiring began to assume alarming proportions. At the end of October the Ministry authorised the purchase of second-hand cars, to cost not more than £30, for the Rescue and First Aid Parties;[7] and some weeks later they asked that all hiring on a whole-time basis should stop and be replaced by part-time hiring or outright purchase.[8] But improvisation and 'self-help' by the services continued, up to the onset of heavy attacks, to characterise this matter. Petrol rationing and higher taxation reduced the number of private cars available, many of the cars bought at low prices proved defective or unsuitable, and no technical guidance was as yet offered by the central or regional authorities about types of vehicles to be bought or methods of adaptation.

---

[1] pp. 213, 235.

[2] F.B. Circular No. 33/1940.

[3] A.R.P. Dept. Circular 202, 29th August 1939; pp. 215, 235.

[4] H.S.C. 31/40, 23rd February; S.R. & O. 1940, No. 236.

[5] Memorandum No. 15, April 1940 which in various editions remained the authority throughout the war.

[6] pp. 236–237.

[7] A.R.P. Dept. Circular 288, 28th October 1939.

[8] A.R.P. Dept. Circular 338, 14th December 1939. This allowed the purchase of lorries costing up to £80.

It is not surprising that in September 1939, as at later stages of the war, senior officials held different opinions as to the degree in which the A.R.P. Service could be described as trained. The Home Office had already built up a large national training structure; but the use made of this organisation depended, more than most matters, on the individual factor. On the willingness, for example, of regional and local officials to attend to this problem; on the energy or availability of the 4,000 or so 'Instructors A.R.P.S.' and the thousands more whom these had trained as local instructors; and on the keenness and capacity of the volunteers who, it is important to note, were under no formal obligation to take part in training.

The two Home Security Schools carried on, maintaining their policy of providing training of a high standard to a limited number of instructors or officials, and extending training to incendiary bomb control and defence against high explosive attack.[1] But the A.R.P. Staff School in London had closed down on the outbreak of war, and attention at the centre to training matters had been suspended. The more enthusiastic units throughout the country began, as noticed earlier, to 'train on duty'. But it was not easy to relate these exercises to the conditions that would actually be faced, or to continue indefinitely what a London official called 'play-acting in public'. Persons appointed by local authorities to supervise training were often of subordinate status. Qualified instructors were still scarce, and supplies of stirrup pumps and other equipment still inadequate.

By the end of 1939 the important bearing of training on the morale of the Service under stand-by conditions had become clear. In the early months of 1940 the Inspector-General's Department at the Ministry was enlarged to include a Training Branch, and Training Officers were appointed in all Regions. A publication in February called 'Basic Training in A.R.P.' consolidated both for the services and the general public the main principles contained in the numerous handbooks and memoranda issued before the war.[2]

At a conference in London in January a new training plan was initiated. This, published in April, was designed, in the words of the Mabane Committee, to 'establish a uniform practice in training throughout the country'.[3] It continued the division of training into individual, collective (or team) and combined; and gave new emphasis to the instruction of higher staff in operational control. It included detailed syllabuses, and advice on refresher training, on the organisation of centres, posts and depots and on training in industry.

---

[1] pp. 209–210.
[2] A.R.P. Training Manual No. 1, 16th February 1940.
[3] A.R.P. Training Manual No. 2, 16th April 1940.

z

The Inspector-General told the Mabane Committee that 'no end of the task (of training) is in sight'. But this committee decided that the new plan had provided clear direction from the centre in this matter; and also proposed regular central and regional inspection. Much responsibility in this sphere now rested on Regions. London Region, it must be added, had been devoting more energy to training since the war than the others, and had already pioneered two important developments. Relying more than formerly on recruits from outside the building trades for its Rescue Parties, it had formed several Regional Schools to develop specialised training for this service.[1] And it had evolved the idea,which was to prove of lasting value, of 'Incident Officers' trained to co-ordinate all operations at the actual scene of an attack.

The new emphasis at the centre on national training was in part responsible for the creation early in April at the Ministry of Home Security of the new office of Chief of the Civil Defence Operational Staff, to which the Regional Commissioner for Bristol, General Sir Hugh Elles, was appointed. His function was defined as that of helping the Regions 'to ensure the operational efficiency of their civil defence services and to develop the necessary operational training'.[2] This step, which was preceded by much discussion between chief officials of the Ministry and certain Regional Commissioners, bears wider interest as the newest of the various attempts already recorded in this narrative to create a Civil Defence General Staff. Stated in other terms, it was the outcome of dissatisfaction felt by some— though by no means all—senior officials in Home Security with the adequacy for civil defence of normal administrative processes, and of the view that, for the purposes at least of operations, the centralising military elements of the structure needed strengthening.

Once heavy attack had started, it must be added, the idea of an operational commander at the centre proved unworkable in practice. Regional Commissioners, in so far as they needed advice on operations, consulted the Minister or his chief officials. This office therefore lapsed at the end of 1940.

---

[1] p. 214.

[2] H.S.C. 61/40, 11th April 1940. Gen. Elles returned to Bristol in September 1940 and was succeeded for a short time by Gen. Sir W. H. Bartholomew.

CHAPTER IX

THE THREAT REDOUBLED

(May – August 1940)

The New Scale of Attack, and Invasion

THE twilight war—and with it the general scepticism about air attack—ended abruptly with Germany's invasion of Denmark and Norway on 9th April. British naval, land and air forces were all strenuously engaged, and for the civilian at home the war had at last come to life. But a series of disasters quickly followed, causing much disquiet over the higher conduct of affairs. On 10th May Germany, through the avenue of the Low Countries, began her long-postponed attack on the West. The same day Mr Churchill became Prime Minister and formed an all-party administration. Addressing the House of Commons, for the first time in this capacity, on 13th May he said, 'We are in the preliminary stage of one of the greatest battles in history', and continued, 'I have nothing to offer but blood, toil, tears and sweat'.[1]

As the German armies made lightning progress it became clear that the threat to Britain had redoubled. The danger of all-out air attack became merged in the greater danger, so remote in experience as to be hard to conceive, of actual invasion. And large-scale assault on civilians and factories from the air was shown to be only one item of strategy in a war which was rapidly abolishing all distinction between military and civilian objectives. The German Air Force, for example, obliterated the centre of Rotterdam on 14th May, killing about 1,000 people, as one item of its activities in support of the army.[2] Enemy parachutists and airborne troops were landing far behind the defenders' front-lines. And German pilots were not hesitating to bomb and machine-gun civilians on the roads as a method of blocking military traffic.[3]

In a broadcast on 19th May Mr Churchill warned the British people of the new situation confronting them:

There will be many men, and many women, in this island who when the ordeal comes upon them, as come it will, will feel comfort, and

---

[1] H. of C. Deb., Vol. 360, Col. 1502.

[2] It was at first reported that no less than 30,000 persons had been killed at Rotterdam.

[3] See e.g., C. D. Freeman and D. Cooper, *The Road to Bordeaux* (1940).

even a pride—that they are sharing the perils of our lads at the front
—soldiers, sailors and airmen, God bless them—and are drawing away
from them a part at least of the onslaught they have to bear.[1]

A week later, on the day before the decision was taken to withdraw
the B.E.F. from France, the Chiefs of Staff reviewed the nation's
prospects on the assumption that French resistance would collapse.
There were three ways, they affirmed, in which Germany could
defeat Britain—unrestricted air attack aimed at breaking morale,
starvation through attack on our shipping and ports, and occupation
by invasion.

The crux of the problem lay in Britain's air defences. If France
fell, the Germans would be free to concentrate their whole air
force against this country. This was thought to consist of nearly
2,000 long-range bombers, 550 dive-bombers, 1,550 heavy and
light fighters and a number of coastal aircraft; and facilities for
expanding this force would be greatly increased. Enemy occupation
of Norway had already exposed north-east Scotland, with its naval
bases, to a larger scale of attack. The greater catastrophe would
enable the enemy, from bases stretching from Norway to Brittany,
to send long-range bombers against any part of the British Isles,
including the approaches to all West Coast, Scottish and Irish ports.
Dive-bombers and long-range fighters could penetrate England to a
line drawn from Cardiff to Grimsby, and short-range fighters could
reach the Home Counties. The enemy's ability to concentrate a very
large number of bombers, with fighter escort, over a big area of
Britain, including the industrial Midlands and all probable landing-
areas on the coasts, would constitute a threat the seriousness of which
could not be overstressed.

To counter these formidable forces Britain could muster a home-
based fighter force of rather more than 700 first-line aircraft, backed
by about 230 in reserves immediately available. The production
of fighters was not keeping pace with losses, and much of this was
concentrated in two cities, Birmingham and Coventry. Although
aerodromes and landing grounds were well dispersed, the R.A.F.
ground organisation had serious weaknesses in relation to the new
scale of attack. What had now become its flanks had inadequate
radar cover; and balloon protection was insufficient even for vital
points. The tactics and equipment of defensive night-fighting were
still rudimentary.

The nation's morale, the Chiefs of Staff affirmed, would under the
circumstances they were considering be subjected to a far heavier
strain than ever before. As regards civil defence, they stated that as
long as 'the present quasi-peacetime organisation' continued there

---

[1] Charles Eade (Ed.), *The War Speeches of the Rt. Hon. Winston S. Churchill* (1951),
Vol. I, p. 184.

was 'no guarantee that this country could hold out'. What they called (somewhat loosely) 'the Home Security Organisation' was not constituted to deal with the problems arising from a combination of heavy air attack, invasion and fifth column activities. It was essential to organise the country as a fortress. In particular, (i) the operational control of all civil defence forces, including the police, should be removed from local authorities, vested in the Ministry of Home Security and exercised through the Regional Commissioners, (ii) all enemy aliens and other doubtful persons should be interned, and (iii) all evacuation or movement of refugees should be forbidden.

As the reader is aware, the conditions for which the Chiefs of Staff were prescribing rapidly became true. The 'deliverance of Dunkirk' was completed on 4th June. On that day Mr Churchill informed the House of Commons and the world that 'we shall go on to the end . . . we shall fight in the fields and in the streets . . . we shall never surrender'.[1] By 18th June the Battle of France was over and Britain stood alone. Mr Churchill thereupon proposed to his compatriots that they should 'brace themselves according to their duties'. In his references in this broadcast to bombing attack he said:

> I do not at all underrate the severity of the ordeal which lies before us; but I believe our countrymen . . . will be able to stand up to it, and carry on in spite of it, at least as well as any other people in the world. Much will depend upon this. . . . For all of us, at this time, it will be a help to remember the famous lines:
>
>> 'He nothing common did or mean,
>> Upon that memorable scene'.[2]

In a full-dress debate on 12th June the Home Secretary concluded his account of civil defence with the remark that this whole problem had 'taken a new turn as a result of the course of development of the war'.[3] Two things of special significance to this narrative were occurring: first, a revival of the nation's spirits, and second, the creation or improvisation of much new machinery for home defence. The gravity of the situation, new leadership, new decisiveness at many points combined to produce the result that the British people now 'passionately attached themselves to the war. This was the great transforming fact, the motive power of all subsequent achievement. A united Government and people made victory their watchword'.[4]

This upsurge of morale was, for the average citizen, accompanied

---

[1] H. of C. Deb., Vol. 361, Col. 796.

[2] Charles Eade (Ed.), *The War Speeches of the Rt. Hon. Winston S. Churchill* (1951), Vol. I, pp. 198–207.

[3] H. of C. Deb., Vol. 361, Col. 1297.

[4] W. K. Hancock and M. M. Gowing, *op. cit.*, p. 209.

by ignorance of all but the broadcast military facts. This ignorance must be underlined in any account of air attacks, and with reference not merely to the summer of 1940 but to all later stages of the war. The demands of security in its special sense, it has already been mentioned, became austere.[1] The machinery, apart from the will, for disseminating information was often deficient. Events in the military sphere might succeed one another with great speed, or be non-existent. For these and other reasons the ordinary British civilian usually had only the broadest knowledge either of the dangers threatening him from the air or of the attacks that had actually been delivered.

The reorganisation of central government which took place during these weeks is not, for the most part, the concern of this narrative.[2] But it must be noted that G.H.Q., Home Forces and its subordinate formations now found themselves potentially 'in the field'. On 14th May the Local Defence Volunteers (soon rechristened the Home Guard) were formed as a supplement for defence of the island to the regular army. In less than eight weeks these volunteers numbered over 1,000,000. They were drawn, it is important to note, from the same classes of male citizens which had volunteered for civil defence. Like the part-time members of civil defence, they received small allowances but no pay. But unlike these, they were (at least in theory) armed, and were subject when on duty to military law and discipline.

The structure of civil defence described in an earlier chapter was not in essentials altered.[3] But it needs to be emphasised, first that the military, and more especially the army, organisation in Britain assumed greatly enlarged responsibilities and authority; secondly, that many civil authorities, central and local, acquired large duties in the sphere of repelling invasion. This threat, the reader must be reminded, took the two broad forms of (i) large-scale seaborne invasion, with the enemy air force acting in support of the naval and ground forces, and (ii) smaller-scale airborne invasion or raids on vital points and elsewhere. In connection with these and with other threats such as sabotage, the Home Office and other civil Departments had new and varied responsibilities in what may either be called 'civil defence' in its broadest sense or 'home defence'.[4]

The functions of the Ministry of Home Security, however, remained those of co-ordinating and administering civil defence against air attack. The important development to be noticed here was the clothing of the Civil Defence Regional Commissioners with

---

[1] p. 299.

[2] See W. K. Hancock and M. M. Gowing, *op. cit.*, Chapter VIII.

[3] Chapter VII above.

[4] p. 301.

new powers, and still more with new functions, in the larger field. The Emergency Powers (Defence) Act, 1940, passed on 22nd May, had extended the powers conferred on the Government at the opening of war to almost complete control over persons and property.[1] Defence Regulation 16A of 31st May empowered Regional Commissioners to issue orders in any Defence Area or to control entry into such an area for hindering enemy attack or protecting the persons and property endangered by such attack.[2] The exercise of these powers, which embraced various specific matters such as the closing of roads, immobilisation of cars and vessels and a curfew, was subject to the control and direction of the Minister of Home Security.

These powers in the event of invasion can only be mentioned to suggest the way in which the Commissioners' scope of activities and responsibilities widened. In the narrower sphere of defence against air attack legal powers were, for the first time, conferred on the Commissioners by Defence Regulation 29A of 31st May.[3] This conferred on 'the appropriate Minister' the express power to direct local authorities in all their civil defence functions under the Acts of 1937 and 1939. The Minister of Home Security, after consulting the Minister of Health, delegated to Commissioners the power to control and direct all operations of the Civil Defence Services in their Regions. This included the power to require the local authorities to co-operate in preparing reinforcement schemes.[4] The authorities were not, however, relieved of responsibility for the local control and efficiency of their services.

A recommendation of the Chiefs of Staff on 19th June for larger immediate transfer of civil control to the Commissioners was not approved by the War Cabinet. Some powers conferred on them regarding shelters will be noticed later. And by a series of Orders during the following weeks all Civil Defence Regions were progressively declared Defence Areas. What must finally be stressed is the expansion of the functions, as distinct from the powers, of Commissioners, particularly in the south and east of the island. In the growing number of home defence or anti-invasion tasks liaison with military commanders naturally assumed much importance and various new forms.[5]

A form, at the highest official level, of such liaison needs special mention, particularly as it continued throughout the war. A body entitled the Home Defence Executive was created under the chair-

---

[1] 3 and 4 Geo. 6, Ch. 20.
[2] S.R. & O. 1940, No. 842.
[3] S.R. & O. 1940, No. 845; H.S.C. 114/40, 2nd June 1940.
[4] See Chapter XIV below.
[5] pp. 311–312.

manship of the Commander-in-Chief, Home Forces, on 11th May, and reformed under the chairmanship of Sir Findlater Stewart early in June. The new chairman combined this office with the post of Chief Civil Staff Officer to the Commander-in-Chief, Home Forces. The Executive was in fact a co-ordinating committee, meeting frequently and attended by representatives of the Ministry of Home Security and many other civil Departments. Its proposals, which usually called for prompt action, were given effect by the ordinary processes of command in the case of the Services and of administrative action in that of the civil Departments. Among its pre-occupations air attack, in the earlier years of the war, ranked relatively small; although after the onset of the blitz the chairman often attended meetings of the Civil Defence Committee.[1]

Widespread but Light Attack

On 10th May a single German plane made the first attack of the war on Britain's mainland by dropping bombs near the villages of Petham and Chilham, a few miles from Canterbury. No casualties or damage resulted. A phase of more offensive reconnaissance by the enemy then opened and continued until early July. While the *Luftwaffe* moved to bases in France and Belgium and regrouped its formations, single or small formations of aircraft penetrated with growing frequency over Britain to reconnoitre ports and airfields, test our defences, provide the enemy pilots with training and cause general disturbance. Though only as a by-product of these pre-invasion activities, the air attack on the civil population had in fact begun.

The reader must here be reminded of the need imposed on this narrative to record the attacks in a summary and mainly quantitative manner. This need does not arise simply from considerations of space. The reader is already aware of the part which planning, administrative action and many other forms of preparation in advance of the event played in civil defence. If time, the consumption of effort and of material resources are the criteria to be followed, these processes, which continued until victory was gained, appear to the historian as the major share of the iceberg, with the assaults actually delivered by the enemy as only that smaller share which appears above the surface. This perspective is further supported by the fact, which is now common knowledge, that the possibilities of attack from the air which the Germans from time to time were fully capable of delivering were considerably larger than those they actually made. If 'what matters most in history is not what happened, but what people said about it when it was happening'[2] and—it may be

---

[1] The Executive was prominent in planning against 'V-weapon' attack; see Chapter XV.

[2] G. M. Young, *Last Essays* (1950), p. 9.

added—thought was going to happen, then the emphasis given by this narrative to administration in its broadest sense is justified.

But the historian of this segment of war has, nevertheless, to face the fact that when a mine-laying German bomber was shot down on 30th April with its mines still on board over Clacton-on-Sea it obviously mattered to the two civilians killed, the hundred and sixty-two persons injured and the owners of property damaged to the extent of £100,000. This, though not a deliberate attack, was the first serious incident in England involving the A.R.P. services, which acquitted themselves with credit.[1] Every subsequent attack which succeeded in causing death, injury, or damage to property in some form mattered to individuals and, usually more remotely, to the State. This appears to be the appropriate place to warn the reader that neither the toll of human suffering nor the physical damage can be adequately measured by the statistics employed in this and later chapters.

For other reasons, arising from the nature of the matter and worth emphasising at this stage, the statistics give an inadequate picture. No two bombs, it is almost certain, ever fell on the same spot; and no two incidents were the same. It is also probably true that no single incident ever looked the same to any two persons who observed it. This carrying of the argument to extremes may serve the purpose of stressing the significance of the activities, including reporting, of the warden, police constable or other man on the spot. The fullest description of any incident was that given *sur place* by the warden reporting, usually by telephone, to his local control centre. Inevitably the subsequent processes of reporting upwards by control centres to Region and thence to the Home Security War Room involved progressive compression. Even if no allowance is made for the factor of error in these transactions, the written summary in the form finally composed at the centre was only a very partial account.

Ministers, Regional Commissioners and senior officials did, of course, often go to the scene of an attack to view the situation for themselves. But Ministers and officials in Whitehall had normally to base their decisions on the summaries and statistics here under discussion. The incompleteness of these must therefore be viewed as a handicap or even (in a political sense) a hazard of modern aerial warfare.

The word 'incident', it must here be remarked, became once war had started another technical term in the field of civil defence. It was generally substituted, as shorter and more attractive, for the word previously printed on wardens' report forms, 'occurrence'. As Mr John Strachey has mentioned, from personal experience as a London warden, 'the word is wonderfully colourless, dry and remote;

---

[1] *The Times*, 2nd May 1940.

it touches nothing which it does not minimise'.[1] The point to be emphasised in the present context is that it covered events ranging in significance from the destruction by enemy bombs of two foxes to the major disaster in March 1943 at Bethnal Green underground station, when 178 people were killed and 62 injured.

During the month which followed 10th May air attack was described by the Ministry of Home Security as more systematic. Bombs, both high explosive and incendiary, were dropped by single or a few enemy aircraft on seven nights. The total was calculated at about 240 H.E.s and 700 I.B.s. The targets were still predominantly on the eastern and southern coasts. Some military objectives, for example at Southampton, were machine-gunned. Only ten or so civilians were injured; and the damage caused was very slight. Middlesbrough was the first industrial town, and Dorman and Long's works the first industrial plant, to be bombed. Catterick was the first airfield to be attacked, and Northallerton the first place on Britain's railway system to suffer damage.

During the next month, from early June to early July, the enemy became more persistent. Raids, though still minor in terms of their effects, were more frequent and more widely spread. From 18th June they began to take place every night, and in early July by day as well. East Anglian airfields, some Midland industrial areas and Aberdeen were now included as targets. On 19th June Cambridge was the first English town (apart from the Clacton episode) to report a serious incident, with nine fatal casualties. On the same night Croydon was the first town in London Region to be bombed. On 28th June the enemy bombed the Channel Islands by daylight, killing thirty civilians and injuring forty. A determined attack by twenty aircraft, which caused some damage, was made on Portland Dockyard on 4th July.

During this month over 2,000 H.E.s and about 5,000 I.B.s were reported. The majority of the former were of the 50 kg. type, with the 250 k.g. type next in importance. A considerable number of bombs had failed to explode; and some delayed-action and some whistling bombs had been used. The toll in human fatality was 150 persons killed and 640 injured. Material damage, though not negligible, was considered by the experts to be slight in relation to the tonnage of bombs delivered. And the accuracy of the enemy's bombing was a good deal lower than had been expected.

Evacuation

The threat, as distinct from the attacks, introduced in May caused large complications, both human and administrative, regarding

---

[1] John Strachey, *Post D.* (1941).

evacuation. Though the schemes, and their consequences, for official evacuation of private citizens in this phase have been fully described by Mr Titmuss, some brief attention to them is required here.[1] The new scheme for official evacuation, now limited to 670,000 children, from London and other target areas announced in February had met with a poor response.[2] The onrush of events in May not merely upset the greater part of this scheme but compelled the Government to order the removal from the new danger areas on the south and east coasts of the London children who had been evacuated there. During May and June about 25,000 children of this class were removed from the coasts of East Anglia, Kent and Sussex.

The next stage was the removal, in all from thirty-one towns, of children who normally lived in these areas to South Wales and the Midlands. This was on a voluntary basis though it was encouraged by the closing of all State schools. New plans to evacuate children of school age, unaccompanied by their mothers, were then hurriedly recast, first for London and Thames-side and then for towns on the south and north-east coasts. By 1st August roughly 213,000 children had been moved from these centres to safer areas. At the end of June a new scheme for moving mothers with children under five years old was introduced. This was known as 'assisted private evacuation', since the onus of finding accommodation lay with the parents while the Government provided free travel vouchers and billeting allowances to the householder.

The main fact which concerns this narrative is the small response of parents affected by this offer until the bombing of London began in September. Most of those, Mr Titmuss concludes, who took advantage of it lived in the coastal areas; and 'during July and August, when the Battle of Britain was being fought and daylight raids were made on many towns, there was no significant demand for the evacuation of children to safer areas'.[3]

The story of movement, and lack of movement, by private citizens during these months must include a few further facts. A considerable number of British parents, according to the same authority, sent their children overseas under the official arrangements which ended abruptly with the sinking of the *City of Benares* on 17th September.[4] About 30,000 civilians from the Continent, a further 29,000 from the Channel Islands and some 10,500 Gibraltarians entered Britain before the end of the year.

Business firms were advised by the Government late in May to

---

[1] R. M. Titmuss, *op. cit.*, Chapter XIII.

[2] p. 328.

[3] R. M.Titmuss, *op cit.*, p. 248.

[4] By 15th August the Children's Overseas Reception Board had approved applications for 19,365 children, 99 per cent. of whom were attending State-aided schools.

take the opportunity of the lull to evacuate staffs from London, though with the familiar proviso that such action should not be taken if it would cause a serious loss of efficiency.[1] Some weeks later, when the policy of eliminating all unnecessary movement was clearly established, the Government discouraged business or other large-scale private evacuation; and emphasised that there was now no intention, except in the case of extreme necessity, of moving the seat of Government from London.

The interaction of the different types of evacuation on the psychological plane had always been evident to those concerned with the problem in Whitehall. By this stage of the war the interaction of evacuation of business firms and of Government staffs had become more pronounced on various other planes. Growing sections of industry, for example, were at work for the Government and the Supply Departments naturally wished their representatives to be close at hand. In spite of changes of policy in this matter, to be noticed later, it seems probable that the movement of firms of any size out of London slowed down. 'The scale of private evacuation' (which of course included more than business), states Mr Titmuss, 'diminished as the war went on at least as markedly as did the volume of official evacuation, and possibly in greater measure.[2]

The removal of the seat of Government or the 'black move', which had hitherto caused such complications, was now abandoned.[3] And it is of interest to record that British Ministers were impressed by the highly unfortunate consequence of the moves of the French Government from Paris to Tours and thence to Bordeaux, both for French morale and for the conduct of official business. The new strategical situation, with the German Air Force establishing bases on the Channel coast, made it obvious that the West Country had become vulnerable to air attack. It was decided that if the Government should be driven out of Whitehall by such attack they would move temporarily to other quarters within the defended area of London. The accommodation earmarked in the West Country was to be used for military and other staffs not required in London.

The problem of evacuating the less-essential Government staffs (the 'yellow move'), which had caused almost equal complications, was now, in its largest administrative and political aspects, resolved.[4] Under the altered conditions the opposition both of certain Ministers and of the majority of the staffs involved appears to have melted away. It became necessary to speed up this type of evacuation for two additional reasons—the great difficulty of finding accommodation

---

[1] pp. 327–328.
[2] R. M. Titmuss, *op cit.*, p. 356.
[3] pp. 326–327.
[4] pp. 327–328.

in London for a rapidly expanding Civil Service, and the increased need to retain premises earmarked in the provinces for the possible later use of more essential branches or Departments. By 5th June a total of some 30,000 officials had been evacuated under the 'yellow move'.

Movement of this character continued on a piecemeal basis to a growing number of centres in the north, west and south of the country. Choice of such centres, it may be mentioned, was one matter about which civil Departments sought the advice of the Home Defence Executive.[1] The grounds for complaint by hotel-keepers and others with property standing empty began to dissolve; though the Press caused the Government concern by wrongly suggesting that the move, for example, of Ministry of Food staffs to North Wales heralded a general move of the Government from London. Problems of transportation, accommodation, billeting and welfare confronting the Office of Works and other Departments, it must be added, continued to prove extensive.

Warnings: the 'Alarm' becomes an 'Alert'

The widespread attack by night caused a prompt reaction by the Government in the matter of warnings. During the last week of June many parts of the country came under red warnings for long periods. War production began seriously to suffer. Night workers obeyed the instructions to shelter, and day workers suffered from loss of sleep. A short experiment by A.O.C.-in-C., Fighter Command in restricting red warnings offered no solution, since factories relied on these to extinguish exempted external lighting, and failing such notification they offered the enemy targets conveniently lighted up.

The War Cabinet decided that, while examination into the possibility of modifying the system proceeded, workers in factories should be asked to continue at work after the red warning and not to seek shelter until they heard the sound of gunfire or bombs. On 2nd July the Home Secretary announced what was, in effect, a considerable shift from a policy of safety first to one of production first. 'In order to defeat any efforts by the enemy to dislocate production in our war industries', he said, 'workers engaged in war production should be encouraged . . . to continue at work after a public air-raid warning until it is clear than an enemy attack is actually imminent in their neighbourhood.'[2]

The next modification was the introduction on 25th July of a 'purple' message as a lights warning. This was to be issued to districts

---

[1] pp. 357–358.
[2] H. of C. Deb., Vol. 362, Col. 660.

in the raiders' track which were not expected to be the object of serious attack; on its receipt all exempted outside lighting was to be extinguished but no other action taken, except the action appropriate to a 'yellow' if that message had not already been received. Since it was necessary for practical reasons to limit the total number of messages to four, the 'green' (raiders passed) message had now to be combined with the 'white' (cancel caution). Siren operators had hitherto sounded the 'all-clear' on receiving 'green', and the new arrangements would, it was foreseen, inevitably sometimes mean the sounding of an 'all-clear' when no public warning (or red) had been given. The new message would allow work inside factories to continue and reduce interference with sleep. Though it would, of course, impede outside work and slow down rail transport.[1]

Neither the Home Secretary's statement nor the new 'purple' warning provided an immediate solution. Reduction of public warnings increased the risk of bombs without warning, which factory workers disliked as much as other people; and workers were insistent that their families should be adequately warned.[2] Protracted conferences between the Government, the British Employers' Federation and the T.U.C. followed, and culminated in arrangements which carry the story of this topic to the opening of the Battle of London in early September.

Public warnings or, as the Prime Minister described them, 'prolonged banshee howlings' were still to be sounded freely. But the red warning, he told Parliament on 5th September, was now to be regarded 'more in the nature of a general alert than a warning of the imminence of danger to any particular locality'.[3] It was also decided by the War Cabinet on 10th September that both the red or 'alert' (as it now was) and the sounding of the 'all clear' should be reduced in time from two minutes to one minute.[4]

The industrial problem, the core of the matter, was to be solved by creating what, in effect, was an industrial warning system within the public one. Roof watchers, described by the Prime Minister as 'Jim Crows or lookout men', were to be trained to give the alarm in factories and similar places when immediate danger was expected at any point. The Royal Air Force began to train A.R.P. Instructors from each Region, who then organised area training classes. This process naturally took time; workers were by no means universally enthusiastic over the scheme, and problems were set for many factories by the fact that their shelters had been sited on the original basis of a five-minute warning period.

---

[1] H.S.Cs. 170, 180, 181/40, 10th, 18th, 19th July 1940.
[2] pp. 317–318.
[3] H. of C. Deb., Vol. 365, Cols. 45–6.
[4] A leaflet, with a message by the Prime Minister, called 'Working after the Siren' was issued at the end of August. (H.S.C. 219/40, 26th August 1940.)

Some other developments, or refinements of the system born from experience, require notice here. After the fall of France it was found that enemy planes operating on or near the coasts caused much disturbance over inland areas included in certain warning districts. Some adjustments to districts were therefore made in September, causing the total number to be increased from 111 to 116. Another development was the institution during these weeks at Fighter Command of a 'sensitive list' of towns which asked to be given early warnings, or red warnings on the approach of single enemy planes. Norwich, for example, had experienced a good many reds without bombs and several minor attacks without any sounding of sirens. As it would defeat the purpose in view to keep towns on this list too long, Regional Commissioners were to be periodically consulted about its revision.

Bogus warning messages were still enough of a nuisance to justify the Ministry addressing a circular on this matter in early June to Chief Officers of Police.[1] The introduction, described in an earlier chapter, of remote control of sirens elsewhere than in London was proceeding.[2] It may, finally, be noticed here that the interference caused by war with the sounds which the public was used to hearing was increased in the middle of June by the prohibition throughout the country of all ringing of church bells except as a warning by the military authorities of parachutist or other airborne attack.[3]

Mention must also be made of the black-out and the topic, related to it in this narrative, of restrictions on various kinds of amusement. Naturally summer, with summer-time added, much reduced the hardships of the black-out for the majority of the public. Members of the Fighting and Civil Defence Services were acquiring some experience of performing their duties in night-raiding under black-out conditions. The next chapter in the history of this matter opened with a request by the Prime Minister in August for a thorough and urgent review of ways in which a policy of 'black-out' might be modified into one of 'blackable-out' in the approaching winter. The conclusions of this will be noted later. But it must be mentioned that they merged in September with plans to elaborate still further the new warning arrangements by creating more effective local alarm systems within the general alert.[4]

The 'Dunkirk spirit' which now pervaded the country manifested itself, among other ways, in considerable demands for the restriction

---

[1] H.S.C. 117/40, 4th June 1940.

[2] p. 319.

[3] H.S.C. 129/40, 13th June 1940. The Control of Noise Order passed on the outbreak of war prohibited all noises, including church bells, which might be confused with air-raid warnings.

[4] See Chapter X.

of racing and other sports.[1] Strong support, for example, was reported from mining districts for severe limitation of the 'dogs'. Though this attitude was now based less on the air threat and more on grounds of industrial output and the need to save foodstuffs and petrol and set an example of abstinence, the Ministers concerned had still to resolve the problem of pursuing such aims without unduly depressing the morale of workers and others. The Home Secretary was averse to violent fluctuations of policy, or return to the severe limitations of the earliest months of the war, in this matter. In the outcome racing was considerably curtailed, though the Derby (for which plans had been made long before) was run at Newmarket with little publicity. Appeals were made to private motorists to refrain as much as possible from using their cars for pleasure. But no important changes were made in the arrangements, outlined in the previous chapter, regarding theatres, cinemas and football matches.[2]

Shelters

Adopting the arrangement of the previous chapter, discussion of shelters may be preceded by brief attention to anti-gas defence.[3] An American journalist reporting day-by-day events in Britain noted that when Germany invaded Denmark and Norway 'gas-masks began to appear again'.[4] The problems in this sphere had become mainly those of maintenance of masks and other equipment through all the stages from production to care by the individual, and of an adequate level of training and of public consciousness of this threat.

The fitting of 'contex' to the millions of masks in possession of the public continued during these weeks to occupy the attention of wardens and others.[5] The inspection initiated in March of these masks, also by wardens, continued at varying speeds up and down the country. By gas-vans, gas-chambers and similar means citizens were invited to test their masks under battle conditions; they were also asked by the authorities to make a habit of wearing their masks for a quarter of an hour each week. The masks of school-children evacuated under the official scheme which had been lost or damaged were replaced without charge. Guidance was issued by the Ministry in July regarding destruction of masks worn by persons with certain infectious or contagious diseases.[6] Supplies of masks for the Civil Defence Services were steadily improving; and those of anti-gas

---

[1] e.g., H. of C. Deb., Vol. 361, Cols. 1368-9, 13th June 1940.

[2] pp. 323-324.

[3] pp. 329-332.

[4] E. R. Murrow, *This is London* (1941).

[5] p. 332.

[6] H.S.C. 159/40, 5th July 1940.

ointment for these Services had been completed. The Home Secretary stated on 18th July that he was about to instruct local authorities which had not already done so to install gas-curtains in public shelters or have these readily available.[1]

A few days earlier the Prime Minister had issued instructions for a general overhaul of gas-masks, adding 'it may well be Hitler has some gas designs upon us'.[2] The Ministry thereupon asked its Regional Principal Officers to take steps to remind the local authorities and the public of the importance of maintaining adequate preparations against this form of attack.[3]

The new course of the war further stressed the need to complete the large, diversified, shelter programme in the shortest possible time.[4] The reduction of official evacuation had already enlarged the obligation on the authorities to provide shelter in the main target areas. After 10th May the enemy's rapid progress caused urgent demands from the public and local authorities in areas hitherto regarded as safe for inclusion in the Government's shelter schemes. What followed was to prove, in the words of a Regional Officer, 'a most difficult period for all concerned with shelter provision'. Apart from certain areas (for example Newcastle Region where miners were available) labour suitable for this purpose was now at a premium. In the south and east there was large-scale diversion of cement and other essential materials to military purposes. Elsewhere supplies of steel for basement-strutting and so on were reported by Regional Officers to have practically vanished.

The Government, while not prepared to admit that existing financial arrangements were a legitimate cause for local delay, took further steps to decentralise approval of schemes. Assistant Chief Engineers from the Ministry were 'planted out' at Regional headquarters with large powers of approval, Regional technical staffs were further enlarged, and responsibility for approving London shelter schemes was transferred in July from the Ministry to London Region. On 1st June the Home Secretary assured Parliament—which was once more showing strong interest in shelters—that he would make full use of the powers conferred on him by Defence Regulation 29A to give local authorities directions relating to their civil defence obligations. Shortly afterwards he delegated to Regional Commissioners the power to give the authorities either general or detailed instructions concerning shelter provision. He asked the Commissioners to concentrate their urgent attention on the most backward areas, to ensure that new construction conformed as far as

---

[1] H. of C. Deb., Vol. 363, Col. 383.

[2] W. S. Churchill, op. cit., Vol. II, p. 569.

[3] H.S.R. 137/40, 29th July 1940.

[4] pp. 332–340.

AA

possible to standard designs and prices and to refrain from issuing formal directions except as a last resort.[1]

Though more than 2,000,000 free 'Andersons' had been distributed by the opening of this phase, a good deal of evidence had accumulated of wastage. Allegations in Parliament and the Press that large numbers had not been erected and that components were lying about and rusting had grown frequent. The scepticism which had prevailed during the winter had undoubtedly caused neglect by the public, and the Government had taken too sanguine a view of the ability of citizens to erect these shelters by self-help.[2] Though some authorities, for example Hackney and other London Boroughs, had organised teams of their employees or volunteers to help householders with erection, these were still the exception. Bristol Region now reported small progress throughout its whole area in this matter, and said that Bristol city had recently had to undertake responsibility for erecting all 'Andersons'.

At the end of May the Government was compelled to act drastically in this matter. All to whom free 'Andersons' had been issued were now compelled under Defence Regulation 23B either to erect and cover them adequately within ten days, or to inform their local authority why they had not done this.[3] If a householder was genuinely incapable of erecting his shelter, the local authority was to do so for him. Otherwise, the authority was to collect the materials, and either issue them to someone else or store them as a reserve.

Much improvement seems to have ensued.[4] And a good deal of redistribution began, which included the delivery of several thousand shelters to the non-specified areas. During the scattered but small-scale attacks of these weeks the 'Anderson' proved even more effective than the authorities had promised. The public, as yet, had little need or inclination to seek shelter beyond their own homes. Those under attack who possessed this type of protection experienced, nevertheless, solid grounds for comfort.

The Government and local authorities were concentrating their efforts regarding domestic shelter on the communal shelters, or structures of brick and concrete to protect twelve or so families from a group of adjoining houses.[5] The Government had undertaken to pay the full cost of materials used on these; while the public surface shelters—which, being of the same design and capacity, were frequently confused with the communal—were only grant-aided. The Parliamentary Secretary to the Ministry of Home Security told

---

[1] H.S.C. 133/40, 13th June 1940.
[2] H. of C. Deb., Vol. 358, Cols. 1359–60.
[3] H.S.C. 111/40, 30th May 1940.
[4] e.g., in Nottingham Region, etc.
[5] p. 335.

Parliament after the fall of France that a very considerable increase had been made in the number of communal shelters in readiness.[1] But this progress was, it transpired later, being made at the expense of a serious and widespread sacrifice of quality. The causes of this need some, necessarily much-condensed, explanation.

Soon after the outbreak of war the Government had given instructions that lime, in the ratio of two parts to one part of cement, should be used as much as possible for mortar used in the masonry of all surface shelters, and the British Standards Institution had issued a lime-mortar specification for this purpose. Such action, the Government hoped, would both help to ease the pressing demands on cement, and also (since lime-producing firms were widely distributed) reduce the demands of the shelter programme on national transport. The Ministry issued new instructions in April 1940 about domestic surface shelters; and some ambiguous wording in these were construed by large numbers of borough engineers and builders as permission to use mortar consisting of lime and sand only, and this in the construction not only of domestic surface shelters but also of communal and public shelters.[2] Though the Ministry issued fresh instructions in July which clearly forbade the use of ungauged lime mortar, considerable damage, as events were to prove, had been done.[3] After some months of bombing it was found that many surface shelters needed strengthening or even rebuilding. In London Region alone well over 5,000 of these had been built with ungauged lime mortar; and in Bristol Region it was found necessary early in 1941 to strengthen, or demolish and rebuild, some 4,000 shelters built in this way.

Much activity was also taking place over public shelters. Though a large number of trenches were ready, this 'most primitive and uncomfortable form of protection' as a Regional Officer now described them, had fallen further from favour.[4] Experience had shown that supplies of lining materials were erratic, that trenches might vary in cost from about 25s. (in Cheltenham) to as much as £5 per head (in Bristol) and that they were difficult to keep waterproof. Chief attention was now being paid to converting all types of buildings. The Government told the local authorities in June that they might quickly provide more public shelters by demolishing derelict buildings above first floor level and strutting their ceilings

---

[1] H. of C. Deb., Vol. 362, Col. 443, 26th June 1940.

[2] Memorandum No. 14, *Domestic Surface Shelters*, 29th April 1940. The instructions themselves mentioned only the use of lime and sand in the preparation of mortar, but they included a reference to the previous B.S.I. specification which showed that a gauging of cement was required.

[3] It was unfortunate that these did not refer to the previous ambiguity but took the form of new instructions.

[4] pp. 336-337.

and strengthening their walls.[1] The need for authorities to give notice before building public shelters on highways was suspended.[2] The heterogeneous assortment of buildings being brought into use for this purpose included, so far as the Government knew, about 250 church crypts and halls, though these were regarded officially as of very limited value as protection.

Attempts were being made to improve the inadequate shelter at London's main railway stations. It was only when Russia's bombing of Finland had confirmed the idea that railway stations would be high on the list of targets that the authorities began to pay much attention to this problem. Though several railway companies had made arrangements for passengers to shelter in their termini they were under no legal obligation to do this. A survey in February 1940 of the shelter in or near fourteen London stations showed that this was totally insufficient for the numbers who would be in the neighbourhood during peak travelling hours. Enough shelters, it was decided, should be provided on station premises for the equivalent of ten minutes' flow of passengers at peak hours; and the borough councils concerned were asked late in May to provide these on the same financial terms as other public shelters. The railway companies, for the most part, co-operated readily in making parts of stations available as shelters, though some councils complained of excessive rent charges. The local authorities began to take active measures. By mid-July work on these shelters was under way in all the important London stations, though this was by no means complete when the Battle of London began in September. The Government had, in the meanwhile, decided that similar action should be taken at some of the principal stations in provincial cities.

The areas not so far specified—or roughly the towns which contained no industry and the rural parts of the country—had, as mentioned earlier, begun to press claims for inclusion in the Government's shelter schemes. Though the Act of 1939 had obliged the counties and county boroughs in these areas to provide some public shelter, no more than a few had done so.[3] An attempt was now made on a limited scale to catch up with this work. For example, the Leeds Regional Commissioner used his new powers to direct the provision of public shelter in certain medium-sized Yorkshire towns; and the Ministry urged other Commissioners to take similar action. The Government, however, made it quite clear that most of the inhabitants of these areas would have to rely mainly on self-help.[4] They gave much emphasis to fresh advice distributed to all

---

[1] H.S.C. 120/40, 6th June 1940.

[2] H.S.C. 144/40, 24th June 1940.

[3] pp. 197-198.

[4] H. of C. Deb., Vol. 362, Cols. 987–90, 4th July 1940.

householders in May in the form of a booklet, *Your Home as an Air Raid Shelter.*[1] This stated that an ordinary soundly-built house would offer very substantial protection; and it gave those unable to build some form of shelter much detailed guidance on the preparation of refuge rooms, the protection of windows and so on. In contrast to the similar but more simple instructions issued at Munich, this, since all adults and children now possessed gas-masks, placed little emphasis on the need for householders to gas-proof their rooms.[2]

In the full-dress debate of 12th June Parliament again showed predominant interest in shelters, though security (in its special sense) now imposed a definite restraint on discussion of this topic.[3] Sir John Anderson stated that the original shelter programme which, as Lord Privy Seal, he had launched in December 1938 had now been achieved.[4] Sufficient shelter of the blast and splinter-proof standard was in readiness up and down the country for some 20,000,000 persons—and he justly claimed this to be 'an outstanding fact'. The central and local authorities had fulfilled their original plans for domestic and public shelters. In the 12,000 factories concerned, and also to a large extent in the mines, shelter schemes had been put into full effect. The Government had completed the standard shelter for their numerous offices in the danger zones. Eight months of respite had given the Research and Experiments Department the time for much further experiment, and also provided Regional staffs and local authorities with valuable experience. But though the original aims had been reached, the sights had now been set higher. The Minister stated that the Government were still pressing forward to improve upon the existing provision, to speed up distribution and to fill various gaps.

He then proceeded to deal with the matter which, it seems undoubted, had been the most controversial issue in civil defence since Munich. The plans for evacuation had since early in 1939 won the confidence of the public; and these, under the unforeseen conditions of months of immunity from attack, had in fact proved too comprehensive. But the Government's basic shelter plan—the provision of widespread, but only moderate, protection—had from its inception been regarded in some quarters as misconceived and totally inadequate. In the six months preceding war the demand for some system of 'deep' or 'strong' shelters had been steadily growing, and after a few months of war this had begun to revive.[5] In December 1939 the unofficial A.R.P. Co-ordinating Committee, which led the

---

[1] H.S.C. 98/40, 22nd May 1940.

[2] p. 163.

[3] H. of C. Deb., Vol. 361, Cols. 1277–1354.

[4] pp. 170-171.

[5] pp. 198-199.

attack on the Government over this matter, had put forward a method of greatly strengthening shelters which came to be known as the building of 'two-stage shelters'.[1] The Government, though not entirely excluding this plan, had emphasised that the immediate necessity was to concentrate on the programme already in hand. Sir John Anderson claimed in the debate just referred to that the Government's basic policy had been fully justified. Had they, he stated, adopted the deep shelter proposals, 'we should at this moment have been in a far worse position . . . than we are today. The country would have been caught with a very limited amount of shelter in course of construction and not completed'. He had again consulted both employers and workers on this issue; and the workers had expressed a definite reluctance to be given better shelter than that available to their families. The experience, already considerable, of warnings was suggesting that the original estimate that anyone would have from 5 to $7\frac{1}{2}$ minutes in which to reach shelters was a good deal too optimistic. The public was also about to be issued with stirrup pumps, in the hope that they would take an active part in preventing fires. And the Minister referred, more openly than he had hitherto done, to the Government's earnest desire to avoid the creation of a 'deep shelter mentality'.

This issue was to revive in new and stronger forms after some months' experience of heavy raiding.[2] But it was, for the time being, closed by the Government's statement early in July that there was no longer time to undertake the construction of any 'two-stage shelters'.[3] The second (or war-time) phase of shelter provision was at this date about to close, and the first phase of widespread shelter use was about to open.

The Services:
the First Taste of Action and of Compulsion

The A.R.P. Services, which in the last resort were but a cross-section of the nation's more mature civilians, shared in the upsurge of morale which took place in May.[4] Stand-by had, after the months of waiting, been succeeded by new stand-to. The scattered light raiding up and down the country caused, as already noticed, a considerable increase of yellow and red warnings. If this warming-up process was still gradual and localised, it was nevertheless progressive. Cambridge Region reported early in June that recent events had 'gingered up' local authorities and the services, whose response to

---

[1] H. of C. Deb., Vol. 361, Cols. 777–8, 4th June 1940.
[2] Chapter XII.
[3] H. of C. Deb., Vol. 362, Cols. 987–90, 4th July 1940.
[4] p. 355.

the demands made on them had been excellent. Incidents, even if minor ones and involving no bombs, provided a welcome change from training in the form of 'play-acting' and lectures. Nottingham Region reported in July that its services had been called out on frequent occasions, that the average turn-out had been very good, and that the new appeal for part-time volunteers had produced encouraging results. The Ministry at the same date informed the War Cabinet that the performance hitherto of the services had been worthy of the greatest praise.

It had become clear, therefore, that this expensive and much-criticised Service did actually function; that the Wardens, Rescue Parties and others were showing a heartening enthusiasm, and that unpaid part-timers were turning out when required for duty in large numbers. Mr Noel-Baker, for example, stated in Parliament, 'this service is alive and inspired by a splendid spirit'.[1]

In terms of manpower and establishments the Service was, nevertheless, beginning to encounter fresh difficulties. And the general picture of enthusiasm and satisfactory turn-out, it soon became apparent, needed decided qualification. The problems, long familiar to the authorities at the centre, of maldistribution and insufficient recruits for particular services arose once more. On 13th May the Ministry authorised Regional Commissioners to use their discretion over proceeding with the reductions of both paid and unpaid personnel laid down, after so much effort, in the circular of 18th April and due to be completed by the middle of June.[2] Paid personnel were no longer to be dismissed except in areas where the Commissioners decided this could be done without impairing the efficiency of the particular service. Superfluous paid wardens were, if possible, to be transferred to another local service which was under strength.

Events and the freedom of action implied in a voluntary service were giving new unreality to the figures of strengths in the files of the Ministry, the Commissioners and the local authorities. The evacuation from Defence Areas on the east and south coasts, for example, was depriving authorities of part-time wardens and others described by Cambridge Region as 'volunteers of the better type, or persons of independent means or with few ties who were able to give plenty of time to their duties and take important parts in the organisation'. Evacuees of this type, including civil servants, who for one reason or another had migrated to safer areas often saw no particular reason for re-entering A.R.P. service.

More serious were the growing claims of the Fighting Forces and industry, and the impact of these on the familiar difficulty of

---

[1] H. of C. Deb., Vol. 361, Col. 1310, 12th June 1940.
[2] pp. 345-346.

maintaining the A.R.P. force at adequate strength in the industrial or main target areas. The Home Guard, formed in the middle of May, seemed for a time a formidable competitor to the A.R.P. Service.[1] In Birmingham and Sheffield, to take two examples, a considerable number of wardens and others applied for enrolment in this more martial organisation which grew, it will be recalled, in under eight weeks to over 1,000,000 men.

The need for workers in industry and the appeal of rising wages were proving a large cause of wastage. Thus the draining away of paid A.R.P. staffs in Birmingham, Stockton and Middlesbrough led the Ministry to sanction a larger establishment in these areas of whole-time Rescue and Casualty workers. Wastage in the vulnerable Medway area with its populous towns of Rochester, Chatham and Gillingham, dockyards and factories gave rise to arrangements of special interest and future significance. Approval was given for the creation of a Kent County Civil Defence Mobile Reserve, consisting of whole-time First Aid, Rescue and Decontamination Parties, to be stationed during attacks just outside the area. Formed and trained at a depot near Deal, the first company of this Reserve was ready for action by the end of August.[2]

The reports of local authorities in many parts of the country, supported by their Regional Commissioners, about wastage now became formidable. Birmingham was concerned over the systematic reduction both of the Rescue and the Wardens' Services; the appeal for new recruits had virtually been a failure, and only compulsion could save the situation. The Manchester Regional Commissioner reported that wastage of all A.R.P. staffs was becoming very serious; the authorities were especially concerned over loss of men and women over whose training much effort and money had been spent. The emergency committee of Warwick County Council was perturbed about losses of trained men and the difficulty of securing new volunteers. Lancashire Boroughs, Nottingham and Reading reported to the same effect. The Chief Administrative Officer of London Region considered that a decision in favour of some measure of compulsion was urgently required.

The Home Secretary told Parliament in June that the total establishment of the A.R.P. services had now been fixed at just under 1,000,000, of which about 180,000 would be paid staffs. This, he added, would produce an annual saving to the Exchequer of between £5 and £6 million. The establishment of the fire services accounted for an additional 200,000; of the auxiliary police for 60,000; of persons engaged in the health and casualty services for 250,000 and those concerned with evacuation for about 100,000. Industry, he

---

[1] p. 356.
[2] *Evening Standard*, 20th August 1940. See Chapter XIV.

continued, had now carried out its responsibilities under the Civil Defence Act in a manner worthy of all praise. Among other things, it had trained in A.R.P. duties and organised in units about 150,000 men and women.[1]

It is clear that the Government still lacked accurate and comprehensive information about the results of the Home Secretary's appeal in April for another 250,000 part-timers, and of the further appeal late in May to all A.R.P. workers to 'stay on the job'.[2] For a variety of reasons, including this lack of data, they were determined to proceed with caution over any steps undermining the voluntary basis of the Service. They believed that in many parts of the country the Service was perfectly happily organised on this basis. And, as the Mabane Committee had concluded, the principle of compulsion would be most difficult to apply to part-time A.R.P. workers.[3]

On 4th July, nevertheless, the Home Secretary stated that he was considering as a matter of urgency how this principle might be applied to areas which had still not succeeded in completing their establishments and reserves.[4] The first wedge in the voluntary principle had, in fact, been driven by Defence Regulation 29B of 4th June which could require persons employed in the police or civil defence to continue in such employment until their services were dispensed with, and empowered the Minister of Home Security to issue Orders 'freezing' the whole-time members of these forces.[5]

The first 'freezing Order' requiring police and firemen to continue in their employment was issued, with some reluctance, by the Government on 20th June; it was also announced that men between 30 and 50 years old might volunteer for either of these forces as an alternative to military service.[6] It then became necessary, on the abundant evidence of wastage of Rescue and First Aid Parties produced by local authorities, to take some action over these. On 9th July the 'freezing' of members of both these parties was introduced, together with reservation of such persons at the age of 30 and temporary deferment of those under 30 until substitutes for them could be found.[7] Then the wastage of paid wardens—most conspicuous in London Region—caused after the opening of the Battle of London a 'freezing' order which will receive attention in a later chapter.[8]

---

[1] H. of C. Deb., Vol. 361, Cols. 1287-8, 12th June 1940.

[2] p. 346.

[3] p. 345.

[4] H. of C. Deb., Vol. 362, Col. 990.

[5] S.R. & O. 1940, No. 906.

[6] Police and Firemen (Employment) Order, 1940, S.R. & O. 1940, No. 1041.

[7] Civil Defence (Employment) Order, 1940, S.R. & O. 1940, No. 1206; H.S.C. 169/40, 10th July.

[8] Chapter XIII.

The conditions of A.R.P. service were in the meanwhile being improved, though at what seemed to many of the rank and file an unduly slow pace. For the central authorities the difficulty of whether whole-time civil defence workers were to be regarded primarily as national defence or as industrial personnel, with the many practical consequences that followed, had now become more acute. How far could the doctrine, enunciated by the Mabane Committee, that 'civil defence is a service and not an employment' be maintained in practice?[1] Considerable difficulty was being experienced in getting the principles of the 72-hour week and of the universal flat rate of pay established. The view of the Ministry that it was necessary for paid A.R.P. workers to adjust their peace-time habits to war-time necessities was by no means always popular.

Other difficulties had arisen over trade union employment and conditions, and over the extent to which the Ministry was to engage in consultation with the unions. Mr Ernest Bevin, the Minister of Labour and National Service in the new Government, argued with success that the unions had a right to be consulted on any questions affecting basic conditions of A.R.P. service. A consultative committee was therefore set up in June of the Departments concerned and representatives of the unions (particularly the Transport and General Workers and Municipal Workers Unions) for regular discussion of these matters.[2]

At the beginning of July the flat rates of pay of whole-time volunteers were increased by 5s. per week for men and 3s. 6d. for women —or to £3 5s. and £2 3s. 6d.[3] Depot Superintendents and their deputies paid less than £5 per week were granted similar increases. The principle of the flat rate of pay had already been modified in favour of three specially skilled men in each Rescue Party and these also shared in the increases. The Minister of Pensions claimed at this date that the Personal Injuries (Civilians) Scheme, which insured not only civil defence volunteers but all gainfully employed persons against enemy action, was working very well; payments had already been made in 5,300 cases of injury, mostly to members of the A.F.S. or the A.R.P. services on practice or patrol duties.[4] More generous provision, promised for some time past, for free meals and refreshments for volunteers was also introduced.[5]

The provision of buildings, vehicles and different kinds of supplies and equipment was improving.[6] Regional Officers reported that

---

[1] p. 345.

[2] H.S.C. 141/40, 24th June 1940.

[3] H.S.C. 157/40, 4th July 1940.

[4] H. of C. Deb., Vol. 362, Cols. 338-40; p. 348.

[5] H.S.C. 161/40, 6th July 1940.

[6] pp. 348-350.

A.R.P. buildings, of the type then considered necessary, were in general acquired and equipped. Nottingham, for example, reported sufficient wardens' posts, a general increase in size of report centres and good regional communications arrangements. Newcastle stated that buildings were almost completed, though little had been done about alternative offices and headquarters. Bristol and Cambridge reported in the same vein. The situation as regards vehicles, as recorded earlier, was a good deal less satisfactory, and improvement continued largely to depend on local self-help and improvisation.

The Home Secretary stated on 12th June that for all practical purposes the issue of essential equipment, including reserves, to the A.R.P. services and the A.F.S. had been completed. This situation did not, of course, prevent continuing mistakes over distribution, and complaints, in varying degree justified, that some particular area or some service within that area had not been supplied with one article or another, and that volunteers were thereby disheartened. Uniforms or overall suits were still so scarce that in July the authorities made a proposal, which they soon had to rescind, to withdraw those already issued to male wardens.[1] The Government had now issued over 100,000 stirrup pumps, which it recognised as the most important item of equipment for citizens at large for dealing with attack by incendiary bombs. This number, however, was still quite insufficient for the needs of the services; and numbers of pumps, which might otherwise have been available to the Government, were being sold on the open market at inflated prices.[2] Various items of the more specialised equipment for Rescue Parties were still in course of development and production.

The new impetus given early in the year by the centre to training and the new machinery at Regions for this purpose were beginning to bear fruit.[3] And, as mentioned earlier, incidents of one sort or another were giving some reality to what, previously, had been mainly exercises of the imagination. Though certain local authorities concluded that raiding or war conditions justified a halt over training, they were soon informed that this was a heretical view. The Leeds and other Regional Commissioners reported, as the summer progressed, a steady growth of training activities. More Regions were following the example of London in creating their own Rescue and other training centres. The local authorities were appointing more and better qualified training officers. Exercises of a combined nature and between neighbouring authorities and even on Regional level were being held more frequently. Some Regions and authorities were

---

[1] p. 349; H.S.C. 190/40, 27th July 1940.

[2] p. 350.

[3] pp. 351-352.

intensifying their efforts to provide A.R.P. and fire-fighting training to the public.

Early in July the Ministry began the issue of a series of A.R.P. Training Bulletins which modified and compressed information previously published in handbooks and memoranda and were of special value to factory and other employers.[1] As experiences of raiding began to accumulate, a steady flow of information travelled from the periphery to the centre, and was there studied and redistributed in various forms. Training in its less formal sense was carried on continuously by means of operational instructions, teleprinter messages, circulars and so on. As the Inspector-General had remarked, no end of the training task was in sight. If the London Group Officer quoted earlier could record that by August of 1940 'confidence in trained ability had long replaced uncertainty' among his services, there were many areas and units more remote from the danger where this was by no means the case.[2]

---

[1] H.S.C. 160/40, 5th July 1940.
[2] R. Bell, *The Bull's Eye* (1943).

CHAPTER X

THE TIDES OF BATTLE

(July 1940 — March 1944)

The Battle of Britain (July – October 1940)

ON 10th July a total of about seventy German bombers attacked Swansea and Falmouth in daylight killing thirty persons and doing some damage to shipping, a power station and railways. A new phase was opening of daylight attack added to the night attack.[1] Though the enemy was still mainly concerned with shipping, ports and the coastal areas he began to penetrate inland more deeply. And though the weight of attack was in general still small, the number of more serious assaults was growing. The German Air Force had entered on its attempt to destroy the Royal Air Force in the air and on the ground as an essential preliminary to sea-borne invasion. The Battle of Britain grew steadily more intense up to the defeat on 15th September of the enemy's immediate ambitions.

The record of the plans, physical expansion and operations in the air and on the ground of Fighter Command and the other active defences falls outside the scope of the present volume.[2] This story of achievement against odds in the administrative sphere, in the factories and in the skies must, so to speak, be assumed in this narrative. It is here necessary, in fact, to go somewhat further and to underline the differences in objective and outlook between these active and the passive defences. The Air Staff and Fighter Command were the source of the Ministry of Home Security's information regarding the attacks which the enemy was liable to deliver either in the distant or the immediate future. The differences just mentioned were accompanied by differences in terminology relevant to the attempt of this chapter to record the tides of battle.

Thus for Fighter Command a 'sortie' was any one enemy aircraft leaving its base; and a 'raid' was any number of hostile aircraft (from one to x) which approached as a single formation. For the passive defences with which this narrative is concerned German aircraft only began to matter when they had closely approached or crossed our coasts. It would be untrue to say that the number of

---

[1] See pp. 358-360.

[2] This will be dealt with in the official series of Military Histories.

379

enemy bombers employed on any particular occasion did not matter
to the passive defences, though they clearly mattered less than to
those whose function it was to destroy them. Numbers mattered in
terms of the bomb-load which (say) twenty Junkers 88s would
probably be carrying and intended to drop, and of the disturbance
in time and space these were capable of creating.

In the summary which follows, therefore, numbers of the attacking
aircraft are often included as some indication of the weight of attack;
though limitations of purpose and space make it impossible as a rule
to specify here the type of aircraft, with its particular bomb-load,
which the enemy used. The number or tonnage of bombs actually
dropped on any particular target, such as a town or factory, it must
be added, was only progressively a matter of accurate calculation.
It is an essential part of the history of the topic that the reporting
of attacks by police, wardens or others contained errors which only
experience and training could hope to eliminate.[1] It was not until
September 1940 that the close scientific study of enemy raids was
begun. The Research and Experiments Department and the Air
Ministry then instituted a system for analysing the data of raids and
'deducing therefrom the enemy's tactics and methods'.[2] This
enterprise, which became known as the 'bomb census', could for
practical reasons be applied at first only to London, Birmingham
and Liverpool. As its value became apparent it was extended to other
cities. But it was not until September 1941 that its field organisation
was operating in all the civil defence regions.

This narrative is at present most concerned not with 'raids' in the
Fighter Command sense but with 'raids' in the popular sense of an
attack accompanied by bombs. It must nevertheless be apparent to
the reader that raids in the former sense had much bearing on the
civil, as well as on the military, defences. Through the warning
system they could alert the civil defence services or the public over
wide areas. And even if no 'yellow' or 'red' warning had been given,
formations of enemy aircraft could be heard. Without the *ultima
ratio* of his efforts—namely bombs—the German attacker could
produce considerable dislocation of industry and transport, wastage of
civil defence effort, loss of sleep and disturbance to the general public.

The following outline of attacks over nearly four years on the civil
population is based on these broad considerations. It is necessary
to add a few further introductory comments. First, that it can offer
no more than a conspectus of the assault, leaving the response and
re-organisation this provoked in the passive defences to be recorded
in later chapters. Second, that its sources are predominantly the
intelligence available to civil defence authorities during the war;

---

[1] pp. 306, 359.
[2] p. 304.

information acquired from enemy documents and otherwise after victory had been won can only be noticed here in cases of particular discrepancy in the figures and usually in the form of footnotes. This is again to pursue the principle that what primarily matters is what people reported as happening, or thought was going to happen. It has been elsewhere pointed out, for example, that a well-known case of miscalculation—the belief that our defences had destroyed 185 German aircraft on 15th September whereas the actual figure was eventually found to be only 60—helped to sustain the morale of Britain's pilots and people.[1]

Thirdly, a summary in so short a space can hardly avoid producing a flattening effect, as well as ironing out much that, at the time, was dramatic. That the storms—for example the 'Big Blitz' of 1940-41— were succeeded by lulls is undoubtedly true. But four years of attacks, measured by the reports continuously received at the centre, assume more the appearance of the ebb and flow of tides. While one area, such as Merseyside or Clydebank, was being attacked London, for example, was enjoying a period of recuperation. Important centres such as Plymouth and Liverpool were attacked for five or more nights in succession, and then given a respite of varying lengths before being attacked again. Hull was being continuously attacked during a phase when activity elsewhere was slight. Many places, of course, were subjected to frequent 'alerts' without ever being bombed.

The Home Security War Room compiled summaries of events, based on reports received from the twelve Regions which were in turn based on reports from local control centres, twice in each 24 hours of the day throughout the war. These, circulated in the Ministry and elsewhere in Whitehall, formed, especially during periods of heavy raiding, the starting point of many types of official action. The war room also issued weekly appreciations which have formed a main source of information about the attacks in this volume.[2]

The German Air Force first-line strength had risen by the middle of August, it was thought, to about 5,400 aircraft. This included 1,550 fighters (some 500 of which were long-range fighters), and a long-range bomber and bomber reconnaissance force of some 3,107 aircraft.[3] The Air Staff also calculated that this first-line strength

---

[1] e.g., by 'Strategicus', *A Short History of the Second World War* (1950). Denis Richards and H. St. G. Saunders, *Royal Air Force, 1939–1945*, Vol. 1 (1953) was published as the present volume was going to press. This states that the figure of 182 German aircraft destroyed on 15th August 'like that of 185 for 15th September, though subsequently shown to be wrong, had an important psychological effect during the battle. For it undoubtedly inspired not only the fighter pilots but the whole nation to still greater miracles of effort.'

[2] p. 306. The War Room at first also issued monthly appreciations, but these were abandoned in October 1940.

[3] p. 354. It was known after the war that in fact the Germans had available for use against the U.K. about 1,400 long-range bombers, 400 dive-bombers and 1,200 fighters, besides reconnaissance and coastal aircraft.

would grow to about 6,500 aircraft in a further year. These large enemy forces now had a considerable part of Britain within range. It had become apparent, for example, that they had established tracks over Devon to the Bristol Channel and up the Welsh Marches to Chester and Merseyside. Fighter Command at this date had fewer than 60 operational squadrons, with an effective fighting strength of some 700 aircraft; first-line strength of these operational squadrons was of the order of 1,000 aircraft.

The American journalist quoted earlier had reported on 25th May that the dropping of a few bombs on the previous night had not caused much excitement, and that 'most people believe that when the Germans decide to bomb it'll be a real blitz'.[1] Onslaught on the scale which this new word suggested was still to be deferred for some months. And it may, at this stage, be emphasised that in civil as in military defence the expected often failed to happen, more especially at the time when the experts considered it to be due; and that the unexpected happened more frequently than the experts were sometimes ready to admit. The experts had, of course, to estimate the enemy's capabilities, and could not be asked, beyond a point, to know his plans. This weakness of all defensive warfare constituted an additional hardship—almost too obvious to mention—on the local authorities (who in the nature of the case could not be so fully informed as those at the centre), the members of the civil defence services and the general public.

The weeks of July, August and early September, seen in retrospect, formed for the passive defences a further period of progressive 'warming up' and preparation. More areas and towns began to suffer sharp attacks, usually by single or small formations of aircraft. Daylight attacks were made in July on Norwich, Cardiff docks, an aircraft factory near Bristol, Air Force stations in Berkshire and Caernarvon and a barracks at Aldershot. The most determined attacks of this month, in each case by about fifty aircraft, were made against Portland and Portsmouth. The enemy was now more persistent in his visits by day, sometimes accompanied by the dropping of bombs, to north-east Scotland, the whole English coastal area from the Tyne to the Bristol Channel and South Wales.

These and the widespread night raiding, though still primarily armed reconnaissance, began to cause heavier loss of life and civil damage. The enemy's efforts now appeared less sporadic and more in the nature of a co-ordinated wearing-down of the defences. It was also obvious that he was providing his pilots with useful training. He consistently maintained his minelaying operations, for example in the areas of the Thames estuary, the Humber, Harwich, Liverpool and Belfast. He was now paying more attention of an undesirable kind

---

[1] E. R. Murrow, *op. cit.*

to the railways, for example in the neighbourhood of Bath, Bristol and Radstock and elsewhere in the West Country. It seemed that he might be leading up to a determined effort, as a concomitant of invasion, to immobilise these railways and so cut off southern from eastern England. Incendiary bombs dropped at this time on the North Kent marshes seemed to have been aimed at the Faversham marshalling yards.

Between 7th and 14th July totals of 960 H.E.s and 534 I.B.s were reported as having been dropped; and the casualties during this period of 234 civilians killed, 278 seriously injured and 395 slightly injured were much higher than those of any previous week. The 50 or so casualties at Portsmouth had been exceeded by 34 persons killed and 21 seriously injured in Aberdeen, as well as some damage to the shipyards, during an attack on the night of 12th/13th when no 'red' warning was sounded. Attacks causing smaller casualties and some damage were made during the next three weeks on Norwich (twice), Swansea, Falmouth, the British Oxygen Company's works at Plymouth, and a factory at Hartlepool.

The totals reported for the month ending 7th August of 2,887 H.E.s and 2,146 I.B.s exceeded those of the previous month; and over twice as many persons, or 304, had been killed and 577 injured. The casualty figures given here and throughout this narrative, it must be stated, refer almost exclusively to civilians. Casualties, that is to say, caused by an incident on a naval or military establishment were usually the affair of the Service Department concerned. There were, however, inevitably cases of death or injury to men and women in the Armed Forces on leave or helping at an incident which came to be included in the civilian figures. Further, the casualty figures, like most others relating to incidents taking place all over the country, only progressively became accurate, and many of those reported during or soon after a raid had later to be revised. The category of 'seriously injured' indicated, in general, admission to a hospital. Some of the air raid victims so admitted might, of course, subsequently die.[1]

The authorities were able to report early in August that no damage of major importance had as yet been caused to war production. The most serious consequence in this sphere was that, discussed in the previous chapter, of interruption of work and loss of workers' sleep caused by the frequency of warnings.[2] The completeness of the black-out, they concluded, was the principal reason for the difficulty the German pilots had so far experienced in finding specific targets inland. The large proportion of bombs dropped during night attacks in fields and open country, though this had heartened the defences, could not at this stage be taken as proof of the ineffectiveness of such attacks. All reports indicated that the civil defence

---

[1] Figures of civilian casualties throughout the war are given at Appendix 2.

[2] pp. 363-365.

services, though the calls on them had still been limited, had acted promptly and efficiently.

Late in July Hitler adopted the practice—which, incidentally, Britain had pursued soon after the opening of war—of dropping leaflets (headed 'Appeal to Reason') behind his enemy's lines. Though the topic does not belong to the present narrative, the effect of these, which were long-winded and badly printed, was probably much the opposite to what he intended. The Ministry of Home Security reported that the public was 'growing steadily more robust' and, when under attack, was developing calmness and a spirit of co-operation. They also reported that the people's morale during an attack was noticeably improved by the effectiveness and (which were not, of course, necessarily the same thing) the visibility and the audibility of both the active and the passive defences.

Marshal Goering declared early in August that the armed reconnaissance of his forces was ending and that air warfare was about to play its prime role against Britain. By the 8th his assaults against the Royal Air Force were much stronger, though bad weather postponed the opening of the main attack until the 13th, when he sent nearly 2,000 aircraft against this country. Two days later, on 15th August, the *Luftwaffe*, believing that they had drawn all our fighter squadrons to the south, sent 65 bombers escorted by 35 fighters to attack Tyneside by daylight, while about 50 bombers approached Spurn Head. At the same time over 800 planes were sent to contain our forces in the south. The result was the largest air battle so far engaged, which embraced five major actions on a front of five hundred miles. In the north-east Spitfires and Hurricanes brought down 23 enemy planes, and the total German losses for the day were 75 as compared with Britain's 34. It was a few days later, after the Air Force had given further evidence of its prowess, that the Prime Minister told Parliament, 'never in the field of human conflict was so much owed by so many to so few'.[1]

Attempting to launch some 1,400 or more aircraft daily against this country, and sometimes sending these by day in mass formations of several hundred, the enemy began to stretch the resources of the active defences to the limit. The total of H.E.s reported and civilian casualties (some 330 killed) for the one week 14th-21st August exceeded those for the month ending 7th August. Damage to R.A.F. aerodromes, aeroplanes on the ground and certain aircraft factories (for example at Croydon and Filton) began to assume serious proportions. In the civilian sphere, which most concerns this narrative, the bombardment assumed new intensity not only in the towns and fields of Kent, Sussex, and other southern counties but over many inland areas.

---

[1] Charles Eade (Ed.), *op. cit.*, Vol. I, p. 240, 20th August.

What the Ministry called 'harassing attacks' were maintained by day and night not only on military establishments but on industry and communications. The offensive reconnaissance by night was continued, more generally accompanied by bombs, and conducted on several nights towards the end of the month by over 200 aircraft. On the 19th bombs from a single aircraft started a serious fire at a South Wales oil storage depot which burned for a whole week and destroyed ten out of fifteen oil tanks. Night raids by small numbers of aircraft causing some damage were made on Liverpool, the Port Talbot docks, Birmingham, Croydon, Boston, Rotherham and Cardiff. An important feature (for example in the raids on Birmingham) was the large number of unexploded H.E. bombs or, as these were officially known, 'UXBs'. Many industrial areas in the southwest, South Wales and the Midlands began to experience long periods of 'red' warnings. Communications, gas, electricity, water, and telephone services suffered serious damage in certain areas. The lessons of raids that were now rapidly accumulating included the facts, (i) that railway damage could be repaired more rapidly than had been thought, and (ii) that the quick repair, though this was less easy, of public utilities was important to the restoration of local morale.

The civil defence services had now come into action on a much larger scale, and the Ministry was getting many reports of their 'skill, enthusiasm and endurance'. Volunteers 'on call' had turned out in satisfactory fashion; and part-timers had turned out too often, pointing the need for better local arrangements. In more than one area members of the Services had been machine-gunned as they worked. 'Incident control', however, was still little developed. The W.V.S. had given most valuable help in maintaining mobile canteens at the scene of incidents and in other ways.[1]

On 24th August the first bombs were dropped in daylight on Central London. That night what seemed the first general attack was made on the capital. Single aircraft dropped high explosive and incendiary bombs on the City, dockland and elsewhere in the East End and on various suburbs.[2] Two nights later the metropolis experienced its first all-night alert. A small number of bombs, causing long periods of warning, then began to descend on London Region each day and night. Bomber Command of the Royal Air Force dropped the first bombs on Berlin on the night of 25th-26th.

The enemy were, in fact, starting to despair of defeating the Royal Air Force and trying to force a way open to London. They began to pursue two major objectives—the gaining of air supremacy,

---

[1] See Chapter XIV.

[2] In fact, these bombs on London were dropped against orders by enemy crews who supposed themselves to be elsewhere.

and the cowing into submission of the Government and people concentrated in London—in place of one. On 7th September Goering
announced to the German people, 'this is the historic hour when
our air force for the first time delivered its stroke right into the
enemy's heart'. The Battle of London, which effectively began on this
day, will shortly be described in some detail. It is only necessary
here to recall that the Battle of Britain continued unabated for some
weeks. Its crux on 15th September formed, in Mr Churchill's phrase,
'one of the decisive battles of the war'. Two days later (though this
fact was naturally not known in Britain) Hitler decided to postpone
the invasion of Britain (operation 'Sealion') at least for some weeks.[1]

The *Luftwaffe* nevertheless persisted with daylight assaults into
October, with 27th September, on which our active defences claimed
to have destroyed over 130 aircraft, as another important date.
Concentrated and vicious attacks were delivered in these weeks on
areas other than London, notably Portsmouth and Southampton.
As the result, presumably, of faulty navigation the enemy dropped
eight bombs, which killed three people, on 26th August on County
Wexford, Eire.

Dover, which had experienced a number of bombing attacks
during the summer, became for the first time on 22nd August the
target for shelling by long-range enemy guns from France. The
shells fell in the centre of the town demolishing several houses and
injuring four civilians. British guns replied and 'shooting matches'
of this kind soon became a regular feature of life in the town; though
it was not until four years later that the most intensive shelling took
place. The Dover civil defence forces were henceforth engaged in
issuing warnings, saving lives and repairing the damage caused by
this form of attack as well as by air bombardment.

The Battle of London (September – November 1940)

The German attempt at a knock-out blow had been expected by
the public to accompany the opening of war; and by those in
responsible positions to form a possible, or even probable, move of
Hitler's strategy some months before war was declared. Its arrival
may properly be dated with the opening of the Battle of London
on 7th September, after almost exactly one year of conflict. It had
already become known, in anticipation, as the *blitz*; and this word
now became almost overnight a British colloquialism for an air raid.
The popularisation of technical terms (of which in its full form of
blitzkrieg or lightning war this was one) during the course of the

---

[1] Hitler's order of 17th September was to the effect that 'Sealion' must be postponed
but might take place in October. On 12th October he renounced the plan for sea-borne
invasion of Britain in 1940.

war was, according to an authority on our language, 'almost startling', and many of these were foreign importations.[1] It may be relevant to add that the people's adoption of this German word probably sprang from motives similar to those which, John Strachey has suggested, inspired the universal description of the enemy in the First World War as 'Jerry'. There was in this, he writes, 'an acceptance of a destiny; of a destiny to resist. There was a refusal to take the panoply of German might at its own valuation.'[2]

This panoply in terms of bombers and other aircraft, in spite of the losses still being inflicted by the Royal Air Force, was formidable. The German Air Force, it must be admitted, had not been primarily built for night bombing operations. But the reconnaissance phase since June had given the enemy's pilots experience of night bombing, and enabled him to prepare airfields, ground organisation and navigational aids for this purpose. Britain's active defences against night attack, whether measured by equipment, techniques or training, were still rudimentary.

The 'Big Blitz', though directed at first mainly against London, became virtually nation-wide and continued with ferocity for roughly eight months, or until early in May 1941. It has already been noticed that it began before the Battle of Britain had reached its crux; and this mingling by the enemy of broad policies and objectives was destined to continue.[3] The fact that this (as it has since become apparent) reflected divided counsels among the enemy's leaders is less relevant to the present narrative than the difficulty it creates for the summary presentation of the various phases of the attacks. To overemphasise the major objectives and targets of any particular phase is to produce one kind of historical distortion. And to pay too much attention to the secondary objectives and targets which the enemy was also pursuing in this phase is to produce another.

A warning to the reader that the divisions of the four years' onslaught as this bore upon the passive defences are by no means water-tight or conclusive therefore seems appropriate here. The Battle of London now under discussion lasted for roughly two months, or until early in November. From 7th September to 2nd November the capital was bombed every night, by a nightly average over these fifty-seven nights of some 200 planes.[4] This continuous attack against the heart of the Empire, though accompanied by some serious raids elsewhere, was probably the enemy's most concentrated effort of the war against any single British target,

---

[1] Eric Partridge, *Usage and Abusage* (1947).

[2] John Strachey, *Post D.* (1941).

[3] p. 386.

[4] German records show an average of 163 bombers used between 7th September and 13th November.

as London, in spite of its size and the variety of its contents, must for the purposes of this volume be regarded. Of the total of 11,700 persons killed in air raids during these two months some 9,500 (or over 4 out of every 5) were killed in London. So in this case the remarks just made about general emphasis need some qualification. The title which heads this section is, in addition, misleading if the reader fails to recall that the enemy returned on many later occasions to make savage attacks on London. Notably, in the big raids of 29th-30th December on the City and of 10th-11th May 1941 on Westminster and elsewhere.

Between five and six o'clock on the evening of Saturday, 7th September some 320 German bombers supported by over 600 fighters flew up the Thames and proceeded to bomb Woolwich Arsenal, Beckton Gas Works, a large number of docks, West Ham power station, and then the City, Westminster and Kensington. They succeeded in causing a serious fire situation in the docks. An area of about 1½ miles between North Woolwich Road and the Thames was almost destroyed, and the population of Silvertown was surrounded by fire and had to be evacuated by water. At 8.10 p.m. some 250 bombers resumed the attack, which was maintained until 4.30 on Sunday morning. They caused 9 conflagrations, 59 large fires and nearly 1,000 lesser fires.[1] Three main-line railway termini were put out of action, and 430 persons killed and some 1,600 seriously injured. After the fire brigades had spent all day in an effort to deprive the enemy of illumination, some 200 bombers returned at 7.30 in the evening to carry on the assault. During this second night a further 412 persons were killed and 747 seriously injured, and damage included the temporary stoppage of every railway line to the south.

On these and the next few nights it seemed to the London public that the enemy bombers could roam at will and attack where they chose without any effective opposition. But on 11th September our anti-aircraft barrage suddenly roared out, causing the citizens to cheer in the streets. General Sir Frederick Pile, G.O.C.-in-C. of Anti-Aircraft Command throughout the war, has recorded in detail the planning, operations, failures and successes of his command.[2] He states that the general supply position of these defences was at this time 'still appalling'; and that 'we seemed as far as ever from solving the great problem of the night raider'.[3] Night fighters and night interception methods were still, by comparison with their later development, embryonic. He nevertheless concentrated guns from

---

[1] Conflagrations were officially defined as major fires which were spreading. Major fires were those requiring attendance by over 30 pumps, serious by 11-30 pumps, medium by 2-10 pumps and small by one pump.

[2] Sir F. Pile, *Ack-Ack: Britain's Defence against Air Attack During the Second World War* (1949).

[3] *Ibid.*, p. 144.

all over the country on London, and instructed them on 11th September to fire every available round. This 'barrage' (which was not properly speaking a barrage) forced the enemy to fly higher, turned him away from entering the inner artillery zone and 'bucked people up tremendously'.

It was, he also records, due to 'the stubborn courage' first of the East Enders and later of all classes and areas in London, that the enemy's largely inaccurate bombing failed to cause any serious loss of morale. Seen from another angle, namely that of a leading civil defence officer in the East End, what ensued were 'eight long agonising weeks. The atmosphere (he later recorded) grew tense with suffering and struggle . . . an immense weariness at the relentless regularity of the attack found its match in a dogged determination to go on, no matter what the cost'.[1]

On 17th September Mr Churchill told the House of Commons that the A.R.P. organisation in all its branches had proved its efficiency, and added, 'our whole system of life and labour is being rapidly adapted to conditions hitherto unknown to modern society'. In secret session on the same day he proposed to the House three measures of adaptation of its own proceedings and business. Namely, a ban in future on the publication of dates and hours of sittings, the advance in time of sittings to the morning and early afternoon and a reduction for the time being in the normal number of sittings. He suggested that Members not otherwise occupied in national service might at this stage do invaluable work in their own constituencies, especially those which had been 'knocked about by the enemy's fire'.[2]

During this week of 11th-18th September the enemy maintained a scale of attack of about 150 aircraft each night, and a number of incidents of an outstanding character took place. In daylight on 11th September an incident occurred which provided an exception, among others, to the general picture of continuous night-raiding. About midday a single German plane dived out of the clouds in what appeared to be a deliberate attack on Buckingham Palace, to which the King and Queen had just returned from Windsor. It dropped six bombs, two in the forecourt, two in the quadrangle, one which wrecked the chapel and one in the garden.[3] In the course of the next few days, and on separate occasions, incendiaries and delayed-action bombs were dropped on the Palace and in its grounds and its vicinity.

The damage in this week to civilian property (as distinct from military establishments, factories and communications) in London

---

[1] R. Bell, *The Bull's Eye* (1943).

[2] Charles Eade (Ed.), *op. cit.*, Vol. I, pp. 260–264.

[3] See W. S. Churchill, *op. cit.*, Vol. II, p. 334.

and elsewhere was in the aggregate considerable, though the Ministry stated that in London Region some of this damage had been 'less hard to bear' in that it had been caused by crashing enemy aircraft. The problem of UXBs—which might or might not be delayed-action or time-fuse bombs—already becoming familiar in the attacks of the previous phase, could now be described as acute.[1] Besides seriously dislocating rail, road and other communications, these made necessary the evacuation for longer or shorter periods of considerable numbers of citizens from their homes. A notable example of this menace was a bomb of 1,000 kg. (about a ton) which was dropped near St. Paul's Cathedral and failed to explode, threatening not only the Cathedral but all the trunk telephone communications with the north country. The officer of the Bomb Disposal Squad of the Royal Engineers who removed this missile was one of the first recipients of the George Cross.

On 17th September the formidable 'parachute mine'—a naval mine with considerable blast effect and of a weight and explosive power never previously carried by aircraft—was dropped for the first time on London Region. Many others followed in the course of the ensuing weeks, and a large proportion of them failed to explode. The task of disposing of these fell on the Admiralty, or more parti-cularly the Land Incidents Section of the Directorate of Torpedoes and Mining. The naval parties who composed this section dealt with large numbers of these mines in London and elsewhere with great courage and efficiency, sustaining a number of casualties in the process. Their work obtained little public notice owing to the paramount need to conceal from the enemy what we knew about the weapons he was using, and the methods by which we were dealing with them.

On a single night in September (18th-19th) the enemy aimed 350 tons of bombs at London—or more than the total weight of bombs dropped on the whole of Britain during the First World War.[2] By the end of this month he had dropped over 10,000 H.E.s and an immense number of I.B.s on London Region. The figures of killed and seriously injured for the whole country had, however, declined from about 6,000 in the week after 7th September to under 5,000 in the next week, about 4,000 in the third week and under 3,000 in the last week of this period. About four-fifths of these 18,000 or so serious casualties had occurred in London. The damage to war production and vulnerable points of different kinds, though not negligible, had been less than was officially expected. But the destruction of civilian property, especially the small houses of the poorer sections of the

---

[1] pp. 360, 385.

[2] p. 11. According to German records the enemy aimed over 250 tons at London on nine other nights in September.

community, had been very great. The worst onslaughts had fallen on Stepney, Poplar, Bermondsey, Southwark, Lambeth, Deptford, Shoreditch, Bethnal Green, Holloway and the ancient City. But heavy damage had also been inflicted on homes and property of many other kinds in Central London and the West End.

On 23rd September King George VI broadcast to his people from Buckingham Palace, 'with its honourable scars', while an evening air raid was in progress. He recalled that with the Queen he had already seen many of the places in the capital which had been most heavily bombed and many of the people who had suffered most. He extended 'a special word of gratitude' to the men and women of the A.R.P. services. And he announced his decision to recognise the deeds of gallantry being performed by creating 'a new mark of honour for men and women in all walks of civilian life'. This would consist of the George Cross, to rank next to the Victoria Cross, and the George Medal for wider distribution.[1]

These few weeks of heavy attack had already formed a pattern in some respects decidedly different from the hypothesis or general picture formulated in advance by the defenders. The most definite difference between the actuality and the anticipation was the enemy's strategy, following his defeat in the Battle of Britain, of continuous night-raiding. Both factors of this equation—that of time, or the continuity of raiding which began about dusk and persisted until dawn, and that of darkness—had many consequences for the passive defences. While it was true that the raiding during the months of May to July had been chiefly by night this, by any standard of measurement, had been light.[2] All-night attacks which were also heavy presented many new problems.

A summary account must probably rate the most serious problem for passive defence as that of shelters and sheltering. The raids produced an immediate desire on the part of a not insignificant section of the London public to go underground to shelter. Many, of course, did this in their own homes, restaurants, hotels or other places where they happened to be; and a volume or more could doubtless be compiled on the habits, psychology and experiences of Londoners of all classes and geographical sections who sheltered in one form or another under these first attacks. What more concerns this narrative is the use that was made of the shelters of various types that had been provided for the public by the Government, and the local authorities.[3] It seems that the public, especially those in the East End who bore the brunt of the earlier attacks and whose homes were often of flimsy construction, quickly sought the various types of

---

[1] *The Times*, 24th September 1940.

[2] pp. 358–360.

[3] pp. 366–372.

shelter which were officially provided, with a preference for any that were underground and public as distinct from domestic.

Though the story of this topic will be told in a later chapter, a few salient facts need mention here.[1] In certain areas the public (as they had done in the First World War) flocked into London's Tube stations, disregarding the Government's announcements that these should not be relied upon as shelters.[2] In the Tubes and in other large underground shelters they at once developed the habit of spending the whole night, thus creating the problem, to be later fully discussed, of the use of air raid shelters as dormitories. By the middle of September the practice of sleeping in London shelters had become widespread. The first census of London's shelterers was not taken until early in November, or almost at the end of the phase now under consideration, and this cannot, for reasons to be later suggested, be regarded as very accurate. It concluded, however, that 9 per cent. of the estimated population spent the night in public shelters, 4 per cent. in the Tubes and 27 per cent. in household shelters; or a total of 40 per cent. It is probable that during September and October these figures were appreciably higher, since experience proved that as the public became used to raiding the number of shelterers steadily declined.

Heavy all-night attack created obvious extra hardships for all sections of the community, including the added fears of not (except on rare occasions) being able to see the attackers, the added difficulties of extricating oneself from a building or taking other steps which might be necessary, and persistent loss of sleep. For the A.R.P. services the extent to which operations would have to be carried on in darkness had not, in training exercises and otherwise, been fully foreseen. Some delay was therefore caused over rescue work, attributable in large part to the difficulty of arranging sufficient lighting. Hand torches or lamps proved generally inadequate, the use of flares was obviously injudicious and unpopular both with the rescue parties themselves and with the neighbouring public, tarpaulin screens were difficult to erect over debris, and the use of motor-cars with screened headlamps might produce congestion at the scene of the incident.

The second most significant unexpected feature of these attacks was the relatively small loss of life accompanied by the relatively high amount of damage to all types of building which they caused. The conception, crudely stated, had been that of a hail of high explosive bombs falling in the streets and other open places and killing or seriously wounding a considerable number of persons. The reality, on the basis of this short experience, was that large

---

[1] Chapter XII below.

[2] It was reported that 177,000 people sheltered in the Tubes on 27th September 1940.

numbers of H.E.s and I.B.s caused relatively few casualties but widespread physical damage, which included the trapping of persons in partially destroyed buildings of all types. The expectation of the authorities on the outbreak of war that 3,000 persons might be killed and 12,000 wounded on a single night and that this rate of losses might continue almost indefinitely had thus, fortunately, not been fulfilled. And the hospital and mortuary arrangements for some 250,000 casualties as a first provision had so far proved excessive.

It followed from this that the calls on the Casualty Services proved much fewer and those on the Rescue Service much greater than had been expected. It was even estimated by the Ministry late in November that 40-50 per cent. of the London Stretcher Parties could be dispensed with without ill effect. Rescue operations, on the other hand, proved both difficult and prolonged. The available parties were almost continuously at work, and the margin of reserve was almost non-existent. The methods and technique of these operations could only be evolved by trial and error. Though the topic will be more fully considered below, difficulties, in addition to manpower shortage, which at once arose included the physical removal of the quantity of debris often involved, the obtaining of reliable information about persons trapped in particular buildings, and the unsuitability or shortage of some of the rescue equipment issued.[1]

A third principal unexpected feature, already briefly referred to, was the quantity of UXBs and UXPMs or enemy bombs and mines which, being fitted with delayed-action fuses, failed to explode when they fell.[2] The UXPMs, it has been noted, were dealt with by naval officers and ratings working under the direction of the Admiralty. The story of administrative preparation for UXBs before and during the twilight phase of the war is one into which it has not been possible fully to enter. The War Office had shown considerable reluctance to undertake permanent responsibility for this matter, and much discussion between this Department and the civil authorities had taken place. An attempt initiated by the Ministry of Home Security soon after the outbreak of war to organise the training of civilians under local authority auspices for bomb disposal had failed; and in February 1940 the War Office had finally accepted this responsibility.[3]

The UXBs dropped in such unexpected numbers formed at this stage, it is probably not too much to say, one of the largest threats to normal civil activities and war production. They immobilised important railway junctions and long stretches of line, blocked main

---

[1] Chapter XIII below.

[2] pp. 385, 390. UXPMs=unexploded parachute mines.

[3] A.R.P. Dept. Circular 239, 10th September 1939; H.S.C. 88/40, 11th May 1940.

roads and approaches to airfields and vital factories, and made it necessary to evacuate many civilians from their homes. Mr Churchill has recorded the special organisation set up in September to deal with this menace, the flow of volunteers to join the Royal Engineers' Bomb Disposal Sections, and his opinion that the overworked epithet 'grim' should have been reserved for their dangerous occupation.[1] But although by the end of October some 7,000 persons were employed throughout the country in bomb disposal, the number of UXBs still to be dealt with remained then and for many weeks to come at about 3,000.

It appears, at least in retrospect to an historical student, that much of importance in civil defence took place in a sphere that (whatever the current official organisation) cannot be satisfactorily classified as either 'operational' or 'administrative' but partook in some measure of both. In this the UXBs posed various problems, first of which, probably, was the detection of the genuine article from the false one. Since the fall of a bomb was often indicated by no more than a hole in the ground, or the effect of an explosion was often hidden, reports of the presence of UXBs much exceeded their actual number; and much time and effort was expended in investigating these reports. In London Region late in September ten 'Bomb Reconnaissance Officers', not necessarily persons with technical knowledge, were appointed with the function of sifting these reports, making inspections and giving authoritative advice. This was the genesis of the special training, which naturally took time and will be more fully described later, of police, wardens and civilian volunteers of various kinds in the detection and reporting of unexploded bombs and shells.[2]

Another problem, related to this one, was that of establishing priorities for the removal of unexploded bombs, real or supposed. Ministers, for example those of Transport and Supply, naturally came into competition with one another in this matter, while the maps in Regional War Rooms and local control centres continued to show an accumulation of UXBs waiting to be removed. This problem was one in which use was made of the co-ordinating machinery of the Home Defence Executive.[3] Regional Commissioners, it was decided, should have overriding authority in settling priorities, and the Ministry of Home Security began the formulation of categories of 'relative urgency' for the removal of unexploded missiles.

The fourth major feature not fully foreseen was the direct consequence of the three just described, though perhaps more especially of the second. The heavy destruction of civilian property, the

---

[1] W. S. Churchill, *op. cit.*, Vol. II, pp. 318–320.

[2] Chapter XIII below; H.S.C. 300/40, 20th December 1940.

[3] pp. 357–358, 363.

evacuation made necessary by unexploded bombs, and continuous night attack created problems of a quite unexpected character and magnitude in the sphere which became officially called 'post-raid services'. The present volume stops short, in the main, at the stage of events which immediately preceded the coming into operation of these services.[1] It is concerned, as the reader is aware, with the forecasts of attack; the planning before the war which concentrated effort mainly in one Department and on particular methods of immediate mitigation; the widening responsibility of this Department once war had started as a co-ordinating agency, and its continuing special responsibility for 'first-line' defence.

The need, which the Battle of London first clearly disclosed, to make arrangements on an unforeseen scale for the care, feeding and rehousing of the general public, the restoration of public services and the revival of industrial production lies, as a general topic, beyond the scope of this volume. This clearly enlarged the responsibilities for co-ordination both of the Civil Defence Committee and the Ministry of Home Security, and much increased the activities relating to air attack of many of the sixteen or so civil Departments with which both these agencies of government were concerned. It constituted, it seems true to say, a further expansion of the scope of 'civil defence' comparable to the expansion already introduced by the unexpected threat of invasion in the previous May.[2]

The chief of these many post-raid services have been described in Mr Titmuss's *Problems of Social Policy* and other volumes in the present series of histories.[3] It is only necessary here to allude to a few of Mr. Titmuss's findings regarding post-raid welfare as the Battle of London presented this complex of problems.[4] When the battle broke on 7th September, he states, 'the relief services in London were overborne'. Rest centre accommodation was available, but with little structural protection, inadequate sanitation and few amenities. No provision was made for a stay of more than a few hours. Blankets, clothing and other essentials were scarce. Feeding arrangements were quite inadequate. Financial provision for the 'bombed-out' was limited. Adequate staff, not only to supervise rest-centres but to perform the many services required of local authorities, was totally lacking. By the end of September, Mr Titmuss states, 'a rest centre population of 25,000 had piled up in London Region . . . of which over 14,000 were in the desperately overcrowded centres run by the

---

[1] The chief exception is the attention paid in Chapter XIV below to the Regional Commissioners' activities regarding post-raid services.

[2] pp. 356–357.

[3] e.g., R. J. Hammond, *Food*; M. M. Postan, *British War Production*.

[4] R. M. Titmuss, *op. cit.*, Chapter XIV.

London County Council'. This total, he adds, was the highest figure reached throughout the war.

The days and weeks which followed 7th September proved turbulent in London official circles concerned with these matters. But order began to replace confusion, and improvement appears to have been steady. In the middle of September the Government appointed a committee under the chairmanship of Lord Horder to investigate shelter conditions.[1] Soon afterwards they appointed Mr Henry Willink a Special Commissioner at London Region to co-ordinate the work of the London County Council, the Boroughs and voluntary bodies in providing assistance for those rendered homeless by the raids.[2] It should here be added, as another of Mr Titmuss's conclusions, that 'it was the voluntary organisations— the Charity Organisation Society, the Society of Friends, the Settlement Workers, the London Council of Social Service and many others—who helped to hold the line during this period while the official machine was beginning to take effective action'. Many individual religious and other bodies, such as St Martin-in-the-Fields and the Central Hall, Westminster, had provided immediate all-night shelter, food and other assistance to the stricken public.

In a letter published in *The Times* on 11th September the Lord Mayor opened a Mansion House Fund to help to relieve the suffering of those rendered homeless or otherwise in distress. This fund financed the distribution of clothing and other essentials by the W.V.S. and other voluntary bodies; and amounted before the end of the war to over £4,700,000. The foundation before the war of the 'W.V.S. for Civil Defence' and its close association at the centre and in the Regions with the other civil defence authorities have been noticed in earlier chapters of this volume. Its many activities all over the country do not, for reasons already stated, fall within the scope of this volume; and these have been fully described in Charles Graves's *Women in Green: the Story of the W.V.S.*[3] But in the present context of post-raid problems two facts may properly be stressed. First, that the organisation, preparations and activities up to this date of the W.V.S. had equipped it to play a leading role when the major test came. Secondly that its work, with W.V.S. centres in every Metropolitan Borough, covered an immense and expanding range of functions, including the provision of mobile canteens, clothing, transport and miscellaneous advice.

The opening of the blitz on London had, as Mr Titmuss records, set going the second official evacuation movement, this time under

---

[1] Chapter XII below.

[2] H. Willink: b. 1894; R.F.A. 1914–19; Nat.&Cons. M.P. North Croydon, 1940–48 Minister of Health, 1943–45.

[3] Published 1948.

battle conditions.[1] The Government proceeded on this occasion more cautiously with their schemes; but caution soon proved to be unnecessary for, as this writer concludes, 'resistance to evacuation steadily hardened as Londoners became familiar with air raids and shelter life'. Instead of a mass evacuation there was now a 'trickle evacuation' through different channels into areas of relative safety according to the circumstances of the moment. Thus during September some 20,500 unaccompanied children were moved out of the Metropolitan area in organised parties, while in December only 760 children were so moved. The total by a year later, or September 1941, amounted to under 60,000. The response to arrangements for evacuation of certain classes of mothers with their children also proved small. The authorities, in addition to further publicising these facilities, now extended the scheme of 'assisted private evacuation' to homeless people of either sex.[2]

During these weeks of intensive attack the Government was considering the feasibility of bringing pressure to bear on institutions such as the Law Courts, professional bodies and selected business firms to move out of London.[3] But practical difficulties, particularly shortage of accommodation, and then reduction in the scale of the raiding, militated against such action. Though information on this matter is scarce, it is probably true that evacuation from London of established private firms and institutions had also now become only a trickle. Records and papers had, in large part, been sent to safe areas earlier in the war. Firms and so on which were bombed out did, of course, move to new premises on London's outskirts. Or join in what, with the growing number and dispersal of factories engaged in war production, had become a scramble for office and housing accommodation in places farther afield.[4]

The post-raid services, or measures to restore the life of the community after heavy attack, were not of course confined to the social services just discussed but included restoration of gas, water, telephones and other public utilities, the repair of roads, railways and houses, and the restoration of war and other production. These extensive activities also lie beyond the scope of the present volume, with the exception that some attention is paid to them in the closer consideration below of the Regional Commissioners' tasks. But it needs notice here that simultaneously with the appointment of Mr Henry Willink, Sir Warren Fisher, formerly the Regional Com-

---

[1] R. M. Titmuss, *op. cit.*, Chapter XVIII.

[2] pp. 360–361.

[3] pp. 361–362.

[4] The important topic of dispersal of war factories, initiated in the autumn of 1940, can be no more than mentioned in this volume. See M. M. Postan, *British War Production* (1952), pp. 164–6, etc., and other volumes in this series.

missioner for Manchester, was appointed as Special Commissioner at London Region to organise the clearance and salvage of debris and to co-ordinate the work of London's numerous authorities in restoring public utilities, communications, houses and other buildings.[1]

In his summary on 8th October of the war situation the Prime Minister paid chief attention to Hitler's attack on the civil population of our great cities, and especially London.[2] 'We have', he stated, 'to organise our lives and the life of our cities on the basis of dwelling under fire and of having always this additional chance—not a very serious chance—of death, added to the ordinary precarious character of human existence.' While warning the nation that savage, indiscriminate, attacks on the built-up areas would probably continue, he hinted at new methods being developed 'to make the wholesale bombing of the civilian population by night and in fog more exciting to the enemy than it is at present'. He himself, as well as Ministers and Members of Parliament, had visited, soon after the event, the scenes of enemy destruction. 'In all my life', he continued, 'I have never been treated with so much kindness as by the people who have suffered most. . . . On every side there is the cry, "We can take it," but with it, there is also the cry, "Give it 'em back".'

It was obvious that effective counter-attack, or the bombing of Berlin and other targets in Germany and the countries Germany had occupied, made it easier for the British public to sustain the onslaught on themselves. The operations of the Royal Air Force Bomber Command can, even less than those of Fighter Command, be summarised in the present volume.[3] These also raise the question of the difference between Bomber Command's claims as estimated at the time and announced to the public, and the more accurate assessment reached after Germany had been entered and victory had finally been gained. But it is clear that Britain's bomber forces were still small and, technically and in every other respect, feeling their way. They had assumed, among other things, that precise identification of targets would be far easier than it proved to be.

It is of interest, perhaps, to add here that the stories, current in Britain at the time, that Goering had flown personally with his *Luftwaffe* over London are now known to have been quite unfounded.[4]

The Prime Minister referred in the speech just mentioned to Ministerial changes in the sphere of civil defence. On 4th October Sir John Anderson became Lord President of the Council. Paying

---

[1] It must be added in this context that the Ministry of Works established a Directorate of Emergency Works to help the Ministry of Health over house repairs.

[2] H. of C. Deb., Vol. 365, Cols. 289-303.

[3] p. 379.

[4] See, e.g., Ewan Butler and Gordon Young, *Marshal Without Glory* (1951); p. 384.

tribute to his contribution (which had, in its latest phase, covered the two years since Munich) to civil defence Mr Churchill said, 'there is no better war horse in the Government'. In his new office Sir John Anderson presided over the Lord President's Committee which, as Professor Hancock and Mrs Gowing state it, 'became during 1941 the most important focus of civil government under the War Cabinet, handling and settling a great deal of the business which the War Cabinet itself would otherwise have had to carry as an additional burden'.[1] Concentrating at first on the largest issues of economic policy, this committee became from early in 1942 increasingly concerned with general home front problems.

Mr Herbert Morrison (hitherto Minister of Supply) succeeded to the double office of Home Secretary and Minister of Home Security, which he continued to hold until the end of the war in Europe.[2] He, in Mr Churchill's words, 'was a Londoner, versed in every aspect of Metropolitan administration'; as Leader of the London County Council for a number of years 'he had unrivalled experience of London government'.[3] At the end of November 1942 he entered the War Cabinet. His transfer to the Home Office and Ministry of Home Security was accompanied by the appointment of Miss Ellen Wilkinson as Joint Parliamentary Secretary to the latter Ministry; at first specially concerned with shelter problems, she also continued in this office until May 1945.[4] Sir George Gater returned at this time to serve as Secretary of the Ministry.

'It was', Mr Churchill has since written, 'no bed of roses which I offered Herbert Morrison'; and also that the Government's 'outlook at this time was that London, except for its strong modern buildings, would be gradually and soon reduced to a rubble-heap'. After some slackening of his effort at the end of September, the enemy's attack of the night of 4th/5th October was as serious in its results as any he had so far delivered. On certain nights of the week which followed the raids reached their peak in the early evening and the 'all-clear' was sounded by two o'clock in the morning. But more usually they continued in a rise and fall of intensity throughout the hours of darkness. Between 9th and 16th October buildings of national importance which were hit and in some measure damaged included St James's and Kensington Palaces, St Paul's, the Royal Courts of Justice, the National Gallery and the Natural History Museum. On 15th/16th October, in a full moon, the heaviest attack since 7th September was delivered by about 400 bombers which dropped over 1,000 high explosive bombs and made a large use of incendiaries.

---

[1] W. K. Hancock and M. M. Gowing, *op. cit.*, p. 220; p. 300.
[2] pp. 99, 106.
[3] W. S. Churchill, *op. cit.*, Vol. II, p. 326.
[4] p. 303.

They succeeded in putting five of London's main railway termini out of action, and interfering with others. The City's water supply was cut off at Edmonton, and 1,800 members of the Pioneer Corps were employed in its restoration. During this night some 430 persons were killed and 900 seriously injured.

During these autumn weeks the enemy succeeded in causing a number of serious incidents in shelters. Though the Tubes and (obviously to a lesser and varying extent) the London underground stations usually gave good protection, single incidents in October killed 7 shelterers at Trafalgar Square, 19 at Bounds Green, 64 at Balham and injured 15 at Camden Town. Public shelters hit, with serious loss of life, included shelters at Stoke Newington and Stepney, the Druid Street Railway Arches in Bermondsey and St Peter's Crypt, Southwark.[1] The London hospitals in which the victims of these and other incidents were being treated were repeatedly hit; in several of these weeks fifteen hospitals suffered loss of life and injury to doctors, nurses and patients and some degree of physical damage.

In the middle of these attacks Parliament debated the whole topic of air-raid precautions (as the chief passive counter-measures were still frequently called).[2] The principal topics on which Members were critical were the apparent ineffectiveness of the active defences; 'bombs without warnings' and other eccentricities (real or apparent) of the warning system; the lack of shelters and of amenities in those that existed; delays in dealing with UXBs, and the inadequacy of various post-raid services. Their criticisms were answered—in a manner which it is not possible for this narrative to suggest and even less to record—by the Minister of Health, Mr Malcolm MacDonald, and the Under-Secretaries of the Home Office and Air Ministry. Parliament, it must be added, had been provided with its own roof-spotters or 'Jim Crows', and when these reported imminent danger to the Speaker, Members descended to shelters which were not particularly safe.[3]

The executive branch of government, in the meantime, had had to take more active steps for its own safety. The evacuation of the seat of government from London had, as already recorded, been virtually abandoned as a plan during the previous May and June.[4] 'Under the bombardment the desire and resolve of the Government and of Parliament to remain in London was unmistakable, and I shared this feeling to the full.' Mr Churchill, recording this fact, also records the short and long-term measures which were now being taken for the

---

[1] See also Chapter XII below.
[2] H. of C. Deb.. Vol. 365. Cols. 390–464, 9th October 1940.
[3] p. 389.
[4] p. 362.

safe working in London of the central government machine.[1] These included the preparation of the 'Annexe' in the New Public Offices overlooking St James's Park, and of a citadel called 'Paddock' for the War Cabinet near Hampstead. It appeared late in October that 'the bombing of Whitehall and the centre of Government will be continuous until all old or insecure buildings have been demolished'. The Treasury, for example, had already been hit and its underground shelter demolished, and some fifty heavy bombs had fallen in the area of the Palace of Westminster and Whitehall.

The task of constructing a number of bomb-proof strongholds in London to house all the essential staffs of various Departments was therefore begun. Lord Beaverbrook, a member of the War Cabinet, was appointed to supervise the execution of this undertaking by the Ministry of Works.

Among other particular concerns of the Government was the danger to London's sewers and water supplies. Early in October the main sewage outfall was in fact destroyed, and all sewage had to be released into the Thames. This problem was nevertheless mastered. The threat of serious epidemics, arising particularly from overcrowded dormitory shelters, was also, and largely through energetic action, averted. A problem, less serious in its consequences but more intractable, was that of transport, especially into and out of the central area. Warnings and actual raids of a minor character in daylight continued, in addition to the continuous severe attack by night, to harass the public throughout October. These interruptions, and damage to the railways and the roads, caused difficulties of travel for which no rapid solution could be found.

The Ministry reported towards the end of October that though 'Londoners are feeling the strain, their spirit as a whole remains high'. The phrase 'London can take it' became current, and there is small doubt that this reflected the reality of the situation. Evacuation, whether under the official schemes or privately, was relatively small, and there was no panic.[2] Morale was naturally improved by the visible and efficient performance of their tasks, both in lulls and during attack, of the Wardens, Rescue and other A.R.P. Services and the police. Also by evidence of energetic official action in such matters as the improvement of sleeping and other conditions in shelters, the decision to call in troops for the clearance of debris, the quick repair of gas mains and so on, and the provision of adequate services for those who had been bombed out.

It is worth, however, emphasising that action in these and other matters often took time. During these eight or more weeks of the Battle of London the shelter provision, the welfare arrangements,

---

[1] W. S. Churchill, op. cit., Vol. II, Chapters XVII, XVIII.
[2] R. Bell, op. cit.; pp. 325, 361.

and the experience in all civil defence affairs of officials, the services and private citizens were not what they subsequently became. Looked at in retrospect, it is probably too much to say that the beginning (as these eight weeks effectively represented for London) was half of the whole. But it formed at least a substantial experience both acquired and overcome.

On the night of 3rd/4th November, for the first time since 7th September, no alarm sounded or bomb fell in London. The following day the Prime Minister, reviewing the war situation, summarised the main results up to that date of the enemy's air attacks.[1] The killed among civilians numbered 14,000 and the seriously injured 20,000, nearly four-fifths of these still relating to London. About 300 members of the armed forces had been killed, and 500 wounded. Much destruction and damage of house property had been caused; though not more than could as yet be covered by the scheme, announced to Parliament two months previously, for full national insurance against air raid damage to property. Only small physical damage had been done to aircraft production and other forms of war production; though as already emphasised time, sometimes substantial, had been lost through the frequency of warnings. The public services of water, fuel, electricity, gas and sewage in London and elsewhere had not, except locally and temporarily, broken down. The 'score' of German bombers and other planes destroyed was about three to each British plane lost.

A change was at this date impending in the policy of Germany's air offensive. The onslaught on Coventry on the night of 14th/15th November introduced a determined attempt to disorganise and subdue the chief industrial centres in the provinces. London, nevertheless, remained in the eyes of the enemy the principal target. And he returned frequently, in varying degrees of strength, to attack it during the following six months.

Dispersed Attack on Industrial Centres in the Provinces, with some Attention to London and the Ports

(November – December 1940)

The German Air Force turned to what, measured by the capacities of modern aerial attack, was a long term plan. London, regarded as the centre of the nation's civil life and of its war effort, had not been subdued. The season for invading Britain had, for the time being, passed. The enemy decided to attempt the systematic disorganisation and destruction of key factories and centres of war production up and down the country. He had been able in the course of the past few

---

[1] H. of C. Deb., Vol. 365, Cols. 1241–1250, 5th November 1940.

months both to improve his navigational devices and to train certain squadrons especially for the task of attacking industrial key points. The continuous growth in the number of such points, and in the total share of the nation's industry devoted to war production, may be brought to the reader's recollection.

Emphasis has already been laid on the fact that the enemy had taken to pursuing several objectives at the same time, or that his major objective was usually accompanied by one or more concurrent efforts which, in retrospect, appear in the light of strategic diversions.[1] During the Battle of London just discussed he had maintained a certain scale of attack against both ports and industrial centres. He was well aware of the dependence of Britain, as she stood alone, on overseas food and raw materials; and his aim of overwhelming London had already been accompanied by attempts to hinder the unloading and distribution of sea-borne supplies and, in lesser degree, interfere with war production.

Thus it is necessary to return slightly in time to record that attacks of varying weight were made during September and October on Merseyside, Manchester and elsewhere in Lancashire, Swansea and Cardiff, several towns in Scotland, Portsmouth, Southampton and elsewhere. Compared with what these towns and areas were to undergo later, these weeks must be regarded as a further period of 'warming up', though at a temperature generally higher than that of the widespread but light attacks of the summer.[2] It is of smaller relevance, however, to this narrative that the total weight of German attack (it was later confirmed) against Britain during these two months proved higher than in several of the succeeding months, than that this scattered raiding further exercised the civil defence services and the public and inflicted casualties and damage in important parts of the provinces.

The enemy (it later became known) defined a 'major attack' as one in which he intended his pilots to drop 100 metric tons or more of high explosive bombs.[3] Somewhat more than this weight of bombs had been dropped on the Liverpool-Birkenhead area during each of the last four nights of August. But while the Battle of London raged in September and October no single provincial town was attacked on this scale. With a few exceptions these attacks never exceeded a weight of about 10 tons. The chief secondary attack of September was directed, usually on about this scale, against Liverpool, which received the enemy's attention fifteen times. This,

---

[1] p. 387.

[2] pp. 358–360.

[3] It will be recalled that on one September night the enemy dropped over 350 tons on London (see p. 390). Since he was still at this stage using mainly 50 kg. or 250 kg. bombs, 100 tons was equivalent to 2,000 of the former or 400 of the latter.

of course, meant that Merseyside was for continuous periods under warning, and that the Control, Wardens and other A.R.P. services were frequently in action. On two nights in the month casualties reached the figures of about 45 killed and nearly as many seriously injured. But on most nights these were much smaller or even non-existent. While damage to civilian property—houses, businesses, and so on—was extensive, that to the docks and other war installations was still relatively small.

In October the attack was more dispersed over the north and the midlands, with southern ports (as they had done in September) receiving the enemy's occasional attention. Manchester was attacked three times (with casualties on the worst occasion of 22 killed and 27 seriously injured); Coventry about six times (with comparable casualties of 30 and 27); Liverpool again about nine times and Birmingham eleven. In the second half of the month the weight of attack on certain of these centres increased. Birmingham, in particular, suffered heavier onslaughts of between 20 and 47 tons. On the night of 25th-26th an attack (though only about 25 tons by weight) caused the city's worst casualty roll to date of some 170 persons killed and 140 seriously wounded. By the following night there were over 300 fires burning in the city, and substantial reinforcements had been sent to its fire brigades by other Regions. Damage to civilian property was already extensive; though, as in Liverpool, that to property directly concerned with the prosecution of the war was not yet serious.

It will be obvious to the reader that individual cases of damage to war production cannot, except rarely, be mentioned in a summary of this nature. Innumerable docks, factories, workshops, railways and other industrial establishments were, as the war proceeded, either 'affected' by air raids (to use a term employed by the Ministry which usually indicated shattered windows, the presence of an UXB or something else not particularly serious), or hit and in some degree damaged. A list of such places which suffered in one or other of these ways in one of the principal raids on London or other cities would fill several pages. But it may here be repeated that the Ministry maintained a department in London specially for the purposes of receiving and collating reports of damage to vital points, and classifying these places and advising on their geographical distribution.[1]

The determined attempt to subdue the provincial industrial centres dates from the onslaught on Coventry on the night of 14th-15th November. Early in the evening of 14th the attack opened with the dropping of considerable numbers of incendiary bombs in the area round the fourteenth-century cathedral. This ancient city, it may be

---

[1] The Key Points Intelligence Directorate; p. 304.

interpolated, had grown by the outbreak of the Second World War to a major centre of the engineering, motor-car and radio industries, with a population of some 250,000. Guided by the extensive fires already in progress, waves of enemy bombers dropped over 500 tons of bombs causing a roughly similar number of incidents in a small area. A shortage of water developed, gas and electricity supplies were completely disorganised and telephone communications broken. Some 18 UXPMs and 200 UXBs added to the confusion. Rescue squads were required in a hundred or so incidents, and since two hospitals were hit casualties had to be sent outside the city. In this raid 554 persons were killed and 865 seriously wounded.

The problems this attack presented to the local services and officials and the Regional Commissioner and his staff will be noticed in later chapters. It was obviously comparable, as an atrocity and in its effects, to the bombing exactly six months earlier of the centre of Rotterdam;[1] and like that event it was used as an occasion by the Germans for the coining of a new word, intended to strike terror into their opponents, *Coventrieren* or to 'Coventrate'. Though all factories were closed on the morning after the raid, the all-important industry of the city was not brought to a standstill. By destroying about 100 acres of the city centre, however, and disorganising utilities, transport and normal life the enemy caused interruptions of war production which it took about two months to amend. Though the people were stunned, their morale was not broken. The King visited the city on 16th November, and the large work of rehabilitation was put vigorously in hand.[2]

Though this attack for the moment overshadowed others, the enemy's raiding now became much more intense. The next night, 15th-16th November, the *Luftwaffe* again attacked London heavily under a full moon, causing death to some 142 persons and serious injury to over 430. All but one of the Metropolitan Boroughs, and 76 out of the total of 95 boroughs in London Region, were bombed.[3] A delayed-action 1,800 kg. bomb (almost the first of this size, which the Germans had christened 'Satan') fell at the G.P.O. sorting office, Mount Pleasant. Buildings hit and in some degree damaged included Westminster Abbey and School, the National Portrait Gallery, Wellington Barracks and four hospitals. At Euston Station

---

[1] p. 353. It is only intended to suggest that these attacks were so comparable to the layman and ordinary member of the British public. Clearly the objectives of the G.A.F. were different in the two cases. It later became known that the enemy crews were briefed to attack specific industrial targets in Coventry—though this fact could only give cold comfort to the owners of shops and homes in the centre of the city and the Cathedral authorities.

[2] *The Times*, 18th November 1940. For the influence of this raid on future British counter-attack see Sir A. Harris, *Bomber Offensive* (1947), pp. 82–5.

[3] This proved to be the largest 'score' in these particular terms of any single attack on London during the course of the war.

three platforms were put out of use, and 25 incidents affecting traffic on the four main-line railways were reported.

Although London was now (though in a strictly limited sense) a secondary objective, raids of some severity were maintained against it each night for over a week. It was not, in fact, until 25th-26th November that the capital enjoyed its first twenty-four hour period since 7th September (or for twelve weeks) free of an air raid warning. But, as earlier remarked, the enemy returned on many occasions during the next six months to make attacks, sometimes severe and sometimes light, on London.

Statistics of enemy raiders, bomb tonnages dropped, casualties caused and physical damage, even if much fuller than any it is possible for this narrative to present, can, of course, only convey a partial account of any air raid or series of raids. For fuller description in this sense recourse must be had to the files of the contemporary Press, collections of articles subsequently republished by journalists, local histories (official and otherwise), memoirs and literature.[1] Though some of such different kinds of publications have been quoted in this history these form, it is needless to say, only a fraction of those which have so far appeared. And it can be asserted with confidence that the number of deliberate accounts of A.R.P. and the attacks which followed on particular localities and institutions, and of more or less incidental descriptions of these in literature, will grow.

Books of this nature, and especially those with a claim to be literature, may describe, besides the attacks, the condition (which was nearly as much a part of the matter) of waiting to be attacked, wondering and living under the black-out and other restrictions in the expectation of future raids. In *Caught*, for example, Henry Green has described the experience of a London A.F.S. station in the long waiting period of the twilight war and then in action in the dock fires.[2] Miss Elizabeth Bowen's *Heat of the Day* serves particularly to record the atmosphere of London at the stage which this narrative has reached, at least as this enveloped the large class working in offices and living (say) west of the City.[3] In this 'heady autumn', as she describes it, the daytime was felt as 'a curious holiday from fear'. The roping off of the streets drew crowds; the diverted traffic streaming past modest windows in side-streets 'set up an overpowering sense of London's organic power, a source which forced for itself new channels'. But there were no holidays and 'fatigue was the one reality . . . the dead made their anonymous presence felt throughout London'. Those left began to try to break down indifference

---

[1] The officially-sponsored booklet on the Big Blitz, *Front-Line, 1940–41* (1942) had a considerable circulation during the war.

[2] Published 1943.

[3] Published 1949.

while there was still time. For 'the garrison' (as she calls the black-coated classes) there was plenty of everything—attention, drink, taxis, most of all space. Two years later, when the war had moved from the horizon to the map, this autumn of 1940 seemed 'more apocryphal than peace'.

This description may be taken, *mutatis mutandis*, for other cities at this stage of the war, or after these had received a certain share of attack and were living in expectation of more. Its psychological analysis—in particular the impression which the Battle of London had created of space—may be linked with the fact that the smaller the city or the target attacked by an equal number of enemy aircraft or weight of bombs the larger the damage, dislocation and moral disturbance which was liable to result. In this summary the reader should bear in mind that an attack by x aircraft on Birmingham or Bristol was not the same as one (say) on Southampton, Plymouth, Banbury, Hull or Swindon.

Birmingham received its heaviest raid so far on the night of 19th-20th November, when some 400 tons of high explosive and nearly 30,000 incendiary bombs were dropped on the city, affecting almost every part of its big area. Over 800 incidents including a large number of fires were caused, and the Rescue Services had to call for aid from outside. Some 450 persons were killed and 540 badly injured. But the story was repeated of much damage to houses, shops and so on but little to establishments, apart from the railways, engaged in direct war work. The enemy now began to attack provincial towns for two or more nights in succession. Thus Birmingham was raided again less severely on 20th-21st and, after a night's pause, once more heavily on 22nd-23rd.

Southampton suffered two sharp raids in these weeks followed by two successive attacks on the last night of the month and the first night of December.[1] Bristol had its heaviest attack so far, a conspicuous example of 'area bombing', on the night of 24th-25th November. About 130 enemy bombers succeeded in killing 196 people and badly injuring a further 140 or so. They created many fires, the extinguishing of which was much hindered by water failures, and did much damage to the principal shopping centres. Before the end of the year this city suffered two more heavy attacks. In one of these the Regional Headquarters received a direct hit, though there were no casualties and work continued in the underground war room.

On 8th-9th December the *Luftwaffe*, possibly as a reprisal for an R.A.F. attack on Dusseldorf, inflicted London with its longest and heaviest raid for two months. Some 400 enemy bombers maintained the attack from early evening until seven o'clock the next morning. They killed some 250 persons and badly wounded over

---

[1] See Bernard Knowles, *Southampton: The English Gateway* (1951).

630, and started over 1,700 fires, including many in the docks. Buildings hit included Westminster Abbey and the House of Commons (though not severely), the Royal Mint, the Royal Naval College and once again a number of hospitals. One bomb fell on Broadcasting House while the nine o'clock news was being read. Though this did severe damage, necessitating evacuation of all except the A.R.P. parties, the broadcasting service was maintained.

The enemy turned back to the provinces, paying serious attention before Christmas to Merseyside again, Manchester, Birmingham, Sheffield, Portsmouth and Gosport, Leicester and other places. Sheffield received its first, and as it proved heavy, taste of attack on 12th-13th December, followed by a second attack three nights later. Though its commercial centre was severely damaged, particularly by fire, most of the industrial damage was superficial. Some 589 citizens were killed and 488 seriously injured in these two raids. Manchester, which compared with Liverpool had so far escaped lightly, was heavily attacked on the nights of 22nd-23rd and 23rd-24th. Much damage was caused by fires, especially in the industrial Trafford Park area, both main railway stations and the chief bus depot were hit, and some 376 persons killed and a rather larger number badly injured.

Probably on account of the weather, the Germans refrained from attack on Christmas Day and for two or three days thereafter. It is of practical significance to add that during the raids of November and December just summarised they had deliberately chosen Sunday nights, when the civil defence services and the public might be expected to be less on the alert, for their heaviest fire attacks on successive cities.

On the night of 27th-28th they resumed raiding in earnest with London as the main target. After attack on the next night on Plymouth and on the following night on Crewe, they returned on 29th-30th to make (as it proved) one of the most spectacular raids of the war on London. It was this attack which 'fired', on a much larger scale than in the reign of King Charles II, the City of London. Six conflagrations enveloped most of this square-mile. At the height of the attack the river Thames was dead low, so that fire-boats could not be fully used and many fires had to be abandoned. The Guildhall was destroyed, and eight Wren Churches burnt out. Guy's Hospital had to be evacuated and eight other hospitals were damaged. The Central Telegraph Office was demolished and three City telephone exchanges in the modern Wood Street building had to be abandoned.[1] Railway traffic was disorganised by the closing of five termini and

---

[1] This building, which was burnt out, also contained the Headquarters P.A.B.X. and hundreds of repeaters for circuits passing through to Faraday Building. This night's attack inflicted the worst blow of the war on G.P.O. telecommunications plant.

sixteen underground stations. The damage at certain of the docks was considerable. Some 163 persons were killed and 509 seriously injured.

Growing Concentration of the Blitz on the Battle of the Atlantic Ports (January – May 1941)

In his Christmas Day broadcast the King said, 'this time we are all in the front line and the danger together', and 'we have surmounted a grave crisis. We do not underrate the dangers and difficulties which confront us still, but we take courage and comfort from the successes which our fighting men and their Allies have won at heavy odds by land and air and sea'.[1] On 17th January Mr Churchill, speaking at Glasgow, warned that 'before us lie many months of having to endure bombardment of our cities and industrial areas without the power to make equal reply'.

After the fire-raising attack on London at the end of December the enemy reverted to widespread raiding and devoted his air, as well as other resources, increasingly to economic blockade. To the growing U-boat scourge, Mr Churchill has written, 'was now added air attack far out on the ocean by long-range aircraft'. The Port of London had been cut down to a quarter of its capacity. The Channel was an actual war area. Air attack had already gravely hampered the sole remaining chief commercial ports on the Mersey, the Clyde and the Avon. 'It was a struggle to breathe.'[2]

Air attack was aimed in growing degree in January on the west and south-west of Britain. Out of fourteen raids in this month in which more than 50 aircraft were over the target, ten were on ports in these areas. A heavy incendiary raid on Cardiff on 2nd-3rd January was effectively met by the fire service. But 167 persons were killed and rather more seriously injured, some damage was done to public utilities, factories and shipbuilding yards, and Llandaff Cathedral was very severely damaged. The following night about 180 bombers maintained an all-night attack against the docks and surrounding districts of Bristol. This killed 142 persons and badly injured nearly as many, destroyed or damaged a number of sheds in the docks, and necessitated the bringing into use of the city's emergency telephone exchange.

It must here be interpolated that the danger and damage to telephone exchanges up and down the country have necessarily received scant notice in this volume. By the nature of their work and the fact

---

[1] *King George VI to his Peoples, 1936-51* (1952).
[2] W. S. Churchill, *op. cit.*, Vol. III, Chapter VII.

that they were usually in the centres of towns, these suffered severely
—in terms both of danger and discomfort to their occupants and
damage to buildings and equipment.[1] Apart from the Wood Street,
London exchange just mentioned, no exchange in the country was
ever abandoned, though emergency exchanges in better-protected
parts of their buildings had often to be taken into use. Besides direct
hits and fire spread from other buildings, such external causes as
damage to street cables often disrupted their working.

On 9th-10th some 300 bombers attacked all Regions except
Scotland with targets which included London, Chatham, Portsmouth, Bristol, Avonmouth, Manchester, Liverpool and Birkenhead.
The next night a particularly heavy raid was made on Portsmouth,
especially its centre and southern district. This caused 194 fatal
and over 200 serious casualties, fires and other damage to the dockyards and the Guildhall which housed the A.R.P. Control, and total
interruption of electricity supplies for two and a half days.[2] The two
following nights forces of about the same size made short sharp
raids on London, starting a number of large fires.

As a consequence of the 'incendiary classic' on London just after
Christmas the War Cabinet had decided on the major step of introducing compulsion (for men only) for civil defence duties.[3] On
31st December Mr Herbert Morrison had announced this fact in a
broadcast, and also appealed for volunteers on a large scale to
form street fire-fighting parties—'fall in the fire-bomb fighters!'
During the two raids just mentioned the amateur fire-fighters
did, in fact, fall in to some effect and mastered the fires quickly,
in spite of many explosive incendiary bombs and continued shortage
of stirrup pumps. These raids caused two serious railway incidents.
A bomb killed 43 persons, most of them waiting passengers, at
Liverpool Street station. Another fell on the Bank underground
station causing the roof to cave in and the blast to travel down the
shaft, and killing 38 shelterers.[4] A block of Lambeth Hospital was
also destroyed, with seven fatal casualties.

Bad weather, including snow, then gave a brief respite. From
15th-18th January the enemy contrived to make substantial attacks
on Derby, Nottingham and elsewhere in the Midlands and to return
to attack Bristol, Avonmouth and Swansea. Then followed two to
three weeks of less activity on the part of the enemy (except for
minelaying) than at any time since the previous summer. But in
mid-February night attack was resumed, mainly against Scotland,

---

[1] e.g., switchboard suites were usually on the top floor of a building used by an
exchange in order to get the maximum amount of light through a central skylight.

[2] Nearly a year was needed to recommission the two damaged generating sets of the
city's power station.

[3] See Chapter XIII below.

[4] See Charles Graves, *London Transport Carried On* (1947), p. 69.

the east coast and aerodromes in East Anglia. This widespread bombing, though on the whole ineffective, occasioned three out-standing incidents. On 13th February a 2,500 kg. bomb at Hendon destroyed 196 homes, made 170 uninhabitable, damaged 400 more, killed 75 people and injured about 445. On the next day a bomb of the same size fell on open ground at Harrow but caused considerable damage to houses. And a bomb which exploded in an archway shelter at London Bridge station caused heavy casualties among shelterers.

With the weather improving, the Germans intensified their attacks on the ports and their efforts to put these and other towns out of action by raids on several successive nights. From 19th February to 12th May (or for the next twelve weeks) they mounted 61 raids employing more than 50 aircraft, and in 33 of these they dropped more than 100 tons of bombs. Of the 61 attacks, 36 were made against English and Welsh western ports, 3 against Belfast, 7 against London, 6 against Hull, 2 against Newcastle, 1 against Sunderland and 6 against other provincial centres. About 80 per cent. of all this effort was therefore directed against ports, and about 60 per cent. against targets in the west and south-west.

On the nights of 19th and 20th February Swansea was attacked by some 60 to 70 bombers, and on the 21st once again though by a smaller force. These followed the pattern, now becoming familiar, of parachute flares succeeded by incendiaries which were in turn succeeded by high explosive. Though the docks and other military targets escaped lightly, the centre of the town suffered severe damage. Though a few thousand people 'trekked' out of the danger zone each night, the population was reported to have 'stood up very well' to the onslaught. Some 14 Rest Centres to accommodate over 2,000 homeless had been opened by 22nd February. The casualty roll was about 230 killed and a similar number seriously hurt.

Cardiff was again bombed, with broadly similar technique and results, on three nights in the first week of March. The shopping and business streets in its centre were badly damaged while the docks hardly suffered at all and fires were quickly brought under control; on the worst night, 3rd-4th March, 57 citizens were killed and 119 badly injured. During the following week the *Luftwaffe* attacked Portsmouth on five nights. On that of 10th-11th their efforts, con-centrated on the dockyard area, met with a good deal of success. Large fires were started in the dockyard and a victualling yard, five naval oil tanks were fired, two magazines exploded and the town's electricity system was badly damaged. On this and the following night 115 persons were killed and 170 seriously hurt in Portsmouth and Gosport.

On 12th-13th the enemy again heavily attacked Merseyside and on the next night (besides a further visit to Merseyside) they for the first time gave Clydeside their serious attention. About 200 bombers concentrated on this area, to which a similar force returned the next night. While the centre of Glasgow escaped lightly, severe damage was caused along the riverside from Govan to Clydebank. Possibly every house on Clydebank was either destroyed or in some degree damaged, and at least half of the 50,000 inhabitants of this area were evacuated officially or otherwise. Rest centres, feeding and other arrangements presented serious difficulties.[1] The Rothesay and other docks suffered severely. The shipbuilding yards, though a number were hit, were not seriously damaged. But over twenty key points, including the Dalnottar oil depot, were hit, civil defence establishments suffered heavily, railway and other communications were badly disorganised, and unlucky hits on water mains seriously handicapped the work of fighting fires. In these two nights some 1,235 persons were killed and 1,029 seriously wounded in the area— figures which raised the national totals (1,874 killed and 2,197 injured) for the current eight-day period to the highest so far suffered.

These attacks confirmed certain conclusions, which were already becoming apparent, regarding the total consequences of the enemy's air blitz, now entering on its seventh month. Damage to vital war production had not yet been serious. But the effect (indirect and otherwise) on less-essential production had been substantial; and that, so far only local and temporary, on morale had not been negligible. Here entered, not merely in relation to Clydeside, the variety of opinion on this topic by those at the centre who had to take action on reports about morale to which reference has been made earlier.[2]

Perhaps it may here be re-emphasised, first that morale was always an imponderable factor, and secondly that the most responsible authorities had no knowledge, except within broad limits, of what the enemy was next going to attempt. But in these Clydeside raids the connection between morale (not only of the area bombed) and the publication of air raid casualty figures acquired new practical significance. It must be recalled that at this stage of the war the Government did not, until a certain period of time had elapsed, announce what precise city or target the enemy had attacked, or publish details of the casualties and damage inflicted.[3] But a few days after these Clydeside raids the official announcement (as an exceptional arrangement) included casualty figures which later proved to be a serious underestimate. Rumour then took the upper hand, and

---

[1] See R. M. Titmuss, *op. cit.*, pp. 313–314.

[2] p. 295.

[3] There was, however, immediate announcement by 'Lord Haw-Haw' and others on the enemy wireless of claims, of varying degrees of accuracy, about the British objectives hit and casualties inflicted.

some lack of confidence in the official communiqués developed. The situation gave a striking example of the handicap, mentioned earlier, imposed on the Government by the inaccuracy (often unavoidable) of the first reports from the scene of an attack.[1]

After discussion in the War Cabinet and the Civil Defence Committees the Home Secretary gave revised figures of the large Clydeside casualties to the House of Commons. The Civil Defence Committee had agreed that it would be advisable in future to avoid publishing casualty figures (and especially early estimates based on first local impressions) of specific attacks. And Mr Morrison informed the House that his action in this case was not to be regarded as creating a precedent.

The *Luftwaffe's* spring offensive, in which it employed a much higher proportion of heavy H.E.s and many parachute mines, began to produce more substantial results. On the night, 14th-15th March, of the second Clydeside attack it delivered bombs on every Region, and in particular on Sheffield, Leeds and elsewhere in the West Riding and on Hull. The shopping centre of Leeds was badly damaged, eight factories in this area were hit, telephone communications almost put out of action, road transport badly disorganised, 64 persons killed and nearly as many badly injured. In Hull 17 people were killed and 22 seriously injured, and in Sheffield the comparable casualties were 14 and 29. Minor attacks were made this same night on London, Southampton, Plymouth, Portland, Tunstall, Merseyside and Tipton.

On the night of 15th-16th, which was foggy, some 115 bombers (about a third of the force deployed on the three previous nights) concentrated on London and the Home Counties. Some thirty London boroughs, mainly in the east and south-east, were bombed, 166 fires were started, some damage was caused to the docks, and about 70 citizens were killed and 120 badly wounded.

A literary classic of the war, Richard Hillary's *The Last Enemy*, which describes London at about this time derives special interest from the fact that the writer was a Battle of Britain pilot and (for the time being) a professional airman.[2] He records his taxidriver remarking, 'Jerry's wasting 'is time trying to break our morale, when 'e might be doing real damage on some small town'. The war, he found, 'was practically never discussed except as a joke'; but Londoners, having shown for long enough that they could take it, 'were waiting on the time when it would be their turn to dish it out'. He describes what it felt like to experience a 'near miss', and to be called upon to help to dig out (with his hands) a victim from a demolished building.

[1] p. 359.
[2] Published 1943.

The catalogue—unavoidable in an attempt to record the attacks of four years in a single chapter—of attacks early in 1941 must be resumed by recording a raid of some weight on the night of 16th-17th March on Bristol. From the reports received at the centre this raid did not appear particularly unusual. Yet some 255 of Bristol's citizens were killed and 145 seriously injured, 168 fires were started, about 6,000 houses were in some measure damaged, the central districts suffered heavily, two public shelters and a church crypt containing shelterers were hit causing serious loss of life and the railways were disorganised. A raid on Hull on this night caused 94 fatal casualties and serious injury to nearly 70 persons and a good deal of damage by fire, and isolated the city for a time from the electricity grid system.

On the night of 19th-20th March London was again the target, some 500 bombers making a six-hour raid which was the heaviest the capital had experienced since the previous October. Some 750 people were killed and nearly 1,200 badly injured. The docks were the principal objective and the heaviest weight of attack fell on West Ham, Poplar and Stepney. Some 1,880 fires, 3 of which were officially classified as conflagrations and over 60 as serious, which the enemy started was a larger number than in any previous raid. In Poplar a shelter and A.R.P. store were set on fire and some 80 people killed in a single incident. Considerable damage was caused to factories and warehouses in the dock areas.

For the two following nights Plymouth was the enemy's main target. On the 20th the King and Queen visited the city, which enjoyed a gala day with bands and dancing on the Hoe. Soon after their Majesties' departure the first of a force of over 150 raiders appeared and the bombs began to fall. Next night over 100 raiders continued the assault.[1] Little damage was done to the large naval and military establishments, but the consequences to the city and its 215,000 inhabitants were severe. The whole area within a radius of 600 yards from the Guildhall was levelled, a large part of the shopping centre was destroyed by fire as the result of a complete failure of water supplies, over 18,000 houses were destroyed or damaged, 329 persons killed, 283 badly injured and some 5,000 made homeless. The two largest hospitals were damaged. The municipal offices were destroyed. These included the A.R.P. Control Room, which was wiped out with all its maps, reports and records of UXBs, though without casualties. Telephone communications were completely disorganised.

Operational control had then to be exercised from Devonport, with the help of military despatch riders and police cyclists. The Royal Navy gave invaluable help to the hard-pressed civil defence

---

[1] German records show 155 and 168 raiders on these two nights.

services, and assisted greatly in establishing post-raid services, for which the provision made beforehand proved quite inadequate.

Bad or indifferent weather over the enemy's bases caused a marked decline in the weight of attack during the latter part of March and the first week of April. Attacks on shipping and mine-laying, especially from Norwegian bases, nevertheless continued unabated. And in these two weeks or so the towns attacked, with some loss of life and damage, included Shanklin, Ipswich, Gloucester, Hull, Yeovil, Bristol, Hythe, Poole, Folkestone, Norwich and Eastbourne. Small numbers of bombs were dropped ineffectively in many other places, ranging from the southern counties and South Wales to Fair Isle north of the Orkneys.

On the night of 7th-8th April heavier attack was resumed with some 370 German bombers ranging over every Region. These paid special attention to Clydeside, where about 50 planes were reported over the districts which had suffered so severely in the previous month, Tyneside and Tees-side, where they achieved little, and Yarmouth, where 20 persons were killed and substantial civil damage was inflicted. This night was also notable for the first raid in any strength on Belfast, where some 100 casualties were caused but the damage, except to one shipbuilding yard, was not heavy.The next night some 250 bombers made the biggest attack on Coventry which this city had experienced since the memorable night of 14th-15th November, and two nights later a smaller force came back to Coventry.[1] Casualties in these two raids were some 475 killed and over 700 seriously injured, besides those—who have had to be statistically disregarded throughout this summary—who were injured in a degree which did not necessitate admission to a hospital. Several aircraft and other important works were damaged, the central police station suffered casualties and damage by fire, the Warwickshire Hospital, King Henry VIII's school and St. Mary's Hall were damaged by fire, and some 50 water mains and many gas mains were cut.

The inhabitants of Coventry and of the many other provincial centres mentioned in this summary may perhaps have pondered in April 1941 on the admonition of Holy Writ that 'here we have no continuing city'. They were naturally unaware of the rather more optimistic view being taken at this date at the centre about the enemy's air offensive against Britain. Widespread raiding suggested an attempt to avoid the casualties lately inflicted by Britain's active defences during concentrated attacks. Attempts to dislocate production by keeping large areas in the north under warning and dropping bombs at many places seemed, at least temporarily, to be the *Luftwaffe's* strategy. In spite of the enemy's improved

---

[1] pp. 404–405.

navigation and accuracy of aim, military damage had not been extensive. And scattered raiding had only 'dented' local morale, in the sense of arousing anger but not despair, and had given the stricken cities opportunity to recover.

During the week of 16th-23rd April the enemy, while continuing to hammer at the western ports, notably Portsmouth, made two more severe assaults on London. These diversions from the main strategy may have been due to recent heavier R.A.F. raids on Berlin. On the night of 16th-17th some 450 aircraft made the heaviest raid so far on the capital, dropping 446 tons of high explosive and 150 tons of incendiaries and causing more casualties— about 1,180 killed and 2,230 badly injured—than in any previous attack.[1] Over 2,250 fires were started; and the centre and south of the metropolis bore the brunt of the attack. Civil buildings, transport and communications were badly damaged. At one stage all Southern Railway termini were closed, several stretches of underground railway were suspended and road services were much disorganised. Though water and electricity supplies were fairly well maintained, gas supplies were severely interrupted.

More than 60 public buildings, including the Houses of Parliament, the Admiralty and the Law Courts, were in some degree damaged. At least 6 churches were destroyed and a further 13 damaged; and 18 hospitals were affected. Among the churches concerned was St. Paul's Cathedral which suffered a direct hit, causing (as it proved) the worst damage inflicted on the Cathedral in the war. In *Saint Paul's Cathedral in Wartime* the reader can find a graphic account of the activities of the Cathedral's Watch both in preparation and under attack.[2] On this particular night a fierce, concentrated, attack appeared to be deliberately made on the Cathedral. A heavy high explosive bomb fell through the North Transept causing much destruction, though 'the Dome almost miraculously remained unmoved and intact'. The whole east end was threatened by a parachute mine, which was ultimately rendered harmless by a naval party.

Three nights later the enemy again attacked London, concentrating this time on the East End and the docks. Casualties were again heavy—over 1,200 killed and 1,000 seriously wounded. Parachute mines and incendiaries caused considerable damage to sheds, warehouses, silos, timber yards, barges, trucks and offices. The Royal Naval College, Greenwich, St. Peter's Hospital, Stepney

---

[1] German records show the much higher figures of 685 aircraft, 890 tons of H.E. and 4,200 incendiary canisters dropped. This attack proved the worst on London of the war in terms of weight of bombs dropped, casualties inflicted and the number of fires caused.

[2] W. R. Matthews (1946). During the First World War a volunteer watch had also kept guard in the Cathedral every night.

(where a serious fire caused casualties among staff and patients), a number of other hospitals, churches and museums were hit or damaged by blast.

After two nights of relative respite the enemy began on 21st April an all-out attempt to destroy Plymouth. On this and the two succeeding nights, and again on the nights of 28th and 29th, forces varying from 100–150 aircraft bombed the city relentlessly. An American journalist, Quentin Reynolds, who had lived through London's battles since September and seen Coventry, Southampton and Liverpool, records 'nothing I had seen prepared me for the sight of Plymouth' after its five nights of attack in seven.[1] More coldly stated than his eye-witness account, nearly 600 citizens had been killed and another 440 badly wounded. To the destruction caused in March was added damage to another 20,000 houses and complete obliteration of the shopping centre. The A.R.P. Control Centre was again hit. The dockyards and other service establishments did not, this time, escape and at one period Devonport dockyards appeared to be a sheet of flame.

The city nearly reached breaking-point, and the Deputy Regional Commissioner, General Lindsay, and the Senior Regional Officer of the Ministry of Health established headquarters at Tavistock to try to restore the life of the community. Quentin Reynolds reported Plymouth as being 'virtually a city without children. Every large untouched building not used as a hospital or feeding centre is a rest centre'. It has earlier been recorded that the March attacks found the post-raid services quite inadequate, and these were considerably handicapped by the fact that Plymouth's hinterland was rural and sparsely populated.[2] Only 10 per cent of the city's food distribution facilities remained, and the problem of the 40,000 or so homeless citizens was acute. Instant help was provided by the 'Queen's Messengers' (Ministry of Food mobile canteens), the W.V.S. and other voluntary and official bodies.[3] It appears that the tablet commemorating the departure of the Pilgrims to Plymouth, Massachusetts, escaped the universal destruction.

Fortunately, the enemy then turned from Plymouth to other targets. On 27th-28th they made a severe attack on Portsmouth, killing over 90 persons and badly injuring 135. During the first week of May they despatched an average of 270 long-range bombers each night (as compared with an average of 202 in the previous September). Belfast was heavily attacked on the nights of 4th-5th and 5th-6th, with casualties of nearly 200 killed and about the same number

---

[1] Quentin Reynolds, *Only the Stars are Neutral* (1942).

[2] p. 415.

[3] For information about these mobile canteens see R. J. Hammond, *Food*, Vol. II n this series.

seriously hurt. The first serious raid on this city of 7th-8th April, which, like the others, is fully described in the official history of the war in Northern Ireland, had been followed by a heavier one eight days later which caused over 750 deaths and 450 cases of serious injury. Greenock was heavily attacked in this week, and (less severely) Barrow-in-Furness, Tynemouth, Paisley, Portsmouth, Sunderland and Torquay.

But the most significant enemy effort of this week was an attack for seven consecutive nights (a record for the provinces) on Merseyside.[1] Even here lack of enemy concentration, or a simultaneous attention to other targets, confuses the historical picture. For example, on 5th-6th May, when the number of German bombers sent against Britain rose to over 400, Merseyside, Clydeside, Belfast and Tyneside shared the honours of being attacked. The Liverpool Docks cover, of course, a considerable area and Merseyside a much larger one. Yet the cumulative effects, in the moral and material spheres, of these nightly attacks began to produce serious results. The toll of casualties was some 1,900 killed and 1,450 badly hurt; and nearly half of the deaths were thought to have been inflicted on the worst night, 3rd-4th May. The homeless in rest centres were estimated at over 70,000.

The destruction of certain records, including those of the 'Bomb Census', made it impossible for the authorities to apportion much of the damage to particular nights.[2] Though the main weight fell on Liverpool, Bootle, Birkenhead and Wallasey also suffered severely. Nearly 70 out of 144 berths were at some stage put out of action, the blocking of road and rail approaches caused much interference to the working of the docks, and tonnage landed was for a time cut to one quarter. The utilities damaged included the two main generating stations of the Liverpool area, and all main trunk telephone routes were cut. The General Post Office and ten hospitals in Liverpool were hit. Over 66,000 houses were demolished or damaged. Mr Churchill has concluded that 'had the enemy persisted the Battle of the Atlantic would have been even more closely run than it was'.[3]

The enemy, fortunately, turned away and delivered his main attack on the 8th-9th on Hull, which had also been a secondary target on the previous night. On these two nights nearly 450 people were killed, 300 seriously injured and some 10 per cent of the population was made homeless. Nearly the whole length of the riverside quay was gutted by fire, and considerable damage was caused to the docks and to food stores. On 8th-9th Nottingham suffered its first heavy raid, when 157 persons were killed and 116 badly injured. The Civil Defence Regional Store was destroyed, severe damage was done

---

[1] This also proved the longest unbroken sequence of serious attacks on any provincial area of the whole war.
[2] p. 380.
[3] W. S. Churchill, *op. cit.*, Vol. III, p. 39.

to several of Messrs. Boots' factories and the University College and Masonic Hall were among the buildings hit.

Soon after eleven o'clock on the night of 10th-11th May the *Luftwaffe* returned in a full moon to attack London on a scale similar to that of three weeks earlier.[1] Some 550 aircraft maintained the onslaught for five hours, mainly on the capital's centre, eastern and south-eastern districts, though in all 75 boroughs were involved. Some 440 tons of high explosive, many parachute mines and large numbers of incendiaries were dropped.[2] The casualties of some 1,436 killed and about 1,800 seriously injured were similar to those of 16th-17th April. Nearly 2,200 fires were started. This attack has outstanding historical interest due to the enemy's destruction by fire of the Chamber of the House of Commons and damage to Westminster Abbey and many other national shrines, religious and secular. The heaviest blows on the Palace of Westminster fell first on the courts and corridors adjoining the House of Lords. Later, incendiaries on the Victoria Tower caused a spectacular and highly dangerous blaze. While the staffs were dealing with these and other fires, incendiaries, probably accompanied by an oil bomb, destroyed the Commons Chamber. Westminster Hall was somehow preserved, in large part owing to energetic action by Mr Walter Elliot, M.P.[3]

Though Westminster Abbey was not seriously damaged, its Deanery was destroyed by fire, and the adjoining Westminster School was badly damaged. Other buildings in some degree damaged included St. James's Palace, the War Office, the London Museum, the Public Record Office, the British Museum, the Mansion House, the Guildhall Art Library and the Tower. Churches damaged included St. Clement Danes, St. Stephen's Walbrook, St. Mary-le-Bow, Holy Trinity, Sloane Street and St. Columba's, Pont Street. The Halls of the Mercers, Salters, Cordwainers, Cutlers and Butchers' Companies in the City were destroyed. Fourteen hospitals, including the Children's Hospital, Westminster, were involved. Much damage was caused to civil defence premises, fire stations and rest centres. The Mayors of Westminster and Bermondsey were killed. All but one of the main-line railway stations were blocked. The Elephant and Castle junction, Southwark, was the scene of a conflagration.

Quentin Reynolds, who graphically reported this raid to the United States, added his belief that on this night 'Britain won the war'.[4] John Strachey, viewing the matter from a somewhat different angle as an active London warden but also writing close to the

---

[1] p. 416.

[2] German records show 507 aircraft over the target and 711 tons of high explosives dropped.

[3] See *The Times* 'Survey of the House of Commons', published in October 1950 on the occasion of the opening of the rebuilt Chamber.

[4] Quentin Reynolds, *op. cit.*, pp. 27–41.

event, wrote 'a sort of invocation to Hitler' advising him to 'make haste'. The British people had had the temerity to survive his bombs. If he continued to leave them living it would be 'thought that there is something in the world that the detonations do not shatter'.[1] For the remainder of May the scale of enemy attack, with the exception of one raid on Birmingham, was slight. Early in June this rose for a time to a level of 100–140 aircraft and Merseyside, Manchester, Salford and Hull received sharp attacks.

The *Luftwaffe* was already moving bomber and other squadrons to support the invasion of Russia. This 'fourth climacteric', as the Prime Minister described it, of the war broke upon the world on 22nd June. Though Britain's Battle of the Atlantic was far from over, the enemy's assault on these islands in direct support of it for the time almost ceased.

Breathing Space (June 1941 – April 1942)

The Prime Minister reviewed London's civil defence services in Hyde Park on 14th July and afterwards addressed a luncheon given by the London County Council.[2] Those in the review, he said, represented 'nearly a quarter of a million organised functionaries and servants in the defence of London'. Lifting the veil on some of the Government's past apprehensions and plans, he admitted that 'when the storm broke in September, I was for several weeks very anxious about the result'. And when the enemy shifted the burden of his assault on to the provinces he and others felt anxiety lest attack 'concentrated on those smaller organisms' should prove more effective than when directed against London.

Britain's survival of this ordeal had impressed every country in the world and, he added:

> I do not hesitate to say that the enormous advance in United States opinion towards making their contribution to British resistance thoroughly effective has been largely influenced by the conduct of Londoners and of the men and women in our provincial cities in standing up to the enemy's bombardments.[3]

He then proceeded to warn the civil defence forces and the nation that Germany, in spite of her preoccupations in Russia, had a bombing force in the West 'quite capable of making very heavy attacks'. Britain's bombing of German cities, ports and industries had been much intensified, and this process would continue 'on a steadily rising tide, month after month, year after year'. This might provoke vehement enemy counter-action. Every preparation had therefore

---

[1] John Strachey, *op. cit.*
[2] Charles Eade (Ed.), *op. cit.*, Vol. II, pp. 20–27.
[3] The United States Lend-Lease Bill had been signed on 11th March 1941.

to be made for attack on an equal, or higher, scale in the forthcoming autumn and winter. To the civil defence forces the Prime Minister stated, 'it is of the utmost consequence that you should regard yourselves as constantly in action'.

In March the British experts had computed that Germany's operational aircraft, in spite of the losses incurred in attacking Britain, might amount to over 5,000 machines.[1] From June 1941 onwards, though the bulk of the *Luftwaffe* was employed in Russia, the Mediterranean and elsewhere, substantial forces of bombers, capable of sudden attack on Britain, were maintained in the West. The threat to Britain these represented was reinforced by the enemy's great facility for moving his forces rapidly from one theatre of war to another. It is pertinent to recall that during this summer, and for some time ahead, British official opinion was decidedly pessimistic about Russia's chances of withstanding the German onslaught. The Ministry of Home Security reported in July that though the *Luftwaffe* was showing the German army's dislike of fighting on two fronts, small bomber and mine-laying forces were almost nightly keeping some part of the British population aware of its existence. A speedy conquest of Russia by Hitler would make possible invasion of these Islands in the autumn. Slower progress in the eastern campaign might be accompanied by a return, at short notice, to 'heavy blockade-bombing'.

Preparations by the passive defences to meet a renewal of heavy attack in the winter of 1941–42 are discussed in later chapters, and need only bare mention here. The topic was considered exhaustively in Parliament on 11th and 12th June.[2] Outstanding among these preparations were the formation in August of the National Fire Service, and consolidation of the widespread fire prevention arrangements into a 'Fire Guard'; efforts to strengthen and multiply shelters, including the invention towards the end of the year of the new 'Morrison' indoor shelter; extension of the principle of the 'interchangeability' of the civil defence services; and extension, by amendment of Defence Regulation 54B, of the powers conferred on the Government and delegated by Ministers to Regional Commissioners, over certain 'post-blitz services'.[3] In a statement on this last development in Parliament on 24th July the Home Secretary stated that restoration of the life of a community after air attack depended on a large number of services 'extending far beyond the civil defence organisation as originally conceived'.

Rather more attention must be given here to developments of the warning system, the black-out and other first-line passive defences.

---

[1] p. 381.

[2] H. of C. Deb., Vol. 372, Cols. 215–304, 371–454.

[3] p. 631–644.

Mention has already been made of official inquiries, inaugurated at the beginning of the Battle of London, into further modification both of the warning and the lighting arrangements.[1] The outcome, so far as warnings were concerned, was first a decentralisation, as an experiment, of responsibility for issuing warnings from Fighter Command Headquarters to certain Fighter Group Headquarters. This action was prompted by the fact that the enemy was deliberately sending one or two aircraft to zig-zag over the country to cause industrial dislocation. In terms both of manning requirements and physical communications this experiment took time to prepare, and was only initiated, with respect to two Fighter Groups, in February 1941. As it then proved a success, the Prime Minister authorised at the end of April the devolution of this responsibility from Fighter Command to all Fighter Groups in the country. This process was completed on 4th July.

Secondly, the idea, also inaugurated at the opening of the Battle of London, of persuading industrial workers all over the country to regard the 'alarm' (i.e. the public warning) as merely an 'alert', and to create local alarm systems within this, had been gradually developed. The roof watcher method had proved, in many cases, limited in its efficiency. After much discussion 'Alarm Officers' were appointed to each Region and 'Alarm Controllers' to many Observer Corps Centres in the country. The function of these Controllers became that of tapping the Centres for news of impending attack and passing this on over Post Office communications either to a central control point or (less usually) direct to the factories.

By the end of 1942 this system embraced much of the vital production of the country and had proved a genuine success. The Birmingham Region Alarm Centre, for example, had begun its operations in March 1941 with 9 alarm schemes and 18 speech and 520 bell recipients. Three years later it was operating 44 schemes with 78 speech and some 1,140 bell recipients, covering about 800,000 industrial workers. In London Alarm Controllers were eventually stationed at 'ack-ack' battery sites and linked with controls in a large number of factories.

Another development of the warning system during this phase (in this case a contraction and not an expansion) was the abolition at the end of October 1941 of the 'yellow' or preliminary warning.[2] This confidential message had become steadily less valued by those to whom it was sent. Heavy raids had caused the A.R.P. services to be constantly on the alert, and the 'purple' message had largely taken its place in hours of darkness.[3] The effort and the cost of disseminating

---

[1] pp. 364–365.

[2] H.S.C. 239/41, 22nd October 1941.

[3] p. 363.

the 'yellow' may be gauged from the fact that in the London Telecommunications Region over 1,000,000 of these messages were passed
in the one month of October 1940 to recipients on the official list. It
was calculated in March 1941 that the abolition of the 'yellows' and
the 'whites' cancelling them would save 59 per cent of the warning
telephone calls. 'Yellows' had put an additional strain on the telephone system since (though supposedly confidential) they had frequently been passed on to persons not entitled to receive them.

The examination begun in August 1940 into possibilities of changing the policy of 'black-out' into one of 'blackable-out' had continued throughout the autumn and winter, and was in essence to
continue until the end of the war.[1] This question was frequently
under consideration by the War Cabinet, advised by a succession of
inter-departmental committees. The experience of eight months'
heavy attack had confirmed the opposition of many local authorities
(for example, the Metropolitan Boroughs) and a large section of the
public to the introduction of more (i.e. higher intensity) street
lighting. At the end of July 1941, the War Cabinet agreed that action
of this kind should be deferred. When, early in 1943, re-examination
of this particular problem was undertaken, scarcity of materials and
labour added further complications to its solution.

Opposition by Members of Parliament and sections of the public
and the Press to the black-out in the autumn of 1941 foundered
against considerable faith in this method of protection by a substantial part of the public. This attitude is illustrated by the conclusions of the report on the Bethnal Green disaster, which occurred
some eighteen months later. Those in charge of this shelter had fitted
appliances to improve the entrance lighting which had been deliberately removed or broken. 'The population', this report stated, 'are
peculiarly sensitive to any display of light in an air raid'.

In official discussions, the Air Staff maintained strong support for
the policy, by now long-established, of stringent lighting restrictions.
As the reader is aware, these were most elaborate in theory and in
application, involving shop window and stall lighting, vehicles of all
kinds, the screening of glare from blast furnaces and so on, and the
lighting of shipbuilding and repairing yards, the railways and
industrial establishments of many kinds. Emphasis on the complexity
of the problem seems not to be out of place here. The technical experts
mentioned in previous chapters were continuing to give advice to
individual establishments, and the authorities were continuing to
introduce various minor relaxations. For example, vehicles were
allowed to use two masked headlights each giving a light of the
maximum intensity previously permitted to one. Higher lighting
standards were allowed to shipyards, factories engaged in the

---

[1] p. 365.

production of landing craft, aerodromes and other constructional works and tractors engaged in night-ploughing.

Sixteen years earlier the first A.R.P. Committee had bracketed the defensive weapon of lighting restrictions with that of concealment by smoke screens, camouflage and other means.[1] The practical application of these subsidiary methods, as already observed, had made little progress by the outbreak of war. But by the stage this narrative has reached the Ministry of Home Security's Camouflage Directorate had reached some maturity of organisation and accumulated a considerable amount of technical information. Its activities from this date, though they met with much success and furnished many cases of interest and entertainment, cannot be adequately recorded in this volume.[2] Up to August 1944 this establishment (to use its own language) 'considered about 16,000 items for camouflage purposes'. Emergency treatment was applied to 562 sites, and specific instructions issued to over 4,000 vital factories and key points and to several thousand less important places or landmarks.

A minute by the Prime Minister at the end of May 1940 had started re-examination of the possibility, discarded by the Air Defence Research Committee before the war, of using smoke screens as a method of concealment.[3] The Prime Minister had requested proposals for action, including the burning of briquettes in cottage fires, and enquired whether it was true that factories were actually obeying the peace-time regulation of limiting their smoke.

Executive responsibility in this matter was, somewhat anomalously, entrusted to the Ministry of Home Security.[4] Part of the reason for this decision was disbelief by the Air Staff, which was maintained for a long period, in the effectiveness of smoke screens as a means of stopping, or even hindering, aimed bombing. Almost nothing was known about screening large areas by this method, so that the Ministry's experiments had to start virtually from scratch. During the earlier phase of heavy attack, or up to the end of 1940, activities were still confined to experiment and provision of the necessary human and other resources. The topic appears to have roused a good deal of inter-departmental fire; and it formed a good example of the Ministry of Home Security's function of co-ordination and attempted reconciliation of many diverging interests, both civil and military.

After January 1941 a phase of rapid expansion in this sphere began, due in the first instance to the formation of a War Cabinet Committee

---

[1] p. 22.

[2] Entertainment consisting in successful deception of the enemy, and sometimes (unintentional) deception of friendly forces.

[3] p. 87.

[4] p. 303.

on Smoke Protection under the chairmanship of Lord Beaverbrook. The Lord President's and three other top-level committees were actively concerned, and a member of the Ministry recorded that 'committee activity was intense'. An historian may in this context claim that committees, which figured so largely in civil defence and receive much attention in this volume, were more than a scaffolding to procure action. By resolving conflicts (as noticeably in this matter) of Departmental opinion and interests they represented action. Doubts on this score may, perhaps, be removed by consideration of the inter-Service rivalries which seriously hampered the German totalitarian war-machine.

During 1941 and the earlier part of 1942 a system of operational control of smoke screens was established, a school to train smoke screen operatives and drivers was created and an organisation was formed to manage a fleet of some 1,500 motor vehicles. The War Cabinet Committee had authorised the use of 'Haslar' generators (which consumed fuel oil and water at the rates of about 85 and 70 gallons per hour respectively, and burnt for 8–9 hours) on a large scale. By the end of 1942 and early 1943 these operations were employing some 500 civilians and over 10,000 members of the Army. The eight or so smoke screens of July 1940 had grown to over 30, covering groups of vital points in such places as Birmingham and Coventry.

In March 1943 (to carry this story beyond the phase with which this narrative is immediately concerned) the Ministry's responsibilities in this sphere were transferred to the War Office and the Air Ministry. The Ministry was then able to claim that none of the establishments protected by smoke screens under its control—for example, at Billingham, Derby, Newcastle and Nottingham—though the object of some attention from the enemy, had suffered important damage.

These extensions and refinements of the defence were developed during ten months which, though not free from attack, can properly be called a breathing space. During June and July 1941 the weight of high explosive bombs in any one raid exceeded 100 tons on only three occasions. On the night of 4th-5th June most of some 95 bombers sent against this country attacked the Birmingham district, killing 12 persons at Darlaston in the Black Country and 16 at Atherstone and doing a good deal of damage to houses over a wide area. Two weeks later about 80 bombers attacked Southampton, killing 12 citizens and seriously injuring 32, destroying or severely damaging over 700 houses, causing some damage to the docks and railways and dropping leaflets on the 'Battle of the Atlantic'. On 17th-18th July a major night attack was made against Hull. This caused 150 fatal and 98 serious casualties, and serious damage both to industrial and private property. Some 3,500 people were made homeless, the trunk telephone exchange had to be evacuated, a number of communal shelters were hit and gas and water supplies were seriously affected.

For the remainder of 1941 there was no further attack of this weight against any British town, and the *Luftwaffe's* sorties by day and night against land targets declined steadily month by month. The enemy's principal objective with their limited air power in the west had become the intensification of mine-laying and attacks on coastal shipping. They also hoped to employ a reduced bomber force more effectively by using radio bombing devices to mount attacks of greater accuracy and concentration.

An effort to do this against Birmingham on the night of 8th-9th July was signally frustrated, since only (as enemy records subsequently proved) 22 of the 88 bombers detailed for this task reached the target and these dropped bombs with little effect. From the aspect of passive defence the most serious attack of this night, intended by the enemy only as a diversion, was inflicted on Yarmouth. Already much-bombed, this town of 50,000 or so inhabitants had suffered 12 fatal and 4 serious casualties two nights before. On this occasion only two persons were killed; but some 120 houses, shops and a church were demolished, and a further 1,000 houses, a fire brigade station, a first aid post, the railway and utility services suffered damage. Another diversionary attack of this night against Plymouth killed two policemen and caused twelve fires and damage to main services.

The Birmingham raid reduced the faith of the enemy in the particular bombing devices they had employed with the consequence, to quote an Air Ministry account, that their 'use of radio aids declined throughout the year'. This may be the appropriate place to remind the reader of the continuous efforts made by the enemy from the Battle of Britain onwards to improve their bombing attacks by the development of radio. The Germans' use of the radio beam, the success of the British in 'bending' this, the enemy's evolution of the *Knickebein* apparatus, British jamming of this and development of radar devices for night-fighters and anti-aircraft guns form a story of much fascination.[1] Though this scientific competition lies outside the scope of this volume, it is nevertheless important to recall that it had continuous bearing both on the enemy's bombing of Britain and on the British counter-offensive against Germany and German-occupied countries.

For those engaged in passive defence, as this narrative has tried to emphasise, what chiefly mattered was the fall of bombs and the death and injury to human beings, physical damage and civil and industrial dislocation these caused. British success in the scientific development

---

[1] See W. S. Churchill, *op. cit.*, Vol. II, Chapter XIX, Vol. III, Chapter III.

of defence at this stage brought some unforeseen consequences, of which the failure of the attack on Birmingham and the suffering caused to Yarmouth formed only one example. On 8th May successful deflection of the enemy's beams had saved the Rolls-Royce works at Derby from their attention, but caused severe bombing of Nottingham and the unloading of many bombs in open country.[1] Early in the morning of 31st May the Germans, through a gross error of navigation, dropped four high explosive bombs on the North Strand and Phoenix Park, Dublin, killing 29 persons and seriously injuring 45.

On the night of 27th-28th July some 60 enemy aircraft raided the south-east, paying special attention to London. Since some of these were twin-engined fighters, many of the high explosives dropped were of light weight although 31 fires were caused. Some 90 persons were killed (about 30 of these in incidents at three shelters) and 111 seriously hurt. In proportion to the weight of attack the damage, especially to houses in the East End, was high. On 12th-13th August an attack of some weight was made on Birmingham.

From this date no attack of consequence was made on any inland town (with the one exception of that by 46 bombers on the Manchester area of 12th-13th October) for the remainder of the year. As the weeks went by and the enemy drove deeper into Soviet Russia renewal of the bombing onslaught on London was deferred. The targets for the reduced enemy forces were predominantly ports on the southern and eastern coasts. Hull was unfortunate enough to suffer two appreciable raids, besides that already mentioned, in July and two more in August; largely owing to the enemy's use of heavy bombs, these five attacks caused nearly 500 serious casualties and considerable damage. Hull's situation on the Humber and proximity to Spurn Head also made it a convenient landmark for the enemy en route to attack other northern towns. It is apposite to quote here the view of a Regional Officer (expressed after the war) that 'the people of Hull have always been aggrieved because few outside Yorkshire recognised that their city was among the most heavily bombed in the country, and some sympathy may be felt with this attitude'.

Hull presented one case of what Mr Titmuss calls 'the singular issue' which faced provincial authorities under repeated air attack, namely the phenomenon of 'trekking'.[2] At this phase about 10,000 people, it was calculated, were leaving the city each night to sleep in its hinterland. Emigration of a similar kind from Merseyside, Plymouth, Southampton and Portsmouth had already caused the Government much concern in the spring of 1941; and they had appointed a Special Commissioner to Reading Region in April to

---

[1] p. 418-419.
[2] R. M. Titmuss, *op. cit.*, pp. 306-309.

assist the Commissioner temporarily in dealing with this problem in the Southampton area.[1] The need for concerted action by the authorities of the cities concerned and of the surrounding country had, Mr Titmuss states, 'received little attention before the spring of 1941'. The problems of restoring morale, at the times and in the places where this was shaken, and of maintaining production and overseas supplies lay at the heart of the matter. The many interesting questions that arose, for example the difficulties of distinguishing between the trekkers and the genuinely homeless and of harmonising local jurisdictions, belong to the topic of the post-raid services. The authority just quoted concludes that, 'the number of individuals concerned in trekking was small in comparison with the total of people made homeless by the attacks on provincial areas during 1940–41'.

Tyneside and Tees-side, particularly Newcastle and North and South Shields, suffered some sharp attacks in the early autumn. On the night of 1st-2nd September, for example, a force of 28 bombers attacked Newcastle for only an hour. But they succeeded in killing 57 persons and seriously wounding a further 64, and in demolishing over 100 houses, making 1,000 citizens homeless and causing several major fires, including one at a goods station which destroyed quantities of flour, sugar and bacon and 85 million cigarettes. On 2nd-3rd October low-flying aircraft killed 67 people and seriously injured 117 at South Shields, causing many fires, shooting down a barrage balloon and machine-gunning a train.

During the last five months of 1941 no raid exceeded about 15 per cent. of the maximum effort in the previous autumn. But despite this dwindling weight of attack, damage in one place or another to houses, industrial property, utilities and the railways, even if small measured on the scale of the national war effort, had its local effects.

The year 1942 opened with night attack by the enemy on the same limited scale as that of previous months. But a relatively new form of attack was introduced by the Germans' use of fighters and fighter-bombers to make brief 'tip-and-run' attacks on coastal towns. Places as widely separated as the Shetlands, Aberdeen, Sunderland, Spittal, Lowestoft, Torquay, Belfast, Aldeburgh, and Dover received a share of the enemy's attention in the form of reconnaissance, machine-gunning or the delivery of a few bombs. While February was in general quiet, fighter-bomber attacks on Channel shipping and coastal towns began to increase at the end of March. On 1st April the Ministry of Home Security reported that the enemy's long-range bomber force in the West was still capable of delivering 'a sizeable night attack' on a selected inland target.

[1] Lord Chatfield, Admiral of the Fleet, and Minister for Co-ordination of Defence, 1939–1940.

'Baedeker Raids' (April – July 1942)

The most significant point to be re-emphasised at this stage is the enemy's failure to renew heavy onslaught on London and other cities during the winter of 1941–42. But though the tide of air attack on Britain had ebbed strongly for ten months there was not, as yet, much happening elsewhere to hearten public morale. By April 1942 the United States had entered the struggle, Russia had shown unexpected capacity for resistance and our air offensive against Germany had increased. But Japan had been conducting a most successful amphibious blitz, British success in the Western Desert had halted, Malta was undergoing a desperate siege and the Battle of the Atlantic was growing more acute.

With the improved conditions of April the *Luftwaffe's* bombing activities against Britain began somewhat to increase. In the first week of the month sharp attacks were made against Dover, Weymouth and works of the Gloster Aircraft Company, causing higher casualties than in any week since early January. Shortly afterwards Grimsby was attacked, and night activities began noticeably to grow. Middlesbrough, for example, was attacked on the night of 15th-16th, when 25 persons were killed and 52 badly injured and some 1,800 houses in some degree damaged.

At the end of April the enemy began an increased effort, particularly in a series of attacks against inland cathedral cities notorious under the name of 'Baedeker raids'. None of these cities was of appreciable military importance or especially large in area or population. The German objects appear merely to have been reprisal (for example for the heavy Royal Air Force attacks at this time on Luebeck and Rostock) and wanton destruction of places of religious, historical and aesthetic value. A scattered attack on the Exmouth region on the night of 23rd-24th formed the prelude to a low-level attack on the next night in good visibility by some 25 bombers on Exeter itself. The enemy, aware that this and other Baedeker cities were not particularly expecting attack and were weakly defended, employed the tactics of dropping bombs of exceptional weight as well as a great number of incendiaries.

Some 80 persons were killed and 55 seriously wounded in this attack; about 6,000 houses were affected and trekking took place on a fair scale. Troops in the area gave help to the Rescue Service and police reinforcements had to be introduced. On the following night, 25th-26th, the largest German force deployed since the previous July attacked the south-west, with Bath and Bristol as its main targets. A second attack on Bath on the subsequent night increased the loss of life and physical destruction in this city.

Bath was neither well-prepared nor well-protected; heavy high explosive bombs caused much damage to ancient houses supported mainly by their walls, and blast effects in these attacks were exceptional. Communications were badly damaged, the central telephone exchange had to be evacuated and the Air Raid Precautions Control Room was hit. On the second night fire-fighting was badly hindered by high winds and low water pressure. As recorded in later chapters the Fire Guard, still a new form of organisation, was overwhelmed by a concentration of incendiaries which were accompanied by machine-gun fire. Police, fire and Air Raid Precautions service reinforcements had to be called for. The Great Western Railway station was put out of action and the line to Bristol was closed. Several churches and hospitals were hit, and over 2,000 houses made unfit for habitation. As with Exeter, a good deal of trekking occurred. Nearly 400 citizens were killed, and a total not far short of this seriously injured.

The attack was then switched to the eastern side of the island with Norwich as the chief target on 27th-28th April and again two nights later. Though Norwich was more accustomed than Bath to the presence of the enemy, the outcome, broadly speaking, was similar. The attacks were well-delivered, and the second added considerably to the destruction caused by the first. Severe damage was done to houses, especially in the poorer quarters, and commercial buildings, utilities and railways. The fighting of fires was hampered, in this case, by demolition of the Waterworks Control Room. About 222 persons lost their lives and rather more were badly wounded.

In between these two raids York was attacked, though less severely. During this raid, however, which lasted only about an hour, 100 high explosives and numbers of incendiaries caused the death of 79 persons, serious injury to another 90 and a good deal of damage. Timbered buildings and narrow streets helped the fire-raising efforts of the enemy which succeeded in destroying the fifteenth-century Guildhall. The neighbouring Air Raid Precautions Control Room had to be abandoned and communications were reduced to the messenger service. The Minster narrowly escaped damage. The London and North Eastern Railway station and a London express standing in it and the telephone exchange were hit.

After more forays in the north-east the enemy returned on the Sunday night of 3rd-4th May to inflict on Exeter what the Mayor is reported to have called the worst calamity which had befallen the city since its destruction by the Danes in 1003. Some 90 aircraft added to the death and devastation of a week earlier in a low-level attack, concentrated in time and space, with high explosive, parachute mines, incendiaries (many of a new type) and machine-guns. A conflagration and many lesser fires overwhelmed the fire-watchers and largely destroyed the city's shopping centre and main east-west artery. Some 163 citizens were killed and 131 badly injured. The Cathedral, though hit, escaped serious damage; but nine churches and various historic buildings, 2,000 houses, the General Post Office and the Public Library (beneath which the Control Room was situated) were destroyed. Though the topic of post-raid restoration plays little part in this volume it must be added that much had been done in this respect when, four days later, the King and Queen visited the city.

The next night a sharp attack on Cowes caused 140 serious casualties (66 fatal) and serious damage to a number of factories and shipyards. A few nights later an attempt by a sizeable force to renew attack on Norwich was ineffective, owing either to a new balloon barrage or to the presence of a decoy site. For the next three weeks or so of dark nights attacks on the Baedeker targets were suspended.

But with the help of a new moon some 80 German bombers made a concentrated attack on Canterbury on the night of Sunday, 31st May-1st June. In essentials this attack was similar in its aims and results to those just recorded. A conflagration and many lesser fires taxed the resources of the defenders almost to the limit, and succeeded in destroying many houses, shops and other buildings, including the Corn Exchange, City Market, Lady Wootton's Green, three churches, two schools, banks, clubs and the main bus depot.

The evidence suggests that the enemy made a deliberate effort to wreck the Cathedral, though this met with little success. A cluster of incendiaries which penetrated the roof were successfully dealt with by fire-watchers and many others burnt themselves out on the ground. But several high explosive bombs in the precincts badly damaged the Library and broke many windows.

The enemy returned to Canterbury, after a sharp attack on Ipswich, two nights later and again on 6th-7th June. But, owing largely to the addition of a balloon barrage to the other defences, these assaults were relatively ineffective. About 45 persons were killed and a similar number seriously injured in Canterbury in these three attacks. A raid on Norwich towards the end of June which killed 14 persons and seriously wounded 11, started over 60 fires (including one at the Corporation Maternity Home) and did a good deal of damage proved the last in the series of Baedeker raids.

In this context, and as a brief interruption to this summary of attack, death and destruction, the historian may introduce a remark on the enemy's motives in omitting Oxford from his Baedeker targets.[1] So far as he is aware no documentary evidence on this problem exists. But speculation has suggested, first that Hitler or his satellites had

---

[1] Cambridge, it has already been noted, had been subject to minor attacks since an early phase of the enemy offensive.

chosen Blenheim Palace as a convenient seat for the Nazi government of Britain. Secondly, and more plausibly, that Oxford was a vital centre of communications for the coming enemy invasion. It is relevant to add that this geographical point had not been overlooked by the British defences. Though Oxford was never bombed (except for one 'stick' near its boundary on the Nuffield Works in 1941) it had served as an important centre for exercises designed to repel the bombing which would inevitably accompany invasion.

From the end of June to the end of July attacks were made on a good many British towns and, though usually small in scale, these cannot be swept aside by an historian as irrelevant. On 21st-22nd June a sharp raid on Southampton killed 34 persons and caused a good deal of damage. Three nights later an enemy force heading for Birmingham actually raided Nuneaton, causing 14 fatal casualties and extensive local damage. Shortly afterwards Weston-super-Mare was attacked on two successive nights, with the loss of 100 inhabitants and serious injury to a further 210 and destruction caused by fire.

Some damage to factories of national importance in Middlesbrough, Billingham and elsewhere was inflicted early in July. Later in this month the *Luftwaffe's* activities increased both in daylight and moonlight. On 22nd-23rd Cromer was attacked with the loss of 11 lives, on the following night Withernsea and on the next night Middlesbrough again. On 27th-28th the enemy began three nights of scattered raiding which affected almost every Region but had the Birmingham area as the main objective. During two of these nights over 170 people were killed and 380 fires started (with the help of new types of incendiary and phosphorus bombs) in Birmingham. But on the third the brunt of the attack fell on Wolverhampton and Walsall; and on the next night a small enemy force killed 24 persons and destroyed at least 70 houses in Hull.

The destruction and damage to vital war industries by the attacks over these four months was small. But from the wider standpoint of the destruction of human life, of the services upon which these various communities depended and of buildings of national significance the enemy's achievement should not be underrated.

'Tip and Run' (July 1942 – January 1944)

By the summer of 1942 the war, for the Allies, had reached its watershed. While the Germans and Japanese continued to advance or to consolidate their gains Allied resources were in no sphere yet adequate for large-scale counter-attack. During the eighteen months with which this narrative is now concerned this attack began in the autumn of 1942 in the West with the victory of El Alamein and the

North African landings. But it was not until the invasion of Italy a year later that the Allied 'approach march' effectively began.

For the British public at home, including members of the civil defence forces up and down the country this, in Miss Bowen's phrase, was 'the lightless middle of the tunnel'. While the preparations and re-organisation described in later chapters went forward,the average 'civil defender' and the average citizen in his role of active defender of his home and place of business against air attack inevitably became bored. As during the twilight war of three years before, preparation for attack which was not (so to speak) visible proved hard to undertake.

The point is worth labouring since, in the aggregate, enemy air activity in this phase was fairly large. The Departments concerned, the Ministry of Home Security and Regional officials were kept occupied, not only with planning and re-adjustment but with the consequences of the enemy's day-by-day intrusions. But the summary of these which it is necessary to present here should not be allowed to obscure the fact that a high proportion of the towns and villages of the country were immune from attack by bombs for the whole of this phase.

'Tip and run' attacks by single or a few aircraft began, it has been noted, early in 1942.[1] But from the summer onwards they became almost the sole form of enemy raiding. For the remainder of this year the only night attacks on any scale were those made at the end of July on Birmingham and at the end of October on Canterbury. Birmingham was raided for two hours on the night of 27th-28th July by some 50 aircraft and for a similar time by a larger force two nights later. Some 170 persons were killed and over 400 badly injured and a good deal of damage was caused by incendiaries on these two occasions. On the night of 31st October some additional damage, though with little loss of life, was inflicted on Canterbury.

From July day activity by enemy fighter-bombers, normally singly and relying for safety on low flying or cloud cover, against specific inland targets increased. These, for example, made 30 raids in July on selected key points and succeeded in causing some damage to 10 of them. Neither the loss of life nor the material damage inflicted on Britain by this strategy during the autumn were, however, serious. In November, the Allied landings in North Africa compelled the enemy to divert more bombers and other aircraft to the Mediterranean.

More numerous and more disturbing to the public concerned were the tip and run raids on coastal towns, mainly in the south, which the enemy maintained through 1942 and most of 1943. These fast low-flying attacks caused, as General Pile has described, much trouble to the active defences, mainly owing to an almost complete lack of

---

[1] p. 428.

warning.[1] On 24th September, to give one example, 7 enemy fighter-bombers made an afternoon attack on the sea-front of Hastings, killing 23 persons and demolishing 8 houses. A few days later a boy's school at Petworth was hit with 31 fatal casualties.

Torquay, Sunderland, Deal, Eastbourne, Grantham and Hartlepool were among places subjected to this type of attack with (quantitatively speaking) more than negligible loss of life. The enemy's objectives were not entirely confined to the coasts. Thus on 19th October some 30 aircraft dropped about twice this number of bombs, accompanied by cannon and machine-gun fire, on five East Anglian counties. On the last day of the year Exeter was revisited and 39 serious casualties caused. Though the harm done by these attacks to military objectives was small, houses and other buildings, railway systems, gas and electricity supplies were frequently damaged.

Air attack on Britain in 1943 was broadly similar in character and effects but progressively smaller in scale. Before recording it in somewhat more detail it will be convenient to consider certain broader aspects of the defences in this phase. In spite of the enemy's pre-occupations elsewhere, his potential scale of air attack on this country remained roughly what it had been for the past eighteen months.[2] So far as the British experts were aware some 500 enemy aircraft capable of making sudden effective onslaught on (say) London remained in the West. It was also a feature of the air threat that the Germans could rapidly withdraw bombers and other machines from some other theatre of war to concentrate against Britain. And the effectiveness of aircraft in terms of speed, range and bombs carried was continuously improving.

For the Government and the Chiefs of Staff and their other advisers these factors were overshadowed in the spring of 1943 by reports that Germany was hastening development of rockets and pilotless aircraft. An account of preparations to meet this threat belongs to a later chapter.[3] But the reader may be reminded that the Ministry of Home Security and other civil as well as military authorities were gravely concerned with it more than a year before the first 'V-weapon' landed on Britain. In the enemy's camp, it has become known, Hitler was now beside himself with fury at the failure of Goering and the *Luftwaffe* to fend off British bombers and make adequate reprisals.[4] And, with most other Nazi leaders and the German people, he was attaching much hope to the *Vergeltungswaffen* (reprisal weapons) as a means of still bringing Britain to defeat.

---

[1] Sir Frederick Pile, *op. cit.*, Chapter XIX.
[2] p. 421.
[3] Chapter XV below.
[4] A. Bullock, *Hitler: A Study in Tyranny* (1952).

The gathering weight of British counter-bombing of Germany must be remarked upon here owing to its double influence, first in provoking retaliation and secondly in heartening Britain's morale.[1] The first '1,000-bomber raid' had been made on Cologne on 30th May 1942. Thereafter the efforts of Bomber Command, like those of the *Luftwaffe*, were dispersed among a number of objectives. But in March 1943, Air Marshal Sir Arthur Harris records, his Command's offensive against the enemy's vitals really got under way and continued on a mounting scale for the following year. In June Mr Churchill told the nation that 'those who sowed the wind are reaping the whirlwind'. In the first half of the year the R.A.F. alone had delivered on Germany thirty-five times the tonnage of bombs which the Germans had discharged on Britain.[2]

The tip and run form of attack set difficult problems in the matter of warning especially as the enemy, flying low over the Channel at a speed of 300 m.p.h. or more, was temporarily able to defeat the radar system. An adjustment, which brought considerable improvement, extended in certain places the decentralisation of the system already under way.[3] Observer Centres in certain southern and eastern coastal areas were linked by direct line with the telephone exchanges from which warning messages were distributed, and the alarm controllers stationed at these were permitted to issue the 'red' warning. The not inconsiderable physical changes needed were quickly carried out by the Post Office.

In the meantime decentralisation of the system on a national basis through transfer of responsibility from Fighter Group headquarters to Observer Corps Centres was being planned. The ever-increasing speed of aircraft made it essential to hasten this process, so as to eliminate delays in transmitting intelligence about the tracks of enemy aircraft and the time taken in transmitting this downwards from Fighter Groups. Transfer of executive responsibility for issuing warnings from the Air Ministry to the Ministry of Home Security was approved by the War Cabinet in June 1943 and effected in the following November. From this date the change-over was progressively introduced in the 36 Royal Observer Corps Centres, and completed by April 1944. The former alarm controllers then became Home Security warning officers.

The prohibition throughout the country of the ringing of church bells except by the military as a warning of air or sea-borne invasion has been mentioned earlier. As has elsewhere been described, Home Guard commanders in certain areas rang bells on their own initiative in early September 1940, thereby causing some confusion. The Prime

---

[1] p. 398.

[2] Charles Eade (Ed.), *op. cit.*, Vol. II, p. 480.

[3] p. 422.

Minister authorised the ringing of church bells on Christmas Day in 1940 and subsequent years, and also after the victories of El Alamein and Tunis. On this second occasion, he has since recorded, 'in London there was, for the first time in the war, a real lifting of spirits'. In this early summer of 1943 the prohibition was first partially and then completely removed.

It is important to allude again here to the continuing efforts to convert a policy of 'black-out' into one of 'blackable-out'.[1] For the ordinary citizen there was small change in the condition, to which he had now grown accustomed, of nearly complete darkness in all public places soon after the sun had set. But for the responsible authorities the matter was one of continuous investigation, especially in its aspect of the hindrance imposed by lighting restrictions of all kinds on war production. In the autumn and winter of 1943–44 a 'removable' was substituted for a 'permanent' black-out in certain factories; some relaxation was permitted to the railways and public utilities, and also in minor degree to churches, civil defence and Home Guard training establishments. As the 'Little Blitz' was launched on London these investigations continued.

Further allusion must be made to the defence, almost as elaborate in application and as permanent in intention as the black-out, against gas attack. The production, distribution and maintenance of masks and other equipment and the training of the civil defence services and the public in this matter, had remained, so to speak, a permanent background to three years of waiting and attacks in which no use of gas had been made by the enemy.[2] In a world broadcast on 10th May 1942 Mr Churchill revealed the apprehensions of the Soviet Government about the Germans' use of this weapon against them; and gave an undertaking that, if they did so, Britain would treat the attack 'exactly as if it were used against ourselves' and use Britain's 'great and growing air superiority in the west to carry gas warfare on the largest possible scale far and wide against military objectives in Germany'.[3]

Three months later Mr Herbert Morrison announced in the House of Commons that the Government no longer regarded the carrying of gas-masks by the public as necessary. The extent to which this practice had decayed may be gauged from his statement that if the carrying of a mask 'was conclusive proof of the good citizenship of the men and women of this country, we should have to come to the conclusion that there were not many good citizens'.[4] The necessity to conserve rubber supplies and reduce general wear and tear of masks

---

[1] p. 423.
[2] See Chapter VIII above.
[3] Charles Eade (Ed.), *op. cit.*, Vol. II, pp. 264–5.
[4] H. of C. Deb., Vol. 382, Col. 785, 30th July 1942.

underlay this decision. The public, however, were asked to keep their masks easily accessible in their homes, and local authorities were told that the Government wished to emphasise 'with all the force at their command' that they did not consider that the danger of gas attack was in any way past.

In an administrative sense, anti-gas measures continued to occupy a good deal of attention. In March 1944, when the possibility of the enemy's use of gas to repel Allied invasion had to be envisaged, the Ministry sent secret instructions to Regions regarding the announcements and instructions to be issued in this event to the public.[1]

The scale of attacks, as previously mentioned, declined steadily during 1943. Shortage of crews and aircraft impelled the enemy to a policy of an increasing conservation of his resources. In March Hitler appointed an *Angriffsfuehrer England* to co-ordinate all technical resources and equipment available for the air attack on Britain.[2] It is not irrelevant to mention here the plan of Marshal Goering of some months earlier, frustrated by Admiral Doenitz, to bomb New York and the Panama Canal; and that air raid warnings were sounded on the Pacific Coast of the United States during 1942.

A measure of the growing ineffectiveness of the enemy's attack was provided by the increasing discrepancy between his propaganda broadcast claims and the reality. In some 354 such claims made early in this year the enemy only possessed the confidence to name towns in 40 per cent. of the cases, and of these only 43 per cent. were correct. The enemy bomb load delivered on Britain declined from some 790 tons in the first quarter of the year to about 420 in the last quarter. Some 2,230 tons of H.E. were dropped on this country in 1943, as compared with some 3,030 tons in 1942.

There was, nevertheless, hardly one period of 24 hours throughout this year without at least one air raid incident. A few concentrated attacks on cities were included. For example, over 100 long-range bombers attacked London on 17th-18th January, paying chief attention to its southern suburbs and dropping a total of about 47 tons of bombs.[3] Two days later a proportion of fighter-bombers which flew in over the coast at 'zero-level' attacked the same general area. The brunt was on this occasion borne by Bermondsey, Deptford and Lewisham, where a 500 kg. bomb penetrated a school and killed many children. In these two attacks 107 citizens were killed and 158 badly injured. Though 8 key points and 5 railway systems were affected, the only substantial damage was to the Surrey Commercial Docks.

---

[1] H.S.R. 43/44, 22nd March 1944.

[2] Colonel Peltz, an ace bomber pilot of 29 in whom Goering had much faith.

[3] German records, possibly through some confusion with the propaganda claims, show a total of 128 tons of bombs.

Cardiff sustained a night attack of some weight on 17th-18th May, when numerous flares were used to light up the railways and docks. Forty-three persons were killed and rather more seriously hurt and considerable damage was done to the main railway station. Soon afterwards Sunderland was the object of two moderately heavy night attacks. In these over 150 persons were killed and over 200 badly injured, a number of residential areas damaged and key points, railways and shipping were affected.

These occasions apart, the attack was predominantly of the tip and run or—as it was sometimes called—'the scalded cat' variety. The worst single incident of the year took place on 3rd March at Bethnal Green Tube shelter when, ironically enough, no attack was in progress on this particular area. A night attack of moderate proportions was being made on London, and warnings had sounded. A woman among the crowd entering this shelter, encumbered by a baby and a bundle, fell, causing those pressing behind her to tumble in a heap and the death by suffocation of no less than 178 persons.[1] Measured by the suffering on even one day in one enemy concentration camp this tragedy, which aroused deep concern in Britain, could appear small. But by less quantitative standards it may appear to future historians —irrespective of any mistakes made by the various authorities concerned—as a conspicuous example of the horror and futility ot war.

The incidents caused by tip-and-run attack declined progressively from 80 in January of this year to 52 in March, 39 in June and somewhat fewer in the autumn months. In December there were only 7. On a geographical computation throughout the year Sussex suffered most severely, closely followed by Kent; and Devon, Hampshire, the Isle of Wight, Dorset and Cornwall were the other counties most concerned. Any list of the towns on which loss of life and damage was inflicted must include Dover, Ashford, Bournemouth, Eastbourne, Hastings, Brighton, Plymouth, Hull, Grimsby and Great Yarmouth.

A conspicuous feature of an attack on the night of 13th-14th June by long-range bombers on Grimsby and Cleethorpes was the number of small anti-personnel bombs (often known as 'butterfly bombs') which caused many of the 163 serious casualties in these two towns. Bombs of this character had first been used by the enemy in October 1940 and (though relatively rare) had given the British defences a good deal of concern. Instructions regarding their treatment had been at once issued to Regional authorities, the police and wardens, and the public had been strongly warned in the Press and by the B.B.C. not to handle them. On the occasions when these missiles were dropped police and members of the civil defence services were

---

[1] See pp. 544-545.

faced with the difficult tasks of estimating their numbers, finding and disposing of them. In the Grimsby-Cleethorpes attacks just mentioned no less than 1,600 unexploded bombs of this type had to be dealt with.

By December the rising weight of Bomber Command's offensive against Germany had still failed to produce the retaliation the enemy threatened. The British authorities and the British public were linking these threats with current enemy propaganda about Hitler's development of formidable secret weapons.

'Little Blitz' (January – March 1944)

Late in 1943 Britain's offensive had in fact caused the Germans to withdraw all the air strength they could spare from the Mediterranean and Russian fronts and marshal this on the Western front for reprisals against this country. Every long-range bomber was taken from Italy, and it was estimated that the *Luftwaffe* could deploy 150 bombers against us on any one night. The year 1944 in fact opened uneventfully. The week of 6th to 12th January provided the first in which there were no incidents of significance since November 1942. But before the month was out activity flared up, and between 21st-22nd January and the end of March, 2,350 tons of bombs were dropped—a tonnage greater than the total delivered in 1943. All but 100 tons of this total were delivered in 15 attacks, 13 of which were aimed at London.

In contrast to the raids of 1940–41 these attacks were concentrated into the shortest possible time, and were noteworthy for a return to incendiary attack which employed every type of fire raiser. In December 20 'firepot bombs' comprised the total fire attack; but in January the proportion of incendiaries to H.E. in weight was one third and in March it rose to one half. Canisters containing hundreds of incendiaries (a large proportion being fitted with an explosive charge) were timed to open near the ground and secure a concentration of fires, while H.E. bombs of up to 2,500 kg. were dropped simultaneously to deter the fire-fighters. This gave the combined London N.F.S. and Fire Guard their first test. The latter were sometimes driven to shelter by high explosives and were overwhelmed by the number of fires, but the shortness of the raids set the task and exposed its dimensions and the N.F.S. were not unduly stretched. Late calls proved, however, an embarrassment and, to obviate delays the observation posts were extended, enabling the firemen to arrive at fires in their incipient stages, and these tactics proved very successful. It was nevertheless estimated that 75 per cent. of the fires were extinguished by Fire Guards.

This Little Blitz was responsible for a quick change in the habits of shelterers. Though in general, after four years of war, morale was not so high as in 1940–41 the population were at first reluctant to take shelter in the same way as before. But the proportion of heavy high explosive bombs was higher than formerly and, weight for weight, the blast was more powerful; and many people, besides those rendered homeless soon sought the shelter of the Tubes. The permanent shelter population of the Tubes rose from a low of about 3,000 to a peak of about 50,000, but more who now went to shelter went on the 'alert' and came out on the 'all clear'. There was also a heavy demand for 'Morrison' shelters, while 'Andersons' and surface shelters were in less favour. Though plans for evacuation of school children were prepared, there was no strong demand for organised evacuation from London.

To guide his attackers to the target the enemy had devised a complicated ambitious scheme for the use of flares, which was subject to frequent variations. The G.A.F. at this stage had to depend on crews with inadequate operational training; and this scheme placed success largely in the hands of pathfinders, so that if the pathfinders were destroyed, the effectiveness of the attack was much reduced. It was doubtless the enemy's intention to build up these attacks, but events on the other fronts and the loss of not less than 150 aircraft with their crews efficiently baulked this intention and the vaunted reprisals faded out at the end of March. The attacks in February, however, proved the heaviest since May 1941 and achieved appreciable success.

Up to the opening of this blitz the chief incident took place on the night of 14th-15th January when a 2,000 ton attack by the R.A.F. on Brunswick enabled two enemy aircraft to escape identification as hostile and to drop 3 H.E.s when no warning was in force. One of these hit a cinema in Croydon, killing 5 people and seriously injuring 33 others.

On 21st-22nd the largest force plotted overland on any night since July 1942 made for London, and dropped some 268 tons of bombs, including more 2,500 kg. bombs than during the whole war up to this date. The attack was made from a considerable height in two phases, and the defences proved so successful in breaking it up that 15 per cent. were claimed as destroyed, and in the first phase only 14 aircraft succeeded in reaching London and in the second 13. As a result there was a considerable spill of bombs over south-east England, and of the 245 incidents of this night 201 were outside London—110 in Kent, 53 in Sussex and 18 in Essex.

On the 28th-29th January some 22 enemy aircraft flew over East Anglia and the south east without accomplishing anything. But on 29th-30th a force estimated at 161 aircraft formed the largest effort since the reaction to our raid on Dieppe on 19th August 1942. The target was London but only 15 enemy bombers reached this area.[1] These, however, were rather more successful than in the preceding week, and 343 fires, including an important one at the Surrey Commercial Docks, were started while casualties numbered 157. There were 60 incidents in Essex, 59 in Kent, 26 in London, and 7 elsewhere. These included 6 railway incidents, damage to 17 key points and the use of a new type of parachute bomb of 1,000 kg.

On 3rd-4th and again on 5th-6th February smaller attempts were made to attack London, but the bombing was of no account except in German propaganda claims. The suspected use of the Heinkel 177 in conjunction with a 'radio target beacon' did, however, suggest that the enemy was infensifying his efforts.

The following week three more sallies were made against London. Only 22 aircraft arrived over the target and most incidents were in the neighbouring counties. On the 12th-13th all the bombs dropped were H.E., half of them being the new parachute bomb; but on the following night a considerable proportion of the load was again incendiaries, though no serious fire situation was caused.

After a lapse of four days the G.A.F. carried out with skill and pressed home a series of attacks on London which proved the heaviest since May 1941, as well as a small-scale operation against southern and south-east England. The London raids took place on 18th-19th, 20th-21st, 22nd-23rd, 23rd-24th, and 24th-25th, and were notable for the increased proportion of aircraft penetrating to the capital, the skilful use of flares, the shortness of the bombing and relatively small enemy losses. Much of the success could be attributed to the anti-radio-location device used; and to route-marking with flares which enabled the enemy to outflank the defences and approach London from various directions. Though no heavy concentration on any one borough seems to have been attempted most were affected, and Battersea, Camberwell, Chelsea, Chiswick, Feltham, Fulham, Hammersmith, Putney, and Wandsworth were particular sufferers.

At Battersea about 3,000 houses in an area of about 20 acres were destroyed or made uninhabitable. At Chelsea a block of flats collapsed under a direct hit and casualties were heavy. At Hammersmith there was damage to the railways, St. Paul's School and four other schools were hit, and the bridge over the Thames was penetrated. In Fulham over 1,200 people were made homeless, there was a 40-pump fire, the telephone exchange was put out of commission and there were 100 incidents on the Control Room board.

---

[1] German records show that as many as 285 aircraft were despatched against London, and that 229 reached the capital.

In spite of the fact that the bombing was concentrated into a period of under an hour in all these raids, an appreciable fire situation arose on each occasion. There was a 70-pump fire at Turnhill Street, E.C., a 50-pump fire at the Isle of Dogs, 40-pump fires at Highgate, Royal Victoria Docks and Fulham, a 30-pump fire at Hatton Garden and a number of others requiring more than 10 pumps[1]. Casualties showed a sharp increase and for the month amounted to 961 killed and 1,712 seriously injured, most of these suffered in the London area.

After a slight recession, which might be attributed to the weather, to R.A.F. attacks on enemy airfields, the high proportion of inexperienced enemy crews or the vigour of the defences, the attacks were resumed in March on much the same scale. London was the chief target on 1st-2nd, 14th-15th, 21st-22nd, and 24th-25th, Hull and north-east England on 19th-20th and the south-west and South Wales on 27th-28th.

On 1st March the German-controlled Radio National announced that 'to-day is the day of the *Luftwaffe*, and it is expected that retaliation will start as from to-night'. But of the 70 aircraft which crossed the coast probably no more than 10 arrived at London and the rest scattered over Hampshire, Sussex, Surrey and Kent.[2] The attack was of poor quality in spite of its description by the enemy as 'the fourth mass attack in the series of nine heavy blows which have hit the British capital since January. . . . The objectives were clearly defined by new target-indicators which made possible the exact placing of H.E. and incendiary bombs. . . . The third wave . . . simultaneously opened their bomb doors at one single word of command and released 280 bombs, thereby destroying an industrial arsenal of military importance'. On these laurels the *Luftwaffe* rested, as it was not until 14th-15th that any appreciable number of aircraft again crossed the coast. On that night at least 100 aircraft were over London and a mainly incendiary attack was inflicted on the central area, though 54 boroughs were affected. Damage to residential property was considerable and widespread and 390 fires were reported.

The next sizeable force crossed the coast on 19th–20th March, dropped most of their bombs harmlessly in east Lincolnshire and north Norfolk and claimed to have attacked Hull, which was, however, untouched. But on the following night a force of about 120 aircraft returned to the attack on London and succeeded in causing 247 fires. There were two fire-zones, one of 50 pumps in Islington

---

[1] See Chapter XI below.

[2] German records show that as many as 164 aircraft were despatched against London, and that 131 reached their target.

and the other of 20 pumps in Tottenham. In the Millwall dock area, Dagenham and elsewhere there were serious fires. Paddington station was hit and other railway damage was sustained, while Lambeth, Croydon and Holborn suffered outstanding house damage. On 24th-25th the activity of about 120 bombers extended over an area bounded by Portsmouth-Oxford-Southwold, and about half this force reached Greater London. In Croydon 81 fires were started and some serious damage done. Beckenham also had 60 fires, while a 70-pump fire in West Norwood and a 56-pump fire in Fleet Street were caused. On 27th-28th some 120 aircraft made a widespread ineffectual attack over an area stretching from Land's End-Cardiff-Reading-Selsey Bill, which the enemy claimed as a heavy raid on Bristol, on which city no bomb fell, though decoys in this area succeeded in attracting attention. An extensive use was made of 50 kg. phosphorus bombs, but some 80 per cent. of these failed to explode.

Enemy activity was then much reduced and it was not until 18th-19th April that about 120 aircraft again crossed the coast to attack London. There were 50 incidents in Cambridge Region, the most serious being a 40-pump fire zone at Romford. At Edmonton the North Middlesex hospital received a direct hit, at Braintree the American hospital was damaged and there was minor damage at other places. The following week under 200 aircraft were plotted overland, mostly over the south-west, and the emphasis was on flares rather than bombs; though this did not stop the Germans from making fantastic claims as to the extent and success of their intrusions. On 29th-30th April about 20 aircraft were over parts of Cornwall and South Devon, and the first use of a radio-controlled bomb was unsuccessfully made against a battleship in Plymouth.

The enemy, aware of Allied preparations to invade Europe, was now concentrating on reconnaissance and efforts to probe points where concentrations of shipping were suspected. In the view of Home Security it was 'undoubtedly to our advantage that these harlequinades have entertained no less than 7 or 8 Regions, thereby giving a much needed stimulus to a civil defence service apt to regard the war as over, in so far as it affected their own personal convenience'. In May widespread activity was reported from Reading Region with incidents at Portsmouth, Poole, Weymouth, Havant, Shanklin and Ventnor. In the Portsmouth-Solent area a smoke-screen and the operation of decoys seem to have been successful, but the enemy's standard of bombing was now very low and he was achieving very little.

On 28th-29th May some damage was done at Torquay and next night two oil tanks at Falmouth were set on fire and were not extinguished until the following night. The harbour also had to be closed owing to suspected mines. From that date until the dispatch of the first flying bomb on the night of 12th-13th June German air activity over Britain was very slight.

CHAPTER XI

THE EMERGENCY FIRE SERVICE

Mobilisation and Stand-by

IT is now necessary to go back in time to carry on the record of the Fire Services from the outbreak of war. Chapter VI has recorded, in brief outline, the planning, initiation and development of the emergency fire services up to the outbreak of war. Men, women and appliances had been added to the fire brigade resources in considerable numbers, and still more auxiliaries and emergency appliances were coming forward. But the organisation for war was largely lacking and the brigades had a very great deal more to do to get their services welded into an effective fire-fighting organisation. Fortunately the enemy gave them time.

Later experience was to show the need for fundamental changes in the operational organisation, but within the limits of the Fire Service structure as it existed at the outbreak of war the brigades were able to make good use of the respite.

The Auxiliary Fire Service was mobilised on 1st September 1939, in company with the other arms of civil defence.[1] Fire stations were now to be manned on a twenty-four hour basis, reserve pumps were prepared for action and towing vehicles were found. Overnight the strengths of many of the brigades multiplied eight or tenfold as the Service braced itself for immediate action.

Administrative arrangements to absorb this sudden influx were, however, often sketchy. As already recorded, a rather restricted view of what would be required in the way of accommodation and amenities had been taken during the planning phase of A.R.P., largely on grounds of economy. When the time came for premises to be occupied, confusion and hardship were sometimes the result. Many of the buildings hastily pressed into use were cramped and unsuitable, supplies of beds and bedding were often scanty or non-existent, and feeding and cooking arrangements were primitive. Moreover, from the point of view of administration and discipline, it was a serious drawback that too many of the auxiliary fire stations

---

[1] A telegram 'Emergency Fire Brigade measures: call out Auxiliary Fire Service and proceed as in Circular of 23rd March 1939' was sent out. This circular dealt with a number of administrative and financial matters, quoted the text of the telegram which would, if need arose, announce the Government's decision to 'mobilise' the Auxiliary Fire Service and detailed the measures which Fire Authorities should then take with all possible speed.

had only room for one or two appliances, so that men and equipment were scattered, and training, supervision and messing arrangements complicated. A vast amount of sandbagging was needed to protect control rooms and crews' quarters, many emergency telephones had still to be installed, many more vehicles to be found and towing attachments to be improvised. Record systems had to be established, arrangements made for paying the thousands of auxiliaries who had reported for whole-time duty, and innumerable small items of equipment and stores had to be hurriedly bought. In fact the first few days of mobilisation were, as one official put it, 'more of a confused scramble than an orderly transition from a peace to a war footing'.[1]

Nevertheless, within a few days most of the stations had settled down to their new routine and auxiliaries showed great ingenuity in making quarters habitable and in preparing posts for action. After much improvisation and many makeshifts, the auxiliary fire stations were equipped and manned, and a considerable fire-fighting force was standing at the ready for fire attacks that were expected daily.[2]

Returns obtained from towns of 50,000 population and over showed that, within a week, more than 4,800 pumps were manned and kept ready for action, and 1,200 more could be got ready for action at short notice. About 40,000 whole-time firemen were at their posts and 34,000 part-time firemen were either on duty or could soon be at their stations on a warning. London had 1,800 pumps manned, as against about 125 peace-time appliances, and there were 8 emergency fire boats in addition to the 3 regular craft.

In the central Departments also a measure of reorganisation was required to meet the war demands. Towards the end of 1939 the Fire Brigades Division of the Home Office, which, as recorded in Chapter VI, had been operating in three main Branches, was reorganised in five Branches, one dealing with general problems, a second with the emergency fire precautions schemes and the others mainly with problems of buildings and stores, and the development, allocation and distribution of appliances and equipment. The Fire Brigades Inspectorate was strengthened by the addition of an Assistant Inspector at each Regional Headquarters, but, even so, its strength was so small in comparison with the number of brigades that, in practice, the Inspectors could give relatively little attention to details of the local organisation, so that progress depended largely on the degree of energy and enterprise put into the work by the local fire brigade officers.

In Scotland, on the outbreak of war, the Scottish Home Department took over the functions of the Scottish Office and created a

---

[1] From a longer version of the history of the emergency fire services prepared by the former Head of the Fire Service Department at the Home Office.

[2] The volunteers' response and the spirit in which they were facing the long hours and discomfort were recognised in a message of appreciation from the King which was circulated to the Services on the 13th September. (F.B. Circular No. 63/1939.)

special Fire Brigades Division which, until 1941, dealt with Scottish fire service matters, in close consultation with the Home Office, from the London Office of the Department.

But although the Fire Service had been quickly at the ready, months were to pass without attack. This respite had two important but contradictory consequences. It gave valuable time for the emergency organisation to settle down and make good its most serious deficiencies. Less acceptably, however, it brought criticism of the Government's alleged over-insurance in civil defence and noisy demands that air raid precautions services should be cut.[1] It was during this period of anti-climax, partly precious breathing-space and partly corroding inactivity, that those four essentials of fire-fighting—men, equipment, water and organisation—completed their transition from peace to the long-awaited conditions of real war.

Mobilisation had found the Service under-manned in comparison with the official estimate of needs.[2] Heavy bombing and serious fires were expected at any moment and on 7th September the Minister of Home Security broadcast an appeal to employers to release as many auxiliary firemen as they could spare for whole-time duty and to release part-time firemen wherever possible when the sirens sounded during working hours. But as the expected attack was postponed and early fears evaporated, instead of strenuous action firemen had to withstand the unexpected strain and discouragement of a long stand-by.

Public criticism of the expense of 'idle' civil defence workers mounted quickly. Coupled with boredom it caused large numbers of trained firemen to resign, many of them to join the Fighting Services. The Government reacted equally quickly to this criticism and in October announced that it had reviewed the whole question of manpower for the civil defence services.[3] As far as the fire services were concerned, the fire authorities were advised on the numbers of 'first line pumps' (i.e. those kept permanently manned) and 'second line pumps' (i.e. those to be manned if and when required) they should maintain, and on the number of whole-time firemen to be kept on the strength to man the first line units and to provide a nucleus for the second line crews. First line pumps were to be from 40 to 50 per cent. of the total complement that had been laid down earlier[4] in the most

---

[1] This criticism and its effects on the civil defence services as a whole are discussed fully in Chapters VII and VIII.

[2] Between 84,000 and 89,000 whole-time auxiliary firemen reported for duty in Great Britain as compared with the Home Office's original estimate of requirements to the Manpower Committee of 150,000. The strength at the end of 1939 was about 60,000 whole-time firemen, 6,000 firewomen and 3,000 youths. In addition, about 130,000 part-time auxiliaries, including 7,000 women and 4,500 youths, were attached to the brigades.

[3] This is discussed generally in Chapter VIII, pp. 342–348.

[4] See Chapter VI, pp. 246, 260–263.

vulnerable areas, from 25 to 40 per cent. in large inland towns and from 25 per cent. down to none at all elsewhere. In Scotland the percentages ranged from 30 to 40 per cent. downwards. All whole-time men in excess of those needed to man the pumps on this basis were to be discharged, and skilled men required in munitions work were also to be released.[1]

On the basis of the specific schemes which the Departments had approved the whole-time strengths could be readily assessed and the necessary adjustments were soon effected. The reductions were not serious and were made for the most part by brigades which on strategic grounds could best spare men. In total they amounted to nearly 7,000 full-time men, but at the same time certain brigades, in particular the London Fire Brigade, where the numbers were con-siderably below establishments, were allowed to recruit additional men to make up the deficiencies. The total authorised full-time establishment after this review amounted to about 63,000 in England and Wales and 4,000 in Scotland.[2] Fire authorities in the main centres of population were also authorised to recruit additional full-time auxiliaries up to about 12,000 men if severe raiding began.

Total strengths were not the whole story, however. Early in 1940 the decision to call up men between 23 and 27 for military service caused some anxiety in the fire brigades, where a higher proportion of young and whole-time workers was necessary than in most other arms of civil defence but where there was still no compulsory service. To meet this situation, when the general age of reservation for auxiliary firemen was fixed at 30, arrangements were made with the Ministry of Labour and National Service for the enrolment of indi-vidual firemen in the Armed Forces to be deferred where numbers were short. These arrangements were extended later on, and by the end of 1940 the deferments covered about 13,000 firemen.

The German victories of April and May 1940, changed the problem of and the public attitude towards service in the A.F.S.,[3] in common with civil defence generally.[4] In May the Home Secretary warned the services that there was every prospect of calls being made on them very soon. In the following month trained auxiliary firemen who had left their brigades were urged to rejoin,[5] and the establishments of many brigades in areas which were now much more vulnerable than

---

[1] F.B. Circular No. 70/1939, 29th September 1939 and Scottish Home Department Circular No. L.73/39, 3rd October, 1939.

[2] There were in addition about 6,700 other men, including former part-time regular firemen now doing full-time duty, and drivers and watch room attendants, as well as 4,200 women and 2,500 youths.

[3] F.B. Circulars No. 14, 15 and 17/1940, and S.H.D. Circulars No. L.26, 30 and 32/1940. In 1941 the age of reservation was lowered to 25.

[4] It was not long before cinema audiences were applauding when the picture of a fireman appeared on the screen.

[5] F.B. Circular No. 69/1940, 1st June 1940.

before were increased. Thus all through 1940 the strength of the fire services was under constant review, inequalities were 'ironed out' and the brigades' establishments settled on a systematic and realistic basis, subject, of course, to the increasing competition for national manpower. For by this time competition with the Armed Forces and industry for young men was becoming acute, and in June, to prevent a serious drain on the manpower of the brigades, whole-time firemen, regular or auxiliary, were no longer allowed to resign without permission.[1] At the same time, in an attempt to fill some of the gaps, it was announced that men between 30 and 50 might volunteer for the Auxiliary Fire Service in place of military service.[2]

To maintain part-time strengths was also a continual problem; part-timers were extremely valuable, especially for night duty, when most of the air attacks were, in fact, later to occur. During the opening phase of inactivity and criticism, many part-time firemen had been lost. In theory, deficiencies in whole-time strengths caused by wastage and economy cuts were to be made good by part-time firemen, but in practice it was difficult to fill the gap satisfactorily with men who were only able to do an occasional turn at the stations.[3] Moreover, the number of part-time workers continued to fall as more of them volunteered for or were called into the Armed Forces. In June 1940, to check this wastage, the Ministry of Labour extended the deferment procedure for whole-time firemen to essential part-time firemen over 25 years of age who were doing at least twelve hours' duty each week.[4] By September 1940, such deferments had been arranged for about 14,000 out of the aggregate strength of 110,000 part-time firemen.

Despite these various expedients, however, the attacks of the autumn of 1940 found the Service still well below the strength the Departments considered necessary to man the fire brigades' equipment.

This same period between September 1939 and the summer of 1940 saw the completion of most of the equipment programme. On mobilisation the brigades had about 14,000 emergency pumps or about 60 per cent of their estimated requirements. But a considerable production capacity had been built up and about 500 pumps were being delivered every week. By May 1940 the pump programme was virtually completed; so that when the heavy attacks began the

---

[1] Police and Firemen (Employment) Order, 1940, S.R. & O. No. 1041, 20th June 1940. F.B. Circulars No. 81 and 86/1940. Scottish Order: Police and Firemen Scotland (Employment) Order, 1940, S.R. & O. No. 1129. S.H.D. Circular No. 4034. These orders applied also to the police. See also p. 375.

[2] F.B. Circular No. 81/1940, 20th June 1940.

[3] Authorised full-time establishments barely permitted all 'first-line' pumps to be manned, which meant that part-timers were relied on for nearly all the 'second-line' pumps.

[4] F.B. Circular No. 83/1940, 22nd June 1940. S.H.D. Circular No. L.110/1940, 24th June 1940.

brigades had as many pumps as they could man, with some in reserve. Nearly 23,000 pumps of various types had been supplied.[1] London for example, had more than 1,200 first line pumps constantly ready for action—about ten times its peace-time complement of major appliances—and these were backed by a larger number of second-line pumps. In the larger cities and towns expansion had been on a comparable scale, though here equipment included a higher proportion of lighter machines. Ancillary equipment, which had caused great difficulty before the war, also became available in the required quantities, and by the end of 1939 all the pumps in the hands of the brigade had their essential gear. Even the particular difficulty of hose supplies was mainly cleared up. When the 'blitz' opened in September 1940, 3,500 miles of hose, including 1,000 miles from Canada and the United States had been delivered to the brigades and, although this was still short of the original quantity planned, the brigades had enough to equip all the pumps they could man and to replace the heavy wastage.

There were nevertheless, certain gaps and shortcomings. Some of these only became apparent under the actual stress of air raid operations; others had deliberately been left unfilled before the war because the cost of the equipment would have been higher than it had seemed justifiable to incur against the contingency of an emergency;[2] and others had not been provided because no satisfactory technique had yet been found. Among the more expensive appliances ordered at this stage were fire boats, to supplement those already in use by the brigades,[3] 100-foot turntable ladders, hose-drying apparatus and canteen vans.[4] The production of some of these items had started before the war, and after war broke out further orders were placed and efforts made to hasten deliveries. The most serious shortcomings, however, during this period of respite were in the supply of towing vehicles and in the organisation of repair and maintenance facilities for pumps and transport.

An important consequence of the concentration on trailer pumps

---

[1] At a later stage more heavy and large trailer pumps were ordered, largely to replace losses, bringing the total orders for fire brigade purposes up to 26,300, costing £4,376,222.

[2] In particular, equipment was needed to improve the arrangements for water supplies. Almost all the steel piping, half the turntable ladders and escape units and all except 1,000 of the standard towing vehicles were ordered after the formation of the National Fire Service in August 1941.

[3] One of the peace-time fire boats of the London Fire Brigade, the *Massey Shaw*, with a volunteer crew of London firemen, took part in the Dunkirk evacuation, making three trips to the beaches. It brought back 96 men and transferred 500 others to larger vessels.

[4] About fifty mobile kitchens and dozens of canteen vans were received as gifts, most of them from Canada. When the attacks came they proved invaluable as a means of getting hot meals to firemen often still on duty at fires, as well as for feeding people made homeless by the raids. The kitchens could provide hot meals for 200 people at a time. See also R. J. Hammond, *Food*, Vol. II.

was the need for separate towing vehicles. Until just before the war, it will be remembered,[1] the policy, which applied to all the A.R.P. services, was to rely mainly on vehicles that could be hired on a part-time basis or could be requisitioned in an emergency. The Treasury had strongly opposed the purchase of new vehicles except for special purposes. As a consequence, when war broke out, the Auxiliary Fire Service had to take part in a general scramble for vehicles. In some areas arrangements broke down completely: sometimes fire authorities had not 'earmarked' enough vehicles, or had chosen vehicles that were unsuitable for towing pumps; sometimes vehicles had to be given up to their owners or to the military authorities. The London Fire Brigade and one or two other brigades had relied mainly on taxi-cabs but these quickly proved unsuitable and expensive to run.[2] For the most part, brigades came to rely on second-hand lorries, light vans and large motor cars.[3] As a stop-gap, these vehicles served the purpose fairly well—they could draw a pump and carry the crew, hose and other tackle. But for many of them, especially the taxis and the private cars, the work was too heavy and breakdowns were frequent, and if raids had followed quickly on the outbreak of war the fire brigades might have found themselves in a serious position.

By the end of 1939 the policy of hiring or requisitioning cars had been more or less abandoned as too expensive.[4] During 1940 about 7,500 vehicles were bought, but second-hand car and van prices were steadily rising and second-hand lorries were becoming virtually unobtainable. All this time these makeshift arrangements were becoming increasingly unsatisfactory; more than ten per cent. of the vehicles were 'off the run' awaiting repairs at the end of 1940 and the Home Office estimated that the rate of replacement would soon run up to 1,000 cars a year. The Department feared that the service was heading for disaster if the policy were not changed soon, and early in 1941 it managed to persuade the Treasury to authorise the purchase of 2,000 two-ton vans with specially designed bodies. This new type of towing vehicle became the standard for the remainder of the war, gradually replacing the private cars and other makeshifts.

---

[1] pp. 236, 237 and 259.

[2] 'London grew used to seeing convoys of squat grey pumps drawn by taxis careering down the street in search of a fictitious fire', said one commentator, '—for following the precedent of Paris and the Marne a quarter of a century before, the taxi-cab was once more pressed into service in the first scramble for trailer-vehicles.', W. Sansom, *Westminster in War*, (1947), p. 121.

[3] Permission to purchase a small proportion (not more than one car for every 10 light-trailer pumps allocated under the local emergency scheme) of the vehicles required was given by the Treasury in August 1939 (F.B. Circular No. 41/1939 and S.H.D. Circular No. L.83/39). This proportion was increased in October to cover the needs of 'first-line' pumps and up to 50 per cent. of 'second-line' pumps.

[4] F.B. Circular No. 94/1939, 14th December 1939. S.H.D. Circular No. L.133/1939. Fire authorities were asked to dispense with vehicles being paid for on the basis of weekly payments and to replace them by purchase. Cf. p. 350.

The servicing of transport and pumps was another problem that caused early trouble. The three Home Office Storage Depots[1] became repair workshops once their reserve of pumps and equipment had been sent out, but they were never intended, and had not the capacity, to provide a regular system of overhaul or even to repair the large numbers of units now constantly 'off the run' for one reason or another, and the local arrangements made by the fire brigade authorities were quite inadequate for the volume of work. In consequence, there was no possibility of keeping the machines under regular overhaul; breakdowns were frequent and repair work accumulated and was long delayed, and much of it had to be entrusted to local garages, often with unsatisfactory results—a situation that was to cause great problems later on when all the equipment was working under strain.[2] Spare parts were an added difficulty, especially when pumps went out of production and manufacturers became increasingly occupied with other war contracts.

The third element in the emergency preparations—increased water supplies—made up some leeway during the stand-by respite. It will be recalled that before the war the question of the allocation of costs for emergency water installations had been a check on progress with the measures worked out for London.[3] In September 1939, only a little of the major installation work had actually been completed, and the postponement of air attack was therefore invaluable. This was complicated and laborious work which inevitably took a long time to finish. By the autumn of 1940 much of the system of emergency mains for London had been laid down, but the scheme was not complete when the heavy fire-fighting of 1940–1941 began. During these early months of the war work also went on all over the country on providing water tanks, dams and fire boats. By May 1940, about 3,000 steel tanks and 12,000 canvas dams were in the hands of the brigades, and measures of many kinds were taken, with varying degrees of enterprise and energy, to improve the supplementary supplies of water. But it was soon to be proved that these achievements were not enough.

The fire brigades had also been making strenuous efforts to develop the organisational techniques of emergency fire-fighting.[4] Schools which were empty or had spare accommodation and many other premises were taken over for training. More telephone lines were installed, control rooms were established and innumerable exercises helped in the evolution of control room procedures and emergency communication schemes. The day-to-day living arrangements for

---

[1] See p. 268.
[2] See p. 462.
[3] See pp. 270–273.
[4] For some of the special factors see pp. 458–460.

firemen at the stations were improved and many stations were provided with canteens where auxiliaries could be supplied with meals free of charge if on duty for twelve hours or more.[1]

Air Raid Fire-Fighting

(a) *The Attacks*

When, almost a year later than expected, the big fire-raising raids finally came, they justified all the preparations that had been made to withstand them. The brigades were not given much chance of feeling their way into the perils and techniques of air raid fighting; the onslaught was sudden and overwhelming and firemen had little opportunity to practise their jobs during small-scale operations.

The last chapter contains a general account of the enemy's air attacks, which summarises their broad strategy and consequences for the public at large. In this chapter, where the main purpose is to trace the development of the emergency fire services after mobilisation and their operations in their combatant role of fire-fighting, some repetition is unavoidable, for it is on their response to the enemy's attacks in their varying phases and intensities that the work of the brigades must be judged. So it must be understood that in the account of the enemy's attacks which follows attention is concentrated almost exclusively on the fire aspects.

Apart from a few early scattered attacks and some raids on aerodromes, the first important fire raids on Great Britain were the series of attacks on oil installations in August and early September 1940. On 19th August, the Admiralty Oil Installation at Pembroke Dock was attacked and the fire burned for 17 days. This was one of the most spectacular fires of the war, and, coming as it did while the emergency fire services were in a comparatively early stage of their war experience, presented them with tasks which seemed at one time almost overwhelming. Six tanks, each of 12,000 tons capacity, were damaged by H.E. bombs, and when the Senior Fire Brigades Inspector (who was sent down by the Home Office to take charge at the fire) arrived, three tanks were alight, three were in danger of firing and thousands of tons of oil in the saucers and moats surrounding the tanks were blazing furiously. The firemen already on the spot were showing signs of exhaustion, water supplies were utterly inadequate and for two more days and nights little progress was made. On the 22nd August, five firemen were caught, and perished, in a great gush of burning oil from one of the tanks, which also destroyed a cottage and farm buildings, and by that time two more tanks had caught fire. Eventually, however, by dint of much gallant

---

[1] The conditions under which meals and refreshments might be provided at the cost of the Exchequer were shared with the Civil Defence Services generally (p. 348).

fire-fighting, in the course of which much oil was drawn off and saved, the firemen,[1] though harassed by repeated air attacks and imperilled by many more surges of burning oil, were able to get the fire in hand, but this was not until the 5th September. On the same day another serious oil fire, at a refinery near Swansea, which had been burning for three days was overcome, mainly by the efforts of the refinery staff.

This day also saw the opening of the concentrated attacks on the oil installations at Thames Haven, Shell Haven and Purfleet. Breached tanks let loose lakes of oil, in which many of the firemen had to work, one at least losing his life when the flames flashed back and overwhelmed him before he could get clear. The attacks on these installations were repeated over and over again. Many brigades were engaged, and London Fire Brigade units which had gone to the assistance of the brigades from Cambridge Region were still engaged on the afternoon of the 7th September, when the enemy opened his great attack on London. As a result of the experience gained in these oil fires new techniques were worked out, supplies of foam and foam-making branch pipes were increased, and a panel of oil experts was set up to help Fire Service Officers on the particular problem of fighting oil fires.

These oil fires were particularly difficult to contend with, but they were something in the nature of a specialist problem, separate from the main air raid fire-fighting, which began in earnest on the 7th September, with the 'London Blitz'. From 13th August 1940, to the first week of September the Battle of Britain was being fought over the South of England and the approaches to London; German planes ceaselessly bombed the aerodromes of the fighter squadrons in an attempt to knock out the capital's protective air screen. On 7th September, however, the enemy began to combine this strategy with direct attack against the Metropolis itself. The fire brigades in and around London were suddenly and dramatically confronted with the sort of situation for which they had been preparing for so long, but on a scale which few of them could have imagined and for which they were certainly unprepared in point of organisation. The local brigades were overwhelmed and all attempts to exercise detailed control of the fire-fighting was soon abandoned. By 8 p.m. on that first day of the London Blitz, the West Ham Fire Brigade alone had called for 500 more pumps; at 11 p.m. there were six extensive fires in and around the London Docks and six in the Surrey Commercial Docks area on a scale that were judged to call for over 1,000 pumps; the Royal Docks were heavily attacked and fires in the vicinity of the Royal Albert Dock and the George V Dock were

---

[1] The number of firemen engaged at the fire, drawn from brigades over a wide area, varied between 300 and 500.

completely out of hand. The heat from the fire at the Surrey Docks blistered paint on a fire boat 300 yards away. Sixty craft were sunk or destroyed on the river during this night, and blazing barges, their moorings having burnt through, drifted down river with the tide and threatened the riverside wharves. There were major fires at Woolwich Arsenal among stacked boxes of ammunition and crates of nitro-glycerine, and among the warehouse fires were pepper fires, rubber, paint, sugar, tea and grain fires, all with their own special difficulties and dangers.

In the main, the brigades stood up well to this first great onslaught. Movement in the streets and dock areas had been very difficult—not only had fires and debris blocked the way but congestion caused by pumps and towing vehicles had impeded the bringing forward of petrol and other supplies. But much gallant fire-fighting had been done and the Chief Inspector of Fire Brigades reported that the devastation would have been much greater if the brigades had not prevented many of the fires from joining up, and he especially praised the work of women at the control rooms. Demands on the London regional reinforcement scheme quickly exhausted all the resources available and early next morning additional pumps had to be brought in from two adjoining Regions.

The next night the attack was renewed in strength on the dock areas, and on North-East, South-East and Central London, but although several serious fires developed, all except one was 'in hand' by the next morning. In the attack on the 9th-10th September serious fires were started in the City and Woolwich Arsenal, the latter being described at the time as half a square mile of danger buildings, containing high explosive shells, well alight and the fire liable to spread to a large magazine.[1] However, by 8.30 a.m. the next morning all the fires were surrounded and under control. On 10th September, in order to give the London brigades some relief during this period of strain, the Home Office Fire Control called in reserves from towns bordering on London Region.

Attacks continued daily, the enemy shifting the main weight of his attack, now concentrating mainly on the docks or riverside areas, now on the City and now on the North-Eastern, North-Western or Southern boroughs and the districts outside the London County Council boundary. After the spectacular failure on 15th September of the great daylight raid on London and of the attempt to wipe out the R.A.F. opposition, the enemy concentrated his main efforts on night attacks.

All through September, October and the first part of November 1940, London, as already recorded, was bombed heavily nearly every night by forces averaging about 200 bombers. The number of fires

---

[1] Sir Aylmer Firebrace, *Fire Service Memories*, (1949), p. 170.

to which the brigades in the London Region were called exceeded 1,000 on four occasions (7th-8th September,18th-19th September, 24th-25th September and 14th-15th October). The London Fire Brigade alone attended over 13,000 fires during September and October 1940; the brigades of East Ham and Croydon attended over 500 fires and eight other brigades[1] attended more than 250 fires.[2] Help under the Regional reinforcement scheme was called for on 381 occasions; West Ham, for instance, needed reinforcement 10 times during these first two months. Only 11 of the 67 brigades in London Region had no occasion to call for help.

After early in November, although London had yet to withstand some of the heaviest raids of all, attacks on the Metropolitan area were less regular as the *Luftwaffe* changed its main objective to the ports and the great munition centres. In September and October there were several raids on Merseyside, Birmingham and Coventry, culminating in the great attack on Coventry of the 14th-15th November—probably the most concentrated and destructive single attack throughout the war on any British city outside London. In the earlier and fairly heavy raids on Coventry the local brigade had been able to hold the fires. On the night of the big raid they succeeded in doing so for the first four hours but before the night was over they were overwhelmed. The attack lasted all night; all telephone lines except one were cut; normal water supplies failed entirely; roads were blocked so that reinforcements found it difficult to get into the centre of the city where the main attack was concentrated and where huge fires were devouring the shopping centre and many of the old timbered buildings clustering around the cathedral.

Birmingham, Bristol, Manchester, Liverpool, Bootle, Sheffield and Southampton each had their turn of heavy air attack. On 19th-20th November in Birmingham nearly 650 pumps were engaged and on 22nd-23rd November more than 850 pumps. On this occassion bombs severed the three trunk mains which brought the City's water supply from Wales, leaving about four-fifths of the City entirely without a piped supply for several days. Fortunately, there was no further raid before the supply was restored. On one occasion in Bristol fires were out of control for some time and on another night in Sheffield two large areas of spreading fires were only held with great difficulty. Merseyside had 44 attacks within three months. In Liverpool there were more than 500 fires from the raids of 20th-22nd December and, at about the same time, Manchester had 600 fires in one night, wiping out many blocks of commercial and warehouse premises.

---

[1] Willesden, Tottenham, Ilford, Acton, Hendon, Barking, Walthamstow and Barnes.

[2] Here and elsewhere in this chapter only fires which resulted in fire calls are taken into account.

During this phase of the attack on the munition centres and the ports, London was still being raided but less frequently and less heavily. On the 8th-9th December there was a heavy attack, producing 1,700 fires in various parts of the Metropolis. On 29th-30th December, however, came the great incendiary raid on the City when the German Air Force made a determined attempt to destroy the City by fire. Out of the 1,460 fires reported, all but 28 were in Central London and the majority were within the City square mile. By 8 a.m. there were big and spreading fires in the City and the situation was serious south of the river in Southwark. Twice during the night Fire Brigade Controls had to be abandoned, in one case some of the men and women only escaping with their lives by means of a tunnel which passed under the burning buildings. More than a dozen large water mains were damaged, including the emergency main from the Thames to the Grand Junction Canal. To add to the difficulties the Thames was at its lowest ebb tide in the early part of the raid; little use could be made of fire boats to get the water ashore, and the situation was exacerbated by an unexploded parachute mine in the river which delayed fire boats from the lower reaches being brought above Tower Bridge. At this period London Region had about 2,680 pumps available, but even these had to be augmented, and the Home Office Fire Control called in 300 pumps and a large number of water-carrying units from other Regions.

More heavy attacks on London occurred during the spring of 1941 —on one night in March there were about 1,900 fires and and on 16th-17th April nearly 2,250 were reported. By this time, however, there was an extensive fire watching organisation which extinguished thousands of incendiary bombs before they could start serious fires. The last large-scale attack on London came on 10th-11th May 1941 when there were again over 2,000 fires in London Region. Fire-fighting operations were hampered, as often before, by extensive interruptions in water supplies and communications.[1] Some of the extensive fires were barely being held the next day, and it was not until twelve days later that the last of the appliances could be withdrawn from some of the fires started on that one night. About 2,500 pumps from brigades within London Region were in action during this raid and 70 more were sent in with reinforcement crews.

After this very heavy raid nearly 1,000 firemen were brought in from other areas to give the London firemen some rest. In the event, however, this proved to be the last of this series of heavy attacks on London; against all expectations, apart from a comparatively light

---

[1] On this occasion 605 of the Metropolitan Water Board's mains were damaged— the largest number in any one raid, and 98 of these were mains of 12 inches diameter or over. Altogether, in the course of the war, the Board had 6,635 of their mains, 875 of them of 12 inches diameter or over, damaged in air raids. (Report of Metropolitan Water Board for 1945-6.)

attack in July, it was in fact the last serious fire-raising attack that the London Fire Brigade had to deal with during the whole war, for before the next attack of any consequence the Brigade had been merged in the National Fire Service.

Meantime, during the early months of 1941, the attacks on the ports had increased—with heavy and repeated attacks on Cardiff, Swansea, Portsmouth, Southampton, Hull and Merseyside (which had attacks on seven successive nights) and in March on Glasgow and Clydebank. In April a series of heavy attacks on Plymouth and Devonport (five of them within nine days) caused fires that overwhelmed the local services and left great areas of devastation, and in that same month Belfast experienced severe raids.

This narrative has mentioned only the big air attacks on London and on the main centres of commerce and industry; these were the main targets for the enemy and all the brigades faced the same problems in their fire-fighting operations though in different degrees. Very many other towns and even remote villages also had to fight air raid fires and had on a smaller scale to contend with similar situations to those experienced in the big centres. Even in completely rural areas part-time firemen underwent long spells of arduous fire-fighting. They had the difficult task of extinguishing aircraft crash fires and sometimes had to fight huge crop or forest fires caused by jettisoned enemy bombs. Moreover, firemen in districts that were not attacked frequently volunteered, with the utmost keenness, to go with their pumps on long reinforcing runs to badly hit areas and fought fires far away from their home stations.[1]

(b) *The Fireman's Job*

Before discussing some of the lessons of these first months of air attack it is perhaps worth considering briefly the peculiar features of fire-fighting under air raid conditions and what these tests of battle involved for the individual fireman. His job in normal times calls for strength, endurance, courage and initiative; he has often to work in punishing heat or choking and nauseating smoke or wet to the skin in a freezing wind, in danger from collapsing buildings or from explosions, handling heavy and intractable lengths of sodden hose and trying to manœuvre his equipment in congested conditions. In air raid fire-fighting there were all these normal risks but there were added even greater hazards and more formidable handicaps. Not only did he have to fight more violent fires at worse odds but he was fighting on the illuminated target of the enemy aircraft overhead; it was common procedure for the enemy to drop high explosive bombs

---

[1] After the first heavy raid on London, when six volunteers were called for in one part-time brigade, every man, including the A.F.S. auxiliaries, volunteered and a free fight occurred before it was settled who should go. Eventually the appliance travelled to London with 13 men clinging to it as best they could.

into the fire areas, and sometimes firemen were even machine-gunned as they worked.[1] As an observer in Westminster wrote:

When they fought, at last, their first fires, the new firemen found them very different from their neat exercises. To begin with, they got wetter than they had ever thought a man could be! Fire is a dry element, but the fighting of it with water soaks the fireman to the skin in the first five minutes. Often then, in the cold of that winter, he was called upon to fight wet and frozen, for a stretch of some fifteen hours without respite. Throughout this period he was the special target of the high explosives that were sent down to stir up the fire; he could not think of cover; the nature of his job kept him out in the open or up against the fire. It is too a particular tradition with London's firemen that they should attack the fire first from *within* the building—not from the safer ground outside. . . . Thus, many of the hours of bombardment were spent enclosed with the dark smoke and the fire between walls dangerously unstable, vulnerable both to the heat of the fire and the shaking up of a near-by bomb.[2]

Apart, however, from the increased personal hazards, the fundamental factor that differentiated war-time from peace-time fire-fighting was the size and intensity of the problem. In normal times fires generally occur singly and the fire brigade organisation can meet the requirements of the situation in men, appliances and water. But under air raid conditions the situation could be immensely different. Houses left empty, with windows 'blacked-out', could mean that fires were not spotted in their early stages, and congestion on the communications system, overlapping and confusion under the tension of air attack could prevent calls getting through to brigades until fires had a good hold or were already spreading. Still greater delays could occur when telephone exchanges were destroyed and cables cut. With communications severed it could become almost impossible for the officer in charge of operations to have any clear picture of the total fire situation—of where the principal danger lay, and of where and in what numbers reinforcements were needed. Delay could also be caused by road blocks, by craters and debris,[3] or by congestion of vehicles and other gear. All these factors tended to be cumulative— a small blockage at any point could soon grow into a worse blockage;

---

[1] The average fireman's reactions were summed up by the Chief of the Fire Staff as— 'grim determination on the siren wailing—tension as the first bombs fell—exhilaration as he left cover to attend to the first fire call—exaltation as the raid proceeded and hell was let loose around him. Then, exhaustion, and, finally, much later, satisfaction— satisfaction at having done a useful night's work.' Sir Aylmer Firebrace, *op. cit.*, p. 183.

[2] W. Sansom, *op. cit.*, p. 121.

[3] During the Coventry raid of 14th-15th November, for instance, reinforcements could not, for a long time, reach the centre of the city where the main attack was concentrated (p. 456).

and fierce fires could spread at a remarkable rate—advancing, for instance, down a street as fast as man could walk.[1]

Movements over long distances under black-out conditions were a great strain on the drivers, and on arrival the reinforcements from outside areas faced new problems; they needed guides to the locality and, later, food and accommodation, all causing further strain on the local organisation. But the most frustrating shortcoming of all was the drying-up of water supplies. Laying out long hose lines is a time-consuming and exhausting business; the lines when established are all too vulnerable[2] and, even when they could be maintained, often supplied water in quantities which were pitifully small in comparison with the quantities required. Firemen and pumps could be successfully brought to the spot only to find themselves powerless because water mains had been damaged and there was no effective alternative supply within reach.

(c) *Review of Emergency Measures*

How did the emergency fire brigade organisation stand up to these great tests? Was it big enough in strength, in equipment, in water resources? Did its communications and control systems work? How did each of the partners in fire-fighting show up under the strain of continued operations?

The first components of the fire-fighting organisation—firemen—were under strength when the heavy attacks began. Recruitment had never reached the Home Office original estimate of manpower needs and still further depletions occurred during the disillusionment of the stand-by period.[3] The fire services and the police shared with the civil defence general services in the various vicissitudes of the competition with the Armed Services and industry for manpower. This part of the problem is dealt with at length in Chapter XIII, but it seems necessary here to refer in anticipation to some of the main developments as they affected the fire services in particular. Although the palliatives of deferment, 'freezing' orders and the alternative of fire brigade service to military service were introduced during the summer of 1940,[4] strengths were well below approved establishments in many important centres. A small but valuable supplement was secured when, by a reversal of the normal flow of manpower, some 4,000 trained firemen who had resigned earlier and enrolled in the Army were transferred to Army Reserve W and returned to the brigades.[5] By the end of 1940 the aggregate margin between establish-

---

[1] Sir Aylmer Firebrace, *op. cit.*, p. 177.
[2] See, for instance, the account on p. 463.
[3] See pp. 447–448.
[4] See pp. 448–449.
[5] F.B. Circular No. 130/1940; S.H.D. Circular No. 6163/40.

ments and strengths of whole-time men was not far short of 10,000.[1] Part-time numbers were also increasingly difficult to maintain, a serious handicap as part-timers were extremely valuable at night when most of the attacks were taking place. It was, in fact, by no means uncommon for the number of pumps manned and available for action in a brigade to be half as many again at night as in the day because of the added strength of the part-timers.

As well as the shortage of actual numbers of firemen there was also a serious lack of officers to take charge of operations when big fires became numerous. None of the brigades had anything like enough officers to go round. In handling these large fires, skill in strategy and tactics was essential; even competent crews with ample equipment and water could fail to deploy their resources to the best advantage without direction from those who could see the situation as a whole. The first and most obvious way to provide more officers was by the temporary promotion of suitable experienced regulars, but this did not go nearly all the way, the officers, or potential officers, being so few in comparison with the enormously expanded emergency Service. There was a valuable reserve of officer material in the Auxiliary Fire Service, but at this stage the A.F.S. was unavoidably lacking in operational experience, especially experience of large-scale fire-fighting. Early in 1940 the London Fire Brigade had introduced a 'unification scheme' under which selected members of the A.F.S. could qualify for officer posts in the regular brigade. Many of these officers rendered excellent service in the heavy attacks which followed, as indeed did A.F.S. officers in other brigades where the relations between the regulars and auxiliaries had been different. In the mean-time, as a stop-gap arrangement, the Home Office established a national roll of Special List Officers—experienced senior officers of fire brigades who were willing to go at any time into any heavily attacked area to take charge on the fireground or even in an emer-gency to take charge of the brigade.[2]

But all these measures were merely palliatives. So long as the Service was divided into hundreds of small units, the problem of control in major fire-fighting situations was insoluble.

On the subject of the second cog of the fire-fighting machine—equipment—there is not a great deal more to be said. On the whole the planning, production and distribution of the many varied items of essential equipment during the pre-war years and during the valuable respite of the stand-by period had resulted in the brigades

---

[1] Authorised establishments now amounted to 87,300 auxiliary firemen, which meant that there was a deficiency of 8,600 men. However, the Home Office believed that establishments would have to be substantially increased in several districts. In London alone something like 10,000 men were needed for 300 first-line pumps and 700 second-line pumps which could not be manned.

[2] Memorandum accompanying F.B. Circular No. 15B/1941, 27th February 1941.

being well equipped for their fight. Yet there were still certain deficiencies to be made good. The heavy attacks on the docks, for instance, found the number and in some cases the type of fire boats inadequate to the occasion. The provision of towing vehicles was still, a problem for some brigades, and nearly all of them suffered to a greater or lesser extent from inadequate arrangements for the repair and maintenance of vehicles and other appliances and from the shortage of certain spare parts.[1] But in general it should be said that the policy of the central purchase of equipment for the emergency service had produced very good results, and an impressive number of major appliances were in the hands of the brigades. Indeed, the problems of the fire-fighters were often those of inadequate ammunition rather than an insufficient quantity of weapons.

The main ammunition for fire-fighting—water—was the third essential in the emergency measures, and it proved to be the most difficult to guarantee. In spite of all the measures that had been taken water shortage was the brigades' most serious handicap. There were many occasions when the mains supply of a city was cut off, or reduced to a little more than a trickle early in a raid, and many others where, though there was less interference with the mains, the supply they gave was utterly inadequate. In such circumstances the supplementary supplies could be drawn upon but their use depended at that time mainly on long hose lines, which were extremely vulnerable and, as already explained, gave at best only a limited supply. The intense frustration felt by the firemen standing with his equipment ready but impotent can readily be imagined.[2]

The quantities of water the fire brigades required seemed enormous, even in a raid on a provincial City, not to mention London. For instance, in the case of an attack on Bristol the Regional Commissioner's estimate was 200 million gallons in the day. The Chairman of the Metropolitan Water Board mentioned in the House of Commons that 100 million gallons might be drawn from their system alone (or lost from fractured mains) in the course of a single raid.

A description of one incident on the night of 10th-11th May 1941

---

[1] In Liverpool, for instance, after nights of heavy attack the tremendous volume of repair and maintenance work for pumps and other appliances, many of them damaged in the raids, was far beyond the fire brigade resources, and Army mobile workshops were brought in to help.

[2] 'The constant failure of the water supply during raids was a continual bugbear to the fireman. He would be nicely in position, a strong hissing jet doing good work, and perhaps saving a building, when suddenly the water would die away, giving, as it does, the impression of retreating resignedly back into its hose. Such failure might be due to a variety of causes. The main might have been disrupted by bombing, the precious water either wasting quietly away into the ground or fountaining high into the air; or the hose might have been burnt through by an unobserved incendiary bomb; or too many pumps might be drawing water from the same main. . . . Perhaps debris had fallen on the hose from a crumbling building and was constricting the supply. Perhaps the pump had been hit—perhaps all sorts of things had happened, and would happen again and again during a raid.' Sir Aylmer Firebrace, *op. cit.*, pp. 178–9.

illustrates the horror and problems of water shortage: it is a summary of a report from the Chief Superintendent of 'F' District in the London Fire Brigade area. Fires, well alight, were discovered at Freeman, Hardy and Willis's shop and warehouse at the Elephant and Castle and Spurgeon's Tabernacle. Ten pumps were called and arrived in five minutes but found all the hydrants dry. One of the pumps was set into a 5,000 gallon dam in the forecourt of Spurgeon's Tabernacle and two jets were got to work but the dam was drained in five minutes 'without making any appreciable impression on fires of such size'. Two pumps were sent to Manor Place Baths (a supply of 125,000 gallons) and three more to a 200,000 gallon supply in the basement of the demolished Surrey Music Hall, St. George's Circus, about one-third of a mile distant. Meanwhile a scaffold dam was erected and pumps were made up to 50, but several more fires had now broken out and bombing was still intense. The fires were beginning to 'get away' said the report 'as, although pumps and men were available at the site, no water was available'. A further relay was arranged with 2½ inch water unit hose from London Bridge—a distance of about one mile and a half. Meanwhile Manor Place Baths had been emptied and a heavy H.E. bomb fell among the pumps at St. George's Circus, killing seventeen of the crews and blocking the only entrance to the water supply. In the meantime more fires had been started here. A fire barge was now ordered to relay water from the Surrey Canal to the Elephant and Castle, and water lines were started from Waterloo and Westminster Bridges, both being about a mile and a half from the fire ground. The relay line from London Bridge was then cut by a collapsed building and the road blocked with red hot bricks. By this time nearly a mile of a second hose line had been laid with great difficulty, but a lorry bringing up a canvas dam for the line to discharge into had driven into a bomb crater in the Old Kent Road, sparks and flying embers had kept burning the hose as it was laid so that much water was lost, and soon after the line was completed it was cut by a bomb. 'The fire was eventually held and controlled just after daybreak with water from the Thames and Surrey Canal, relaying through approximately nine miles of hose'.

It is, of course, difficult to say categorically to what extent more effective emergency water supplies could have reduced the damage done by these early fire raids. There was a climax in some of the concentrated incendiary attacks when no brigade, whatever its resources in men, appliances and water, could have hoped to prevent fires spreading in closely built high risk areas, such as those in the heart of many of our big cities.[1] Nevertheless it can hardly be denied

---

[1] This point was reached many times in German cities when uncontrollable fire hurricanes developed after concentrated incendiary bombing. See for instance *Fire and the Air War*, edited by H. Bond, pp. 99–102.

GG

that if the measures on water supply which were to be taken later in 1941 and in 1942 had been in full effect during the 1940 and 1941 fire raids, a great deal of property which was destroyed could have been saved.

The remaining element in fire-fighting to be reviewed is the system of communications and administration which bound together all the other elements and directed their effective deployment. How efficient in operation were the systems of central and local organisation, ranging from the individual communications arrangements of the various brigades to the national use of reinforcements? Was the structure of the Fire Service adequate and responsive to its tasks?

During the big fire raids there were many instances of communications breaking down and of lack of knowledge of the overall fire situation causing uncertainty and confusion at headquarters. Sometimes the telephone services on which the brigades normally relied failed completely because exchanges were destroyed, lines were cut by bombs, switchboards were put out of action or control room installations themselves were damaged or destroyed. The lads who had been recruited and trained as cyclist messengers rendered gallant service on many such occasions, but they could only cope with a fraction of the message work; and at this period observation posts, from which fires could be spotted and their positions fixed irrespectively of the telephone system, though in use already in some brigades, were far less developed than they came to be after the National Fire Service had been instituted. Moreover, when the raids began, control room procedure and practice were often too cumbersome or too slow to meet the strain. Even under the most favourable conditions it was difficult during a heavy raid to keep any effective record of fires reported, of appliances at each fire and of appliances still required; it was practically impossible when there was any serious interruption in the normal means of communication.

In addition to the local and regional control systems there was also the Home Office Fire Control, linked by direct lines with the Regional Headquarters; it acted as an intelligence centre for the country as a whole, and was responsible for directing the movement of inter-Region reinforcements when a Region required more reinforcements than the Regional Commissioner could call upon.[1] During the heavy fire-fighting of 1940–1941 it often happened that reinforcements had to be drawn from considerable distances—from the Midlands to London or from the North of England to South Wales. These movements needed very careful planning. When the enemy switched his attack, as he often did, from one part of the country to another, pump crews from the North might be in the South and crews from the South in the Midlands or Wales. There was at least one stage of the blitz

---

[1] See Chapter VI, pp. 275–277.

when brigades in nearly every part of the country had been called on to such an extent and so many pump crews were in transit or resting after arduous duty that the Fire Control Room was hard put to it to find uncommitted crews that could be called upon without depleting local resources to a dangerous extent.

Much valuable, and sometimes bitter, experience was gained by the brigades during these first months of serious attack. In some areas relatively little attention had been paid, for instance, to such important problems as the control of concentrations of appliances on the fire ground, the handling of incoming reinforcements, the organisation of large-scale water relaying and measures for supplying food and petrol to units at work, and for relieving, feeding and resting firemen who had been on duty for long periods. And even where attention had been given to these matters the scale of the operations was often greatly in excess of any provision that had been made or thought necessary. In matters like this the experience gained in one area might clearly be used as warning and guidance to others. Accordingly, in December 1940, the Home Office and Scottish Home Department began to issue a series of notes on actual fire-fighting operations. In addition, all fire authorities were asked to review their emergency arrangements and to report by the end of the year on the measures they had taken to improve them. To supplement and reinforce these instructions, meetings of fire brigade officers were called in every Region and addressed by senior officials from the Departments.

All the conditions that had been experienced under actual air attack, it was claimed, had been foreseen and prepared for. It was, however, the combination of these conditions on the scale recently experienced that produced such overwhelming problems, only to be overcome by careful planning and thorough preparation. Fire authorities were asked to reconsider their arrangements under a series of heads and to report on the measures they proposed to adopt. The needs included (1) better measures for dealing with incipient fires—the enforcement of the Fire Watchers' Order and the Clearance of Lofts Order, the organisation of supplementary fire parties and the strengthening of fire parties in factories, shops, etc.; (2) improved organisation in control rooms,[1] which should be staffed in the main by A.F.S. personnel and women, as 'generally speaking the place for officers with experience of fighting large fires is in control at the fires and not in control rooms'; (3) the decentralisation of the fire-fighting reserves; (4) the institution of 'Special List Officers';[2] (5) a review of

---

[1] On the broad principle that each local fire station should be responsible for sending out appliances up to the limit of its resources, keeping Divisional and Headquarters Controls informed how its resources were engaged.

[2] See p. 461.

telephone facilities and the systematic use of messenger and observation post arrangements to supplement the telephones; (6) the organisation of alternative control rooms; (7) the extension of emergency water supplies and of arrangements for long relays of water; (8) an improved organisation for handling reinforcements, including the prior selection of rendezvous points where incoming units could report, be deployed to fires and bases where they could be rested and fed; (9) improved arrangements for providing food and drink for men engaged at fires; (10) the preparation of plans to obtain assistance from the military where practicable; and (11) a review of arrangements for ensuring the maintenance of petrol supplies for pumps at fires and of bulk reserves.

These instructions amounted for the most part to little more than stressing measures already dealt with in Home Office and Scottish Office circulars and memoranda, but on the particular problem of water supplies a different approach was urgently needed. The huge quantities of water required, the vulnerability of mains supplies and of hose lines as these great attacks developed made it clear that more radical measures than those taken so far were essential. The real need was for a system of immense capacity *distributed throughout the more vulnerable areas and independent of the normal piped supply.* Towards the end of 1940 the Home Office, assisted by the Regional Works Advisers, drew up detailed plans on new and more systematic lines, and fire authorities were advised of the proposals in February 1941.[1] There were to be two main developments: (1) the provision of tanks or water basins that would allow 250,000 gallons per 100,000 population in high risk areas, and (2) the use of emergency mains of 6 in. steel piping laid on the surface.

The water basins that were to be provided could be constructed in many different ways: by excavating in clay soil, by building tanks of wood, concrete or brick above ground level, by erecting steel tanks from components produced in bulk or (and this was usually the most effective way in cities that had already been heavily attacked) by converting the basements of bombed buildings into water storage tanks. The Home Office placed new orders for large numbers of steel water basins and for 100 miles of 6 in. steel piping. The piping was to be in lengths of about 20 feet and with each mile of piping there would be about 150 special components—half and quarter lengths, bends, tees, valves, collecting and outlet heads, joints, etc. To begin with about 60 miles of the piping was held in lots of from 1 to 3 miles at different points under the control of Regional Headquarters and used as emergency mobile reserves; the remaining 40 miles were laid down as semi-permanent emergency pipe lines fed from a river, canal

---

[1] F.B. Circular No. 7A/1941, 5th February 1941, and S.H.D. Circular No. L.27 R/41, 15th February 1941.

or other large supply to supplement water facilities in high risk areas. The piping quickly proved its value. It was relatively invulnerable to high explosive bombing; shocks which fractured cast iron mains laid below ground hardly disturbed steel piping on the surface or merely caused the joints to give a little; even red hot debris from burning buildings could fall across the pipe lines without interrupting the flow of water. Even if the line was broken by a direct hit, repairs could be carried out with the special components held by the brigades. This policy of above-ground steel piping was to be developed much further later on in the war, when the fire services had passed under direct central control.[1]

In the meantime and in addition to these new measures, work had also been continuing in London to complete the system of emergency mains carrying unfiltered water. An additional 24 inch main connecting the West End main with one of the dry mains in Hyde Park was also being laid. The plan for a main from the City to the East End proved very difficult to carry out and work was not completed until early in 1942.

But while these steps were being taken to improve the handling and organisation of the existing system of fire brigades, doubts were growing as to whether more fundamental administrative changes were not necessary. The main shortcomings of the Fire Service during these months of strain were those that sprang from the division of control among more than a thousand local government units, the very limited resources in officers, men and appliances available to most of the separate units and the inevitable unevenness in efficiency and raggedness in co-ordination. Although the emergency measures had been centrally planned it was a question of Home Office *advice* rather than of *orders*, and the execution by individual authorities showed great variation. Some brigades were short of vehicles, having perhaps, only one towing vehicle for every three pumps; one city omitted to provide any towing vehicles in its dock area, the pumps being pushed to the fires by hand with the hose and gear piled up on top. One important seaport refused to provide its fire officers with cars, an alderman being reported as saying that he 'was not going to have officers gallivanting about the place in cars', though they had to supervise many widely separated fires; this same city had provided no alternative fire control room.[2] Local authorities were often loth to amalgamate their brigades with those of their neighbours. In one case there were three towns packed tightly together with confused, interlocking boundaries, the whole area containing important, vulnerable national risks but the authorities were most unwilling to combine and

---

[1] pp. 494-495.
[2] Sir Aylmer Firebrace, *op. cit.*, p. 184.

regarded all suggestions for a joint scheme with hostility and suspicion.[1]

Though many of the initial shortcomings had been overcome long before the heavy attacks were over, the principal weaknesses were inherent in the system. Experience of air raid fire-fighting and anticipation of what might lie in the future called for a new assessment of whether the current organisation was equal to the demands which might be made upon it. The Home Office estimate of the menace of the light incendiary bomb had not always been shared in other quarters, but by now it was realised on all sides that incendiary bombs were the most effective of aerial weapons. The raids on London in December 1940 and May 1941 and the attacks on Coventry were the genesis of the R.A.F. policy of saturation incendiary bombing;[2] and in turn attention was focused on the possibility of still greater menace to the cities of the United Kingdom in the future. 'The experience of all raids, including our own photographs of what we are doing in Germany', said the Parliamentary Secretary to the Ministry of Home Security later, 'shows that the biggest single problem while a raid is actually in progress is the problem of fire'.[3] Moreover it was cumulatively the most destructive agent in city areas.[4] The enemy still retained a fair-sized bombing force in the West and no one knew whether a Russian collapse would free the forces engaged in the East for a fresh all-out attack on Britain. From 1941 onwards, therefore, fire defence measures were given a greater emphasis in civil defence planning and a greater share in its total resources. The most important developments were to be the nationalisation of the fire services and the compulsory civilian fire guard plan.[5]

The National Fire Service: (i) Its Planning

Thus it became clear that, though the fire-fighting services had stood up to the great fire raids with courage and tenacity, their efforts

---

[1] Sir Aylmer Firebrace, *op. cit.*, p. 203.

[2] 'The Germans again and again missed their chance, as they did in the London blitz . . . of setting our cities ablaze by concentrated attack', wrote 'Bomber' Harris. 'Coventry was adequately concentrated in point of space, but all the same there was little concentration in point of time, and nothing comparable to the fire tornadoes of Hamburg and Dresden ever occurred in this country. But they did do us enough damage to teach us the principle of concentration, the principle of starting so many fires at the same time that no fire-fighting services, however efficiently and quickly they were reinforced by the fire brigades of other towns, could get them under control.' Sir Arthur Harris, *Bomber Offensive*, p. 83.

[3] H. of C. Deb., Vol. 390, Col. 1648, 30th June 1943.

[4] A post-war investigation claimed, for instance, that photographic studies of damage in Germany indicated that ton for ton incendiaries were 4.8 times as effective as high explosive bombs on residential areas and smaller industrial and mercantile property. *Fire and the Air War*, edited by H. Bond, p. 80.

[5] The fire guard plan is described in detail in Chapter XIII.

were greatly handicapped by weaknesses inherent in the local fire brigade organisation.[1] The Government's policy on civil defence was to rely on local authorities to organise and operate the various services, subject to general directions from Whitehall and to a certain amount of closer supervision by the Regional Commissioners. But air raid fire-fighting was often on a scale quite out of proportion to the scale of even the larger local government units, not to mention the many small units in the fire services, and fires paid no attention to the niceties of local government boundaries. Despite the various steps taken during the months of heavy attack to integrate and improve the emergency fire brigade organisation, nothing had been achieved that really went to the heart of the matter. The principal sources of weakness were the piecemeal character of a system operated at the level of local government through hundreds of separate units, the smallness of most of the units and the unevenness of their organisation.

What seemed to be needed was something every military organisation regarded as an essential—unity of command exercised through operational units organised and adapted for the functions they had to perform. Over 1,600 brigades of all sorts and sizes, with independent control and leadership, however well they might work individually or even co-operate locally, were too heavily handicapped to face a ruthless enemy. Larger units under single command and operating with speed and flexibility were vital to secure full efficiency. Standardisation in ranks, uniforms, training, operational technique, orders and messages would prevent much confusion when reinforcements were brought in from other districts. Officials at the Home Office had become impressed by the weaknesses in organisation and were considering the best methods of securing greater efficiency from the total resources; and early in 1941 suggestions were being made in Parliament and the Press that the fire services should be reorganised on 'regionalised' or 'nationalised' lines.[2] 'No Army' said *The Times* of 5th May 1941, 'could fight efficiently with nothing between a commander-in-chief and company commanders; and the Government ought to consider at once whether the army of fire-fighters should not be given a less localised organisation and status'. By the time this article appeared, however, the Government had already

---

[1] It is interesting to note that during the war Germany also nationalised its fire services which had previously been run by local authorities.

[2] A series of letters to *The Times* opened with one from Lady Astor of 4th April 1941, after she had witnessed a heavy raid on Plymouth. She claimed that local fire-fighting organisations were totally inadequate to deal with the effects of thousands of incendiary bombs dropped simultaneously, and criticised the measures taken by the Government, including in particular the question of water supplies. *The Times* followed with two special articles on 23rd and 24th April on 'Lessons of the Raids' recommending the energetic training of fire guards, more equipment and particularly large reserve water supplies. Letters from Admiral T. P. H. Beamish (26th April) and others urged the nationalisation or regionalisation of the fire services.

decided to take the brigades under direct control and were working out the best technique.

A few days before the article in *The Times*, the Lord President of the Council had forwarded to the Home Secretary a summary of representations he had received on the reorganisation of the fire brigades. The Home Secretary considered these arguments along with a memorandum from the Head of the Police and Fire Brigades Divisions of the Home Office. The latter claimed that the fundamental failing of the existing system of small units was that no Chief Officer had nearly enough officers of his own on whom he could call in case of need. What was required, it was argued, was some system of unification of the smaller brigades so as to form larger units. This would be a radical change, involving legislation. Could it be undertaken in war-time? After considering the cases put before him, the Home Secretary decided that one possible solution would be the merging of all county district fire brigades under the county councils, and as a first step he called a conference of Regional Commissioners to discuss this suggestion.

In the meantime, however, the officials saw many disadvantages in the proposal to set up County Fire Brigades. County boundaries were often inconvenient; areas such as Birmingham and Manchester, for instance, each with their satellite towns, should clearly be considered as a whole, but in both cases they straddled at least three counties. County Councils in England and Wales, and most of those in Scotland, had never been fire authorities and had no experience in this field; they were, moreover, already heavily burdened with other emergency work. Apart from those in London, there were no officers with experience in county brigade organisation. This proposal would involve the creation of 60 separate new fire authorities in addition to the 83 county borough brigades which would continue to operate. It would certainly not achieve a unified officer system, which should be one of the objects of any reorganisation. The more the Home Office officials considered the proposition the more convinced they became that the County scheme could not achieve the ends desired, and that the proper course was to free the fire services completely from what they had come to regard as the hampering shackles of local government control and bring them under the direct and unified control of the Secretary of State himself. They recommended, therefore, that, instead of proceeding with the County scheme, the Home Secretary should ask Parliament for powers to take all the fire brigades in England and Wales under his own control and carry out whatever reorganisation he decided upon through the agency of his Department and his Regional organisation, and without the intervention of the county councils or any of the fire authorities. In the course of a midnight conference on the night of 28th-29th April, the officials' arguments prevailed, and when the Home Secretary met the Regional Commissioners on the following morning the plan he put to them was no longer the reorganisation of the brigades under the county councils but, instead, a plan to take all the brigades under direct central control. The Regional Commissioners welcomed the proposal, and it was submitted to and approved by the War Cabinet on 8th May 1941.

As yet the fire authorities themselves knew nothing of what was afoot. The first step was to inform them of the decision, obtain their agreement on the financial aspects and their co-operation in bringing the plan to fruition. Accordingly the Home Secretary and the Secretary of State for Scotland met representatives of the local authorities at conferences on the 10th and 12th May; these were followed by further conferences at which the financial implications were discussed.[1] By no means all fire authorities were in agreement with the scheme, but they bowed to the inevitable and most of them accepted it with good grace. On 13th May, the Home Secretary announced the Government's decision in the House of Commons.[2] While paying 'a very sincere tribute of admiration for their conspicuous personal courage and skill', to the regular fire brigades and the Auxiliary Fire Service, the Home Secretary explained that the Government was convinced that to meet air attacks on the scale that had been experienced, 'a drastic change of organisation must be made'. On the same day circulars explaining what had been decided were issued from the Home Office and the Scottish Home Department to all the fire authorities.[3]

This was not, however, to be a permanent reorganisation. In view of the controversy which developed later regarding the return of the fire brigades to local authority control, it is worth noting that the Home Secretary recorded at the time: 'I think it is (also) necessary to bear in mind that, while it would clearly be out of the question to return to the present basis of organisation when the war is over,

---

[1] In this respect the plan involved a sort of reversal of the usual relationship—a grant from local authorities to the Exchequer instead of the other way about. The Exchequer would undertake the whole cost, in the first instance, and sums were to be paid to the Exchequer from local rates representing 75 per cent. of the current cost of the regular brigades (which had hitherto not been subject to Exchequer grant) or in the case of authorities that had not yet carried out their obligations under the Fire Brigades Act, 1938, and established an efficient fire brigade, the like proportion of the produce of a two-penny rate (representing the reasonable cost of providing a local service on a modest scale). The normal payment could be adjusted where the expenditure for the standard year could be shown to be exceptionally high or exceptionally low. (F.B. Circular No. 39/1941. S.H.D. Circular No. L.71/41.)

At this time the annual cost of the regular fire brigades was about £3,000,000 per annum, while the emergency fire services were costing about £27,000,000, of which about £21,000,000 was already being borne by the Exchequer. The burden transferred from the rates to the Exchequer was therefore relatively small.

[2] H. of C. Deb., Vol. 371, Cols. 1082-5, 13th May 1941.

[3] F.B. Circular No. 39/1941. S.H.D. Circular No. L.71/41.

the fire brigades will presumably then pass back to local authority administration on some basis, though with much closer supervision than hitherto'. . . . In the House of Commons he said, 'It is certainly my very definite view that after the war the fire-fighting forces should again be a local authority service;[1] and later, 'I frankly admit that I gave an absolute promise that the brigades would go back to local government after the war. I did not say they would go back to the same authorities . . . I am bound to say . . . the experiment of a National Fire Service has taught us a good deal, and we must not be unwilling to think again when we come towards the end of the war as to what it would be right to do in the national interest'.[2]

Thus this important issue was speedily settled. The decision to alter the organisation in so revolutionary a way when air attacks might be resumed at any time was a courageous one. Moreover, the Departments had had as yet little time to consider ways and means. There were no precedents to guide them, no previous experience on which they could call; everything would have to be worked out from first principles. Speed was the essence of the problem and the Home Secretary set three months as the period within which he desired the new Service to be constituted.[3]

It is not often that a completely new administrative and operational organisation has to be planned at speed from the foundations upwards, and a brief summary of some of the more important elements that had to be provided may be helpful to the reader. In the first place, the Secretaries of State had to be given their new powers—to supersede or adapt all current fire brigade legislation, to set up the new Service and provide for the transfer of the functions, responsibilities, property and liabilities of the fire brigade authorities to themselves. And there was, of course, the financial side of the transaction to be settled with the Treasury and the local authorities.

The constitution and organisation of the new Service had to be prescribed in every respect. In this branch of the work ideas had often to be readjusted on matters of substance or detail as the work went forward, but the general pattern, swiftly sketched out in the earliest planning, was adhered to in the main. Among the many varied issues to be settled were the name of the new Service, the distribution of powers and responsibilities between the Secretary of State, the Regional Commissioners and the Fire Service Officers; the definition of the size, area and boundaries of the main Fire Service

---

[1] H. of C. Deb., Vol. 371, Col. 1429, 20th May 1941.

[2] H. of C. Deb., Vol. 390, Cols. 1737–8, 30th June 1943.

[3] The establishment of the National Fire Service was 'one of the quickest administrative revolutions that ever took place', in the view of the Home Secretary. (H. of C. Deb., Vol. 390, Col. 1726, 30th June 1943.)

formations ('the Fire Forces') and the subordinate formations within them; and the system of ranks and their respective titles, rank badges and uniforms and the system to be followed in matters such as appointments, promotions and the disciplinary system. Conditions of service had to be prescribed anew for all members of the Service, regular and auxiliary, whole time and part-time, pensionable and non-pensionable, whose current rights and obligations would disappear with the fire brigade legislation.

Buildings had to be found for the new main and subordinate headquarters, a complete communications system established to link the new administrative and operational units, and a new mobilising system prescribed to secure appropriate attendances at fires and reinforcements when necessary. The administrative system, of course, had to be entirely revised, with new personal records for all members of the Service, catering arrangements for the stations, a purchasing organisation and stores for food, station necessaries, uniforms etc., and a complete system of financial accounting and control.

Even training had to be taken up afresh. Obviously, training would have to be provided for the new entrants to the Service, for the thousands of women who would be recruited to staff the new controls and for many officers who would have new and quite unfamiliar tasks to undertake; but, more than that, it was necessary to ensure that the firemen from different brigades followed the same drill in handling their gear and that those serving in the smaller brigades who had had experience only with a limited range of appliances were made familiar with all the principal appliances and types of equipment in use anywhere in the Service.

Answers had to be found to all these questions, and many more; and all had to be set out in the shape of Regulations or Instructions which were to govern the actions of all concerned in the building up of the new Service. And when all this had been done it amounted to no more than the preparation of the 'blue print'. It was still necessary to find the officers to carry out the work. They had to be selected from the Fire Brigades or from elsewhere and posted wherever it was judged they could render the most effective service.

The Act giving the Secretaries of State the necessary statutory powers (Fire Services (Emergency Provisions) Act)[1] received the Royal Assent on 22nd May 1941. The Act gave the Secretaries of State almost unlimited powers to carry out by Regulations the unification of the fire brigade services. They were enabled to take such powers as they required to constitute the new organisation as they chose, to suspend or modify the powers of local authorities and require them to obey their directions, to exercise the local authorities' powers or use their property on behalf of the Crown, to transfer the

[1] 4 and 5 Geo. 6, Ch. 22.

members of their fire brigades to the service of the new organisation with or without their consent, and generally to provide for such other matters as they thought necessary for the co-ordination, unification or improvement of the fire services.[1]

The Act was thus in very general terms; it was the Regulations that were to be of cardinal importance, for they would provide the detailed foundation on which the structure of the new Service would depend. The first and principal batch of Regulations, applying to the whole of Great Britain, were made by the Home Secretary on 5th August 1941.[2] Through an oversight, which illustrates the abnormal pressure of war on the administrative machine, these Regulations were not laid before Parliament until nearly three years later.[3]

In the meantime there was considerable reorganisation in the Home Office. The transformation of the Department's relations with the fire services carried with it a corresponding transformation of their functions and responsibilities, and brought to an end the arrangement by which both police work and fire service work in the Home Office were grouped together under one Assistant Under-Secretary of State. A new Fire Service Department, based on the existing Fire Brigades Division, was organised in six Divisions (soon increased to seven) under the Assistant Under-Secretary of State (Sir Arthur L. Dixon) who had previously had charge of both Police and Fire Brigades Divisions.[4] A professional Fire Staff and Inspectorate, paralleling the administrative Divisions, was set up, with Commander A.N.G. Firebrace, Chief Officer of the London Fire Brigade, who had been transferred to the Home Office for special duties in the previous December, as Chief of the Fire Staff and Inspector-in-Chief. Mr. B. A. Westbrook, who had previously served as Fire Adviser and Chief Fire Brigades Inspector, became Chief Engineer and Technical Officer. There was corresponding reorganisation in the Scottish Home Department, with Mr. A. B. Craig, Chief Officer of the Bromley Fire Brigade, appointed Chief Technical Adviser to the Department. In June 1941, a Fire Service Council,

---

[1] At a later stage the Secretary of State's statutory powers were extended for certain purposes by Regulations made under the Emergency Powers (Defence) Act, 1939, on the strength of a provision (section 2) which had been included in the Fire Services (Emergency Provisions) Act; for example, by the Defence (National Fire Service) Regulations of the 5th August 1941 (S.R. & O., No. 1133) which empowered the Secretary of State, *inter alia*, to provide for the employment of members of the N.F.S. in Northern Ireland and on ships at sea.

[2] The National Fire Service (General) Regulations, 1941. S.R. & O., No. 1134. A little later separate sets of regulations were made to give effect to the financial settlement and to preserve certain pension rights.

[3] See Herbert Morrison, *Government & Parliament* (1954), pp. 320-4.

[4] With the special rank of Principal Assistant Under-Secretary of State, which was revived for the purpose. He reported as before to the Home Secretary through the Secretary of the Ministry of Home Security. (See p. 248.)

on analogous lines to the Army or Air Council, was constituted to supervise the reorganisation of the Service.[1]

The primary unit of operational control and administration in the new National Fire Service was to be the individual Fire Force. Each Fire Force constituted a single unified command extending over a prescribed area, the Fire Area, under a single officer, the Fire Force Commander. The Fire Force Commander's powers were derived from the Regulations and were subject to directions given by the Secretaries of State and, in England and Wales, to certain authority vested in the Regional Commissioners.

Under the original Regulations, England and Wales were divided into 33 Fire Areas and Scotland into 6. The Fire Areas varied considerably in size and still more in the number of appliances and firemen within them. In settling the Fire Areas the main objective had been to bring the whole of each important urban or industrial fire risk under a single command[2]. On the other hand Fire Areas should not be so large as to prevent effective supervision from a single headquarters. Local government boundaries were a secondary consideration. Several important high risk areas such as Tyneside, Tees-side, Merseyside and greater Manchester could readily be organised into single Fire Areas; other areas such as Lincolnshire, Northamptonshire, Derbyshire, Essex, Norfolk and Suffolk readily lent themselves to treatment on a county basis, subject only to very small adjustments. But greater Birmingham, and some of the agricultural areas with scattered towns, gave more difficulty, and in two to three cases the original scheme had to be altered after a longer or shorter trial. London Region was originally constituted as one Fire Force, but here also changes became necessary at a later date. The maps on the following pages show the Fire Forces as they stood in 1944.

Within each Fire Force, there were to be the following principal subordinate formations:

Division, typically comprising 100 pumps
Column   ,,   ,,   50   ,,
Company ,,   ,,   10   ,,
Section   ,,   ,,   5   ,,

---

[1] The Home Secretary took the chair and other members included the Parliamentary and Permanent Secretaries, Ministry of Home Security, the head of the Fire Service Department, the Chief of the Fire Staff, and a representative of the Scottish Home Department. (No corresponding body was considered necessary in Scotland.) The Fire Service Council met first on 16th June 1941 and afterwards at fairly frequent intervals while the reorganisation was being worked out, but when the National Fire Service was established the Council soon ceased to take any significant part in its control and met only occasionally until August 1944.

[2] A principle which representatives of the Department had urged on the Riverdale Committee, but which that Committee had not seen their way to adopt in their proposals for the peace-time service.

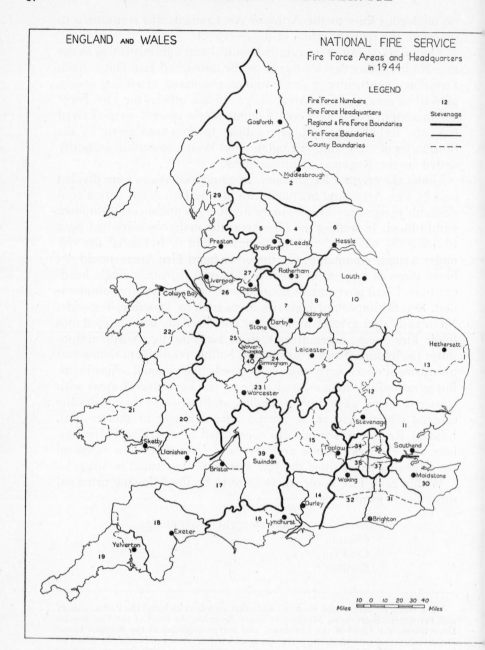

ENGLAND AND WALES

NATIONAL FIRE SERVICE
Fire Force Areas and Headquarters
in 1944

LEGEND
Fire Force Numbers   12
Fire Force Headquarters   Stevenage
Regional & Fire Force Boundaries
Fire Force Boundaries
County Boundaries

NATIONAL FIRE SERVICE
Fire Force Areas and Headquarters
in 1944

SCOTLAND

NORTHERN

Inverness

NORTH EASTERN

Aberdeen

EASTERN

Dundee

WESTERN
No 1

Edinburgh

Glasgow

Paisley

SOUTH EASTERN

WESTERN
No 2

LEGEND

Fire Force Areas	SOUTH EASTERN
Fire Force Headquarters	Edinburgh
Fire Force Boundaries	——
County Boundaries	– – – –

10   0   10   20   30   40
Miles   Miles

Officer ranks were to be created to take charge of each of these tiers, with an additional rank, Senior Company Officer, where necessary[1].

It was proposed at one stage that the rank designations should be quasi-military in their terms, but fairly soon functional designations specific to the Fire Service were adopted. After much discussion on such issues as officer ranks for women and ranks for fire officers at Regional Headquarters, the Regulations set out the following ranks:

Men	*Women*[2]
Chief Regional Fire Officer	Senior Area Officer
Fire Force Commander	Area Oficer
Assistant Fire Force Commander	Group Officer (in charge of
Divisional Officer	roughly 250–300 firewomen)
Column Officer	Assistant Group Officer (for
Senior Company Officer	roughly 50 firewomen)
Company Officer	Leading Firewoman (for roughly
Section Leader	10 firewomen)
Leading Fireman	Firewoman
Fireman	

The selection of officers had also to be reorganised. There were many new officer posts to be filled and it was essential to make the fullest use of talent in the Auxiliary Fire Service as well as of the experience in the regular brigades. There was now one promotion ladder. Previously each fireman had been limited in his prospects of promotion by the scope in his own brigade; now he could get as far as ability and experience justified. The essence of the problem, however, was that the tasks for which the officers had to be chosen were in many respects quite different from anything that fire brigade officers had undertaken hitherto, and quite unprecedented in the degree of initiative and responsibility involved. Officer selection, it was decided, would be organised on a national plane, and a Central Selection Board was set up to consider candidates for the three senior ranks.[3] Appointments to the rank of Divisional Officer

---

[1] The number and distribution of subordinate formations was left to the decision of the Fire Force Commander, but average requirements might be of the order of 1 Divisional Officer, 2 Column Officers, and 10 Company Officers per Division, with a sufficient number of Section Leaders and Leading Firemen to provide the necessary complement in the several reliefs.

[2] Regulation 6 (2) of the National Fire Service (General) Regulations, 5th August 1941. Later Regulations abolished the rank of Senior Area Officer and added four new women officer ranks—Chief Woman Fire Officer, Regional Woman Fire Officer, Assistant Area Officer and Senior Leading Firewoman.

[3] The Chairman of the Board was the First Commissioner, Civil Service Commission, and other members were Fire Service representatives and outside members from industry and trade unions. A member of the Scottish Fire Commission was present when there were candidates from Scotland. In the case of the ranks not dealt with by the Central Selection Board, the procedure in Scotland was rather different. The Secretary of State made appointments to the ranks of Divisional Officer and Column Officer and a Scottish Board interviewed candidates for these ranks.

and below were to be made by Regional Commissioners (who generally worked with a Regional Selection Board) and by Fire Force Commanders. Staff employed on administrative duties were in future to lose their 'civilian' status and to become uniformed and subject to the same conditions of service as operational firemen and firewomen. Thus there was created a system of ranks which applied throughout the Service and which could be universally understood and recognised. The Home Office believed that this element in the reorganisation made a major contribution to the building up of efficiency both in administration and on the fire ground.

By the end of June 1941, administrative preparations for the transfer were fairly well advanced and 1st July was fixed as the date from which the Treasury would assume financial responsibility, subject to the appropriate payments from the local authorities.[1] These authorities provided inventories of the premises, appliances and equipment in the possession of their brigades on 1st July. On 17th July, a statement of the main features of the new Fire Service organisation was issued through the Press and the B.B.C.

Most of the officers to fill the posts of Chief Regional Fire Officer and Fire Force Commander had been selected by the third week in July and they were now briefed by the Head of the Fire Service Department and the Chief of the Fire Staff with a sketch plan of the new Service and told of the immediate tasks that lay before them. On 24th July, they were ready to proceed to their several headquarters to set about the construction of the new operational and administrative formations. However, very few headquarters did in fact exist. The selection of officers had advanced much faster than the selection of the buildings to accommodate them, their staff and their equipment. The only headquarters buildings in existence were those of the old fire brigades, which rarely bore any relation to the requirements of a Fire Force protecting, perhaps, a county or more and comprising several thousand firemen and firewomen.

The task of finding the necessary buildings, adapting them and providing control room and telephone facilities devolved in the main on the Ministry of Works and Buildings and the General Post Office. Unfortunately for the N.F.S. this search for accommodation took place at a very difficult time; almost all suitable premises were already occupied by the military authorities or other Government Departments. Many Fire Force Commanders had, therefore, to begin their work in cramped and makeshift accommodation, at least one of them in the cells at a police station.

The National Fire Service (ii) Its Establishment

Subject to the Regulations made under the authority of the Fire

---

[1] F.B. Circular No. 57/1941, 28th June 1941 and S.H.D. Circular No. 4498.

Services (Emergency Provisions) Act, the general corpus of instructions which governed the whole life of the National Fire Service took the form of 'Regional Memoranda', sent to Regional Headquarters only, and 'National Fire Service Instructions', sent to both Regional Headquarters and Fire Force Commanders. From May 1942, matters relating to conditions of service, welfare, etc., were dealt with separately in 'General Fire Force Instructions', which received a wider circulation than the 'National Fire Service Instructions', and technical matters and advice on operations and training were dealt with in a series of 'Operations and Training Notes'.

Soon after the Regulations were made, the Departments issued a series of National Fire Service Instructions dealing with some of the fundamentals of the new Service—the powers of Fire Force Commanders,[1] the Fire Force organisation,[2] mobilisation in response to fire calls, including the introduction of standard messages and the maintenance of reserves of pumps at the call of Regional Commissioners,[3] and fire brigade property and works, with important instructions on emergency water supplies.[4] Other instructions soon followed on the appointment of administrative staff, conditions of service, discipline, and finance and accounting.[5] The appointed day for the final transfer was fixed for 18th August,[6] and every Fire Force Commander was given the text of a Fire Force Order to be issued in his Fire Area on that date.[7] From then responsibility for the administration and control of the Fire Service and the conduct and efficiency of its members passed from the local authorities to the Home Secretary and the Secretary of State for Scotland. To signalise the institution of the new Service the Secretaries of State issued Orders of the Day to all ranks.

Now, in place of the loose-coupled fire brigade services, with their hundreds of separate units, there was to be a close-knit organisation of between 30 and 40 Fire Forces, each constructed on similar lines, with identical training, system of ranks and operational procedure, and each able to put substantial fire-fighting forces on to the fire ground anywhere in its area. Alternatively, a Fire Force could despatch to a stricken area elsewhere a self-contained body of

---

[1] National Fire Service Instruction No. 1/1941.

[2] N.F.S. Instruction No. 2/1941.

[3] N.F.S. Instruction Nos. 3 and 4/1941.

[4] N.F.S. Instruction No. 5/1941.

[5] N.F.S. Instruction Nos. 6, 7, 9 and 11/1941. The Regulations relating to pensions (S.R. & O. 1941, Nos. 1267, 1268 and 1270-74, and the Finance Regulations (S.R. and O. 1941, No. 1269) were issued on 18th August 1941.

[6] S.R. & O. 1941, No. 1381. No general announcement was made, however, until 14th September 1941, to avoid giving the enemy information which might be useful to him.

[7] N.F.S. Instruction No. 8/1941.

reinforcements with pumps, water units, control vans, wireless cars, repair vans, canteen vans or mobile kitchens and staff officers, water officers, mobilising officers and staff capable of taking over much of the operational responsibility from the local officers and staffs if they should be exhausted and unable to carry on.

This type of organisation, moreover, was to persist all through the war, moulded by directions from the centre, and guided also by the Regional Commissioners and the Chief Regional Fire Officers, to meet the varying exigencies of the time. There was, for instance, the build-up till towards the end of 1942 and beginning of 1943, when the total strength, whole-time and part-time, reached nearly 350,000 men, women and youths; this was followed by the gradual reduction in numbers and concentration on the South and East Coasts towards the approach of D-day, and finally came the continuous contraction to something approaching a peace-time complement, at about one tenth of the peak figure. After the war, outside the period covered by this history, most of the essential characteristics which had been impressed on the Fire Service in these few years were carried over into the County Fire Brigade system established by the Fire Services Act, 1947.

The National Fire Service: (iii) Organisation

The first phase in the story of the National Fire Service after its establishment in August 1941, covers the period to the peak of its development about the beginning of 1943. It was a period largely free from operational strain and during it a complicated organisation was built up. Instructions, advice and the laying down of a standard practice were evolved on such different subjects as the selection and equipment of buildings for operational and administrative purposes, the provision of accommodation for personnel, catering, medical services, discipline, uniforms, record systems and finance. Much of the work, though cumulatively vital, was long and detailed and it would be of little interest to the general reader to take him through these mazes of official administrative endeavour. Certain aspects of this work should, however, be considered further: they are mainly concerned with the structure of the national fire-fighting machine and with each of its cognate parts, and with the chain of command which directed and integrated the whole.

The structure of the National Fire Service was that of a pyramid with the Home Office and the Scottish Home Department at the top, sloping down to the Fire Forces and widening to the smaller formations within the Fire Forces at the bottom. The Regional Commissioners and the Chief Regional Fire Officers fitted in between the Home Office and the Fire Forces, though in some respects the functions of the Regions were less clearly defined than those of the other units in the chain of command.

In the Fire Service Department, with the Principal Assistant Under-Secretary of State at its head, there was a broad division of responsibility between the administrative staff and the two professional Sections, the Fire Staff and the Inspectorate. On the administrative side there were two Assistant Under-Secretaries of State, one with general charge over the Divisions dealing with problems of organisation, staffing, conditions of service, discipline, records, etc., and the other over those dealing with appliances and equipment, supplies, buildings and supplementary water. The Fire Staff, with an original establishment of 22 officers (including two women) worked out, in co-operation with the administrative staff, technical plans concerned with personnel, training, exercises, operations and improvements in technique. The Inspectorate, originally 6 in number but soon increased to 12, with 3 women Inspectors, was concerned with watching and assisting in the execution of these plans by the Fire Forces, by comprehensive general inspections, conferences and visits. Especially in the early days the Inspectors could do much to ensure that the mass of written instructions were understood and followed with a reasonable degree of uniformity. Also at the centre was the Home Office Fire Control Room, now responsible, under the Chief of the Fire Staff, for directing the movement of reinforcements between one Region and another. In each Region the movement of appliances and men within the area of a Fire Force was now under the full control of the Fire Force Commander and their movement between one Fire Force and another under the control of the Regional Commissioner. The regional reinforcement schemes were thus completely superseded and lapsed with the disappearance of the fire brigades.[1] The Fire Control Room was still quite separate from the Home Security War Room, though both controls were in close touch and intelligence work was co-ordinated between them.

The next level after the Home Office was that of the Regional Headquarters. Certain functions were conferred by Regulation on the Regional Commissioners, including some disciplinary powers and the appointments to intermediate ranks; though they also exercised certain powers by delegation, their N.F.S. responsibilities were different from those they possessed with regard to other arms of civil defence. On most civil defence questions the Minister laid down a general policy which the Commissioners implemented with the local authorities; but the establishment of the National Fire Service, bringing the fire services under the Secretary of State's direct control, introduced a new relationship. In the initial stages especially, many of the directions issued from the Home Office on matters such

---

[1] F.B. Circular No. 83/1941.

as conditions of service, mobilisation of appliances and other operational procedures in which a high degree of uniformity was necessary, were specific and detailed and by no means confined to broader issues of policy. Questions also arose regarding the operational responsibilities of the Fire Force Commanders and the close relationships which the Fire Service Department established with the officers responsible for all branches of the Fire Service work. Some Regional Commissioners questioned the Departments' procedure in these matters, and in May 1943 a memorandum was circulated defining the distribution of powers and functions between the Home Office, the Regional Commissioners and the Fire Force Commanders; and, although the document in no way changed the rather independent status of the Fire Service, it went some way toward preventing future friction. At the Regional Offices in England and Wales the Chief Regional Fire Officers exercised a wide range of functions, comprising direction, supervision and advice in proportions which varied from one Region to another, and they acted also as an invaluable link between the Service and the Home Office on innumerable administrative and operational problems.[1]

The next level below the Regional Headquarters was that of the Fire Forces. It has been mentioned earlier that when the National Fire Service came into operation, England and Wales were divided into 33 principal formations or Fire Forces, each corresponding to a Fire Area, and Scotland into 6, a distribution which, with a few changes and minor adjustments, held good for the rest of the war.[2]

The average number of Divisions in a Fire Force was four; the highest (after the single London Fire Force had been divided into five) was seven. Each Fire Force Headquarters had its operational and administrative staffs. The former included staff officers for general duties and one or more Water Officers and Communications Officers and a Control Room Staff, and there was a small staff on corresponding lines at each Divisional Headquarters. On the administrative side the Home Office considered that, as the Fire Areas would embrace, on an average, the territories of forty fire authorities, they would be too large to allow of all administrative functions stemming from headquarters, at any rate in the transitional period when personnel, appliances and property were being taken over and redistributed and record and accounting systems were being built

---

[1] There was at first some difference of opinion at the Home Office as to whether Chief Regional Fire Officers should have a senior rank to that of Fire Force Commander, since the Fire Force was to be the primary organisational unit. However, the Regional Officer was given a specific senior rank. See p. 478.

[2] In May 1942, London Region, previously a single Fire Force, was divided into 5 formations. A few other changes in boundaries were also made later in some other Regions, and adjustments in the number of Fire Forces were made at a much later stage still, when the strengths of the fire services were being reduced. In particular the London Fire Forces were reduced from 5 to 4.

up. They arranged, therefore, for much of the administrative work to be carried out at Divisional Headquarters, and some essential records to be kept at both Divisional and Fire Force Headquarters, as a safeguard against one or other of the Headquarters being destroyed. Fire Forces were to have a Chief Clerk at their headquarters with five branches under him—finance, establishments, stores, catering and transport—and a corresponding organisation was also to be established at Divisional level.[1] This decision inevitably meant a certain amount of duplication of staff at each level.[2]

By the end of 1941 the aggregate administrative staff of the N.F.S. amounted to about 940. The staffing arrangements were kept under constant review, and early in 1942 the allocation of responsibility for the administrative work was being reconsidered with a view to concentrating more of the work at Fire Force and/or Regional Headquarters. The Department was encouraged to press on with this work by questions asked in the course of an inquiry by the House of Commons Select Committee on National Expenditure.[3] The Committee found that so far as operational efficiency was concerned, the change-over to a national basis had brought great advantages, especially with regard to the mobilisation of outside aid for raided towns, the universally recognised chain of command and the increased potentiality for further improvements. They also accepted the Home Office view that many of the local authorities' criticisms of the size of the operational staff at Fire Force and Divisional Headquarters had been misconceived. But on the question of the system of administration the Committee was more critical. It considered the three tier system adopted in England and Wales— with administrative branches at Divisional, Fire Force and Regional Headquarters—unnecessarily expensive in money and manpower, and it found the record system unduly elaborate. The Committee felt sure that administrative staffs could be reduced and compared the machinery in England and Wales unfavourably with the simpler plan which had been followed in Scotland. It recommended therefore that the plans for the centralisation of administration, on which the Department was already working, should be speeded up. Some adjustment in strengths followed this criticism; the bulk of the administrative and clerical work was concentrated at Fire Force Headquarters, and later still some of the administrative functions were transferred thence to Regional Headquarters.

---

[1] In Scotland there was a much simpler Divisional organisation, all finance work, for instance, being concentrated at Fire Force Headquarters.

[2] It was estimated for instance, that the average Fire Force Headquarters would need between 25 and 40 subordinate administrative staff, while Divisional headquarters would need about 20, though London and Manchester Regions estimated their requirements to be considerably higher.

[3] Thirteenth Report from the Select Committee on National Expenditure, Session 1941–2. H.C. 105 of 1942.

The establishment of the new N.F.S. formations involved the creation of an entirely new system for mobilising fire service units. There was now a complete chain of control, from the Home Office Fire Control through the Regions, Fire Forces, divisional and sub-divisional controls to the fire stations, which could be called into play to any extent that circumstances might require. At each stage information, instructions, reports of calls to fires and requests for reinforcements would be passed in either direction according to pre-arranged procedures. Detailed instructions were issued and amended as experience or exercises suggested improved methods. Training and practice produced a high degree of skill among control room staffs in what, under attack, was a very exacting job. But the instructions on the subject were complicated and were several times revised and it seems doubtful whether a complete, or even the best practicable solution of this problem had been attained before the air attacks came to an end and the Service had only to concern itself with peace-time fire situations.

The whole communications system had, of course, to be reorganised to meet the needs of this new chain of command. Under the old arrangements there was little need for direct telephone lines between the headquarters of local brigades; now direct telephone communication from the Fire Force Headquarters to Divisional Headquarters and thence to subsidiary formations and to Regional Headquarters, would be essential, as the nerve system of the whole organisation. All this involved immense work for the Communications Directorate of the Home Office, working in collaboration with the General Post Office. To supplement telephone services in an emergency the observation post system and messenger services were further developed. The use of wireless for fire service communications was only at an early stage when the National Fire Service was established. In the autumn of 1941, however, the Treasury approved a proposal for 50 Fire Service wireless schemes within the next twelve months. By 1943, 22 of these schemes were in operation.[1]

So far this account of the establishment of the National Fire Service has concentrated on the construction of the machine and the interrelation of its various components. But the organisational and administrative issues of building up an integrated national service out of an uneven conglomeration of local brigades were not the only problems to be solved. There still remained the many technical problems concerned with the handling of the three constant elements of men, equipment and water. The provision of each of these partners in fire-fighting has been described earlier at different stages during

---

[1] The absence or insufficiency of two-way radio equipment for communications is criticised in a survey on *Fire and the Air War* for the National Fire Protection Association, U.S.A., edited by H. Bond, p. 108.

this story. It now remains to consider what changes were wrought by the nationalisation of the Service on each of these items.

Reorganisation did not, of itself, involve any great change in the number of firemen; the primary objective was not to expand the Service but to make more effective use of existing resources. But a measure of redistribution of personnel was now possible and could be undertaken with advantage. Under the previous system there could be little guarantee that local strengths corresponded to requirements viewed as a whole. Now men could be posted to wherever they were most needed. Whether the Service would need to be expanded or reduced would depend partly on the experienced or anticipated form and scale of the enemy attack and partly on the competition for manpower from the Fighting Services and industry. It was, of course, inevitable that reorganisation should involve certain increases in staff—to do the administrative work previously done by local authorities, to cope with the much larger problems of supply, maintenance of buildings and equipment that followed nationalisation and to operate the new network of controls—but it was hoped that a large proportion of these new staffs would be women.

When the National Fire Service was born heavy air attacks had ceased; any assessment of the proper strength of the Service had to be based not on current experience but on advice from the Chiefs of Staff on the enemy's potentialities for the future. The advice given was that attacks would begin again before long, possibly in an intensified form, especially when the time for the invasion of the Continent drew near. The Fire Service would need, therefore, to have crews for most, if not all, of its major appliances. For this the Departments estimated that about 103,500 whole-time firemen would be needed,[1] the light appliances to be manned in the main by part-time firemen.

Early in August 1941 the Departments had obtained Treasury consent to increase the full-time establishment to 102,000; allowing for wastage this would have involved the addition of 56,500 new male recruits by June 1942; and another 27,400 women were also needed to staff the new controls and serve as drivers, etc. By this time the National Service Act had introduced the principle of conscription for civil defence, but the extent to which these powers should be used took a long time to settle. Eventually, in November 1941, the Home Secretary asked the War Cabinet for an allocation of 30,000 men for the N.F.S., in addition to some 14,300 men who had already been posted under the National Service Act machinery,[2] and the Cabinet

---

[1] This estimate did not allow for certain new developments that were being undertaken, such as the formation of salvage squads.

[2] Numbers forthcoming under the National Service Act machinery were always disappointingly low. Almost the only men posted for whole-time service were those who, when called up, were already part-time firemen or the few who expressed a preference for the Fire Service. Compulsory posting was not favoured until after February 1942, and even then it was used very sparingly.

approved an allocation of 22,000 (19,200 for England and Wales and 2,800 for Scotland). But these figures were never attained. Peak strengths of whole-time firemen (about 100,000) were reached early in 1942.

The role of women in the Fire Service was completely changed by nationalisation. About 5,250 firewomen were serving as whole-time auxiliaries in the old fire brigades, 3,000 of them in London, but there was little specific organisation for their training, supervision or welfare and there were few women officers. Manpower shortages, however, soon demanded a reorientation of view regarding the work that could be done by women. 'The fact that certain duties have hitherto been performed exclusively by men, and that their assignment to women might be a shock to professional feelings', declared one of the first of the National Fire Service Instructions, 'should not be allowed to stand in the way of any change which might release fit men for fire-fighting duty'. And again 'the experience of the ambulance and emergency canteen services has, for instance, shown that women drivers are as able and as willing to face danger as are men'.[1] The number of women now began to increase rapidly. They were employed in control rooms and station watch rooms, on nearly every branch of administrative[2] and clerical work, in stores and workshops, as cooks, as drivers for cars, canteen vans and stores vans, and as despatch riders. By May 1942, the women had acquitted themselves so well that it was laid down that, wherever practicable, every sub-divisional control should have, in addition to women telephonists etc., a woman Mobilising Officer, rather than a man, in charge.[3] By the end of 1941 there were about 20,000 whole-time firewomen in England and Wales and 1,120 in Scotland, but 'mobile' women were now becoming very scarce, and six months later the strengths were only 26,500 and 1,500, as opposed to the 33,100 required for England and Wales and 3,350 for Scotland. Their broad distribution among the various duties is indicated by the following figures showing how the Home Office estimate was made up:

Staff for control rooms (over 3,000 stations) and control units	10,750
Administrative and clerical . . .	6,500
Cooks and mess room staff, canteen van crews	7,160
Stores	1,800
Car drivers, despatch riders and messengers	4,200
Miscellaneous	2,700
Total for England and Wales . .	33,110

---

[1] N.F.S. Instruction No. 15/1941. Many examples of their courage and determination are on record. See, for example, Sir Aylmer Firebrace, *op. cit.*, Chapter XXVI.
[2] One woman officer acted as Chief Clerk in a Fire Force for four years.
[3] N.F.S. Instruction No. 51/1942.

The National Fire Service also inherited from the brigades a part-time strength of about 110,500 men, 6,750 women and 8,300 youths. They came from every walk of life. They had their own conditions of service and their own *esprit de corps*, which took different forms in different areas and even in different stations in a single Fire Force. In the more rural parts of the country the part-time 'retained' firemen had been the mainstay of the fire brigades; in some brigades there was a strong family element, with the officership almost a matter of settled succession. In some the training was good and the men keen and public-spirited, but others were distinctly easy going. In some towns there was a strong volunteer element, the firemen being drawn to a large extent from business and professional walks of life. In the aggregate, of course, the part-time elements of the Auxiliary Fire Service out-numbered all the rest. The assimilation of such a heterogeneous element into the organisation of the N.F.S. was by no means the least of the formative problems.

The number of part-time firemen decreased for a while, but the recruitment of women and youths increased. Part-time firemen could not be required to serve without their consent outside their former fire brigade area, and returns obtained soon after the institution of the N.F.S. showed that, while about 10,000 men out of 66,000 covered by the return were prepared to go anywhere on reinforcing runs and about double that number were willing to go anywhere within their new Fire Force Areas, rather more than half were not willing to go outside their former brigade areas. In practice, however, no great difficulty appears to have arisen from the existence of this restriction. The contribution made by part-time men and women to manning the pumps and the controls varied a great deal. In December 1941, returns showed that, on the average, 30 per cent. of the part-time firemen reported for duty when air raid warnings sounded; about half the part-time firemen did duty at their stations for 48 hours a month or more, though in London the proportion was much higher.[1]

It remains to mention two additions to the resources of the Fire Service, one from Canada and the other from industrial firms at home. The idea of a contingent of firemen from Canadian municipal fire brigades joining in the fight against Hitler's incendiary weapons was first mooted after a visit of Mr McKenzie King to this country in 1941 and was taken up enthusiastically. The firemen, all volunteers of course, came from over 100 fire brigades and numbered at the peak strength 400 officers and men, 70 per cent. of them professional

---

[1] In three of the London Fire Forces more than 90 per cent. of the part-time men did more than 48 hours duty a month. This, it may be noted, reflected a special form of organisation which had been adopted in the London Region, for, though the number of part-time firemen in the Region was relatively small, the firemen had their special stations which they made a special point of manning, and attended very regularly for duty in most cases.

firemen. The main body of the Corps of Canadian Fire Fighters arrived in August 1942. They served in four detachments at Portsmouth, Southampton, Bristol and Plymouth. The last of these built their own 10 bay station (which was opened by the Duchess of Kent), and 20 of their number joined the Overseas Contingent.[1] The Corps returned to Canada towards the end of 1944, after a farewell parade in Trafalgar Square on the 16th November 1944.

The Works Brigades which became 'affiliated' with the N.F.S. did not, as a rule, attend fires beyond, or at any rate far beyond, the premises in which they served; but they were assimilated so far as possible to the N.F.S. as regards training and were subject to inspection by N.F.S. Inspectors, and their officers might qualify for N.F.S. rank. The arrangement, though bringing no direct addition to the N.F.S. strength, was indirectly an advantage as tending to ensure high standards of fire protection at important industrial establishments.

A concomitant problem on the personnel side was the training of new recruits and, even more important, the standardisation of training of firemen taken over from the brigades. Standard drills were essential if confusion, danger and delay were to be averted when the men from different brigades came to work together. There were also many gaps and deficiencies in the training of men from the smaller brigades, and there were many new techniques to be learnt in the operation of the new control room system and the reorganised chain of command. Moreover, the experience gained in the large-scale fire-fighting during the 'blitzes' showed the need for a higher standard of officer training and for certain kinds of specialist training. Systematic physical training was also regarded as essential for both firemen and firewomen.

The training programme took shape in a three-tier organisation based on (1) fire stations, (2) residential Regional or Area Training Schools and (3) the National Fire Service College. Altogether this amounted to a major undertaking. Its results were in proportion, for the training that was carried through contributed as much as anything to the transformation of the fire services of the country that was accomplished in these few years during which the National Fire Service was in being.

One of the earliest of the Home Office plans, which was being formulated even before the N.F.S. had been brought into existence, was that for a Fire Service College. In the Department's view, some such institution would be essential, as a centre where their training policy could be given practical effect and, so to speak, be radiated out in all directions throughout the Service. It would be used, for instance, for the training of officers, various specialists and the instructors who would have the task of carrying through the various aspects of the

---

[1] See p. 498.

training programme up and down the country. Suitable buildings were found at the Ocean Hotel at Saltdean, near Brighton, and the College was opened in the autumn of 1941, with Brigadier C. C. Hewitt, D.S.O., M.C. as the first Commandant. Brigadier Hewitt had had a long experience of Army training and brought to the task personal qualities which had much to do with the success the College became and the distinctive contribution it made to the efficiency and *esprit de corps* of the Service.

For the rest of the training programme, Training Schools were to be established in every Fire Force, and by the spring of 1943 there were no less than 72 Regional and Area Training Schools established in requisitioned country houses and similar places, including 27 for women, as well as over 100 Divisional and Sub-Divisional Training Schools, mainly on fire station premises.

At a later stage, when it became impossible to spare women from the controls, their training was carried on by teams of instructors who went to the various stations; and for part-time firemen serving at stations where suitable accommodation was lacking, 'travelling schools' were provided—taking not only the instructors but also the schools to the students instead of the other way about.

In February 1942 a Standard Drill Book prepared by the Fire Staff was issued.[1] The Fire Staff also undertook the preparation of a Manual of Firemanship. This was a text book dealing with all branches of the firemen's profession, brought out in a series of volumes, which not only became the foundation of much of the training in the N.F.S. but has given the Fire Service a work of reference of permanent value on all aspects of the fireman's work.

Throughout this extensive programme of work the Fire Service College served, as was intended, as the focal point of all the training. Early in 1942 courses for women were introduced, more especially on the many aspects of mobilising and control room work, and the College became a co-educational establishment on quite a considerable scale. By the end of the war some 360 courses of one kind or another had been held and 10,400 students, including 170 from the Army and foreign Fire Services, had passed through the College.

A complete system of physical training, 'fitness training' as it was called, was worked out and brought into regular use throughout the Service, based in the case of firemen on a modified Army system and for women on the methods of the Central Council of Recreational Physical Training.

One further aspect of the College work deserves special mention because of the importance of its influence on the work of the post-war Service: that is the development of a specific fire prevention doctrine

---

[1] Later in the year a slightly amended edition was placed on sale by H.M. Stationery Office (N.F.S. Instruction No. 58/1942, Item 8). Revised editions followed later.

and body of experience and the acceptance of this work as part of the responsibilities of the Fire Service as a whole. Before the war, while some fire brigades, notably the London Fire Brigade, had well developed branches for fire prevention work[1] there was no generally accepted policy or practice, and outside the great cities very little of this work was done. The question of introducing a course at the Fire Service College was raised soon after the College had been opened. As the Chief of the Fire Staff put it 'we want to breed fire preventionists—there are very few of them about', but for some time it was not found possible to make a start. Eventually, in July 1944, a conference of representatives of the Fire Staff and the Fire Service College met at the College to review various proposals which had been made and the first course for fire prevention officers was opened by the Head of the Department in September of that year. The initiation of this course undoubtedly constituted a landmark in this important aspect of Fire Service work. The course, originally 3 months, was extended to 5 months, and other courses followed. Fire Prevention Officers who had received the College training were given a place in every Fire Force, and the Fire Prevention Departments then established are now perpetuated in the post-war fire brigades. Yet another valuable branch of fire brigade work, that of salvage—the art of minimising the incidental damage that may be caused, by water and smoke, in the course of fire-fighting—which is now a regular part of fire brigade practice, was also worked out in somewhat the same way.

So far as equipment was concerned the pump programme and the production of most of the other important items had been virtually completed before the National Fire Service took over. Most of the items still needed were for special purposes, including, in particular, equipment for improving water supplies. Fire boats, for instance, had been very valuable in the big raids on London and the ports, but it had been found that rather more sea-worthy craft were necessary. In September 1941, therefore, the Home Office arranged for the production of 20 craft of improved type, and later it also acquired a few sea-going fire boats.[2] By 1944 the total number of

---

[1] The term 'fire prevention' is used here in the sense in which it is commonly used in the Fire Service, as including study, training and instruction in all manner of measures calculated to reduce the risk of fires breaking out, in the home, ships, industry, agriculture or anywhere else. It is not to be confused with the special use to which the term was put during the war in connection with civilian fire watching and the fire guards. (See Chapter XIII.)

[2] These craft rendered invaluable services in salvaging or putting out fires in ships which had been bombed at sea, e.g., after D-day. On other occasions the N.F.S. put their trailer pumps on craft provided by the Admiralty and attacked the fires in that way, as in the case of the *Lucellum*. This was a tanker carrying about 5 million gallons of oil and petrol which had been bombed, set on fire and abandoned by her crew. The firemen boarded the ship, manoeuvred pumps on board and after a long and arduous struggle extinguished the fires in the tanks and many other parts of the ship, which was saved and brought into port.

fire-boats and barges available in the N.F.S. had risen to about 330.

Although there was not much difficulty by this time in the supply of essential appliances and equipment, their repair and maintenance was quite another matter. The scale of the problem was considerable. The National Fire Service had become responsible for more than 22,000 pumps and more than as many vehicles of various kinds, to the value of some £10 million, as well as correspondingly large quantities of other equipment. As already recorded, the repair facilities available in most districts were inadequate and unreliable, and there was a serious danger of the Fire Forces finding themselves under-equipped in a raid because of immobilised equipment. A national scheme to improve this situation was worked out soon after nationalisation.[1] There was to be a central workshop for each Fire Area and a workshop for each Division or group of Divisions, supplemented by repair vans working from Area workshops and service vans working from Divisions.[2] Garages and other premises had to be requisitioned, more mechanics found and officers appointed, the craftsmen required to staff the workshops and vans being found in the main from firemen already serving in the N.F.S.[3] The organisation thus brought into being not only succeeded in gradually overtaking the accumulated arrears of work but also established a sound standard of maintenance for all equipment throughout the remaining life of the National Fire Service. The three Home Office depots[4] were also fully occupied with design and development work on all manner of N.F.S. appliances and equipment.

The reader may wonder what became of the vast quantities of pumps and other emergency equipment with which the fire brigades and the National Fire Service had been provided. Much of it was, of course, used up or destroyed in the course of the fire-fighting: but much remained over at the end of the war. About 1,700 self-propelled appliances (pumps, escape carrying units and water tenders) and 3,000 trailer pumps were retained in the Fire Service and transferred to the new fire authorities in 1948, for use until they could be replaced by machines produced to new post-war designs. About 500 self-propelled units, 830 unmounted heavy pumps and over 4,000 trailer pumps were taken into store: and yet other pumps and great quantities of steel piping and other equipment were sent to the liberated countries or were sold.

---

[1] The Home Office secured the services of Mr. J. H. Williams, Equipment Engineer to the London Passenger Transport Board, to assist in this work.

[2] N.F.S. Instruction No. 103/1942.

[3] A scheme for additional pay for skilled and semi-skilled firemen employed as mechanics was arranged after consultation with the Trade Unions through the Civil Defence Services Joint Consultative Committee.

[4] See pp. 268 and 452.

The workshop mechanics were not the only craftsmen who now found an opportunity to practise their trades in the N.F.S., for it was soon necessary to initiate a programme of building construction, reconstruction and repair. This need arose in a number of ways, partly because redistributions of strength called for additional station accommodation, partly to provide sleeping and messing accommodation when it was decided to introduce the 48/24 hour duty system (i.e. 48 hours on duty followed by 24 hours off), partly to provide accommodation for the women who were added to the station staffs and partly to improve the existing accommodation where reasonable amenities were lacking. Cumulatively, all this amounted to quite a considerable undertaking, and much of the labour was provided by bricklayers, carpenters, painters and other craftsmen in the N.F.S. who, like the mechanics, drew additional pay at rates arranged in consultation with the trade union representatives.

Unreliable water supplies, it will be remembered, had been one of the most serious handicaps during the heavy raids of 1940 and 1941, and in consequence new and more systematic measures had been taken early in 1941 to supplement the supplies already available.[1] With the institution of the National Fire Service the Exchequer became responsible for the cost of all this new work and it was now possible to decide on and carry through a comprehensive national plan.[2] The country was divided into areas of three categories: Category A areas comprising high risk districts of the Metropolis and 53 important cities and towns, including 17 in Scotland; B areas consisting of the lower risk parts in these places and other important centres with populations of 100,000 or more and the university towns; and C areas, the rest. In A areas where water was not already available in virtually inexhaustible supply, the objective was to provide supplies of the order of 1½–2 million gallons per square mile (later increased to 4 million gallons in London), the supply to be distributed in units of 50,000–500,000 gallons spaced, if possible, not more than about a quarter of a mile apart; these larger basins were to be supplemented by smaller basins (5,000–20,000 gallons) up to about 20 per square mile, to serve as relaying points and provide an immediate supply at points of special risk. In B areas there were to be smaller tanks (on the average 10,000 gallons) with one or two larger basins per square mile. C areas were to be covered normally by adaptations of natural supplies at relatively small cost. All this work was to be organised regionally. There were to be three main lines of development: (i) the further construction of water basins in basements of bombed buildings or built up on ground level, and of

---

[1] See pp. 453–458, 460, 462–464.
[2] N.F.S. Instruction No. 5/1941.

smaller steel tanks; (ii) the laying of six-inch steel pipe lines to link the water basins with major supplies of water and with one another; and (iii) the placing of borehole pumps for drawing supplies from rivers or docks to bridge or ground level.

The first estimates of the requirements for this new programme showed an aggregate storage capacity of about 440 million gallons, to cost nearly £2¾ million, but by November 1941 the estimate had risen to 484 million gallons at a cost of £3½ million, plus nearly £1 million for 420 miles of steel piping, £300,000 for borehole pumps and another £1 million for special schemes in invasion areas and London.

All through this period additions were being made to the system of emergency water mains in London,[1] and borehole pumps, drawing up water from the Thames independently of the tides, and discharging into 20,000 gallon tanks, were installed on 22 road and railway bridges in the London area.

But even the programme just described was by no means the final word. The 'Baedeker' raids in the spring of 1942, shortly to be described, fully confirmed the value of the surface pipe lines and water basins laid out on a systematic plan. The enemy having now turned his attention to targets of secondary importance to the national economy, often undefended but very vulnerable to incendiary attack, the whole question of water supply had to be looked at from rather a different angle. In May 1942 it was decided to extend the earlier scheme to 100 more centres (66 of them in the A category), involving the provision of more tanks and another 300 miles of piping. And later, when the enemy had begun to use the anti-personnel incendiary bomb designed to counter the efforts of the fire guards, the Home Office stepped up the programme of tanks and piping yet again. Most of the piping was used to construct semi-permanent pipe lines leading from inexhaustible or very large supplies of water to strategic points in high risk areas, discharging into tanks or ending in 6-way outlets to which hose lines could be coupled. These new mains formed really important additions to normal water supplies. They were much less vulnerable to high explosive bombs than the cast iron underground mains, and on more than one occasion enabled the fire services to carry on effective operations when mains supplies had been completely cut off. Altogether, more than 1,000 miles of steel piping was provided. Some miles of the piping was held in reserve and organised in mobile units with special carriers for emergency laying; and teams of firemen acquired great skill in handling it. In one competition, for instance, a team of 17 men laid a 1,000 feet line of piping, erected a 5,000 gallon dam and had a pump discharging about 1,000 gallons of water a minute into the dam within 7½

---

[1] See also pp. 271–273, 467.

minutes; and another team of 19 men laid a mile of piping, weighing 40 tons, in 45 minutes, with pumps and dams in position.[1]

The tank and basin programme had, however, its own particular problems—the shortage of raw materials and labour, the need to requisition land, the breeding of mosquitoes, and the use of tanks as rubbish dumps by the public. And it had its applications to peaceful purposes, for there were occasions, notably in the drought of 1944, when the N.F.S. were able to put their extensive equipment and manpower to good use in helping farmers or even water undertakings by pumping or carrying water to replenish ponds which had gone dry or, in much larger quantities up to millions of gallons, reservoirs which had fallen to dangerously low levels.

The National Fire Service: (iv) In Operation

During 1942 and early 1943 the National Fire Service attained its peak of development; whole-time firemen reached about 100,000 early in 1942, whole-time firewomen nearly 30,000 early in 1943, while part-timers reached 220,000 (153,000 men, 48,000 women and 18,500 youths) towards the end of 1943. Ironically enough, however, after the establishment of the National Fire Service in 1941 incendiary raids declined both in number and intensity. During the three months allowed for the complicated transfer of the Service and during the months of settling down that followed, there were very few attacks on any scale. There were attacks on Manchester, Tyneside, Tees-side and Hull, but the main enemy activity was taking the form of 'tip and run' attacks on coastal areas, causing some fires but rarely of great intensity. The first real tests of the new Service did not come until the spring of 1942 with what became known as 'Baedeker raids', a series of attacks on cathedral cities.[2]

The cathedral cities were obviously vulnerable to fire-raising attack, which doubtless contributed to the enemy's choice of them for these reprisal raids. Exeter, Bath, Norwich, York, Canterbury and Ipswich were attacked on one or more occasions between April and June 1942. There were also many sharp attacks on South coast towns, a few on the Midlands and one on Weston-super-Mare. The resources of the N.F.S. were adequate to these attacks, though in some instances emergency water provision had still not gone far enough. At Bath, Exeter and Canterbury the fires had to be fought wholly or mainly with the emergency supplies. Notwithstanding this handicap, at Exeter and Canterbury in particular large spreading fires were held in areas of old, congested buildings with much wood in their construction and where there was no thoroughfare

---

[1] Sir Aylmer Firebrace., *op. cit.*, p. 217.
[2] See Chapter X, pp. 429-432.

wide enough to be of use as a fire-break—feats of fire-fighting which would have been impossible without organisation such as the N.F.S. supplied and enough experienced officers to carry out the Fire Force Commanders' plans.

The National Fire Service had been designed to take the strain of heavy fire-fighting. But although the risk of future raids could not be ignored, the lull that had accompanied the reorganisation continued. Meanwhile the overall planning of war operations was moving into the offensive phase and the amount of insurance carried for passive defence had to be carefully scrutinised. The problem was to release as many men as possible to help mount the attack and yet to be in a position to contend with raids that could come at any time and in any place.

Cuts in the National Fire Service began early in 1942. The first measures were to release a number of skilled tradesmen to industry and younger men to the Services, amounting in all to about 20,000. In October the manpower budget for the following year called on the Civil Defence Services to give up some 75,000 men and women; the Fire Service share of this was 14,000. From now onwards there was a steady decline in numbers, calling for economies in administration and for a certain re-deployment of the strength still available.

In order to compensate for the prospective reduction in whole-time numbers[1] it became necessary to try to strengthen the part-time element in the National Fire Service. This was done by withdrawing the right of part-time members to resign[2] and by empowering the Ministry of Labour to direct men and women to do part-time service in civil defence.[3] Hitherto no part-time establishments had been laid down, but once direction was introduced it was necessary to agree target strengths with the Ministry of Labour. The strengths agreed—200,000 men, 57,000 women and 28,000 youths—were never by any means achieved. By August 1942 only 4,000 part-time recruits had been found; for it was by now becoming increasingly difficult to find men who could be expected to do duty at fire stations in addition to their normal work and who were fit enough for fire-fighting. Shift work interfered with attendance and sometimes there was competition from the Home Guard. However, by the end of 1943 part-time strengths in the N.F.S. reached their peak figure of 220,000 which has just been mentioned.

All this time the N.F.S. had been sharing with the Civil Defence General Services in a variety of activities supplementary to their primary functions, as mentioned later in this narrative. In particular

---

[1] See Chapter XIII.

[2] National Fire Service (General) (No. 2) Regulations, 22nd January 1942. S.R. & O. No. 125.

[3] Regulation 29BA of the Defence (General) Regulations, 18th December 1941. S.R. & O. No. 2052.

they carried on at fire stations many forms of productive work for various industries, made great quantities of toys for children, helped in the running of savings weeks and organised lectures, discussion groups and correspondence classes for members of the Service. And the Service organised a Benevolent Fund which has devoted large sums to the assistance of disabled firemen and the orphans of firemen who lost their lives.

One piece of reorganisation carried out early in 1944 was a change in the structure of the London Fire Forces into two separate branches. This was done in anticipation of attacks on London with Hitler's new weapons. One branch, the 'Home Cover Force', with about 12,000 men and women, was to man the regular fire stations, deal with all the lull-period fires and those caused by small-scale enemy attacks; the second branch, the 'Task Force', consisted of about 15,000 men and women, organised in 14 mobile divisions of 100 pumps each. The latter had no territorial responsibilities, were housed as far as possible in large units and were trained to develop physical fitness and readiness for any demand which might be made on them; they also received special training in rescue work, as did contingents in other Fire Forces in the threatened areas.

Once the Baedeker raids were over, the main enemy attack was again limited to comparatively small scale raids on towns near the Eastern and Southern coasts. In the autumn of 1942 the Air Staff's estimate of the future tactics of the enemy was that low flying 'tip and run' raids under cloud cover were likely to continue and possibly increase in intensity, that heavy attacks on targets not far from the coast were probable, especially where anti-aircraft defence was thin, and that raids might well be predominantly incendiary in character. To deal with these possibilities steps were taken during the summer of 1943 to reinforce some of the coastal towns from inland areas.

By now, Allied preparations to invade the Continent, with the concentration of vehicles, equipment and stores and the risk of violent attacks from the air when the invasion was launched, made it necessary to reinforce districts in the south of England on a large scale. Detailed plans were worked out in consultation with the naval and military authorities. The reinforcements for the south were provided by reducing by approximately one half the whole-time fire-fighting strength north of a line from the Wash to the Severn and transferring 11,450 firemen and firewomen, with 1,240 pumps and other appliances, to districts in the south—an operation which acquired the code name the 'Colour Scheme' because of the manner in which the districts were distinguished in the plan of operations. The large reductions of strength in the northern areas involved a drastic reorganisation of the fire-fighting arrangements in those areas, which was later extended to the whole country as the overall strength of the Service became progressively reduced.

About the same time some 2,000 firemen were specially trained and equipped and organised into five self-contained fire fighting units or 'columns', ready to go overseas with the armies, and fire-boat flotillas to reinforce fire-fighting resources at the Continental ports were also established.

It was part of this plan that the firemen, if called upon, would go overseas as members of the N.F.S., preserving their civilian status, and this condition involved the Department and the military authorities in innumerable problems and technicalities. It required also a new set of Regulations[1] to authorise the employment of the N.F.S. overseas in Europe 'where it appears to the Secretary of State that their employment will promote the success of any operations of war undertaken by His Majesty's forces'—which expression was to be construed as including forces of an allied Power serving under the same command as any of His Majesty's forces.

As things turned out, only one of the columns (Column 4) was called upon to go overseas—with the United States Army. This column, some 540 strong, embarked at Tilbury on the 25-26th January 1945, and eventually reached the Rhine, on one occasion leading the U.S. column as it marched into Germany. Its stations extended for a time approximately over the area Frankfurt—Cologne—Namur—Verdun. It was afterwards transferred to 21 Army Group, bringing with it marked commendation from the commanding officer under whom it had served, and was stationed in and around Antwerp until its return to this country in the following July.

In the meantime the National Fire Service had become involved in the Fire Guard Plan. This celebrated measure, which is discussed in detail in Chapter XIII, affected the N.F.S. in several ways, for it was intended that if and when the Plan reached its full development the fire guards rather than the telephone should be the principal medium through which the N.F.S. was to be called to fires. The main features, so far as the N.F.S. was concerned were, in brief,[2]

(a) The Fire Guard Sector Points, block points and assembly points were to be manned at night or in such part of the specified period as the Regional Commissioner might have directed, or in the day time on an alert or fall of bombs or gunfire.

(b) During the Fire Guard Plan period, calls for Fire Service

---

[1] National Fire Service (Employment Overseas) Regulations, 12th June 1944. S.R. & O. No. 675.

[2] N.F.S. Instruction No. 23/1943.

assistance were to be made by the fire guards normally by messenger, but by telephone if this had been arranged.

(c) Originally the initial message was to give only the address of the block point or assembly point to which the appliances should be despatched, followed, if need be, by a repeat call with a brief situation report, but later instructions left rather more discretion to the fire guards.[1]

(d) Fire guards were to work in close co-operation with the National Fire Service in various ways, in addition to dealing with incendiary bombs and fighting incipient fires, e.g., by supplying information as to water supplies if the National Fire Service crew had come from a distance and was not familiar with the ground, assisting in handling hose, hose ramps etc., and relieving the Fire Service crews for damping down etc.

It was, of course, quite out of the question to bring a scheme of this sort into operation without a great deal of preparation, involving on the one hand the detailed definition of areas and the training of fire guards and on the other a radical alteration of the Fire Service procedure—measures which were neither simple to work out nor capable of being put into operation quickly. And it would have been fatal to surrender the accustomed method of getting fire calls to the fire stations unless and until the new organisation was sufficiently well developed and reliable to take its place. Discretion was therefore left to the Regional Commissioners to say when the change in reporting procedure should be made in any given area. For one thing, the change necessitated a complete revision of the internal fire station procedure for handling the messages and despatching appliances to the fire ground, and the preparation of these new instructions gave rise to many fresh problems, much discussion and some controversy.

Whether all this effort would have been justified by the results it is impossible to say with any certainty, for the scheme was fated never to come into general operation. Even where it was brought into operation and tested under air raid conditions, during the local but concentrated attacks on London shortly to be noticed, this was never on a scale sufficient to test the system thoroughly. But, judged from the Fire Service point of view, such evidence as is available does not seem very favourable.

The National Fire Service: (v) The Closing Years of the War.

The final phase of the National Fire Service was one of transition and varied activity. It saw the launching of the Allied attack on the

---

[1] N.F.S. Instruction No. 63/1943.

Continent and the successful advance towards Germany. It opened with a series of sharp attacks on London that were known as the 'Little Blitz' and with attacks on Hull, Bristol and Weston-super-Mare. Later came the flying bomb and rocket attacks on London and South-Eastern England. For the N.F.S., it was a period demanding complicated redistribution of strength to reinforce the areas affected by the preparations for D-day or vulnerable to the new weapons and to provide the contingent to go abroad. And at the same time there were the continued cuts in strengths, all of which involved a turmoil of reorganisation—the selection of officers and men for release, the recasting of the administration of the Fire Forces and much more.

The 'Little Blitz', from mid-January to April 1944, followed two and a half years of almost unbroken lull in the London area[1]. Late in 1943 the penetration of single raiders to the London area increased and nights became noisy with the great anti-aircraft barrage that had been built up. On 21st January came the first of the fairly short but severe raids on London. A high proportion of incendiary bombs were dropped and the enemy was now using new incendiary weapons. There were the firepot bombs (a mixture of explosive and thermite incendiaries), the phosphorus bombs (of 50 and 250 kgs. containing a sticky mixture of phosphorus and rubber) and various other anti-personnel devices. In comparison with the worst fire raids of 1940 and 1941 these attacks were limited both in area and time and the fire services were well able to cope with them. No fire situations got out of hand and many fires were nipped in the bud by the new army of civilian fire guards.

The flying bomb and rocket attacks on London and South-Eastern England lasted from June 1944 until March 1945, with a slackening of the attack during August when the flying bomb launching sites in France had been over-run and before the rockets began to fall. This form of attack was quite different in character from any previously experienced.

These bombs rarely caused fires, and when they did the fires were usually on a small scale and easily extinguished. The National Fire Service in the London area had by now a well-developed system of observation posts, which proved extremely valuable in locating the fall of flying bombs and rockets, and regularly sent out 'flying columns' of pumps and a turntable ladder to all flying bomb incidents, with their accustomed express speed. They were often first on the scene and able to start on rescue operations; and their help was the more valuable because of the special training in rescue work which the 'Task Force' firemen had received, with the threatened V-weapon attacks in view. They were also able to render invaluable assistance

---

[1] See Chapter X, pp. 439–444.

in the salvaging of furniture and other property, with 'first aid' repairs to roofs, using the tarpaulins which they normally used in 'salvage' work during fire-fighting operations, and generally helping to 'clear up the mess'.

The fire services had by now been engaged for some four years in active emergency operations taking many forms and with varying degrees of intensity and strain. Examples of gallantry, determination and self-sacrifice had been innumerable, and casualties severe. In the course of the war 793 firemen and 25 firewomen had lost their lives and more than 7,000 had been more or less severely injured, the great majority of these casualties being directly due to enemy action. The awards for gallantry included 2 George Crosses, 90 George Medals, 194 British Empire Medals and 395 commendations.

From this point the N.F.S. turned more and more to the task of adapting itself to the changed conditions and preparing for the transition to its peace-time strength and status, whatever that might prove to be. Cuts in the N.F.S. were continuing all through this period of attack by pilotless weapons. For the second half of 1944 a cut of 24,000 was planned but before the end of the year the number was stepped up to 44,000.

But the reductions lagged behind and were less severe than in the Civil Defence Services generally, for the N.F.S. had a permanent service to be provided for after the war. Strengths had to be retained for the time being considerably in excess of those that would be required later on, because of the exceptional fire risks created by the vast quantities of war-like equipment and materials in transit or in store. All this involved a lot of complicated sorting out. Some members of the Service were keen to stay, with an eye to permanent employment, while others who were in it only as a war-time duty naturally wished to be released as soon as possible. Towards the end of 1944 plans were made to reduce current establishments (now 85,600 men and 25,000 women) by about half. By the middle of 1945 whole-time strengths were down to 52,000 and by the end of the year to 31,500.[1]

Decisions on the control and structure of the post-war service had yet to be taken. As to its scale, the Home Office believed that, whatever system were eventually adopted, the whole-time strength of the Fire Service would need to be about 18,000 men, and the N.F.S. was being reduced to about double this assumed post-war strength, to provide material from which to select the men who were to be retained. As to the structure of the future Service, the Home Secretary had given a pledge that it would not be permanently run by the

---

[1] The annual cost of the N.F.S., which reached about £32 million at the peak, was now down to about £15 million.

State but would return to local control again.[1] Nationalisation had proved so successful in many ways that hopes were entertained in some quarters that the N.F.S. could be retained in being. The local authorities, however, were vigorous in their demands to have control of the brigades. After much consultation and discussion a Fire Services Bill was presented to the House of Commons early in 1947,[2] transferring the fire services to the councils of the counties and county boroughs. It became law in the following July, with effect from the 1st April 1948. The selection of the county and county borough councils as fire authorities meant that the number of local fire brigade authorities in England and Wales was reduced to 146—not much more than a tenth of the pre-war figure. In Scotland the fire services were returned to local authority control on the 16th May 1948 and there was an even more substantial reduction in the number of brigades than in England and Wales. Glasgow was empowered to maintain its own brigade, but to cover the remainder of Scotland the Act provided for the establishment of Joint Committees to control 10 fire brigades, the constituent local authority of each being a Joint Committee which was scheduled in the Act. The number of fire brigades in Scotland was thus reduced to 11, from a possible maximum figure of 228 before the war. The Central Departments retained a close interest in training and research; an Exchequer grant (albeit much less than the local authorities hoped for) was introduced and a system of regular inspection was inaugurated. In a word, the parochialism which had been the bane of the pre-war service in many areas had disappeared for good.

It lies beyond the purpose of this volume to attempt comprehensive assessment of the place of the National Fire Service in fire service history. But several aspects of the reorganisation have been mentioned as having had lasting influence, and some brief recapitulation seems fitting.

The most important permanent contributions, apart from the replacement of the hundreds of small brigades by the larger units, can probably be summarised as first, the development of a Service as against a purely local fire brigade consciousness and, secondly, the replacement of heterogeneity by system, emanating from greater central advice, supervision and inspection, and an Exchequer Grant. It remains to be seen how far the development of a Service as against a local consciousness and other centralising tendencies will prove lasting; but as to the speed and thoroughness of the transformation under the stress of war in a remarkably short time there can be no doubt.

---

[1] pp. 471–472.
[2] H. of C. Deb., Vol. 435, Cols. 1422–1520, 27th March 1947.

The 'system' introduced by war-time nationalisation has left its influence on almost every aspect of Fire Service organisation. It applies, for instance, to the system of ranks, established for the Service as a whole and universally understood; to the conditions of service of all ranks; to training, with the Manual of Firemanship and the Standard Drill Book as guides, and the Fire Service College; to the extension thoughout the Service of experience of fire-fighting equipment and techniques formerly out of the reach of most of the small brigades; to the development of innumerable operational and administrative practices for mobilising appliances and salvage work, records for personnel, accounting and stores, an effective organisation for the maintenance and repair of appliances, all of which could be, and have been, carried over with relatively small readjustments beyond the life of the N.F.S. itself, and, last but not least, to the development of a body of fire prevention doctrine and practice common to the Fire Service as a whole.

These developments towards uniformity suffice to show that the experiment of a National Fire Service has had profound influence on post-war Fire Service organisation and work.

CHAPTER XII

SHELTERS

EARLIER chapters have shown that, because of an exceptionally late start, the shelter problem at the outbreak of war still assumed large proportions; but that all concerned then made good use of a further eight months' respite despite the new difficulties caused by scarcity of materials. When attacks began in earnest a Home Security official was able justly to claim that the country possessed 'a very respectable amount of shelter'.

In more statistical terms, some 17,500,000 persons (it was estimated) of the 27,500,000 or so in the 'specified areas' had been provided at the public expense with domestic and public shelter. Shelters were available in factories and offices in these areas for another 5,000,000; and a small number of householders had provided them on their own account. Over 2,300,000 'Andersons' had been distributed. Citizens not eligible for these could resort to strengthened basements, trenches, some specially built surface structures or any accessible modern buildings. Though there was not enough shelter for everyone, there was more than enough for those wishing to shelter in what, when the programme had been framed, were thought to be the threatened areas.

The transformation of the war in April–May 1940 had, however, exposed to attack the remaining one-third or so of the population which, at this date, had few domestic or public shelters. It must, nevertheless, be recalled that a large part of this minority lived in rural areas or in residential towns not regarded as very likely targets. Agitation had, however, at once arisen in such places for inclusion in the Government's various shelter schemes, and some progress had been made in doing this[1].

Some Effects of Attack

Previous chapters have shown how far in the earlier years of war the tonnage of bombs dropped by the enemy fell short of what had been expected. But appreciation of the test, in a structural sense, to which shelters were put also requires some attention to the weight of the individual bombs employed. In designing shelters, the 500 lb (250 kg) medium case bomb had been adopted as the standard; though it had been recognised that the enemy might use a proportion of heavier bombs.

[1] See pp. 367–372.

During the attacks of September 1940—May 1941 the large majority of high explosive bombs dropped by the Germans were, in fact, of 50 kg or 250 kg weight. The Research and Experiments Department estimated that the number of heavier bombs and mines was only about 1 per cent. of the total up to the end of 1940, and only 5 per cent. from then until August 1941. These proportions included, however, a few 1,000—2,500 kg bombs, and nearly 4,000 parachute mines of 500 kg or 1,000 kg (an unexpected weapon). In later attacks, for example the 'tip and run' and 'Baedeker' raids, the total weight of attack much declined but the proportion of heavier bombs steadily rose. In 1942, these represented about one-third of the total; in 1943 over 12 per cent.; and in 1944 (excluding 'V-weapons') nearly 20 per cent. In the 'Little Blitz' of this year the proportions of exceptionally heavy missiles—the 1,400 kg ('Fritz') the 1,800 kg ('Satan') and the 2,500 kg ('Max')—were much higher than formerly.[1]

The early scattered raids showed that 'Andersons' were most effective, and this was fully confirmed by the later raids on London and the provinces. The tensile character of their structure allowed it to spring back to its original shape after being distorted, and the covering of earth prevented damage from splinters. 'Andersons' properly sited and covered were usually undamaged by 50 kg bombs falling 6 ft. away or 250 kg bombs falling 20 ft. away, and their occupants suffered no more than shock. Occasionally, they resisted bombs falling even nearer. But those which were insufficiently covered or had fronts or backs unprotected were sometimes severely damaged even by bomb splinters.[2]

Brick and concrete surface shelters had proved, on the whole, less successful. Experience showed that the effects of blast and of bombs exploding underneath these structures had been over-estimated. But they proved liable to penetration or distortion by groups of splinters and they could be seriously damaged by earth shock caused by the movement of earth displaced by bombs. Many stood up remarkably well, even to these forces. But there were instances of surface shelters collapsing which, in some places, produced a whispering campaign about their safety.

Most of the faulty shelters were those built after the outbreak of war with mortar containing much lime or even, as a result of the ambiguous instructions issued in April 1940, of lime and sand only.[3] Other inferior materials and faulty workmanship were responsible

---

[1] These were German sobriquets. The 'Satan' was nearly 9 ft high without the tail.

[2] The Research and Experiments Department prepared three early appreciations of the results of air raids—on 11th July 1940 (based on the experience of minor raids on coastal towns); 26th September 1940 (after raids on London and provincial cities); 23rd January 1941 (after four months of intensive raiding).

[3] p. 369.

for some catastrophes. Yet there was also a defect in the design of the surface shelter. The roof slab was not fixed firmly to the walls and was likely to be raised and to crash down again on to the shelter if the walls were shifted by surface earth-movement. This was serious, since after the spring of 1940, when steel shortage became acute, local authorities had relied to an increasing extent on surface shelters, which represented a big proportion of the total shelter in many places.

The performance of trenches varied much, according to the method of construction. Some lined with wood or even with concrete slabs proved very vulnerable, as the roof was easily lifted and the sides pushed in. But many of reinforced concrete resisted bombs falling only 8 ft away. Small strutted basements held debris loads very successfully. In fact, experience showed that strutting was unnecessary in small houses, since the amount of debris produced if the house collapsed was not likely to cause fatal casualties in an unprotected basement. But the basements of large non-framed buildings, widely used for public shelters, were not very satisfactory since they offered large targets with the risk of heavy casualties. The R. and E. Department had been aware of these defects in trenches and strutted basements in the spring of 1940; but that was an unpropitious time for introducing modified designs. Buildings with steel frames stood up excellently to the effects of bombing and gave good shelter not only in their basements but in higher floors as well.

The London public, in spite of instructions to the contrary, had as in the First World War flocked to the Tubes when raids began. Apart from a small number of incidents, these gave a very high degree of protection.[1] The combination of circumstances which could lead to a disaster, except in stations with less than 25 ft cover, was so improbable that there seemed to be no technical justification for prohibiting the public use of Tubes as shelters.

Though experience thus revealed weaknesses in construction of some shelters, on the whole they withstood the ordeal well and many gave better protection than was expected. The most serious challenge to shelters during the 1940–41 attacks came not from the weight of the attack but from its form. Shelter (like other) policy had been based on assumptions that raids would be spread fairly evenly over what were considered the vulnerable areas, would usually be made by day and would be short, with about seven minutes warning. When they came, the raids proved to be either short daylight attacks with little or no warning, or long attacks in hours of darkness.

---

[1] *On the State of the Public Health during Six Years of War, Report of the Chief Medical Officer of the Ministry of Health 1939–45* (H.M.S.O. 1946) gives a list of Tube stations damaged by enemy action and the casualties caused in them during the whole of the war.

The effects of the long night raids were the most spectacular. In London especially some people quickly formed the habit of going to shelters at dusk and staying there until morning. Thus shelters designed to be occupied only for short periods became 'dormitories'.[1] The authorities had been so preoccupied with the primary task of making shelters safe that they had paid little attention to amenities. This tendency had been intensified by the fact that shelter responsibility had been borne in Regions mainly by technical staffs, and in local councils by borough engineers.

In the earliest phase the situation was made worse by the tendency of the public, notably in London, to congregate in certain shelters, usually the larger public ones, leaving others almost empty. Motives for this were various, and difficult to assess. Public shelters might be favoured because they were more comfortable to sleep in than 'Andersons' which were often damp, or surface shelters, which were very cramped if occupied for long. Often, people sought companionship. Underground shelters were generally the most popular, since shelterers felt safer and slept better when they could not hear bombs or gunfire.

Brick and concrete surface shelters were usually the least favoured, particularly the communal type introduced in March 1940. These lacked privacy and had none of the amenities of some of the larger public shelters. In spurning them the public were also influenced by the doubts already mentioned about their safety, fostered in some places by the leaders of the 'deep shelter' agitation.

Public preference did not always coincide with safety or with comfort. Some of the most popular London shelters were unhealthy railway arches, such as the Tilbury Arches in Stepney, that had been used as shelters in the First World War but gave little protection, and the basements of large badly constructed buildings. The Ministry discovered (more in sorrow than in anger) that the public showed 'a strong tendency to be irrational in their choice of shelters'. Many things at first combined to detract from the effectiveness of the available shelter and to jeopardise the principle of dispersal.[2]

Conditions in London's large public shelters in the early days of the blitz varied considerably. There is no doubt that in some, people spent nights of almost unbelievable squalor and discomfort. Few shelters had bunks, and the inmates tried to make themselves more comfortable and to stake a claim to the limited space by bringing bundles of bedding, sometimes hours before a raid was likely

---

[1] pp. 512–522.

[2] A Research and Experiments Department memorandum, dated 23rd January 1941, went so far as to say that, as a result of all these factors, the number of casualties had not been reduced by more than 10 per cent. by the existence of shelters.

to begin, thus increasing congestion and creating serious hygienic problems. After the first raids many people bombed out of their homes began to settle down to a permanent life in shelters.

Lighting was rarely very bright and some shelters still had none. The majority had no heating and only inadequate ventilation; many were damp. Sanitary arrangements were hastily improvised and usually inadequate, since there were as yet no arrangements for disposing of sewage. There was rarely any provision for regular cleaning or for medical attention or inspection. Although behaviour in shelters was on the whole good, there were inevitably shelterers who were drunk, noisy, verminous or who otherwise interfered with the comfort, and particularly the sleep, of others.[1]

In other shelters, general conditions were much better. Some people had provided themselves with chairs, camp beds and even iron bedsteads, stoves or electric fires, candles or hurricane lamps and water. But these amenities inevitably reduced the available space. The more enterprising shelterers at once made arrangements for cleaning shelters and so on. In the London Tubes heat and light were already provided; but normal first aid equipment and sanitary arrangements were quite inadequate to meet the new demands, and there were no welfare arrangements and no food.[2]

It would, of course, be wrong to suggest that these conditions affected a majority of the population, even of London.[3] Many did not use any orthodox shelter but remained all night in their beds, or at least in their homes. It is impossible to calculate with any precision the numbers who used shelters, even in the larger towns. In London a periodical count was made of shelterers, usually once a month; but this took place on a single night which was not necessarily typical. In addition, the population was continually fluctuating owing to evacuation, the call-up to the Forces and war damage. The first shelter census in Metropolitan London, taken early in November 1940, showed that 9 per cent. of the estimated population spent the night in public shelters, 4 per cent. in the Tubes and 27 per cent. in household shelters—in all, only 40 per cent. in any kinds of official shelter. In September and October this proportion was probably a good deal higher. Later, as the London public became accustomed to raids, the figures dropped.

Liverpool was the only other city in which people slept in public shelters on a scale comparable to London. In Birmingham the practice was adopted early in the blitz, but a short respite from raids caused the numbers to fall; in Manchester the numbers were

---

[1] There were also reports of behaviour of this kind which turned out on investigation to be merely scandalmongering.

[2] Estimates of the peak number of shelterers in all London Tube stations (reached towards the end of September 1940) vary between 120,000 and 160,000.

[3] Shelter occupation is discussed in R. M. Titmuss, *op. cit.*, pp. 342 ff.

always small. In some places, notably Portsmouth, Southampton, Plymouth, Hull, Merseyside, Clydebank, Swansea and Bristol (and to a far lesser extent London) a proportion of the public adopted the practice of 'trekking' nightly to the surrounding countryside.[1]

All-night raids also removed one of the arguments against 'deep shelters', namely difficulty of access; since many people did not wait for a warning before going to a public shelter but automatically spent the night there. And the demand for such shelters, which had caused the Government frequent embarrassment since 1938, was naturally stimulated by raids. Yet there was no guarantee that the enemy would not change their tactics. If they turned to making short night raids, and people lost the habit of shelter-sleeping, accessibility would again become of prime importance and deep or bomb-proof refuges constructed at enormous cost might become useless.

Daylight raids also falsified some previous assumptions of shelter policy. After the fall of France, these occurred after much less warning than had been expected; and were often so short and frequent, that persons in factories and offices could not try to reach outside shelters each time the siren sounded without serious interruption of their work.

Financial and Administrative Aspects

Financial aspects of civil defence in war have so far been little noticed, except in relation to the high cost of the Services and the strong public criticism of this cost during the twilight war.[2] It will be recalled that the incidence of charges for civil defence as a whole as between the Exchequer and local authorities had proved a serious bone of contention during pre-war years of preparation. Before the outbreak of war the Government had undertaken fully to reimburse the pay of the 320,000 or so whole-time A.R.P. volunteers.[3] But this action had not appeased a proportion of local authorities and their spokesmen in Parliament who continued to maintain that the Exchequer should assume responsibility for all civil defence 'services'—in the broader sense which embraces not merely human organisations but all functions performed.

The financial prominence among these which shelter construction and maintenance had assumed from the start, and was to continue to assume, is a justification for some broader reference at this stage to financial issues. Once war had broken out, estimates were indefinitely suspended and Parliament gave the Government Votes of

---

[1] See R. M. Titmuss, *op. cit.*, Chapters XIV–XVII; pp. 427–428.

[2] Chapters VII and VIII above.

[3] p. 341. The Government had also promised to reimburse the cost of hiring premises and vehicles used for operational purposes.

Credit or block sums. Scrutiny of expenditure was conducted on behalf of the House of Commons by the Select Committee on National Expenditure, which covered during the course of the war a huge field of inquiry. It was also the concern of the Public Accounts Committee, composed of Members of Parliament, and of the Comptroller and Auditor-General. All of these institutions found cause to comment from time to time on civil defence expenditure, particularly on air raid shelters.

In the Appropriation Accounts for 1941–42 (the first year in which this appeared as a separate head) the cost of materials and new construction of shelters was over £26 million out of a total spent on civil defence of £155 million. This was only exceeded as an item by some £40 million spent in pay to the Services, and was more than the cost of the new National Fire Service. For 1939–40 (to refer back somewhat) the cost to the Government of civil defence equipment and materials, which included shelters, had been some £27 million out of a total of £51 million; for 1940–41 the comparable figures were £20 and £105 million.[1]

In October 1940, soon after the opening of the London blitz, the Government took the major step of undertaking that the full cost of materials and labour used in building and equipping shelters of all types should in future be borne by the Exchequer.[2] This was the consequence in part of the confusion and difficulties caused by the different financial arrangements, noticed in earlier chapters, for different types of shelter, and in part of the need for quick large-scale action to repair the deficiences in shelter provision which heavy attacks had revealed. The Government, however, took care to emphasise that their decision implied no criticism of previous financial arrangements and was only intended to remove obstacles to the rapid future increase and improvement of shelters.

Many local authorities, however, were still not satisfied with the general partition of the financial burden. The review of this, promised within three years by the terms of the 1937 Act, began in the autumn of 1940 and continued through 1941.[3] It is impossible, in a single volume devoted to civil defence, either to enter into details of this controversy or to draw much conclusion of value about its significance. The local authorities' main demands may, however, be summarised as follows:

First, that reimbursement by the Exchequer of the cost of constructing shelters should be retrospective. This was in effect (to quote an informal gloss on an official file) 'the wise virgins growing

---

[1] Civil Appropriation Accounts 1939 (H.C. 12), Civil Appropriation Accounts 1940 (H.C. 14) and Civil Appropriation Accounts 1941 (H.C. 27).

[2] H.S.C. 249/40, 1st October 1940.

[3] p. 106.

discontented when the neglect of the foolish virgins was more hand-somely compensated than their wisdom'. Those who had gone ahead in this matter during the past few years felt penalised *vis-à-vis* the less far-seeing and active. They pointed out that the sum involved, about £9 million, was negligible in relation to the total cost of shelters. This argument appears somewhat to have embittered dealings between the central and local authorities in a phase when co-opera-tion was of particular importance. It was the theme of a number of Parliamentary statements during this winter and of a debate in April 1941.[1] Though the Government stood by its decision, the issue was intermittently revived, especially by the Metropolitan Boroughs. It must here be added that the cost of maintaining shelters remained on a grant-aided basis throughout the war.

The local authorities also wanted both aid towards the salaries of normal administrative and technical staffs now spending much of their time on civil defence; and reimbursement of the wages of employees seconded to the Rescue and Decontamination Services. These problems revolved round the difficult question of defining what constituted the 'additional expenditure' imposed on the author-ities by their civil defence function. The outcome of the general financial review, which included these matters, was presented to Parliament in May 1942.[2] This included agreement by the Govern-ment to make a supplementary grant in respect of 1941–42 and any subsequent year to the administrative costs of authorities where certain conditions obtained.

Emphasis must be given here to the large-scale administrative work devolving on the Home Office and on Regions concerning the financing of civil defence, and especially the settlement of grant claims.[3] A section of the Home Office Finance Division was respon-sible for administering A.R.P. grants which, once the blitz had started, embraced considerable sums for the clearance of debris and repair of roads and eventually included the work (transferred from the Shelter Division) on industrial shelter grants. It is no reflection on this section to record that in his report on 1941–42 the Comptroller and Auditor-General stated that there was considerable delay in settling grant claims and that some of these for 1937–38 were still outstanding. Also that the procedure for examining claims by local authorities for reimbursement of Fire Guard subsistence allowances (which grew two years later to an annual sum of £8.5 million) was not, by peace-time standards, very thorough. In view of the man-power shortage, he concluded, this was unavoidable.[4]

---

[1] H. of C. Deb., Vol. 368, Cols. 662–3, 30th January, Vol. 369, Col. 355, 25th February, Vol. 370, Cols. 1770–1800, 10th April 1941.
[2] Cmd. 6356; H.S.C. 124/42, 15th June 1942.
[3] pp. 303–304.
[4] Civil Appropriation Accounts (Unclassified Votes) 1941 (H.C. 75).

Mistakes, it has been noticed, had arisen in the twilight war owing to uncertainty over the precise degree of financial delegation by the Ministry to its Regional Officers.[1] These were sometimes repeated, again with special reference to shelter expenditure, after the Government had decided in the autumn of 1940 to modify its attitude to 'deep shelters'.[2] In the report just mentioned the Comptroller and Auditor-General gave some striking instances of tunnelling and other costly local schemes started either through misunderstandings at Regional level, or without full approval.

The shelter problems which emerged under the stress of heavy attack and will shortly be discussed at more length were constantly reviewed by the Civil Defence Committees and by a new Standing Committee on Shelter Policy under the chairmanship of the Ministry of Home Security's Parliamentary Under-Secretary.[3] From the aspect, which this narrative has tried to suggest, of the volume of administrative work which civil defence involved it is worth adding that the Ministry's Shelter Department now experienced big changes in both the quantity and character of its tasks. It became necessary to enlarge Regional administrative and technical staffs concerned with shelters, and one London Commissioner, Admiral Evans, undertook special responsibility in this sphere. The Research and Experiments Department's Technical Intelligence Division and other branches began to accumulate a substantial amount of data about raids and their effects on various types of shelter.

At the same time experiments were continuing by the Department of Scientific and Industrial Research, the Ministry's research stations at Leamington and Compton Verney, the Research Department (Woolwich), the Porton Experimental Station and on various sites lent for particular tests. In this work, the R. and E. Department was advised by the Civil Defence Research Committee and other bodies referred to in Chapter V of this volume.

Problems of 'Dormitory Shelters'

Soon after the opening of the Battle of London the Government appointed a small committee under Lord Horder's chairmanship to examine shelter conditions, with particular attention to public health.[4] Paying night visits to East End shelters, the Horder committee made a verbal report within four days and a formal report before the end of September. They thought the chief of the many

---

[1] pp. 310, 333.

[2] pp. 530-532.

[3] H. of C. Deb., Vol. 365, Cols. 495–568, 10th October 1940.

[4] Its members, besides the Chairman, were the Chief Medical Officer of the Ministry of Health, the Chief Engineer of the Ministry of Home Security, the Chief Warden of Bethnal Green (Sir Wyndham Deedes) and a representative of the W.V.S.

problems all-night raids had created was gross overcrowding; and though they had no criticism in principle of dispersal, they doubted if it would always be feasible to persuade people to shelter near their homes. They thought the situation aggravated by the fact that no single local official was responsible for the many aspects of shelters. They gave special attention to conditions inside shelters, recommending regular cleaning and inspection, adequate sanitary equipment and first aid posts and the appointment of marshals in the larger shelters. The Horder committee remained in being throughout the Big Blitz and up to October 1941.[1]

After this committee had reported the Ministry told London authorities it was preparing designs and arranging to supply materials for bunks to be installed in large public shelters, and asked them to begin immediately to provide chemical closets in all public shelters (at Government expense) and to arrange for these to be emptied and shelters to be cleaned daily. For shelters holding 500 or more people it recommended a box of first aid equipment. It also promised guidance about ways of keeping order in shelters and of providing light and warmth in the coming winter.[2] The Chief Medical Officer of Health asked Medical Officers of the Metropolitan Boroughs to inspect shelters in their areas. Principal Officers of other Regions were kept informed of the efforts being made in London, and asked to encourage areas where heavy raiding was already developing to take similar steps.[3]

Local authorities throughout the country were again urged to help householders to ensure that 'Andersons' would not be made unusable by flooding and were given more advice about this. It was even suggested that, in exceptional circumstances, it might be advisable to remove these shelters and erect them indoors.[4] In an attempt to make 'communal surface shelters' more popular, the Ministry had already modified its ruling that the persons using these should be responsible for making them comfortable, and had told local authorities that they might, if this could be done cheaply and easily, provide them with seating and some internal lighting.[5] Contracts were later placed for wire netting sufficient for about 1,000,000 bunks. But the size of many of these shelters made them wasteful of space when used for sleeping, and in October it was

---

[1] Some of their supplementary recommendations were published, with a summary of their first report and of the action taken on it, in two White Papers—Cmd. 6234, November 1940, and Cmd. 6245, December 1940.

[2] H.S.R. 175/40, 28th September 1940; London Regional Circular No. 203, 27th September 1940.

[3] H.S.R. 175/40, 28th September.

[4] H.S.C. 247/40, 28th September.

[5] H.S.C. 201/40, 1st August 1940. Sanitary conveniences could not be provided in standard types of communal shelter because of shortage of space.

decided that in places subject to heavy night attack new communal shelters should measure at least 12 ft. 6 in. by 4 ft. 6 in. inside. Minimum dimensions were also given for new individual surface shelters.[1]

When these early and not very ambitious decisions were made, the Government's shelter responsibility was divided between the Ministry of Home Security and the Health Departments. Home Security dealt not only with designs and construction, but with fittings, including bunks, sick bays, medical aid posts and sanitary arrangements. The Health Departments were responsible only for questions directly related to public health, such as appointment of doctors and nurses, medical inspection and measures to prevent spread of disease. Local authorities were subjected to delays caused by the need to consult both Departments about the insides of shelters. The process would have been simplified if the Minister of Health had followed the Minister of Home Security's example in delegating some shelter powers to Regional Commissioners, who could then have acted as channels of communication between both Ministries and the authorities. But the difficulties went deeper than this. The flood of problems which arose when shelters became dormitories had almost submerged the Ministry of Home Security's headquarters and Regional staffs, and many of the new tasks were quite outside their previous experience.

Early in 1941 the Government decided to introduce, so far as possible, single responsibility for the insides of shelters. Home Security was to remain responsible for shelter numbers, location and construction. But the Health Departments took over ultimate responsibility for all other shelter questions—matters of health in the widest sense, including sanitation, bunks, stoves, lighting and ventilation, canteen accommodation and public order.[2] The Minister of Health delegated many of these functions to Regional Commissioners, whose shelter staffs were reinforced by Ministry of Health officials.

A new London Regional Commissioner, Alderman Charles Key, was in January given special responsibility for shelters on behalf of both Ministers.[3] His shelters branch included medical advisers, an inspectorate and welfare staff. The first helped medical officers of health to examine shelters. The inspectorate continued the general inspection initiated in the autumn and by the end of March 1941 had visited public shelters—a total of over 1,800—in every local authority area in the Region.

Meanwhile, the Government's appeal 'to the authorities had been followed by directions which eventually extended to all the

---

[1] H.S.R. 188/40, 21st October 1940.

[2] For information on shelter canteens see R. J. Hammond, *Food*, in this series.

[3] Admiral Evans now turned his special attention to civil defence personnel. (See p. 512.)

problems which shelter occupation produced. This large central administrative effort which must now be described should not obscure the considerable work done by local authorities, voluntary bodies of all kinds and the shelterers themselves to improve conditions. Though it is impossible here to begin to describe the contribution of particular voluntary bodies, that of St. Martin-in-the-Fields may be mentioned as typical of many, religious and secular. As soon as the Battle of London opened people of all sorts and conditions came from all parts of London to shelter in the six large vaults which, at the request of Westminster City Council, the authorities of this church had made available as shelters. Sleeping facilities for some 600 persons—many of whom became 'permanent' shelterers in the crypt—a canteen and recreation of various kinds were, step by step, provided.

It should not, in addition, be assumed that the central Government's directions automatically produced results. The energy and efficiency which local authorities brought to this task varied much. Even the best were hampered by shortages of materials, and by the fact that much of the labour available to them had to be used to repair bomb damage. When materials and labour were available it was often necessary to delay work on bunks, lighting and so on until shelters had been strengthened.

Because so much had to be done, attention was often concentrated first on the biggest, most notorious, shelters—a tendency probably encouraged by the Ministry of Health's concern with the danger of disease. There was thus often a large time-lag before instructions had appreciable effect. As detailed records were being sacrificed, at all levels, on the altars of action the central authorities often found it difficult to keep check of progress. Though London authorities furnished the Region with information on the basis of which reports were regularly prepared for the Minister,[1] outside London there was no regular shelter inspectorate and similar reports were not prepared until after the middle of 1941.[2]

First supplies of standard bunks for public and communal shelters were ready in early December 1940. These were produced in bulk on Government contract and delivered in sections for local erection; most were of wood (in three different designs) but there were also two types of steel. They were usually arranged in three tiers with the middle one made to drop down as a back to the lowest, which could be used as a daytime seat.[3] Some authorities, chiefly in central London, had already begun to provide locally-made bunks, but the numbers rapidly increased when central supplies became

---

[1] L.R.C. No. 226, 31st October 1940.
[2] H.S.R. 188/41, 24th July.
[3] H.S.R. 210/40, 15th November.

available.[1] By the middle of January nearly 400,000 had been installed in London Region, and by the end of April well over 600,000. Even so, in many shelters people still had to stand or sit on the floor, and in some parts of the country bunks were still being fitted in the following autumn. Later, special bunks were designed for 'Andersons' in areas where people habitually slept in shelters.

The lighting in most public shelters was at first insufficient for reading or any social activities. At the beginning of 1941 authorities were asked to provide brighter lighting, but to arrange for this to be dimmed when people wanted to sleep.[2] Adequate lighting was essential to cleanliness, and a special effort was made to ensure good lighting throughout the night in closets and medical posts.[3]

Heating shelters adequately was more difficult. At first it was merely suggested that shelterers should provide themselves with hot water bottles or hot bricks.[4] But if people had to concentrate on keeping warm by such means they were able to do little else, and after a few weeks' raiding shelters that were exceptionally cold and damp—notably, surface and trench shelters—began to be deserted while the warmer ones became overcrowded. Small coal-burning 'Cura' stoves (consisting of a rectangular iron box lined with fire brick and a cylindrical cast-iron pipe to carry the fumes through the roof) were introduced into surface shelters and trench shelters holding fifty or more people in one compartment.[5] These, though an improvement on previous methods, proved difficult to use and clean and produced unpleasant fumes. Electrical heating was obviously dangerous before shelters had been made dry, and was limited by equipment shortages. But after the spring of 1941 this was permitted in shelters holding fifty or more persons not already supplied with stoves, and on the whole it was much more popular.

The ideal ventilating arrangement through some air-conditioning system was usually impracticable. Simple extraction or impulsion fans were sometimes fitted in basements, but most shelters were ventilated merely by openings which could be varied according to the weather.[6] Without elaborate apparatus shelters could not be both adequately ventilated and made gas-proof. When attacks began gas curtains, which could be dropped to cover all openings, had been fixed in many shelters; but after a few months of night raids with no gas attack no more of these were fitted and some were removed.[7]

---

[1] By 15th November bunks had been installed for over 53,000 people in London.

[2] L.R.C. No. 284, 16th January 1941.

[3] Ministry of Health P.R.O. Circular 30/41, 23rd June; L.R.C. No. 327, March 1941.

[4] H.S.R. 175/40, 28th September.

[5] H.S.R. 220/40, 6th December and H.S.R. 229/40, 14th December.

[6] H.S.C. 3/41, 30th January; Ministry of Health P.R.O. Circular 26/41, 14th June.

[7] H.S.C. 194/40, 26th July.

The urgent problem of providing simple sanitation was dealt with quickly, and by mid-October closets had been installed in almost all London's public shelters. Arrangements for emptying closets presented a more difficult and a continuing problem. In the spring of 1941 authorities were told they might instal water-borne sanitation in the larger new shelters, and in large existing ones where arrangements were unsatisfactory.[1] Shelterers in converted basements and communal shelters had to rely on the lavatory facilities of near-by buildings. There was usually no attempt to provide washing facilities for all the occupants of a shelter. Instead, public baths were opened early enough in the morning for the use of those who had no time to go home. In the spring of 1941 the Government found it necessary to allow authorities to engage extra staff for cleaning; but it was not always possible to find such staff, and cleaning often remained a difficult problem.

The Ministry of Health was particularly concerned with the possibility that the dormitory use of shelters might cause epidemics. Medical Officers of Health could isolate shelterers found suffering from infectious diseases and send them home or to hospital after a raid was over. Ambulances were provided for these and for other, including maternity, cases.[2] Local authorities had to ensure that doctors would be available to deal with illness or accidents, and a nurse (preferably trained) was needed in each large shelter.[3] By the middle of January, 150 medical posts had been set up in London's large shelters and 25 more were serving groups of smaller shelters; many more were set up during the next few months.[4] In the confusion which often accompanied heavy raids many people injured by bombs came (or were even brought on stretchers) into shelters, imposing a heavy strain on these posts, and special efforts had to be made to ensure that raid casualties went straight to first aid posts or hospitals.[5]

Body vermin never became so large a problem as had been expected. Shelter wardens had power to deal with obviously verminous shelterers, and were given short courses at the School of Hygiene and Tropical Medicine. In London most of the shelterers who proved infested were the habitual sleepers on the Embankment. A special

---

[1] Ministry of Health P.R.O. Circular 12/41, 1st March; L.R.C. No. 319, 1st March 1941. This concession was later applied to school shelters which were used by the public at night.

[2] On the State of Public Health During Six Years of War, Report of the Chief Medical Officer of the Ministry of Health, 1939-45 (H.M.S.O. 1946). During the flying bomb attacks, when the hospitals in London were able to cater for only the more serious diseases, special shelters or bays in larger shelters had to be set aside for people suffering from minor infectious diseases.

[3] Ministry of Health Circulars 2190, 30th October 1940; 2216, 22nd November 1940.

[4] Ministry of Health Circular 2203, 12th November 1940.

[5] L.R.C. No. 374, 22nd May 1941; P.R.O. Circular 25/41, 6th June 1941.

shelter, the 'Hungerford Club', with bathrooms and cleansing facilities was organised for them by voluntary workers under Westminster's medical officer of health. Bed bugs were more of a menace; for though people were soon stopped from keeping their bedding continuously in shelters, they often left it by day in bug-ridden stores. A few boroughs met the problem by establishing bedding stores, or by treating bedding with hot air disinfectors. In many shelters mortar joints and crevices had to be coated with special paints and the air sprayed with insecticides.

All-night shelterers, especially those without time to go home in the morning, needed food and hot drinks, and at first arrangements for these were most haphazard. But in late October, after some voluntary organisations had successfully supplied regular food for a week to certain shelters, many London boroughs began arrangements for shelterers to obtain light refreshments at modest prices.[1] At first this food was supplied by caterers or voluntary bodies, but later local authorities began to provide it themselves.[2] By mid-November arrangements had been made to feed some 150,000 shelterers; though at the beginning of December this facility was only available in about a sixth of the public shelters in London Region. By the end of April, however, food was being supplied in most of these shelters. The Government then asked authorities outside London to take similar steps where public shelters were used for sleeping or were likely to be used if air attack was intensified; and canteens were still being installed in some provincial shelters in 1942.[3]

The Ministry of Food appointed some inspectors to advise caterers and ensure hygienic methods, but was reluctant to exercise control over types of food, feeling that these should depend on popular demand which varied considerably in accordance with local tastes and traditions. A committee under Lord Horder's chairmanship considering this question in June 1941 agreed that a dictatorial attitude should be avoided. But on its recommendation the Ministry set out to stimulate interest in food values by means of leaflets and posters in shelters.

Even after the necessities of health, food and minimum comfort had been arranged for, there was much scope for useful work. Special problems were created by the presence in shelters of the old, nursing mothers, babies and adolescents. After a little experience of raids shelterers became more used to bombs, but less patient with the boredom of long hours spent in such surroundings. Many individuals and organisations had engaged in welfare work before

---

[1] Ministry of Food Circular, 22nd October 1940; L.R.C. No. 222, 24th October 1940.

[2] Ministry of Food Circular, 29th November 1940.

[3] Ministry of Health P.R.O. Circular 16/41, 24th March 1941.

the central or local authorities entered this field. But their efforts tended to be unevenly distributed and were occasionally, for example in the much resented practice of 'shelter slumming', misdirected.

The Ministry of Home Security approached welfare activities with some apprehension lest shelters should be made too attractive and the dispersal policy endangered. It soon, however, became clear that since large numbers were determined to congregate in shelters, it was better to accept the situation and help sustain morale by furnishing entertainment and education. In November 1940 a 'Central Advisory Committee on Entertainment and Instruction' in shelters was formed in London from bodies prepared to organise shelter activities and employ their own funds.[1] It was suggested that each local authority should appoint a committee or single officer to supervise arrangements in its area. Authorities were asked to be cautious about entertainments by professional artists, confining these to the early evening and not announcing them beforehand or allowing them to be given more than once a week in any shelter.[2]

By the new year books such as 'Penguins' were being circulated by public libraries, two hundred L.C.C. classes (e.g. on current events and dress-making) were being held in the larger shelters, E.N.S.A. was providing weekly concerts in about twenty shelters, the Pilgrim Players were giving performances, chiefly in crypt shelters, and the British Drama League had been approached by Bethnal Green and West Ham for help in organising shows. Classes and entertainments were also being held in a few shelters in Bristol and other large cities.[3]

Meanwhile, the Ministry had been discussing shelter welfare with various bodies and collecting names of voluntary workers who were prepared to help. In January 1941 a full-time Regional Welfare Adviser was appointed for London.[4] In March the Committee on Entertainment and Instruction was reconstituted as a Welfare Advisory Conference. Thirteen Metropolitan Boroughs eventually appointed shelter welfare officers, though only two of these special appointments had been made by the end of the Big Blitz. By the end of June 1941 twenty boroughs had formed shelter welfare committees

---

[1] It consisted of representatives of London C.D. Region, the Ministry of Health, the Board of Education, the Ministry of Information, the L.C.C., the County Boroughs of East Ham, West Ham and Croydon, the Council for the Encouragement of Music and Arts, the Entertainments National Service Association, the W.E.A., the British Institute of Adult Education. Representatives of other bodies—e.g., the British Drama League and the Middlesex County Council—were added later.

[2] L.R.C. No. 248, 28th November 1940.

[3] Two members of the Horder Committee who visited shelters in Bristol at the end of 1940 reported that one large shelter was used entirely for entertainment for 24 hours on end. The fears that entertainment in shelters might be abused were evidently not without some foundation.

[4] Mrs. M. A. Creswick-Atkinson, a member of the W.V.S. and of the Horder Committee.

including representatives of voluntary organisations.[1] Most large shelters had also set up informal committees of shelterers.

Activities naturally varied from shelter to shelter. They included W.V.S. story-corners for toddlers, children's play centres (many organised by the L.C.C. and the 'Save the Children Fund'), boys' and girls' clubs, advice to parents on child care and so on. Such activities, starting in shelters, were often extended outside them after heavy raiding had ceased. Attempts were also made to stimulate the work of non-residential clubs for adolescents by providing them with shelters for use during the evenings and, if necessary, as dormitories.[2] But the division of families was unpopular with shelterers, many of whom had resisted efforts to segregate the sexes and to arrange special children's bays when bunks were being allotted.

The preservation of order in shelters clearly presented special problems. Sometimes, early in the blitz, shelterers had formed voluntary committees to reduce overcrowding by allocating places. In October London authorities introduced a ticket system for all dormitory shelters by taking a census of occupants and inviting applications for tickets.[3] Such a system could help towards a more even distribution of London's shelterers; and the Government proposed that tickets should not be given to those with their own household shelters in satisfactory condition.

General responsibility for keeping order in shelters fell on the Wardens' Service. At first this was undertaken by part-time wardens, often helped by people living near the shelter.[4] These helpers, usually called 'shelter marshals', had nothing except an arm-band to distinguish them from the shelterers. Later, some paid wardens were engaged to look after large shelters, first in London and then in provincial towns.[5] The title 'shelter marshal' was dropped, and everyone engaged on these duties (whether part or full-time) was called a 'shelter warden' and regarded as a member of the Wardens' Service. These wardens were given powers to enforce order in shelters by a new Defence Regulation (23AB) issued in December.[6] They could direct any inmate to use a particular part of a shelter and refuse to admit or expel anyone who might be dangerous or offensive to others or whose presence might cause over-crowding. These wardens also helped to prevent property in shelters from being pilfered and shelters being misused when empty.

[1] L.R.C. No. 350, 8th April 1941.

[2] H.S.C. 12/41, 11th January 1941.

[3] L.R.C. No. 218, 19th October 1940.

[4] At St. Martin-in-the-Fields young men of the Peace Pledge Union undertook this work.

[5] H.S.R. 175/40, 28th September 1940 and L.R.C. No. 207, 3rd October 1940; Home Security Broadcast 0927, 4th December 1940.

[6] S.R. & O. 1940, No. 2064; H.S.R. 225/40, 12th December 1940.

Similar problems to all these arose in London's Tubes; but they were complicated by the fact that the needs of travellers had always to be the first consideration.[1] In the early days of the blitz the rush-hour traffic had dispersed before dusk. But it was clear that when the days grew shorter there would be danger of congestion on the platforms, and in December the Government reaffirmed its decision that the Tubes must always first be available for essential traffic.[2] In practice, traffic was able to continue unimpeded despite the presence of shelterers; and it is doubtful whether any serious attempt could have been made to dislodge the shelterers, especially after amenities had been introduced.

Action had been quickly taken to supplement sanitary arrangements in stations; the L.P.T.B. provided chemical closets, and local authorities were responsible for emptying these daily. As platforms were below the sewer level, this proved a laborious and insanitary task until experts of the Ministry and the Board were able to devise means of using the compressed air available at stations to force the sewage up to a higher level where it could be discharged directly into the sewers. By early October the Board had installed (at Government expense) sewage ejector plants in 29 stations and this work was in hand at another 47. Progress was then delayed by difficulties in obtaining labour, tanks and fittings and by the end of June work was still held up at several of the 81 stations in use as shelters. The L.P.T.B. also cleaned the permanent way and provided iron baskets for refuse, and local authorities cleaned and disinfected platforms each morning. The police helped to clear the stations early enough for cleaning to be finished before the heavy morning traffic began.[3]

When heavy raids began voluntary workers, including many members of the Red Cross, gave first aid treatment to shelterers in certain stations in improvised 'posts' of a few feet of platform fenced off by benches. Later, local authorities set up first aid points in stations and arranged for the constant attendance of trained first aid workers.[4]

At the end of October, the Board had agreed that bunks might be installed (at Government expense) on platforms provided they did not hamper traffic. The design chosen was a steel three-tier frame with wooden slats for the bottom berth and steel mesh for the two upper ones. The parts were at first sent direct from the manufacturers to stations; but when it was found that there were delays

---

[1] See Charles Graves, *London Transport Carried On* (L.P.T.B., 1947).

[2] In November the L.P.T.B. placed an ex-General Manager of the Tube Railways in charge of all the work arising from the use of the Tubes as shelters.

[3] L.R.C. No. 203, 27th September 1940.

[4] Ibid.

in delivery, wooden and steel beds were assembled in a Home Security depot at Ealing and delivered complete in twenty-four hours to stations which had received the necessary steel frames. By the end of February 1941 bunking had been completed in all but three stations. Some of the bunks showed early signs of wear due to defective materials, and it was found that many steel mattresses had been placed upside down. Bunks led to a system of place reservations, bringing to an end the day-time queues of shelterers outside the Tubes.

The Board itself undertook to supply light refreshments to shelterers in stations; and by mid-December these were available for all Tube shelterers. Some stations were equipped with electric hotplates and urns, and food and drinks prepared with these were distributed to other stations by special train. Welfare organisations naturally did not have the same scope in the Tubes as in other types of shelter. But communal enterprise among Tube shelterers resulted in knitting and sewing parties, story-telling groups for children, libraries and 'advice bureaux' on personal problems.[1]

Soon after the onset of heavy night attack the Government had enquired whether parts of the Tube system other than the platforms could be made available for shelter. The Holborn-Aldwych section had already been closed to traffic and offered as shelter to the Westminster City authorities. In October the Board made a schedule of other parts of the system which might accommodate 4-5,000 people. Though some of these had to be rejected on technical grounds, the South Kentish Town, City Road and British Museum stations and the extension to the Bethnal Green Tube not yet brought into use were adapted by the Board (at Government expense) and leased to the appropriate authorities as shelters; and spaces in addition to platforms were made available at several other stations.

Immediately night raids began people, carrying bundles of bedding, congregated in the shelters provided for passengers in subways and vaults under the platforms of London's main-line stations.[2] The railways feared at first that there would not be enough shelter for passengers, particularly when the evenings lengthened and raids would probably coincide with peak travelling hours. But it began to transpire that there would be fewer passengers during these hours than had been expected, since many workers had begun either to leave for home before raids began or to sleep in their offices and factories. Local authorities in whose areas these shelters were situated began to equip sections not needed for passengers as dormitories for the public, and to sub-divide some of them so as to reduce the risk of mass casualties.

---

[1] L.R.C. No. 248, 28th November 1940.
[2] p. 370.

Strengthening and Multiplying Shelters

While tackling these 'dormitory' problems, it was also necessary to deal with shelters which were proving structurally unsatisfactory, notably surface shelters built with inferior materials. The Ministry's instruction regarding these of July 1940[1] was followed in October by a prohibition of the inclusion of any lime in mortar used for surface shelters during the winter months. Some authorities who had experienced misfortune with these shelters had already stopped using mortar containing lime, but many had only been prevented from doing so by the continuing shortage of cement.[2] In April 1941, when the cement position had eased, prohibition of the use of mortar containing lime was indefinitely extended.

So far as surface shelters already built were concerned, the best course seemed to be to attempt to strengthen those that were moderately satisfactory and to close any that were obviously unsafe. In December 1940, authorities were given detailed instructions for strengthening or partially rebuilding shelters built with mortar containing lime, and were also told about methods of remedying dampness.[3]

In March 1941 the Ministry decided that all public and communal surface shelters built with mortar of lime and sand only should be closed or, if they were visibly unstable or the site or materials were needed for other purposes, demolished.[4] Shelters built with lime-cement mortar were to be examined, and if necessary also closed or demolished. These instructions did not apply to individual surface shelters which, being smaller, were stronger. The closing of shelters of these types roused strong public criticism.[5] Many local authorities were unable to offer alternative shelter near at hand; and some who protested it was unreasonable to condemn all lime-mortar shelters without distinction were later allowed to retain any which their engineer could certify as satisfactory.

The cost of strengthening or demolishing shelters was usually borne by public funds. The Government urged local councils to force contractors, if necessary by legal action, in cases where there was clear evidence of faulty workmanship or poor materials, to make good defects at their own expense. Some contractors did, in fact,

---

[1] p. 369.

[2] The provisional allocation of cement for shelter works for October was less than half the estimated minimum requirement.

[3] H.S.C. 290/40, 11th December 1940. In London Region it was reported that very few of these shelters were bad enough to be demolished, but repointing was necessary in most areas.

[4] H.S.R. 53/41, 5th March; L.R.C. No. 329, 11th March 1941.

[5] For example see H. of C. Deb., Vol. 370, Cols. 304-5, 20th March 1941.

rebuild the shelters, but many were able to use technicalities in their contracts to escape this obligation.[1]

Though the worst instances of these shelters collapsing were usually due to poor materials or workmanship, an effort was made to improve the design. In a new design prepared by the R. and E. Department in December 1940, the walls were constructed of ferro-concrete, brickwork or hollow concrete blocks reinforced with vertical steel rods, the vertical reinforcements being tied to the roof and, wherever possible, to the floor. This meant that if a bomb exploded near at hand the shelter could move bodily without breaking. In addition, a bituminous felt damp-proof course was provided at ground level to increase the shelter's resistance by allowing it to move slightly in a horizontal direction, and also to help to keep it dry; and the roof was designed to overhang the walls.

This improved design was used for all new public and communal shelters. New individual surface shelters were constructed in reinforced brickwork and provided with a bituminous damp-proof course.[2] Further research made it possible to apply many of the new design's merits to existing shelters by adding a new outer or inner 'skin' of reinforced brickwork or concrete keyed into the old brickwork. Public and communal shelters built with lime or lime-cement mortar were strengthened in this way first, especially those that had been closed because the mortar was unsatisfactory.[3]

Though the Government had intended that these improvements should be followed by a widespread publicity campaign, this was not thoroughly under way before the end of the Big Blitz. A new attempt was, however, made to encourage the public to use communal and domestic rather than public shelters.

Methods were devised of strengthening trenches with pre-cast concrete linings; but new trenches were lined whenever possible with 'in situ' ferro-concrete, which had proved very successful.[4] More sub-divisions were made in certain basement shelters where too many people were sheltering in each compartment, and emergency exits communicating with adjoining basements were often provided. The various types of strutting were improved; and because of the danger of bombs penetrating pavement lights many of these were cut off from basement shelters by a heavy vertical wall either flush with the building line or inside it. Local authorities already had power to close any unsatisfactory shelters they had provided, and in May 1941

---

[1] H.S.R. 114/41, 19th May; H. of C. Deb., Vol. 370, Col. 171, 23rd April 1941.

[2] H.S.C. 290/40, 11th December 1940.

[3] H.S.R. 193/41, 29th July 1941. A number of brick surface shelters strengthened in various ways and a reinforced concrete shelter conforming to the latest design were tested with 250 kg. bombs at Richmond Park in June 1941. Further tests were made during the autumn and winter.

[4] p. 506.

Defence Regulation 23AA empowered them to prevent the public from using unsafe or unhygienic shelters in private premises.[1]

Surface shelters, trenches and strengthened basements had been provided extensively, on the Government's advice, for workers in factories, offices and shops. These shelters clearly ought to have been strengthened in the same way as those provided by local authorities. But because this would have meant further burdens on owners or employers who had already fulfilled their obligations under the Civil Defence Act, it was decided that, though these should be advised to improve their shelters, they should not be laid under a legal obligation to do so.[2] Many new industrial shelters provided at this time qualified for Exchequer grant.[3] No grant was paid towards capital expenditure on improving existing shelters; but the cost of some of the minor improvements recommended, for example measures to reduce dampness or replace defective mortar, was classed by the Inland Revenue as revenue expenditure and qualified for income tax allowance. In addition, considerable financial relief could usually be obtained for capital expenditure under the terms of the Finance Act, 1941.[4]

When providing extra shelters the logical course was to concentrate on types which were proving both structurally sound and popular.[5] Though the Government hoped it would eventually be possible to achieve more dispersal by encouraging people to use domestic shelters, the most vocal immediate demand was for more public shelters. Large steel-framed buildings, which were resisting the effects of bombs exceptionally well, were particularly suitable for this purpose, but these were used in the main for factory and office staffs. Though the owners of private buildings could be compelled to allow members of the public to shelter, this power had not at first been applied to industrial and commercial premises.[6] At the end of

---

[1] H.S.R. 119/1941, 26th May.

[2] In July 1941 Factory Inspectors began to encourage factory occupiers to strengthen existing shelters wherever possible, particularly any constructed with mortar containing a high proportion of lime, and to use the revised designs for any new shelters. In November local authorities were asked to encourage the owners of commercial buildings to take similar action.

[3] See p. 533.

[4] 4 and 5 Geo. 6, Ch. 30, Section 19. This introduced a new income tax allowance for exceptional depreciation of buildings or plant provided after 1st January 1937 by a trader for the purposes of his trade. This allowance was also used to assist employers whose staffs had increased and who had provided extra shelter after fulfilling their obligations under the Civil Defence Act; and those who provided shelter voluntarily in newly specified areas in premises where less than fifty people were employed. These two complications had previously been the subject of long negotiations between the Ministry of Home Security, the Treasury and the Inland Revenue Department. Similar allowances were also available in respect of Excess Profits Tax and National Defence Contributions.

[5] For the control exercised by the Ministry of Works over the Government's building programme including shelter and other civil defence construction see C. M. Kohan, *Works and Buildings* (1952) in this series.

[6] A.R.P. Dept. Circular 216, 31st August 1939; Defence Regulation 23(1).

September 1940, however, local councils throughout the country had been given power to make industrial and commercial shelters available to the public as shelters outside business hours.[1] In practice, this source of shelter was to some extent limited by the need to ensure that normal work was not interrupted, for it was still assumed that 'safety first' for the individual was less important than the defeat of the enemy's attempt to dislocate the life of the country.[2]

Government departments were urged by local authorities and the public to make a similar contribution by admitting shelterers at night to their basements, though it was officially expected that this shelter would be needed to an increasing extent during the winter as sleeping accommodation for Government staffs. Also, strict precautions had to be observed when admitting people to some Government offices. Most of the shelters in Government buildings in Central London remained closed to the public, though some in branch offices in outer London and the provinces were used at night as public dormitories.

Though even the upper floors of steel-framed buildings gave good protection, the public almost always preferred underground shelters and much of the extra dormitory shelter took the form of basements. For example, by mid-October 340 extra basement shelters with accommodation for 65,000 people had been acquired in London. During the next months the number steadily increased, until by March 1941 most of the basements that remained could be opened to the public only by seriously interfering with the activities of the regular occupiers.

While responding to the demand for more public shelters, the Government gave fresh evidence of its steadfast belief in dispersal by arranging for the manufacture of a limited number of new 'Andersons' to be issued to certain authorities, who were this time responsible for delivery to those householders most in need of them. About 184,000 were produced in the last two months of 1940 and the first quarter of 1941, but it became necessary to abandon production after March because of acute steel shortage.[3] Extra curved sheets were distributed to extend the smallest 'Andersons', which had proved too small to sleep in. Some 123,000 pairs of these sheets were produced by the end of March, and a further 160,000 or so after the beginning of June.[4] All the new shelters were of the standard size, large enough for six people.

---

[1] S.R. & O. 1940, No. 1750, 27th September 1940. Local authorities were at the same time empowered to ensure that the basements of tenement houses would be available for shelter to the tenants of upper floors.

[2] School shelters had been built with the aid of a grant of 50 per cent. from the Board of Education. But in January 1941 it was decided that the full cost should be reimbursed on condition that the shelters should, if required, be made available outside school hours to the general public.

[3] p. 334.

[4] H.S.R. 199/40, 30th October 1940.

Experience of raids also led to the introduction of an entirely new type of household shelter. 'Andersons', though structurally satisfactory, had not originally been intended for sleeping and became in many cases unfit for winter occupation. Domestic surface shelters were very cramped when used for sleeping and were in some places not popular, and strengthened domestic basements had been neither very successful nor widely used.[1] After night raiding had ceased to be a novelty, many people preferred to stay in their houses rather than to go out of doors even to their own domestic shelters. The 'Anderson', it will be recalled, had at first been envisaged as an indoor shelter.[2] Since many people were now determined to remain in their homes, it had become necessary to introduce some indoor shelter which might reduce the risk of injury from falling masonry and furniture. The fact that many who had hitherto sheltered under their staircases or furniture had been rescued unhurt from the wreckage of houses suggested that extra protection might be given by a light structure on the ground floor. To devise such a shelter was intrinsically simple; but the Research and Experiments Department, asked to tackle the problem very quickly, found it necessary, owing to shortage of materials and difficulties of mass-production, to make various designs.

By the end of 1940 two designs had been produced. The first, later known as the 'Morrison' shelter, had a rectangular steel framework 6 ft. 6 in. long, 4 ft. wide and about 2 ft. 9 in. high. The sides were filled in with wire mesh, the bottom consisted of a steel mattress and the top was made of steel plate an eighth of an inch thick, fastened to the framework by bolts strong enough to withstand a heavy swinging blow.[3] The shelter, which could be used as a table in the daytime, could accommodate two adults and either two young children or one older child, lying down.[4] Experiments showed that it would carry the debris produced by the collapse of two higher floors. But it gave no lateral protection and was intended to be placed on the ground floor, so that it would be shielded by the walls. Although this shelter gave less protection than a properly covered 'Anderson', it gave considerably more than the average house. A second design, with a curved top, was afterwards abandoned owing to manufacturing difficulties.

'Morrisons' were easily erected and were not, of course, subject

---

[1] Materials for strengthening domestic basements ceased to be centrally supplied in January 1941, and local authorities then had to rely on the resources of local contractors.

[2] pp. 187 ff.

[3] The plates were thicker and more cumbersome than was necessary for protection, but they were conveniently available having been imported for another purpose.

[4] The original height of 4 ft. (which gave more headroom) had been reduced to make the shelter more suitable for its purpose.

to flooding.[1] They met the needs both of places subjected to all-night bombing and of those where occasional raids made reasonably good, accessible, shelter desirable. They had the advantage, to become of much significance later, of being easily moved. The Prime Minister showed great interest in these shelters the first of which, in fact, were erected in No. 10 Downing Street.[2] In January 1941 the Cabinet approved the manufacture of 400,000, providing protection for perhaps 1,200,000 people.[3]

An attempt was now made to help householders not eligible to receive free shelters. Shortage of labour and materials made it difficult for them to construct their own, and though they had been given the opportunity to buy 'Andersons', the response had not been good and these, in any case, were in short supply. When serious raids began, large numbers of people had been without domestic shelter. Yet the position was anomalous, since there was nothing to prevent them from using public shelters. It was now decided to raise the income limit of householders entitled to free shelters to £350. People still ineligible for these could either buy a 'Morrison' for £7 12s. 6d., or have one of the other standard types of individual shelter constructed for them by the local authority at cost price.[4]

The Government decided to concentrate supplies of 'Morrisons' in the most vulnerable areas, and first deliveries were made in London and a few other towns at the end of March.[5] The shelters, like the 'Andersons', were manufactured on Government contract, but authorities were responsible for storing the parts (which arrived from several different sources) and distributing them to householders.[6] In February contracts had been placed for 270,000 shelters, and another order for the same number was placed in April (thus exceeding the 400,000 originally approved). Two further orders for 270,000 were placed at the end of July and the end of September.

---

[1] Instructions were given in a pamphlet, *How to put up your Morrison shelter*, on sale to the public.

[2] One with a flat top and one with a curved top were erected in No. 10 Downing Street. The Prime Minister was at first inclined to favour the curved design but he afterwards recognised the advantages of the flat top, which would allow the shelter to be used as a table, and gave his approval to both designs.

[3] It was estimated that each 'Morrison' would use over 3 cwt. of steel, and that about 65,000 tons would be needed for the 400,000 shelters. This proved to be an underestimate since the table shelter, as finally designed, actually weighed 4.43 cwt.

[4] H.S.C. 87A/41, 10th April 1941. The price of the 'Morrison' was later reduced to £7, a refund being made to people who had paid the higher sum. There was no hire purchase system, as there had been for 'Andersons'.

[5] Under the new classification of areas, described on p. 534, those in the most vulnerable group were given first claim on the supply of 'Morrisons'.

[6] L.R.C. No. 320, 3rd March 1941; H.S.C. 64A/41, 8th March 1941. The railways at first allowed a reduction in standard rates for carriage, as they had done for 'Andersons'. But from October 1941 'Morrisons' became subject to a new flat rate introduced for the railway traffic of each Government Department, irrespective of the type of goods or the distance carried and including collection, delivery and incidental services. (S.R. & O. 1942, No. 151, 28th January 1942.)

When the first designs were being prepared, a two-tier model for the use of large families had been suggested and rejected. Though in April 1941 the Research and Experiments Department produced such a design it was feared that its introduction might dislocate arrangements for distributing the table shelter, and the decision to manufacture this model was not taken until the autumn.

Though distribution of 'Morrisons' started too late for much benefit to be derived from them during the Big Blitz, those which underwent this test emerged remarkably well. In April 1941 the Research and Experiments Department undertook to test indoor shelters of various designs being placed on the market by private firms; certificates were issued for those which reached the required standard and if a specimen had weaknesses the manufacturer was given advice about re-designing.

In June a revised version of *Your Home as an Air Raid Shelter* was issued with the title *Shelter at Home*.[1] This included information about three types of shelter which could be put inside refuge rooms—the 'Morrison', a commercially made steel shelter, and a timber-framed structure designed by the Ministry of Home Security. Some technical consultants were already offering reduced rates to householders for advice on preparing refuge rooms, and some local attempts were now made to compile lists of consultants willing to give free service to people unable to pay a fee.[2]

New types of protection had to be devised for workers in factories and offices who found it impracticable to use existing shelters during short and frequent daylight raids. In September 1940, leaflets were distributed containing a message from the Prime Minister asking employers and workers in essential industries to continue to work after the siren, and explaining that arrangements would be worked out between managements and workers for an industrial warning system within the framework of the public system and for special methods of protection to reduce the risk of casualties.[3] The length of the industrial warning by roof-spotters varied considerably, but not more than fifteen to twenty seconds could be guaranteed, which meant that workers could not reach shelters situated over about fifty feet away. In September, after inspecting factories in London, the Ministry gave advice on methods of improvising suitable protection in various types of buildings.[4] For example, floor area of workshops should be divided up as much as possible by dwarf walls, machinery, benches or stacks of products behind which workers could shelter when danger was imminent. If the roof was of light

---

[1] p. 371.

[2] H.S.C. 135/41, 12th June 1941.

[3] pp. 364, 422.

[4] Memorandum No. 16, *Emergency Protection in Factories* (H.M.S.O. 1940).

construction, some form of covering could be given at each work-place by use of existing fixtures or materials being manufactured. Advice about the protection of glass was included. The Inland Revenue agreed, after some hesitation, to regard the cost of most of these measures as revenue expenditure, while cases of especially elaborate measures would be considered on their merits.

Probably the most essential of these measures were those against flying glass from windows, skylights and glass partitions shattered by blast. On 16th November the Minister of Labour issued an Order compelling occupiers of factories employing more than 250 people to safeguard workers from this risk.[1] Scrim and similar net-ting, glass substitutes, bricks, timber and roofing materials suitable for this purpose could be obtained without much difficulty. But supplies of the most effective material—small-mesh wire netting— were limited. Firms were urged to deal immediately with all glass which could be removed or treated with other materials.[2] An arrangement was later made with the expanded metal industry for preference to be given to certain orders; supplies of wire netting were then reserved for vital factories and small-mesh expanded metal was officially recommended as a substitute in less vital factories and offices.[3]

Deep Shelter Policy Revised

Most of these measures, taken as a result of battle experience, conformed with the dispersal principle. But the Government's decision, closely linked with this principle, not to provide 'bomb-proof' shelter was still often being challenged, and the deep shelters agitation naturally received stimulus from the attacks.[4] By the end of September 1940 its development was causing the Government real concern. Though entangled with politics, and especially with Communist Party activities, it was gaining support from the more moderate Press and from many inspired only by desire for the public safety. Despite publication of the Hailey Report there was still much confusion of thought about the Government's policy, some-times misinterpreted as an objection in principle to safe shelter. Moreover, the public had removed one of the chief objections to deep shelters—the difficulty of quick access—by developing the habit of all-night sheltering. By October the whole question had to be urgently reviewed.

The Cabinet decided at the end of this month that though deep shelters could not be anywhere extensively provided, a new system

---

[1] Factories (Glass Protection) Order, 1940, S.R. & O. No. 2013.
[2] Ministry of Labour and National Service Circular No. 845262, 21st November 1940.
[3] H.S.R. 23/41, 23rd January 1941.
[4] pp. 371–372.

of tunnels linked to the London Tubes should be bored and tunnelling authorised in the provinces where, with the aid of natural features, this could be done economically.[1] The decision as regards London was clearly influenced by the fact that the public had already turned many Tube stations into dormitories. Deep shelters in natural tunnels and caves would not, as the Home Secretary had emphasised in Parliament on 9th October, be an innovation.[2] But hitherto, though the Government had approved a small number of projects of this kind strongly pressed by particular local authorities, it had generally viewed them with small enthusiasm.

Besides those already provided by local authorities, some 'natural' shelters had been contrived by collective initiative or as a result of individual enterprise. For example, from 12–15,000 people, many from the East and South East of London, sheltered during the autumn raids in caves at Chislehurst, Kent. These had been provided with electric light and water by two private citizens (one of whom held the lease of a section of the caves formerly used for cultivating mushrooms), and the shelterers subscribed money for cleaning, sanitary arrangements and so on and appointed 'captains' to keep order. After some agitation in Parliament and the Press structural improvements were made at Government expense and bunks and a medical post installed. The shelter was eventually taken over by the local authority, though an effort was made to maintain the 'self-help' spirit among the shelterers.

In January, 1941 it was decided not to attempt to construct heavily protected surface shelters for the public, since these would need much labour and materials and cost about £25 per head. The Government had no intention of generally abandoning the dispersal and moderate protection policies, and the amount of bomb-proof shelter would still be relatively very small. But what there was of this would no longer be intended only for key workers but would be available without discrimination to protect what a member of the Government bluntly called 'unselected lives'.

By the end of 1940 preliminary plans had been made for the L.P.T.B. to construct, at Government expense, two parallel tunnels, 16 ft. 6 in. in diameter and 1,200 ft. long, underneath the platforms and tunnels at each of ten Tube stations.[3] The tunnels, divided into two decks, would include kitchens, first aid posts and sanitation

---

[1] Home Secretary's broadcast on Civil Defence, 3rd November 1940. Mr Herbert Morrison had succeeded Sir John Anderson as Home Secretary early in October.

[2] H. of C. Deb., Vol. 365, Cols. 457 ff.

[3] The stations were: Clapham North, Clapham South, Chancery Lane, Goodge Street, Camden Town, Oval, Stockwell, Clapham Common, St. Paul's, Belsize Park. The last mentioned was not selected until April. Leicester Square had been suggested but had the disadvantage of being an interchange station. Considerable delay was experienced at St. Paul's as the result of a warning by the Dean and Chapter that the shelters might affect the Cathedral's foundations.

and be entered through existing station entrances. They would accommodate about 9,600 shelterers at each station, at a total cost estimated at £1.5 million—or from £15–16 per shelterer. It was agreed that the Board should be given the option of taking these tunnels over for a system of express trains at the end of the war.

When work began it was expected that the first shelter would be ready in July 1941. As will later be noticed, miscalculations and labour difficulties caused postponement of this date until nearly a year after the big blitz was over. As with most deep shelter projects, its cost also proved to have been much under-estimated.

Following examination of the possibility of boring tunnels in the chalk hills of South London, schemes were made for shelters in Bostall Woods, Woolwich and Jack Cade's Cavern, Blackheath. Both of these were abandoned at the end of 1941 since they would have involved diverting labour from the strengthening of existing shelters. The Government began inquiry into the possible use of mines as shelters, and the Mines Department gave Regional Commissioners lists of disused mine drifts in various parts of Britain.[1]

Experience of bombing, it has been noticed, caused stronger protection to be provided for the Government.[2] In September 1940, the Cabinet decided to continue in Whitehall until it was bombed out or communications broke down; and this decision was reaffirmed the next February after many bombs had already dropped within a thousand yards of the Cenotaph. In the late autumn of 1940 part of the New Public Offices in Whitehall was much strengthened, and early in 1941 a thick concrete slab was added to give the sub-basement of this building extra protection. During the first half of 1941 the Government built some strong steel-framed buildings in central London and four 'fortresses,' which came to be popularly known as 'citadels'.

Distribution Changes

The character of the raids necessitated two important changes in distribution. The obligation to provide shelter was extended to factory premises throughout the country (which involved extension of the 'specified areas'); and the attempt to give roughly equal protection to the general public throughout all vulnerable areas was much modified.

Industrial shelter had been compulsory under the 1939 Act only in areas specified at that time as vulnerable or in premises individually specified. In August 1940, however, the Trades Union Congress adopted the view that as the whole country had become

---

[1] H.S.C. 284/40, 22nd November 1940.
[2] pp. 400–401.

liable to attack workers in other factories which had no shelter were undergoing an unreasonable risk. Specification of the whole country, which the T.U.C. suggested, seemed to the Government too extreme a step, as there were still many areas where raids were unknown. Yet though the authorities would have preferred to exclude factories in remote districts from this obligation, it was found in practice to take too long to sort these out. On 1st November, therefore, occupiers of all factories employing more than fifty persons not covered by existing Orders were warned they would be expected to provide shelters. The requirements of the 1939 Act were then formally applied to all these factories (and to commercial buildings which included factories) by specifying whole areas or individual premises.[1]

The areas hitherto specified had been mainly industrial centres of some size. Almost all industrial districts were now included, and the opportunity was taken to consolidate boundaries. Commercial buildings in these areas came within the scope of the new Order, though no such buildings were specified individually. Government offices with staffs of over fifty in the new areas had also to be provided with shelters.

It was essential that new factory shelters should be near actual places of work. They were expected to conform as far as possible to the standards of the shelter Code;[2] but where this was impracticable occupiers were advised to adopt the emergency measures recommended for factories whose more substantial shelter was relatively out of reach.[3] On the whole, those now put under this obligation responded more slowly than those whose factories had been specified in July 1939. This was chiefly due to shortages of labour and materials and the difficulties of construction work after attacks had begun.

Before May 1940 the Government had set out to provide a roughly equal standard of public protection throughout the areas then thought to be vulnerable. But when supplies of labour and materials began to decrease it became impossible to supply even free domestic shelters to all newly specified areas, and much less to provide universal heavier protection.[4] Moreover, equality of protection appeared less justified when the heaviest attacks were found to fall, in fact, on a limited number of areas. The most logical course seemed to be to concentrate resources on areas already under heavy

---

[1] S.R. & O. 1940, No. 2210, 31st December.

[2] pp. 193-194.

[3] Shelters conforming to the Code were eligible for the usual Exchequer grant if they had already been provided voluntarily or were provided within three months of the Order making them obligatory. Emergency protective measures were usually eligible for an income tax allowance.

[4] H.S.C. 163/40, 6th July 1940.

bombardment and a few others which appeared highly probable targets. In the spring of 1941, therefore, the Ministry divided the country into three types of area: (1) those which had suffered intense and repeated bombing and some of similar national importance which had so far escaped, (2) those of considerable size and importance and dense population, and lesser centres in the East, South East, South and South West which seemed particularly liable to attack and (3) the rest of the country, including the bulk of the old non-specified areas and many of those originally specified.[1]

Maximum effort was concentrated on the first group, which was given first claim on 'Morrisons', and provided as quickly as possible with a reserve of shelter in steel-framed buildings in an attempt to make public shelter of some kind available for about 25 per cent. of those without any household shelter. In the second group similar measures were attempted but given lower priority, and only about half as much public shelter was considered necessary. In the third group the ideal plan would have been to provide everyone with shelter near their homes. But since this was impracticable, the best course seemed to be to aim at a small amount of well distributed protection which would cater for the minority who chose to leave their homes at night and could also be used as public shelter by day[2].

This classification of areas was used to apportion the inadequate labour and materials. Thus in April 1941 it was estimated that over the next six months it would be possible to undertake shelter works of a value of £12 million employing a force of only about 40,000 workers. Portions of this force were allocated to different Regions, which were expected to devote them solely to areas in the first two classes. In the third class only local labour, which was liable to be removed by the Ministry of Labour without notice, was allowed.[3] London Region, to keep within its allocation, had to reduce its estimated requirements of new construction by 50 per cent. and of shelter improvements by 30 per cent.

This sub-division of the country related only to public and household shelters. The obligation to provide shelter still extended to all factories throughout the country and to commercial buildings in 'specified' areas, which included some areas in the third, least vulnerable, category.[4]

---

[1] A small number of areas which had not been specified in 1939 were, however, included in the first two groups.

[2] H.S.R. 68/41, 27th March 1941.

[3] H.S.R. 97/41, 25th April 1941.

[4] It was decided, however, that shelter should not be provided in Government offices situated in any areas in the third category, even if these were 'specified'. Government offices situated in the small number of areas in the first two categories which were 'unspecified' were dealt with on their merits. The construction of shelter was not usually authorised in these areas unless they were likely to be subject to day-time raids.

Response Grows at the Circumference, 1941 – 42

By the middle of May 1941 the Government had thus made a substantial effort to fit shelter policy to the pattern of attack. The most urgent problems raised by all-night use of shelters had been solved; and, in London at least, most of the weaker shelters had been strengthened or closed. But the more ambitious welfare activities had hardly begun. Many shelters still had to be strengthened, and more were needed. Work on new Tube tunnels in London and on most of the natural deep shelters elsewhere had only just started, and the new system of distribution had scarcely been tried out.

Much remained to be done in the next few months especially in the provinces, and since raiding was greatly reduced conditions favoured progress. But the official atmosphere of urgency remained; for though this phase appears in retrospect as a breathing space the authorities were engaged in much preparation for a renewal of heavy attack in the autumn and winter. It was not until the spring of 1942 that the scale of shelter activity at all levels was much reduced.

Activities were still seriously hampered by labour shortages. By the end of July 1941 it was clear that the allocations made to Regions in April would have to cover work on other civil defence needs besides shelters, such as strengthening report centres and providing static water supplies. Regional Commissioners were advised to place shelter work last in order of priority. In October it was decided that new shelters should only be built in the least vulnerable areas in exceptional circumstances;[1] and it was clear that even in the main danger zones there would have to be considerable reduction in the number of workers.[2] Two months later, however, the Ministry of Labour agreed not to ask local authorities to dismiss men surplus to their quota employed on civil defence works until it had made definite arrangements to transfer them to other employment.

Because of labour shortage most local authorities, even in the more vulnerable areas, concentrated mainly on remedying structural defects in existing shelters and making them more comfortable to sleep in. By the end of September 1941 most public and communal shelters built with lime mortar had been examined and, if necessary, temporarily closed. Meanwhile, some of these, especially in London,

---

[1] But the classification of areas was at the same time slightly modified, certain areas in the third category being partially up-graded. (H.S.R. 255/41, 10th October 1941.)

[2] H.S.R. 253/41, 10th October. It was shortly afterwards announced (H.S.R. 255/41, 13th October) that shelters and other civil defence building work might, where appropriate, be scheduled under the Essential Work (Building and Civil Engineering) Order (S.R. & O. 1941 No. 822). It was at first proposed to schedule particular building firms engaged on this work, but it was later decided that sites should be scheduled instead. (H.S.R. 59/42, 11th March 1942.)

were being strengthened by the new method introduced at the end of July.[1] By the end of November some local authorities in the provinces had been able to turn to the less urgent task of strengthening surface shelters built with cement mortar. Work on surface shelters was usually given priority, as these were more likely to be used as dormitories. But in January and February 1942, when bad weather hampered other work, much was done to trenches and basements, though many trenches constructed in 1938 and 1939 had to be abandoned because of the high cost of strengthening them. Local authorities also encouraged householders to erect baffles to protect entrances to their 'Andersons'.[2]

By the late autumn most of the work necessary to prevent serious dampness in trenches and surface shelters was finished, and further deficiences could be dealt with by improved heating and ventilation. In the country as a whole, the large majority of 'Andersons' had been made watertight.

Towards the end of May 1941 the Minister of Health had urged authorities outside London to prepare for heavy attacks in the following winter by providing sanitation, lighting, heating, ventilation and bunk fittings as soon as possible in all public shelters, even if the public were not at present using these to sleep in.[3] Because of labour shortages, however, most authorities could do little more than improve the arrangements for keeping public shelters clean and orderly.[4]

Cleaning of shelters was now transferred in some places from county councils to districts which, since they were the normal sanitary authorities, were often better equipped for this task.[5] In October authorities were empowered to inspect premises where bedding used in public shelters was stored and order this to be disinfected. Infestation in shelters rarely reached serious proportions; though during this autumn certain shelters in Hull and London were reported to be verminous, and one London Tube where this trouble was severe had to be temporarily closed to shelterers. Coventry set up its own 'Hungerford Club', a basement shelter with a bath for vagrants. Local authorities also renewed efforts to educate shelterers in health matters by posters, leaflets and films produced by the Central Council for Health Education.[6] A Ministry of Health poster, 'The British Public is not to be sneezed at', was also used for this purpose.

---

[1] See p. 523. More guidance about ways of strengthening communal shelters was given in H.S.R. 321/41, 2nd December 1941.

[2] H.S.R. 248/41, 1st October. Local authorities were afterwards given permission to erect baffles themselves in exceptional circumstances. (H.S.R. 289/42, 5th November.)

[3] Ministry of Health P.R.O. Circular 23/41, 23rd May 1941.

[4] Ministry of Health P.R.O. Circular 46/41, 26th September 1941.

[5] Ministry of Health P.R.O. Circular 46/41, 26th September 1941 and 81/42, 4th May 1942.

[6] Ministry of Health P.R.O. Circular 52/41, 10th October 1941.

In November the Ministry of Home Security attempted to end the considerable confusion still existing over shelter wardens by announcing that shelters where five hundred or more people might congregate could be provided with a full-time paid warden, but that those with a smaller population (i.e. the large majority) would have to rely on unpaid part-timers.[1] By the end of October, more London Boroughs had appointed welfare officers, thirty welfare committees were functioning and six others were ready for action if needed. More attention was now being given to welfare in communal surface shelters, often with help from the W.V.S. In the provinces, where there were fewer very large shelters, welfare arrangements were usually less organised, though in this autumn some large authorities began to appoint shelter superintendents. After the big blitz ended the London inspectorate had continued their systematic inspection of public shelters, and by early 1942 were able to turn their attention to communal shelters.

Provision of bunks, heating, lighting and so on was also hampered in this phase by bad weather; and the progress of bunking was seriously affected by delays over production. The demand for bunks for public and communal shelters had increased considerably in the summer of 1941;[2] and more were now needed owing to a decision that they were to be installed in domestic surface shelters used regularly for sleeping and in all 'Andersons'.[3] By the end of October less than half the bunks needed had been delivered to local authorities; and though the rate of delivery then increased, in mid-December supplies still fell far short of requirements. By about March 1942, however, most of the areas classed as vulnerable had received enough bunks.

The work of installing heating and electric lighting in public shelters proceeded slowly during this autumn and winter, and heating was also provided in some communal shelters.[4] In December, after six people in Great Yarmouth had suffered carbon monoxide poisoning as a result of misuse of 'Cura' stoves, the Ministry of Health issued another warning about the danger if flue-pipes were not fitted firmly and cleaned regularly, and drew authorities' attention to a scraper which could be used to remove the deposit which formed inside the pipes.[5]

The visible efforts to deal structurally with communal surface shelters and the installation in these of bunks and electric heating combined to make them more popular than they had been in the

---

[1] H.S.R. 296/41, 18th November 1941; p. 520.

[2] Ministry of Health P.R.O. Circular 46/41, 26th September 1941.

[3] Ministry of Health P.R.O. Circulars 33/41, 24th June and 37/41, 11th August 1941.

[4] Ministry of Health P.R.O. Circular 69/42, 28th January 1942.

[5] Ministry of Health P.R.O. Circular 62/41, 6th December 1941; p. 516.

past. Investigations in twelve Metropolitan Boroughs about September 1941 suggested that people had gained more confidence in the safety of these shelters. Some Boroughs had made successful efforts to persuade those entitled to use them to develop a personal interest in keeping them clean and tidy.[1]

Despite labour shortages a small number of new shelters, chiefly communal and domestic, were built in some more vulnerable areas, usually to replace timber-lined trenches and defective surface shelters or to make up for the space taken in existing shelters by introduction of bunks and other amenities. 'Morrisons' were distributed in growing quantities to householders without any domestic shelter in this summer and autumn, and were especially valuable for supplementing shelter in areas where no labour was available.[2] By the end of October over 500,000 had been distributed and many applications were still being received. It was decided that 1,000 two-tier models should be manufactured as an experiment and given to large families in areas where table shelters were being distributed.[3] These were 4 ft. 3 in. high, and would hold two beds fitted one above the other. Families with a table shelter could exchange this for a two-tier model; and those not eligible for free shelters could buy one for £9 15s. od. or obtain one in exchange for a table model and payment of £2 15s. od. Further orders for these shelters made in February and March 1942 brought the total up to nearly 10,000.[4]

In December allocations of steel to all Departments had to be reduced and orders for the manufacture of some 100,000 'Morrisons' were suspended. When the position was reviewed in February it was estimated that 'Morrisons' still in the manufacturers' hands should be more than sufficient to meet outstanding requirements.[5] There were also about 100,000 in Regional reserves and some authorities had received more than they had asked for. But it was realised that if production entirely stopped it would be most difficult to resume it, and the cancelled orders were therefore replaced, though the rate of output was reduced so that production would continue until August 1942.

---

[1] By November 1941 the Ministry had produced a poster designed to popularise surface shelters, but it was decided to hold this in reserve until heavy raiding was resumed. (H.S.R. 315/41, 28th November 1941.)

[2] At the end of November it was agreed that 'Morrisons' might be supplied in certain of the least vulnerable areas to people whose communal shelters were constructed with lime-mortar and could not be strengthened because of shortage of labour. (H.S.R. 314/41, 28th November 1941.)

[3] Two 'Morrisons' (or one 'Morrison' and one 'Anderson') were already being supplied in some places to householders whose families were too large for a single shelter. (H.S.R. 196/41, 2nd August; 228/41, 9th September 1941.)

[4] The actual number was 9,300; these counted towards the total number of 'Morrisons' authorised—i.e., 1,080,000.

[5] H.S.C. 24/42, 7th February 1942.

Besides other distribution, 'Morrisons' were being issued to house-holders exposed to undue danger by the fact that they lived within a thousand yards of an aerodrome.[1] Special arrangements were also necessary in some small towns and villages, principally in the Tunbridge Wells and Cambridge Regions, chosen by the military authorities as 'nodal points' for anti-invasion defence. Civilians in these places, where there was usually little air raid shelter, would be expected to stand firm in an invasion. It was decided in the spring of 1941 to provide free shelters for the total population likely to remain in these 'points' in the two Regions mentioned, though progress in doing this was slow.

By the autumn more nodal points had been designated in these and other Regions; and all such places were divided into three classes (according to the time they might be expected to hold out and other factors) and the supply of free shelters restricted to the first class. Free shelter was also provided for many of the inhabitants of certain places called 'vulnerable defiles' situated on important lines of communication.

Shelter for these various places usually took the form of surplus 'Morrisons' and 'Andersons'. For example, in December 1941 13,000 'Andersons' and 10,000 extension sheets were transferred from local authorities' stocks. Difficulties were created by population increases due to the return of evacuees, and by the up-grading of some nodal points in the lower classes to the first class.

Some more local authorities took advantage of the Government's changed attitude towards deep shelters.[2] Thus early in 1941 Surrey County Council began to bore five tunnels in the chalk of the North Downs. Steps were taken to sub-divide and strengthen the roofs of caves cut in a sand bed in Nottingham and used for shelter since the start of the blitz. Tunnelling at Tranmere Quarry, Birkenhead was begun in the spring of 1941 and by February 1942 a third of this tunnel had been lined and lighting and bunks installed; another tunnel at Birkenhead begun in December 1941 was nearly ready at the end of May. Though the Government had no general inten-tion of providing special shelter for 'trekkers' they approved, some-what reluctantly, in June 1941 a project for tunnels in Portsdown Hill for 3,000 of the 30,000 trekkers from Portsmouth.[3] In December they agreed to the adaptation of an existing tunnel at Egg Buck-land, Portsmonth for a similar purpose.[4]

---

[1] It was decided in the autumn that this arrangement should not be applied to decoy aerodromes, as the Air Ministry requisitioned houses within four hundred yards of the site and provided shelter for occupied houses between four and eight hundred yards away. Requests for 'Morrisons' from people living near anti-aircraft gun and search-light sites, etc. were also refused.

[2] pp. 530–532.

[3] These tunnels were later extended to accommodate 5,000.

[4] This particular scheme was subjected to protracted delays.

As early as February 1941, however, the Government was looking with diminished favour on local deep shelter projects. Conditions in some tunnel shelters—notably those at Ramsgate, which an observer described as the equivalent of a gipsy camp—revived fears that widespread deep-shelter mentality might develop. Apprehension also grew over the cost of tunnelling schemes, since even where natural conditions seemed most suitable it was found that after boring the tunnels needed lining to support roofs and reduce dampness.[1] A few tunnels, for example the Ouseburn Culvert at Newcastle, were already having to be partly closed because of structural defects. In January 1942 the Ministry of Home Security announced that it was most unlikely that further deep shelter proposals would be approved, save in exceptional circumstances.[2]

By the early summer of 1941 it had become clear that the new London Tube shelters would take much longer to construct and be more expensive than had been expected.[3] In August work on the whole of the St. Paul's site and on half the Oval site was abandoned. At the end of November it was decided to abandon the second half of the Oval site, and to make no attempt to provide means of communication between the tunnels and station platforms. Nevertheless, the first tunnel was not ready until March 1942. By the end of May another was half-finished and available for use by about 4,000 people, and two more were sufficiently advanced to be able if necessary to shelter about 3,000 persons each.

The eight of these shelters eventually completed cost £2¼ million, and since standards of accommodation had been raised they were considered adequate for only 8,000 persons apiece. Thus the cost per head was more than £35, or well over twice the original estimate.

In November a committee under the chairmanship of the retiring Lord Mayor of London, including representatives of the L.C.C. and L.P.T.B., was formed to undertake the management of these shelters in co-operation with London's Regional Commissioners.

Contraction

Long before the spring of 1942, when practical shelter work had to be severely reduced, the central administrative organisation concerned had shrunk considerably. In June 1941 the two divisions of the Ministry's Shelters Department had been amalgamated and much reduced in size.[4] Though central administrative effort had to some extent taken second place to nation-wide application, a heavy

---

[1] The tunnels in Surrey (an extreme example) cost more than twice the original estimate, despite the fact that one of the sites was abandoned.

[2] H.S.R. 21/42, 28th January 1942.

[3] pp. 531–532.

[4] See pp. 303, 512.

burden rested on the staff who remained. The head of the Shelters Division expressed concern lest its size should be determined by a conviction that everything regarding shelters was 'over bar the shouting'. It was, nevertheless, becoming clear that only a small share of the nations' resources could in future be spared for air raid shelters.

Early in April 1942 it was announced that the allocation of labour for civil defence works would be reduced from an existing level of 40,000 to 30,000 by the middle of May and 20,000 by the end of June, when it would be completely withdrawn;[1] though in practice men working on shelters would not be dismissed until the Ministry of Labour had arranged for them to be transferred to other essential work.[2] It was at first feared that after June local authorities would have to rely for shelter work on whatever labour might be provided by an elaborate 'garrison' scheme being prepared by the Ministry of Works and Buildings to secure enough building labour in towns of 10,000 inhabitants and over for demolition and clearance, maintaining services and repairing air raid damage.[3]

However, a complete remodelling took place of the system of allocating mobile building labour, which became almost entirely engaged in work sponsored by the Service and Supply Departments.[4] A special allocation was, however, made for certain shelter works, which included shelter in the most vulnerable nodal points, four tunnels in Birkenhead, Newcastle and Plymouth, the new London Tube shelters and new shelters in a few other important places.[5] Strengthening and installing amenities in shelters liable to be much used in the most vulnerable areas also continued, though for this councils had to rely on local labour. In the least vulnerable areas all shelter work was banned entirely, with the exception of simple maintenance work which could be carried on by the local authorities' staffs.

By late October 1942 all the 'Morrison' table shelters ordered had been manufactured and a reserve of about 2,000 accumulated.[6] Distribution of these had been gradually extended even to the least vulnerable areas; weekly demands varied between 4 and 14,000 and

---

[1] H.S.R. 85/42, 8th April.

[2] H.S.R. 102/42, 8th May 1942. It had been estimated at the end of 1941 that with the present labour force it would be possible to complete about 70 per cent. of shelter work outstanding at the end of August 1941 by the end of March 1942; and that if the labour allocation for the following three months was cut to 38,000 the work would be virtually complete by the end of June.

[3] H.S.R. 123/42, 1st June 1942. See C. M. Kohan, *Works and Buildings* (1952) in this series.

[4] H.S.R. 149/42, 23rd June 1942.

[5] H.S.R. 300/42, 27th November 1942.

[6] The last order for 'Morrison' two-tier shelters was placed in April 1942. The rate of production of these had been exceptionally slow and aroused much public criticism.

now were increasing as a result of 'tip and run' raids on coastal towns and elsewhere which often gave people no time to reach public shelters or even 'Andersons' at the bottom of their gardens.[1] In existing circumstances, however, the production of more 'Morrisons' could hardly be justified. Rather than continue distribution to meet all routine requirements, it seemed wiser to create reserves in different parts of the country which could be sent quickly to any place which might be heavily attacked in future. At the end of November distribution ceased in London and (with a few exceptions) in the Midlands and North-West.[2] Issues to people living close to aerodromes and to nodal points and so on were also stopped by the end of this year.

This decision, together with labour shortage, meant it was out of the question to replace or supplement shelters in the 'tip and run' areas by 'Morrisons', or indeed by any other protection suited to this type of attack. Public anxiety was nevertheless growing over attacks of this kind on a number of schools, such as that on a boys' school at Petworth which caused 31 fatal casualties. Some schools were therefore supplied with 'Morrisons' which could be placed singly in the smaller class-rooms, or 'Andersons' to be erected immediately outside entrances or close to class-room walls so that children could pass directly into them.

During the winter of 1941-42 the Ministry had been collecting data about surplus local stocks of 'Andersons'. By August 1942 there was still a considerable overall surplus of these, and it was decided to extend distribution to all areas in which 'Morrisons' were being supplied (except defended places, which were receiving special treatment).[3] This meant that after distribution of 'Morrisons' was stopped in certain areas at the end of November, 'Andersons' were still available. Some 'Andersons' were also used as huts for training Fire Guards and for storing ammunition.[4]

During the last months of 1941 the numbers sleeping in public shelters had steadily declined. Though the intermittent raiding from the spring of 1942 again caused much resort to this practice, more people now preferred domestic shelters. Nearly all the medical posts in London shelters were closed and doctors made weekly instead of nightly visits. Shelter inspections ceased to be a matter of routine, though occasional visits were made to ensure that shelters would be ready if raids began again. Welfare work was now extended outside

---

[1] These demands were partially met by transferring 'Morrisons' from the reserve held by London Region. See pp. 432–438.

[2] H.S.R. 298/42, 26th November 1942.

[3] H.S.R. 189/42, 10th August 1942. 'Andersons' were not however issued in areas where they were likely to need waterproofing.

[4] Surface shelters which had not been equipped or were defective were used for similar purposes. (H.S.R. 31/43, 15th February, 61/43, 31st March 1943.)

the shelters; for example, parties of London shelterers visited the Zoo and went swimming in the Serpentine.

A large problem now arose of preventing unoccupied shelters from being misused, and complaints about damage and theft of fittings had become frequent by the autumn of 1941. In December some authorities locked shelters during the day and quiet periods, giving keys to the wardens' post or to the police so that shelters could be opened immediately the sirens sounded. They usually kept a few shelters open at night for those who wished to sleep there regularly, even when there was no alert.[1] One of the more successful devices for locking shelters was a strong inside bolt which could be reached from outside through a hole covered by a glass door secured by a padlock; wardens or police could open the shelter by unlocking the padlock and drawing the bolt, but in an emergency shelterers could break the glass door. Pilferers found it more difficult to remove such fixtures though there was, of course, nothing to prevent them from breaking the glass, and sometimes the doors themselves were smashed or entirely removed. It sometimes proved necessary to use a special device for locking up lamp bulbs in shelters.

The Press and various organisations co-operated with local officials in campaigns against these offences. Ministry of Health inspectors were very successful in some of the worst areas in encouraging women shelterers to undertake cleaning and looking after the shelters. Though by the end of 1942 this situation was improving, complaints were still frequent that the penalties imposed were inadequate and in January 1943 the Home Office asked magistrates to take a serious view of these offences. The possibility of making a special Defence Regulation was considered, but this could hardly be justified as offenders could be punished under the existing law for almost every kind of damage to shelters.

The fact that shelters had to be kept closed still caused uneasiness to Parliament and the public, and early in 1943 the Government reminded authorities of the importance of ensuring that people would have quick access to them in an emergency.[2] It was in this period that many householders began to use domestic shelters as stores for bicycles, garden tools and other belongings. Unless this was likely to cause deterioration or was undertaken for profit no attempt was made to prevent them. One A.R.P. Controller in Scotland, however, was officially asked to take 'all possible steps' to prevent a householder from using his shelter as a hen-house.

The numbers sleeping in London's Tubes also began to fall off soon after the Big Blitz ended. The L.P.T.B. suggested in July 1941 that some stations should be closed to shelterers, but the Government

---

[1] Ministry of Health P.R.O. Circular 63/41, 9th December 1941.
[2] Ministry of Health P.R.O. Circular 104/43, 19th February 1943.

would not accept this risk at that time. But twelve months later shelterers were temporarily excluded from thirty-nine stations and parts of two others where they caused most inconvenience to traffic. Stations within easy reach were kept open as shelters, and skeleton staffs were retained in those closed so that they could, if necessary, be opened during alerts. The closing of stations roused strong public criticism, and in June 1943 it was arranged that they should all be opened automatically in the event of an alert and should remain open for the next three nights, or if necessary longer. The next month, when alerts in London became more frequent, a number were permanently re-opened. In the autumn, however, bunks not needed for ticket-holders were removed from some stations where they were causing inconvenience.

In the spring of 1943 the Board urged the Government to take further steps, now that the enemy was using heavier bombs, to protect the Tubes from flooding from water-mains, sewers or the Thames. Watertight doors had been fitted at a number of stations before the blitz to safeguard them from the first two dangers. But a disaster at Balham Station in October 1940 when a number of shelterers were overwhelmed by liquid debris had shown that risk still remained. After technical experts had examined certain stations, the Ministry decided that the risk was not great enough to justify closing any of them to shelterers and a proposal to install floodgates in two of them was later abandoned.

Flooding from the Thames was a more serious danger. For though sections of the Tubes under the river could be cut off by floodgates from the rest of the system when the sirens sounded, this did not eliminate the risks of a bomb breaching an under-river Tube before floodgates were closed or of the floodgates being damaged. Nonetheless, the Government concluded that some of these risks would have to be accepted and rejected an elaborate L.P.T.B. scheme in 1943 for installing more floodgates and watertight doors in certain low-level passages at a cost of about £25,000. The Ministry was more concerned about the risks of five of its new Tube shelters being flooded, and special floodgates to protect these were installed at a cost of about £3,000.

About this time, when the public expected reprisals for heavier R.A.F. raids on Berlin, there was a serious disaster at a large shelter adapted from a Tube station under construction at Bethnal Green. On the night of 3rd March 1943, large numbers of people descending a dimly lit staircase into the shelter after the siren had sounded were subjected to sudden pressure from those behind them, alarmed by a salvo of anti-aircraft rockets. A woman who had nearly reached the bottom fell and blocked the stairway which, according to the magistrate who investigated the incident, was 'converted from a corridor into a charnel house in from ten to fifteen seconds'.[1] The disaster again focused attention on the difficulty of controlling crowds at the entrances to large shelters, which had been one of the Government's strongest arguments against deep shelters. It was also a grim reminder of the conditions which could ensue if people lost self-control in an air raid, though in this instance no bombs had dropped. The entrance to Bethnal Green station was immediately altered and walls were erected around entrances to other Tube stations.

Many London authorities then examined entrances to large shelters, particularly those with descending stairways, and where possible installed crush barriers and sliding gates and saw that stairways were adequately lit and fitted with handrails.[2] The disaster made a deep impression on public opinion, and prompted a few local councils to produce ambitious schemes for strengthening shelters to eliminate the risk of injury and panic, most of which proved quite impracticable owing to scarcity of labour and materials.

In the spring of 1942, when the first of the new tunnel shelters under certain stations was nearly ready, the New Tube Shelter Committee had urged the Ministry to open the shelters, or parts of them, to give staffs and the public experience of using them.[3] This idea also appealed to the L.P.T.B. since it would enable shelterers to be transferred from other Tubes where they were causing some inconvenience. But as maintenance costs would be high and the new shelters were not really suitable for intermittent raids, the Government decided to keep them in reserve.

In August, when seven were almost complete and provided with bunks and amenities, the Ministry agreed that skeleton staffs should always be available in these so that Tube shelterers could be transferred to them if heavy raiding was resumed and the Tube system became seriously overcrowded.[4] But the shelter committee was still dissatisfied, since the decision to transfer shelterers was to be taken by the Regional Commissioner and not by the stationmaster or shelter superintendents, and there would be no arrangements for allocating places in the new shelters in advance. This controversy, which attracted much public attention, continued throughout 1942 and 1943, and on several occasions the New Tube Shelter Committee threatened to resign.

Meanwhile, the Government was discovering other uses for this underground accommodation. At the end of 1942 part of the Goodge St. shelter was made available for General Eisenhower's London headquarters, and later two others were adapted for use by the

---

[1] See p. 438. This disaster caused the death by suffocation of 178 shelterers.

[2] H.S.C. 70/43, 19th April 1943.

[3] pp. 531-532, 540.

[4] At an eighth station, Belsize Park, tunnelling was completed but floors had not yet been erected in all sections and there were no bunks.

operational staffs of Government Departments. A section of one shelter was used each night as a hostel for American troops, and sections of the other four were used by British troops at week-ends. At the end of 1943 it was decided that all these new Tube shelters should be temporarily held in reserve to be available if needed as extra 'citadel' accommodation.

Mobilising Reserves

The preparations starting in 1943 to meet the new challenge of V-weapon attacks are recorded later in this volume.[1] Notice of some of the efforts to provide suitable shelter in areas likely to be attacked by this method is nevertheless appropriate here. For these proved of much value during the 'Little Blitz' of early 1944 which, apart from being concentrated on London, was not essentially different from the earlier attacks.

It was assumed that to be effective in attacks by pilotless aircraft or long-range rockets, shelters would have to be easily accessible. Yet a review of London shelter in the summer of 1943 had shown that large numbers still had no domestic shelter, and that many thousands would be unable to reach a public shelter quickly. Though the obvious solution to the problem was the 'Morrison', production of these had stopped twelve months before; and in order to build up a reserve issue had been discontinued in various areas, including London. At the beginning of October it was decided that another 100,000 'Morrisons' should be manufactured and that the reserves held in Scotland, the North of England, the Midlands and North Wales should be moved to the vicinity of London and to the Reading and Tunbridge Wells Regions, from where they could, if necessary, be used to supply London.

Large-scale redistribution of 'Morrisons' and the procurement of new ones called for a substantial administrative effort. Nonetheless, most reserves were transferred during the autumn, and by the end of January 1944 some 12,000 had deen distributed to London householders. At the beginning of this year, however, preparations for the Allied invasion of Europe began to choke the railways with more important traffic, and it became impossible to transport new shelters from manufacturers in the north of England. This difficulty, combined with delays in the production of spanners and nuts, meant that no new shelters could be delivered before late February or early March, when it was expected that the V-weapon attacks would have begun. Arrangements were made for some to be shipped coastwise to London; but in mid-February the contract for the remaining 'Morrisons' (about 20,000) was cancelled.

---

[1] Chapter XV below.

The 'Little Blitz' had meanwhile begun.[1] In February another 17,000 'Morrisons' were distributed to London householders; and it was estimated at the end of this month that these shelters in reserve in London, with those which could be transferred from other Regions and new ones nearing completion, totalled over 100,000. Redistribution was controlled by the Shelters Division, which received applications from local authorities and put them into touch at once with a Regional store or another authority which could meet their needs. Thus supplies usually began to arrive on the day after the request, and in a few urgent cases deliveries were arranged on the same day. Some London authorities undertook to store more shelters than they would need, so that supplies would be ready for others with less storage space. At no time during these raids did stocks of these shelters held in London Region fall below 27,000. But these reserves were quickly absorbed after the V-weapon attacks began in June, and special steps had then to be taken to replace them.

During the 'Little Blitz' many people began again to sleep in public shelters, and at the end of February the Cabinet considered opening the new Tube shelters to the public. It was once again decided, however, to hold these in reserve, on the grounds that they might be needed for operational purposes and that there was already enough shelter of a fairly high standard for the people of London. Parliament was told of this decision on 29th February.[2]

---

[1] See pp. 439-443.
[2] H. of C. Deb., Vol. 397, Cols. 1249–1251.

CHAPTER XIII

ADAPTING THE CIVIL DEFENCE SERVICES

Manpower

THE manning of civil defence and the adjustments of the
disheartening 'stand-by' period and of the first months of
scattered air attack have been described in previous chapters.[1] Before continuing with the story of civil defence manpower
from September 1940 onwards, it is perhaps worth recalling the
two important principles of recruitment and organisation that had
so far been taken as axiomatic: first, that civil defence was a volunteer service, comprising a core of whole-time paid volunteers
reinforced by a much larger body of part-time unpaid volunteers;
secondly, that it was a local service, organised by local authorities
for the protection of local communities. The first of these principles
had already suffered severe attack by the issue of 'freezing orders'
in June and July 1940[2]. The solvents of total mobilisation and of
actual air attack were soon to erode these early principles yet further.
Stage by stage—through 'freezing orders' for whole-time and part-
time workers, through compulsory enrolment under the National
Service Acts and the compulsory recruitment of part-time personnel
—the volunteer principle was cut away, to be largely replaced by
the principle of universal responsibility and universal participation.
Stage by stage too, though much less completely, civil defence ceased
to be a purely local service and central government, generally through
the Regional Commissioners' organisation, came to play a larger
role. The cracks in local organisation came from such developments
as the substitution of a National Fire Service for the locally run
fire brigades and Auxiliary Fire Service, the recruitment and control
under the National Service Acts of a national civil defence force and
the creation of mobile reserves under Regional control. The first
section of this chapter will trace the change in civil defence from the
volunteer stage to the establishment of compulsion, and from its
parochial beginnings to its maturity as a more national service. It
will also describe the difficulties confronting the civil defence services

---

[1] Chapter VIII, pp. 340–352; Chapter IX, pp. 372–377.
[2] See Chapter IX, p. 375.

548

in contending for manpower against the vital demands of the Service and Production Departments in an increasingly competitive labour market.

(i) Reservation and Compulsion

Although alleged overstaffing had been the first problem of civil defence strengths, it was not long before the wastage of trained men began to cause concern. As early as February 1940 arrangements had to be made to reserve and defer auxiliary firemen,[1] and some of the younger men in the Rescue Parties, and in June and July the first 'freezing orders' were issued.[2] The onset of heavy raids in September 1940 quickly revealed the need for further protection of civil defence strengths.

By September, the Wardens' Service was in trouble in London. During June and July 1940, one-tenth of the London paid male wardens had already been lost;[3] and the situation was serious when, in September, London became the main target of the *Luftwaffe*. Temporary deferment attangements for London wardens over 30 were, therefore, negotiated,[4] and in October they were 'frozen'.[5] In February 1941 the deferment arrangements were extended until the following autumn to prevent the loss of 6,000 trained wardens under 41 years of age.

When the question of the deferment of the London wardens came up again at the end of August 1941, the situation was critical; out of 16,953 paid male wardens, 2,370 were under 35 and there could be no hope of saving them from the call-up; another 3,403 were between 35 and 40, so that if all up to 40 had to go some 35 per cent. of London's most active paid wardens would be lost. London's experience of air attack had led to a reassessment of the value of the warden and a rejection of the earlier belief, still held in other Regions, that this was a job for older and part-time volunteers.[6] 'The idea that existing wardens can be effectively replaced by new-comers, as if it were merely a matter of manpower of one sort or another, is quite unreal', declared the London Regional Commissioner.

London now proposed a compromise: they suggested that the age of reservation for wardens should be lowered and that for Rescue

---

[1] See Chapter XI, pp. 448-449.

[2] See Chapter IX, p. 375.

[3] 632 to the Armed Forces, 992 to other causes, e.g., industry, out of a total of 16,926.

[4] At first deferment was approved until 31st December 1940; later the deferment arrangement was extended until September 1941.

[5] Civil Defence (Employment) (No. 3) Order, S.R. & O., No. 1839, 16th October 1940.

[6] The importance which wardens acquired under the test of experience is discussed on pp. 564-570.

and First Aid Parties raised. This would involve the reorganisation of their services on a basis of greater interchangeability and would in fact release more manpower.[1] Some of the duties of first aid and rescue parties would be combined and the wardens trained to undertake simple rescue and first aid duties from their local posts. This compromise was adopted for London Region—the age of reservation for whole-time members of the Rescue and First Aid Parties was raised from 30 to 35, and whole-time District Wardens, Deputy District Wardens and Post Wardens over 30 were retained, as well as all other whole-time wardens over 35. By this bargain London Region kept its invaluable 3,400 men wardens over 35 while the call-up gained some 13,700 men from the other branches as against the 5,700 men who would gave been released had the full force of the cut fallen upon the Wardens' Service.[2]

The volunteer principle, already undermined by the issue of various 'freezing orders', suffered its next set-back in connection with recruiting. 'The men and women of the civil defence organisation have stood their ground splendidly', Mr Herbert Morrison had reported to the War Cabinet in December 1940, 'but there are gaps in the ranks—gaps that are dangerous in "blitz" conditions. I ask my colleagues to decide that a firm plan shall be adopted whereby those gaps can be filled and remain filled'. The Fire Service was the most seriously affected. It was usually able to deal with heavy and recurring attacks so long as they were fairly dispersed but there was a danger that it might be overwhelmed by heavy and concentrated attacks; even on the basis of present establishment it was short of 6,000 men, mainly in the target areas, but it was estimated that 10,000 men were needed to bring the service up to efficient strength. The civil defence general services also needed new recruits, especially younger men for their rescue and casualty services and the police estimated that they might require another 10,000 men. The first measure intended to provide these new recruits came in January 1941 when it was announced that men over 30 registering for military service could opt for full-time service in the Police War Reserve, the Auxiliary Fire Service or the First Aid Parties.[3] But as it was unlikely that this measure alone would solve the problem

---

[1] See pp. 573–576.

[2] It is interesting to see the following comment from the Regional Commissioner for London on 9th August 1944, when making a report to the Minister of Home Security for the period to 30th June 1944, and including observations on the period of the flying bomb attacks up to 3rd August 1944—'The strain on manpower has been felt chiefly in the Wardens' Service with its predominance of part-timers. I have never been more convinced of the value of the bargain struck in the autumn of 1941, when we gave up our Rescue and Stretcher Party men under 35 and kept our wardens between 35 and 41, with a few key men under 35'.

[3] H.S.C. 11/41, 8th January 1941, and attached pamphlet C.D.R.1. Acceptance for these services would put a man in a reserved occupation. He would be liable to be posted away from home but in that case would receive a subsistence allowance.

the War Cabinet also agreed to compulsory enrolment, a need quickly confirmed by the two registrations of the 11th and 18th January 1941, when only 400 men opted for civil defence.

During early 1941, a Bill was drafted to cover both option for service in civil defence and the application of direct compulsion to recruitment. It was a delicate task to achieve a proper balance between the civil defence conscript and the civil defence volunteer on the one hand, and between the civil defence conscript and the army conscript on the other; issues of comparative status, conditions of service, pay and discipline were important in both directions. In order to make the best use of the conscript reinforcements, it was proposed to 'nationalise' this part of the Service by making these recruits entirely mobile and servants of the Crown instead of any local authority. The Bill struck at both the original principles of civil defence organisation; for conscription not only attacked the volunteer emphasis but also brought in its train the erosion of local responsibility.

The Act received the Royal Assent on 10th April 1941.[1] During the Commons debate the Minister of Home Security emphasised that friction between conscript and volunteer would be avoided and that there was no question of regarding the volunteer principle as a failure;[2] indeed, the amazing success of civil defence on a voluntary basis was 'one of the greatest things in history'. The Bill had not been brought in because the volunteer principle had failed but because circumstances had changed and pressure on manpower was becoming acute. 'I do not want to say a word or do a thing that will kill the spirit of voluntary, unpaid public service', he said. 'The democracy of our country owes a great deal to it and our democracy will be a poor thing when nobody will do anything for the public interest unless he gets something out of it.'[3]

The Act declared certain civil defence services—the Auxiliary Fire Service, the Police War Reserve and later the Civil Defence Reserve—civil defence *forces*.[4] All these forces received recruits through the Act but never as many as were asked for. The National Fire Service got 24,400 men, mainly in 1941, but the Civil Defence Reserve was allotted only 260 recruits. National manpower shortages, with limited and decreasing allocations to civil defence, prevented any extensive use of this machinery. The Act was, however, the means of obtaining some valuable manpower for the fire services in an increasingly rigid market.

---

[1] National Service Act, 1941. 4 and 5 Geo. 6, Ch. 15.

[2] H. of C. Deb., Vol. 370, Cols. 161-162, 603-670, 19th and 26th March 1941,

[3] H. of C. Deb., Vol. 370, Cols. 657-660, 26th March 1941.

[4] This was done by Statutory Rules and Orders—S.R. & O. 1941, No. 775 for the Auxiliary Fire Service and S.R. & O. 1941, No. 1567 for the Civil Defence Reserve. The Police War Reserve was covered in 4 and 5 Geo. 6, Ch. 15, Sect. 12 (1).

(ii) A Share in the National Manpower Budget

As yet this account of civil defence manpower has been mainly concerned with administrative action taken within the services to preserve and strengthen their various establishments. But it is also necessary to set these problems in the wider context of national manpower resources. Until the end of 1941, and apart from the early stand-by period, the Ministry of Home Security had been able to obtain Cabinet support for most of its proposals to retain and acquire personnel. From the autumn of 1941, however, the demands of civil defence came under more critical scrutiny; along with all other claimants for manpower, it had to accept allocations of labour to fit an overall distribution of national resources planned to win the war.

By the middle of 1941, economic mobilisation for an all-out effort was well under way and manpower had become a key factor. The problem now was to balance the rate of intake into the Fighting Services against the maintenance of a labour force adequate to equip the Services and meet the minimum needs of the civilian sector. If the full demands of the Armed Forces and civil defence were to be met over the next twelve months, said the Minister of Labour in August 1941, it would involve the withdrawal from industry of something like 1 million men and the redistribution of about $2\frac{1}{4}$ million men and women, with inevitable and serious interference in industrial production. Changes on such a scale would be possible only if the nation was prepared to give up 'not only amenities but many things that had been looked upon as almost necessities', and if there were 'throughout the nation a new sense of urgency about the release of men of military age for service in the Forces and the transfer of other manpower to vital work'.

The first task was to fix manpower ceilings for the Services on the basis of their strategic needs, and then to achieve the most efficient balance between the supply of and demand for labour for all other purposes. The 1941 Manpower Survey was the first comprehensive war-time attempt at labour budgeting; it tried to estimate the requirements of labour for essential purposes for the period July 1941 to July 1942, and to distribute the available manpower in the most effective manner. At this stage the demands of the Services, including those of civil defence, tended to be regarded less critically than later on, and the main problem was to apportion the balance between the different sections of production. There was, however, a total deficit in supply of more than 360,000 men if the authorised strengths of the Services and civil defence (which was now demanding an additional 67,000 full-time workers) were to be met. A drastic programme to increase the supply of manpower was, therefore, planned. It involved the replacement of the shelter of reserved occupations by a system of individual deferments, the lowering of the call-up age to 18½ and the recruitment of large numbers of women into industry and the Services. The Minister of Labour was also contemplating measures to impose on all men and women between 18 and 60 some form of national service.

In the light of these great developments, it was clearly necessary to review the manning of the civil defence services. The Minister of Home Security claimed that the policy of his Department so far had been 'to make as few inroads as possible upon the diminishing resources of manpower available for active service with the Forces and to exploit to the fullest extent the time and training of men and already in civil defence'. The case of the civil defence services for labour had always received a sympathetic hearing up to now, and its demands for reservation, 'freezing' orders etc., had usually been satisfied. But the autumn of 1941 was to mark a watershed in national manpower policy. The strategic slant of the war economy was changing; preparedness to meet the attack and hold the line was giving way to active preparations for the offensive. As a contribution, the Minister of Home Security believed that the civilian population was ready, within reason, 'to sacrifice some loss of efficiency in the ministrations of passive defence' if the nation's war effort was proportionately increased in other directions. Although there were already serious manpower deficiencies in certain arms of the Service, it was proposed to deal with these shortages in the main by reorganisation and the fuller use of available resources. A programme on these lines was accordingly approved by the Cabinet. It included the continued deferment of key personnel and the recruitment of men into the fire and police services under the National Service Act, plus a series of economy measures, such as the intensive application of interchangeability to training, the further development of mobile reserves and the compulsory enrolment of part-timers.[1]

The first of these economy measures was the extension of the principle of interchangeability among the different branches of the general services.[2] First steps in this direction had been taken early in 1941 when training in each other's work was offered to Rescue, First Aid and Decontamination Parties. Later, alternative training was made compulsory so that reinforcement from one branch to another could be easily effected.[3]

Mobile reserves, the second line of economy, had first appeared as an operational technique designed to meet the special problems

---

[1] Other minor measures to be taken included variations in shifts, increased hours of work for women and the use of personnel during stand-by periods on other duties.

[2] This development is discussed more fully on pp. 573-576, and also in connection with training on pp. 577 ff.

[3] See 577.

of the Thames Estuary.[1] They were, however, clearly economical in the use of manpower, and as early as April 1941, Sir William Beveridge had written to the Ministry of Home Security: 'Every conceivable economy will be imperative . . . I hope that in any civil defence service in which you can rely upon mobile reserves serving more than one city in place of immobilisation of local reserves in every town of the country you will try to do so'. By the autumn such economies were even more important and they were extended. Mobile reserves were to be sited in convenient central positions in the Regions, ready to serve groups of areas needing reinforcement; this would allow local authorities, especially those that did not seem to be primary targets, to manage with lower establishments. The mobile reserves, which would be under the control of the Regional organisation, would normally consist of detachments sent in rotation from the areas served, though in exceptional cases personnel might be recruited through the National Service Act, 1941 or by permanent transfers from local authority units.

The third line of action was to strengthen part-time establishments. The national plan had always been based on part-time workers, trained and ready to withstand an attack on their own neighbourhood and strengthened by a professional core of whole-time workers. If part-time strengths became too depleted some districts might be unable to contend with even moderate attacks. About one-quarter of a million workers had been lost from the total civil defence establishment between the outbreak of war and June 1941;[2] the loss of whole-timers had now been stopped but in many areas the part-time establishments were in jeopardy. So far the position of part-timers had remained unchanged—they were voluntarily re-cruited and were free to resign. Two complementary measures to alter this were now discussed; first, compulsory enrolment to increase the total strength,[3] and secondly, the 'freezing' of those already enrolled.

As far as the first of these measures was concerned, the Minister of Home Security already possessed powers to enrol men and women for compulsory civil defence duties, though as yet he had only used his powers in connection with fire guard duties.[4] The Minister now suggested, however, that the Ministry of Labour should take on any

---

[1] p. 374. The organisation of mobile reserves is discussed in detail in Chapter XIV.

[2] Moreover the $1\frac{1}{2}$ millions that remained (this figure excludes the police) included about 200,000 'other enrolments' or volunteers who had not undertaken to do the usual 48 hours' duty per month but who on enrolment signified their willingness, if available, to undertake duty when called upon.

[3] An alternative suggestion was to use the fire guards for civil defence duty. An order covering the compulsory enrolment of men between 16 and 60 for fire guard duties had been issued in January 1941.

[4] S.R. & O. 1941, No. 70, 18th January 1941. See p. 593.

extended use of these powers; this was already directing persons to other forms of part-time national service and was the only Department that could judge the claims of directees to be exempted. In December 1941 the War Cabinet approved this proposal and the Ministry of Labour became responsible for the direction of any person in Great Britain to take up part-time police, fire guard or civil defence duties. Not until the following March, however, were local authorities called upon to submit their wants for part-timers so that directions could be issued to meet them.[1]

Having arranged to introduce new blood into civil defence it was now equally important to see that existing volunteers were not lost. The 'freezing' of part-time workers had been considered and rejected during the summer of 1940 when the Orders retaining whole-time members of the service were issued. But by the end of 1941 the demands for part-time manpower were infinitely greater and the market infinitely smaller. Now there were the competing claims of the Home Guard, Observer Corps and the Fire Guard, and the long hours being called for in industry. To lose the great band of trained volunteers, many of whom had been heroes of the blitz, was inconceivable, yet it was rather embarrassing to recognise their invaluable services by forcing them to remain. While not wanting to antagonise these original voluntary workers, the Ministry of Home Security could not risk heavy resignations. It was accordingly arranged that volunteers would be entitled to resign within a fortnight of the imposition of the new 'freezing' order, and that those who resigned would be released as soon as substitutes had been found for them. Resignation could only be a gesture, however, as release would not absolve them from redirection into civil defence work under the new compulsory enrolment orders. The 'freezing' of part-timers was approved by the Cabinet in December 1941; on 22nd January 1942 an Order was issued requiring all Civil Defence workers over 18 to continue in that employment until their services were dispensed with by a local authority or a Regional Commissioner.[2]

Naturally enough the Government had been reluctant to impose compulsion on men and women who, at the height of the raids, had uncomplainingly borne so much of the heat of the day, unpaid and on top of their normal days work. Mr Herbert Morrison made this clear:

> Please understand this: we have no doubts of you—your loyalty or your patient readiness to hang on. In view of your record, those

---

[1] H.S.C. 63/42, 21st March, 1942.

[2] Civil Defence (Employments and Offences) (No. 3) Order, S.R. & O., No. 123, 22nd January 1942, announced to local authorities in H.S.C. 12/42, 22nd January 1942.

doubts would be absurd. But the population of the country is facing great changes and disturbances. The needs of war demand that the Government should tell increasing numbers of people that they must go to such-and-such a place, or do such-and-such a job. All this is essential for victory. But it is impossible for Civil Defence to carry on amid these upheavals unless it too has the men and women to enable it to do its job. The movement of great numbers of people from place to place, from job to job and from no job at all into the Services or war work will mean in any case that the Civil Defence Services are going to have a hard time in keeping up their strength. And it's essential that the necessary strength should be kept up . . . You part-timers are important in every area, you are the key factors in a great many, while in some you are the whole show. We are not prepared, whatever may happen to run the risk of losing you.[1]

But in spite of these attempts to soften the blow, the measure was not popular. Volunteers felt that they had been badly treated, and to add to their grievance, there were suspicions that the compara-tively new service, the Fire Guard,[2] was being better treated than the civil defence general services.

Thus, by the beginning of 1942, two fundamental modifications had been made in the original plans for civil defence. Firstly, the creation of mobile reserves had removed a part of the service from the jurisdiction of the local authority and transferred it to that of the Region. This, together with the 'nationalisation' of the Fire Service in August 1941[3] and the recruitment of the Civil Defence Reserve under the National Service Act, 1941, was in direct contrast to the original doctrine of civil defence as a local authority service, recruited and organised by the local authority primarily for its own protection. Secondly, the introduction of compulsory enrolment for civil defence duty and the 'freezing' of volunteers destroyed much of the original volunteer principle. Voluntary local service alone could not be relied upon as a weapon firm enough to be matched against the strains of total war. Nevertheless the spirit of voluntary part-time service in one's own locality, with its inevitably informal discipline, remained a central feature of civil defence throughout the war.

During 1942 expanding war industries made ever increasing demands on labour. Side by side with the War Cabinet's anxiety to make the best use of manpower, civil defence workers themselves were often keen to make their own direct productive contribution. Many who had been 'frozen' wanted to be released for work in industry; one factor was of course higher wages, and the boredom of long stand-by periods was another. Some units began to do

---

[1] Broadcast after the 9 o'clock News, 22nd January 1942.

[2] See pp. 590 ff.

[3] This is discussed fully in Chapter XI.

munitions and other work at their posts and depots.[1] This 'out-work' grew up sporadically, especially between June and December 1941 when enemy action was slight. But 'out-work' could not be a universal solution; depots were not always suitable for industrial work and appropriate work was not always available. By the early months of 1942, therefore, there was considerable pressure both from within the service and from outside to release civil defence personnel for industrial work.

In April the Ministry of Home Security presented to the Cabinet a plan for the release of civil defence workers to industry. The needs of industry it was argued had high-lighted the question of whether it was necessary to maintain the stand-by of such large numbers of whole-time personnel. The time had come 'to replace defensive thinking by an offensive will to victory', involving 'the acceptance by the civil population of a reduced degree of cover in passive defence'. Complete immunity from danger was impossible; the question was, what could be 'properly sacrificed in order to transfer into war productive industry considerable numbers of those now immobilised in civil defence'. The Minister was prepared to take drastic measures. In the civil defence general services he was willing to accept a cut of up to one-third in the whole-time strength, in the fire service of up to one-sixth and in the police service of some 7,000 young policemen. Such steps could only be justified, however, if the Ministry of Labour could fill the gap by producing more part-timers. As the maximum duty that could be required from part-timers was 48 hours a month, complete replacement would involve finding six times as many part-time workers as the number of whole-time members released; but by the further development of interchangeability and the use of mobile reserves it was hoped that such large numbers of replacements would not be necessary. In addition, trained whole-time workers released would not be completely lost—they would still be required to do part-time service and many of them would be subject to recall in an emergency.[2]

To release such a large proportion of whole-time workers, especially in the more populous districts, was undoubtedly something of a risk. The Air Staff, however, believed that the preoccupations of the *Luftwaffe* on the Russian Front were likely to prevent any immediate resumption of heavy raiding. In any case, they thought, the enemy could not mobilise for attacks in less than about six weeks,

---

[1] Amongst the work successfully done was the manufacture of toys and furniture for the war-time nurseries under a scheme organised by the Nursery Schools Association.

[2] Defence Regulation 29B was amended to cover their enrolment for part-time duties even if they moved from their original district for their war industry jobs; it also provided for the recall of released civil defence personnel to these duties in an emergency. An administrative arrangement was made with the Ministry of Labour whereby men released to industry under H.S.C. 88/42 would not become subject to the call-up and so would remain available for recall to civil defence.

time enough (it was optimistically stated) to allow for much to be done in training new part-time entrants.

Local authorities were told of these proposed releases in the famous Home Security Circular 88 issued on 14th April 1942—a circular that marks the beginning of a steady decline in numbers of whole-time workers until there remained only a cadre of first-line permanent personnel to stiffen the part-time strength.This predominantly part-time body was to be supported by the highly trained mobile reserves which could be sent by the Regional Commissioners as reinforcements. To reach the all-over reduction of one third in the whole-time strength of the general services, some authorities in less dangerous areas would have to make drastic reductions, even to the extent of releasing all their whole-timers.[1] In other districts economies could be achieved by reorganisation and the amalgamation of duties.[2]

Some authorities, especially those experiencing tip-and-run raiding, were reluctant and therefore rather slow to implement such rigorous cuts. In addition, the part-time substitutes that the Ministry of Labour was to find were not forthcoming in the numbers needed; the Home Guard had first priority for men between 18 and 41, and a large number of directees were claiming exemptions. One Ministry of Labour official complained that 'on the average some 10 persons are selected for consideration before one is found who can definitely be recruited'. In Manchester it was reported that ineffective directions were as high as 43 per cent.; while at Bootle 75 persons were directed into the Wardens' Service but after exemptions for sickness, long hours in vital industry etc. had been granted, the number actually taking up duty was only 15.[3] Even where enough part-timers could be found their quality varied. Essex commented that their directees, though numerous, were often unwilling and stuck so closely to the letter of the law in the hours they put in, that it would take three to four months to give them even basic training; Newcastle on the other hand had nothing but praise for their directees.

---

[1] Regional Commissioners were asked to proceed on the basis that for each Region as a whole the average proportion of whole-time personnel to the existing establishment should not exceed the following fractions of that establishment:

	Cat. A areas	Cat. B areas
Rescue and First Aid Parties combined	$\frac{1}{3}$	$\frac{1}{4}$
Report and Control	$\frac{1}{3}$	$\frac{1}{3}$
Wardens Service	$\frac{1}{8}$	$\frac{1}{10}$

Areas in Categories C and D were to release as far as possible *all* whole-time personnel.

[2] In London Region, for instance, 21,914 persons left the whole-time strength of 76,341 between 1st January 1942 and 31st August 1942. Much of this reduction was achieved by the combination of the light rescue and stretcher parties into light rescue parties. This smaller but more compact body would still be entirely adequate, it was believed, to meet attacks on the scale hitherto experienced.

[3] The Ministry of Labour, however, commented that the situation in Bootle was not typical for the N.W. Region, where up to 12th September 1942, 5,951 persons had been directed into part-time civil defence work.

It was soon apparent that the original replacement ratio of 6 : 1 could never be achieved. In July 1942 a revised establishment for local authorities outside London set the ratio at 3½ to 1, and even at this lower level deficiencies were soon considerable. But the Ministry of Home Security was not unduly worried; it believed that, with certain exceptions, the existing strengths were sufficient for the services to function effectively, provided that (as they expected) air raids were not persistent or on a heavy scale. Events were to prove their optimism well-founded. Apart from the Little Blitz of early 1944 aimed mainly at London, no great tests were imposed on the services until the flying bomb raids later in that year, when the attack was sufficiently localised to allow reinforcement from unaffected areas.

By September 1942, of the 32,000 men and women that should have been transferred to industry, only 22,000 had gone. The discrepancy of 10,000 was accounted for by 'the inevitable time lag between selection and starting work in new employment; the reluctance of local authorities to make releases before replacement by part-timers',[1] and discussions about who should be released, since some of the people concerned were of low physical standard.[2] By the end of October, however, it was claimed that reductions up to the approved amount had been reached in most Regions. Some 34,914 persons had left up to 31st October 1942, and replacements in part-time workers amounted to 118,566.

Hardly had these economies been carried through than more far-reaching sacrifices were demanded from civil defence. In October the War Cabinet was considering the latest Survey on Manpower and was preparing a new Manpower Budget for the period June 1942 to December 1943. Vast new demands for labour by the Supply Departments, especially for aircraft production, and the seemingly unlimited needs of the armed forces for an offensive war, had to be matched against a limited and rapidly diminishing supply of manpower. Resources did not match existing programmes. To bridge the gap between supply and demand—a gap of nearly a million persons—curtailment of activities on the civil front was inevitable, and it was even necessary to cut the armed forces. In the light of such immediate strategic considerations as the U-boat peril, the decline in the menace of air attack and the plans for mounting the Continental offensive, the Prime Minister suggested the proportions in which the 'cut' should be shared: the land war to sacrifice

---

[1] Progress in transferring whole-time personnel was reported to be slow in most Regions and the reverse process—the direction of part-time workers to replace them—was making hardly any headway at all.

[2] Many of those released were neither of the age nor the physique to be put to industrial work. There was even the suspicion that some authorities were getting rid of their 'bouches inutiles' and retaining the men who would have been the most use in industry.

54 per cent., the air war 28 per cent., the Admiralty 7 per cent. and the civil defence services 10 per cent. of the gap. For the first time, the direct effect of turns in the manpower screw on the formulation of programmes was visible all along the line.

Although the other Departments were prepared to weather the proposed losses, the Ministry of Home Security, the Ministry of Health and the Scottish Home Department felt obliged to urge a reduction in their contribution. Considerable cuts had already been made in the National Fire Service, the police force, and especially in the civil defence general services. The Departments thought, however, that it would be feasible to reduce the numbers in civil defence by 75,000, as opposed to the 100,000 suggested. Even so, this reduction could only be agreed to 'in pursuance of a policy inevitably involving substantial risks of impairing national security for which the Cabinet as a whole accepts responsibility'. An important proviso was also made: the reduction of 75,000 should be made on the actual working strengths of the services, allowance to be made for future wastage and, subject to changes in the war situation, strengths be kept at the new levels.[1] The Cabinet accepted this case and agreed to temper the wind to the already shorn lamb of the civil defence services; it also urged that a proportion of those released should be available for recall in serious emergency.

Local authorities were told of these new cuts in April 1943.[2] The general services for the country as a whole were to be reduced in strength by not less than one-quarter of the number by which they were reduced during the year 1942. This was an overall aim and the Regional Commissioner would tell each area what proportion of the cuts they were to bear. Authorities were also asked to avoid, as far as possible, asking for part-time substitutes for the personnel released, who would themselves remain liable for part-time service.[3]

When the Cabinet again reviewed the manpower situation in May 1943, it was estimated that whole-time civil defence workers had been reduced by 50,000, leaving a further 25,000 to go by the end of the year. But by now the changing pressure of war operations was calling for new adjustments in manpower. The U-boat peril remained a major preoccupation, but an increasingly important part was being played in the anti-U-boat war by air power. Some additions to the manpower allocations of the M.A.P. and some

---

[1] The cut, in fact, after taking into account arrangements outstanding for withdrawals to industry meant a reduction of 64,000. Once numbers were down by 75,000 to the new approved establishment of 308,600, recruitment would be necessary to offset normal wastage and keep the services at this minimum strength.

[2] H.S.C. 61/43, 3rd April 1943.

[3] The Ministry of Labour was anxious that calls for part-time civil defence service should be kept to the 'absolute minimum' because of the hardship involved for many people, especially married women, who had already done long hours of work in essential industry employment.

corresponding reductions in the Admiralty allotment at the expense of their building programme were, therefore, among the changes approved by the Cabinet. Civil defence manpower also came under scrutiny again, and the Minister of Home Security was asked what further reductions could be made. He replied that 'notwithstanding the sacrifices that the civil defence services have already made and the risk that further reductions may lead to avoidable disasters in particular areas', he would agree to a further reduction of 15,000 paid workers by the end of the year, bringing their full-time strength down to 293,600.[1]

The Ministry thought it unnecessary, however, to insist on specific cuts in local establishments; the promised further releases of 15,000 could in the main be achieved automatically by wastage. Outstanding reductions were to be shared: 3,000 from the National Fire Service where, it was estimated, it could be achieved by normal wastage if recruitment was not reopened; 8,000 from the Police Force, who undertook to reduce gradually the number of War Reserve Constables by the release of younger men to the Armed Forces; and 9,000 from the civil defence general services where reductions could be achieved by normal wastage plus the releases to industry that had already been agreed with certain Regions.

In the autumn of 1943 the Manpower Budget for 1944 was being prepared. By the end of the year mobilisation would be almost complete. The total intake from all sources in 1944 would not replace ordinary wastage and there would be a deficit of 150,000 on essential demands even if no more men and women were called up for the Services. The situation in 1944 presented a new problem which could not be solved by proportionate cuts in the demands of the Service and Supply Departments but required a fresh review of the uses to which available manpower should be put. The problem, said the Prime Minister was no longer one of closing the gap between supply and requirements. Our manpower was now fully mobilised for the war effort. We could not add to the total; on the contrary, it was already dwindling. All we could do was to make within that total such changes as the strategy of the war demanded. One of two alternative assumptions had to be made for the purposes of manpower planning —that Germany would be defeated by the end of 1944 or that the European war would continue until well after 1944.

For the Manpower Budget it was decided to work on the basis that

---

[1] Certain provisos were, however, made. 'Those services in which bodily vigour and staying power are needed should be the last to be affected by the further sacrifice.' Young women in Fire Service control rooms and the police service should be retained as far as possible; no further regular police should be allowed to go nor police auxiliaries under 35 years of age; and it would be unwise to weaken the civil defence rescue services by releasing their younger men. It was also important not to release civil defence personnel until industrial vacancies awaited them and the reductions should be made as far as possible from the less vulnerable areas.

maximum effort must be made during 1944 and that Germany would be defeated by the end of that year, though a subsidiary estimate on the situation in 1945 was also made in case the European war continued. The recommendations of the Manpower Committee were presented to the War Cabinet in November. A minimum intake into the Services was considered inevitable, and it was essential that some important civil industries should receive a net increase of labour. Reductions for the Supply Departments and again for civil defence were inevitable. The Committee therefore proposed a further cut of 50,000 in civil defence personnel,[1] adding that presumably any cut decided upon would have to be operated so as to maintain the defences of London and the South East.

Again the Ministry of Home Security and other Departments concerned with civil defence felt obliged to resist. They pointed out that the services were now at a very low level and that the Cabinet should take into account the possibility of heavy air attacks on the ports, assembly points and communications for the European offensive. There was also the new threat of long-range rocket attack which, if it materialised, would certainly involve the need for military assistance, but would, even so, call for a substantial number of civil defence personnel with experience in fire-fighting and rescue work. And when British forces eventually went overseas might they not be well advised to take with them contingents of the National Fire Service? The Minister of Home Security therefore thought these proposed new cuts dangerous to the well-being of the population and warned his colleagues that the Government as a whole must be prepared to accept responsibility for any breakdown in civil defence organisation. If, nevertheless, the reductions were approved, he made certain stipulations about the timing and distribution of the releases.

The Cabinet felt compelled to uphold the Manpower Committee's proposals. Since 1940-41 the risk of heavy and sustained air attack had receded and, with manpower so short, the question was whether the nation was not carrying too heavy an insurance against such risks. The Vice-Chief of the Imperial General Staff thought it unlikely that air attack would be resumed on a large scale—the relative air superiority of the Allies was growing and our air offensive had compelled the enemy to concentrate on the production of fighters rather than of bombers. It was accordingly agreed that the 50,000 cut in the civil defence services should be sustained but that the reduction should take place between 1st April and 30th September 1944, and not during the first half of 1944 as had at first been suggested. As one measure of insurance, however, permission was given, where

---

[1] Under reductions approved earlier the total civil defence establishment was to be 294,000 by the end of 1943; this new cut would bring the numbers down to 244,000.

strengths were very deficient, to recall whole-time members of the services who had been conditionally released to industry and to invite part-time members to volunteer for whole-time duties, if and when required.

When in June 1944 the flying bomb attacks finally came, soon to be followed by the rocket, the restricted target area made it possible for depleted civil defence services to be reinforced from other Regions. This final spasm of strain was, however, comparatively short-lived. By September, the war situation had improved sufficiently for big reductions to be made in all Regions other than London and those in the south and east.[1] In the less vulnerable Regions the following principles were adopted: substantial reductions in the unit establishments of all services, the release of whole-time personnel without obligation to continue part-time duties, substantial reductions in part-time strength, the reduction of maximum hours of stand-by duty for part-time workers and (with certain exceptions) the abandonment of the continuous manning of posts and depots. A small percentage, about 5 per cent. of whole-time staff, was to be retained in the higher posts for winding-up duties.[2] This, for most of the country, was the virtual disbandment of civil defence. But there was no need to worry about these reductions, said the Minister of Home Security—'the scale of preparedness' had been 'adapted consistently to meet the danger of attack'.[3] A month later, it was possible to say that 'without under-rating the will of the enemy to injure this country . . . the progress of the war makes it no longer necessary in London, or in Regions so lately near enemy occupied territory, to maintain the same scale of preparations as hitherto'; similar, though slightly modified, instructions to reduce establishments were therefore issued as for the rest of the country.[4]

By the end of 1944, the civil defence services had been cut to the bone, and except in the National Fire Service the average age of those remaining was high and their standard of physical fitness often low. Working now on the assumption that the European war would continue until 30th June 1945, the War Cabinet approved a further scheme for the redistribution of manpower. The civil defence services were to lose 94,000 during the first six months of 1945, and a further 52,000 in the third quarter of the year, which would leave them with about 100,000 men, or only the permanent members of the police and fire services.

At the end of April 1945 arrangements for the complete disbandment of the war organisation of the civil defence services were

[1] i.e., all Regions other than Cambridge, London, Reading and Tunbridge Wells.
[2] H. S. C. 115/44, 19th September 1944.
[3] H. of C. Deb., Vol. 403, Col. 441, 28th September 1944,
[4] H. S. C. 128/44, 20th October 1944.

announced.[1] An 'appointed day' was about to be named, after which the civil defence organisation would no longer be needed for the purposes of the war. Information was given on the revocation of the various Orders on 'freezing', reservation, compulsory duties, and on how releases were to be arranged and many other points of administrative procedure. A few days later, the 'appointed day' was named as 2nd May 1945,[2] and the machine began the final stages of its unwinding.

Adapting the Services (i) Experience and Manpower Economies Bring Realignment

Considerations of permitted establishments and later of manpower allocations set the ultimate limits of manoeuverability for the civil defence services. Actual numbers were not, however, the whole story; there remained the questions of organisation and deployment. Did the balance between the various specialist arms make the most effective use of the manpower available? How far did the pattern of organisation planned in peace-time serve to meet the tests of actual operations? What deficiencies or shortcomings were revealed, and how were the services adapted to contend with this experience?

The first thing which must be said is that pre-war planning proved on the whole well balanced; the actual attacks presented few problems that had not been in some measure expected and prepared for in training and exercises. Unforeseen problems inevitably arose, but comparatively few called for major adjustments of method or organisation. The main features which proved in greater or less degree unexpected were the very few casualties in relation to physical damage; the large amount of rescue, repair and clearance work necessary; the high number of unexploded and delayed action bombs; the enemy's introduction of land mines; the difficulty of knowing about the occupants of damaged buildings and so being able to assess and find casualties, and the extent to which operations had to be carried on in darkness. Heavy attacks also revealed underestimation of the difficulties of controlling and reporting incidents, of the need for mutual support between local authorities, and of the scale of the problems of fire-fighting and of the post-raid needs of stricken areas.[3]

Many of the adjustments that had eventually to be made involved the largest and most individual branch, the Wardens' Service. This service, created in 1937, had remained throughout one of the most popular. The warden's primary task was to report incidents

---

[1] H. S. C. 35/45, 26th April 1945.

[2] H. S. C. 40/45, 30th April 1945; pp. 670–672.

[3] See pp. 394–396.

and then to inform the specialised services. In fact he did very much more, and could exercise almost any function. Besides carrying out his original tasks of reporting the fall of bombs and guiding people to shelter, he quickly became the handyman of the A.R.P. services. Wardens stopped innumerable fires by dealing promptly with incendiary bombs; they gave help of every kind at the scene of disaster, assisting the rescue parties and giving first aid to the injured; the senior men controlled and directed operations; they looked after homeless people and took them to rest centres, and more and more the general public looked to them for guidance and help. During the blitz the wardens assumed such prominence and soon became so inextricably linked with the other services in the public mind that many thought of A.R.P. as the Wardens' Service. 'We do not think that anyone realised before the battle began the extent to which the Wardens' Service was pivotal' declared the London Regional Commissioner. 'The wardens' days are constantly occupied with multifarious duties and it is they who, when the attack comes, are always first on the scene and themselves do much first aid and rescue work. But most important of all is that they are the tried, trusted and experienced leaders of the people in whose locality they live, and that in the battle directed not against material things but against the spirit, the example of steadfastness and courage thus given to ordinary people by other ordinary people has been decisive'. How important the warden had become was clearly demonstrated when, as has been mentioned earlier, London Region was prepared to give up more men in its first aid parties to make sure of retaining its wardens.[1]

One side of the wardens' activities that soon needed some amendment concerned their duties in public shelters. Continuous raiding by night produced a profound change in the anticipated use of shelters. Instead of being merely a refuge they became dormitories where people went for a night's rest. Under this strain the arrangements of the part-time shelter warden or unpaid shelter marshal often broke down.[2] Volunteers could not be expected to take a long period of duty—often lasting all night—and then go to work in the morning. In October 1940 London Region took on additional wholetime wardens to act as shelter wardens; the basis was one additional warden per shift of 12 hours for every public shelter habitually used by 500 persons or more, and two per shift for those habitually used by 1,000 or more; for 2,000 or more special arrangements were made. Other Regions with areas of high vulnerability made similar arrangements. The duty of these shelter wardens was to preserve order in the shelters and they were regarded as part of the Wardens' Service. At

---

[1] pp. 549–550.
[2] pp. 520, 537.

first they had no legal power to enforce order and there were many complaints of the misuse of public shelters. In November after the question had been referred to the Home Policy Committee a set of rules for shelterers was drafted and a Defence Regulation issued investing the shelter warden with new powers to keep order.[1] Since conditions varied from Region to Region the power of rule-making was delegated to the Regional Commissioners. In London paid shelter wardens were to be subject to all the obligations of the ordinary Wardens' Service and would receive the full training of a warden and thus be interchangeable, but this was not universal and in some places the shelter wardens were quite independent of the Wardens' Service. Later, however, in the interests of manpower economy, the policy of interchangeability of full-time shelter wardens and other wardens was extended to all areas, and the number of whole-time and part-time wardens to the expected population of each shelter was laid down. The investment of shelter wardens with semi-police powers in shelters while control outside remained in the hands of the police worked smoothly.

In this matter the position was happier than that which persisted over incident control. In November 1939 London Region had developed a scheme to train selected wardens to be sent from local control centres to take charge of all A.R.P. operations, except fire-fighting, at any major incident.[2] The Incident Officer was not to supervise the technique of rescue and first aid work but, with the help of wardens acting under his orders, he was to see that the services required were there, that vehicles were parked conveniently, that parties did not impede each other and that the control centre was kept fully informed of progress. It was soon clear that the Incident Officers' position *vis-à-vis* the police would have to be clarified. In London Region two important principles were laid down: first that the police, who had statutory duties and the power of enforcement, must take general charge of the situation and make every effort to maintain public order and traffic control; secondly, that the Civil Defence Incident Officer, though working in co-operation with the Fire Service, would have no control over that service but would confine himself to the supervision of the A.R.P. General Services. In London, therefore, the arrangement was that the police kept the ring within which the Incident Officer directed the operations of the A.R.P. services and a Fire Officer those of the fire services, and on the whole this arrangement worked quite well.

Some doubts about functions, however, persisted and in May 1940, after discussions between the Home Office and the Ministry of Home Security, a memorandum was issued laying down the

---

[1] Defence Regulation 23AB, S.R. & O., 1940, No. 2064.
[2] p. 352.

general principles of responsibility for the police, the Fire Service and the A.R.P. services for the country as a whole. A senior police officer was considered the best person to be an Incident Officer and to assume the general direction of the other services, whose own officers would be present to relay the necessary instructions. This senior police officer should establish an Incident Officer's Post and report this to the A.R.P. Controller as well as to the police authorities; he was to be responsible for intelligence, for determining the priority of operations and for seeing that regular reports of progress were made to report or control centres and to the proper police station. Since, in other Regions besides London, wardens as well as police were being trained as Incident Officers, the memorandum assumed that there might well be an Incident Officer for the A.R.P. services besides the senior police officer present at an incident.

This arrangement caused a good deal of friction between the police and the A.R.P. authorities. On the one side the Chief Constables were often sensitive to any indications that the non-police Incident Officer might want to take control. On the other side the A.R.P. services felt that the police knew little or nothing about A.R.P. yet wanted to interfere. Where there were sufficient senior police officers trained in the duty the arrangement worked, but where a local constable attempted to oust from control a more capable warden interference was resented. Nevertheless, it was insisted that incident control should remain a responsibility of the police, and as more people outside the ranks of the police continued to be trained in this, the problem persisted.

By the spring of 1943 the police seem to have been convinced that those in charge of civil defence, at any rate in the Regions, were anxious to keep them away from the position of Incident Officer. On the other hand, the A.R.P. services were saying that in some Regions the police had refused to allow civil defence personnel to undergo incident control instruction and that wardens had been ordered off the site of an incident. The matter was brought up at a meeting of the central conference of Chief Constables on 6th May 1943, when it was agreed that the Incident Officers' Service should be regarded as a civil defence service, but that except in London it should be under the control of the Chief Constable. There should, however, be specialised training both of wardens and police and a pool of trained personnel in every district. The conference agreed that responsibility for selecting and despatching the Incident Officer should rest with the Chief Constable, but that once this officer reached the scene he was to be responsible to the Controller in charge of the operations of the General Services.

The Incident Officer it can be seen was a splinter—albeit a polished and specialised splinter—from the Wardens' Service;

another such splinter was the Bomb Reconnaissance Officer. At the beginning of the war there were still differences of opinion over who was responsible for disposal of unexploded missiles. In September 1939 local authorities were informed that these would be dealt with by Royal Engineers attached to each Command;[1] a few days later, on the initiative of the Army Council, they were told that they themselves must shoulder this duty. Each R.E. squad was to be replaced by three civilian volunteers who would undergo a short course of instruction at a military depot.[2] But for one reason or another the provision of training was postponed, the War Office being unwilling to retain responsibility and the local authorities feeling unable to assume it. Finally, the War Office reluctantly agreed that the military should deal with unexploded missiles and the War Cabinet ruled that this responsibility should rest in all cases with the Army. This decision was however modified when parachute mines were dropped on land; these were considered to be a job for the Navy.[3]

Before unexploded missiles could be dealt with they had to be found and this work naturally devolved on police and wardens. Frequently the only thing to indicate an unexploded missile was a hole in the ground, and missiles on the surface were not always easy to recognise in the mass of debris scattered by explosions. The most serious aspect of the whole matter was the time spent by the few Bomb Disposal Squads in investigating false alarms. By December 1940, they had on their books awaiting investigation and disposal over 3,000 unexploded missiles, all causing work to be held up, traffic diverted or houses evacuated. It was clear that there would have to be special machinery for sifting reports.

The Army remained responsible for training in bomb reconnaissance. Local authorities and Chief Constables were asked to select a number of wardens, policemen and control centre staff for training as Bomb Reconnaissance Officers who would have the duty of deciding whether a reported unexploded bomb was genuine, and if and when police might relax safety precautions. All Army Commands undertook this training and the presence of qualified Bomb Reconnaissance Officers in the ranks of the civil defence services, the police and industry helped to solve a most difficult problem.

This training, too, filtered down to the ordinary wardens, who had to sift the reports which brought out the Bomb Reconnaissance Officers. One type of bomb reconnaissance in which all wardens were concerned resulted from the use by the enemy, between March and August 1942 and again in the middle of 1943, of small anti-personnel ('butterfly') bombs. To prevent accidents from any that

---

[1] A.R.P. Dept. Circular 239, 10th September 1939.

[2] Ibid.

[3] See p 393.

might be unexploded, every bomb from every container had to be accounted for and wardens were called on to help Bomb Disposal Squads and search parties by showing where these bombs or containers had been reported.

During the heavy raids of 1940 still more duties were progressively added to the warden's numerous tasks. His training having embraced methods of dealing with incendiary bombs, it was expected that the warden would tackle incipient fires pending the arrival of the fire services. When, in many areas, the public formed themselves into unofficial fire parties, the wardens were asked to encourage and help to train them. But as will be described later in this chapter the comparatively few unofficial fire parties proved quite insufficient to cope with the great fire-raising raids of December 1940, and in January 1941 the Minister of Home Security had to call upon the public to fall in as fire-fighters. Volunteers were asked to see their warden immediately and the Wardens' Service had not only to supervise and train these parties and record the stirrup-pumps and sandbags issued to them, but also to be responsible for reporting the number of incendiary bombs dropped in each raid. When in August 1941 fire watching was made compulsory and the Fire Guard formed, the Wardens' Service still played a great part in training the new service; and even after the promulgation of the Fire Guard Plan in 1943 the Fire Guard Organisation remained in some areas part of the Wardens' Service.[1]

Yet another aspect of the wardens' work was their knowledge of the whereabouts of trapped casualties in damaged buildings. To begin with, lack of knowledge about whether or not there were people in bombed buildings delayed rescue work or alternatively led to rescue parties wasting valuable time looking for casualties that did not exist. To meet this difficulty wardens were asked to maintain a complete census of occupants of buildings in their areas and of where they sheltered at night. After serious raids wardens often set up an inquiry point, to which members of the public looking for missing relatives and friends could be directed. By combining both sources of information it was possible to assess the total number of people, including residents, visitors and passers-by, likely to have become casualties. Not only were rescue operations helped but parties could often be released much earlier for more urgent duties elsewhere. This procedure was later formalised and Incident Inquiry Points with considerably extended functions became usual at all important incidents. The W.V.S. ultimately became responsible for manning many of these.

The collection of information about trapped casualties became increasingly important in the relations between wardens and rescue

---

[1] pp. 601–605.

parties. Wardens were on the spot and during the heavy raids they did a good deal of rescue work without equipment or training. It was difficult to stop them, but there was some fear that more harm than good might result. Opinion was divided in the Ministry of Home Security on whether or not the wardens should be trained in rescue work. They had so many other duties that complete inter-changeability was impossible. On the one side there was the feeling that any policy that economised in manpower was desirable; on the other was the view that wardens were better employed in collecting information about likely casualties. This division of opinion, coupled with some Treasury reluctance to provide extra equipment, was the main reason why for the next two years wardens were not encouraged to do rescue work. In London, as a result of the formation of light rescue parties out of the stretcher parties, wardens got some simple rescue equipment in the autumn of 1942, and in other Regions wardens were given rescue training. When the rescue and first aid parties were finally amalgamated at the beginning of 1943, qualms about the dangers of the wardens doing rescue work faded before the practical certainty that they would continue to do this work, and it was finally accepted that they should be properly trained and equipped. So that wardens should not be diverted from their other work no general scheme was launched, but the Ministry would consider proposals if local training arrangements had been made. Equipment was to be confined to leather gloves, shovels and debris bins. It was emphasised, however, that rescue work was quite secondary to the normal work of wardens, and that it was just as important for them to keep the public from walking over debris which might collapse.

Thus the Wardens' Service, the first link in the chain of command, was progressively adapted to meet new responsibilities.[1] But between the warden and those directing the tactical deployment of the various services lay the nerve centres of the Report and Control Centres. This headquarters service was a key one, since on the accurate appreciation of the wardens' reports depended the proper deployment of forces and often the rapid rescue of trapped casualties. It was also an intelligence branch responsible for collecting and collating information on many matters of the utmost importance to the Armed Forces and other Government Departments. One of its important duties was to collect and plot all information concerning damage to essential services, such as gas, electricity and water,

---

[1] An Association of Chief Wardens in London Region was formed in May 1942; and a Wardens' Advisory Council, representative of all Groups in the Region, met each month thereafter under the chairmanship of one of the Regional Commissioners. These bodies promoted the general welfare of the Wardens' Service, and participated in the framing of various London civil defence plans including the invasion defence plan for Greater London, the Fire Guard Plan and arrangements for Incident Control.

together with the current position in rest centres and other amenities so as to enable technical officers to assess the position quickly and to decide on priorities of treatment. To begin with there was often a tendency towards over-elaboration in control rooms, and the devising of complicated mapping and recording systems. Experience soon showed that only the simplest systems survived under the pressure of attack; also that it was important to allow only essential officials to be present during raids.

One of the most serious problems for the Report and Control Centres was that of maintaining communications. They received their information by telephone and in many of the more serious raids the telephone system either partially or wholly broke down, while in several instances the Centre itself was hit and put out of action. The answer to these problems lay in the provision of an alternative Centre and the organisation of a more adequate Messenger Service.

To provide the latter the Civil Defence (Outdoor) Messenger Service was reorganised in June 1941[1] to supplement the telephone service and to replace telecommunications which had broken down. Messengers were kept at all operational centres as well as at rest centres, information centres and mortuaries. A certain number were provided with motor cycles and the remainder as far as possible with cycles, though bad bomb damage often made any alternative to a 'runner' impossible. Though some adults were enrolled, the service largely consisted of boys and girls. They were accepted at 15 years, but were not to be employed out of doors in raids until 16 and then, in the case of girls, only with their parents' permission. After 18 there was no restriction. Boys of the Sea Cadet Corps, Army Cadet Force and Air Training Corps could be enrolled on special conditions agreed with the Departments concerned.[2]

As far as the provision of alternative Control Centres was concerned authorities were advised in September 1941 to collaborate with the Post Office in setting up duplicate centres, preferably outside the target area. These were to be provided with a small staff, to be kept continually in the picture and ready to take over at a moment's notice should the main Centre go out of action.[3] In certain target areas the Regional Commissioner formed a local committee of the police, the Fire Service, the local authorities, the Post Office, the Fighting Services, utility undertakings, railway, port and dock authorities, and Government Departments to exchange information on the means of communication available and consider any alternative arrangements necessary. An important function of this com-

---

[1] H.S.C. 146/41, 28th June 1941.
[2] H.S.C.s 65/42, 23rd March 1942, 111/42, 21st May 1942, 38/43, 1st March 1943.
[3] H.S.C. 192/41, 2nd September 1941.

mittee was to arrange for an information centre to which, after heavy raiding, details could be passed as to the new addresses of firms and so on which had had to move.

On the wardens' reports to the Control Centres depended the deployment of the specialist services, one of the chief of which was the Rescue Service, trained to render immediate first aid to wounded and to rescue trapped casualties. As already mentioned, one of the most unexpected features of the heavy raids was the large amount of rescue, repair and clearance work necessary. Rescue operations could be long and arduous, involving great strain and danger to personnel whose training had inevitably been unrealistic. In a heavy attack all available parties were continually at work and the margin of reserve to meet emergencies was tiny. Some relief was gained by drawing a sharper distinction between rescue operations and clearance, and by the employment of military and other labour on the latter. But in some cases actual rescue operations seemed to lag and it was suggested that there was a tendency to regard trapped casualties as 'bodies' much too soon, though when casualties were known to be alive this acted as a great incentive to the parties. In the early days there was sometimes undue concentration on the technical aspects of shoring up buildings, and common-sense rescue measures were overlooked. Further, the equipment issued to rescue parties proved in some respects unsuitable and co-operation with the salvage service in loading debris was not close enough. Fortunately, casualties were not nearly as heavy as had been expected, though even so it was felt that the size of the Rescue Service should be increased. One of the easiest ways of increasing the numbers in Rescue was by training some of the men of the other specialist branches in this work. As early as 1938 it had been suggested that the personnel of the Decontamination Service should be trained in rescue work and this issue was revived in March 1940 by the Mabane Committee.[1] At the Ministry of Home Security there was increasing awareness of the need to foster interchangeability. With some experience of heavy raids, the Mabane Committee met in October to discuss the problem, among others, of aid to the rescue parties.

To meet the difficulties of debris clearance, one suggestion was the formation of a corps of unskilled labourers who could be called out when needed and who would work under the supervision of a Rescue Party leader. This proposal did not meet with much favour, however, chiefly because it would mean that the labourers would have to be paid industrial rates and the rescue parties civil defence rates for doing the same job. Moreover, with the increasing demand for manpower it would be wasteful to have numbers of able-bodied men,

---

[1] pp. 345–346.

probably of military age, standing by. Military assistance had been given in London Region, but this could obviously be only a temporary measure.

Between October and the end of the year views on how the rescue parties could be augmented became clearer. Now it was planned that there should ultimately be a composite force made up of rescue parties, first aid parties and decontamination squads. Here lay the germ of the later formation of units of the Civil Defence Reserve and the amalgamated rescue and first aid parties. But for the moment there was no question of compelling men of one service to do the work of another, which would have involved a new Defence Regulation exercising compulsion on volunteers. Nor was any idea of formal amalgamation put forward. It was decided instead to propagate the idea by offering training in the others' work to each of the branches.

There were however, some misgivings on the advisability of mixing personnel of the rescue parties and the first aid parties. The men were often of a very different type both socially and physically. There was the danger, it was argued, that the first aid parties would think the rescue men 'toughs' and the rescue men call the first aiders 'cissies'. The first aiders were often men from shops and clerical professions, while the rescue men were usually builders, artisans and labourers. Any form of direction was ruled out. So far as the decontamination squads were concerned, compulsion was felt to be specially undesirable as most of the men were local authority employees who had been told that in the event of gas raiding they must undertake decontamination work and who had therefore not exercised the same freedom of choice in joining the civil defence services as other volunteers. Persuasion therefore seemed still to be the right solution and in February 1941 Regional Officers were told that it had been decided to offer additional training to the rescue parties, the first aid parties and decontamination squads, so that the first two could do each other's work; rescue parties were also to be trained in decontamination and decontamination squads in rescue work.

This was the beginning of the introduction of the principle of interchangeability—the first of the manpower economy measures that have been mentioned earlier in this chapter.[1] The principle was to be developed much further as the war went on. It was increasingly recognised that a composite force was more likely to be operationally efficient than groups of specialists, and if one man could do three functions saving in manpower would be achieved.

In May 1941 the doctrine was carried further by an Order in Council which provided for the direction of members of one service to perform work normally done by the other services, including

[1] See p. 550.

training.[1] The Minister of Home Security explained to the War Cabinet that this Regulation was desirable because interchangeability would result in further resources being available if each man not needed for a particular duty was competent to reinforce another service that might be exceptionally pressed. Under the National Service Act, 1941 (in which men liable for military service might be called up for civil defence) men posted to a particular civil defence service might be called upon to perform the duties of another service, either in the locality in which the men were first posted or elsewhere. Men called up for civil defence would be working side by side with existing volunteers. The new Regulation would therefore apply this principle of interchangeability of functions to the existing volunteer whole-time personnel, except that the liability to perform duty outside the area of their own local authority would be limited to occasions when parties or detachments were being sent to another area for mutual support.

The formal combination of the two services could only be made as part of the general reorganisation of the whole of the civil defence services. By the early months of 1942, it will be remembered, it had been agreed that the civil defence services must contribute to national manpower shortages by releasing a large number of whole-time personnel to industry.[2] One of the measures for accomplishing these releases was by the extension of interchangeability, particularly in the rescue parties and the first aid parties, where there was still a large proportion of whole-timers.[3]

In May 1942 it was finally decided that the Rescue Parties and the First Aid Parties should be combined into one service—the Civil Defence Rescue Service. Each party was to consist of ten men including a driver, which would enable the party to divide neatly into five for operational purposes, since it had been found that only limited numbers could be effectively employed at many small incidents. Heavy raiding had shown that fewer first aid parties were needed, so that the number of men for the new service was calculated as being equivalent to the existing Rescue Service plus half the existing number of the First Aid Party Service. Much had to be done in providing the combined service with new equipment and vehicles.

At this time the unit establishment of the Rescue Service, excluding London, was 57,000 men and of the First Aid Party Service 60,000 men. The proposed new service was, therefore, to be 87,000 men or 8,700 parties of 10 men each. There were three views about

---

[1] S.R. & O. 1941, No. 743, 30th May 1941.

[2] See pp. 552–559.

[3] It may be remembered that London Region had already absorbed its First Aid Parties into the Rescue Service.

the proper size of the party: one was that ten men was the lowest number that could act efficiently, another supported the London system of light and heavy parties of five and ten men respectively, while the third view favoured a standard party of seven with a reduced amount of equipment. When the three alternatives were considered further the general opinion was that, outside London, it was essential to have a standard unit. The main reason for this was that during a raid a Controller could not usually tell from the reports received whether a light or heavy party should be sent out. The general impression was that many incidents could be dealt with quite adequately by seven men, provided that they were fully trained in both rescue and first aid. To begin with there was some fear that more parties would mean more party leaders, and more party leaders less good leaders. But a meeting of administrative staff and technical experts finally decided in November 1942 that the normal size of the rescue party should be seven including the driver, though authorities who wished to retain parties of ten could do so with the permission of the Regional Commissioner.

This reduction in the size of the party meant a reduction in the amount of equipment carried, particularly as regards heavy chains and lifting tackle, though a certain amount of new equipment was now wanted, including a new type of jack, remote breathing apparatus and flood lighting sets. A difficult problem was to find enough vehicles to make the increased number of parties self sufficient; the old vehicles for ten men were too large and other lorries and light vans were very scarce. These new plans were passed by the Treasury early in 1943 and local authorities were advised of the amalgamation of the two services.[1]

Amalgamation on the whole was most successful; indeed it regularised much that had already been practised. There was some anxiety among First Aid Parties, however, that the omission of any reference to casualties from the title of the new service might obscure one of its most important functions, and medical officers of health feared that good first aiders might lose their skill by doing rescue work. There was indeed a danger of this happening, for in most cases the service was under the supervision of the borough surveyor, though he was supposed to work in close liaison with the medical officer of health. Moreover, the standard of first aid training was later simplified for the new service. In general, however, the balance between rescue and first aid was properly maintained. Perhaps the clear line of demarcation between them should never have been drawn, since operationally rescue and first aid were inextricably mixed and one could not be successful without the other.

Early in the war there had been concern about the lack of First Aid

---

[1] H.S.C. 16/43, 27th January 1943.

personnel and the question of reservation had been considered.[1] There was, therefore, considerable relief when the big raids did not bring the heavy casualties expected and the number of first aid parties proved quite adequate. The functions and organisation of the Ambulances and First Aid Posts did not alter and except in remote rural areas the Mobile First Aid Units were seldom used. Light Mobile Units, consisting of a doctor, trained nurse and a couple of auxiliary nurses did, however, prove of considerable value in supplementing the work of the First Aid Parties at large incidents. One most important early lesson of the blitz was that too much first aid on the spot was undesirable and that casualties should, wherever possible, be sent to a hospital or first aid post without delay.

The development of interchangeability between specialist branches was the first of the measures to economise manpower mentioned earlier in this chapter.[2] To build and maintain a completely adequate defence force was beyond the country's capacity and it had soon become a question of making the best use of the resources available. The demand for labour for national service of all kinds was such that even before the attacks of 1940–41 were over, it was recognised that the risks inherent in an undermanned civil defence must be faced.

The second most important method of achieving economy in civil defence manpower was to be the use of mobile reserves. Instead of attempting to bring up to an ideal strength the separate services of each local authority, groups of areas would be covered by a mobile reserve made up of personnel detached, permanently or in rotation, from local authority services or recruited through the National Service Act, 1941. This development is discussed in the next chapter as an aspect of the work of the Regional Commissioners.

(ii) Training

When serious air attacks began in 1940 the training acquired by civil defence volunteers throughout the country was varied and patchy. It may be recalled that early air raid precautions training had concentrated on the menace of gas and that it was not until the middle of 1939 that training in incendiary bomb control and methods of dealing with high explosive bombs began to be generally introduced. The stand-by period of the war then provided the opportunity to make good deficiences, but in many areas the discouragements of the 'twilight war', the scarcity of training supervisers and the dearth of stirrup pumps and other equipment hindered real progress. By the end of 1939 the Ministry of Home Security had become very conscious of the importance of training in maintaining the morale of the service under stand-by conditions,

---

[1] See pp. 374–375.
[2] See pp. 553 ff.

and a headquarters training branch was established and training officers appointed in all Regions. During the early months of 1940 the issue of a new training plan[1] and the organisation of Regional training schools were designed to establish the 'uniform practice in training throughout the country' recommended by the Mabane Committee. The appointment in April 1940 of a Chief of the Civil Defence Operational Staff concerned with national operational efficiency gave emphasis to the need for progress in training.[2]

The next few months saw considerable activity in training schemes at the local authority level. Rescue Service schools had been set up in many Regions, anti-gas training was well advanced, more attention was being directed to training in technical subjects and exercises were being held all over the country. In the absence of actual experience of bombing attacks lantern slides of bomb damage in foreign countries were used to illustrate the situations which might be encountered,[3] and in August 1940 the first civil defence training films were produced.

In the summer of 1940 widespread air attacks began, and thereafter training could be based on actual experience. One of the first surprises of operational experience was that casualties were much lower than forecast; first aid parties were less in demand than expected and what casualties there were required the minimum of first aid and a rapid removal to hospital. On the other hand the Rescue Service found itself severely strained.

To ease the burden the Ministry began to think in terms of some combination of duties and modification of training for both branches. In February 1941, rescue, first aid and decontamination squads were given the opportunity to train in each others' duties, and in May interchangeability between these branches was made compulsory.[4] Regional Rescue schools were to train the leaders of the parties in each others' work and the leaders were to carry the training back to their units. Experience of the heavy raids had shown that much of the previous rescue training was inadequate and unrealistic; two new schemes of training were therefore drawn up, including the new subject of searching for casualties or what was later called rescue reconnaissance. By the end of 1941 70 per cent. of the rescue parties had been trained in first aid and it was being suggested that the separate entity of these two services should be abolished. It was not until the early months of 1943, however, that the complete amalgamation of the rescue and first aid services was achieved.

One early and important lesson of the raids was that the fire

---

[1] A.R.P. Training Manuals Nos. 1, 2, 16th February, 16th April 1940.
[2] H.S.C. 61/40, 11th April 1940. See p. 352.
[3] H.S.C. 109/40, 29th May 1940.
[4] See pp. 573–574.

menace had been greatly under-estimated. Incendiary bombs dropped in large numbers in built-up areas needed something more than the fire brigade services, namely an army of fire-fighters who might eliminate the bombs before serious fires could develop. This meant intensified training in fire-fighting not only for the civil defence services but also for the general public, and the great fire raids at the end of 1940 made this problem most urgent. The establishment of a civilian fire guard organisation to contend with this menace is discussed later in this chapter.

Practically every raid provided some new experience, exposing a weakness in procedure or requiring a new technique for counter-action. Faced with these problems the civil defence services had to think quickly. Improvisation was the order of the day and various remedies were designed and tried out. Reports of experiences, the lessons learnt and the measures taken began to be circulated and compared. From these reports the Training Branch compiled circulars for the Home Office schools and issued a series of A.R.P. Training Bulletins.[1] The schools relayed information to ex-pupils and the Regions to training officers and instructors by circulars and conferences.

As the raids increased the need for much more specialised training in certain duties became apparent; two of the most essential of these were incident control and bomb reconnaissance, the administrative development of which has been traced earlier.[2] Roof-spotters also needed training in aircraft recognition; local courses were held towards the end of 1940 and later this training was continued in the many roof-spotters clubs which were formed.[3] At the beginning of 1941, while so much attention was being concentrated on fire-fighting, training officers were advised that the Government was still of the opinion that gas would be used. Charts of war gases were issued; refresher courses for anti-gas instructors were started; the instruction of further Gas Identification Officers (including persons nominated by private concerns) undertaken and more public anti-gas courses were organised.

One continuing problem for the Ministry throughout the war was how to keep the vast army of civil defence informed on such security matters as the methods of dealing with new enemy weapons. It was essential that the services should know about these weapons immediately, but secrecy was also vital so that the enemy should gain no information that would help him to frustrate our defence measures. The procedure adopted when a new weapon was identified was to give all Regional Headquarters a brief description and instructions

---

[1] H.S.C. 160/40, 5th July 1940.

[2] See pp. 566–569.

[3] H.S.C. 162/42, 15th August 1942.

on how to handle it. This information was then passed on to Chief Constables and A.R.P. Controllers, who in turn passed it down to those members of their services who might be concerned. The Department also prepared a series of confidential training pamphlets, and from time to time additions and amendments were made to assist all training officers to keep their services up-to-date. The first of these was issued in December 1940 and in the following February a series of confidential Fire Prevention Bulletins was started to help local authorities in the training of their fire-fighting parties.[1] Later, in response to suggestions made by employers, a series of Industrial Bulletins was issued.[2]

In the early months of the war local training officers had a difficult task; pressed from Headquarters to run more and more courses they were confronted not only with a lack of facilities and often a shortage of instructors but were hampered by the fact that there was no compulsion on part-time volunteers to accept training. Most local authorities soon found that a training officer with no other responsibilities was essential and the number of staff dealing solely with training began to expand at all levels. Courses for training officers spread from Region to Region and many new training schools or centres were started either for general training or for specialist functions. Sometimes mobile units with a gas chamber and incendiary bomb hut were used to train thousands of persons who could not attend a local centre. In one Region the Regional Training Officer set up a travelling 'circus', spreading the lessons of raids and holding 'bandstand' exercises on post-raid procedure; in another the Ministry of Information loud-speaker vans were used to train the public in dealing with incendiary bombs.

Once the heavy raids began general training arrangements were inevitably disturbed. As much rest as possible for personnel was essential, instructors often had to be used as Incident Officers and formal exercises were reduced. Individual training suffered particularly and untrained persons had to acquire their knowledge by personal experience or from paper. After May 1941 general training, now stiffened by experience, revived. But it was not always easy, after nine months of raids, to retain interest and to pull training together again. As one officer wrote 'there is no doubt that training is rusty and there is evidence of the very dangerous feeling that we are well tried under fire and that to go back to the kindergarten is both undignified and unnecessary'. Efficiency, keenness and tone depended in no small measure on the A.R.P. Controller. There were still local authorities who had not appointed a training officer, yet the Ministry was calling for an expansion of training to cover

---

[1] H.S.C. 52/41, 25th February 1941.
[2] H.S.C. 180/41, 21st August 1941.

a great variety of subjects—fire-fighting, bomb reconnaissance, incident control, rescue, reporting, roof-spotting, new weapons and invasion duties.

Although anti-gas exercises were still staged, the main pre-occupation of training officers at Regional and local authority level since the beginning of 1941 had been the problems of fire-fighting. This was given a new emphasis when, in August 1941, the Fire Guard was inaugurated as a separate service allied to the Wardens' Service.[1] Regions were now urged to set up their own training schools for Fire Guard Staff Officers, the courses to cover individual, team and tactical training. Before the end of the year many had done so and others followed in the early part of 1942. Some Regions established residential schools and offered training facilities not only to their own Staff Officers but also to those of other Regions; in others special courses for Staff Officers were held where possible; while in the Bristol Region, in addition to a residential school, a travelling 'Fire Prevention Circus' toured the Region advising local authorities on methods of organisation, and giving publicity to the need for training. Courses at the Regional schools were confined to the senior instructors who quickly qualified to train the rest of the Fire Guard service. Further assistance was given by the issue in March 1942 of 'The Fire Guard's Handbook' and in April of a new edition of 'Incendiary Bombs and Fire Precautions'.[2] Progress was inevitably uneven—the Regions had no power to coerce the local authorities and they in turn had no real power of compulsion over the Fire Guards. In many areas the training of the Fire Guards lagged and when the new service was put to the test by the 'Baedeker' raids many weaknesses were exposed. In August 1942[3] new Orders made it compulsory to provide training for all Fire Guards in their 48 hours' part-time service and a training syllabus was issued covering not only the characteristics of incendiary bombs and the use of appliances, now including some light trailer pumps, but also the operational use of Fire Guard parties.[4]

The policy of reducing the numbers of whole-time personnel and replacing them by part-time workers posed many difficulties in connection with training. To begin with part-timers were not com-pelled to accept training and in most cases they were only available in the evenings, by which time the paid instructors had done their day's work and were either too tired or required extra pay for giving further instruction. As the proportion of part-time personnel to whole-time personnel grew, therefore, so the overall standard of

---

[1] See pp. 596 ff.

[2] A.R.P. Handbook No. 14; A.R.P. Handbook No. 9.

[3] S.R. & O. 1942, Nos. 1654 and 1655.

[4] H.S.C. 162/42, 15th August 1942; A.R.P. Handbooks Nos. 13 and 14.

training declined. This was especially so with the vast numbers enrolled under the Fire Prevention Orders. People who had been working all day were disinclined to turn out for training in the evenings and a number of night inspections of fire prevention arrangements at business premises in March 1942 showed that the majority of Fire Guards were entirely untrained. In reporting this the Inspector-General said that it was difficult to see how the situation could be improved until it was made compulsory to take training.

In January 1942 a successor to the A.R.P. Staff School, which had closed down at the outbreak of the war, was established by the opening of the Civil Defence Staff College at Stoke D'Abernon, Surrey. Its first object was to give senior local officials instruction in the higher organisation and administration of civil defence and to keep key men and women fully informed of lessons learnt in the raids and of improvements in operational techniques. At first the College only accommodated twenty-two students, but later it could take fifty. The scope of the training also expanded; syllabi were constantly under review and special courses were run for Chief Constables, Industry, Borough Engineers and Surveyors, Medical Officers of Health, Training Officers, N.F.S. and members of the W.V.S. Later the College became almost international in character, its students including officers, both civil and military, of most of the Allied nations. During the three and a half years of instruction 112 courses of twenty different types were held and these were attended by 4,899 officers and students, no less than 1,386 being from the Allied forces. When the College first opened the country still lay under the threat of invasion and the emphasis was on the many civil problems that invasion would present. The great importance of the post-raid aspects of civil defence required knowledge not only of the normal functions of the Civil Defence Services but also of those of many other services and early courses were framed to meet this need. Later on much attention was paid to incident control. In February 1944 the College undertook the entire training of British and United States army officers in the organisation and operational control of passive air defence, and finally a number of Allied nationals were trained in the basic principles needed for the reorganisation of civil defence services when their countries were liberated.

Throughout 1942 the training programme of the civil defence services was expanding, both in subject matter and in the personnel involved. In May the W.V.S. decided to train their members in basic civil defence measures.[1] In August the War Office introduced a similar scheme for the Home Guard[2] and Regional Training Officers

---

[1] H.S.C. 104/42, 22nd May 1942.
[2] H.S.C. 170/42, 28th August 1942.

and local authorities were asked to help with instructors, equipment and accommodation. Among other developments during this year were special courses in anti-gas measures for N.F.S. personnel,[1] for equipment officers at Ministry of Home Security Regional Stores, for civil defence drivers at Ministry of Labour Training Centres, for Gas Identification Officers and for Bomb Reconnaissance Officers. To the subjects being taught were added new types of bombs, new techniques in decontamination, the rescue of crews from crashed aircraft, and the duties of the civil defence services in case of invasion. Handbooks and memoranda were revised and a comprehensive Rescue Service manual issued.

In August 1942 part-time civil defence service became compulsory for women thus adding a further class in need of training. Regions were urged to speed up local authorities' lagging fire-fighting training programmes, as at the end of September only about 30 per cent. of the local authority Fire Guards had completed their theoretical and practical training and about 15 per cent. their tactical training. A week's course for Regional Fire Prevention Training Officers was held in London in January 1943, and the Regions and authorities soon found it essential to have one officer responsible for this side of the work.

At this time many Regions lacked a central school where all subjects could be taught and still relied on *ad hoc* schools set up for a course or courses in a particular subject. The Ministry now proposed that each Region should set up a permanent Regional School to train umpires in civil defence exercises, Controllers or other officials in invasion work and in the organisation of post-blitz exercises, senior wardens in incident control, and to provide instruction for equipment officers, physical training instructors, and party leaders in the specialist branches. It was not intended that the courses at Regional Schools should replace the Civil Defence Staff College, but rather that the grade of officers attending them should extend to lower levels than at the Staff College. The cost of the schools was to be borne by the Government, but a standard daily fee was set for students which ranked for grant in respect of any students sent by local authorities. The Regions were responsible for finding a floating staff of instructors and lecturers according to the subject of the course, while equipment was obtainable through official channels.

These Regional schools were gradually established but, pending their opening, those Regions without one continued to rely on *ad hoc* courses. This applied particularly to the training of the Fire Guard, which had scarcely become accustomed to its link with the Wardens' Service when it was disturbed by the entirely new training inherent in the new Fire Guard Plan. It had been expected that occupiers

---

[1] H.S.C. 119/42, 8th June 1942.

or street party leaders would make themselves responsible for the tactical training of their fire guards, but in practice this had not been done.[1] To hasten the new training special Fire Guard Instructors' courses were held at Falfield and Easingwold, the successful candidates being qualified to instruct at Regional or local authority schools or centres.[2] A new syllabus of training for fire guard instructors was issued in June and, after the publication of the Fire Prevention Orders of July, a completely revised syllabus of Fire Guard Training set out the subjects to be taught and the persons qualified to teach them.[3] The Fire Guard was now to be linked with the National Fire Service and members of the latter were asked to give instruction in certain subjects to Fire Guard Officers, who would then relay it to the other ranks. The new Orders finally made it compulsory for all fire guards to undertake training, and from this time to the 'stand-down' all Fire Guard Training Officers were fully employed in bringing the Fire Guard to a state of efficiency. A series of Fire Guard Training Notes, some special films and refresher courses helped instructors to keep up-to-date and to build up a common doctrine of training.

In August 1943 it was decided to raise the quality rather than the quantity of civil defence instructors; a new syllabus for instructors revised that drawn up in 1939 and covered a course of training in anti-gas ($16\frac{1}{4}$ hours), elementary high explosives ($4\frac{1}{2}$ hours) incendiary bomb control (11 hours) and general ($7\frac{1}{2}$ hours). Candidates were to be of a standard of intelligence capable of absorbing teaching quickly and of sufficient personality to enable them to impart the instruction to others. The Instructors who conducted these courses were themselves required to attend refresher courses.[4] That refresher courses for training officers were a constant necessity may be judged from developments in the latter half of 1943. The handbook 'Training in First Aid for Civil Defence purposes' was amended as regards instruction on crash injuries; an atlas of coloured photographs of typical air raid injuries was published; additions to 'Notes on the detection and reporting of unexploded missiles' and 'Objects dropped from the air' were made; a new training mixture to simulate mustard gas was produced; lantern slides and films dealing with debris tunnelling and clearance, the 'butterfly' bomb, and 'A fighter has crashed' were made available; decontamination squads were trained in the treatment of contaminated foodstuffs.[5]

---

[1] H.S.C. 129/43, 10th July 1943.

[2] H.S.C.s 88 and 104/43, 18th May and 12th June 1943.

[3] H.S.C. 150/43, 8th September 1943.

[4] H.S.C.s 145/43, 26th August 1943.

[5] A.R.P. Handbook No. 10. H.S.C.s 137, 185, 187, 195, 218, 226 and 37 of 24th August, 25th and 28th October, 8th November, 4th and 17th December 1943 and 31st March 1944 respectively; Training pamphlet No. 7.

To keep abreast of all these developments post-graduate refresher courses were held at Falfield and Easingwold. Regions pushed forward their preparations for opening comprehensive schools and by January 1944 ten of these were in operation. The selection of courses depended largely on the needs of the moment, but generally the main emphasis was on the training of Incident Officers and Fire Guard Officers and on bomb reconnaissance, with particular reference to the small anti-personnel bomb.

Since the Regional mobile units were analogous to the Civil Defence Rescue Service, use was made of training facilities at head-quarters of Regional columns, not only for members of the Rescue Service but also increasingly for members of the Home Guard and the Armed Forces. This was particularly the case in Scotland where between 1941 and 1945 no less than 16,000 members of these Forces (including Allied forces) and of the Home Guard were trained in rescue work and incident control at the three Rescue Service schools.

The Civil Defence Rescue Service was composed of a large number of part-time members, who had only a limited amount of time at their disposal for instruction. To meet their needs in January 1944 three new courses in basic and operational training were designed covering some eighty hours of instruction in first aid, rescue reconnaissance and rescue work to be spread over several months.[1] In August a National Civil Defence Rescue School was opened at the headquarters of the Regional Column unit at Sutton Coldfield providing accommodation for twenty-four students.[2] Its main purpose was to train rescue instructors who would carry out every kind of rescue training required by the civil defence organisation. The courses lasted about three weeks and covered the whole field of rescue work, including the handling of trapped casualties. The first to attend were the Operational and Training Officers of Regional Column units, and these were followed by the heads of the local authority Rescue Services and officers in industrial and commercial concerns in charge of rescue services.

As the date of the invasion of Europe approached, the demand for training for the forces of the Allied nations in passive air defence, incident control and rescue work expanded and the services of the civil defence training organisation were freely called upon. At the end of March 1944 the Regional Commissioner of the Tunbridge Wells Region reported that 'during the quarter the Region has become a civil defence training camp'. Over 1,000 military personnel received instruction in civil defence work, much Home Guard training was carried out as well as the training of R.A.F. ground staff and

---

[1] H.S.C. 10/44, 12th January 1944.
[2] H.S.C.s 70 and 77/44, 25th May and 13th June 1944.

of Allied forces. Port services and merchant ships' crews were given special courses in anti-gas measures.

Meanwhile the steady reduction of the civil defence services went on, and to provide against the expected enemy reaction to invasion every possible source of assistance had to be sought. Women and the Home Guard were almost the only sources left. Simple basic training was now extended to train all the Home Guard in rescue work and the W.V.S. in wardens' duties and some of the duties of incident control, particularly that of conducting incident inquiry points. To help make a little go a long way rescue training was also provided for wardens, members of the N.F.S. and personnel from industry.

By the spring of 1944 the lull for most of the country had lasted a long time. Work was hard, people were tired and the necessity of constant turning out for training was no longer obvious. Training Officers did what they could to counteract natural apathy by trying to make training more interesting through such means as competitions, demonstrations, quizzes and films. In places challenge cups were presented, and competition for them not only encouraged efficiency but also proved of interest and enjoyment for the competitors. It is noteworthy that in Scotland the Rescue Challenge Cup was won by a team from the north of Scotland which had never experienced raiding. The state of efficiency of the services depended, as always, on the personal enthusiasm of the individual. That this was still widespread was evident from the willingness of so many to come to the assistance of the south during the attacks by flying bombs and long-range rockets, and from keen competition to be selected for the overseas column.

The enemy did not react as expected to the invasion, and the keyed-up state could not be maintained indefinitely. Part-timers became reluctant to give time to further training and this gradually slackened and practically ceased when in September drastic reductions of civil defence personnel were ordered and the training of fire guards in all deprescribed areas stopped.[1] The Civil Defence Staff College and the Regional schools continued to hold courses for instructors, and training in Passive Air Defence, incident control and rescue work was carried on for military personnel and others going overseas. But in December formal training of the civil defence services came to an end.

(iii) Conditions of Service

Less obviously urgent than issues of tactical realignment and operational training, problems of working conditions and welfare proved, nevertheless, continuous. From the beginning the status

---

[1] H.S.C. 115/44, 19th September 1944.

and treatment of civil defence workers were influenced by the volunteer principle. Civil defence was seen not as a regular job but as a voluntary service performed in one's own locality. As a consequence, authority could sometimes develop a rather parsimonious attitude towards some of its responsibilities and a tendency to trade on the patience of a willing horse. As the war went on, however, more and more attention was paid to questions of working conditions, pay, accommodation and recreation. It began to be realised that even the volunteer spirit could be daunted if authority demonstrated too cavalier an attitude towards the welfare and comfort of civil defence workers, and that morale and efficiency could not be kept at full stretch among men and women who were uncomfortable and bored.

Certain improvements in hours of duty, sleeping accommodation and arrangements for meals and the limited issue of overalls were introduced during the early stand-by period.[1] By July 1940 a consultative committee of officials and trade union representatives had been set up and pay increases with special rates for some skilled men had been negotiated along with more generous provision for meals, accommodation and equipment.[2] In October 1940 the Mabane Committee was again considering matters affecting civil defence personnel, among them reservation and deferment, measures for enforcing discipline, possible sources of recruitment and schemes for clothing, subsistence allowances, compensation and funeral grants.

From the outset the organisation of the A.R.P. services had, with some exceptions, been based on equality of rank and rates of pay. To meet the increased cost of living basic pay was raised in July 1940 by 5s. 0d. per week for men and 3s. 6d. a week for women and again in February 1941 by the same amounts (bringing it up to £3 10s. 0d. for men and £2 7s. 0d. for women).[3] By the early months of 1941 'freezing orders' and compulsory enrolment had put a different complexion on the position of volunteers and the Government had to face up to fresh responsibilities. More consideration had to be given to questions of clothing, equipment, food and compensation for loss of wages.

On the advice of the Mabane Committee, it was agreed to introduce an ordered scheme of pay for certain intermediate ranks in the civil defence services,[4] new terms of compensation for injury were published,[5] travel concessions granted[6] and negotiations put in hand

---

[1] H.S.C. 155/40, 3rd July 1940; pp. 347–348.
[2] See Chapter IX, p. 376. H.S.C. 141/40, 24th June 1940.
[3] H.S.C. 47/41, 10th February 1941.
[4] H.S.C. 126/41, 31st May 1941.
[5] H.S.C. 139/41, 20th June 1941.
[6] H.S.C. 149/41, 4th July 1941.

for the payment of subsistence allowances.[1] Among other improvements were arrangements for the supply of meals to part-time volunteers or payment of cash in place of meals under certain conditions, sick leave concessions and the issue of an annual free railway voucher to whole-time personnel to ensure them a holiday in peaceful surroundings.

A suggestion to grant proficiency pay was discussed for three years before it was announced that from 1st January 1944 paid personnel would receive extra pay in respect of each year of completed service up to three years: 1s. 6d. per week for the first year, 3s. 6d. for two and 7s. od. for three;[2] in March it was announced that they would receive gratuities after the war. In August 1944 basic pay was raised to £4 os. 6d. for men and £2 16s. 6d. for women. Earlier in the year the rank of certain supervisory grades had also been raised.[3]

The provision of uniforms was a matter that for long caused heartsearching. On the one hand there was the view that a personal issue of uniform was a matter of justice to the volunteer, necessary for identification purposes and the development of *esprit de corps*; on the other hand the Ministry was reluctant to spend large sums of money in providing a free issue to each of the vast number of workers involved. During the spring and summer of 1940 the first issues of the A.R.P. blue cotton overall were made to certain branches of the service, the remainder still being provided only with a steel helmet and an armlet.[4] But the advent of heavy air raids soon made the question of waterproof and protective clothing acute. A cotton uniform was little protection against the weather and permission was, therefore, given to use anti-gas oilskin jackets and gum-boots for outdoor duty, while rescue men were issued with groundsheet capes and leather boots.[5] Later groundsheet capes were issued to the First Aid Parties and Messenger services and waterproofs to wardens and the Ambulance Service.[6] Towards the close of the Big Blitz in the spring of 1941 most A.R.P. personnel were still wearing blue cotton overalls over their own sweaters and under their own greatcoats. During the next few months, however, a Welfare and Comforts Fund organised by the W.V.S. began to provide knitted clothing.[7] And in May 1941 the issue of genuine uniforms of blue serge, overcoats, berets and boots for whole-time members of the services and

---

[1] H.S.C. 256/41, 11th November 1941.
[2] H.S.C. 60/44, 29th April 1944.
[3] H.S.C. 5/44, 15th January 1944.
[4] See p. 349.
[5] H.S.C. 253/40, 5th October 1940.
[6] H.S.C. 278/40, 9th November 1940.
[7] H.S.C. 285/40, 12th November 1940.

for part-time members undertaking not less than 48 hours' duty a month, began.[1]

Apart from the fundamental questions of money, food and clothing the day-to-day comfort of the civil defence forces raised many difficulties. The original conception of depots and posts had not visualised any lengthy occupation and quite ignored the social life of the Service. Events soon falsified this conception. Even on duty reasonable standards were often difficult to find. In 1939 the first consideration had been to provide gas cleansing stations, through which contaminated persons would pass without delay[2]; for the warden any space with a telephone, some blast and splinter protection and room for his equipment was considered enough. If this could not be conveniently found in an existing building, £50 (or in exceptional cases a maximum of £75) could be spent on a small post.[3] It was realised, however, that rescue and first aid party personnel might be working on a 24 hour relief basis and would need messing and sleeping accommodation. This would be arranged at or near the depots in existing local authority buildings, many of which were already protected.[4]

At the beginning volunteers endured these conditions and discomforts reasonably cheerfully. A few concessions and much local improvisation offset the severity of the first winter. Not until January 1941 however, was it decided that personnel should have the same standard of protection, both for their posts and sleeping accommodation, as the general public.[5] Fresh consideration was also given to the provision of bunks and the air space necessary per person.

In the lull following the heavy raids some physical recreation, occupations and entertainments for personnel standing by were organised and there was a growing realisation that civil defence workers needed more than just a roof over their heads. In November 1941 the Ministry of Home Security emphasised to local authorities the great importance, from the point of view of morale, of facilities for recreation, handicrafts and education. With the assistance of the Central Council for Physical Recreation, the Comforts Fund scheme was extended to cover general welfare activities, especially recreational activities and handicrafts.[6] A pamphlet 'Physical Recreation for Civil Defence Workers' was issued, Regional sports advisers were appointed and local authorities were encouraged to make similar appointments.

---

[1] H. of C. Deb., Vol. 371, Cols. 1565–7, 22nd May 1941.

[2] A.R.P. Dept. Circular 56, 27th March 1939.

[3] A.R.P. Dept. Circular 101, 4th May 1939; p. 348.

[4] A.R.P. Dept. Circular 134, 7th July 1939.

[5] H.S.C. 16/41, 3rd June 1941.

[6] H.S.C.s 262/41 and 275/41, 22nd November and 8th December 1941.

The Comforts Committee also interested itself in education and made a grant to the Workers' Educational Association to help it organise talks and lectures.[1] Discussion groups were encouraged and Regional Commissioners asked to help train leaders for them.[2] In 1944 a Discussion Group Bureau was established to act as a clearing house for the dissemination of information about the movement and to prepare material.[3] With so many extensions of its work the name of the Comforts Fund was changed to the Civil Defence Welfare Fund.

Responsibility for the welfare of the members of the Civil Defence General Services rested however with the local authorities, and the interpretation of this responsibility inevitably varied up and down the country. Some of the original posts and depots proved quite unsuitable and offered real hardship. The dirt and discomfort that might be tolerated in the face of heavy air attacks became a scandal when these had passed, and a series of reports on the still unsatisfactory standards of sleeping, sanitary facilities and cleanliness to be found in some posts and depots so impressed the Minister that he issued an appeal to all authorities setting out minimum standards that should be observed.[4] It was pointed out that the services were now being reinforced by men and women enrolled under some measure of compulsion, who might lack the readiness to accept poor conditions usually shown by the original volunteers. Discomfort would seriously impair efficiency, and local authorities were urged to call upon a central supply of equipment now established to remedy deficiencies.[5]

The matter of amenities assumed particular prominence when, in 1942, women became liable to compulsory enrolment for fire guard duties at business premises. These premises were of all kinds and were often quite unsuitable for women to stay in overnight. The earlier Business Premises Order required occupiers to provide 'reasonable amenities' for Fire Guards, but in spite of many requests this requirement had never been defined. But in September a memorandum was sent to all local authorities setting out the amenities and minimum standards.[6] This dealt with the questions of sleeping accommodation, washing and sanitary conveniences, bedding, meal facilities, duty and recreation rooms, and suggested that a responsible woman officer should be appointed (either whole-time paid or part-time unpaid) with the rank of Fire Guard Assistant

---

[1] H.S.C. 105/42, 19th May 1942.

[2] H.S.C. 96/43, 28th May 1943.

[3] H.S.C. 17/44, 5th February 1944.

[4] H.S.C. 122/42, 15th June 1942.

[5] Ibid.

[6] F.P. Leaflet No. 3/42 and H.S.C. 183/42, 24th September 1942.

Staff Officer to supervise amenities for women Fire Guards. Should this provision involve the occupiers of the business premises in special expense, this could be included in allowed expenses for taxation purposes.

One other aspect of conditions of service that must be briefly mentioned is that of discipline. The A.R.P. forces, it will be recalled, were subject to no formal disciplinary code, and in spite of many suggestions to alter the position this remained true to the end of the war. The Mabane Committee believed that a solution to disciplinary difficulties lay in the institution of graded ranks to attract leaders, to maintain authority and to protect the interests of the members rather than in the establishment of a formal code.

In January 1941, however, the compulsory enrolment of part-timers[1] made it necessary to introduce powers to give directions in accordance with the new Order. This was done in April by the Civil Defence (Employment and Offences) Order which made any member of the Civil Defence Services liable to a fine of £10 or a month's imprisonment for disobeying a lawful order or for being absent from duty without reasonable cause.[2] The institution of proceedings under these regulations was in effect the only procedure whereby disciplinary action could be taken, but for a variety of reasons local authorities were chary of taking this step. Dismissal, in view of the shortage of personnel, was normally an unsatisfactory procedure and not acceptable to local authorities, while the trade unions were opposed to stoppage of pay or indeed to any disciplinary code at all. Although the absence of such a code occasionally caused difficulties, civil defence was pre-eminently a service which depended on the loyalty, common sense and goodwill of all concerned; that very few persons were found guilty of offences suggests that these qualities were sustained.

Fire Prevention and the Fire Guard

Although during the thirties public and indeed official imagination had tended to revolve around the horrors of gas and high explosive attack, it was soon clear to the planners that the light incendiary bomb was an equal, if not greater, danger. While steps were taken to help meet this menace—in the development of the emergency fire services[3]—it was realised that the task might well prove too big to be left entirely to these professional forces. With the possibility of widely scattered fires breaking out in large numbers the Home Office had begun to think in terms of amateur help. The threat

---

[1] S.R. & O. 1941, No. 68; p. 551.
[2] S.R. & O. 1941, No. 455.
[3] These are described in Chapter VI.

of widely dispersed fires was later reinforced by other motives for extending citizen participation. From 1941 onwards, as the civil defence services were drained of every able-bodied man that could be spared, it became more and more urgent that comparatively unskilled but universal assistance should be organised. How could the householder, the factory or shop worker and the part-time A.R.P. worker be further employed to redress the balance?

In 1936 the fighting of fires *at the early stages* was visualised both by the Riverdale Committee and the A.R.P. Department of the Home Office as a duty that could be assigned to a branch of the Wardens' Service.[1] The Fire Brigades Division had different views; they felt that the brigades were most competent to deal with fires and proposed instead an Auxiliary Fire Service and a system of street patrols based on fire stations and, where necessary, 'fire posts' manned and equipped for elementary fire-fighting.[2]

Backed by a study of the Spanish Civil War, the Incendiary Bombs Committee decided that the small incendiary bomb was likely to be the enemy's most dangerous weapon and that the public should be trained to deal with it. Courses in this subject were not, however, started at Falfield and Easingwold until January 1939. A few months before the war ten temporary schools were hurriedly opened in the Regions to train instructors.[3]

Meanwhile, this Committee had evolved the stirrup pump with a 'dual purpose' nozzle as a fire-fighting appliance.[4] In the first quarter of 1939, 50,000 of these pumps were ordered for delivery to wardens' posts; later in the year a further 50,000 were authorised, and local authorities were permitted to draw on this issue for the protection of A.R.P. buildings.[5] By the outbreak of war, however, only about 9,500 pumps had been delivered; by June 1940 local authorities had received some 86,000.

In April 1940 an issue of stirrup pumps on loan had been arranged for fire authorities, who became responsible for the selection and training of volunteers for informal supplementary fire parties.[6] Thus a beginning was made with the supply of pumps to members of the public with some guarantee that they would know how to use them and the issue of a further 75,000 was then authorised. But public opinion demanded more. The Civil Defence Act, 1939 placed on individuals and industrial concerns responsibility for providing protection for their premises. Equipment was however expensive and difficult to find—varieties of pumps could sometimes be

---

[1] See Chapter III, p. 71.
[2] Memorandum on Emergency Fire Brigade Organisation, 23rd February 1937.
[3] See Chapter V, p. 210.
[4] See Chapter IV, pp. 147-148.
[5] pp. 213, 235.
[6] F.B. Circular No. 33/1940, 19th April 1940.

bought but the supply was small and the price high and there was much criticism therefore of the Home Secretary when in a broadcast he urged 'every householder to get a stirrup pump and to learn how to use it'. In August after much discussion it was decided to provide local authorities with pumps to be sold to the public at £1 each. As output was still limited and slow, certain priorities had to be observed and the vociferous demand was only partly met. Moreover, when the incendiary attacks became severe at the end of the year this supply had to be diverted to the police, wardens, organised fire parties and the Home Guard. Twenty-thousand stirrup pumps were distributed to police authorities and 1,500 to agricultural districts for the protection of crops. Although pumps were delivered to wardens' posts, fire-fighting was not among the formal duties of a warden, whose job was to report fires and summon help. But in many districts householders organised informal street fire parties and wardens were urged to encourage this movement and to hand over pumps to reliable persons. It is impossible to assess the number in the hands of the public during the Big Blitz, but there is no doubt that this was quite inadequate. As late as June 1942 there was still an outstanding demand for about 95,000 pumps.

Even in the summer of 1940 no one clearly visualised the need for an army of civilians to help the professional brigades and the A.F.S. in the task of fighting fires. At Regional Headquarters fire prevention was in the sole hands of a Regional Fire Brigade Inspector. There was still apathy and refusal fully to acknowledge the fire menace. Local authorities were often slow and unco-operative and sometimes resented outside advice, particularly from Whitehall. Planning was therefore hesitant.

The first Fire Watchers Order of September 1940 was quite inadequate.[1] It applied only to premises in which more than 30 persons worked, to warehouses of more than 50,000 cubic feet and to saw-mills or timber yards containing more than 50,000 cubic feet of timber. The Order required that at such premises a person should be present at all times to detect any fire and to summon assistance. But the Order was too loosely drawn. Watchers were difficult to obtain, applications for exemption were numerous and premises outside the scope of the Order were just as inflammable. When in the latter half of 1940 raids increased in intensity the enemy's strongest weapon was his opponent's unpreparedness. Fire prevention was in its infancy, equipment was scanty and there were few street fire parties in business districts. Parties often fought without training or leadership, and in some places strengths were reduced by a nightly exodus. For instance, after a raid at the end of November 1940 Southampton counted 9,600 unoccupied shops

---

[1] S.R. & O. 1940, No. 1677.

and houses. Fire-fighters were further handicapped by restrictions on the power of entry to premises. Consequently on 19th October 1940 the power of entry already granted to auxiliary firemen by Defence (General) Regulations, 1939 was granted to air raid wardens and members of any recognised voluntary fire-fighting party and later this was extended to the Home Guard, members of a fire-fighting party organised by a local authority and to constables.[1]

The Civil Defence Committee also took the view that it was 'not possible to organise a satisfactory system, even with the use of compulsion, on the basis of private effort alone'. Compulsion for fire prevention duties had been under discussion for some months. But the raids of the autumn of 1940 culminating in the great incendiary attack on London on 29th-30th December spurred the War Cabinet to agree on 31st December to the principle of compulsion for part-time civil defence duties. That night the Minister of Home Security broadcast an appeal for volunteers to form street fire-fighting parties and announced at the same time the forthcoming introduction of compulsion.

On 15th January 1941 new Regulations[2] gave the Minister of Home Security powers to compel persons of both sexes within prescribed ages to perform part-time civil defence duties. In pursuance of these powers he replaced the Fire Watchers Order with the Fire Precaution (Business Premises) Order[3] and made the Civil Defence Duties (Compulsory Enrolment) Order.[4] Local authorities or other 'appropriate authorities', which included all Government Departments, were now required to make adequate arrangements for detecting and combating fires in prescribed business and industrial districts, and men between 16 and 60 residing in such areas had to register for possible part-time fire prevention duty. Women and youths were encouraged to volunteer for these duties. The maximum period for compulsory service was limited to 48 hours per month.[5] In England and Wales the local authorities for the purposes of these Orders were the borough and district councils, but county councils were to co-operate in the organisation of voluntary street fire parties through the Wardens' Service.[6] In Scotland the local authorities were county councils and all town councils. Compulsory enrolment would apply only when the Regional Commissioner was satisfied

---

[1] S.R. & O. 1940, No. 1873; S.R. & O. 1941, No. 170; S.R. & O. 1941, No. 1248; S.R. & O. 1942, No. 634.

[2] Defence Regulations 26A, 27A and 27B.

[3] S.R.&O. No. 69, 18th January 1941.

[4] S.R.&O. No. 70, 18th January 1941.

[5] Defence Regulation 27A.

[6] H.S.C. 21/41, 18th January 1941.

that volunteers were insufficient.[1] Many areas were in fact prescribed and a large number of persons became liable for fire prevention duties.[2]

Training of these new fire watchers was in the hands of the Fire Brigades, the A.F.S., the Wardens' Service or experienced members of Supplementary Fire Parties. Parties were organised as a unified service, but how they were employed depended largely on local circumstances.[3] At private business premises the members of the fire parties were trained by their own instructors, while Government employees were largely trained by Ministry of Works Fire Training Instructors. The Business Premises Order also required the occupiers of premises to provide adequate equipment. For the use of the fire parties enrolled by local authorities there was a free issue on loan of stirrup pumps, sandbags and, in certain cases, steel helmets, and armlets bearing the initials 'S.F.P.' were provided, but parties had to provide receptacles for water from their own resources.[4]

These Orders were not, however, a success. Local authorities found them complicated and most of them were reluctant to apply for the unpopular power of compulsory enrolment; and in a number of cases when they did apply it was not authorised by Regional Commissioners on account of the anomalies and deficiences in the Orders. Confusion was caused by the multiplicity of 'appropriate authorities' and by the absence of a statement of the individual's legal responsibility. The unwillingness of independent businessmen and of Government Departments to co-operate in joint schemes was often a further source of weakness. Even the responsibility of the Regional Commissioner was not clear, and the lack of overall direction was felt. Some county scheme-making authorities, though responsible for the Wardens' Service, were excluded from any concern in the fire-fighting organisation and from the power of compulsory enrolment given to other local authorities, and thus hereditary feuds between some local authorities and the county were exacerbated. Few local authorities had any adequate staff organised and trained to deal with these new tasks that had been added to the heavy burdens already resulting from air attack. Enrolments were, therefore, often delayed and large scale evasion occurred. The Orders also put many difficulties on occupiers; joint schemes were hard to arrange and differing rates of subsistence allowances paid to fire

---

[1] H.S.C. 26/41, 28th January 1941.

[2] Members of the Home Guard, armed forces, civil defence services were not subject to these Orders; mental defectives and blind persons were exempted (S.R. & O. Nos. 69 and 70, 18th January 1941). Appeals for exemption on the grounds of medical unfitness or exceptional hardship, including long hours on vital work, could be made to a Military Service (Hardship) Committee. H.S.C. 26/41, 28th January 1941.

[3] H.S.C. 26/41, 28th January 1941.

[4] Ibid.

watchers caused some discontent. Authorities often found it difficult to find extra fire guards for business premises, where fire watching was uncomfortable and unpopular. In places, too, it could be dangerous; it was said that in Hull fire watchers said good-bye to their families and left their wives weeping. A report on conditions in Portsmouth and Southampton recommended publicity campaigns to persuade those taking part in the nightly exodus to perform their fair share of fire-fighting duties in the town.

These Orders of January were framed to apply to business and residential premises in prescribed areas, but there were some districts which by their nature required special consideration. There were, for instance, special Orders for men working in the City of London, where fire watching duty was given precedence over enrolment elsewhere.[1] In the same way fire prevention measures had to be found for the Palace of Westminster. Throughout most of the Blitz the Palace was far from being well protected. The first two Orders did not apply to it, and even in March 1941 there were doubts as to where responsibility lay. Appeals to the staff and Members of Parliament in March and April failed to produce enough volunteers and the Ministry of Works had to ask the police and the London Fire Brigade to improvise small parties. In April it was decided to appoint a full-time A.R.P. Officer but before this organisation was in being, on 10th-11th May, the House of Commons Chamber was destroyed, Westminster Hall severely damaged and two police constables killed. On 30th May compulsory fire watching duties were imposed on men between 18 and 60 working at the Palace.[2]

The following year the Business Premises Order was extended to any building 'the preservation of which or of the contents of which appeared to be in the public interest by reason of their historic or national character'.[3] To deal with the problem of empty houses, the Fire Precautions (Residential Buildings) Order compelled occupiers to see that certain windows were left unobscured, that water was available and that an authorised person should have keys to be able to enter quickly.[4]

But it was soon obvious that uniformity had not been achieved. In some areas the fire parties were organised by the Wardens' Service, in others by the local fire brigade and in others they were under the direct control of the local authorities. Further adjustment was necessary and became imperative when in August 1941 local

---

[1] S.R. & O. 1941, No. 538; S.R. & O. 1942, No. 1269; S.R. & O. 1942, No. 2288.

[2] Defence (Palace of Westminster Fire Prevention) Regulations, 1941, S.R. & O. No. 757.

[3] Fire Prevention (Historic Buildings) Order, 1942, S.R. & O. No. 1352.

[4] S.R. & O. 1942, No. 241.

authorities lost control of the fire services and the National Fire Service was established.[1]

Now it was decided that supervision of the part-time fire parties called for the creation of new posts and that these should form part of the general Wardens' Service. In August it was laid down that in future all persons performing fire prevention duties should be known as 'Fire Guards' and wear an armlet bearing that title instead of 'S.F.P.'.[2] Where the fire prevention organisation was already linked to the Wardens' Service little change was required, but in other cases special adaptation was necessary. For the first time a series of whole-time posts for leaders of different grades was created, and where these could not be filled by volunteers payment was authorised.[3]

Chief, District and Divisional Wardens were now responsible for the organisation of the Fire Guards, and to help them Fire Guard Staff Officers, Fire Guard Assistant Staff Officers, Head and Senior Fire Guards were appointed from the ranks of the wardens. The Fire Guard Staff Officers' function was the organisation and allocation of the available Fire Guards, the organisation of depots or places of assembly, and administration and inspection. At the depots a Fire Guard Depot Superintendent prepared rotas of duty, maintained discipline, organised sleeping and feeding accommodation and looked after equipment. A Senior Fire Guard supervised about 600 Fire Guards in the area of one or more wardens' posts, while a Head Fire Guard had charge of a group of some 8 Senior Fire Guards.

Although the introduction of the name 'Fire Guard' and an officered service was helpful, the organisation still remained complicated by the division of responsibility between various 'appropriate authorities' and the obscurity surrounding the position of Fire Guards at business premises. Generally the new arrangements were received by local authorities without enthusiasm. The Slough Trading Estate can provide an example of the problems that could arise. This was in the area of Slough Borough; it had a roof area of about 4½ million square feet, and housed 227 firms, which together employed about 18,000 men and women and constituted an exceptional fire risk. The 227 firms being engaged on various forms of work, the 'appropriate authorities' for fire prevention purposes included Slough Town Council, the Ministries of Labour, Aircraft Production, Supply and War Transport and the Admiralty. All these had their own ideas and methods of organising their Fire Guard and only after considerable controversy was it agreed that the single authority for fire prevention should be the Ministry of

---

[1] See Chapter XI.
[2] H.S.C. 174/41, 6th August 1941.
[3] Ibid.

Aircraft Production. But the handling of the task and interpretation of the Fire Prevention Orders by this body did not go smoothly and there were a series of complaints, strikes, petitions and summonses up to the relaxation of fire watching in 1944.

In September 1941 two new Orders replaced those of the previous January.[1] One extended the application of the original order to premises previously exempt and added to the duties of the occupier in respect of the organisation, equipment and training of Fire Guards. The other provided for the compulsory enrolment of men who performed fire prevention duties at business premises for less than 48 hours in 4 weeks to do a substantial part of the balance where they lived.[2] These Orders, still complicated and burdensome, brought little relief to local authorities already harassed by manpower shortages. In all areas to which the Business Premises Order applied fire prevention duties were compulsory on all male householders; but the investigation of the flood of claims for exemption, rising to 75 per cent. of those registered, caused much work and the drafting of Fire Guards from the local authorities' pools was very difficult. Both the Orders provided for exemption on the production of a certificate that the bearer was engaged in 'vital work for exceptionally long hours'. Superficially the phrase appeared reasonably succinct, but in practice it was difficult to define 'vital work' or 'exceptionally long hours'. Once granted, a certificate might last too long and permit the avoidance of duty without justification. The Orders involved a multiplicity of elaborate forms, while accounting for subsistance allowances caused much trouble. After long complaint, subsistance allowances were officially standardised, but anomalies persisted and the cost to the Exchequer gave rise to criticism. Some local authorities were annoyed that these allowances were only grant-aided and thought they were too high and granted only as a sop to the T.U.C. One Region complained that the cost was greater than that of the rest of the civil defence services put together.

Registration was conducted by the Ministry of Labour and National Service but the documents were drafted by the Ministry of Home Security and were not always fully understood by the Labour Exchange managers. There were also delays due to the pressure of work in passing the papers from the Ministry of Labour and National Service to the Town Clerk's department and thence to the Fire Guard office, and there were so many means of obtaining exemption that it was said 'that anyone not a congenital idiot could easily evade fire guard duty, and in any case a congenital idiot was

---

[1] Fire Prevention (Business Premises) (No. 2) Order, 1941, S.R. & O. No. 1411. Civil Defence Duties (Compulsory Enrolment) (No. 2) Order, 1941, S.R. & O. No. 1412.
[2] H.S.C. 201/41, 17th September 1941.

entitled to exemption'. Early attempts at enforcement suffered from lack of a uniform policy, reluctance to institute proceedings which might be dismissed on a legal technicality and the widely differing penalties imposed. To co-ordinate enforcement the Minister asked local authorities to obtain the agreement of the Regional Commissioner before instituting proceedings.

The problems continued to be acute and solutions had to be found. Already the number of persons involved in the administration of fire prevention measures was growing fast and this was augmented in October by the institution of the National Advisory Council for Fire Prevention and its subsidiary regional councils. It was composed of representatives of employers' associations, the T.U.C., local authorities, the Scottish Office, the Home Office and the Ministry of Home Security. Liaison with all Government Departments was maintained through a Fire Prevention (Operational) Committee and with the Regions through the Regional Advisory Councils. In November 1941 at the second meeting of the Operational Committee the vice-chairman suggested that a 'stage had been reached when the complexities of the Fire Prevention Orders were so great that a drastic simplification was called for if further progress was to be made'.

As we have seen earlier, in this latter part of 1941 national manpower shortages were presenting many problems. In December a new Defence Regulation empowered the Minister of Labour and National Service to direct persons to whole or part-time service in civil defence.[1] As at this time and subsequently the threat of invasion tended to loom larger than the danger of fires from bombing attacks, the Fire Guard often suffered in the allocation of manpower from competition with the Home Guard.

From August 1941 until the 'Baedeker' raids of the following early summer there was a lull in air attack which gave an eight months breathing space to the organisers of the new Fire Guard. The 'Baedeker' raids and the first real tests of the fire guard organisation began on 24th April with a low level attack on Exeter. Incendiary attack was concentrated, and though the 11,000 fire guards were brave and efficient they were hampered by machine-gun fire, narrow streets and inaccessible roofs. Arrangements in Government premises were below standard and the attitude of some 'appropriate authorities' made co-ordination difficult. Lack of organisation and knowledge of fire control allowed fires to spread and caused the loss of 2 out of every 3 buildings ignited. On the next two nights the target was Bath, which had been considered a 'safe' town and perhaps for that reason was found virtually unprepared. Training was inadequate and equipment defective; in many buildings there were

---

[1] Defence Regulation 29BA (S.R. & O. 1941, No. 2052); see pp. 555-556.

no fire guards at all, and lack of leadership contributed to an exodus of fire guards on the second night. The attacks then shifted to Norwich, where again on two nights in April and on 1st May concentrations of incendiary bombs presented problems beyond the powers of the fire guards. They did all that was possible in the business areas, but the street fire parties lacked leadership and in some cases left the city.[1]

Late in April a short attack was made on York and though the Minster was undamaged the Guildhall was gutted, largely owing to handicaps imposed by the narrow streets. On 3rd May a return visit was paid to Exeter, and then cathedral cities were unmolested until the last day of the month when the first of three attacks was made on Canterbury. About 6,000 incendiaries were dropped, mostly from a low level, and caused an impossible situation for the fire guards. They were, however, a credit to their training and organisation and displayed great gallantry. A party remained throughout the raid on the roof of the cathedral and successfully dealt with a cluster of incendiaries. The next night an insignificant raid was made on Ipswich and in the next four days two more visits were paid to Canterbury.

These raids focused attention on the inadequacy of fire prevention measures. The results of compulsory enrolment for business premises had been slow, painful and disappointing both in quantity and quality, so that in many cases local authorities had not enough fire guards in their 'pools' to enable them to make good the deficiences.

In May 1942, an Order was made applying the principles of the Business Premises Order to Government premises and the Minister of Home Security, supported by the Minister of Labour and National Service, announced that he proposed to introduce compulsion for women.[2] The Lord President's Committee felt that this should apply only to business premises; the Trades Union Women's Advisory Committee thought it should apply also to residential areas, while the Trades Union Council affirmed 'their complete objection to the conscription of women for fire-fighting, whether for business premises or private premises'.

However, the plan proceeded and three new Orders were issued containing a number of provisions designed to ensure that every person who was not performing some other form of part-time service should be liable to perform fire guard duty under their local authority.[3] Authorities were empowered to hold supplementary registrations from time to time; the exemption from enrolment of the

[1] See pp. 429-432.
[2] S.R. & O. 1942, No. 839; S.R. & O. 1942, No. 2397.
[3] S.R. & O. 1942, Nos. 1654, 1655 and 2397.

voluntary street parties was withdrawn and for the first time a limited scheme for the compulsion of women between 20 and 45 was introduced. Certain exemptions were granted on account of family or household duties or war work and, as far as possible, women were not to serve outside residential districts.[1] To offset the shortage of personnel and in the hope of improving discipline, training was made compulsory for all fire guards.[2]

Though the withdrawal of exemption from street fire parties gave local authorities the power to post them away from their parties or to another service, authorities were warned that their Fire Guard Organisation could not be satisfactory until every block of buildings was covered either by a street fire party or by fire guards organised to conform with the Business Premises Order. Experience had shown that where Head and Senior Fire Guards were careful to build up a proper system of leadership through Street Fire Party Leaders and Street Captains these parties formed a valuable fire prevention force. It was, therefore, emphasised that stress should be laid on the selection of officers for the street fire parties and the establishment of a recognised chain of command.[3]

These orders met with a mixed reception, but the balance of opinion was distinctly unfavourable. In places the compulsion of women was welcomed, in others it was disliked and in all areas the duty put upon occupiers of providing 'adequate amenities' proved very difficult. Women were most reluctant to do duty at business premises, very often because of the discomfort and uncleanliness of the accommodation, and they resented being conscripted from volunteer street parties. A high proportion applied for exemption. One Region claimed that their view that compulsion for women for business premises would not repay the labour involved was confirmed by experience. The London Regional Commissioner in his report for November 1942 stated that out of nearly 1,300,000 women registered about 66 per cent. claimed exemption, and Reading Region wrote that registration by the local authorities only secured about one quarter of the women available. Dealing with these claims involved endless clerical labour at a time when every form of manpower was scarce and when local authorities and Regional staffs were already hard pressed. Another bitter source of complaint was the number of men who managed to evade full fire guard duty, and from all sides it was urged that women should not be liable for duty at business premises until all available men were fully employed.

The view of one Region that 'no branch of war-time legislation

---

[1] H.S.C.s 157/42 and 165/42, 7th and 19th August 1942.

[2] See p. 583.

[3] H.S.C. 158/42 and Annex, 11th August 1942.

has resulted in so complex and cumbersome an administrative machine' was endorsed by many local authorities and by October it was necessary to take steps to remove some of the causes of complaint. The Minister decided to introduce extensive changes in the fire prevention system. Amendments to the various Defence Regulations and Orders and the issue of a new Order to give him power to apply special schemes in specially prescribed areas were proposed in the House of Commons on 17th November. Knowing these amendments were in preparation and hoping soon to have some of their burdens lightened, local authorities were slow to issue any instructions; provisions of existing orders were ignored and progress halted except as regards the training of those already enrolled. But between the promise of the new orders and their appearance came a long exasperating delay.

The Orders establishing the Fire Guard Organisation were complicated by a certain amount of dual control and confusion in the chain of authority. Responsibility for fire prevention lay with district councils but responsibility for the Wardens' Service of which the Fire Guard now formed a part rested with the county councils.[1] While in some areas this worked quite well, in others it led to endless difficulties. By now enemy bombing tactics were concentrating more and more on incendiary attack and an adequate Fire Guard with the closest working arrangements with the N.F.S. was of supreme importance. In December 1942 a Regional Commissioners' conference considered four alternative solutions: (*a*) that the Fire Guard should become part of the N.F.S.; (*b*) that responsibility for fire prevention should be transferred from the district councils to the larger scheme-making authorities who would then control the Fire Guard through the Wardens' Service; (*c*) that Fire Guards should be made a separate service under the administrative and operational control of local authorities, and (*d*) that Fire Guards under all local authorities should be made a separate service under the administrative and operational control of the local authorities with officers solely responsible to the local authorities and with the Fire Guard Staff Officer reporting to them and not to the Chief Warden.

In February 1943 the Minister announced that for England and Wales he favoured alternative (*d*). But there would, of course, be the closest possible co-operation with the N.F.S. The duty of implementing this decision then passed to the Regional Commissioners. If they were satisfied that the association of the Fire Guard with the Wardens' Service was working adequately then there was no need to disturb the *status quo*, but their decisions were to rest on consultations with the local authorities.[2] On 18th February full

---

[1] H.S.C. 176/41, 14th August 1941.
[2] H.S.C. 23/43, 4th February 1943.

particulars of the new 'Fire Guard Plan' were sent to all local authorities in England and Wales who were urged to achieve close liaison between the Fire Guard and N.F.S. in all areas prescribed under the Fire Prevention Orders.[1]

For Scotland it was decided to continue the existing arrangement under which the Fire Guard formed part of the Wardens' Service. The greater part of the remainder of the Fire Guard Plan was adopted in Scotland, and every effort was made to improve the liaison with the National Fire Service. The use of telephones for summoning assistance from the N.F.S. to air raid fires was, however, always allowed in Scotland and runners were used only where, under air raid conditions, they provided a quicker service.

The Plan was to operate only during the hours of darkness, i.e. from half an hour before to half an hour after black-out. In effect the fire guards, though under the control of the local authorities, became the scouts of the N.F.S. The unit area of the reorganised force, the division, was the area served by each N.F.S. station. This area was divided into Sectors, each under a Fire Guard Sector Captain, and each sector was sub-divided into Street Party areas under Party Leaders in residential areas and Blocks under Block Leaders in business premises areas. In each division there was a point to be manned immediately after an alert, on the fall of bombs or if there were gunfire. Each of these points formed part of the chain linking the Fire Guard Sectors with each other and with the N.F.S. In England and Wales all messages had to pass through these points and the duty of summoning N.F.S. assistance by messenger lay entirely with the Fire Guard Sector Captains. Only outside the Plan hours should the police, the wardens or members of the public summon N.F.S. assistance. While the Plan was in operation the duties of detecting and fighting fires and of summoning assistance were in the hands of the Fire Guard. Sector Captains could send Fire Guard reinforcements to other sectors to operate under the orders of the Sector Captain of the area involved, but if the N.F.S. was summoned all Fire Guards on the fire ground would come under the orders of the senior N.F.S. Officer present.[2] To avoid delay or duplication a standard message form was prescribed which would give a sufficiently definite picture of the fire position to the N.F.S. while imposing the least amount of additional duty on the Fire Guard Leaders.[3] It was also part of the Plan that the N.F.S. should look to the fire guards to show them the best way to enter buildings, the position of party walls, water supplies, etc., to help with the hose and to relieve N.F.S. crews by damping down fires.[4]

---

[1] H.S.C. 29/43, 18th February 1943.
[2] Ibid.
[3] H.S.C. 120/43, 16th August 1943.
[4] H.S.C. 29/43, 18th February 1943.

Where the Plan did not operate it remained the duty of wardens to report fires to the nearest fire station by the quickest available means.

In April 1943 detailed instructions regarding the organisation and administration of the Fire Guard as a separate service were issued.[1] At the head of this service a local authority officer replaced both the Chief Warden and the Fire Guard Staff Officer. He had the title of Fire Guard Officer and might have a deputy and be assisted by an Assistant Fire Guard Officer, both also local authority officers. The other ranks of the existing Fire Guard were also abolished and replaced by whole-time paid Fire Guard Area Officers, part-time unpaid Area Captains, Sector Captains, Block Leaders and Street Party Leaders. In place of the depots, reserve centres were to be set up under the general charge of the Area Officers or Captains, but with a Centre Superintendent in immediate charge.

In general, officers holding appointments under the existing organisation were readily transferable to analogous posts in the new service. The Plan, however, fixed the number of sectors in each area and in some cases it was not possible to absorb all the existing officers. Where this occurred they were to be asked to take subordinate posts in the new service or be retained in the Wardens' Service. To supervise amenities, it was suggested that women should be appointed as Assistant Fire Guard Officers or Fire Guard Inspectors (Amenities). The appointment of paid Training Officers or Inspectors as well as unpaid Area Instructors was also authorised.[2] In May and June special training courses were started at the Ministry of Home Security Schools and Regional Schools for Fire Guard Training Officers and local instructors.[3]

When the Plan (set out by the Ministry in a 72-page memorandum which achieved fame, if not notoriety, in civil defence circles) was published local authorities looked askance at the prospect of re-organisation and re-training. Nevertheless, by the end of June a fair amount of preliminary work had been done and many schemes submitted for approval. It was not, however, until 20th September— ten months after the Minister's statement in the House of Commons —that the Orders legalising the new Plan came into operation.[4]

The Plan consisted of 2 parts; Part A provided for the organisation,

[1] H.S.C. 63/43, 9th April 1943.

[2] H.S.C. 129/43, 30th July 1943.

[3] See p. 583.

[4] The new Plan was given a legal basis by the Fire Guard (Local Authority Services) Order, 1943; the Fire Guard (Business and Government Premises) Order, 1943; the Fire Guard (Medical and Hardship Exemptions) Order, 1943—all under the Defence (Fire Guard) Regulations, 1943 (S.R. & O., 1943, Nos. 1043, 1044, 1045 and 916). On 9th August 1943 copies of these Orders, together with the Explanatory Memorandum, were circulated to all local authorities (H.S.C. 133/43, 9th August 1943; Scottish Home Department Circular No. 5430).

leadership and mutual support of fire guards and Part B for a systematic method of summoning N.F.S. assistance during or just after attack. Part A was obligatory in all prescribed areas but Part B was only applied by direction of the Regional Commissioner. The age limit for compulsory service for men was extended to 63, and voluntary enrolment was limited to men between 16 and 70 and and to women between 18 and 60. The classes entitled to exemption were scheduled. No conscientious objection to fire guard duties was recognised and certain aliens were also made liable for duty. Local authorities were responsible for the appointment of officers and for the discipline and training of all enrolled fire guards. The Minister could prescribe an area as a 'special area' and then all persons working there who were liable would be enrolled and exempted from duty elsewhere, but if it was an exceptionally vulnerable area women would be excused. At business and Government premises fire guard duties were to be performed by a fixed team and all surplus fire guards made available to the local authority's pool. Women were only liable to inclusion in these teams if there were not enough men available.[1] When there was no enemy activity only one fire guard need keep awake and even this precaution could be relaxed by the Regional Commissioner. The aim of these Orders was to secure the best protection where this was needed combined with the fullest relaxation elsewhere.[2]

These Orders, needing as they did an explanatory book of 72 pages, encountered a great deal of criticism. One Region described them as 'about as long as the Book of Genesis and quite as difficult to swallow'; another as 'unnecessarily long and obscure'. There was widespread feeling that the Business and Government Premises Orders were too complicated and that instead of reducing the burdens of occupiers they involved much new work. The Local Authority Services Order required fresh registrations but many Town Clerks reported that the registration notice was quite unintelligible. In any case the registration did little to increase resources. New exemptions enabled many women to withdraw, and local authorities in most Regions had to search National Registration records for those who might be evading duty. There were still too many people entitled to submit schemes, and too many 'appropriate authorities' with whom the Fire Guard Officer had no right to interfere. The Plan demanded manpower and equipment now beyond the country's resources. One Region gauged its need at 4,236 Sector Captains, 4,500 Sector Clerks, 3,000 Block Leaders, 13,000 Street Party Leaders and 60,000 messengers every night.

The large number of bodies between whom responsibility was

---

[1] H.S.C. 153/43, 13th September 1943.

[2] H.S.C. 182/43, 21st October 1943.

divided made it impossible to obtain accurate statistics on personnel. The Inspector-General's Department estimated that in August 1942 the strength was approaching six million, and incomplete information in reports by Regional Advisory Councils for Fire Prevention suggest a figure of over 5,600,000 at the end of December 1943.[1] But by then the peak had been passed; during 1943 registrations had not been able to check the leak from the Fire Guard to other fields. In London Region in September there was a deficiency of over 160,000 below the minimum standard requirements. It was impossible to set up the Reserve Centres necessary and difficult to find suitable persons to act as Sector Captains, Block or Street Party Leaders. But even so, this civilian army was still a colossus and to equip it was an enormous undertaking after the drain of four years of war. For the Fire Guards themselves, establishment as a separate service stimulated morale and Fire Guard Officers benefited by their new independence and authority. Though it was difficult to maintain interest in a new system and in training at this stage of the war, new methods and the issue of certificates made training more popular and, after a slow start, Fire Guards generally achieved a high standard of efficiency—just when this ceased to be urgently required.

But the personnel also had their grievances. By the force of circumstances they were being saddled with more directions, more training and longer hours just when other civil defence services were being progressively reduced, and there was some restiveness regarding the requirement of 'daylight watching' and the 'wakeful watch'. Regional Commissioners had wide powers to grant relaxations, but in vulnerable areas a high standard of preparedness had to be maintained and these duties were irksome. Inequalities and delay over medical exemptions, variations in exemptions granted on account of 'long hours' and in subsistence allowances, loss of wages, lack of transport, lack of distinctive uniform and above all lack of amenities continued to be sore points. The employment of women Fire Guard Officers led, however, to an improvement in amenities.

One of the best points in the Fire Guard Plan was that it brought the local authorities into closer contact with the N.F.S.; and as this service had by this time established good co-operation with many of the works' fire brigades a new cohesion in fire prevention was developed. By September 1943 the Plan was in operation in some 150 areas—about 1/5th of the total in which it was to be applied—and by December Regions were able to report considerable progress

---

[1] Addressing the National Advisory Council for Fire Prevention on 12th April 1945 the Minister of Home Security spoke of 'a gigantic Fire Guard Service, so large that the full total of its members has never been computed, but which may, at a conservative estimate, be given as round about the five million mark'.

in training. The divorce of the Fire Guards from the Wardens' Service had removed the friction caused by division of responsibility between county and district councils.

While this development was going on and while the Plan, even where it was in operation, was still experimental it was subjected to a sharp test. In February 1944, the enemy adopted a new technique and launched a 'Little Blitz'—directed almost entirely at London.[1] The attacks began with path-finders guiding the rest of the attacking force to the selected target. The bombers, on arrival at the marked target, used every kind of fire-raising bomb and interspersed these with high explosive bombs of up to 2,500 kg. The raids were short but sharp. The small incendiaries, which comprised over 50 per cent. of the tonnage dropped, were dropped in large containers timed to explode near the ground and cause a high concentration of fires in one place, while the high explosives were intended to drive fire parties to shelter. The peak of this blitz was reached with five raids from 18th to 25th February and the N.F.S. were called on to deal with anything from 150 to 650 fires each night. To counter this new technique it was necessary for the defenders to extinguish incendiaries with the utmost speed.[2] In areas specially liable to this form of attack all relaxation of the fire guard system was at once withdrawn, and for all areas a new Fire Guard leaflet set out revised instructions for dealing with incendiary bombs. To deprive the enemy of his guiding light these were to be tackled immediately and the use of sandbags was introduced to smother bombs which could not be quickly extinguished by other means.

In London Region the areas attacked included both those in which the Fire Guard Plan was in operation and those in which it had not yet been adopted. It is not reasonable, therefore, to put all the blame on the Plan for the complaint of the N.F.S. that they were often not summoned soon enough. However a modification of that part of the Plan which dealt with the summoning of N.F.S. assistance was at once undertaken. Owing to a reorganisation of the N.F.S. in certain areas, the number of Sectors in proportion to the number of N.F.S. stations had increased and some Sectors were more than half-a-mile from the nearest station. Sector Points were, therefore, classified and certain classes were allowed to use the telephone to call the N.F.S.—a step much welcomed by the local authorities. The message form was also simplified and use could be made of special tallies, known as 'N.F.S. Discs', which contained all the essential information in the message form[3] The N.F.S. then sent a

---

[1] See pp. 439-443, 500.

[2] H.S.C. 54/44, 7th April 1944.

[3] H.S.C.s 63 and 64/44, 18th May 1944.

unit to the Block or Assembly Point where it received particulars of the fire situation; if any further reinforcements were needed it was the duty of the senior member of the N.F.S. present to summon them.

Fire Guards, however, could never be present in sufficient numbers to deal with close concentrations of incendiary bombs and delay in summoning the N.F.S. was more or less inevitable. But by this time the N.F.S. had a well developed system of observation posts and were often able to despatch pumps to the scene directly incendiary bombs had fallen. On arrival the N.F.S. officer took charge of the fire-fighting operations. The Fire Guards, however, achieved the excellent record of extinguishing 75 per cent. of the fires without the assistance of the N.F.S.

Though the 'Little Blitz' petered out in April 1944 development of the Fire Guard Plan proceeded and the enthusiasm aroused by the improved training scheme spread from the officers to the Fire Guard generally. By the end of June the Regional Advisory Councils were able to report that in most Regions the establishment of the Plan was complete and training well advanced. But the war situation was now encouraging the public to look for lighter burdens in civil defence duties, so that when the last Fire Guard Orders still contained instructions on the maintenance of the 'wakeful watch' it was felt to be unnecessary insurance. Apart from certain coastal areas and London Region there was by May 1944 complete relaxation of daylight fire watching at business premises for which the Ministry of Home Security was responsible, and a wide measure of relaxation where other Government Departments were responsible. Complete relaxation was opposed by the War Office and London Region. Others pointed out that training could be carried out more easily in daylight, while the Treasury feared that relaxation might be criticised as a means of depriving Fire Guards of pay.

Although the 'orthodox' raids stopped in April, the attack by flying bombs started shortly after D-day and it was necessary to keep the Fire Guard Plan going during the Allied advance through Northern France. By the end of August these areas had been liberated, the advance through Belgium was progressing and the enemy's ability to attack this country was daily weakening. On 6th September, therefore, the Government announced its intention to make immediate substantial reductions in civil defence organisation in all areas except London and south and east England.[1]

For the Fire Guard this relief was effected either by the 'deprescription' of an area, in which case the Fire Guard Organisation ceased to exist, or by a complete relaxation of fire guard duties in prescribed areas in parts of the country unlikely to be attacked. Everywhere there was complete relaxation of fire guard duties in

---

[1] H.S.C. 115/44, 19th September 1944.

daylight, and in those parts of the country unlikely to be attacked this was also extended to the black-out period. For the latter areas the operation of the Plan was suspended from 12th September, but it remained in force in the east and south coastal Regions and certain coastal districts in other Regions. The Regional Commissioners were given discretion to deprescribe any area or any premises in an area, but they could also prescribe or leave prescribed certain premises in a deprescribed area. Fire Guards in this case would then be on call and not in attendance. Government and Service Departments dealt with those premises for which they were responsible, but if they decided to continue fire guard duties they could not call on the local authorities to make up any deficiency in establishments.

Where the Orders were only suspended local authorities were advised to maintain the nucleus of an administrative staff, the Fire Guard Reserve Centres and Depots and their equipment. They were also to take the necessary steps to inform the public and the Wardens' Service that the Fire Guard Plan was suspended and that the responsibility for reporting fires had reverted to the Wardens' Service, and to see that all leaflets, posters, press notices and signs concerned with the Plan were withdrawn.

In the deprescribed areas the operation of the Fire Guard Plan was automatically terminated and any directions previously issued under the Fire Precautions (Residential Buildings) Order, 1942 or Clearance of Lofts Order, 1942 were withdrawn. The whole Fire Guard was disbanded, and the Wardens' Service resumed the procedure in force before the Fire Guard Plan was established.[1] On 2nd May 1945 the whole war organisation for civil defence was disbanded.

Thus ended the Fire Guard—a huge force of civilians upon whose ordinary life a tedious and often dangerous task had been superimposed. It suffered severely from growing pains, and was just coming into sight of its goal as a fire-fighting force when the need for it passed. No doubt the promise shown in the 'Little Blitz' would have been fulfilled if later tests had arisen. In all Regions lives were risked and casualties suffered—those for London being 484 killed and 1,022 severely injured—and it is remarkable that out of these millions faced with such a complexity of Orders and forms only 9,794 men and 469 women were found guilty of offences relating to the Fire Guard Orders. The transformation from 'a shovel, a bucket, and a length of garden hose' to the elaborate Fire Guard Plan had been achieved in spite of large administrative difficulties and perpetual shortages of personnel and equipment. It had involved the creation at all Regional Headquarters of large Fire Prevention

---

[1] H.S.C. 136/44, 17th November 1944.

Departments with a whole hierarchy of officers and staff.[1] Other 'appropriate authorities', local authorities and businesses had had to find extra staffs to carry out their obligations. It had imposed immense burdens on all responsible for organising the service, interpreting the stream of instructions and carrying through constant changes. The cost was prodigious,[2] but since the service was never fully developed or tried out the question of whether this was justified cannot be answered.

---

[1] p. 311. Administration of the N.F.S. and Fire Prevention accounted for most of the expansion of Regional H.Q. staffs after 1941.
[2] 'The Cost of Civil Defence', Appendix XI.

CHAPTER XIV

THE REGIONAL COMMISSIONERS AT WORK

The General Picture

UNLIKE some other European countries the United Kingdom had, before the war, no tradition of systematic regional devolution of the authority of the central Government; the devolution of powers over some of the internal affairs of Scotland and Northern Ireland was exceptional. There were some departments of the central government that provided services which involved detailed administration and which therefore made local offices necessary—the employment exchanges of the Ministry of Labour are an example. But for the most part the central government regulated the life of the country in a more general way; it determined policy and exercised general supervision. The detailed administration of most publicly provided services was left to the multitude of authorities that comprised the local government of the country. Whitehall and local councils maintained direct contact and there were no intermediaries between them.

It was inevitable that war should change this system. There was an immense growth of detailed administration by the central government and most Ministries found it necessary before long to establish strong regional organisations. This, of course, meant that there also had to be close co-ordination between the regional organisations of different Ministries. In the system of regional government that grew up, there were two main foci. One was the Regional Board where problems of output in each region were dealt with by the representatives of the production Departments and the Ministry of Labour. The other was the Civil Defence Regional Commissioner, who is the concern of this chapter.

The Regional Commissioners' position was quite different from that of any other regional officers. For, as we have seen, one of the chief reasons for the pre-war decision to appoint Commissioners was the fear that communication might become impossible between areas subjected to heavy air attack and the central government in London.[1] If that should happen, the Regional Commissioner

---

[1] See Chapters V, VII above.

concerned would act as the representative of the government as a whole and would have complete authority and power of decision. The responsibility and prestige of the Regional Commissioners were exceptional, and as token of this the Commissioners were appointed by Royal Warrant and not by a Minister.[1]

In the event, communications between London and the provinces were never interrupted—neither by the air attacks that had been foreseen before the war nor by invasion, which had not been foreseen but which was an ever present threat from the summer of 1940 onwards. And one Regional Commissioner said at the end of the war that he was 'pretty well certain that Whitehall would have got through whatever happened'. Be that as it may, the need for the Regional Commissioners to exercise their supreme functions never arose.

In the pre-war plans it had been laid down that until or unless it became necessary for the Regional Commissioners to take over wide powers of direct government, their function would be to ensure that the civil defence plans of the various Departments and of the local authorities were properly co-ordinated. This work of co-ordination was, as we shall see, to become very important, especially after the severe air raids in the autumn of 1940.

But besides being co-ordinators the Regional Commissioners and their staffs became, owing to the unforeseen character of the first months of the war, important as agents of the Minister of Home Security. It will be remembered that long before the war the A.R.P. Department had seen the need for a regional staff to keep watch over the civil defence preparations of local authorities, for it was manifestly impossible for officers in Whitehall to have close contact with the 250 or so scheme-making authorities.[2] Regional Inspectors had therefore been appointed. When war came the regional inspectors, now known as Senior Regional Officers, were ostensibly the men who were the regional administrative representatives of the Ministry of Home Security. In practice, however, they, together with the engineers and other specialist officers, were absorbed into 'Region', the regional headquarters of which the Commissioners were the heads. Thus responsibility for regional administration became in practice vested in the Commissioners; one example of this is the way in which circulars from the Ministry of Home Security in London were addressed to the Principal Officers of the Regions and not to the Senior Regional Officers. Thus Regional Commissioners became involved in the administration of every aspect of civil defence. They were of course the heads of the operational headquarters of their Regions. And they

---

[1] See p. 308. For lists of Regional Commissioners see pp. 179–180 and Appendix 1. A map of the Regions will be found facing p. 309.

[2] See pp. 55, 65, 113, 180–183.

were responsible for seeing that the authorities in their Regions received and fulfilled instructions from London on all the important questions discussed in the preceding chapters of this book—manpower, shelters, fire prevention, the training, welfare and organisation of the civil defence services and, to some extent, fire-fighting.

The need to see that the central Government's plans for the civil defence services were faithfully carried out and to provide local authorities with advice and help for this purpose undoubtedly accounted for the great bulk of the work that passed through the Regional Commissioners' offices. If a separate book were to be written about the Regional Commissioners, their activities in relation to all civil defence functions would have to be studied. Any attempt to do so here would duplicate much of the detail already recorded in other chapters of Part II of this book. For the sake of economy therefore only two examples of the detailed work of the Regional Commissioners will be examined. One is an example of regional administration of civil defence services: the organisation of mutual support between local civil defence forces and of mobile reserves leading to the formation of the Civil Defence Reserve. The second example illustrates the other main function of the Regional Commissioners—co-ordination; here the organisation of post-raid services has been chosen.

Before plunging among the details of these two examples it may be useful to list some of the other jobs that the Regional Commissioners performed. These were of great variety. Another most important example of the Regional Commissioners' co-ordinating functions could be found in the preparations against invasion and for D-day. Without the Commissioners, helped as they were by the attachment of military and police liaison officers to their headquarters, co-operation between military and civilian authorities would have been infinitely more uncertain than it was. The preparations against invasion played a large part in the lives of the Regional Commissioners for many months, but since the subject falls outside the scope of this book this mention must suffice. The preparations for D-day did not spread over so many months but they were equally exacting for some of the Commissioners; the Commissioners in the southern Regions did much to facilitate the flow of troops to the ports and to ensure at the same time the continuance of normal life.

The Regional Commissioners' services as a centre of co-ordination were also most useful when whole areas had to be evacuated in order to be used for battle training and when military help was needed to gather the harvest. Again, the Commissioners could do a good deal to co-ordinate the many welfare bodies at work in their regions. The Commissioners' duties of direct administration did not extend far beyond the operations and organisation of civil defence which are dealt with in this book. There were however a few other such duties—for example, the administration of the bans on visitors to coastal areas and the administration of regulations about the closing of shops in winter.

Quite often other miscellaneous functions attached themselves to the Commissioners simply because of the prestige and status of their position and of the ability of the individuals who held the posts. Thus Commissioners often helped to smooth out difficulties, such as colour bar difficulties, that were connected with the arrival of American troops. A Regional Commissioner might be found helping to seek out accommodation for a sudden influx of men into Portsmouth and Southampton to work on the synthetic harbours needed for D-day. Or he might be found helping to provide auxiliary labour for gas works during the winter cold period. Or he might approach the Board of Education because children destroyed route and bridge military classification signs. Moreover, Regional Commissioners had special responsibilities regarding morale, and commented in their reports to Whitehall on such diverse influences on morale as the incidence of tax on small incomes, the dissatisfaction about the high wages paid to unskilled workers and the 'debunking' of the newspapers' vogue for astrologers.

There was one leading question concerning the Regional Commissioners that caused much official as well as public discussion from time to time. Were their powers adequate? When the decision to appoint Commissioners had first been announced there were some fears that they would be 'dictators'. When the air raids came, however, criticisms were not so much of an excess of power as of a deficiency.[1]

When the Regional Commissioners and other officers at the Regional headquarters acted as the administrative agents of the Ministry of Home Security in London, the question of powers was not difficult. The Ministry had the power to see that the air raid precautions of the local scheme-making authorities were adequate and it was simple enough to delegate administrative functions concerning shelters, the civil defence services, fire prevention and so forth to Regional officers. A great deal of the detailed administrative work on these subjects was done in the Regions, though it should be noted that the limits within which Regional officers could authorise expenditure were usually narrow.

The chief problem over powers arose in connection with the very important function of the Regional Commissioners that will be considered later in this chapter—post-raid services. Here it was most important that Regional Commissioners should work very closely

---

[1] See e.g., articles in *The Times* of 16th May 1941 and in *The Observer* of 18th May 1941. Also H. of C. Deb., Vol. 372, Cols. 215–304 and 371–454. See pp. 308, 357.

with the Regional representatives of other Government Departments and with the local authorities in a great variety of subjects.

There was clearly no question of giving Regional Commissioners formal power over the Regional representatives of other Departments—unless communications with London were severed. For each representative was constitutionally responsible to his own Minister in London. If Regional representatives had not wished to co-operate with the Regional Commissioner or to fall in with his suggestions, the Regional Commissioner would have had no authority in reserve save an appeal to the Minister of Home Security in London, who would then have discussed matters with the Minister of the regional representatives concerned. In practice, however, such situations arose very rarely, for in general the Regional Commissioners and the Regional representatives worked together happily and very well. During the twilight war some representatives were undoubtedly sensitive about interference; but soon frequent meetings between the Regional Commissioners and all the senior representatives generated an *esprit de corps* that began to cancel suggestions that the Regional Commissioners were meddling with affairs that did not concern them. Once heavy raiding had begun, the position of the Regional Commissioners, though it was not defined and was often a matter of convention, was welcomed for practical reasons; without these men co-ordination of post-raid services would have been infinitely more difficult than it was.

The same informal understanding that grew up between Regional Commissioners and the Regional representatives of other Departments governed, for the most part, the relations between the Regional Commissioners and local authorities.[1] But the authorities differed widely in efficiency and there was obviously scope for friction between some of them and the Regional Commissioners. As we have seen, the Ministry of Home Security thought it desirable in 1940 to give the Regional Commissioners some legal authority over local authorities.[2] The powers delegated by the Minister of Home Security to Regional Commissioners under Defence Regulation 29A could be used to adjust areas, to transfer civil defence functions from one authority to another or to determine the persons by whom civil defence functions should be discharged. This was all very well as far as it went, but in co-ordinating the work that was necessary to restore the life of a community after a concentrated raid the Regional Commissioners were concerned with many local authority activities that would not legally come within the definition of civil defence functions. Here Regional Commissioners had no power to give general directions to local authorities; they had to rely solely on their personal authority.

---

[1] In London Region an informal Town Clerks' Co-ordinating Committee proved most successful throughout the war in promoting good relations with local authorities.

[2] See p. 357.

For much the greater part of the Regional Commissioners' work this personal authority was enough. Some local authorities might resent the intrusion of the Regional Commissioners but most of them were co-operative, especially after air raids began, and in general sanctions against them were not needed.[1] Ministers, when they discussed the extension of the Regional Commissioners' powers, found themselves in something of a dilemma. A small minority of local authorities might be difficult to control but any general interference that went further than persuasion might lead to 'a dangerous break up of the spirit of co-operation and goodwill among the local authorities'. Ministers, strongly supported by some Regional Commissioners, were very averse to recommending any increase in powers which might antagonise the local authorities. They felt that general powers of coercion must be confined to Ministers. When however, the legal experts further examined Defence Regulation 29A they doubted whether it gave Ministers power to issue directions to local authorities over the whole field of civil defence. In the summer of 1941, therefore, the necessary powers were given to Ministers by an amendment to Defence Regulation 54B;[2] this made it possible to issue directions to local authorities over the widest possible field of activity. At the same time it was agreed that the powers should be fully delegated to Regional Commissioners on the understanding that they would not be used without previous consultation except in cases of extreme emergency.

Thus for the later years of the war the Regional Commissioners had in reserve all the necessary powers over local authorities. They were, however, very little used; the new powers under Defence Regulations were never used. In practice the position of the Regional Commissioners remained one of informal, not formal, authority. The war had brought a revolutionary, if temporary, innovation to the relationship between central and local government and it was typically British that the innovation, the new rules of the game, were not codified on paper. The arrangements by which the Regional Commissioners functioned were not necessarily logical, but they had the great merit that they worked.

---

[1] The welcome accorded to the Commissioner's activities depended in large measure on the size and status of the local authority. Difficulties, for example, arose at one time between the Commissioner and the almost metropolitan city of Birmingham.

[2] Defence Regulation 54B gave power to require a local authority to perform such functions as might be thought necessary in the interests of public safety, the defence of the realm, the maintenance of public order, or for the efficient prosecution of the war, or for maintaining supplies or services essential to the life of the community. The new amendment (S.R. & O. 1941, No. 1038) conferred powers to give directions to local authorities as to the detailed execution of measures which might be considered necessary whether they related to civil defence functions or to matters falling within the wider field covered by Defence Regulation 54B.

Mutual Support

In the years from 1940 onwards, probably the most important tasks confronting the Regional Commissioners in the sphere of administration of the civil defence services were the organisation and encouragement of local schemes for mutual support and the development of mobile reserves.

The principle of mutual support had been enshrined in the Air Raid Precautions Act of 1937. For the Act enjoined local authorities charged with functions under the Act 'to assist each other where possible in making provision for the protection of persons and property from injury or damage in the event of hostile attack from the air'. In a few Regions—London, Birmingham and Nottingham —the pre-war plans did include well organised schemes for grouping local authorities under Group Controllers who could divert forces from one area to another in case of need.[1] But in most Regions either no progress was made with organising mutual support schemes or else there were very loose pacts of mutual assistance between neighbouring authorities.[2] Some of these, for example in Leeds Region, were made on the basis of excluding any Regional assistance. Progress was equally slow in the first months of the war, and early in 1940 the whole problem was studied carefully by two committees. As a result, the Ministry of Home Security sent out a circular to local authorities embodying clear guidance on the organisation of mutual support.[3]

Hitherto the Regional Commissioners had not played much part in the organisation of schemes as they had no power to instruct local authorities in their duties in providing mutual support. Now, however, the Commissioners were brought into the centre of the picture; it was made clear that local authorities should take no action on the basis of the circular other than what was prompted and approved by the Regional Commissioners. Specific powers were still not to be conferred on the Commissioners but it was assumed that local authorities, out of good sense no less than self-interest, would accept direction from the Commissioners.

The main point in the circular of April 1940 was the establishment of a chain of control leading from local Report Centres and Control Centres to Regional Headquarters and thence to the Ministry of Home Security. Each centre forming a link in the chain was, in the first instance, responsible within its own area for controlling the movements of mobile A.R.P. parties and dealing with damage up to the limit of the local resources available. If those were insufficient, application for additional help had normally to be made

---

[1] See pp. 184, 186.

[2] The scheme for mutual support between fire brigades is described in Chapter VI.

[3] H.S.C. 69, 22nd April 1940.

to the next higher Centre. The next step was to ensure that each Centre had adequate information on which to base its decisions, and the circular pointed out that such information must include details of the resources available for mutual support movements, particulars of any damage and the extent to which each sub-area needed reinforcement. It was of equal importance that there should be reliable facilities for the intercommunication of the information, and it was stressed that the organisation must be capable of functioning even in the event of extensive damage to telephone communications. Finally, emphasis was placed on the value of training to ensure the smooth working of these arrangements under active service conditions. Accordingly, it was recommended that the staffs of Centres at all levels of control including Regional Headquarters should take part in carefully thought-out practice exercises.

On the basis of these main principles the local authorities were advised of the types of organisation most suitable to meet varying local conditions. Through them all ran the constant themes of co-operation and adequate control together with the necessity of linking operationally with Regional Headquarters. There would then be established not a series of isolated arrangements between neighbouring or groups of authorities, but a balanced scheme linking together through the medium of the Regional Commissioners' H.Q. both the local agreements of the county town or rural area and the wider reinforcement schemes of the big cities. It was still considered that in the first instance not more than one third of the resources available should be moved on reinforcement duties from an area; but the authorities were warned that the Regional Commissioner might find it impracticable to treat this limit as a hard and fast rule in all circumstances.

This outline of the strategy of reinforcement was supplemented within a month by an equally clear picture of the tactics to be employed. The advice was given in the form of an A.R.P. Training Manual which dealt in detail with the essential points arising on the assembly, movement, deployment at the incident, and return to their home depot of mobile A.R.P. parties engaged on reinforcement duty.[1]

When the first series of heavy and concentrated attacks on individual cities came in the autumn and early winter of 1940, they gave the first severe practical tests of mutual support and reinforcement. The operational reports showed that the basic plan had emerged with credit; but it was only to be expected under the stress of these early raids that the movement and deployment of reinforcing parties would reveal mistakes, for example the practice of sending

---

[1] H.S.C. 87, 11th May 1940, A.R.P. Training Manual No. 2B, 'Reinforcements'.

reinforcement units piecemeal into the middle of the battle area. These early shortcomings, however, did not detract from the soundness of the planning of the spring of 1940. In fact, with but one or two minor amendments of detail, the plan that had been drawn up then withstood the tests of the whole war. A notable feature of both the early and the later operations was the readiness with which local authorities near or far from the scene of action responded to calls for assistance. Controversies, doubts and difficulties that had arisen during the planning stage were not in evidence when the time for action arrived. Civilians from the cities, country towns, and villages went gladly into action as organised forces to reinforce hard pressed neighbours or more distant cities in the fight against air attack.

A typical reinforcement move consisted of a number of stages. The local authority under attack appealed for aid through the planned channel of control. The responding local authority or authorities assembled from their depots the number of mobile civil defence parties required. The assembly was usually concentrated at a particular starting point in each area. The parties then moved in convoy or, if necessary, as individual units to a pre-arranged rendezvous point on the outskirts of the city under attack. From there, they went into action under the directions of the receiving local authority. The move into action did not necessarily take place immediately on arrival at the rendezvous point. If the existing forces were very hard pressed the extra assistance would probably be required urgently and the incoming help would be sent to incidents within the city as soon as possible. But there were often advantages in holding back reinforcement until daylight; it was possible then to make a better appreciation of the situation and the assistance could be used to relieve men and women exhausted by their night's work. In the great raid on Coventry in November 1940, for example, the reinforcements were brought during the night to the outskirts of the city and held there until dawn, when they were immediately moved into action. The manner and timing of the deployment of reinforcements could not, however, be the subject of hard and fast rules; it was an important tactical operation that remained the responsibility of the local authority receiving the assistance. Through the medium of its Control Centre the authority at the receiving end had first hand knowledge of the progress of the raid, the damage suffered, the probable number of casualties and the needs of its civil defence services. On completion of their work the reinforcing parties were rested, re-assembled and then returned to their own areas.

Reinforcement moves were supported by the careful organisation of all the detailed items necessary to their success. The issue of standing orders on transport, equipment, rations, movement in convoy and of daily routine orders which earmarked the parties for duty call that day, all played their part in the arrangements for putting the wheels for reinforcement into motion. On the call for action, drivers and officers in charge of parties were given written instructions as to the route to be followed and the place of rendezvous at their destination. Previous training in map reading and routeing helped them to become familiar with the likely journeys they would be called upon to undertake. The organisation had to cover also the reception of reinforcements. Rendezvous points had to be found with suitable parking spaces so that the vehicles could be reasonably dispersed, responsible officers had to be selected to take charge at each of the points and a system of communications had to be arranged with the Control Centre. Reliable guides had to be available to meet reinforcing parties and later, as circumstances required, pilot them into action. In addition, adequate welfare arrangements were necessary for the care of personnel both before and after their turn of duty. The foregoing details are no more than an outline of the work entailed in the organisation that was necessary at all levels of control to provide for the efficient working of these schemes under heavy attack.

The lessons drawn from the first series of attacks covered, as we have seen in earlier chapters, more or less the whole civil defence organisation. The opportunity was taken not only to give guidance and advice based on recent practical experience, but also timely reminders of the state of readiness and planning expected generally. There was no complacency in reviewing the results of the first operations. The Ministry of Home Security proceeded immediately to examine with a critical eye the operation of mutual support schemes along with other aspects of the civil defence services in action. The Regional Commissioners, in their role of commanders in the field, were in a position to contribute to this examination valuable lessons drawn from their experiences in combating the results of heavy assaults. The Ministry in turn was able to sift the evidence from a number of sources, to give Regional Commissioners the benefit of guidance based on as wide a field of experience as possible and to make suggestions for improvements where weaknesses had been revealed. During the period of heavy raiding this was a continuous process. The conclusions of the Ministry, covering the whole field of civil defence, were circularised usually in the form of conveniently headed notes—aptly termed 'Lessons of Intensive Air Attacks'. Included in these notes were the lessons which had been learnt from the experience of reinforcement operations. Some were matters of detail which more training and exercises would resolve, but there were also problems which proved more obstinate.

One of these problems was provided by the opening stage of a reinforcement move—that is, the appeal for assistance. This stage, in common with the others, had of course been the subject of exercises; but it was so much a matter of judgment that it was usually difficult in an exercise to simulate with any degree of realism the conditions faced by an A.R.P. Controller in an actual raid. The problem here was twofold. Firstly, there was a certain tardiness, and in some instances even reluctance, to ask for assistance. Secondly, it was necessary to try and obtain in the appeals for assistance closer estimates of the numbers of reinforcing parties that were needed. The first difficulty was partly due to the understanding that calls for reinforcements should not be made until the whole of a local authority's own parties were deployed. The reluctance on the part of some authorities to ask for help could be ascribed equally, perhaps, to civic pride in their own resources and to ignorance of the fact that, although each local civil defence organisation was designed to take the initial shock of a large scale attack it was not intended to carry on long operations without outside assistance. Whatever the reasons for the delay or reluctance to ask for assistance it was essential that doubts about procedure should be removed. Accordingly, it was stressed that the need for assistance must be anticipated and that there were great advantages in issuing preliminary warnings that this might be required.

The second problem, which was the absence of a yardstick for estimating the quantity of assistance required, was more difficult to solve. No rule of thumb method was possible, for the circumstances of heavy raids on different cities obviously could not fall into uniform measurable patterns. The tendency in asking for assistance had been the rather natural one of over-estimating requirements. In some instances, indeed, messages to Regional Headquarters had asked for all possible help without any further indication of what was required, with the result that more parties arrived on the scene than could usefully be employed. In spite of the difficulties it was most important to achieve a greater degree of accuracy, for the answer to the call for all possible help meant that valuable resources in manpower and transport that might be required with equal urgency elsewhere were immobilised until it was discovered that their services were not needed. It was equally inconvenient when authorities asked for two or three parties to be sent, and then as the need for further assistance became apparent repeated the request at more or less irregular intervals until the total requirements were met; organising assistance in this piecemeal fashion made the task of Regional Headquarters much more difficult. The better procedure was for authorities to wait a short while until a close appreciation of the situation could be obtained and meanwhile to issue a preliminary warning that outside help would probably be wanted. Regional Headquarters, through information received from

Home Security War Room, were sometimes able to help Controllers by giving them news of the slackening of attacks and of the possibility that the enemy forces were withdrawing. This information was of considerable value in assessing the outside help necessary.

Another more intractable problem was the important matter of the welfare of the men and women in the reinforcements. The normal drill provided that they should travel with blankets and emergency rations sufficient for an absence of 12 hours. If their services were needed for a longer period, then it was the responsibility of the local authority receiving the assistance to provide meals and sleeping accommodation. After early experience of operations it was urged that a mobile canteen should be available at the rendezvous so that reinforcements after a long, and possibly cold, drive could be forti- fied with a hot drink and some food before going into action. In the more densely populated areas reinforcements usually had not very far to travel and they were able, on completion of their turn of duty, to return to their own depots for a period of rest. Apart from the provision of incidental food and drink their welfare did not, therefore, present much difficulty to the receiving local authority. Where, how- ever, reinforcements had travelled long distances to more isolated towns or areas the receiving authority had to accommodate and feed them. If the reinforcements made a longish stay on duty, it was very desirable that they should have an adequate base from which to work and proper facilities for food and rest. Early planning had suggested that they could be attached to a regular civil defence depot and have the use of the facilities available there, or that public buildings should be used for sleeping accommodation or, exception- ally, that billeting should be used. Under conditions where the resources of an area were not too heavily taxed, any of these sugges- tions would doubtless have provided an adequate solution to the problem. The devastation of a heavy raid was another matter. Depots were put out of action either by being hit or through debris or unexploded bombs; other resources for shelter suffered equally and food supplies and cooking arrangements were often partially or completely disrupted. It was imperative, therefore, to find a solution that would enable the reinforcements called to these more isolated towns and areas to be fed, housed and rested without undue depend- ence upon the resources they had come to assist.

An effective solution to the problem was found in the idea of esta- blishing reception camps on the outskirts of these particular towns and areas. The difficulty of finding suitable accommodation was surmounted by earmarking in advance public buildings or other premises. They were not diverted from their normal uses and structural alterations were kept to the essential minimum. If not available already, cooking stores and utensils were installed on the premises together with stocks of beds, bedding and kindred equipment. The camps were under the control of Regional Headquarters, but usually the local authority for whose benefit the camp was being established supervised the arrangements for the alterations that were necessary, earmarked staff to run the camp and opened it up when required. In the majority of the camps there was no ready-made domestic service and the Women's Voluntary Services or perhaps womenfolk of the local civil defence workers stepped into the breach and carried out the domestic duties. It is interesting to note the variety of buildings now pressed into service to provide this essential accommodation. They included public baths, large country houses, schools (including at least two of the well-known public schools), a tea garden, a village inn, a race course, sports clubs, golf club houses (particularly in Scotland), hotels and even a boat house. However diverse they may have been they fulfilled their function of providing a stable base from which reinforcements could work, and on completion of their turn of duty find adequate food and rest. Furthermore, they fitted quite easily into the reinforcement plan of campaign. The rendezvous points for the town or area were fixed near to the camp and on arrival the reinforcement columns were guided the further short distance into the camp. Here they dumped their kit, were given hot drinks and if necessary fed; they were then in good shape to go into action.

Thus, with the basic strategic plan and tactics as a sound foundation, the schemes of reinforcement and mutual aid were adjusted, improved, and developed in step with the experiences and lessons learnt from the first months of heavy raiding.

The Civil Defence Reserve

The first proposal for a self-contained Regional mobile reserve had been made before the war by the Regional Commissioner for Tunbridge Wells. This Region consisted of the counties of East and West Sussex and that part of the county of Kent outside the London Region;[1] it had a large central rural area with the main centres of population distributed round the periphery. If these centres of population should be attacked one after the other so that they could not help each other, other assistance would be distant and would take some considerable time to reach the scene of action. For example, if there were a concentrated attack on the three Medway towns— Chatham, Rochester and Gillingham—and assistance from elsewhere were needed, it would take hours to arrive from such places as Sevenoaks, Tunbridge Wells and Brighton. It seemed to the

---

[1] In March 1941 the Region was extended to include that part of the county of Surrey outside the London Region.

Regional Commissioner, therefore, that a central mobile reserve was needed. The Commissioner and some of the local authorities concerned continued to urge this need on the Ministry of Home Security after war broke out. Early in 1940 the Ministry examined the problem of the Medway towns and agreed that without a central reserve it would be difficult to reinforce the area quickly if it were heavily bombed.[1] The principle of a reserve was therefore approved and the Kent County Council worked out a scheme for a reserve of three companies with a complement of 200 persons per company. The reserve was to be self-contained and was to consist entirely of whole-time personnel trained to work in rescue, first aid, decontamination and ambulance duties. By October 1940 one of the three companies had been established at a large manor called Betteshanger near Deal and the experiment was already proving worthwhile.

It was found that the reserve gave the opportunity for continuity in training and was therefore a means of attaining a high standard of efficiency. Moreover the corporate life of the unit and the interest of the men in their duties fostered an admirable *esprit de corps*. The bearing and efficiency of this first company at some of the earliest serious air raid incidents in the county were commended by the authorities who had called for their help.

In the autumn of 1940 arrangements therefore went ahead for establishing a second company of the reserve in Kent. At the same time the Tunbridge Wells Regional Commissioner proposed that a company should be established in West Sussex. The reason for establishing one here was that there were very few whole-timers in the Sussex civil defence services,[2] and the Regional Commissioner was anxious that the county should have a nucleus of whole-time reserve parties and ambulances ready to go wherever they were needed.

At the same time that the new companies were established, adjustments were being made to the composition of the first company. The most interesting adjustment was the proposal to increase the number of Rescue Parties and reduce the number of First Aid Parties. Experience in all heavily-raided areas had shown that while there had been plenty of First Aid Parties, there had been too few Rescue Parties. It was proposed that in future each Rescue Party should consist of four skilled Rescue men and four First Aid men, the latter being trained in the less technical side of demolition, shoring, etc. This was a first step towards the general utility parties of ten men each (including the driver) that later became the standard operational party unit of the Civil Defence Reserve.

By the close of 1940 three self-contained mobile units had been

---

[1] p. 374.
[2] Most of the areas were graded 'C'.

established. In the spring of 1941 two further proposals for the extension of these reserves to other areas were made to the Ministry by the Select Committee on National Expenditure and the Reading Region respectively. The Select Committee, when discussing the ways of supplementing the deficiencies in the Rescue Service, said 'a third possible solution to the problem of adequately manning the Rescue Service is by way of a mobile reserve of whole-time workers centrally located which can be rapidly moved into any of a number of areas which may be attacked. This arrangement has already been adopted in one Region where special circumstances make it peculiarly appropriate and has been found successful'. The Committee suggested that by means of such reserves 'the local Rescue services might justifiably be less strongly manned than would otherwise be safe'.[1] The Ministry of Home Security in replying to this suggestion said 'the question of mobile reserves is being further explored for areas where vulnerable towns have to rely on reinforcements of rural districts, e.g. Plymouth, Southampton, and Portsmouth. Mobile regional reserves create special problems of their own in accommodation, organisation and officering, and hitherto it has been felt that arrangements for mutual support sufficiently met the case'.[2] It is clear from this reply that though the Ministry recognised the value of reserves in special cases, it was as yet reluctant to depart from the principle of mutual reinforcement between local authorities.

At the end of April 1941 the Reading Region submitted a proposal to the Ministry for the formation there of a Regional reserve. The reason given was that recent heavy raids on the Region had shown that adequate reinforcements close at hand were badly needed. This need was now the more urgent since there was a serious shortage of whole-time personnel in the Rescue and First Aid Party Services in the more vulnerable parts of the Region as well as serious difficulties in recruiting both paid and unpaid personnel. This applied particularly to both Portsmouth and Southampton. Moreover these two towns were grouped together for reinforcement purposes and since they were in isolated positions urgent reinforcement from outside the group was difficult; the surrounding areas were rural with civil defence services which, even at full strength, were not very great.

The case for the extension of mobile reserves to other areas was carried a stage further when in June 1941 the Inspector-General reported to the Ministry of Home Security Planning Committee that he was anxious about the civil defence services in the South Coast towns, particularly Southampton, Portsmouth and Plymouth. In all three places there was a progressive decline in the numbers of

[1] Fourteenth Report from the Select Committee on National Expenditure, Session 1940–1941, Section 28, H.C. 86.

[2] First Report from the Select Committee on National Expenditure, Session 1941–1942, Appendix 2, Section 14, H.C. 20.

volunteers. In the Portsmouth Rescue Service numbers had dwindled from 170 to 20 and in Plymouth all services were only 50 per cent. of their original strength. This decline was due to a variety of causes, but three main reasons were advanced—migration of the population due to destruction of houses, unwillingness to sleep in the towns at night and the loss of employment. There was, however, the growing shortage of manpower to consider as well. The lack of volunteers meant that an additional strain was being put on the whole-timers and this was not made any better in the Rescue Service by the continuous employment of the men on such work as the clearance of debris and first aid repairs to houses. The Inspector-General commented on the lack of training as a result of this extraneous employment. 'In both Bristol and Plymouth', he said, 'it was frankly admitted that no attempt had been made to improve the technique of the Rescue Party Service at all. And the same applies to Portsmouth. Apart from lack of training there is also the point that depot routine cannot be properly established, the men have little chance of proper recreation and the conditions in many of the depots are definitely bad and in some cases demoralising'.

With such a serious shortage of men and women it was obvious that those there were must be fully trained and strengthened by some kind of corporate spirit. One of the remedies suggested was the formation of mobile reserves. These would be composed of conscripts enrolled under the National Service Act, 1941. It was pointed out that not only would the training be better, but it would be easier to look after the men; a comparison was made between the high standard of the men at Betteshanger and the average type of Rescue man. It was suggested that the proposed Reserves should be under the control of Regional Headquarters and that a maximum complement of about 200 in any one unit would be sufficient.

On the 29th July the Ministry of Home Security's Planning Committee agreed in principle to the formation of reserves and decided that the Regional Commissioners should be asked for their views. The Committee also established one very important point. Namely, that it was preferable to have a reserve manned by parties sent by the local authorities for a period on a rotational system rather than one specially recruited and permanently stationed in the manner of the Kent County Reserve. For the former method would be a means of improving the services throughout the Region.

So far the establishment of mobile reserves had been discussed mainly in terms of the operational difficulties likely to arise in certain areas if they were subjected to heavy air attack and of the necessity for the provision of some additional resources beyond those normally available under local reinforcement schemes. There was now, however, another factor which was equally important and ultimately became even more important: the shortage of manpower. This subject has been discussed in the last chapter. It is sufficient to stress here that from the spring of 1941 onwards the need for economy of manpower played an ever increasing part in the development of the mobile reserve from a force designed to meet special local conditions to one Regionally organised and designed for inter-Regional reinforcement.

Before a general survey was made of the desirability of forming mobile reserves the Ministry dealt with the more immediate anxiety of the Inspector-General—that is, the lack of adequate civil defence forces at Southampton, Portsmouth and Plymouth. As we have noted the Reading Region had submitted to the Ministry a suggestion for a Regional reserve to provide, primarily, reinforcement to the two first named towns. This suggestion was now approved and in consultation with the Ministry the Region went ahead in the search for suitable premises and the organisation there of a unit of the mobile reserve. Bristol Region, which was responsible for Plymouth, had no proposals before the Ministry, but within a short time plans were in hand and approved for the formation of a mobile reserve to be located at a place within convenient reach of Plymouth and the neighbouring district.

The establishment of these two new units marked a permanent departure in methods of control from those already established in the Tunbridge Wells Region. In the latter case the units of the reserve, although sponsored by the Regional Commissioner, were organised and directed by the county scheme-making authorities of the areas it was their main purpose to assist. The new units, however, were planned at a time when the insufficiency of trained men and women was an ever increasing danger. It was a natural step forward, therefore, to regard the new units as Regional forces available for immediate reinforcement to all parts of a Region and to place their organisation and administration directly under the Regional Commissioner.

The growing shortage of manpower made voluntary recruitment to the new units virtually impossible. Recourse had to be made, therefore, to new methods. The unit in the Reading Region was manned, apart from a small permanent staff group, by parties of whole-time civil defence personnel sent in rotation by the local authorities in the Region for a period of a month. While at the unit they received intensive training in rescue, first aid and decontamination and were organised into general utility parties of ten men each. This system had much to commend it, but it was impossible unless the local authorities had sufficient available strength in whole and part-time personnel not only to send a quota of whole-timers to the unit but to retain adequate numbers to meet the first stages of a fairly sharp air attack. In the Bristol Region this condition did not exist. The establishments and strengths of the civil defence forces in the areas primarily to be served by the mobile unit were so low already that it was impossible to reduce the number further by drawing off men for rotational training. The unit, therefore, was recruited in the main by permanent transfer from local authority services elsewhere and by conscription under the National Service Act, 1941.[1]

In October 1941 the Ministry took the first step towards making the mobile reserve a national force. It asked those Regions which had not already done so to consider the desirability of forming in their areas 'regional mobile reserves of the principal mobile services'. This request was based not only on the difficulty of maintaining the existing numbers of part-time and whole-time personnel, but also on the longer term consideration that by the formation of these reserves further economies in manpower might be achieved. For example the Regional reserves would make it unnecessary for numbers of separate authorities to maintain small local reserves with limited arrangements for mutual support; this was subject, of course, to the important tactical consideration that sufficient forces must be available locally to take the first shock of a major attack until Regional reserves arrived. The Regions were asked to consider the formation of reserves under two sets of circumstances—firstly, where a group of more or less vulnerable authorities formed natural geographical units and secondly, where isolated target towns were dependent for immediate help mainly on rural areas without strong resources.

This request to the Regions did not immediately bring forth proposals for a wide expansion of the mobile reserve. Action for the time being was confined to the areas whose problems we have examined earlier and to one new Region—Manchester. Manchester Region had for some little time been concerned with proposals to establish a mobile reserve to assist Barrow-in-Furness, a further example of a vulnerable area isolated from effective help.

At this stage the Ministry of Home Security did not know how far the mobile reserve idea would develop. As a first instalment it was envisaging the establishment of about a dozen units, and the Treasury agreed that the Ministry could go ahead and staff and equip this number without seeking specific approval for each case.

The development of the mobile reserves brought various problems. One was transport, for reliability of transport was obviously essential to a mobile force. The earlier transport of the County mobile reserves had of necessity been improvised and adapted from whatever vehicles

---

[1] The Minister of Home Security signed two Orders, one under Section 12(1) of the Act declaring the Civil Defence Reserve to be a civil defence force for the purposes of the Act, and the other under Section 3(1) of the Act designating the Minister of Home Security as the prescribed authority for the Civil Defence Reserve.

could be obtained at the time. The initial planning for the new Regional units had contemplated the use of ex-War Department lorries. But these would in any event have had to be equipped with new bodies for civil defence use and it seemed that the adaptation of reconditioned vehicles would not be worth the expenditure involved. It was decided therefore to supply the units of the mobile reserve with new lorries equipped with special bodies designed for the specific job of carrying a general utility civil defence party of 10 men plus equipment of about two tons in weight.

The expansion of the mobile reserve also brought a standard definition of the nomenclature to be used. Under the National Service Act, 1941 the Civil Defence Reserve had been declared a civil defence force.[1] This statutory title, Civil Defence Reserve, did not apply to any particular unit but represented the organisation which comprised all the separate units then being established under the control of the Regional Commissioners. So far as each Region was concerned, it was decided that the units therein of the Civil Defence Reserve should be known collectively as the 'Regional Column.' A special shoulder title was devised for the staff and permanent members of the Civil Defence Reserve. It consisted of the initials 'C.D.R.' with the number of the Region in Roman numerals underneath and the words 'Regional Column' in crescent shape forming the base of the title. The County mobile reserves, as we have seen earlier, were not under the control of the Regional Commissioner and their official titles were Kent County Civil Defence Mobile Reserve and West Sussex County Civil Defence Mobile Reserve.

In April 1942 the Ministry of Home Security decided that as part of a scheme to enable whole-time members of the Civil Defence Services to make a more active contribution to the general war effort,[2] the Reserve should be further expanded. It was proposed that wherever practicable the remaining whole-time personnel in the mobile services should be organised in Regional mobile reserves. Thus the principle of a mobile composite force was being used now mainly as a means of saving manpower; the achievement of more fluid and greater operational efficiency had become an important but subsidiary aim.

The translation into action of this expansion of the Civil Defence Reserve presented some difficult problems and took time. Premises had to be found, adapted, and often supplemented for their new purpose by temporary buildings. Failing that, sites had to be developed and complete hutment camps built to house the new units of the Reserve. At the time the plan for further expansion was agreed the available building labour force in the country had already been

---

[1] p. 551.
[2] See pp. 553–554.

allocated for some months ahead and materials, particularly steel, were as scarce as ever. Labour and materials remained indeed a matter of concern during the whole course of the building programme. Not only was the scheme in competition for available resources with the urgent needs of other Government Departments, but a nice balance had to be maintained with other schemes of work falling within the Ministry's own field of action. The construction for the National Fire Service of static water installations and fire stations, workshops and buildings, the building of alternative control centres and extra shelters, and the reconstruction of civil defence buildings damaged or destroyed by enemy action claimed their share of materials and labour. Although, later in the year, most of the projects for new mobile units received the blessing of category A priority from the Ministry of Production there were still some disappointing delays in bringing new units into commission.

The aim of the new construction programme was at least to double the previously planned establishment of about a dozen units. It was not merely a question of distributing the units evenly over the Regions but of siting them according to the relative vulnerability of areas and the availability of personnel. In London, for example, large reserves of civil defence personnel were near at hand and help could be provided quickly by the normal mutual assistance arrangements without the aid of a Regional Column. Similarly in Wales the Regional Authorities did not propose to establish a Column as they considered existing arrangements adequate.

By January 1943 fourteen units, covering nine Regions, had been formed or work had begun on their selected premises. A future programme of another twelve units was under consideration. This programme with the addition of two more units was pressed forward to completion during the course of the year and the spring of 1944, making a final establishment of twenty-eight units covering ten Regions. The units varied in size from three to five operational groups, plus a commensurate staff group. This amounted in all to an active force of 110 operational groups. In the building up stage, however, the delays in the completion of the units and the inevitable difficulties of finding the manpower limited the number of personnel to not much more than 50 per cent. of the approved operational establishment. Later, as the new units came into full commission, the position improved considerably and operational strength increased to well over 90 per cent. of the approved figure and even reached 100 per cent. for a short period. The peak figure of numbers employed was reached in the summer of 1944 when a total of about 5,800 men and women were engaged at the units on staff and operational duties. Of that number just, over 5,000 were permanent or rotational members of the operational groups.

At the same time as the Civil Defence Reserve was being expanded by the opening of new units, the control within the units was being built up gradually on common standards of administrative and operational procedure. The first essential was to ensure that the establishment of each unit, although varying in size, fell within a standard pattern. A model establishment was prepared, therefore, which organised the units on a group basis.[1] With this standard organisation operational groups could be moved with a minimum of teething troubles, not only from one unit to another within their own Regional Column but to any other unit in the country. This was put to a successful practical test in the summer of 1943 and again, but on a much larger scale, in the early spring and summer of 1944 when groups were moved from as far afield as Lancashire and Yorkshire to units and bases in the southern counties in expectation of heavy attack on the Allied build-up for invasion.

Post-Raid Problems

Co-ordination of civil defence services was one of the chief functions of the Regional Commissioners. This function was most valuable when problems of reconstruction and rehabilitation arose after a city had suffered a concentrated and devastating raid. Within the limits of the present volume it is not possible to tell in detail the story of the preparations for dealing with these problems. The full story belongs not only to the Ministry of Home Security, but to the many other major Departments of State who between them made up the relief forces upon which towns and cities relied to guide and bring them assistance in their hour of trial. During an air raid the Ministry of Home Security, by virtue of its control of the civil defence services, shouldered the main responsibility for the conduct of operations; but when the raiders passed signal had been given and it was possible to see the damage and loss suffered in the raid, the term civil defence acquired a new and much wider meaning. It connoted then not only the battle forces, but all the forces of reconstruction and restoration. A glance at Appendix VII will show the number of Departments that had responsibilities in post-raid operations and the diversity of services or supplies for which they were responsible. One of the main lessons of the Coventry raid was the need for much closer co-operation between services for which the Ministry of Home Security was not directly responsible, e.g., public health, food, industrial production, information services, housing and repairs to gas and water services.

To the Ministry of Home Security, however, fell the duty of co-ordinating all measures dealing with after-raid problems. At the centre, co-ordination of the work of Departments was achieved

---

[1] See Appendix VIII.

through the Civil Defence Committee and its Executive Sub-Committee and by direct consultation between Departments. At the Regional level a senior officer controlled the service provided by each Department and he received his orders from the headquarters of his Department. At the same time he co-operated with the other Regional representatives under the general direction of the Regional Commissioner. The latter was, as we have seen, specially charged with the duty of co-ordinating all civil defence measures and in so doing he was authorised to 'exercise such authority and control as may be necessary for their due and efficient execution'.[1] To the Regional Commissioners, therefore, fell the heavy responsibility of co-ordinating at Regional level plans for the welfare of the population and the restoration of all civil and industrial services after severe air attack. In this task, they had to collaborate closely not only with the representatives of the central government but also with local authorities, the voluntary services and representatives of industry and public utilities.

Needless to say the post-raid problems were greatest in size and continued longest in the London Region. The Senior Regional Commissioner indeed took part in every meeting of the Civil Defence Committee through the winter of 1940–41. And special steps were necessary in London, such as the appointment of two Special Commissioners to deal with the problems of caring for the homeless and with salvage, the clearance of debris and the restoration of public services.[2] But all Regions had some considerable experience of raiding, and when one or several severe attacks were launched suddenly on towns more concentrated in area than London's sprawling mass the post-raid problems were often more difficult than in London.

All heavy air raids left certain common problems behind them— damage to and destruction of property by fire and blast, damage to public utility services, the need to remove masses of debris and to demolish dangerous buildings that hindered relief work, the presence of unexploded bombs, the dislocation of transport, feeding difficulties, and the care of the population, in particular of the homeless. But although there were certain common factors in all post-raid scenery, there was also an infinite variety of conditions. There was no standard pattern of devastation that could be analysed and dissected so that counter plans could be made accordingly. For example, in one town the civil defence organisation might itself escape unscathed while in another this might suffer casualties, loss of premises, records and equipment. Similarly, the supplies of gas or electricity or both might escape damage in one area and be

---

[1] In the Royal Warrant of Appointment. See p. 308.

[2] See pp. 396–398; also R. M. Titmuss, *op. cit.*, p. 258.

destroyed in another and so on. How then was the problem to be met and dealt with? The lessons of the early bombing showed that some improvisation would always be necessary, but they showed also the advantages of previous planning. An early memorandum by the Ministry of Home Security for the guidance of the Regional Commissioners gave due weight to the need for improvisation, but stressed that the more plans could be worked out and concerted beforehand and the details arranged so as to enable important action to be taken, the quicker could the situation be restored to as near normal as possible.

In the course of pre-war preparations the Government Departments, local authorities, public utilities and industry had of course made provision against some of the features of post-raid dislocation. If they were responsible for materials and/or commodities, reserve supplies had been placed strategically throughout the country. If they were responsible for services, e.g. the public utilities, the authorities carried extra stocks of spare equipment and repairing materials and they had usually arranged some measure of mutual support and pooling of resources. But though there had been some planning to help the life of the community to recover after a severe raid, many of the needs were not, indeed often could not be, foreseen until the bombs fell.

Intelligence

One very important function at all times of the Regional Commissioner's headquarters was the provision of intelligence.[1] The Regional War Room was a centre for the collection of information from A.R.P. Controllers about all incidents due to enemy activity in the Region and the steps taken to deal with them. Full information about the number of bombs dropped, their location, and the damage caused was reported by A.R.P. Controllers to Regional Headquarters as soon as they received it. Information regarding fires was reported by Regional Headquarters to the Home Office Fire Control. On the basis of this, twelve-hourly situation reports were compiled and transmitted by teleprinter to the Home Security War Room which in turn formed the basis of twelve-hourly summaries of enemy raiding activities over the whole country prepared by the Ministry. Even when a Region was subject merely to random bombing by a few enemy planes, the collection of this information at Regional Headquarters served a great many purposes. There were, for instance, Government Departments which were very much concerned with the effects even of sporadic or light raiding. For example the Divisional Food Officer would want to know if a food depot had been destroyed and the Regional representative of the Ministry of

---

[1] pp. 306, 311

Works if one of his stores had been affected. This information was furnished to each Department usually through the respective liaison officers; at Regional Headquarters it was clearly very useful that there was in each Region one separate authority controlling his service.

When heavy raiding occurred in the Region, the Regional War Room fulfilled the function not only of an intelligence centre but also of a centre of operational control; it was in fact, for the time being, the battle headquarters of the Region. An area subject to heavy bombing would in the first instance obtain assistance from neighbouring authorities in accordance with the pre-arranged reinforcement schemes. In a really heavy raid, however, such help might not prove adequate and the next step would be for the authority to appeal to the Regional Commissioner for further aid. The strengths and dispositions of all civil defence services in a Region were recorded and tabulated in a convenient form in the War Room and it was the responsibility of the Regional Commissioner to arrange, when required, for the necessary assistance to the raided area to be supplied from the resources of other authorities. In 1942 and later years the units of the Civil Defence Reserve formed a valuable addition to the resources of the Regional Commissioner.[1]

It was possible for a Region to suffer heavy raiding in the sense that widespread attacks were being made more or less simultaneously on a number of places. Although the collective damage might be appreciable there was probably no one individual incident that warranted any special post-raid arrangements being made. A number of Government Departments might be affected but, generally speaking, raids of this character were regarded as a routine matter for which adequate plans had been made in advance by the local authority and the other agencies concerned. On the other hand, heavy raiding might mean a concentrated attack on a limited target area. In that event the early reports received from the area would give the War Room staff some indication of the enemy's intentions and the position would be watched closely. Although the detailed procedure varied in the Regional war rooms, it was usual at that stage to warn a senior officer or the Regional Commissioner of the possibility that a concentrated attack was developing. Similarly, the senior Regional Officers of the other Government Departments would be kept informed. Officers of the other Government Departments, if they were not already present, would proceed immediately to Regional Headquarters to receive information of the raid as it arrived and was mapped in the War Room.[2] During the actual progress of the raid it

---

[1] His part in the direction of Fire Service reinforcements has been referred to earlier in Chapters VI and XI.

[2] Systems of reporting, communications, and recording the intelligence received on maps and in other ways in War Rooms became highly elaborate and occupied large staffs who worked under heavy pressure during big raids.

was often possible to put in train the relief measures which would be
necessary at daybreak.

Advanced Regional Headquarters

If it was not the Regional Headquarters' town which was under
attack the problem was to establish, when the raid was over, a convenient means of ready contact with the local authority. It was
essential from the point of view of co-ordination, quick decisions
and immediate action that responsible representatives from Regional
Headquarters and the Regional offices of the other Government
Departments should proceed immediately to the scene of action. It
was usually found that the most convenient method of operating was
to set up an Advanced Regional Headquarters where not only the
regional representatives could be housed but also, if necessary, representatives of the local authority, industry and, if military assistance
had been asked for, the military commander.

There was a subsidiary problem of communications in connection
with Advanced Regional Headquarters. A heavy concentrated
attack meant more often than not that telephone communications
with the devastated area were cut off entirely or so reduced that
communication by that means was virtually useless for conducting
urgent business. Ideally, in these circumstances, Advanced Regional
Headquarters should have been set up on the outskirts of the affected
area and the intervening gap bridged by despatch rider. When the
experience of a number of the early raids had been sifted this was one
of the points put forward for the consideration of the Regional
Commissioners. Occasionally, however, other considerations were
more weighty. One town, for example—Southampton—suffered
devastating attacks on two consecutive nights and a rather dazed
population was trekking at dusk, in some strength, into the surrounding countryside and returning to their homes in the morning.
Naturally, the trekkers presented a problem and appeals were made
asking them to stay put. In this instance, although telephone communication was entirely cut, the Advanced Regional Headquarters
was set up in the centre of the town. The Regional Commissioner in
his report said: 'in this case it would have been a mistake to set up
headquarters outside the town even if thereby better communication
with the outside world could be obtained, for the reasons that we
should have laid ourselves open to the charge of staying in a safe
area and asking people to return to the town'. The second reason
put forward by the Commissioner for keeping to the centre of Southampton was the need to keep in the closest touch with local officials
and departments. This shows the difficulty, when sifting the experiences of these heavy raids, of drawing conclusions that had a general
application. For in this instance, the Regional Commissioner set

greater store on quick personal access to the officials responsible for getting the life of the town going again than on quick communication with the outside world and the resources on which he would probably have to call.

The Morning After

After a heavy raid the obvious first step towards reconstruction was to find out the extent of the damage; for then all the officers responsible for materials, services or any details that would contribute to restoring the life of the town could be made aware at the outset of their problems. On the morning following the raid, therefore, the officials of the local authority and the representatives of central Departments, utilities and other interests would make a tour of the raided area to obtain an appreciation of the damage as it affected their particular Department or authority. The situation indeed often resembled a small child's jig-saw puzzle. Each individual piece made a picture and if they were linked together the separate pictures both fused into one composite picture and were shown in their proper perspective to the whole. In the same way the individual appreciations of the job to be done after a heavy raid had to be put together so that a composite picture was obtained. The various Departments and other interested parties would then see how their respective responsibilities fitted into the operation as a whole. Not until then was it possible, with any degree of success, to achieve coordination of the work necessary for reconstruction.

The essence of the job was speed. The action necessary to bring succour to a devastated town could not wait upon the production of carefully compiled composite reports, and yet to achieve the greatest success the individuals had to work as a team. The solution was to hold a daily conference of representatives of Government Departments, the local authority, the W.V.S., voluntary bodies, utilities, industry and other interests. It was usual, immediately following upon the attack, for the Regional Commissioner or his Deputy to confer with the local Emergency Committee about the need for outside help and for the establishment of arrangements to secure effective control. The committee would then convene the first of the daily conferences and summon the representatives of their own services and of any other interests within the town whose attendance might be needed. Regional Headquarters would summon the representatives of the Government Departments and of other outside agencies.

The 'Regional Commissioners' Conferences', as they became generally known, proved one of the most successful institutions in civil defence. The Commissioner or his Deputy would attend the first meeting when the complete picture of the raid would be quickly reviewed. Tasks for dealing with the situation would be allotted and priorities of work agreed. The task of the Regional Commissioner was to ensure that the steps being taken were effective, to use his influence to bring in any necessary extra aid and to satisfy himself that the forces of restoration had a firm grip on the job to be done. There were naturally no hard and fast rules about these meetings, at which formalities were usually kept to the minimum. The Commissioner, if he did not attend later meetings, would ensure that he was kept fully informed of the progress of the work, would use his discretion in giving directions if this did not seem satisfactory, and would approach Ministers on matters requiring the further aid of the central Government. Whether or not circumstances warranted the daily presence of the Commissioner, representatives of Regional Headquarters and of Government Departments would remain in the area in close contact with the local authority until outside assistance was no longer required. Sub-committees would sometimes be formed to deal with special phases of the work.

The reports of one or two of the Regional Commissioners are of interest in illustrating this method of post-raid procedure. In May 1941, for example, the Liverpool and Bootle areas suffered air attack on seven consecutive nights.[1] On the first night it started with a comparatively light attack on Liverpool. On the second night a sharp attack was made, mainly on Liverpool, and the Regional Commissioner for Manchester reported that though the raid was not on a scale which demanded the holding of a conference, he thought it desirable to send over a Regional officer to establish a miniature Advanced Regional Headquarters, which would keep Regional Headquarters in close touch with developments. On the following night a very heavy attack was delivered on Liverpool and Bootle and the following morning the Regional Commissioner held his first conference in accordance with the normal procedure. The Inspector General of the Ministry of Home Security attended one of these Liverpool conferences and he reported, 'the conference I attended was extremely businesslike, each person having made his report was at once released and the whole proceedings only took an hour, although there must have been upwards of 50 to 60 people present'. The next three attacks were not so heavy, but on the seventh night Bootle suffered a very severe attack. The Regional organisation, however, was already in the field as a result of the earlier attacks and it was but a question of extending the area of its activities and if necessary the size of the organisation to cope with these further misfortunes. As a result of experience in this series of raids the Regional Commissioner expressed the opinion that Advanced Regional Headquarters had proved an essential piece of machinery;

---

[1] p. 418.

after a day or two it was put in charge of the Deputy Principal Officer, and it worked very successfully.

A second example illustrates the elasticity that was necessary in post-raid procedure; to insist on the full drill in every case would have hindered rather than helped the work of reconstruction. Sheffield, on on the night of 12th-13th December 1940, suffered a concentrated air attack lasting nine hours. There were 6-7,000 people homeless and 1,100 casualties, of which nearly 300 were killed, but practically nothing in the great mass of factories engaged in essential production along the Don Valley was touched. This was the key to the situation; an industrial city had suffered a devastating raid but its factory buildings and machinery remained undamaged.

In this Region (Leeds), before the Sheffield raid, it had been arranged that after a heavy raid there should be an immediate meeting of all concerned—local authority officials, Government Departments and the Commissioner and his staff. This meeting had been arranged to take place automatically at 11 o'clock on the morning after a raid without any special summons. The meeting duly took place on 13th December and made it possible to obtain immediately a clear picture of the situation and to prevent any confusion or overlapping in the tasks of dealing with the effect of the raid and restoring normal conditions. The situation was so well in hand that the Commissioner did not think it necessary to establish Advanced Regional Headquarters or to attend further conferences after the first day. Thus in this instance the post-raid procedure was launched in the usual way by the Regional Commissioner, but circumstances made the more elaborate arrangements unnecessary.

Military Assistance

On most occasions when the planning of civil defence for major operations was being reviewed in official papers in the pre-blitz period, the conclusion was reached that when the civil defence services were stretched to the utmost in any area the only available further source of reinforcement would be the military. This was the obvious solution to the dire need for manpower which was anticipated during and after heavy raiding. We have noted already that the Mabane Committee reached the same conclusion when considering the resources of manpower available to combat a major attack. It is doubtful, however, whether in any of this planning the full extent of the aid necessary from the military authorities after a major attack was really appreciated.

On their appointment in March and April 1939 the Regional Commissioners had been informed *inter alia* that military assistance would be available for reinforcement of the civil authorities; but the arrangements made for this shortly before the war reflected the concern of the authorities at this time with the problem of panic and were based almost entirely on the assumption that it would be required by the police. The War Office issued a pamphlet called *Civil Defence; Notes for Troops employed on assistance to the Civil Authorities in respect of Air Raids* which gave excellent guidance on the probable action necessary by the troops, but with one small exception dealt with situations involving law and order. The exception was important, however, inasmuch as it contributed towards the much wider conception of civil defence developed under the experience of attack. After noting that the engineer, signals and technical branches would be used primarily in meeting the requirements of other troops assisting the civil authorities it added, 'they can, however, be regarded as an ultimate reserve, to be used for the maintenance of essential civilian services or for repairing civil communications when the civil resources are exhausted or the local situation is so urgent as to demand their immediate employment'. This then was the first step, outside strict police duties, towards the massive aid which later was given so promptly and generously by the military authorities.

These earlier arrangements, although restricted in scope, were the means of providing a ready channel of communication between the civil and military authorities. The scheme provided that in certain areas local detachments of troops would be earmarked to be at the immediate call of the police in the area, and the Chief Constables were advised to make contact with the officers in command of local units. If greater assistance was required the police authorities had to make application through the military liaison officer at Regional Headquarters. At that level it was envisaged that a Regional reserve of troops would be at the disposal of the Regional Commissioner and that consultations would take place about their distribution.

During the months up to May 1940 no further guidance on this matter seems to have been issued to the Army Commands, except for instructions covering police and security matters. During this period, however, most Regional Commissioners made extensive arrangements by personal consultations with military commanders on matters of joint interest. Although instructions from the centre were restricted in scope the Army commanders had some latitude in framing their Home defence schemes. A measure of progress was made, though not to the same degree in all Regions, in providing for military assistance to cover such jobs as rescue, first aid, demolition, ambulance driving and stretcher bearing. With the fall of France and the threat of invasion in the summer of 1940 the military commands, particularly on the eastern and southern seaboards, became too overwhelmed with new duties to pay much attention to A.R.P. commitments.[1]

In October 1940, after bombing had begun in earnest, G.H.Q.

---

[1] See Chapter IX.

Home Forces put the military forces more unreservedly at the disposal of the civil authorities—subject of course to any paramount military considerations. They issued to all Home Commands the following instruction: 'Recent heavy bombing has considerably strained civilian resources in some areas. Subject to the limitations of operational roles and training, the Commander-in-Chief wishes military forces to give as much help as possible where damage has been caused to civilian property by bombs. Such help should be given in consultation with the civilian A.R.P. Services concerned'. It was now left to the Regional Commissioners to make the necessary arrangements with the G.O.C.-in-C. concerned for the implementation of this assistance as and when it was required. This instruction was followed a month later by the further concession that in the event of a breakdown of communications or in cases of exceptional urgency A.R.P. Controllers could make direct calls on local military commands for help.[1] This followed similar arrangements that had been made a little earlier, enabling Chief Constables and Chief Officers of Fire Brigades also to make direct calls for military assistance. In all these arrangements it was stressed that this assistance must not be sought where the needs of the situation could be met by local civil defence resources or by reinforcement schemes. The Regional Commissioners remained, however, the main channel for invoking military assistance.

Thus up to the time of the concentrated attack on Coventry the detailed arrangements for military assistance had been mainly matters for discussion between individual Regional Commissioners and the G.O.C.-in-C.s concerned. The Coventry raid of the 14th-15th November 1940 changed the picture almost overnight. Military assistance was invoked and the situation report from the Regional H.Q. at 6 a.m. on the 15th November stated that 600 troops had been sent to assist the police with control and to help with the removal of debris. Less than a fortnight after the raid, a military inspection of the work in progress at Coventry was able to report that there was close liaison between the officer commanding the troops and the civil authorities, and that the latter were able to give clear general directions as to where and how military help could be given. The inspector's only grumble at this stage was that the troops were mostly doing unskilled work and that civilian labour might by then have been mobilised for this purpose.

The military authorities' impressions when they arrived on the scene immediately after the raid had, however, been much less favourable; they had submitted urgent representations to the Ministry of Home Security about the need for greater co-ordination

---

[1] The Home Guard was now included in the military forces available for assistance to the civil authorities.

by the civil authorities in the repair and reconstruction of the public utility and transport services and the need for working out in advance detailed arrangements for using military assistance. Some of the immediate impressions about the inadequacy of co-ordination were justified; indeed it would have been remarkable if all the arrangements for dealing with the aftermath of a raid of hitherto unexampled concentration had gone smoothly. Other impressions of the military were due to misunderstandings. But the important point that emerged was the need for more detailed planning of the use of military forces in advance. New instructions were immediately issued to military commands by G.H.Q. Home Forces and to Regional Commissioners by the Ministry of Home Security.

The civil instruction detailed the work on which military assistance would be given. It had been accepted previously that soldiers would be available for rescue work, aiding the police and helping feed and succour the civil population. Now, in the light of the experience of Coventry, the scope of their activities was widened considerably. It was decided that soldiers would be available for clearing debris, or repairing roads, bridges, gas, water or electricity supplies and telephone communications. This was subject to the proviso that the work was beyond the immediate resources of the civil authorities, and that military assistance would only be forthcoming until adequate civil resources became available. This was, of course, eminently reasonable as while soldiers were engaged on these duties their training came to a standstill.

The responsibility for calling for military help over this much wider field was placed firmly with the Regional Commissioners. The direct local call for assistance remained, but was restricted to police duties and help in feeding and succouring the civil population. The instruction gave details of the procedure to be adopted in calling for assistance and of the interchange of information which would be necessary on such matters as billets, tools and equipment for work and transport. It stressed the necessity for clear information on the tasks to be carried out and their order of priority. This could only be achieved, of course, if the local authority carried out a quick reconnaissance of the damage in collaboration with the other interested agencies. The local authority should appoint one officer to give the required general directions to the Army officer in charge.

The instruction not only outlined a definite procedure. More important still, it asked Regional Commissioners to proceed forthwith to make arrangements, on the lines described, with the local authorities of towns in their Regions where, in the event of heavy raids, military assistance might be required. Bristol Region adopted an interesting variant of the 'invasion committees' of East Anglia and elsewhere for this purpose. It set up Defence Committees with representatives of the Fighting Services and of all local interests in every local authority area.[1]

On the military side, the Commands were ordered to make specific plans in advance, for example by listing units and the particular areas they would be available to assist, earmarking R.E. officers who would be placed in charge of the work, and arranging transport, the supply of tools etc. This instruction to the Commands was followed a few days later by a further one which linked more closely with the new planning being undertaken by the Regional Commissioners. It was based on the advantages to be gained from a thorough knowledge by military units of the towns in which they might have to work. Military commanders were told to consult the Regional Commissioners about the towns likely to need assistance and then to make a reconnaissance in each town of all aspects affecting their probable duties. This was good planning. The Regional Commissioners, the military, and the local authorities had now the opportunity to hammer out plans in advance which would reduce to a minimum the risk of delay and of misunderstanding when the moment for action came.

The pattern of military assistance given to bombed towns followed more or less regular lines, subject of course to variations in accordance with the nature and distribution of the damage. Generally the troops' first jobs were police duties, the clearance of debris and the demolition of dangerous buildings. These were followed by more specialised help to the public utility services and in the repair of damage to factories etc. A review of the assistance given by the military to certain towns will best illustrate the field of activity covered.

We have seen that in Coventry 600 troops were in the town on the morning following the raid. Twenty-four hours later the number had increased to 1,100 and further increases over the following days brought the number eventually to 1,800; it remained at that strength for over a month. From then on soldiers were withdrawn as work was completed or as civil labour became available in replacement. Further numbers were supplied in another way by the temporary release from the Army of 1,200 slaters and tilers specifically for work at their trades in Coventry. The following are some of the jobs which the soldiers performed in that city. First in order of priority was the clearance of debris on the main traffic routes and the demolition of dangerous buildings which enabled the area to be opened up to the essential repair services. At the same time the Chief Constable asked for the help of traffic control men and the request was met by the despatch of 120 special troops who remained at his disposal for eight or nine days. Next came assistance in repairs to the public utility services and communications. The restoration of the water

---

[1] See Gen. G. M. Lindsay, *The War on the Civil and Military Fronts* (1942).

supply was aided by the laying of temporary mains, and of electricity by the temporary repair of sub-stations and general help to the city's electrical engineers. Help was given also in the clearance and temporary repair of blocked and damaged sewers. Telephone communications were seriously affected and here military assistance was given by provision of despatch riders, of wireless sets for communication with adjacent towns and by help to the G.P.O. with the restoration of main trunk lines and priority service local lines. There followed first aid repairs to key factories, probably the most important of all the jobs that the military undertook in this devastated city. Of more immediate interest to the civilian population was the provision of field kitchens and the inauguration of a soup service. Troops also helped in the salvage of foodstuffs.

These various forms of assistance made up an impressive record of service that was repeated in varying degrees in many areas that suffered heavy attack. The period of working in the different cities varied considerably, but in the majority of cases it was only a few days. As may be expected, a notable exception to this general rule was made in the case of London. In October 1940 over 13,500 troops were sent in and they remained at or near that strength for many months.

The appeal for military assistance for London was made at the same time as the first steps undertaken to organise a special civilian force to deal with the aftermath of air attack in the Region. By the late autumn of 1940 the civilian force had been built up to approximately 27,000 workmen engaged on road and public utility services and about 17,000 working on debris clearance and salvage. In addition, the military force remained at full strength. The military authorities, however, were pressing for a reduction in the number of troops engaged in order to meet the manpower demands of their own Service. The military assistance had been invaluable and generously given and arrangements were made as soon as possible for the gradual reduction of the number of troops engaged. Later in 1941 the military authorities agreed to earmark a special force of Royal Engineers and Pioneers to reinforce the civil defence services should the renewal of large scale attack necessitate this.

Although this assistance to London outweighed in numbers that given elsewhere, the immediate help afforded by the military authorities was particularly valuable to the smaller towns with more slender resources. The Navy, for example, played a large part in fighting the severe attacks on Plymouth of April 1941 and restoring the life of the town. A brief account of the aid given to Southampton in December 1940 will illustrate the type of help afforded to places of similar size.

On the consecutive nights of the 30th November and 1st December 1940 Southampton suffered attack with incendiary bombs followed by high explosive and oil bombs for about four to five hours. The weight of each attack fell on an area north of the docks roughly one mile from north to south by about half a mile in width. This area was devastated. Water and gas mains were put out of action and telephone communication was cut completely. The area included some large factories which were damaged and the main shopping centre of the town which was destroyed. Immediate military assistance was given to the extent of 1,000 unskilled troops and 600 Royal Engineers together with a medical team of 3 doctors and 30 stretcher bearers. Later, 24 cooks were sent in with the necessary stores to provide an emergency feeding service for two thousand men engaged at the docks. The pattern of military assistance followed the procedure with which the reader is already aware—first, help to the police in cordoning off the main area of damage and then the clearance of debris and demolition of dangerous buildings to enable the other services of restoration to play their part. With the aid of one thousand troops the main roads were cleared, at any rate for one-way traffic, by 4th December. Pending the arrival of skilled civilian reinforcements from other towns, the Royal Engineers helped in repairing the water and gas mains and supplied tanks and water carts to carry water for domestic use to areas deprived of the mains supply. Immediate assistance with feeding was given by the issue to the local authority of 4,000 rations for the homeless.

It is clear that in Southampton as elsewhere close co-ordination between civilian and military authorities was achieved. This was one side of the wide general system of co-ordination for dealing with the aftermath of air raids successfully evolved by the Regional Commissioners.

The two detailed examples in this chapter of the Regional Commissioners' organisation at work have been sufficient to show how indispensable this proved. Even under the heaviest attacks communications between London and the Regions were never severed, so that no Commissioner ever exercised his full powers. But the civil defence services could not have been administered, trained or operated without regional grouping and decentralisation of authority from Whitehall. Not even the largest county borough could have stood up to a severe blitz on its own resources; still less could it have co-ordinated the Departmental agencies, military and other outside authorities indispensable for its recovery. By his presence on the spot during or soon after a heavy raid the Regional Commissioner often helped to steady morale and spur on the civil defence services. It must also be emphasised that he was not only the representative of Whitehall in his Region, but became at least equally the representative of his Region to Whitehall.

As the war drew to a close there was a general feeling that extensive regional representation of the central government had come to stay. It was equally well recognised that the post of Regional Commissioner would not outlive the war. The Regional Commissioners, it was generally acknowledged, had performed a most difficult task with distinction. But they had been appointed to deal with emergencies and conditions bred by war, and once these disappeared so would the need for the Commissioners. All the Commissioners and their Deputies resigned in the first half of 1945.

CHAPTER XV

THE NEW CHALLENGE OF 'V' WEAPONS

(April 1943 – May 1945)

Planning Against New Weapons

THE first serious intimation that the enemy was planning to use new long-range weapons against Great Britain came in April 1943. There had already been reports, the first as early as November 1939 and others during 1942, that the Germans were developing rockets for military purposes and that long-range rocket trials had taken place along the Baltic coast. Although much of the information was still nebulous and contradictory, by April 1943 military intelligence had enough evidence to justify informing the Chiefs of Staff of a threat which clearly had such extensive implications both for the defence of the country and for the security of the projected invasion of the Continent. The Chiefs of Staff Committee in turn agreed that the Prime Minister and the Minister of Home Security should be informed; they recommended an investigation to establish the facts, and if necessary to devise counter-measures. Mr Duncan Sandys, Joint Parliamentary Secretary to the Minister of Supply, was put in charge of this enquiry.

Throughout his investigation, which lasted from April to November 1943, Mr Sandys could call upon the intelligence machines of all three Services and the advice of many leading scientists and engineers. The work fell into two main parts: first, establishing the character of the threat; second, devising counter-measures. Although it might have been preferable to assess the danger before embarking on counter-plans, the time factor made it essential that the two activities should go on concurrently.

Mr Sandys submitted his first interim report to the Chiefs of Staff Committee on 17th May. He had not found the evidence conclusive, but it was sufficient for him to urge that an intensive effort should be made to obtain further information from agents on the Continent, from prisoners of war and by air reconnaissance. As well as this intelligence activity the Chiefs of Staff Committee agreed that experimental stations in Germany and suspicious works in North-West France should be bombed, that methods of tracing projectiles and the possibility of diverting them should be studied, and that the Ministry of Home Security should consider what special civil defence measures would be needed should heavy attacks eventually materialise.

Two inter-departmental committees were now set up. The first was to consider technical measures such as radio location, a rocket watch system, the possibility of giving warning of the rockets' approach and methods of destroying them; it quickly recommended the provision of a small amount of special radio location equipment. The second committee, under the chairmanship of Sir Findlater Stewart and reporting to the Home Defence Executive, considered matters of more direct concern to this volume.[1] It was to advise on the possibility of deceiving or confusing the enemy on the effect of his fire, on policy regarding public warning, measures for security and censorship and the necessity for special passive defence arrangements.

The first report of Sir Findlater Stewart's Committee was made to the Chiefs of Staff on 27th June 1943. This reviewed all the major problems of civil defence including control of the press, announcements to the public, accommodation for the homeless, the evacuation of priority classes from London, the warning system, the provision of additional 'Morrisons' and the strengthening of surface shelters in London, and the re-organisation and re-deployment of the services to strengthen vulnerable areas. The Ministry of Home Security was asked to investigate these recommendations and to make detailed proposals for carrying them out.

But there was still very scanty knowledge as to the true nature of this new weapon and there were sharp divisions of opinion among Ministers and officials about the seriousness of the threat. There were those who believed that rocket attacks of the type suggested were either scientifically impossible or hopelessly impracticable. Lord Cherwell, for instance, believed that the long-range rocket story was a deliberate hoax, perhaps a hoax behind which the enemy wished to conceal some other project, such as the development of pilotless aircraft; he felt we should not confine our efforts and attention to the rocket, thus blinding ourselves to the possibility of other developments.[2] Mr Duncan Sandys on the other hand was convinced of the rocket danger. He had accumulated further evidence which, though not completely consistent, contained sufficient common basis to lead to the conclusion that the rocket existed. From a variety of sources an alarming picture of the weapon had been

---

[1] See pp. 357–358.

[2] It should be remembered that at this stage attention was focused almost entirely on long-range rockets, and that the use of pilotless aircraft, or flying bombs, had hardly been contemplated.

pieced together—it seemed that it might be about 38 feet long, 7 feet in diameter, and weigh up to 60 tons with an explosive charge of 5–10 tons; it was believed that the rocket's range was between 90 and 130 miles. From this data the Ministry of Home Security made tentative calculations on the effect of an attack on London by rockets with an explosive charge of 10 tons. A single rocket might damage property over an area of 650 acres, and cause complete or partial demolition over a radius of 850 feet and serious blast damage over a radius of 1,700 feet. Casualties from each rocket might amount to 600 killed, 1,200 seriously injured and 2,400 slightly injured; one rocket each hour for twenty-four hours might result in 10,000 killed and 20,000 seriously injured.

Although uncertainty persisted, the potentialities were sufficiently disturbing to call for immediate action. In July the Prime Minister recommended that it would be prudent to concentrate reserves of 'Morrison' shelters in London and to continue the strengthening of surface shelters; he did not, however, think the danger was sufficiently defined to justify allocating more steel for shelters. Although he believed that the peril might never materialise he favoured taking some additional civil defence measures, and planning a heavy counter-attack by air on the points of origin of these weapons. The Prime Minister did not, however, think that any serious diversion of effort should be made until there was more definite evidence that this danger was imminent.

By the end of August considerable progress had been made in civil defence preparations. A draft public announcement and censorship arrangements had been approved; a warning system had been devised; plans were complete to evacuate 100,000 of the priority classes from London at the rate of 10,000 a day and 20,000 from Gosport, Portsmouth and Southampton; reserves of 'Morrison' shelters were being concentrated in the London area and near Portsmouth and Southampton. The Home Secretary, however, was not satisfied that these measures were enough; he would be happier, he said, if he could have a further 100,000 'Morrison' shelters constructed and if he could press on more quickly with the reinforcement of surface shelters.

Meanwhile, in the field of active defence, attacks were made by the R.A.F. on suspected rocket production centres. The heaviest of these was on 17th August when nearly 600 aircraft dropped about 2,000 tons of bombs on the German experimental station at Peenemünde.

At first, the investigation into possible new weapons had been directed almost entirely to the rocket. During the summer of 1943, however, reports of 'an air mine with wings' and pilotless aircraft began to suggest that the enemy might be developing two long-range weapons—a rocket and something akin to our own Queen Bee (a radio controlled light aircraft developed by the R.A.F.). By the end of August reliable reports had been received making it clear that some form of pilotless aircraft was just as real and immediate a threat as the rocket. In September the Chiefs of Staff Committee, at Mr Duncan Sandys' suggestion, agreed that his work should be confined to long-range rockets and other similar projectiles, while investigations into the development of jet-propelled or gliding bombs, pilotless aircraft and jet-propelled aircraft should be undertaken by the Air Ministry.

On 11th September the War Cabinet considered the need for a revival of the plan (known as the 'black move') to evacuate a proportion of the staffs of Government Departments from London.[1] The numbers now involved in such an exodus of the war-expanded Departments would be high, and difficulties of communications, transport, accomodation and billeting again seemed overwhelming; it was, therefore, agreed that the more practical course would be to devise measures such as 'citadel' accommodation to enable essential work to continue in London. The production of the further 100,000 'Morrison' shelters and the work on the reinforcement of street shelters proposed by the Home Secretary were also authorised.

On the reality and the dimensions of the danger of rocket attack there were still strong and conflicting views: Lord Cherwell and some other scientific advisers continued in their disbelief of the rocket menace, while in Mr Duncan Sandys' view there was a possibility of an attack on London with rockets equivalent to some 2,500 to 10,000 tons of bombs during any single week in November or December. The Defence Committee discussed the evidence on both sides very thoroughly on 25th October. It was agreed that the House of Commons should be told in secret session of the chain of events connected with the rocket threat and the steps which had been taken to deal with it; the Scientific Committee[2] that had been investigating the technical possibilities of rocket attack was to continue its studies; concentrated attacks were to be made on suspicious installations in Northern France; photographic reconnaissance was to be intensified; more consideration was to be given to the question of public announcements and warning arrangements.

By November there was fairly unanimous agreement that a rocket of the range and size suggested could be constructed though there was still division about the urgency and degree of the danger; the

---

[1] See pp. 324–328, 362, 400.

[2] In view of Lord Cherwell's disbelief in the rocket a scientific panel had been set up to decide whether such a rocket was a possibility. The report of this panel was considered at the Defence Committee (Operations) meeting on 25th October 1943. It concluded that rockets of the type reported on were a practical proposition and set out the possible performances of these weapons.

most general view was that this project must involve such difficulties that a number of years might be involved in research and development. Nevertheless it was agreed that the planning of counter measures must proceed. On the question of the maintenance of the machinery of government it was agreed that deep Tube shelters should be used for extra 'citadel' accommodation. A new long-range rocket warning system had now been worked out and tested; a continuous watch for rockets was being maintained at eight selected Radar stations. The Home Secretary recommended to his Cabinet colleagues that further reductions in the strengths of the civil defence services should be postponed until the situation on rocket attack had become clearer, and it was agreed that, while the substantial cuts approved should stand, they should take place between 1st April and 30th September 1944 instead of in the first half of the year.[1]

The War Cabinet considered all these aspects of the problem in the middle of November. It concluded that no serious attack by rockets or pilotless aircraft was likely before the end of the year, questioned the desirability of giving the public a special warning after each rocket was launched, and ruled that while no public announcement should yet be made, certain officials might be warned in confidence of the future possibilities. By this time Ministers felt that the special enquiry stage had passed and the separation of research into rockets and pilotless aircraft was no longer tenable. It was agreed, therefore, that the Air Ministry should now take over the responsibility for all these investigations, now given the code name 'Crossbow'.

In the middle of December the Chiefs of Staff Committee reported that, disregarding the consequences of bombing counter-measures, they considered it possible for the enemy to launch a full-scale attack by pilotless aircraft in February 1944 or a smaller-scale attack during January. As far as rockets were concerned, they found little positive evidence of quantity production. By December therefore development of the 'flying bomb', despite its late start, had overtaken that of the rocket. For some time there had been confusion between the two weapons. During the last three months of 1943, however, evidence began to mount on the flying bomb and on the 'ski sites'[2] from which the Germans planned to launch it; the flying bomb had now replaced the rocket as the more immediate menace. A vigorous R.A.F. attack against the ski sites began on 5th December. Up to the end of 1943 'Crossbow' had been primarily an intelligence

---

[1] See Chapter XIII, pp. 561–563.

[2] A number of these emplacements were discovered in Northern France from October 1943 onwards. They each had a concrete platform some 30 feet long and 12 feet wide with an axis aligned on London, with two rectangular buildings and one square one, and three buildings shaped like skis. In a fortnight of photographic reconnaissance 29 ski sites were identified, and agents reported 80 more.

problem; now that there had been positive identification of this weapon and the means of launching it, the main burden of the problem could be passed to the operational staffs.

On the civil defence side, the War Cabinet decided that the principal newspaper editors could be informed in confidence of the present position; that the Home Secretary might bring the civilian administration aspects of 'Crossbow' before the Civil Defence Committee; that additional plans to evacuate priority classes from Bristol, Cardiff, Dover and Plymouth should be prepared and that, in the allocation of accommodation in deep Tube shelters, priority must be given to the maintenance of the machinery of government. The Civil Defence Committee, on being consulted for the first time at the end of the year, advised against evacuation for possible targets other than London, Portsmouth and Southampton and was doubtful about the advantage of a special warning system.

Strongly conflicting opinions existed among Ministers on the probable scale of attack. Early in February 1944 the Chiefs of Staff gave a new estimate. They recommended that preparations should be based on the assumption that the attack by pilotless and other aircraft might amount to a first blow of between 550 and 625 tons of high explosives over a period of ten hours or, if the enemy was prepared to deplete his bomber resources before the Continental offensive, to between 700 and 900 tons; after this, sustained attacks might be expected of between 45 and 55 tons or 70 to 130 tons during each 24 hours. The worst of the expected attacks were, therefore, equivalent to about one and a half times the weight of the heaviest raids on Britain so far experienced. This estimate was at best an 'instructed guess'. The War Cabinet decided that while the attacks on the 'Crossbow' sites should be continued, the situation did not call at that stage for the expenditure of further money and resources on increasing our passive defence measures.

In the middle of March the Air Ministry again revised their estimated scale of attack in the light of the latest evidence on the enemy production of flying bombs, the number of launching sites and the effectiveness of our bombing counter-measures. Making no allowance for the success of our active defences, they now calculated that the tonnage falling on Greater London might be in the order of: (1) 5 'blitz' attacks in the first 15 days, each being equivalent to 160 tons of blast bombs over a period of 10–12 hours, at intervals of 48 hours; (2) subsequently, 5 attacks in the next 15 days, each equivalent to 80 tons of blast bombs over periods of 10–12 hours, at intervals of about 48 hours. As concentrated R.A.F. attacks could be directed against the small number of sites capable of operating, this scale of attack for the first 30 days could not, they thought, be sustained at anything like these rates. All this added up to a much more hopeful picture than many previous prognostications. The maximum scale of attack should not now exceed something between one-third and one-half of the previous estimate; and if British bombing counter-measures continued with their present success even this scale would diminish after 1st April.

Meanwhile civil defence measures to protect and reassure the population in those areas likely to be attacked were being further discussed and amended. The desirability of a special air raid warning system for rocket attacks was a difficult question to decide. The Ministry of Home Security had devised a system for vulnerable areas by which warning would be given by the simultaneous firing of a number of maroons; the noise of these short sharp explosions would be accompanied by whistles and red flares shooting up to about 1,000 feet, the flares burning for about 8 seconds and being visible by day or night. This signal, based on radio detection from the firing points, would be given as far as possible for each missile and would give at the most about one minute's warning. There were, however, a number of arguments against such a system. The period of warning would be so short that casualties might be caused by a rush to shelter, production would be interfered with and the special warning might itself affect public morale more adversely than no warning. To begin with the Ministry of Home Security tended to the view that the advantages of this system outweighed the dis-advantages; but later, when the flying bomb rather than the rocket had become the immediate menace, it concluded that a separate rocket warning system was inadvisable. As for flying bombs, their speed was not so much faster than that of aircraft; the normal warn-ing system was therefore adequate.

As far as shelter policy was concerned, orders had been placed in September 1943 for an additional 100,000 indoor table shelters and existing stocks were moved into the areas of probable attack. Difficulties of manufacture and transport had led to poor deliveries of 'Morrisons', and it seemed unlikely that more than half of the additional shelters ordered would be available by the time attacks were likely to begin. As the remainder would probably arrive too late to be of any use, contracts for the shelters were to be reduced by about 25,000. On the question of deep Tube shelters it had been agreed earlier that priority in the allocation of space would have to be given to the essential machinery of government. The Ministry of Works worked out a plan to shelter those government staffs not already provided for in the strengthened basements of their own steel-framed buildings. All shelter plans, the reader will recall, were given valuable impetus by the resurgence of 'conventional' attack on London and the south in the 'Little Blitz' of early 1944.[1]

[1] See pp. 546–547.

On evacuation, a scheme known by the code name of 'Rivulet' was ready for the voluntary evacuation of school-children, mothers and young children and expectant mothers from London, Southampton, Portsmouth and Gosport in a minimum of ten days. This scheme could be operated whether the attack was due to 'Crossbow' weapons or to exceptionally heavy 'conventional' raiding.

In active counter-measures the early months of 1944 saw much progress. The heavy raid on Peenemünde of the previous August and subsequent attacks on other production centres and on the launching sites in France delayed the bombardment of London by many months. In March 1944 the Germans were forced to abandon most of the original launching sites rendered useless by Allied bombing and to start constructing alternative sites of simplified design. This breathing-space afforded by the counter-measures was of vital importance. The rockets, for instance, might well have begun to fall early in 1944 instead of in September, by which time the launching sites in Northern France had been over-run and the projectiles had to be fired with much loss of accuracy from improvised positions in Holland, nearly twice as far from London.

This same period saw much development of the active defences against flying bomb attack. There were to be three defence belts—a balloon barrage on the outskirts of London, a gun belt just beyond that and then a fighter aircraft zone. Valuable supplies of electronic predictors and radio proximity fuses for the gunners were obtained from the United States.

In all, nearly fifteen months passed between the first minute to the Prime Minister from the Chiefs of Staff Committee in April 1943 and the opening of flying bomb attack in the middle of June 1944. Looking back on this period of preparation Mr Churchill summed up: 'Not a day was wasted. No care was lacking . . . The whole story may stand as an example of the efficiency of our governing machine and of the foresight and vigilance of all connected with it.'[1]

The 'V.1.' Attacks

On the night of the 12th-13th June the first pilotless aircraft fell at such scattered points as Cuckfield in Sussex, Swanscombe near Gravesend, Platt near Sevenoaks and Bethnal Green. The only casualties were at Bethnal Green where six people were killed and nine seriously injured. At the Chiefs of Staff Committee meeting the following morning bombing counter-measures were discussed. As yet only seven days had passed since D-day; although no extensive diversion of aircraft from the Continental bridgehead seemed desirable until heavier attack developed it was agreed that the four

[1] W. S. Churchill, *op. cit.*, Vol. V, p. 213.

sites believed to be connected with supply should be heavily bombed and that all launching sites should be attacked whenever effort could be spared.

Three days later a heavy and sustained bombardment by the new weapon began. In the first twenty-four hours 151 pilotless aircraft were reported by the defences, 144 crossed the coast of England and 73 reached the London area. On the morning of 16th June the Home Secretary made a statement in the House of Commons. Attacks on this country by pilotless machines—the enemy's much vaunted secret weapon—had begun. Counter-measures had already been taken against these missiles and would be applied with full vigour. Since it was most important not to give the enemy any information which would help him in directing his fire the Government decided that raids directed against areas south of a line from the Wash to the Bristol Channel would only be reported as having occurred in Southern England.[1] The Cabinet agreed that guns and balloons not already in position should be deployed according to a pre-arranged plan; counter-bombing was to begin on as big a scale as possible so long as the battle in Normandy did not suffer, and the general public were to be encouraged to carry on as normally as they could. On 19th June the Cabinet ruled that in future these weapons should be described as 'flying bombs' instead of 'pilotless aircraft.'

During the next two weeks the attack continued at the rate of about 100 flying bombs a day. Of these, fighters were bringing down about thirty per cent. and the static defences some eight to ten per cent., but more than half the bombs which crossed the coast were reaching Greater London. In the first fortnight about 1,600 people were killed, 4,500 seriously injured and 5,000 slightly injured; over 200,000 houses were damaged to a varying extent. Although the total weight of high explosive dropped was much less, the rate of casualties during this first fortnight was as high as that of September 1940, the worst month of the 'Blitz'; the proportion of persons killed to those seriously injured was, however, much lower. The reason for this high injury rate was that the flying bombs did not come only at night when people were under cover but fell at all times throughout the day. As for the damage to houses, the superior blasting power of the flying bomb was causing much greater destruction to property than the same weight of bombs had caused in previous bombing. It was estimated that if damage at the rate experienced during the first fortnight were to continue for two months as many London houses would suffer as had done so during the nine months of the 'Big Blitz'.

Although the weight of this attack was by no means yet up to some of the more alarming estimates of the previous nine months, it was sufficient to cause the Government considerable concern. The Home

---

[1] H. of C. Deb., Vol. 400, Cols. 2301–2303, 16th June 1944.

Secretary justly claimed that after five years of war the people were not as capable of standing up to the strain of air attack as they had been during the winter of 1940-41. If flying bomb attacks were to be supplemented by rocket attacks, the civil defence machine, now much weaker in numbers than during the 'Big Blitz', might prove unable to cope with them and a serious deterioration in the morale of the civil population might set in. Mr. Morrison urged therefore that these attacks should be treated as a major element in the war strategy and that priority should be given to vigorous counter-measures. The War Cabinet agreed that more steps should be taken to mitigate the effects of these attacks. Fresh efforts should be made to improve the amenities in public shelters and to encourage the maximum use of shelters at night so that workers could get some undisturbed sleep; the highest priority should be given to the repair of damaged houses and labour should be brought in from other areas for this work; plans for the evacuation of priority classes should be reviewed to ensure that they could be operated at short notice; everything should be done to provide emergency feeding facilities and adequate accommodation for the homeless. On 6th July the Prime Minister made a comprehensive statement in the House of Commons on the flying bomb position. He described the fifteen months of intelligence reports and the planning of counter-measures before the attack had opened. He thought it was essential neither to underrate nor to exaggerate the importance of this new form of attack. Members of the House might, however, be surprised to learn that the total number of flying bombs launched had killed almost exactly one person per bomb. The Prime Minister went on to mention the various measures on repairs to houses, casualty services, shelters and evacuation that had been and were being put into action. Strong counter-attacks against the launching sites and also targets in Germany would continue to be made. There could, however, be no question of allowing the 'slightest weakening of the battle in order to diminish in scale injuries which, though they may inflict grievous suffering on many people and change to some extent the normal regular life and industry of London, will never stand between the British nation and their duty in the van of a victorious and avenging world'.[1]

Although no disturbing effects on morale were evident during the early weeks of this new attack, the Government was aware of the great strain under which people in the areas under attack were now living and working. As the attacks were likely to continue, the most effective way to ease this tension was by doing everything possible to reduce the number of bombs getting through to the capital. From about the middle of July the offensive against 'Crossbow' targets was therefore increased and the anti-aircraft and

---

[1] H. of C. Deb., Vol. 401, Cols. 1322–1339.

fighter defences reorganised. It should be added that the highly mobile deployment from all over the country of the anti-aircraft defences, and the performance of these A.A. units after some three years (in many cases) of 'waiting inactivity', formed one of the outstanding defensive campaigns of the war.

Meanwhile the Civil Defence Committee was considering the measures planned to follow the opening of flying bomb attack. Although a large number of bombs were falling in London and the South-East and were causing considerable damage and casualties, the total effect was different both in degree and in form from what had been expected. In addition, the defence measures of anti-aircraft guns, fighter aircraft and balloons were proving more effective than had been anticipated. The immediate evacuation of priority classes and the extensive use of London's deep shelters were much less urgent than the planners had imagined and action to put these plans into operation was, therefore, postponed. On the other hand the damage to houses and other buildings was much greater than anticipated and the need to organise first aid repair squads became an unexpectedly pressing problem.

The movement of school children from the affected areas did not start until 3rd July, three weeks after the attacks had begun. There had, however, been a large amount of private evacuation, and by the beginning of July there was some criticism about the absence of an official scheme. One reason for delay was the need to prevent undue pressure on the railways which were heavily involved in moving supplies to the Continental bridgehead. Registration for the evacuation of school children opened on 1st July and for mothers and young children on 8th July. By 17th July some 207,000 of the priority classes had registered and nearly 170,000 had been evacuated. Private evacuation however, had taken place on a much more extensive scale; by the third week in July it was believed that some 530,000 persons had made their own arrangements to leave London. Just over a month later it was estimated that 1,450,000 had left, of whom 275,000 were persons sent out under the official scheme. Government policy was to encourage the priority classes and those without work to do to leave the areas under attack and to stay away.[1] By the end of August, however, there was a considerable flow back from the reception areas—a movement that was to continue steadily even when the rocket attack began.

The flying bomb attacks caused large new demands for 'Morrison' shelters. At the outset the stock of these shelters in London was

---

[1] Private evacuation of people with no essential work to do able to leave London at their own expense would 'assist our affairs' said the Prime Minister, and while no compulsion would be introduced every mother who wanted to take her child to safety or send her school-age children to the country would have the chance to do so. (H. of C. Deb., Vol. 401, Cols. 1322–1339, 6th July 1944.)

about 68,000 and by the first week in July less than 25,000 of these remained and the daily demand amounted to about 6,000. The Ministry of Home Security was therefore asking other Regions to transfer to London any stocks they had in hand, as well as any shelters, including 'Andersons', they could collect from householders prepared to surrender them. Although demand was now dropping, on 17th July the Civil Defence Committee decided to place orders with manufacturers for a further 100,000 shelters, but there were break clauses in the contracts in case the situation altered radically.

The new Tube shelters which had been partially earmarked for Government staffs were not opened during the first three weeks since there was no real demand for them; there was no need to use them for civil servants and the numbers sheltering in the ordinary Tube stations were falling.[1] To begin with it was agreed to hold these shelters in reserve in case of worse things to come, but on 9th July the first one was opened and soon after two more were put into operation. They were available only to ticket holders, and tickets were issued to existing Tube shelterers and to local authorities, especially for people made homeless by the raids. The Ministry of Home Security had feared both that the opening of these new deep shelters might cause discontent among those who could not use them and that it might be difficult to get people out of them during the day. However, after six weeks of their use it reported that there was no sign of any 'deep shelter mentality'. By September, space in the deep shelters could be allocated at weekends as billets to troops on leave, and in October two of the shelters were closed.

While evacuation and deep shelters had produced fewer difficulties than expected, the damage to houses was much more serious and had become, in fact, the biggest civil problem of the new form of attack.[2] Three weeks after these attacks began there was a back-log of 194,000 houses awaiting repairs; over 20,000 were being damaged each day, and in spite of a labour force of 33,000 men arrears were mounting at the rate of 6,000 houses a day. The War Cabinet urged that every effort should be made to bring in more building labour; powers of direction were used but difficulties arose from lack of billets and amenities for the drafted men. By the middle of July the labour force had been increased by about 10,000 and the average rate of repairs now exceeded the daily rate of damage. The repairs carried out by these squads were, however, only first aid measures to enable people whose houses were not

---

[1] See pp. 531–532, 540, 545–546, 651.

[2] This is described in greater detail in *Works and Buildings* by C. M. Kohan in this series of histories, pp. 222–235.

seriously damaged to use them again. On 7th September it was reported that arrears of damaged houses were down to some 27,000, but most houses repaired had only received a 'field dressing' and with winter approaching it was going to be necessary to deal with some of the longer-term repairs soon. During the nine months of flying bomb attack, which included also six months of rocket bombardment, some 29,400 houses were destroyed and 1,255,000 damaged but repairable in the London area, and 2,200 destroyed and 165,000 damaged but repairable elsewhere. Though the physical damage to war factories and vital communications was comparatively small, many public buildings such as churches, hospitals and schools once again appeared in the casualty lists.

During these first months of flying bomb attack some modifications were made in the warning system and the black-out, relaxations were made in fire guard duties and, in the interests of morale, measures were taken to improve supplies of beer in bombed areas. As regards warnings, it was quickly agreed to sound the alert only when batches of flying bombs were arriving, and later a system of roof-spotters giving imminent danger warnings was organised by local authorities; most factories and firms already had their own spotters who could advise when taking cover was necessary, thus reducing interruption of work to a minimum.

In all, the flying bomb attacks on Great Britain lasted from 12th June 1944 to 29th March 1945.[1] The first and most important phase was from 12th June to 5th September 1944. Most of the bombs launched during this period were from sites on the coast of France between Dunkirk and Etretat. During this phase some 6,725 flying bombs were reported by the defences, 3,463 were destroyed by guns, fighters and balloons, and 2,340 reached the target area. Casualties in London and elsewhere amounted to 5,475 killed and 15,918 seriously injured. London south of the Thames bore the brunt of this bombardment, especially the boroughs of Croydon, Wandsworth, Lewisham, Camberwell, Woolwich, Greenwich, Beckenham and Lambeth. But a large number of bombs fell short of the target in 'bomb-alley' in Kent and many in rural areas of Sussex, Surrey and Essex; and a high proportion of those brought down by the A.A. and fighter defences fell in Kent.

By the middle of August there was a general feeling among those responsible for operations that ascendancy was being achieved over this weapon. Despite bombing of sources, the weight of attack had remained fairly static but the counter-measures had notably developed. Only 17 per cent. of the bombs reported between 16th

---

[1] For their distribution, by counties and by months, see Appendix V. During the main phase of the offensive the majority of bombs directed at London crossed the coast between Cockmere Haven and St Margaret's Bay.

August and 5th September fell in the Greater London area, compared to 33 per cent. during the previous month and 44 per cent. during the first five weeks. By the beginning of September the launching areas in North-Eastern France were over-run by the Allied advance; this ended the first and main phase of the attack although it was not the end of the flying bombs. When the launching sites were lost the Germans still had an alternative means of launching the bombs—from aircraft. As early as July and August they had made some use of this method to attack Britain from the east, and once the land sites were put out of operation they strove to develop it. There was a brief lull for a few days when the last land sites were captured; but on 16th September the attack was re-opened from air-launching units in Germany. This new stage in the offensive presented the British defences with special difficulties. Although he was unable to send over as many bombs the enemy had greater mobility for he was no longer tied to fixed ramps; our anti-aircraft belt had to be moved and difficult gunnery problems were caused by the bombs flying at lower heights than previously. During this phase of air-launched bombs from 16th September to 14th January 1945 some 638 bombs were reported by the defences; 403 of these were destroyed by guns or fighters and only 66 reached the Greater London area.[1] Most of this attack was directed against London. But other centres also became targets including Manchester, against which 30 flying bombs were launched on Christmas Eve, 1944, though only six of them came down within ten miles of the centre of the city, and Oldham, Lancs., where on the same night 27 people were killed and 37 seriously injured.

The last spasm of flying bomb attack came between 3rd and 29th March 1945 from launching sites in Holland. The Germans had by this time increased the range of the weapon. However, counter-measures had also made such progress that during this last phase of the campaign, of the 125 flying bombs which approached this country 87 were shot down by A.A. guns and 4 by fighters, and only 13 bombs reached London.[2]

How did the people of London and the South-East stand up to the flying bomb attacks? How effective were the depleted but re-organised civil defence services?

Two weeks after the opening of the new offensive a Cabinet Committee reported that civilian morale remained 'wonderfully good' though there were 'unmistakable signs of weariness'. It was natural that the attack should have its disturbing effects. In contrast to the regular routine of the Blitz when danger was

---

[1] Report by Air Chief Marshal Sir Roderic Hill to the Secretary of State for Air, 17th April 1948. Supplement to the *London Gazette* of 19th October 1948, p. 5601.

[2] Ibid., p. 5603.

concentrated during the hours of darkness there was now no relief from danger at any hour of the day or night. The automatic nature of the pilotless weapon, the purely arbitrary destruction of a bomb that might fall anywhere at any time and with no particular target in view, seemed to many, much worse than 'orthodox' bombing. There was much nervous strain involved in listening to the 'buzz-bombs' or 'doodlebugs', watching them and waiting for the engine to cut out. Flying glass was a special danger and people were warned to take cover on the sound of a bomb diving or the engine stopping, and later on the sounding of imminent danger warnings. The vast damage to houses inevitably caused great domestic upheavals. To begin with there was a definite decline in production in London, due to an increase in the rate of absenteeism, to loss of time in actual working hours through workers taking shelter and to lowered efficiency through loss of sleep and anxiety. The extension of the industrial alarm system and the increase in the labour force repairing damaged property, however, soon reduced these early signs of disturbance. Within a few weeks evacuees were returning to London, shelters were less full and most people were going about their normal tasks as usual.

For the civil defence services the new weapon demanded new tactics. In many ways these attacks were much easier to contend with than ordinary bombing. Firstly, most of the incidents were isolated, so that services could be directed in strength to the affected area without constant competing demands on the personnel at every turn. Secondly, the fall of the bombs could be spotted within a matter of seconds by high-placed observation posts either by night or by day, so that rescue and first aid squads could be on the spot very quickly. Thirdly, the penetrative power of this weapon was slight so that incidents rarely involved the complications of broken gas, electricity or water mains, and there was also little tendency for fires to break out. On the other hand the bombs could fall at any time in crowded thoroughfares; the proportion of casualties in the streets was much higher than ever before while the proportion of trapped casualties was lower. At night time, since there were no German eyes above, the use of artificial light was less restricted and searchlights could be used for rescue work.

By now the numbers in the civil defence services had been substantially reduced[1] but the restricted area of attack made it possible to bring in reinforcements from unaffected districts. The need for a close network of civil defence posts had now largely gone, and instead a system of flying columns was organised and directed to each incident from observation posts. In Westminster, for instance, there were such posts on the high tower of the Victoria Coach Station and

---

[1] See Chapter XIII, pp. 562–563.

on top of the London Transport Offices in Broadway and elsewhere. Within about three minutes of a flying bomb falling, a flying column of heavy and light rescue vehicles, ambulances and a mobile aid post could be directed to the scene. At day-time incidents loud-speaker vans were sometimes used to control the sight-seeing crowds which obstructed the ambulances and rescue vehicles. After the immediate needs of rescue and first-aid had been met, other facilities were brought in. It was often found better to bring in mobile canteens, bath and laundry units rather than to make the people concerned go to the facilities. The large number of houses damaged by each bomb called for speedy action if the need for providing a vast amount of rest centre accommodation was to be avoided. First aid repair squads were, therefore, quickly sent to the perimeter of the damage, and arrangements for furniture removal and storage took an important place in post-raid procedure. The National Fire Service observation posts were used similarly to secure prompt despatch of N.F.S. 'Task Force' units.

Dover, it must be added here, suffered in September its most severe shelling of the war. The enemy guns across the Channel fired 16 in. and A.P. shells by day and night into the town keeping it under almost continuous alert. Owing to the cave-shelters casualties were small, but hardly one house in the centre of the town escaped damage. For a time normal life almost stopped and for several days no deliveries of bread or milk could be made. Folkestone, Ramsgate and Deal were also shelled though on a much smaller scale.[1]

Long-Range Rocket Attacks

While the flying bomb attack held the centre of the stage the Government had also to bear in mind the possibility of worse to come. So far the attack on London had been made by only one of the two weapons that the Germans had developed for long-range bombardment. It will be remembered that the early rumours of the new 'retaliation' weapons had been restricted to long-range rockets; not until some months later was it learnt that the first danger was to be the pilotless aircraft.[2] The menace of the rocket was still, however, most serious, and although technical difficulties had delayed its arrival, it was clear that the Germans were still hoping to play this trump card. Flying bombs had caused less disruption to civilian life and morale than had been feared, but a new and heavy attack by rockets might bring grave repercussions.

Some early reports on the rocket had spoken of a gigantic weapon weighing seventy to eighty tons and carrying a warhead of some

---

[1] Some 2,226 shells fell on Dover during the war and on the worst day, 26th September, nearly 60. On occasions shell-warnings lasted for 13 hours.

[2] See pp. 646-649.

ten tons of explosive which would descend on London with little or no warning. Fortunately these proved to be exaggerated as well as premature. During 1944, however, more precise evidence on weight, the method of launching, performance and organisation to control the operation of the rocket began to come in from Polish agents, from reports about a rocket which accidentally fell in Sweden and from prisoners of war. It seemed that the enemy had brought the lighter 'A4' rocket to an advanced stage of development, though there were still some technical difficulties. An estimate submitted to the War Cabinet's Crossbow Committee in July spoke of a much lighter rocket, weighing perhaps thirty to forty tons with a warhead of five to ten tons and a range of 150 miles. It was believed that the Germans had produced about 1,000 of these rockets which could be launched from fairly simple and quickly improvised sites. Although there was no reliable information about the movement of projectiles westwards from Germany, 'it would be unwise', said the report, 'to assume that a rocket attack is not imminent'.

This information came as a bombshell to the War Cabinet. The rocket menace, a major concern of the Government during the summer and autumn of 1943, had receded into the background during the past few months. Although the first half of 1944 had seen much activity in rocket intelligence work, the evidence had been so incomplete and unsubstantiated that little had been done to keep the War Cabinet informed as stage-by-stage the puzzle was pieced together. It was not, in fact, until July that a picture of any coherence emerged. When the flying bomb attack began in June, the question naturally arose as to whether this might be supplemented by rocket attack. The answer, given in the July report to the Crossbow Committee, that the Germans had already produced a substantial number of rockets which might be directed against us very shortly surprised and disturbed the War Cabinet. The planning of counter-measures now began again in an atmosphere that had much of the urgency of the anxious months of 1943.

The Home Secretary, responsible as he was for the protection of the civil population and for the maintenance of their morale, tended to see the position at its worst. If 1,000 rockets were fired against London, he said (on a basis of calculations made by the Research and Experiments Department of his Ministry which assumed a 7 ton warhead), about 18,000 people would be killed and possibly three times as many injured; a single rocket might demolish or render uninhabitable all houses within a radius of 400 yards of its impact. So far the civil defence services were coping satisfactorily with the flying bomb attacks, though house repairs were well in arrears. If, in addition to the flying bombs, rockets were to arrive at all frequently, civil defence resources would be quickly exhausted, hospital services might be swamped and police, transport and emergency services for accommodating and feeding evacuees might be overwhelmed by an exodus of people from the capital. In a memorandum to the War Cabinet the Home Secretary urged that rocket attack should be regarded as an almost certain major effort by the Germans to avoid sheer defeat. He believed that the rockets might well affect the conduct of military operations. We had boasted rightly of our air superiority and military strength. We would be expected to use our resources to eliminate attacks on the Metropolis by the new weapons as we had virtually eliminated raids by ordinary aircraft. He asked for a decision from the War Cabinet on the vital issue of evacuation, the policy on which would, as on former occasions, determine what was done in other spheres of civil defence.

The War Cabinet accepted the Home Secretary's recommendations and agreed that immediate action should be taken. Responsibility for preparations to meet the rocket attack was allocated to various Ministers and groups of Ministers. This work was to be supervised and co-ordinated by a new Ministerial Committee, known as the Rocket Committee and later as the Rocket Consequences Committee. The Committee met first on 3rd August and considered questions of evacuation, including possible mass refugee movements and the establishment of reception centres and feeding stations at the fringes of the Metropolitan area to provide for refugees on foot, the removal of some Government Departments from London, the dispersal of important industries and key production units, the emptying of hospitals and the feeding of workers remaining in London.

While the plans had to allow for the rockets causing great disturbance in the normal life of the capital and a certain amount of unorganised exodus, the Government's policy would still be to urge Londoners to stand firm. It was not seriously believed that they would do otherwise. In contrast to pre-war fears of vast crowds of panic-stricken refugees, it now seemed to the Government that the people who had withstood the Blitz and the flying bombs would hold fast under this new form of attack. In the meantime, however, it would be wise to encourage the evacuation of mothers and children and other priority classes before the rocket attack began, and to this end the Prime Minister made a statement in the House of Commons on 2nd August. In spite of fantastic German stories of London being in panic under a perpetual pall of smoke and flames as a result of the flying bomb attack, he said, the morale of Londoners could be judged by the fact that many of the evacuation trains had come back to London as full as they went out. 'While a daring and adventurous spirit' was to be commended, this needless risk and movement should be discouraged. It was still possible that the Germans would try to bombard us with long-range rockets, and he did not want to minimise the ordeal to which we might be subjected, except to say that he was sure it was one we would be able to bear. The Government strongly advised those for whom official evacuation facilities had been provided, and others with no war duties in London who could make their own arrangements, to take the opportunity of leaving the capital 'in a timely, orderly, and gradual manner'.[1] The evacuation areas were now to be extended to include 27 boroughs and urban districts around the Metropolitan area and all mothers with children of school age or under, as well as the usual priority classes, could now participate.

Throughout August planning went on vigorously. In drawing up their schemes for the possible effects of the latest and most alarming of Hitler's weapons, the Government had now to steer an uneasy course between encouraging those who had work to do in London to stand fast and at the same time preparing to contend with some degree of unorganised exodus. It might well be a mistake, for instance, to repeat too often the Prime Minister's exhortation that all with no definite work to do should leave, lest this should undermine the confidence of those who ought to stay. When the rockets began to fall it might be difficult to achieve an orderly evacuation of the priority classes and of personnel engaged on Government work if the railway stations were besieged by refugees. On the sheer mechanics of transport it was difficult to formulate any scheme which would avoid congestion at the stations without involving a certain amount of prior publicity and this might injure the stand-fast policy and be objectionable on security grounds. A scheme was worked out by the Ministry of Health whereby travel vouchers at a flat rate of 5/- per adult could be issued by local authorities to would-be refugees giving them the right to a place on a train that could take them out of the danger area. To handle those moving out of London by road, it was estimated that temporary accommodation in rest and reception centres within forty miles of London should be provided for a maximum of 700,000 people.

As well as planning to evacuate the priority classes and to deal with any general exodus, it was also necessary to co-ordinate arrangements to move a certain number of civil servants and key industrial personnel. If the rocket attack caused serious dislocation in London, it would be vital to maintain the machinery of Government and to prevent major disturbances in the production drive. There were now about 130,000 persons on the headquarters staffs of Government Departments in London; of these 20,000 were in poor

---

[1] H. of C. Deb., Vol. 402, Cols. 1476–1478, 2nd August 1944.

buildings, approximately half of which were without shelters. 'Citadel' accommodation was available for not more than 8,500. An evacuation of about 85,000 civil servants was, therefore, visualised, while the remainder, other than those in well-protected accommodation, would have to be dismissed or 'stood off'. As far as the movement of vital industry from London was concerned the principle was accepted that only production which was unique or nearly unique, or of special importance to current operations or largely concentrated in the London area should be interfered with. The moves were to be of personnel rather than of plant, with workers going to reception factories in safer areas. The Ministry of Production estimated that it might be advisable to evacuate some 65,000 key workers, and these with their families might amount to an organised dispersal of about 160,000 persons.

The evacuation of patients from London hospitals was begun immediately and was in progress throughout August. By the end of the month 15,734 patients and staff had been evacuated and 28,249 beds were vacant to receive rocket casualties; at a few hours' notice a further 8,179 beds could be made available by discharging patients to their homes.

Schemes were also drawn up by the Rocket Consequences Committee for the maintenance of amenities in London. The most important of these was concerned with the organisation of labour for first aid repairs to buildings, demolition and clearance and the restoration of essential services. The existing labour force could be supplemented by the Armed Forces so that up to 120,000 men could be brought into action for this work. It was agreed that military direction should only be used in connection with demolition and clearance and the maintenance of essential services, while house repairs should continue to be organised under the existing arrangements. Plans were also made for the emergency feeding of workers remaining in London, and for the control of information about rocket attacks.

But hardly had all these schemes been worked out than the atmosphere of expectation which had produced this urgent activity changed. During the second half of August two new factors emerged to alter future prospects. Firstly, the latest intelligence reports pointed to a much less destructive weapon than had been described in the estimate given in July.[1] Secondly, the rapid advance of the Allied armies threatened to drive the Germans from those areas of Northern France from which it was presumed that a rocket attack would be launched. By the end of August the scientific experts reported that, while the Germans might still try to launch the rocket against us, 'the still existing technical defects, the relatively small warhead, the

---

[1] The total weight of the rocket was now given as approximately 12 tons with a warhead of one ton.

increasing difficulties of supply and our threat to the operational area' led them to believe that 'the magnitude of the threat' was small. The latest appreciation of the possible weight of attack from a combination of rockets and flying bombs amounted to a bombardment less than twice as heavy as the worst week of the flying bomb attack. On 1st September the Rocket Consequences Committee agreed that, as it was now increasingly unlikely that there would be bombardment of London on a scale sufficient to warrant exceptional remedial measures, plans to put these into effect should so far as possible be kept on a paper basis.

During the next few days the situation improved still further. On 6th September the Vice-Chiefs of Staff reported that all areas from which flying bombs or rockets might be launched against London had been, or were about to be, occupied by Allied troops—'there should be no further danger to this country from either of these causes, except for the possibility of the airborne launching of flying bombs.' On the following day the Home Secretary obtained the approval of the War Cabinet for the suspension of all preparations and such evacuation schemes as were actually being carried out, except where, as was the case with some of the arrangements for the dispersal of London production, it would be more trouble to reverse what was being done than to complete it. Civil defence preparations were now being swamped by a wave of optimism that was in sharp contrast to the sober urgency with which the Rocket Consequences Committee had begun its work just over a month earlier. On 7th September Mr Duncan Sandys, in a lengthy review to the Press of the attacks that had taken place, felt able to speak of the Battle of London being over 'except possibly for a last few shots'.

Such complete optimism was, however, somewhat premature; the battle was, in fact, by no means over. During the next six months, over 1,000 rockets and nearly 500 flying bombs were still to fall in the United Kingdom. The rocket attack began on the very day after Mr Sandys' press statement. At about twenty to seven in the evening of 8th September Londoners travelling home from work or preparing their evening meals were startled by a sharp report rather like a clap of thunder. The first rocket had fallen at Chiswick, killing three people and seriously injuring another ten. Sixteen seconds later another rocket fell at Epping but did little damage. During the next ten days rockets arrived at scattered places in South-Eastern England at the rate of about two a day.

The rockets were of the type and weight that the latest Air Intelligence reports had forecast. The radar stations set up to detect the firing of rockets from France had not proved very effective in plotting the rockets fired from Holland, and there could be no question of operating a warning system until their techniques had been improved considerably and their deployment changed.[1] While the situation on land was so promising, and as rockets seemed to be only a little more destructive than flying bombs, the Chiefs of Staff did not think any elaborate counter-measures justified and they advised against any announcement to the public that they were under rocket attack at this stage.

The scale of attack against the United Kingdom did not, as yet, warrant counter-measures involving any diversion of force from the offensive against Germany. However on 8th September the first rocket reached Paris, and soon afterwards other French and Belgian towns began to suffer attack. Rockets, and shortly afterwards flying bombs too, had become not only strategic weapons directed against civilians but also—as shorter distances gave greater accuracy —tactical weapons in the overseas military operations.

On 17th September the Allied airborne operation against the lower Rhine at Arnhem caused German rocket firing troops to move eastwards, and for a week no more rockets fell in Great Britain. On 25th September, however, Norwich became the target, and from that date until 12th October, 36 rockets fell in this area though none fell in the city itself. The attack on London was resumed on 3rd October and for the next few weeks the capital received an average of two or three rounds a day. During November the scale of attack rose—the average number of rockets arriving rose to four a day, and at the end of the month to six a day. Much less could be done than in the case of the flying bombs by the British active defences. The rockets could not be intercepted by aircraft, guns[2] or balloons, and their firing points were mobile and difficult to trace. However, fighter-bomber sweeps and armed fighter reconnaissance against suspicious points in the firing areas were increased during November and probably helped to diminish the attack on London towards the end of 1944. By the middle of December the scale of attack was down to an average of four rockets a day and by the end of the month to three-and-a-half.

Although the German effort against London was by now lower than in previous weeks, the Home Secretary suggested to the Chiefs of Staff on 22nd December that more powerful counter-measures— in particular heavy bomber attacks on the launching areas—should be applied against the Hague area. But the Chiefs of Staff were

---

[1] On 25th September 1944 it was reported that up to date, the performance of the radar and sound ranging units had been such that, if warnings had been based on it, only once out of 16 times would the warning have been followed by an incident in London and only once out of 6 times by an incident anywhere else, and that, moreover, on three occasions between 14th and 18th September incidents had occurred where no warning could have been given.

[2] Towards the end of 1944 and during the early months of 1945 there were experiments in the use of anti-aircraft artillery to fire at approaching rockets and explode them in the air.

strongly opposed to this suggestion—first, the attacks would mean heavy loss of life among Dutch civilians and damage to Dutch property without achieving anything more than a temporary interruption of rocket firing, and second, the bombing effort could not be spared from other more vital targets—and it was agreed that no radical change should be made in the policy of counter-measures.

From the angle of civil defence, the rocket attack was very little different from the flying bomb attack. Rockets had a greater penetrating power, caused more violent devastation immediately around their point of impact and were more likely to damage public services than flying bombs. On the other hand the area affected by their blast was smaller. No important new civil defence problems arose; the civil defence services had been able to meet the demands made on them, there had been no undue pressure on shelter accommodation and no rush of evacuees out of London. The repair of damaged property continued to be a major task but on much the same scale as before. There was no call for a new evacuation scheme, and anxiety was felt by the Government, not about a disorganised exodus of refugees, but because such large numbers of people were pouring back into London when so many houses, schools and other buildings had been damaged. In the middle of November, for instance, when the rocket attack was fairly heavy, it was estimated that the population of London was only 8 per cent. lower than it had been at the beginning of the flying bomb attacks; by January it was only five per cent. lower and was rising at the rate of 10,000 a week.

During January and February the number of rockets increased again. Moreover the accuracy of fire seemed to have improved and a higher proportion were falling during the day. On 26th January there were seventeen incidents, thirteen of them in the London area, the highest so far recorded in one day. Casualties during this period increased sharply—the weekly casualty list was twice as high as during December.

By now the radar stations were detecting a large number of rockets early enough for warnings to have been sounded in the London area if a warning of fifty to sixty seconds had been acceptable to the civil defence authorities. It was, however, decided to investigate the possibility of warnings of up to four minutes, and in the meantime to continue without public warnings.

Intensified fighter-bomber attacks in February and March were followed by a perceptible slackening in the rocket offensive. Unfortunately a number of serious incidents kept the casualty lists high. One of the worst of these was caused by a rocket falling on the morning of 8th March on Smithfield Market, killing 110 people and seriously injuring 123. The German offensive came to an end on 27th March, when the one thousand, one hundred and fifteenth rocket to fall on this country or within sight of shore, fell at Orpington, Kent. On 2nd May on receipt of a report from the Joint Intelligence Sub-Committee that there was no longer risk of flying bomb attack and only very slight chance of rocket attack, the Chiefs of Staff approved the discontinuance of all counter-measures.

The rocket campaign had lasted for seven months. During that time the Germans fired at least 1,300 rockets at London and some 40 or more at Norwich. Five hundred and eighteen rockets fell within the boundaries of the London Civil Defence Region. Two thousand five hundred and eleven people were killed and 5,869 seriously injured in London, and 213 killed and 598 seriously injured elsewhere.[1] The casualty figures would have been substantially lower but for a number of unlucky incidents in which rockets chanced to hit crowded buildings. Among the worst incidents were direct hits on a crowded shop in Deptford on 25th November 1944, on Smithfield Market, and on a block of flats at Stepney on 27th March.

Problems of the Services

The last two chapters have traced the concentration of effort after January 1943 on forming the Civil Defence Reserve, and the development of the Fire Guard Plan. As a result of the former process a nucleus was being given a thorough operational training, while the Plan provided training in fire prevention for an enormous civilian body. The 'Little Blitz' of the early months of 1944 provided a test for this Plan, and although the test proved only a short one useful experience was gained. When preparations for the invasion of Europe gained momentum determined interference by the German Air Force was expected. The civil defence services, especially in the south and south-east, were therefore braced for action.

The arrival of the flying bomb, and later the long-range rocket, cannot be said, therefore, to have caught the civil defence services off balance. These weapons required a change of tactics; but both were in important ways easier to deal with than the previous bombing.[2] The fall of flying bombs and rockets could be rapidly spotted. Incidents were more isolated, and much greater concentration of the necessary services at each incident was possible. The approaches to the scene and the water and gas mains were not so likely to be damaged, nor fires to be caused. Flying columns of mobile units, rescue parties and ambulances were held at readiness and dispatched as soon as the locality of an incident was reported and this remained

---

[1] Report to the Secretary of State for Air by Air Chief Marshal Sir Roderic Hill, Supplement to the *London Gazette*, 19th October 1948. The final casualty figures were slightly higher (see Appendix II).

[2] See pp. 659–660, 667.

the standard method of dealing with the results of attacks by V-weapons.

While much had to be done to recast plans for shelters, warnings, and evacuation, the biggest civil problem turned out in practice to be the repair of houses. The amount of debris caused by the V-weapons was enormous and the manpower available to deal with it was limited. The rehabilitation of homes was a vital factor in the maintenance of morale, but while the attack remained intense the toll of urgent demolition and essential first aid repairs mounted steadily. Forces to cope with this were sought in various directions and reinforcements were brought in from Regional Columns and any other available source from Regions not under attack. In Essex, for example, the Works Regulating Centre set up for 'Overlord' proved very valuable for mobilising labour for first aid repairs.

The continuous nature of the V-weapon attacks involved constant manning of civil defence posts in all the vulnerable areas with long hours or duty for both whole-time and part-time personnel. This was borne willingly and cheerfully, but volunteers to reinforce the Wardens', Report and Control and Rescue Services in London and the south-east were asked for from other Regions. The response was immediate and no Region approached had any difficulty in providing enough volunteers to take a share of duty in the vulnerable areas. Even though the arrangements by which whole-time wardens could be sent to London for reinforcement did not apply to Scotland, 122 part-time Scottish wardens as well as 173 whole-time members of the Rescue Service did voluntary duty in London. The Fire Services too, were heavily reinforced from other areas.[1] The C.-in-C., Home Forces instructed all Home Guard commanders to place a generous interpretation on the conditions under which the Home Guard could support the civil defence services, and required all members not needed for other duties to turn out with street Fire Parties covering their homes. In Tunbridge Wells Region especially heavy calls were made on the W.V.S. as the result of flying-bomb attack; mobile canteens fed rescue workers and members of the Housewives' Section helped to clear and put in order the many houses damaged by bombs and blast. It is worth mentioning that in these last few months the civil defence services made use with some success of trained dogs to locate casualties buried under debris.

'Stand-down'

As the Allied invasion progressed the enemy was driven farther into Europe and his air potential so reduced that the threat to this country from piloted aircraft diminished daily. Even during the period of the attacks by V-weapons, most of the country beyond the

---

[1] See Chapter XI.

target areas in the south and south-east was considered immune from further attacks from the air.

On 7th September 1944, therefore, further relief from fire guard duties was authorised in many parts of the country[1] and on 15th September it was decided to make immediate substantial reductions in the civil defence organisation in all Regions except Cambridge, London, Reading and Tunbridge Wells.

This involved the release of the bulk of whole-time personnel in all services without any continuing obligation to undertake part-time service; a substantial reduction in part-time strength; and the reduction of maximum stand-by duty of part-time personnel at posts and depots whether by day or night, subject to certain necessary exceptions, to 12 hours in every four weeks.[2] At the same time further instructions were sent out on matters connected with the discharge of officers of the Fire Guard Service under local authorities, whose areas were to be deprescribed or subject to complete relaxation of fire guard duty.[3]

In October it was decided to extend the scope of these reductions to the remaining four Regions. The scale of preparation in these Regions had necessarily to be higher than elsewhere, so that the reductions were not quite so drastic and variations in practice were permitted.[4] A circular was also sent to all Regions instructing them to reduce forthwith to a care and maintenance basis all except eleven of the operational units of the Civil Defence Reserve.[5] The establishment of these remaining operational units was amended. Applications for release were invited; if the numbers not seeking release were sufficient to complete the new unit establishment, all applicants could be released without delay. If all who wished to go could not be released, the principle of 'first in, first out' was to be adopted—with some modifications to give priority to those such as building trade workers urgently required to meet industrial needs.

If the numbers wishing to remain in the units were above the requirements of their Region, they could be offered transfer to another Region. Shortly after the issue of this circular an Overseas Column with a strength of 1 Headquarters Group and 4 Operational Groups was sent overseas for service in north-western Europe and a depot to provide it with replacements was set up as part of the operational establishment of the Steventon Manor Unit of the Southern Regional Column.[6]

---

[1] H.S.R. 97/44, 7th September 1944; pp. 607–608.

[2] H.S.R. 101/44, 15th September 1944; p. 563 above.

[3] H.S.C. 116/44, 19th September 1944.

[4] H.S.C. 128/44, 20th October 1944.

[5] H.S.R. 107/44, 20th October 1944.

[6] H.S.R. 107/44, 20th October 1944. This Column rendered distinguished service, which it is not possible to describe here, in countering the 'V-weapon' attacks on Antwerp and elsewhere and training Allied military and civilian forces.

The Minister of Home Security decided in October that in the Bristol, Cardiff, Birmingham and Manchester Regions all local authority areas, except those where it was essential to be able to restore fire guard protection without delay, should be deprescribed under the Fire Guard Orders—the Regional Commissioner and local authorities fixing between them a convenient day for the coming into effect of the legal instruments.[1]

As a result of the releases and discharges from the civil defence services formal training may be said to have ceased by December and over much of the country Civil Defence was at a 'stand easy' stage. The sudden flying bomb attack on Lancashire served however, as a reminder of the importance of ensuring that the services, particularly the report and control centres, were kept in a state of operational efficiency.[2]

But this proved only a flash in the pan and the services continued to release members. The total whole-time paid staff, which at 30th September had been 217,742, was at 31st January 1945 down to 146,467, and it was planned that by 30th April there would be a further reduction to 125,520.

The first months of 1945 saw the departure of many of the 'captains and kings' of civil defence; by the end of March eight of the Regional Commissioners had resigned. Throughout these months a spate of circulars dealt with the release of premises; the fate of shelters, posts, depots, cleansing stations and administrative centres; the collection and disposal of vehicles, equipment and records; grants, gratuities, post-war credits and other financial matters.

On 26th April appeared a circular describing the action to be taken to wind up the war organisation of the Civil Defence General Services when the Government decided that this was no longer needed.[3] This included the disbandment of the Civil Defence Reserve, and Regions were urged to release members as soon as possible and to close down Regional Column unit headquarters with all possible speed.[4]

Almost immediately came the announcement that the 2nd May had been selected as the 'appointed day'. On this day new Orders came into operation revoking the greater part of the Civil Defence (Employment and Offences) Orders and transferring to the Minister concerned the powers conferred on the Regional Commissioners by those Orders which remained in force. On this day all anti-gas precautions were relaxed,[5] the arrangements for the provision and

---

[1] H.S.R. 114/44, 17th November 1944.
[2] H.S.R. 2/45, 17th January 1945.
[3] H.S.C. 35/45, 26th April 1945.
[4] H.S.R. 18/45, 30th April 1945.
[5] H.S.C. 42/45, 30th April 1945.

maintenance of shelters were discontinued,[1] and all restrictions on every class of lighting throughout the country, except for some coastal areas, were removed.[2]

The many processes of winding up a war organisation of the size of civil defence could not, however, be done in a day. Though all whole-time personnel were given two months' notice to take effect on 1st July, some officers of the Civil Defence Reserve remained after this date to help in disbanding the Reserve, and in many Regions temporary staff had to be employed to help local authorities to deal with various matters, which included investigating and taking steps to deal with over 1,000 suspected unexploded missiles in all parts of the country.

On 15th May local authorities were asked to consider terminating the appointment of their Emergency Committees and A.R.P. Controllers as soon as the progress of winding up the civil defence organisation made their services redundant.[3] On 31st May those functions of the Minister of Home Security which it was desired to retain were transferred to the Secretary of State for Home Affairs, and the Ministry of Home Security ceased to exist.[4]

Throughout May ceremonial disbandment parades were held up and down the country, and finally on 10th June in Hyde Park a farewell parade of representatives of the civil defence services of all Regions was reviewed and addressed by King George VI.

His Majesty described the civil defence services as 'a great host of men and women of whom those present are but a fraction'. And he told those on parade that, 'the call of duty, the spirit of comradeship, the sense of high purpose are as necessary in the future as when the citizen armies of civil defence were gathered together'.[5]

All members of the civil defence services with three years' service or more were entitled to the Defence Medal. The ribbon of this, it may be added, was composed of green, intended to symbolise the green fields of Britain, orange, to suggest the flames of the blitz, and two black lines to recall the black-out.

Two months after His Majesty held this review the first atomic bomb used in warfare was dropped by Allied forces on Hiroshima. The modifications this event introduced into the plans and technique of passive defence are no concern of the present volume. It is sufficient to add that with the passage of the Civil Defence Act, 1948 the rebuilding of civil defence in Britain began once again.[6]

---

[1] H.S.C. 43/45, 1st May 1945.
[2] H.S.C. 44/45, 1st May 1945.
[3] H.S.C. 55/45, 15th May 1945.
[4] H.S.C. 62/45, 31st May 1945; S.R. & O. 1945, No. 612. The post of Minister of Home Security was not formally abolished until 1st April 1946.
[5] *The Times*, 11th June 1945.
[6] 12 and 13 Geo. 6, Ch. 5.

Appendices

APPENDIX I

Civil Defence Regional Commissioners

Region	H.Q.	Regional Commissioners (April 1939 and subsequent changes)[1]	Special and Assistant Commissioners, Deputy Commissioners, District Commissioners for Scotland[2] (All shown below were D.R.C.'s unless otherwise stated)
1. Northern	Newcastle	Sir Arthur Lambert	Mr J. J. Lawson; Col. C. J. Pickering
2. North Eastern	Leeds	Rt Hon. Lord Harlech Gen. Sir W. H. Bartholomew (March 1941)	Sir Charles McGrath; Mr E. Dunn; Mr O. G. Willey; Gen. Sir J. Brind
3. North Midland	Nottingham	Lord Trent	Mr H. A. S. Wortley; Mr C. R. Keene
4. Eastern	Cambridge	Sir Will Spens	Lord Eltisley; Earl of Cranbrook; Major-Gen. A. C. Fuller
5. London	London	*Senior R.C.* Capt. Euan Wallace (May 1940-January 1941) Sir E. Gowers (January 1941) *Joint R.C.s* Sir E. Gowers (to January 1941) Admiral Sir E. Evans Mr C. W. Key (January 1941)	*Special Commissioners:* Sir Warren Fisher; Rt Hon. H. U. Willink Lt-Gen. M. G. H. Barker
6. Southern	Reading	Mr Harold Butler Sir Harry Haig (January 1942)	*Assistant Commissioner:* Lord Chatfield Sir W. M. Goodenough; Mr R. H. Bernays; Gen. Sir I. Vesey; Mr W. Asbury; Major-Gen. R. J. Collins
7. South Western	Bristol	Gen. Sir H. Elles (except April-Sept. 1940) Sir Geoffrey Peto (April-Sept. 1940)	Sir Geoffrey Peto; Major-Gen. G. M. Lindsay; Mr H. M. Medland *Supernumerary D.R.C.s:* Sir John Shelley; Col. E. H. W. Bolitho

8. Wales	Cardiff	Rt Hon. Lord Portal *Joint R.C.s* Col. Sir G. Bruce } (January 1940) Mr R. Richards	Capt. Geoffrey Crawshay; Mr R. Richards; Mr P. Morris; Miss E. Owen
9. Midland	Birmingham	Earl of Dudley	Mr S. J. Grey; Major G. Dennison; Mr G. Archibald; Mr G. S. Lindgren
10. North Western	Manchester	Sir Warren Fisher Sir Harry Haig (April 1940) Lord Geddes (January 1942) Mr H. W. Shawcross (July 1942)	Mr J. R. Hobhouse; Col. T. Blatherwick; Sir F. Hindle; Prof. R. S. T. Chorley
11. Scotland	Edinburgh	Rt Hon. T. Johnston (September 1939) Earl of Rosebery (February 1941)	Earl of Airlie; Earl of Rosebery; Mr W. Quin *District Commissioners:* Edinburgh: Sir W. Y. Darling; Sir Gilbert Archer Glasgow: Sir Cecil Weir; Sir Stephen Bilsland Dundee: Sir John Phin Aberdeen: Mr Alexander T. Morrison Inverness: Col. The Hon. I. M. Campbell
12. South Eastern	Tunbridge Wells	Lord Geddes Rt Hon. Viscount Monsell (July 1941)	*Assistant Commissioner:* Earl de la Warr Viscount Knollys; Mr A. G. Bottomley; Mr H. W. Shawcross; Lt-Cdr E. B. Green

[1] The first Regional Commissioners were appointed in April 1939, and are also listed on pp. 179–180 above. Five of these served in the same Region throughout; the others, through death or resignation, were replaced in the manner shown. The last Commissioners resigned during February–June 1945.

[2] The Assistant Commissioners held office for special purposes for short periods only. Special Commissioners were appointed for London only in the autumn of 1940, and held office for several years. Deputy Commissioners are shown in the order of their appointment. Most Regions had two such Commissioners in office simultaneously, including one specially concerned with Fire Service matters. Scottish Districts also had Deputy Commissioners.

For the Regional areas see the Map facing p. 309 above.

APPENDIX II

Civilians killed and injured in Great Britain by enemy action 1939–1945

(Compiled by Ministry of Home Security from police and medical reports)

1.

	Killed			Admitted to Hospital (in most cases seriously injured)			Slightly Injured			Treated at First Aid Posts and Mobile First Aid Units (estimated one-fifth sent on to hospital)[1]
	London	Elsewhere	Totals	London	Elsewhere	Totals	London	Elsewhere	Totals	
3rd Sept. 1939–6th Sept. 1940	257	1,441	1,698	441	1,848	2,289	33,756	20,264	54,020	54,700
7th Sept. 1940–31st Dec. 1940	13,339	8,730	22,069	17,937	10,303	28,240				
1941	6,487	13,431	19,918	7,641	13,524	21,165	13,236	20,880	34,116	43,775
1942	27	3,209	3,236	52	4,096	4,148	63	7,097	7,160	8,719
1943	542	1,830	2,372	989	2,461	3,450	1,015	4,412	5,427	6,598
1944	7,533	942	8,475	19,611	2,378	21,989	33,212	6,343	39,555	41,116
1st Jan. 1945–9th May 1945	1,705	155	1,860	3,836	387	4,223	7,560	1,202	8,762	10,835
Northern Ireland	—	967	967	—	678	678	—	1,793	1,793	—
	29,890	30,705	60,595	50,507	35,675	86,182	88,842	61,991	150,833	165,743

[1] Source: *Report of the Chief Medical Officer of the Ministry of Health 1939–1945.*

APPENDIX II (*contd.*)

2. The 146,777 civilians killed, missing believed killed or seriously injured can be sub-divided as follows:

Men: 67,661, Women: 63,221, Children under 16: 15,358, Unidentified: 537.

3. Civil defence workers on duty (the General Services and the Regular and Auxiliary Police and Fire Services) suffered 6,838 casualties (2,379 killed and 4,459 seriously injured), which are included in the previous total. Of these 6,220 were men, and 618 women.[1]

4. The proportions of casualties attributable to the enemy's chief weapons have been estimated as follows:

	Killed	Seriously Injured	Total
Bombs . . .	51,509	61,423	112,932
Flying bombs . .	6,184	17,981	24,165
Long-range rockets . .	2,754	6,523	9,277
Cross-Channel bombardment .	148	255	403
	60,595	86,182	146,777

5. The foregoing figures, derived from Home Security sources, need some explanation. More especially as they seem a striking example of the difficulties under the conditions of the Second World War of presenting human affairs (in this case the sombre affairs of death and serious injury) in accurate statistical form.

The Registrar-General's returns give the larger figure of 62,464 civilians killed in Great Britain by enemy action. But this, unlike the Home Security figure, includes the Home Guard (1,206 of whom died of wounds, injury or illness due to their service),

[1]Cmd. 6832 of 1946

APPENDIX II (*contd.*)

merchant seamen dying in Britain as a result of enemy action of any kind, and civilians killed by the enemy at sea. Neither figure is restricted to casualties caused directly by bombing; and the conclusions on the whole matter reached by Professor Titmuss (*Problems of Social Policy*, Appendix 8) deserve quotation:

The Home Security statistics do not include a proportion of the deaths of persons who were injured by enemy action and subsequently died. The Registrar-General's returns do, assuming that death certification gives precedence to the initial injury, and in so far as deaths occurred before the end of the German war. Then again, the former include civilians killed by cross-channel shelling, by machine-gunning from German aeroplanes, by exploding anti-aircraft shells and as a result of other defending action. But the Registrar-General's figures are wider in scope, for they include in addition civilian casualties caused by sea-mines, crashed Allied aircraft, Army manoeuvres and battle exercises, train and vehicle accidents caused by enemy action and other deaths due to operations of war.

Another reason for the difference between the figures is that death registration could not be carried out until identification was completed. In many instances, bodies—and parts of bodies—were not recovered for a long time, and identification was delayed for weeks or months. Where no remains were found, it was necessary to establish the fact that the missing person had been on the spot at the time of the 'incident' before registration could be effected and satisfactory evidence produced. All this meant delays before death registrations were made.

The injury statistics are likely to underestimate, rather than exaggerate, the number of civilians injured by war operations in general and air bombardment in particular. The chief reason would appear to be that an unknown number of seriously injured people (and some whose injuries were first thought to be slight but later were found to be serious), and a large number of slightly injured people, never went to a hospital or first-aid post and were consequently omitted from official records. In addition, numbers of first-aid posts were bombed and records destroyed, while in times of stress injuries were attended and not recorded. The distinction between seriously and slightly injured is somewhat thin, for the method of recording often varied from hospital to hospital, and by no means all hospital cases were, in reality, seriously injured. The figures must simply be accepted as showing the order of magnitude of casualty rates.

6. Professor Titmuss estimates the ratio of killed to all injured for the whole war at 1:3.9. Home Security data for a large number of towns during 1940–41 showed this to be usually between 1:3 and 1:4. In London Region alone it has been calculated at 1:3.6 during 1940–43, and 1:7 during the V-weapon attacks of 1944–45.

APPENDIX III

Estimated tonnages of bombs, flying-bombs and long-range rockets reported falling on the British Isles

	Bombs Excluding I.B.s & A.P.s	Flying-Bombs (War-head)	Long-Range Rockets (War-head)	Total (Metric Tons)
3rd September 1939 to 6th September 1940 ⎫ 7th September 1940 to 31st December 1940 ⎬	34,970	—	—	34,970
1941	22,176	—	—	22,176
1942	3,039	—	—	3,039
1943	2,232	—	—	2,232
1944	1,960	5,731	390	8,081
1st January 1945 to 8th May 1945 . .	16	92	664	772
Total . . .	64,393 [1]	5,823 [2]	1,054 [2]	71,270

[1] Though the tonnages or numbers of incendiary bombs dropped in particular raids have sometimes been given in the text these were often in practice incalculable. No reliable total can therefore be given for these or for armour-piercing bombs.

[2] Since the war-heads of both flying-bombs and rockets were about one ton these figures are equivalent to the numbers reported to have fallen.

APPENDIX IV

Major night attacks on United Kingdom cities and towns from 7th September, 1940 to 16th May, 1941

Target Area	Number of Major Attacks[1]	Tonnages of H.E. Aimed
London	71	18,291
Liverpool-Birkenhead . .	8	1,957
Birmingham . . .	8	1,852
Glasgow-Clydeside . .	5	1,329
Plymouth-Devonport . .	8	1,228
Bristol-Avonmouth . .	6	919
Coventry	2	818
Portsmouth . . .	3	687
Southampton . . .	4	647
Hull	3	593
Manchester . . .	3	578
Belfast	2	440
Sheffield	1	355
Newcastle-Tyneside . .	1	152
Nottingham . . .	1	137
Cardiff	1	115

[1] The enemy's definition of a 'major attack', i.e. one in which 100 tons or more of high-explosive bombs were successfully aimed at the target, has been adopted for this table.

APPENDIX V

Total numbers of flying-bomb and long-range rocket incidents reported

Table 1—By Counties

Counties	Flying Bombs	Long-Range Rockets
London (Region)[1] .	2,420	517
Kent	1,444	64
Sussex .	886	4
Essex	412	378
Surrey . . .	295	8
Suffolk . .	93	13
Hertfordshire . .	82	34
Hampshire . . .	80	—
Buckinghamshire . .	27	2
Norfolk . . .	13	29
Berkshire . . .	12	1
Bedfordshire . .	10	3
Lancashire . . .	8	—
Yorkshire . . .	7	—
Cheshire . . .	6	—
Cambridgeshire . .	5	1
Northamptonshire .	4	—
Oxfordshire . .	4	—
Isle of Ely . . .	3	—
Derbyshire . . .	3	—
Huntingdonshire . .	2	—
Lincolnshire . .	2	—
Durham . . .	1	—
Nottinghamshire . .	1	—
Leicestershire . .	1	—
Rutland . . .	1	—
Shropshire . . .	1	—
Total . .	5,823[2]	1,054[2]

[1] London Region received 41 per cent. of flying-bombs, and 49 per cent. of long-range rockets.
[2] 271 of these flying-bombs and 4 of the long-range rockets fell in the sea.

APPENDIX V (*contd.*)

Table 2—By Months

	Flying Bombs	Long-Range Rockets	Relevant Operations in North-West Europe
1944 June . . .	1,435	—	Allies land in Normandy Cherbourg captured
July . . .	2,453	—	Caen captured
August . . .	1,450	—	Paris liberated
September . .	87	34	Brussels and Antwerp captured Boulogne captured
October . . .	131	91	Calais captured
November . .	101	144	Walcheren captured Flushing captured
December . .	74	121	Battle of the Ardennes
1945 January . . .	33	220	
February . .	—	232	Belgium cleared of the enemy
March . . .	59	212	Allies cross River Rhine
	5,823	1,054	

APPENDIX VI

Attacks on London compared with those on Provincial Cities and Towns

FROM the beginning to the end of the war London was a target of the highest importance, and there is no question that in the event it was harder hit, measured both in number of attacks and number of casualties, than any other British city. Throughout the war it had 101 daylight attacks and 253 night attacks, a total of 354, by piloted aircraft. It was attacked at some time during the day or night, with the exception of only two twenty-four periods, for the whole of September, October and November 1940. London received 41 per cent. of the attacks by flying-bombs, and 49 per cent. of those by rockets. There were in all 1,224 alerts in Central London, an average of one every 36 hours.

Provincial cities and towns which suffered more than 50 attacks were:

	Number of Attacks (Cross-Channel shelling included)		
	Day	Night	Total
1. Dover	76	49	125
2. Great Yarmouth	25	72	97
3. Folkestone	56	27	83
4. Hull	6	70	76
5. Hastings	54	21	75
6. Lowestoft	27	47	74
7. Romford	4	68	72
8. Portsmouth	15	57	72
9. Plymouth	13	58	71
10. Margate	30	40	70
11. Liverpool	—	68	68
12. Southampton	18	49	67
13. Southend	10	57	67
14. Portland	28	38	66
15. Eastbourne	39	27	66
16. Ramsgate	37	26	63
17. Gillingham	22	38	60
18. Bristol	5	51	56
19. Birkenhead	—	52	52
20. Birmingham	—	51	51

London suffered over 80,000 of the estimated total for the country of 146,777 fatal and serious casualties. Outside London, only Birmingham and Liverpool suffered more than 5,000 such casualties.

APPENDIX VII

Functions of Government Departments in post-raid work

The main subjects arising after heavy raids, and the division of responsibility for them, in England and Wales.

	Central Department	Regional representative	Local agent responsible for action
Welfare of homeless	Ministry of Health	Senior Regional Officer	Local authority
Evacuation	,, ,, ,,	,, ,, ,,	,, ,,
Rehousing	,, ,, ,,	,, ,, ,,	,, ,,
First aid repairs to houses	,, ,, ,,	,, ,, ,,	,, ,,
Disposal of dead	,, ,, ,,	,, ,, ,,	,, ,,
Repairs to sewers	,, ,, ,,	,, ,, ,,	,, ,,
Casualty services, including hospitals	,, ,, ,,	,, ,, ,,	,, ,,
Repairs to water undertakings	,, ,, ,,	,, ,, ,,	Local authority or undertaking
Civil defence services	Ministry of Home Security	Regional Commissioner and staff	Local authority
Clearance of debris	,, ,, ,,	,, ,,	,, ,,
Salvage of furniture	,, ,, ,,	Regional Salvage Officer	,, ,,
Military aid and disposal of U.X.B.s	Ministry of Home Security and Home Forces	Regional Commissioner	Military Commander
Law and order	Home Office	Regional Police Staff Officer	Chief Constable
Repairs to Roads	Ministry of Home Security and Ministry of Transport	Regional Commissioner and Divisional Road Engineer	Local authority
Traffic control	Ministry of Transport and Home Office	Regional Transport Commissioner and Regional Police Staff Officer	Chief Constable
Demands on transport (road and rail)	Ministry of Transport	Regional Transport Commissioner, and Railway Companies	—
	Ministry of Supply	Area Transportation Officer	—
	Other Departments	Regional representative	—
Communications	G.P.O.	Regional Director, G.P.O.	Local officials
	Ministry of Transport	Regional Transport Commissioner	—
	Ministry of Home Security	Senior Regional Officer	A.R.P. Controller
Emergency feeding arrangements	Ministry of Food	Divisional Food Officer	Local authority
Mobile canteens for civilians	,, ,, ,,	,, ,, ,,	—
Food salvage	,, ,, ,,	,, ,, ,,	Food Salvage Officer
Food shops	,, ,, ,,	,, ,, ,,	Food Executive Officer
Decontamination of foodstuffs (gas)	,, ,, ,,	,, ,, ,,	Local authority

APPENDIX VII (*contd.*)

	Central Department	Regional representative	Local agent responsible for action
Emergency tobacco supplies	Board of Trade (Tobacco Control)	Area representative	—
Relief of distress schemes	Assistance Board	Senior Regional representative	Area Officer
Claims for injuries, etc.	Assistance Board and Ministry of Pensions	Senior Regional representative and Chief Regional Officer	Local officials
Information to the public	Ministry of Information	Regional Information Officer	Emergency or local information officer
Repairs to war production factories	Emergency Services organisation	Area Officer, Ministry of Aircraft Production	Local Reconstruction Panel
Repairs to other factories	Board of Trade and Ministry of Works and Buildings	Area Officer and Assistant Director of Emergency Repairs	Area Officer and Assistant Director of Emergency Repairs
Repairs to shops other than food shops	Board of Trade and Ministry of Works and Buildings	—	—
Repairs to gas undertakings	Board of Trade	Regional Gas Engineering Adviser	Gas undertaking
Salvage of insured commodities	,, ,, ,,	Insurance official	Owner of goods and assessor
Salvage of raw materials	Ministry of Supply	Area Officer	—
General services for emergency repair work and supplies	Ministry of Works	Assistant Director of Emergency Repairs	Emergency Works Officer
Labour supply and unemployment insurance	Ministry of Labour	Divisional Controller	Employment Exchange Manager
Petrol supplies	Petroleum Dept.	Divisional Petroleum Officer	—
Voluntary Social Services	Various Depts.	Officers of voluntary organisations	Officers of voluntary organisations

APPENDIX VIII

Civil Defence Reserve

1. Units were normally made up of three to five Operational Groups plus a Staff Group.

2. Each Operational Group consisted of 40 to 50 persons:

Four Civil Defence General Utility Parties each of 10 men, inclusive of Leader, Deputy Leader, and Driver. All the personnel including the driver were trained in Rescue, First Aid and Decontamination.

Two Despatch Rider Messengers, i.e., 1 to every 2 General Utility Parties. Ambulances, each with 1 driver and 1 attendant—also trained, as far as possible, in Rescue, First Aid and Decontamination, and in the driving of all the Unit's vehicles, especially the General Utility Party vehicles. Despatch Rider Messengers were also trained to perform telephone switchboard duties.

3. A Staff group comprised:

Commandant, Adjutant and Quartermaster, O.C. Training and Operations, Senior Group Officer and Chief Instructor, Group Officers (who also acted as Instructors), Instructors, Deputy Quartermaster, Matron, Driving Instructor, Stores Superintendent, Mechanics, Chief Clerk, Clerks, Shorthand typists or typists, Domestics. Variations within this framework were necessary according to the size of the Unit and to suit local circumstances.

APPENDIX IX

H.S.W.R. WAR DIARY

The following is a *selection* of messages received in Home Security War Room from London Region only during three hours of the attack on London of 11th May, 1941.

Time of origin	Form of message	In or out	Subject	Message No.
0036	Teleprinter	In	SOUTHWARK. H.E. Borough Road blocked. Mains damaged. WESTMINSTER 0004. H.E. Dolphin Square. No cas. LAMBETH 2325. H.E. Norwood Road blocked. BETHNAL GREEN 2350. H.E. Roman Road. Mains dam. ISLINGTON 2342. Heavy incendiary attack. H.E. at Stonefield Road. ST MARYLEBONE 2340. H.E. Wells Street. ST PANCRAS 2350. H.E. H.E. at HARROW and I.B.s at CAMBERWELL, TWICKENHAM, FELTHAM and HAMMERSMITH.	13
0040	,,	,,	POPLAR 2358. East India Dock No. 12. Half dock on fire.	14
0045	,,	,,	POPLAR 2359. South West India Dock Office wrecked by H.E.	15
0050	,,	,,	POPLAR 2359. Cootes Barge Road to right of S.W. India Dock entrance. 12 barges alight.	17
0055	,,	,,	STEPNEY 0020. Part of No. 9 warehouse boundary wall opposite No. 8 St Catherine Dock destroyed by H.E.	18
0055	,,	,,	WESTMINSTER. H.E. approx. 0027. Westminster Cathedral. Further details not yet available.	19
0102	,,	,,	HOLBORN report fire at British Museum, Gt Russell Street. No further details yet.	22
0116	,,	,,	CITY 0005. I.B.s on P.L.A. H.Q. Trinity Square. Fires extinguished. BETHNAL GREEN 2350. I.B.s. Fires. HAMMERSMITH 0018. 3 H.E. 20 casualties, including 18 trapped. WANDSWORTH 0015. 3 H.E. Wardens Post damaged. Casualties. LAMBETH 0005. H.E. 6 casualties. 0014. H.E. Westminster Bridge Road blocked. Bombing at CROYDON, BERMONDSEY, BARNET.	28
0145	,,	,,	WEST HAM 2350. No. 25–27 Sheds, Royal Albert Dock fired by incendiaries. Fairly extensive damage to export goods.	38
0158	,,	,,	SOUTHWARK. H.E. River wall bank, side near power station; river wall damaged. Tide now rising. Possibility of flooding.	46
0200	,,	,,	WESTMINSTER 0024. I.B. Children's Hospital, Vincent Sq., Fire.	47
0230	,,	,,	WESTMINSTER 0155. 3 H.E. Chambers of Houses of Parliament.	59
0232	,,	,,	ST PANCRAS 0010. 3 H.E. Charlotte St area. 10 casualties. ISLINGTON 0037.	61

APPENDIX IX (*contd*)

Time of origin	Form of message	In or out	Subject	Message No.
			10 H.E. across borough. Property and mains dam. Many casualties. L.M.S. Railway Bridge at Corsica St dam. and in dangerous condition. No report of effect on Railway traffic yet.	
0241	,,	,,	POPLAR 0055. P.L.A. report H.E. on mine-sweeper H.M.S. *Goatfell*. Believed direct hit.	64
0247	,,	,,	POPLAR 0115. P.L.A. report owing to damage to impounding station, S.W. India Dock, all power including high tension off.	67
0244	Telephone Fire Control	,,	20-Pump fire at Railway Goods Yard, Silverthorne Road, Clapham, WANDSWORTH. 60-Pump fire at Westminster Hall, WESTMINSTER.	70
0300	Teleprinter	,,	BERMONDSEY from 2358 onwards. Heavy attack by H.E. and I.B.s especially in Rotherhithe area. Much damage to dwelling houses and business premises. Casualties unknown. CHISLEHURST 0106. H.E. Valliers Wood Road, casualties trapped. WESTMINSTER 0017. H.E. Bruton Street. Casualties. WANDSWORTH 0057–0123. 6 H.E. and many I.B.s. Damage to dwelling houses, flats and church. Casualties.	81
0325	,,	,,	H.M.S. *Tower* lying Cherry Garden Pier, BERMONDSEY, has received direct hit. Many casualties.	88
0326	,,	,,	ST PANCRAS. H.E. 0255. De Gaulle's Headquarters, Gordon St, 10 casualties, some trapped. Headquarters partly demolished.	89
0334	,,	,,	ST MARYLEBONE 0040. 3 H.E. Fire and damage. ST PANCRAS 0035. 13 H.E. Widespread damage. At least 60 casualties. PADDINGTON 0055. 2 H.E. Casualties trapped. LAMBETH 0040. 3 H.E. 18 casualties. Considerable damage.	93

APPENDIX X

Numbers employed in the Civil Defence and Police Services in World War II

(Thousands)

	Whole-time											Part-time										Total of Whole-time and Part-time
	A.R.P. Services[1]		National Fire Service[2]		Casualty Services[3]		Regular Police		Auxiliary Police[4]		Total	A.R.P. Services[1]		National Fire Service[2]		Casualty Services[3]		Auxiliary Police[5]		Total	
	M	F	M	F	M	F	M	F	M	F		M	F	M	F	M	F	M	F		
1940 June	108.7	14.9	72.2	4.7	14.9	33.0	64.4	0.3	31.9	0.2	345.2	719.4	136.9	161.6	8.9	46.7	134.2	159.3	0.6	1,367.6	1,712.8
1941 "	110.1	16.8	96.8	5.4	14.5	36.0	64.4	0.4	38.2	0.3	382.9	759.2	148.3	159.4	10.0	47.2	122.2	156.2	0.7	1,403.2	1,786.1
1942 "	88.7	17.6	107.7	28.5	9.3	30.7	60.4	0.4	36.8	3.6	383.7	739.6	137.3	129.9	11.1	39.7	95.2	145.3	1.6	1,299.7	1,683.4
1943 "	66.5	11.7	93.8	30.7	7.1	21.8	51.6	0.4	34.1	5.0	322.7	773.4	167.1	214.8	47.0	47.5	116.6	145.0	1.9	1,513.3	1,836.0
1944 "	56.9	10.0	86.6	24.1	7.1	17.8	48.9	0.4	25.3	4.6	281.7	799.4	179.8	231.9	54.6	49.8	114.2	138.9	1.9	1,570.5	1,852.2
1945 "	—	—	46.2	10.6	—	—	46.8	0.4	18.6	4.0	126.6	—	—	102.9	25.2	—	—	103.6	1.3	233.0	359.6
PEAK STRENGTHS	112.3a	19.4b	108.6b	32.2c	15.2d	37.9e	64.5f	0.4f	39.5h	5.0c	407.7c	802.5i	179.8i	234.9i	54.6j	51.2d	137.0d	160.5d	2.0i	1,576.9i	1,869.1k

[1] Civil Defence (General) Services: wardens, rescue and first-aid parties, report and control centres, messengers.
[2] Until September 1941 regular fire brigades and Auxiliary Fire Service. Including Works Brigades.
[3] Emergency ambulance service and first-aid post service.
[4] Police War Reserve, First Police Reserve, Special Constables, and Women's Auxiliary Police Corps, but excluding civilian employees. From September 1941 the Police Auxiliary Messenger Service is included.
[5] Special Constables and Women's Auxiliary Police Corps, but excluding civilian employees. From September 1941 the figures relate to persons enrolled for employment. From September 1939 to September 1941 the Police Auxiliary Messenger Service is included.

	Date of Peak		Date of Peak		Date of Peak		Date of Peak
a	December 1940	e	December 1941	i	March 1944		
b	March 1942	f	March 1941	j	June 1944		
c	March 1943	g	June 1941	k	December 1943		
d	September 1940	h	September 1941				

APPENDIX XI

The Cost of Civil Defence, 1939–1946

1. *Public Civil Defence Services*
   (a) borne on Central Funds £928,305,000 (96%)
   (b) borne on Local Funds £40,125,000 (4%)

   £968,430,000

2. *Other Services (Industry and Commerce)*
   (a) borne on Central Funds £25,765,000 (44%)
   (b) borne by Industry and
       Commerce . . £32,366,000 (56%)

   £58,131,000

   Grand Total £1,026,561,000

Note—These figures are a reasonable approximation of the cost of Civil Defence for the seven financial years 1939/40 to 1945/46 inclusive.

APPENDIX XI (*contd.*)

ANALYSIS OF EXPENDITURE

1. *Public Civil Defence Services (including Emergency Fire Brigade Services)*

	Expenditure borne on Central Funds	Expenditure of Local Authorities eligible for grant aid (Average rate 75%)
	Thousands £	
Civil Defence Schools	356	—
Research, etc.	1,474	—
Civil Defence Equipment and Materials . . .	76,007	—
Respirator Factories, Storage, Inspection . . .	3,056	—
Vehicle Repairs, etc.	212	—
Evacuation and Miscellaneous (Home Office) . .	58	—
Protective Services	2,718	—
Evacuation (Ministry of Health) net . . .	126,331	—
Casualties and Disease (Ministry of Health) net .	138,786	—
Local Authorities' claims for Civil Defence expenditure	275,769	144,708
Local Authorities' claims for Auxiliary Fire Service expenditure:		
Grant aided services	—	15,793
Pay and allowances	22,216	—
Other expenditure	800	—
National Fire Service:		
Pay and allowances	106,112	—
Other expenditure	46,750	—
Fire-fighting Appliances and Equipment (A.F.S. and N.F.S.)	15,712	—
Civil Defence Gratuities and Post-War Credits . .	11,177	—
	827,534	160,501
Less Receipts	19,605	—
	807,929	—
75% grant on 160,501 . . .	+120,376	−120,376
Centrally borne	928,305	Locally borne 40,125

2. *Other Services (Industry and Commerce)*

Thousands £

Shelters in Factories, Mines, Commercial
Buildings, etc.   .   .   .   . (*a*) 22,000 (Grant at 35%)

Anti-Glare and Camouflage   .   .   12,263
Protection of Vital Services .   .   .   23,868

(*b*) 36,131 (Grant at 50%)

Total (*a*) and (*b*) 58,131

Index

INDEX

INDEX OF PLACE NAMES

S.O. Code No. 63-111-3-13*